The Railway Station

THE
RAILWAY
STATION

○

A Social History

JEFFREY RICHARDS

AND

JOHN M. MacKENZIE

Oxford   New York

OXFORD UNIVERSITY PRESS

1986

Oxford University Press, Walton Street, Oxford OX2 6DP
Oxford New York Toronto
Delhi Bombay Calcutta Madras Karachi
Kuala Lumpur Singapore Hong Kong Tokyo
Nairobi Dar es Salaam Cape Town
Melbourne Auckland
and associated companies in
Beirut Berlin Ibadan Nicosia

Oxford is a trade mark of Oxford University Press

British Library Cataloguing in Publication Data
Richards, Jeffrey
The railway station: a social history.
1. Railroads—Stations—History
2. Railroads—Stations—Social aspects
I. Title II. MacKenzie, John M.
385'.314 HE1035
ISBN 0-19-215876-7

Library of Congress Cataloging in Publication Data
Richards, Jeffrey.
The railway station.
Bibliography: p. Includes index.
Railroads—Stations—Social aspects.
I. MacKenzie, John M. II. Title.
TF300.R53 1986 385'314 85-21642
ISBN 0-19-215876-7

Set by Rowland Phototypesetting Ltd.
Printed in Great Britain by
Butler & Tanner Ltd.
Frome, Somerset

For Our Friends:

Janice and John Brooke
(Scorton 'Central', closed 1 May 1939),

Wendy and Stephen Constantine
(Galgate, closed 1 May 1939), and

Christine and Eric Evans
(Hornby, closed 16 September 1957),

whose homes regrettably can
only be reached by car

Preface

THIS book had two points of departure. One was when the authors, ostensibly on a trip to see the border abbeys of Scotland, found themselves enthralled by an entirely different ruin. This was the railway station at Melrose, which dumbfounded us by its elegance, its ingenious use of a difficult site, and its tragic dilapidation since the closure of the 'Waverley' line from Carlisle to Edinburgh. The second was the magnificent 'All Stations' exhibition, seen in London in 1981, and the accompanying book of the same title. We were prompted by that exhibition to survey the literature on railway stations more closely, and it became apparent to us that, although a number of books had been published on the architecture of railway stations in Britain, Europe, and the United States, none had attempted to survey the incidence of the station world-wide. Little, for example, had been written about the stations in Asia, Africa, Australasia, and Latin America. Even more notably, no one had attempted to write the social history of the station, examining not only its architecture, but also its role in the arts, society, politics, and warfare.

Between us, we have a fairly considerable experience of railway stations, having visited them, used them, and admired them in several European countries, in North America, Eastern and Southern Africa, South and South-East Asia, as well as the British Isles. We each grew up in cities greatly influenced by railways, respectively Birmingham and Glasgow, where we have seen much-loved stations of our youth destroyed. Moreover, it seemed a suitable moment to celebrate the railway station. Throughout the world, stations were subjected to a period of drastic destruction in the 1960s and 1970s. In many cases this awakened the affection of communities for their stations and led heritage and conservation bodies in several countries to agitate for station preservation and, where closure could not be avoided, reuse. Perhaps a wide-ranging survey might now serve to mark a turning-point in the fortunes of the railway station.

In examining the social history of railway stations we were concerned to treat them not as inanimate objects, but as living, breathing places which, better than any other building type of the last 150 years, reflected the societies around them, public buildings which people used in all sorts of ways and whose significance they instantly recognized when depicted in the theatre, the cinema, paintings, photographs, poetry, novels, and travel works. For this reason we have chosen to allow other voices to tell part of the story, to illustrate through quotation the central, but often differing, role of the station in so many societies and so many lives. In this we follow the sage advice offered by Rudyard Kipling to Henry Chappell when he embarked on a railway book in 1924: 'Make the platform speak. It should have some tales to tell.'

Generally the past tense has been used throughout the work, even of those stations which happily survive. This was done partly to avoid a mixture of tenses when writing about a variety of stations, partly because we are unsure of the survival of some stations, particularly those in remoter parts of Siberia, Africa, and Latin America. Moreover, although the destruction rate has slowed down, some stations will almost certainly disappear while this book is in the press.

We are all too painfully aware that there are omissions and neglected areas in this study but, given the size and scope of the undertaking, coverage has perforce to be representative rather than comprehensive. In general, the division of labour saw J.R. take responsibility for Britain, Europe, and the arts, and J.M. take responsibility for the rest of the world, though in many cases the contributions of each author have merged into inseparability. If the book appears partisan, it is because it has been written in the spirit ascribed by Lord Byron to the historian William Mitford: 'Labour, learning, research, wrath and partiality.'

Many people have helped in the preparation of this work. Firstly, we would like to thank all the kind members of station staffs who have helped us on our journeys. Librarians at the Canadian, Australian, and Zimbabwean High Commissions, the Royal Commonwealth Society, the Imperial War Museum, the India Office, the British Film Institute, the British Library, and the University of Lancaster Library have been most helpful. In particular, the staff of the inter-library loans office at Lancaster have dealt with our importunate demands for rare books with great courtesy and patience. The National Film Archive and the Archive Film Agency (Leeds) facilitated the screening of rare feature films. The photographic collections of the India Office, the Royal Commonwealth Society, and the Crown Agents were made available to us by Pauline Rohatgi, John Falconer, and Don Jarvis respectively. The public relations officers of the railways of British Columbia, New Zealand, Queensland, South Australia, West Australia, and Zimbabwe supplied useful information (and in one case, New Zealand, a wealth of valuable material), as did Omer Lavallée, Archivist of the Canadian Pacific Railway, Brien Brothman of the National Archives of Canada, and A. J. Schouten of the National Capital Commission of Canada. We owe particular thanks to Marcus Merriman, who generously loaned materials from his collection on American stations, and to Henry Finch, who provided books, slides, and much information on Latin American stations. Thanks are also due for advice and assistance of various kinds to Anthony Tuck, Nigel Dalziel, Rory Miller, Tony Fielding, Austin Woolrych, Richard Taylor, Gillian Hartnoll, Rachel Hasted, Allen Eyles, Derek Smith, Bob Geoghegan, George Tulloch, Graham Bartram, Philip French, Richard Dunn, John Illingworth, Stephen Constantine, Gordon Inkster, Philip Levy, Alex MacKenzie, Elaine Burrows, Joyce Storer, Norman McGilrray, Gordon Entwisle, Christopher Wood, and Geoffrey Parker.

In choosing the illustrations we have deliberately avoided the familiar and sought to highlight the unfamiliar.

Acknowledgements

The authors and publisher gratefully acknowledge permission to reprint copyright material as follows:

Harry Aland: from *Recollections of a Country Station Life* (Anderson Keenan Publishers Ltd., 1980).

George Arliss: from *George Arliss By Himself* (1940). Reprinted by permission of John Murray Publishers and Little Brown & Co.

Christian Barman: from *Next Station* (George Allen & Unwin Publishers Ltd., 1947).

Len Bedale: from *Station Master* (1976). Reprinted by permission of Pennine Publications Ltd., Sheffield.

Hilaire Belloc: from *On Nothing & Kindred Subjects* (1908). Reprinted by permission of A. D. Peters & Co. Ltd.

Vera Brittain: from *Testament of Youth*. Reprinted by permission of the literary executors, Virago Press Ltd. and Victor Gollancz Ltd.

R. Broad and S. Fleming (eds.): from *Nella Last's War: A Mother's Diary 1939-45* (Falling Wall Press, 1981).

Karel Čapek: from *Intimate Things*. Reprinted by permission of Dilia.

G. K. Chesterton: from *Tremendous Trifles* (1909). By permission of Miss D. E. Collins and A. P. Watt Ltd.

Lady Chorley: from *Manchester Made Them* (Faber & Faber Ltd., 1950).

Carl W. Condit: from *The Railroad and the City* (1977). Reprinted by permission of Ohio State University Press.

Frances Cornford: 'Parting in Wartime' from *Collected Poems*. Reprinted by permission of Century Hutchinson Ltd.

Bernard Darwin: from *War on the Line: The Story of the Southern Railway in War-Time* (British Railways Board, 1946).

Michael Deakin and John Willis: from *Johnny Go Home*. Copyright Michael Deakin and John Willis 1976. Reprinted by permission of Elaine Greene Ltd.

Lawrence Durrell: from *Justine*. Copyright © 1957 by Lawrence George Durrell, renewed 1985 by Lawrence George Durrell. Reprinted by permission of E. P. Dutton, a division of New American Library, and Faber & Faber Ltd.

T. S. Eliot: from 'The Dry Salvages' from *Four Quartets*. Copyright 1943 by T. S. Eliot; renewed 1971 by Esme Valerie Eliot. Reprinted by permission of Harcourt Brace Jovanovich Inc., and Faber & Faber Ltd.

Léon-Paul Fargue: 'Deserted Station' and 'The little station with short shadows . . .' from *Poèmes*. Copyright Editions Gallimard 1944. Reprinted by permission of the Publisher.

Brian Fawcett: from *Railways of the Andes*. By permission of the Literary Executors of the late Brian Fawcett.

Michael Flanders and Donald Swann: from *The Songs of Michael Flanders and Donald Swann*. Copyright the Estate of Michael Flanders and Donald Swann. By permission.

Philip Henderson: 'Night Express' from *First Poems* (1936). By permission of Mrs Belinda Henderson.

Alan A. Jackson: from *London's Terminal* (1969). Reprinted by permission of David & Charles Publishers; from *Semi-Detached London*. Reprinted by permission of the author.

J. R. Kellett: from *Railways and Victorian Cities* (1979). Reprinted by permission of Routledge & Kegan Paul plc.

Peter I. Lyaschenko: from *History of the National Economy of Russia*, ed. W. Chapin Huntington, trans. L. M. Herman (American Council of Learned Societies).

Frank McKenna: from *The Railway Workers 1840–1970*. Reprinted by permission of Faber & Faber Ltd.

Thomas Mann: from *Death in Venice*, trans. H. T. Lowe-Porter. Reprinted by permission of Martin Secker & Warburg Ltd. and Alfred A. Knopf Inc.

Henry Maxwell: 'Dusk on a Branch' from *Railway Rubaiyat* (The Golden Head Press Ltd., 1968).

Carroll Meeks: from *The Railroad Station* (1956). Reprinted by permission of Yale University Press.

George C. Nash: from *The LMS at War* (British Railways Board, 1946).

O. S. Nock: from *Britain's Railways at War 1939–45*. Reprinted by permission of Ian Allan Ltd.

Roger Price: from *The Modernization of Rural France* (1983). Reprinted by permission of Hutchinson Publishing Group.

Marcel Proust; from *Remembrance of Things Past*, trans. Scott Moncrieff and Terence Kilmartin. Reprinted by permission of Chatto & Windus Ltd., and Random House Inc.

Siegfried Sassoon: 'Morning Express' from *Collected Poems*. Copyright 1918, 1920, by E. P. Dutton & Co., copyright 1936, 1947, 1948, by Siegfried Sassoon. Reprinted by permission of Viking Penguin Inc., and George Sassoon.

Karl Shapiro: 'Troop Train' from *Poems 1940–1953*. Copyright 1943 and renewed 1971 by Karl Shapiro. Reprinted by permission of Random House Inc.

Jack Simmons: from *The Railways of Britain* (1968). Reprinted by permission of David Higham Associates Ltd.

Albert Speer: from *Inside the Third Reich* (1970). Reprinted by permission of George Weidenfeld & Nicolson Ltd.

A. J. Taylor: quoted in Alan Delgado, *The Annual Outing and Other Excursions* (1977). Reprinted by permission of George Allen & Unwin (Publishers) Ltd.

Paul Theroux: from *The Old Patagonian Express*. Copyright © 1979 by Cape Cod Scriveners Company. Reprinted by permission of Houghton Mifflin Co. and Gillon Aitken.

David St John Thomas: from *The Country Station* (1976). Reprinted by permission of David & Charles Publishers.

Leo Tolstoy: from *Anna Karenina*, trans. Rosemary Edmonds. Reprinted by permission of Penguin Books Ltd.

Eric Treacy: from *Steam Up*. Reprinted by permission of Ian Allan Ltd.

George Edgar Turner: from *Victory Rode the Rails*. Copyright 1953 by Macmillan Publishing Co., renewed 1981 by George R. Turner and William E. Turner. Reprinted by permission of Macmillan Publishing Co.

Adrian Vaughan: from *Signalman's Morning and Signalman's Twilight* (1984). Reprinted by permission of John Murray Publishers.

John K. Walton: 'Railways and Resort Development in NW England' from *Ports and Resorts in the Regions* (1980). Reprinted by permission of Eric M. Sigsworth.

Keith Waterhouse: from *Billy Liar*. Reprinted by permission of David Higham Associates Ltd.

J. R. Whitbread: from *The Railway Policeman* (1961). Reprinted by permission of Harrap Ltd.

Elizabeth A. Wilmot: from *Meet Me at the Station* (Gage Publishing, 1977). By permission of the author.

Thomas Wolfe: 'The Railroad Station' from *Of Time and the River*. Copyright 1935 by Charles Scribner's Sons, copyright renewed © 1963 Paul Gitlin, Administrator CTA. Reprinted by permission of Charles Scribner's Sons and William Heinemann Ltd.

Emile Zola: from *La Bête humaine*, trans. Leonard Tancock. Reprinted by permission of Penguin Books Ltd.

While every effort has been made to secure permission, we may have failed in a few cases to trace the copyright holder. We apologize for any apparent negligence.

Contents

Illustrations

The Slow Train

Miller's Dale for Tideswell . . .
Kirby Muxloe . . .
Mow Cop and Scholar Green . . .

No more will I go to Blandford Forum and Mortehoe
On the slow train from Midsomer Norton and Mumby Road.
No churns, no porter, no cat on a seat
At Chorlton-cum-Hardy or Chester-le-Street.
We won't be meeting again
On the Slow Train.

I'll travel no more from Littleton Badsey to Openshaw.
At Long Stanton I'll stand well clear of the doors no more.
No whitewashed pebbles, no Up and no Down
From Formby Four Crosses to Dunstable Town.
I won't be going again
On the Slow Train.

On the Main Line and the Goods Siding
The grass grows high
At Dog Dyke, Tumby Woodside
And Trouble House Halt.

The Sleepers sleep at Audlem and Ambergate.
No passenger waits on Chittening platform or Cheslyn Hay.
No one departs, no one arrives
From Selby to Goole, from St Erth to St Ives.
They've all passed out of our lives
On the Slow Train, on the Slow Train.

Cockermouth for Buttermere . . . on the Slow Train,
Armley Moor Arram . . .
Pye Hill and Somercotes . . .
Windmill End . . . on the Slow Train.

MICHAEL FLANDERS AND
DONALD SWANN

Introduction

The Mystique of the Railway Station

THERE is perhaps no more potent or dramatic symbol of the Industrial Revolution than the railways. Although the precise nature of the economic change the railways wrought is still debated, their impact cannot be gainsaid. They epitomized technological advance—a new method of transporting people and goods speedily and in bulk, of unifying nations and, in the words of the celebrated epigrammatist Sydney Smith, 'abolishing time, distance and delay'. The Victorians equated the railways with progress and civilization. Their coming was hymned in art and literature on a scale of imagination and power which the steam train's unromantic supplanter, the motor car, wholly failed to inspire.

The mood of enthusiasm and pride which the railways inspired is nowhere better summed up than in Ned Farmer's poem 'King Steam':

> Hurrah for the Rail! for the stout iron rail,
> A boon to both country and town,
> From the very first day that the permanent way
> And the far-famed fish-point was laid down.
> 'Tis destined, you'll find, to befriend all mankind,
> To strew blessings all over the world;
> Man's science, they say, gave it birth one fine day
> And the flag of King Steam was unfurled.[1]

Great were the claims made by contemporary enthusiasts like E. Foxwell and T. C. Farrer:

Many, if not most, of the distinctive phenomena that constitute 'the nineteenth century' are directly due to railway speed; that is, we can scarcely imagine the possibility of their development in the absence of railways.

These phenomena included 'the unexampled diffusion of wealth'; 'uniformity of prices'; 'an "independence" of manners'; 'the "realistic"

tendency in art and behaviour'; 'the unprecedented growth of population'; 'the astounding cheapness of most necessaries'; 'the universal
and sometimes frenzied spirit of competition'; the ending of feudalism
and the introduction of freedom. Nor was this all:

There are bigger things left. Who can help being struck by the *tolerance* of our
age . . . The incessant shuttle of railway speed, the myriad daily encounters of all
sorts and conditions of men owing to this cheap expedition, the resulting flux and
murkiness in place of definite conviction, the unambitious content as long as one
can find some *modus vivendi* amongst such heterogeneous diversity—this peculiar characteristic of the time (its weakness and its strength) is the special outcome
of express trains. From this restless diffusion of men arises a growing *complexity*
of social problems; no more of the simple parish under despotic government.
Now all our various programmes interact—we are no longer autocrats on our
own instrument, but have to observe *orchestral* behaviour . . . Then there is hope
in the air, a new optimism, fed chiefly by perpetual motion . . . This healthy tone
has been bred not only by the daily influence of the railways, but by the annual
practice of 'going to the seaside' or making a tour, a practice undreamt of before
railways, and now endemic . . . So that standing on the platforms of our great
inland stations, we watch a salutary stir in the ebb and flow of restless men; we
see men under treatment by Motion, and know there is a chance for them. Over
every railway station the flag of Hope waves bright, while day after day the
befriending express moves in and out on its errand of health. What the sea does
once a year to freshen individual lives our railways are doing every day for the
national life, in a way less picturesque but none the less effective.[2]

For all the fact that some of these claims need to be modified in the light
of historical research, there can be no doubting that the nineteenth
century was pre-eminently 'The Railway Age'. The railways were, as
Charles Dickens noted with some distaste, ubiquitous:

There were railway patterns in its drapers' shops, and railway journals in the
windows of its newsmen. There were railway hotels, coffee-houses, lodging-
houses, boarding-houses; railway plans, maps, views, wrappers, bottles,
sandwich-boxes and timetables; railway hackney-coach and cabstands; railway
omnibuses, railway streets and buildings, railway hangers-on and parasites, and
flatterers out of all calculation. There was even railway time observed in clocks,
as if the sun itself had given in.[3]

The central focus of all this railway activity was, however, the railway
station. Here it was that Foxwell and Farrer's 'flag of Hope' metaphorically waved. Here was where people met and mingled, where books
and newspapers were delivered, where goods and foodstuffs arrived.
Here was the gateway to the seaside, to the country, to the wider world.

Much has been written on railway routes and rolling stock. But the railway station has only tardily gained recognition for its contribution both to the railway system in particular and to culture and society in general. In every major city, the tracks terminated in a station. There arose great, echoing halls of glass and iron, colonnaded, canopied, buttressed, and turreted, living temples to the worship of King Steam.

Théophile Gautier said of them: 'These cathedrals of the new humanity are the meeting points of nations, the centre where all converges, the nucleus of the huge stars whose iron rays stretch out to the ends of the earth.'[4] It is a view that was fully justified in a wide-ranging exhibition 'Le Temps des Gares', originally conceived and executed by Jean Dethier at the Pompidou Centre in Paris in 1978 and subsequently presented throughout Europe in such places as Milan, Brussels, Berlin, and Madrid. It ran at the Science Museum in London from May to September 1981 under the title 'All Stations'. The exhibition catalogue, illustrating and analysing its rich array of paintings and photographs, models and mock-ups, artefacts and ephemera, made a major contribution to understanding the multi-faceted role of the railway station both in our lives and in our dreams. This study seeks to build on the foundations thus laid and to take the assessment of the importance of the railway station a step further.

At its most basic level, the railway station was the nineteenth century's distinctive contribution to architectural forms. It combined within itself in eloquent reflection of the age which produced it both a daring and innovative modernity and a heroic and comforting traditionalism. The modernity came in the technological skill which went into the production of the train-sheds, the great single- and double-span roofs, for which unsung engineers solved complex structural problems of weight and distribution with breath-taking brilliance and boldly utilized the new materials, iron and glass, to construct the naves and transepts of the cathedral stations. The frontages were the work of the architects and they worked not in new styles but in revival styles—Gothic, classical, Renaissance, baroque—to comfort and reassure those concerned about the newness of it all. For though it is hard for us to credit it now, many people believed that if you travelled faster than—say—30 miles an hour, you might actually burst and be scattered across the railway lines.

But revivalism in architecture did not mean lack of imagination or inventiveness—quite the reverse: it meant a prodigal outpouring of both. The end-products of this explosion are—or were until recently—all around us. Everyone knows the fantastical splendours of that fairy-tale citadel called St Pancras and the lost magnificence of the Euston Arch, but beyond them in the rest of Britain stood other wonders: the medieval Gothic abbey that was Richmond Station, the handsome Jacobean mansion that was Stamford East, the elegant French Renaissance château of Southport Lord Street, the trim Alpine hunting-lodge that was Kendal, the airy Edwardian summer-house that was Wemyss Bay. Their very names were grand and allusive—Carlisle Citadel, Hull Paragon, Bristol Templemeads, Lancaster Green Ayre, Cheltenham Lansdowne. Abroad, too, imagination took wing. In New York the Baths of Caracalla served as the model for Pennsylvania Station and Alexandre Marcel's designs for Bucharest Central evoked the architectural flights of fancy of Piranesi. In Paris, first the Gare de l'Est and later the Gare d'Orsay became the standard station-forms for their respective generations, models of perfection which others strove to emulate.

Nineteenth-century forms and styles held sway until the 1920s when they were replaced by their horrendous antithesis—Functionalism. Under this dispensation, stations became bare, square boxes, with—in the words of Sir Edward Elgar—'no soul, no romance, no imagination'. They were, in short, fitting products of the era of plastic, concrete, and neon—flat, boring, sterile, and styleless. It is perhaps appropriate that in an age which can design its high-speed trains to resemble aeroplanes and its low-speed trains to resemble buses, its stations should equally have no identifiable association with the railways. The symbol of the new age is the new Euston, an all-purpose combination of airport lounge and open-plan public lavatory. It tells us a good deal about the relative values of the nineteenth and twentieth centuries that where the Victorians modelled their stations on cathedrals and palaces, Modern Man models his on shopping centres and office blocks.

As railway systems all over the world have contracted, so the great stations have been threatened and in many places destroyed. In Britain some 4,000 stations have gone out of use since the 1960s, and many of them have vanished altogether—swept away with a callous disregard for our architectural heritage that takes the breath away. British Rail themselves, the guardians of this heritage, gave a blockbusting philistine lead by demolishing the Euston Arch, an act somewhat akin to tearing down Salisbury Cathedral or Windsor Castle. But the Americans followed suit by levelling Pennsylvania Station, New York. The men guilty of these outrages did not even have the excuse of their European counterparts, who could sometimes claim that wartime bombing had flattened the great stations which they were replacing.

In all of Britain's great cities, majestic terminals went out of use and lay for years rotting like gigantic beached whales in the noonday sun

—Manchester Central, Liverpool Exchange, Birmingham Snow Hill, Glasgow St Enoch's. Country and suburban stations have been closed wholesale and even those still surviving are often covered in graffiti, wrecked and vandalized beyond recognition. There is clearly now an urgent need for a Historic Stations Trust to remove those treasures that remain beyond the reach of the hammers of the destroyers, both official and unofficial, so that at least part of this precious heritage may be handed down to future generations.

The station is an endangered species and conservation is of the essence. The Third World, particularly Thailand and Malaya, has set a notable example in the restoration and preservation of stations. Many are the new uses to which old stations are being put here and abroad —museums, theatres, markets, restaurants, sporting halls, cultural centres. Some of our more charming wayside stations have been sold off as private houses. All chintz curtains and birdcages in the windows, many of them are the homes of old railwaymen who sit by the fire, dreaming of Gresley Pacifics and Stanier Jubilees. And yet—and yet—for all this earnest and worthy work of conservation, the life has gone irrevocably out of these stations. Without the ebb and flow of passengers, the arrival and departure of trains, they have in a very real sense ceased to be. For steam was the breath which animated them, and that breath has been stifled. Now they are being embalmed—dutifully and reverentially, as befits faithful but defunct servitors of mankind.

The closing of a station intangibly but significantly diminishes the spiritual life of a country and its people, for it brings down the curtain with devastating finality on a stage which has seen a thousand dramas, comic and tragic, played out and has mirrored the changing moods of the nation, has etched itself into the working lives of some, the emotional lives of others. Robert Lynd summed this up well when he reported his feelings on listening to a radio broadcast of the arrival of the last mail train at Dublin's Broadstone Station before its closure in 1936:

How tenderly everybody spoke of it during the broadcast! How haunted with memories of happiness it seemed! Old servants of the railway company came into the signal-box from which the broadcast was given and spoke of the closing of the station as if for them it was the end of a world. Never again would the Galway mail arrive there in its midnight glory. Never again would a signalman give the signal that all was clear. A banquet-hall deserted—Broadstone Station would henceforth be only that to thousands for whom it had for long been associated with happiness—the happiness of the day's work, the happiness of companionship, the happiness of simply being alive on a fine day. There was a note of exile in the voices of the old railway servants who came to the microphone to say goodbye to the station . . . Ruskin would surely have been surprised if he had been told that a time would come when railway stations, like lakes and mountains, would become a part of the imaginative life of men, and when the sounding express engine no less than the sounding cataract would rouse in them a noble delight. He would have been still more surprised if he had been told that the closing of an old railway station would one day move men to sadness no less than the demolition of a Gothic church or the violation of a landscape. Yet how natural it is! Life is brief, and the removal of a long-tolerated equally with a long-loved landmark alters and injures the world in which we have been happier than we have deserved to be.[5]

It is worth considering that in part at least the malaise of modern society is the result of ill-considered and reckless policies of demolition and redevelopment. The fate of stations can be taken as symptomatic of this trend. It is a commonplace to talk of the young being alienated. Why are they? One reason could be because all around them are utterly characterless, uniform, boring, and unmemorable buildings—nothing for them to stand and stare at, to wonder at and dream of—as there was in the heyday of the great stations. Concrete underpasses and plastic shopping precincts are not the stuff that dreams are made of. For older people, the familiar landmarks of their lives have been bulldozed, leaving them bewildered and uncertain. The big city station from which they saw off their loved ones to war, from where they left for their honeymoons and holidays, where they kept their romantic trysts under the station clock, has been obliterated or at the very least altered out of all recognition. People may still have their memories but their certainties have been undermined. As Sir John Betjeman said: 'Railway stations are most important in giving places an identity.'[6] Like the town hall, the central library, the cathedral, the station is one of the nodal points of the community, a vital element in its public consciousness.

This was not just true of towns and cities. It was true too in the country. The country station was a crucial factor in the lives of the inhabitants of rural areas. As David St John Thomas wrote in his evocative memoir of the British country station: 'In most areas for at least two full generations all important comings and goings were by train.'[7] Hilaire Belloc, writing of his local station in Sussex in 1908, spoke for all the users of rural stations:

What is more English than the country railway station? I defy the eighteenth century to produce anything more English, more full of home and rest, and the nature of the country than my junction. Twenty-seven trains a day stop at it or start from it; it serves even the expresses. Smith's monopoly has a bookstall there; you can get cheap Kipling and Harmsworth to any extent, and yet it is a theme for English idylls. The one-eyed porter whom I have known from childhood; the station-master who ranges us all in ranks, beginning with the Duke and ending with a sad, frayed and literary man; the little chaise in which the two old ladies from Barlton drive up to get their paper of an evening, the servant from the inn, the newsboy whose mother keeps a sweetshop—they are all my friends.[8]

The station was one of the hubs of village life—a centre of news, gossip, and advice, the home of bookstall and telegraph office. Its disappearance has been followed in many cases by that of the village shop, the village post office, even the village pub—the slow, inexorable process of rural decay. It is a decay that became inevitable when the infamous Beeching Plan substituted the crass motif of economic viability for that of communal need, and ripped out the steel vertebrae of the nation, leaving whole areas more isolated than they had been at any time since the eighteenth century. The country railways, of course, never made a profit; they could not by their very nature. But they provided a vital social service and their closure was a disastrous token of things to come.

What was it about the station that was so fascinating? The station was truly a gateway through which people passed in endless profusion on a variety of missions—a place of motion and emotion, arrival and departure, joy and sorrow, parting and reunion. There are countless individual stories encapsulated in the photographs of migrant workers arriving at Continental stations or commuters pouring into the London termini, of the Jews being herded on to trains headed for the death-camps, or of armies departing for half a dozen different wars—the brave, cheerful, youthful faces of a nation's young men heading off for the rendezvous with destiny.

James Scott in his *Railway Romance and Other Essays* observed: 'It is mainly the human interest to be found in and about a railway station which is the secret of its fascination.' Scott summed up with fine rhetorical finality the maelstrom of conflicting emotions and experiences a station represents:

What of the passengers and their friends! Who may fathom, much less portray, the thoughts and emotions surging within their minds and hearts? The grief and pain of separation, the hopes, the fears, the loving care, the prayers, the joys, the trust! How ill-concealed by some in affected gaiety of mood; how patent in others who do not attempt to conceal! Here are soldiers and sailors, with troops of acquaintances to see them off. There are some boys and girls going away to school, their fathers and mothers filling up the moments of waiting with many injunctions in order to shut out their anxieties which their children must not see. At another place a wife is bidding good-bye to a husband whom duty calls hence.

Elsewhere an only son and brother is setting out into the great world to win a name and place. In the corner of another carriage there sits, his face screened by a magazine, some lonely soul who has no one to bid him adieu at this end of his journey or welcome him at the other. At another compartment a happy wedding party is assembled, and amid merriment and showers of confetti the 'happy pair' are getting a good send-off. These and a hundred other scenes one may witness at the departure of an important train such as this. There may be tears, or mirth, or calm demeanour, but in all the life of feeling runs high . . . A railway station speaks of epochs of decision in life, a parting of the ways, cross-roads in conduct. Shall we embark upon this adventure; shall we definitely declare our hand; shall we make a break in habit; or a departure from principle? Are we fleeing from Nineveh and duty, or going where Love and Right beckon us? As we wait at the station are we still counting the cost, and weighing consequences in the balance? Are we making a sacrifice in going away? Have we left a clean record behind? When the train has borne us away and we settle into our corner, have we feelings of remorse or satisfaction? Where will the journey's end be?[9]

There are those who have made a close study of various aspects of platform life. Bishop Eric Treacy was a connoisseur of station farewells:

What an interesting study of farewells a railway station affords. There are those who scorn any demonstration of affection in public. As the train leaves, with an unnatural casualness they will separate with never so much as a pressure of the hand; others there are who, oblivious of the world around them, stand gazing into each other's eyes, spending their last few moments clasped in each other's arms—matching a succession of last kisses—to separate with a look of bewildered agony on their faces. Then there is that numerous class of people for whom 'seeing people off' is a bit of an outing, not one minute of which is to be lost. So they stand cheerfully by the carriage window revealing in loud voices the personal secrets of the wretched traveller, who winces as he realizes that he has to travel two hundred miles with a carriage full of strangers who know his family history, how prone he is to chills if he wears a damp vest, what he has to do when he arrives at his destination.[10]

The platform was also a happy hunting-ground for observers of social nuance. Henry James, confessing in 1905 to a passion for London railway stations, gave as his reason:

The exhibition of variety of type is in general one of the bribes by which London induces you to condone her abominations and the railway-platform is a kind of compendium of that variety. I think that nowhere so much as in London do people wear—to the eye of observation—definite signs of the sort of people they may be. If you like above all things to know the sort, you hail his feet with joy; you recognize that if the English are immensely distinct from other people they are also socially—and that brings with it in England, a train of moral and intellectual consequences—extremely distinct from each other.[11]

A typical example of such observation can be seen in Alfred W. Arthurton's account of the day's work at Paddington Station in 1904:

Life as seen from the platform at Paddington is most varied and one cannot help thinking that an official who spends most of his time there must gain a vast knowledge of human nature . . . On the arrival or departure of the King and Queen crowds of loyal subjects—mostly ladies—besiege the barriers which have to be erected on the platform, whilst the entrance to the station and the railings overlooking the Royal waiting room are thick with those who would catch a glimpse of Royalty . . . A fine 'Henley week' considerably increases the summer receipts of the Great Western Railway. This is the time for a foreigner to see English youth and beauty at its best . . . Another great event from the Paddington point of view is 'Ascot week'. Again the departure slope is packed with hansoms waiting to discharge their fair occupants, and again the ladies' dresses are a sight not to be missed . . . At another time the platforms are full of youngsters on the way to 'Lords' for the Eton and Harrow match. Before the train stops every door is opened and all try to get out at once, with the result that not a few alight on their faces. Every boy charters a hansom and the spectacle of a mite of ten or twelve years, with stick and blue ribbon bow complete, gravely trying to fold his arms on top of the hansom doors above which scarcely more than his top hat is visible is an amusing one . . . A scene of quite different character is the departure of 600 or 700 of Dr. Barnardo's boys and girls to their new homes in Canada. These have no near friends or relatives to part from, and the future is bright for each; but all the same, a lump comes in one's throat as the train steams out of the station amid cheering and the strains of 'Auld Lang Syne'. Every Thursday during the summer 'specials' are run conveying thousands of children to and from the country. The 'Fresh Air Fund' brings joy to many a childish heart by affording a stay in what seems like another world for a whole week. Vanloads of youngsters, each child properly labelled with name and destination, are brought to the station and dispatched to various places on the Great Western system . . . Today, a crowd of Polish Jews, exiled from their native land, pass through Paddington on their way to America. Pending the departure of the Birkenhead train they bestow themselves in a waiting room set apart, or roam the platforms. Whole families are there with all their worldly possessions . . . Another day a gang of convicts, chained together and bearing the mark of the broad arrow, clank along the platform en route for Portland, Dartmoor or Warwick . . . And so it goes on. The scene is continually changing, and from dawn to dark an endless procession of men and women pass before us, intent on business or pleasure.[12]

The station as a point of departure literally and metaphorically took on a particular intensity for the post-First World War generation of young British literati. Private foreign travel had been restricted by the war. But

after the war, there was a great literary diaspora—to Italy, the South of
France, California, the Far East. It was a flight from the chill of the
trenches, shortages moral and material, rain, cold, and influenza, the
twin banes of puritanism and philistinism, to the sun, to liberation sexual,
social, and artistic. W. H. Auden and Christopher Isherwood, D. H.
Lawrence and Graham Greene, Norman Douglas and Evelyn Waugh,
Robert Graves, Harold Acton, Osbert Sitwell, and Lawrence Durrell, all
packed their bags and decamped gratefully and sometimes for good.[13]

It was the last great age of travel—by ship and by train—before the
joys and mysteries and individualism of travel were overtaken by the
bland, pre-packaged age of tourism when daily long-distance flights, with
their second-rate movies, plastic food, and attendant jet lag, replaced for
ever the slow boat to China and the stopping train to Samarkand. It was
the last age when the railway station was an essential ingredient of every
traveller's itinerary: point of departure, point of arrival, point of contact
en route with everyday life as it teemed and flowed outside the protective
cocoon of the train. The Second World War put an end to this age as
surely as the First World War began it. Thereafter tourism replaced
travel, the masses were unleashed upon the Continent, package-tour
operators and entrepreneurs got to work to ensure that everywhere from
Zagreb to Zanzibar looked, felt, and smelt exactly the same, and the
aeroplane turned Atlantic crossings and transworld flights into the
merest commuting, as mechanical and regular and unremarkable as
catching the 6.10 from Waterloo to Surbiton.

But the point of departure was more than merely physical. It involved a
metaphysical change, as T. S. Eliot observed in 'The Dry Salvages':

> When the train starts, and the passengers are settled,
> To fruit, periodicals and business letters
> (And those who saw them off have left the platform)
> Their faces relax from grief into relief,
> To the sleeping rhythm of a hundred hours,
> Fare forward, travellers! not escaping from the past
> Into different lives, or into any future;
> You are not the same people who left that station
> Or who will arrive at any terminus,
> While the narrowing rails slide together behind you.[14]

Sometimes this departure is final. There is a fearful symmetry on
occasion in the association of the station and death. Count Leo Tolstoy,
whose tragic heroine Anna Karenina threw herself under a train, himself
died in 1910 at the remote Russian country station of Astapovo. Emile

Verhaeren, the Belgian poet who had vividly chronicled the impact of the railways on the countryside, was killed in an accident at Rouen Station in 1916. Bishop Eric Treacy, 'The Railway Bishop', died while photographing trains at Appleby Station on the Settle–Carlisle line in 1978. Indeed the railways began with a notable death. William Huskisson, President of the Board of Trade, was run down and killed at Parkside on the inaugural run of the Liverpool and Manchester Railway in 1830. It was an event, akin to the sinking of the *Titanic*, that rocked society at a moment of supreme self-congratulation and brought home to a people intoxicated with science and progress the existence of an admonitory Deity. A tablet erected to his memory announced sonorously that Huskisson,

singled out by the Decree of an Inscrutable Providence from the midst of the Distinguished Multitude that Surrounded him, in the full pride of his Talents and the Perfection of his Usefulness, met with the Accident that Occasioned his Death; which deprived England of an Illustrious Statesman and Liverpool of its Most Honoured Representative; which changed a moment of the Noblest Exultation and Triumph that Science and Genius had ever achieved into one of Desolation and Mourning, and striking Terror into the Hearts of Assembled Thousands brought home into every Bosom the Forgotten Truth that 'In the Midst of Life we are in Death'.[15]

The association of station departures with death and transfiguration (cf. the Stations of the Cross?) is but one aspect of a wider concern with identifying the particular mystique of the station. It is a problem which has occupied the minds of those whom Canon Roger Lloyd has dubbed 'station saunterers' ('the railway lover counts no time wasted which he spends sauntering on a good station').[16] Many of them have come to the conclusion that the role and atmosphere of the station large and small is essentially ecclesiastical. G. K. Chesterton, a self-confessed station saunterer, celebrated the station as a temple of tradition, a comforting source of continuity in a world increasingly dedicated to change:

The only way of catching a train I have ever discovered is to miss the train before. Do this, and you will find in a railway station much of the quietude and consolation of a cathedral. It has many of the characteristics of a great ecclesiastical building; it has vast arches, void spaces, coloured lights, and above all, it has recurrence of ritual. It is dedicated to the celebration of water and fire, the two prime elements of all human ceremonial. Lastly, a station resembles the old religions rather than the new religions in this point, that people go to it. In connection with this it should also be remembered that all popular places, all sites actually used by the people, tend to retain the best routine of antiquity very much more than any localities or machines used by any privileged class. Things are not altered so quickly or coarsely by common people as they are by fashionable people . . . If you wish to find the past preserved, follow the million feet of the crowd. At the worst the uneducated only wear down old things by sheer walking. But the educated kick them down out of sheer culture. I feel this profoundly as I wander about the empty railway station, where I have no business of any kind. I have extracted a vast number of chocolates from automatic machines; I have obtained cigarettes, toffee, scent, and other things that I dislike by the same machinery; I have weighed myself with sublime results; and this sense not only of the healthiness of popular things, but of their essential antiquity and permanence is still in possession of my mind.[17]

A similar ecclesiastical peace was the principal quality that Karel Čapek detected in Czech country stations:

There are little stations threaded on the lines like beads on a rosary; they stand in the solitude like places of pilgrimage, far from the profane noises of the world; they are the real chapels dedicated to the silent ceremony of Waiting. They are led to as a rule by a country lane with a straggling row of trees; the longer it is the more profound and lasting is the silence which embraces the pilgrim who comes to the station to wait . . . We who are waiting shuffle from one foot to the other and cough under our breath like worshippers in a chapel; we are dressed in clean clothes and depressed in a Sunday sort of way . . . 'Mummy!' says the piping voice of a little girl. 'Be quiet' her mother reproves her in a whisper. 'Mummy, when will the train come?' Be quiet, little girl, we have to wait for the train to come. If you aren't as good as if you were in church, the train won't come, and we shan't go away in it to the ends of the earth.[18]

In this context, then, it is entirely appropriate for Canon Roger Lloyd to speak of the quietude of Marylebone Station in London:

It is essentially peaceful and when some rather fussy penitent told his father confessor that he could find nowhere in London where he could meditate in quiet and peace, he was astonished to hear the caustic answer: 'Have you tried Marylebone, my son?'[19]

It is possible to extend the metaphor almost *ad infinitum*. For if the station is seen as cathedral or chapel, it can also be seen to possess in its heyday a Bible every bit as imposing and sometimes even as impenetrable as the Authorized Version (*Bradshaw*), incense (steam), and liturgical chanting ('The train now standing at platform 3 is . . .', 'Close the doors and stand clear', 'All change'). In some countries nature imitates art and makes this fancy reality. In Tsarist Russia, icons were often placed in railway-station waiting-rooms and in Greece there were shrines at stations where the traveller could light candles to protect him on his journey. The ceiling of the Great Hall at the old Euston Station was deliberately modelled on that of the church of St Peter *extra muros* in Rome.

Somehow sensing this connection, clerics have been drawn as if by a magnet to the rails. Bishop Eric Treacy of Wakefield, who had an engine named after him, was a tireless photographer of and writer about railways. Similarly prolific and passionate in their dedication were Canon Roger Lloyd, author of, among other works, *The Fascination of Railways*, Canon Reginald Fellows, researcher into the history of *Bradshaw*, Canon Victor Whitechurch, creator of the fictional railway detective Thorpe Hazell, and Revd Wilbert Awdrey, author of the much-loved children's books about Thomas the Tank Engine and his friends. Archbishop William Temple when headmaster of Repton had a complete mental recall of Bradshaw and would set as an imposition for an errant boy the best way of travelling from Great Yarmouth to Exeter or Penrith to Ipswich without touching London, complete with changes and times. He would then correct it from memory. It was therefore entirely fitting that, in the celebrated Ealing comedy about the last age of steam, *The Titfield Thunderbolt* should be driven by the local vicar and fired by a visiting bishop.

Not sauntering but fanatically rooted to their hallowed places at the end of the 'Up' main platform in most big stations are to be found the train-spotters, living proof of George Orwell's observation that the English are a nation of collectors, in this case of train numbers. They stand, men and boys of all ages, come rain, come shine, oblivious of the seasons, clad in the regulation uniform of their breed—the anorak—with Thermos flask of coffee, spam sandwiches, bulging notebooks, and a well-thumbed Ian Allan Guide, the Bible of their cult. Incomprehensibly, there seem to be as many spotters now in the days of dull diesels and anonymous electrics as there were when we were train-spotters in the last years of steam and the trains bore names like *Bihar and Orissa, Baroda, Indore, Drake, Camperdown,* and *Barfleur*, names redolent of history and tradition, summoning up fragrant images of far-off places and the martial rattle of distant centuries.

As far as we can tell, no work has yet been done on the psychology of the train-spotter. But a number of possible motivations suggest themselves. The sexual connotation of trains is well known, particularly trains entering tunnels. Is this obsessive watching of trains sliding in and out of stations to be construed, in the child, as a substitute for sex and, in the adult, as a desire to prolong childhood indefinitely and avoid coming to terms with mature sexuality? This gives us the concept of the train-spotter as voyeur, permanent observer rather than regular participant.

But perhaps a more likely interpretation is to be found in the aspect of the hobby known as 'copping', the keeping of lists of trains seen. Is this a desire to provide order and system in a disordered universe, to give life an encompassable finite purpose? That would account for its appeal to males of all ages, and equally explain the absence of females, whose finite universe has traditionally been provided by the home, housework, and the shopping.

A third possibility is the acquisition of knowledge for its own sake in a complex modern society which values experts and regularly validates a person's standing by assessing his expertise. A boy who can demonstrate a wide range of train-spotting knowledge has cachet with his fellows, a cachet that as adolescence burgeons may well be transferred from engine numbers to the macho teenage lore of pop groups, cars, types of beer, and seduction techniques. But these are murky areas into which the unwary amateur ventures at his peril. Perhaps we should draw a veil over further speculation and simply describe train-spotting as one of those lovable British eccentricities, like garden gnomes, toy soldiers, strong tea, and talking about the weather.

Whatever the religious, psychological, or sexual significance of the station, more powerful and directly ideological forces may be at work, using the station to convey a political message. At the very least, a station often mirrors the national ethos. One cannot but be struck by the Spanishness of Toledo Station or the Dutchness of Amsterdam or the clean, bold, heroic lines of Helsinki Central, with its guardian giants so redolent of the spirit of Norse saga. On another level, the station, with its timetables, tickets, uniformed staff, and ubiquitous clocks, is an inherent supporter and encourager of discipline and order. The often-heard statement that Hitler and Mussolini made the trains run on time can be seen—in this context—as a profoundly political one. The word 'station', which originally meant simply a stopping-place, has acquired over the years a more disciplinary, structural, and organizational connotation. It is no coincidence that the most common applications of the word after railway station are police station and military station. It is also not inappropriate that the word has come to be applied to a person's position in society, with the clear implication that 'getting above your station' is somehow wrong and dangerous. All this conduces powerfully to the maintenance of the status quo.

Stations have functioned as election platforms on the whistle-stop tours of American presidents, as venues for revolutionary meetings in, for instance, Russia, and as targets for terrorist bombs, such as at Bologna. In wartime, stations have been since the days of the American

Civil War an essential element in the transportation of men and materials and consequently a military target of the first importance. Most self-consciously of all, stations have been used to glorify the regime, either through the prominence accorded to photographs of leaders like Mao or Lenin in the central stations of Peking and Leningrad or the installation of national and party banners and symbols as in the stations of Nazi Germany. The names bestowed on stations equally convey a message. In the nineteenth century Queen-Empress worship was attested in the creation of stations called Victoria in London, Manchester, Sheffield, Nottingham, Norwich, Swansea, and Bombay. Nationalist aspirations can be seen reflected in the renaming of the Dublin terminals after Irish revolutionary heroes (Connolly, Pearse, Heuston). Great military victories are recalled in London's Waterloo Station and in Paris's Gare d'Austerlitz. The very architectural styles themselves may be proclaiming a message. The stately Victoria Terminus, Bombay, 'The St Pancras of the Orient', embodies the imperishable spirit of the British Raj. At Metz, in German-occupied Alsace-Lorraine, a station was built which with its German Romanesque frontage, Teutonic warrior statues, and stained-glass images of Charlemagne deliberately aimed to stress the current political status of the province. Milan Station, designed in what one critic called 'a megalomaniac delirium', remains a monument to the ambitious and grandiose aspirations of Italian Fascism.

Emile Zola declared that 'our artists must find the poetry of stations as their fathers found that of forests and rivers' and the station has been securely enshrined in every aspect of art and culture.[20] The reality of it, the sights and sounds, the mystique and drama of the station have been filtered through the imagination of the artist. Painters have responded enthusiastically, from the meticulous realism of Frith's panoramic Paddington to the delicate impressionism of Monet's Gare Saint-Lazare, from the distorted heat-haze imagery of Dali's Perpignan Station to the lonely, austere beauty of Vlaminck's station in the snow.

Poets have apostrophized stations great and small, from London Liverpool Street to Adlestrop. In fiction, the station has been a source of solace and joy to E. Nesbit's railway children, and the scene of suicide for Tolstoy's Anna Karenina. It has been the starting-point for many a vintage Sherlock Holmes adventure—'London Bridge Station, cabby, and don't spare the horses'. The great Continental stations, Paris, Stuttgart, Vienna, Budapest, Bucharest, Constantinople, have been the beginning and ending and *en route* stopping-places in the wealth of literature inspired by that acme of railway luxury, the Orient Express, the train on which James Bond once shot a man for ordering red wine with his fish.

But it is the cinema which has blended all these different forms together to create potent and resonant imagery, a visual and aural imagery of powerful locomotives, billowing smoke, clattering rails, and melancholy train whistles, allied to the ideal dramatic potential of a mixed group of passengers thrown together by circumstance for the duration of the journey. Image after image of the station in films crowds into the memory. But it is perhaps David Lean's film of Noël Coward's *Brief Encounter* which lingers most forcefully in the mind. In this film it was at Carnforth Station in Lancashire, amid the bustle of comings and goings and the steadily hardening rock-cakes of the buffet, that the entwined lives of that most English and most gentle pair of lovers Trevor Howard and Celia Johnson reached crisis point.

On a perhaps less exalted level, the station has passed into folklore. For it was while changing trains at Reading Station that T. E. Lawrence lost the original manuscript of *The Seven Pillars of Wisdom*. It was while waiting for a train on Uxbridge Station that the sight of a poster for the Tower Furnishing Company inspired W. S. Gilbert to write *The Yeomen of the Guard*. Noël Coward was inspired to write the song 'London Pride' while standing on the platform of a London station on the morning after a particularly bad blitz and seeing Londoners going about their business 'gay and determined and wholly admirable'. The prolific popular novelist Nat Gould claimed to choose the names of his villains from the stations listed in *Bradshaw*, thus giving birth to such memorable characters as Newton Heath and Miles Platting. The station has given its name to an anxiety state, defined by Cyril Connolly as *angoisse des gares*: 'A particularly violent form of Angst. Bad when we meet someone at the station, but unbearable when we are seeing them off; not present when we are departing ourselves, but unbearable when arriving in London, if only from a day in Brighton.'[21] The station has even provided a Liverpudlian euphemism for coitus interruptus—'to get off at Edgehill'—Edgehill being the last station before Liverpool Lime Street.

Since the First World War the railways in the developed world have been in decline, their role usurped by motor transport and in particular the car. But the car has inspired no great architecture and no great art. It has conferred few benefits. It has given its owners a greater degree of mobility than they hitherto possessed but the social and environmental cost has been considerable. The centres of our old cities have been ripped apart to make way for it. The countryside has been buried under layers of concrete to facilitate its movement in ever greater numbers. Six thousand people a year are slaughtered on British roads alone, an exercise in socially sanctioned mass murder which causes comparatively little comment. The motor car is socially divisive in that while 50 per cent of the population of Britain have access to a car, the remaining 50 per cent do not and they are always the underprivileged sections of the community: the old, the young, the poor.

The difference between car and train can be summed up quite simply. The motor car is private transport, available only to its owner and his immediate circle. The train is public transport, available to the community at large. One measure of a civilized and compassionate society is the extent of its provision of public transport. Violence, materialism, and the self-centred pursuit of success at any cost are often the hallmarks of the car-dominated society, as classically exemplified by the United States, in much of which country there is virtually no public transport and the car reigns supreme, consuming lives and environment with equal ruthlessness.

It would be foolish to pretend that 'The Railway Age' was perfect. It had many faults. But it was an age which saw the slow, sure, and steady progress of social improvement and it was an age of hope, of optimistic belief in the future, unashamed aspiration for better days and better conditions in the world. The great stations stand, if they do still stand, as towering monuments to that belief, public meeting-places where faith in the perfectibility of man by his own ingenuity and the blessing of a divine providence was daily affirmed. In this respect, the oft-quoted cathedral metaphor is not inapt. Stations were cathedrals of the new technology. They were also places of hope, faith, and inextinguishable humanity, embodiments of that spirit that Charles MacKay captured so well in his poem 'Railways 1846':

> Lay down your rails, ye nations, near and far—
> Yoke your full trains to Steam's triumphant car;
> Link town to town; unite in iron bands
> The long-estranged and oft-embattled lands . . .
> Blessings on science and her handmaid Steam!
> They make Utopia only half a dream;
> And show the fervent, of capacious souls,
> Who watch the ball of progress as it rolls,
> That all as yet completed or begun,
> Is but the dawning that precedes the sun.[22]

1

The Station in Architecture (1)
Britain and Europe

THE railway station more than any other building epitomizes the spirit of the nineteenth century, in its mating of technology and architecture, industry and art, in its conscious appeal to the splendours of the past and its confident striving towards the vistas of the future. It was the nineteenth century's most distinctive contribution to building types and that century was to see the creation of the majority of the most memorable and pleasing railway stations.[1]

Many of the earliest railway stations were not purpose-built. Initially railway practices, arrangements, even rolling stock, were modelled on those of the old stage-coaches they were superseding. In the north-east of England, where railways began, old coaching inns, in for instance Shildon, Sedgefield, and South Shields, doubled as railway stations. The terminal of the Stockton and Darlington Railway at North Road, Darlington, was until 1842 a converted goods warehouse. Middlesbrough's first station was initially a dilapidated coach-shed and the Close Station at Newcastle upon Tyne was part of a disused riverside mansion. An assortment of sheds, huts, and barns, invariably scruffy, draughty, and uncomfortable, was the story elsewhere.[2]

The two earliest purpose-built stations were the termini of the world's first passenger service, the Liverpool and Manchester Railway. Both Manchester Liverpool Road and Liverpool Crown Street stations, opened in 1830, were essentially two-storey classical-style town houses, probably the work of the same architect, whose identity remains undiscovered. They followed a linear plan, oriented to the departure platform, and access to the railway line was controlled by the building, which contained the company's offices and waiting accommodation for the passengers. In form and style they set the pattern for the first generation of purpose-built station buildings.[3]

The basic elements of the station were already clear and have never changed. These are platforms for the trains, a reception and waiting area for goods and passengers, and the necessary offices for the issue of tickets and the dispensing of information, the accommodation of staff, and the relief of various human needs and functions.

Overall the station fell into two main parts: the train-shed, which was the functional area and presented the major design and engineering challenge, and the frontage, which was the public face of the railway and gave scope for the architect's imagination. The result was at its best the perfect fusion of continuity and change. As *Building News* declared in 1875: 'Railway termini and hotels are to the nineteenth century what monasteries and cathedrals were to the thirteenth century. They are truly the only representative buildings we possess.'[4] So, like the great cathedrals of the Middle Ages, stations became one of the wonders of the age. 'When Euston was first built', reported a Victorian commentator in 1896, 'it was regarded not as a railway station but as a spectacle. Visitors used to flock to it in omnibuses and examine it with the careful scrutiny of sightseers.'[5] This is not surprising, for the nineteenth century was an age which loved spectacle, in its paintings, in its theatre, and in its buildings. It was also an age of empire—not just in the concrete, narrowly political sense. It was imaginatively true also in commerce and industry, in religious and intellectual life, and in the arts. Art invariably embodies the spirit of an age and the spirit of the nineteenth century was one of exuberance, grandeur, self-confidence, and self-esteem. For European nations, everything was happening on a grand scale: industrialization, urbanization, colonization. The world was Europe's oyster. Public buildings came increasingly to reflect the size and spectacle of it all. They were the expansive visions, translated into wood, brick, stone, iron, and glass. For, as William Bodham Donne noted: 'To touch our emotions, we need not the imaginatively true, but the physically real. The visions which our ancestors saw with the mind's eye, must be embodied for us in palpable form ... all must be made palpable to sight, no less than to feeling.'[6]

The rise and rise of the railways, with the progressive increase in the volume of passengers and goods carried, led to modifications in the basic ground-plan of stations, particularly terminals. The earliest form was the one-sided station, in which arrival and departure took place on the same side. The first Manchester and Liverpool Stations and the earliest stations at St Petersburg (1837), Potsdam (1838), Vienna and Amsterdam (1839) adopted this form. But in Britain the last great one-sided station was Newcastle Central (1850), after which the form disappeared. In Germany it continued for much longer. By the middle of the nineteenth century, however, twin-sided stations, where arrival and departure took place on opposite sides, were the norm. The most important

examples of this type were London Euston (1839), Liverpool Lime
Street (1849), Paris Gare Montparnasse (1852), Paris Gare d'Austerlitz
(1862), London King's Cross (1852), London Paddington (1855), Vienna North (1856), Vienna West (1860), and Copenhagen Central (1864).
But twin-sided stations became a problem, with the increasing volume of
traffic necessitating extra intermediate platforms and presenting difficulties of access. This was resolved by the head-type, where arrival and
departure was through a head-building at the end of the tracks. This
came to dominate in the last years of the century. The French designed
the model head station, the Gare de l'Est (1852), long regarded as the
finest station in the world. The two-sided station continued to be built
throughout the 1870s, particularly in Italy and Central Europe, though
many of them had pseudo-heads, blocks built across the end to link the
wings where the main entrances were. Nevertheless its greater flexibility
ensured the eventual triumph of the head-type and many railway companies killed two birds with one stone by building a hotel to serve as
station frontage.

Where the British station developed with characteristically pragmatic,
forthright, and sometimes undisciplined adventurism, the French were
as ever busy drawing up rules, theories, definitions, and philosophies of
station-building. It was academic theory that was to define the two great
periods of French station-building which produced in the Gare de l'Est
and the Gare d'Orsay terminals which came to be regarded as definitive
types. Auguste Perdonnet published in 1856 an influential four-volume
analysis of station theory and design, the first of a number of significant
French studies.

The great train-shed, one of the glories of the nineteenth century,
lasted just as long as the century itself. It was the triumphant and majestic
application of the techniques perfected by Joseph Paxton for the Crystal
Palace (1851), an arching rib-cage of iron to support a skin-covering of
glass, admitting light but excluding the elements. It was a brilliant and
classically simple construction, which created a formal beauty of line and
curve, and facilitated constantly changing patterns of light, shade, and
steam. It was a tribute to that engineering genius which made Britain the
foremost industrial power in the world and which made engineers chiefs
in the pantheon of heroes of the new industrial age, celebrated in works
like Samuel Smiles's *Lives of the Engineers*.[7]

Sir John Dobson's Newcastle Central, begun in 1846, was the first
major station to apply the form, after which rival companies in their
unending struggle for supremacy and prestige strove to achieve ever
larger roof-spans. A single span of 211 ft. was achieved at the London

and North-Western Railway's Grand Central Station, Birmingham (later renamed New Street) in 1854. The Great Western Railway's Paddington (1854) attained 238 ft. St Pancras train-shed, described in 1868 as 'the greatest in the world', was 700 ft. long, 100 ft. high, and 240 ft. wide. But the companies strove on, ringing the changes in design, from pointed to rounded to curved to semicircular to double, seeking ever larger spans: Hanover (1879), 282 ft.; Frankfurt am Main (1888), 549 ft.; Leipzig (1915), 964 ft. In some stations the train-shed became the central feature, an eye-catching shape dwarfing an insignificant frontage: thus, for instance Manchester Central (1880), 210 ft., and Liverpool Central (1874), 169 ft. Despite John Ruskin's strictures ('Such works as . . . the iron roofs and pillars of our railway stations . . . are not architecture at all'), it is now generally admitted that not only are they architecture but they are also works of art.[8] Eloquent testimony of this is to be found in John Gay's magnificent photographs of London terminals, depicting, for instance, the forest of columns, arches, and metallic tracery supporting the roof of Liverpool Street Station and the perfect form and line of Brunel's 'all interior, all roofed-in' Paddington, achievements that could leave only the most die-hard curmudgeon unmoved.

Stylistically the railway station was the epitome of the aesthetic doctrine of picturesque eclecticism. This doctrine strove above all else for visual effect. Revelling in colour and contrast, drama and dissonance, boldness and individualism, it was the architectural legacy of Romanticism. Romanticism liberated the imagination, exalted the emotions, gloried in mystery and fantasy, dreams and visions. It was the appropriate mode for an age of spectacle and empire. The railway station became a focus for an outpouring of this feeling. It can thus be seen to stand as the architectural counterpart to the other key artistic expressions of the age, the panoramic canvases of John Martin, Edward John Poynter, and Lawrence Alma-Tadema, toweringly romantic and imaginative recreations of the temples, palaces, baths, and amphitheatres of the ancient world, and the novels of Walter Scott, Harrison Ainsworth, and Bulwer-Lytton which evoked a monumental and teeming past of medieval castles, Tudor mansions, and unbridled Gothic imagination. The railway station, in its incarnation as latter-day cathedral, castle, and caravanserai, was yet one more gigantic stage on which drama could daily unfold, casts of thousands could cavort, and modern technology could display its marvels and miracles.

Carroll Meeks, the doyen of station architecture historians, discerns four distinct periods in the era of picturesque eclecticism—the emulation of one style (1830–50), the synthesis of many (1850s), the take-off to creativity (1860–90), and finally megalomania (1890–1914). Initially, as might be expected, the classical form prevailed—the station as Greek or Roman temple—with Amsterdam Willemspoort (1843), Newcastle Central (1850), and Huddersfield (1850) notable examples. But perhaps the most memorable example of the classical mode in station architecture was Euston's Doric Arch, designed by Philip Hardwick (1850). As Christian Barman wrote in 1950:

The railway builders were moved by the spirit of the conqueror and nowhere is this spirit more clearly visible than in the portico of Euston. Moving south-wards for the attack on London we can see that they understood the greatness of their mission. And so when finally they had invaded the greatest city in the world, they built the portico at Euston to proclaim as a memorial their victory to posterity. For this portico, though designed in the manner for porches attached to buildings, is by virtue of its starkly isolated position a genuine military *arc de triomphe*.[9]

Its demolition in 1962, still the most wanton act of vandalic savagery in what has become a century of architectural barbarism, signalled con-clusively the end of the age of giants and the arrival of the age of pygmies.

The big city stations of the nineteenth century reflected to the full the Victorians' unashamed belief in monumentality. In the case of the railway companies, it was a belief derived from a number of sources. In the first instance it stemmed from an understandable utilization of familiar forms to furnish a reassuring and acceptable face for the new means of loco-motion and thus allay the fears of travellers for whom speed was a new and potentially alarming phenomenon. It was the beneficent by-product of competition between companies, each trying to outdo its rivals in visible splendour and architectural might. It stemmed too from the desire of an *arriviste* industry to gain respectability and prestige, from the adoption of the idea of the station as civic adornment, a public building worthy to rank with the town hall, the assize court, and the public library. No expense was spared to produce a station worthy to stand beside the other civic buildings. A reported £690,000 was spent on Dresden Station (1898), £1,300,000 on Cologne (1894), and £1,700,000 on Frankfurt (1888).[10] Even quite small companies parted with large sums to ensure that at the end of the line the fare-paying public would be greeted by an imposing terminal. Both the Maryport and Carlisle Railway Company and the notoriously impecunious West Lancashire Railway contrived to build handsome Tudor-Gothic mansions at Maryport and Southport (Central) respectively.

The feelings that the companies set out to instil with such buildings

—admiration, respect, and confidence—are perfectly mirrored in the comment of Dionysius Lardner in *Railway Economy* (1850):

It is impossible to regard the vast buildings and their dependencies which constitute a chief terminal station of a great line of railway without feelings of inexpressible astonishment at the magnitude of the capital and the boldness of the enterprise which are manifested in the operations of which they are the stage. Nothing in the history of the past affords any parallel to such a spectacle.[11]

The classical phase of station-building was overtaken in Britain by the Italian villa style, which became so popular, particularly for country stations, by 1844 that the *Illustrated London News* could say 'the style has been called Italian; it might be designated more properly an English railway style'.[12] At its grandest it produced the Italian *palazzo*: Chester General (1848) or Dublin Amiens Street (1844). Gordon Biddle, author of the definitive study of Victorian stations in England and Wales, has observed:

There is no question that well designed Italianate lent itself admirably to that display of powerful dignity which the railways were currently trying to achieve. Full advantage was taken of sloping ground, or . . . a broad forecourt, to increase the effect. Nowhere was this better achieved than at Shoreditch in 1840, where Sancton Wood built the Eastern Counties Railway terminus on arches above street level. At the end of the spacious triple-arched trainshed a heavily corniced three-storey frontage block was built at the head of twin flights of balustraded stairs rising to the entrance on the first floor. In front, a broad cab-drive, also balustraded, swept round in a wide semi-circle setting off the entrance to perfection.[13]

The arch motif, classically seen at Euston, is the symbol of the triumph of the railways, the arrival, consolidation, and dominance of the new mode of transport. It takes the form not just of arched entrances, as at Brussels Midi (1869), Zurich North-East (1873), and Budapest East (1881), but also of arched lunette windows which define the building they pierce, as in the Paris stations Gare de l'Est (1852), Gare Montparnasse (1852), and Gare du Nord (1864), and at London King's Cross (1852). The arch was to remain one of the important station motifs but it was to be matched and surpassed by the tower. The tower, like the spire, a symbol of aspiration, the striving for greater achievement, supersedes the complacency of the arch, to epitomize an era of expansion, competition, and further advance. It also had a functional role. The dominant type of station in the early period tended to be long and low, and 'picturesque theory' condemned such buildings as monotonous. The application of towers dramatically broke up the monotony, as in Francis Thompson's Chester General and P. C. Hardwick's Royal Great Western Hotel, Paddington. Monotony was a cardinal sin for Victorian architects, just as it is the predominant defining characteristic of modern architecture.

During the 1860s came the take-off to creativity. Meeks writes:

Stations ... embodied the triumph of the picturesque eclectic aesthetic in complex massing, bolder asymmetry, pointed vaults and towers. Eclecticism had escaped from the control of the revivalists into its more creative synthetic phase. Verticality was in unchallenged supremacy in England and America. On the Continent, station architects tended to be more restrained than their English-speaking colleagues, more prone to arches than towers, but they were not unaffected by the new aesthetic and clung to it longer.[14]

The finest product of this take-off period was St Pancras Station, whose frontage was provided by the Midland Grand Hotel. St Pancras was the undisputed King, or more properly Queen-Empress, of stations. 'St George for England, St Pancras for Scotland' went the joke, unconsciously bestowing on the station a symbolic national status—something Sir Thomas Beecham also did when he declared Elgar's First Symphony 'the St Pancras among the symphonies'. Both jokes contain, as jokes frequently do, an essential truth, seeing St Pancras as the symbol of an empire at its height and of an age of aspiration and achievement.

Sir George Gilbert Scott, a passionate exponent of the Gothic style, had been forced against his will and to his lasting fury to provide an Italianate design for the Foreign Office at the insistence of the Prime Minister, Lord Palmerston. Commissioned by the Midland Railway Company to design the St Pancras Station Hotel, he poured all his fervour, invention, and imagination into his designs. Completed in 1876, the hotel was extolled in its day—one commentator called it 'the most perfect in every possible respect in the world'—and came to be vilified in the twentieth century as a monument to Victorian bad taste.[15] Now it is once again receiving its due meed of praise. Alan A. Jackson, in his careful, thorough study of London termini, expressed the new revised standpoint:

With its castellated fringes, scores of dormer windows (each with finial), its myriad pointed-arch windows below the cornice, the multitude of chimneys on its steeply-pitched roofs, and its every corner marked by spirelet or pinnacle, the Midland Grand Hotel was one of the finest and largest examples of high Victorian secular Gothic. From the elaborate *porte cochère* at the West end, the 565 foot frontage curved back and round to parallel the Euston Road, terminating in a 270 foot spire-capped clock tower which was a worthy rival of that of

Barry and Pugin at Westminister . . . Over the elevations, Edward Gripper's patent bricks were varied with dressings in several different kinds of stone, and red and grey Peterhead granite. Frontage and skyline together offered a treasury of delights and surprises.[16]

St Pancras typifies on the grandest scale the tendency for big city stations to be fronted by hotels. As Donald J. Olsen has written: 'With the possible exception of Canada, Britain has seen a closer relationship between railways and hotels than any other country.'[17] This association was far from being universal. In Spain, for instance, no railway station had a hotel attached and passengers often had a long distance to travel from stations to reach their ultimate destination. The first British railway company to provide hotel accommodation was the London and Birmingham at Euston in 1838–9. The arch was already built, so the hotel was constructed in two separate buildings, the Victoria Hotel and the Euston Hotel, each side of the entrance. Basically an unremarkable set of Regency terrace houses, it was notable only for having 350 windows. Initially the two wings were linked by a tunnel, but in 1880 they were joined by a six-storey addition. The railway company always intended to lease the Euston as a first-class hotel but tried at first to run the Victoria itself. This was eventually leased too. In 1843 the Corsican hotelier Zenon Vantini leased them, achieving such success that he went on to establish the first railway refreshment room at Wolverton. At the other end of the London and Birmingham line, part of the Birmingham terminal, Curzon Street Station, was converted into the Queen's Hotel in 1839.

The station hotels at Euston and Curzon Street were exceptions in the 1830s but by the 1840s hotel accommodation had become an essential part of the planning of new railway stations. Among the first was the Midland Hotel at Derby Trijunct Station. Begun in 1840, it was designed for the North Midland Railway by the station's architect Francis Thompson. Built of fine red brick, it was modelled on a country house, set in its own grounds and boasting an ornamental fountain in the forecourt. The initial necessity for building railway stations on the outskirts of towns caused other companies to adopt the country-house model, with the idea that passengers would spend the night there before beginning their journey or after arriving. It is precisely this sort of arrangement—'rooms had been taken there because they were to start by an early train on that line in the morning'—that leads to a fraught dinner party for Clara Amedroz and the two rivals for her hand at the Great Northern Hotel, King's Cross, in Anthony Trollope's *The Belton Estate* (1865).

From the 1850s, with stations moving to inner-city sites, station hotels assumed palatial aspects and the railway companies set the standard for others to follow. Lewis Cubitt's Great Northern Hotel at King's Cross (1854) was a modest Regency crescent. But P. C. Hardwick's Great Western Royal Hotel, which opened in the same year to provide the frontage to Paddington Station, was perhaps the earliest major building in Britain to show marked French Renaissance influence. Its external grandeur was matched by an enviable internal efficiency, facilitated by the most up-to-date equipment, including fireproof staircases, electric clocks, and an elaborate system of bells. It is interesting to observe how frequently the French style prevails not just in the building of hotels but in the whole 'architecture of pleasure' in Britain. It is as if somehow the puritanical, work-obsessed British associated the idea of 'pleasure' with the saucy, sinful Continent.

The High Victorian hotels shared the exuberance of the stations proper. The full monumental style with towers, chimneys, spires, and mansard roofs was represented by the South-Eastern Railway's terminal hotels at Charing Cross (1864) and Cannon Street (1866), both designed by E. M. Barry, and Alfred Waterhouse's magnificent Lime Street Chambers, Liverpool (1867). Gilbert Scott's Midland Grand Hotel, St Pancras (1876), enjoyed the distinction of being the most expensive of all railway hotels, charging 14 shillings a night for a room, dinner, breakfast, and attendance in 1879.

The passing of the Limited Liability Act in 1863 made the 1860s a boom period in hotel building and there was a considerable amount of resort station-hotel building. Notable examples included the gloriously Gothic Duke of Cornwall Hotel next to Plymouth Station (1863) and the yellow-brick Italianate Zetland Hotel (1862) at Saltburn-by-Sea. Built next to the station, with direct access from it and with rooms at economical prices, it was a deliberate attempt by the Stockton and Darlington Railway Company to facilitate the development of the resort.[18]

From the 1860s the companies increasingly used standardized designs for their country stations, partly for economy and partly to promote a corporate image after a series of company amalgamations which had produced the great conglomerates which were to dominate the railway scene until the 1923 grouping. But many of these stations were pleasingly executed. The London, Brighton and South Coast Railway built a series of sedate two-storey Italianate villas along the Sussex coast. The Great Western Railway built a series of French Renaissance style miniature châteaux with two or three flat-topped pavilion roofs decorated with intricate iron trellis-work. The Furness Railway favoured Swiss-chalet type stone and timber buildings. On the Settle and Carlisle line, the Midland Railway opted for single-storey buildings, with twin-gabled pavilions, linked by a central section that housed a recessed waiting area. A not dissimilar design was used by the Highland Railway in Scotland.[19]

In many cases the use of local materials imparted to country stations a distinctive regional flavour. Jack Simmons recalled them:

a tile-hung front at Oakley Station, west of Basingstoke; knapped flint at Trowse, by Norwich; Midland brick on the Syston and Peterborough line, at Brooksby, Oakham, Manton . . . pretty Broseley tiles to enliven the waiting-room at Shrub Hill station in Worcester; the diaper of blue bricks (a local speciality) on red in the North Staffordshire's Elizabethan stations; fierce and unrelieved Accrington brick at Bolton, and elsewhere up and down Lancashire.[20]

While big city stations in Britain were adopting French Renaissance or Gothic styles, Germany was creating its own distinctive form, which combined the ground plan of the French station with the form of a Romanesque cathedral. Early examples were Munich (1849) and Karlsruhe (1842). Berlin rebuilt many of its stations in this style, notably the Stettiner Bahnhof (1876) and Anhalter Bahnhof (1880). The former, with its three curved arches under a curved roof, flanked by twin towers, was truly the idealized epitome of the station as medieval cathedral. A second group of stations opted for a free version of *cinquecento* baroque—Berlin Potsdamer Bahnhof (1872), Mannheim (1876), Budapest East (1876), Zurich (1871), and Brunswick (1848). The Italians during the same period, aiming for a distinctive national style, succeeded in producing at Turin, Trieste, Naples, Milan, and Rome a series of unremarkable and uninteresting stations.

The 1890s saw the triumph of megalomania as size took over and passengers and tracks increased in number. The station for the new age was Victor Laloux's Gare d'Orsay in Paris, whose opening was timed for the 1900 Paris Exposition. It was reached by two miles of track through a tunnel along the banks of the Seine from the Gare d'Austerlitz. It utilized electric trains and there was no smoke. In consequence there was no train-shed. Vestibule, waiting-rooms, and concourse were all in one and topped by a graceful vault with ample skylights. Enormous archways provided the entrances and the total bulk was increased by a hotel. The Gare d'Orsay like the Gare de l'Est before it was regarded as *the* model station and strongly influenced others, notably Hamburg (1906), Copenhagen Central (1911), and the two New York stations, Pennsylvania and Grand Central. Some, however, have found the so-called 'Beaux-Arts' style, for all its academic rigour and perfection of proportion to be too correct, bloodless, and buttoned-up when set against the free-flowing eclecticism of some other contemporary stations.

The absence of a train-shed from the Gare d'Orsay was symptomatic of the change about to overtake station-building. The era of the great train-shed more or less ended with the Great War. Its final phase was dominated by German stations. The new Frankfurt am Main station, completed in 1888, was planned to replace and combine the functions of three existing Frankfurt stations on a single site on the city outskirts. It had a triple train-shed, designed symbolically to perpetuate the identities of the three regions formerly served by the three redundant terminals. The single head-house at the end symbolized the new unity of the German State. More ominously its size and capacity also took into consideration future military needs. Its style inspired a new family of glass-roofed stations, notably Cologne (1894), Basle (1904), and Hamburg (1906). But Hamburg was the last of the great glass train-sheds. For in 1904 Lincoln Bush patented the Bush shed and installed the first at the Hoboken station of the Delaware, Lackawanna and Western Railroad in 1906. These sheds were low, single spans of rein-forced concrete, covering two lines of track and half a platform on each side. They were cheap to install, economical to maintain, and by 1914 twelve stations had them. The Bush shed was in turn supplanted by an even more abbreviated form, the butterfly shed, which covered only the platforms. It was the decisive end of an imagination whose bounds had been set wider and wider, the doom of the crystal palaces of the rails, the ferrovitreous stables of the champing iron horses. As earthbound con-crete replaced shimmering glass, so crude functionalism was to supplant soaring aspiration.

It was not to be long before the same truncation of aspiration, the same deadening of the imagination affected frontages too. There was, how-ever, a late flowering of the picturesque in Europe, an orchidaceous *fin de siècle* efflorescence. In Central Europe this showed the influence of Art Nouveau and a generation of stations appeared with soft curves, voluptuous domes, rounded arches flanked by pylons, surmounted by statues, urns, and spheres, and decorated with filigree intricacy. These were the high-class European courtesans among stations, glittering, sensual, elegant, veritable Mata Haris and Lola Monteses among ter-minals, the architectural equivalents of Zola's Nana, Manet's Olympe, and Dumas *fils*'s Camille, complete with fans, pendants, and feather boas rendered in stone. They were also regularly penetrated day and night by a variety of trains of different lengths and sizes. Georg Frentzen's

Bucharest Central (1895) and Cologne (1894) and C. F. Müller's Dresden (1898) stood out in this group. But this 'naughty nineties' flavour reached even the stolid and respectable Low Countries. Louis de la Censerie's Antwerp Central (1899) was a courtesan made good, like one of those Edwardian showgirls who married into the aristocracy. The curving shapes are there but she is in her Sunday best, positively dripping in spires, swags, pilasters, finials, and coats of arms, the better to proclaim her respectability and superiority. But then the Low Countries were prone to the occasional architectural brainstorm, such as the remarkable Saint-Pierre Station, Ghent (1912). It is an Oriental mirage, a full-blown castellated and minareted North African Bey's palace. Surmounted by a slender clock-tower, which summoned the Belgian bourgeoisie to rendezvous with the trains as surely as any muezzin summoning the faithful to prayer, it looks for all the world as if it has been transported by some mischievous jinn on a magic carpet. But it can perhaps be seen as an architectural expression of that scented *fin de siècle* fascination with the Near East that produced in this period such works as Massenet's opera *Thaïs* and Strauss's *Salome* and the luxuriant novels of Pierre Loti and Pierre Louys.

However, many of the new stations began to feature a strongly marked nationalism as the assertive spirits of rival nations jostled with each other and advanced their claims for continental dominance with increasing stridency. This bugles-and-banners stridency, drowning out the elegant salon music of pre-war Europe's Indian summer, culminated inexorably in the Great War and the subsequent rise of Fascist dictatorships. The volkist spirit, matrix of the future Nazism, is detectable in the heavily Teutonic exteriors of Karlsruhe (1913), Oldenburg (1915), and Stuttgart (begun in 1911, completed in 1928). All of them look to have been constructed from set designs for Fritz Lang's cinematic version of the *Nibelungenlied*, one of the favourite films of the Führer: rough-hewn temples and folk-moot halls embodying an exaltation of the primitive Teutonic spirit.

But nationalist styles were springing up everywhere. In Scotland, stations like Aboyne and Dundee Caledonian Station were built in the distinctive Scottish baronial style. But in recognition of Scotland's turbulent history, the Norse barn style was adopted for the far northern stations of Thurso and Wick. In Spain, the Madrid, Saragossa and Alicante Railway created a series of handsome two-storey *palacio* stations, topped by prominent decorated clocks (Carthagena, Murcia). They achieved a masterpiece in the Moorish style in the Plaza de Armes Station, Seville (1901), an element of the Iberian past also alluded to in the Moorish elements on the grand Romantic façade of Lisbon's Rossio Station.

Copenhagen Central (1911) was strongly nationalist. A long, low, red terracotta building, it featured steep-pitched roof and clock-crowned central tower, rising above a graceful colonnaded entrance and flanked by smaller turrets. It had all the rugged grandeur of the sea-girt castle of a medieval Danish warrior-king. In Belgium, Bruges Station (1889) was designed in Flemish Gothic style, half castle and half cathedral. Solid, castellated, and colonnaded for much of its length, it suddenly takes off into a free-flowing fantasy of spires and spirelets, as if two different architects' designs had got mixed up on the drawing-board.

In Holland, P. J. H. Cuypers's handsome Amsterdam Central (1889) set a fashion for Dutch Renaissance. Elsewhere, other architects built in similar style stations at The Hague (1893), Groningen and Nijmegen (1894), and the magnificent castle-station at 's Hertogenbosch (1896). In Tsarist Russia, two different traditions stood side by side, as befitted a country straddling two continents. There was a fondness for the strict classical style, as seen in Moscow Kiev Station, affirming a desire to be recognized as a fully-fledged European power. But in the design of Moscow's Riga and Yaroslavl Stations, Russia looked to the other strand of her heritage—the East, producing veritable Oriental fantasies. These stations embodied heady dreams from the steppes of Central Asia, the palaces of Tartar Khans, rich, ornate, barbaric, a fitting arena for Polovtsian dances and processions of the sirdars.

The best known of this nationalist group, finished in 1914 but not put into use until after the war, is Eliel Saarinen's Helsinki. Hailed as a modern masterpiece, it drew on the basic elements of nineteenth-century picturesque—towers, pavilions, arches, and vaults—but gave them a distinct Scandinavian feel and line, the spirit of the sagas, as embodied in the gigantic statues at the entrance. Perhaps the most overweening statement of nationalism in station architecture, however, is Milan Station, begun in 1920 and opened in 1930. With its 700-feet-long façade and 600-feet-long *porte cochère*, it is the last word in grandiose monumentalism. Encrusted with statues, pillars, and reliefs, it looks like a huge wedding cake in stone. Inside, the booking hall was 210 ft. long, 110 ft. wide, and 140 ft. high, with glass roof, stained-glass windows, and multicoloured marble walls. Candelabra flanked the staircases leading to the main concourse, which was 700 ft. long and 72 ft. wide, decorated in rose Baveno granite and polished Travertina. The whole thing had the feel of a palace of some mad potentate, a train-obsessed latter-day equivalent of Ludwig of Bavaria, perhaps.[21]

The Great War more or less put an end to the era of the great station
and with it the period of the pre-eminence of the railways. The system
had reached its greatest extent in route mileage and the grand stations
had all been built. What station-building remained was increasingly to
reflect the functional, geometrical approach, stressing cubes and cylinders and glorying in reinforced concrete. There was more to it than just a
change of style. The Great War had witnessed the death of a world and
a world order. The age of palaces and cathedrals, of ancient dynasties
and stratified aristocracies, of emperors and imperial proconsuls, of
gaudy uniforms and chivalric orders, the world of the Habsburgs, the
Hohenzollerns, the Romanovs, and the Elphbergs had crumbled. In
England revolution had been avoided by the widening of the magic circle
to admit the bourgeoisie. Public schools created a ruling élite, brewers
entered the peerage, and the middle classes travelled by train. They
clothed themselves in the respectability of ancient forms, just like the
railways. In the ruins of the world of age-old aristocratic dominance and
comfortable bourgeois certainty, a new world stirred. The age of the
common man dawned. A new style was devised for the new age. It
emerged as flat, functional, unadorned, lacking in scale or grandeur, and
glorying in the new materials—concrete, plastic, and steel. There were
new sources of inspiration. Where the palace, the temple, and the
cathedral had inspired their Victorian predecessors, British station-
builders of the inter-war years chose more 'democratic' models—the
cinema (Surbiton), the bank (Exmouth), and, with unintended irony, the
garage (West Monkseaton). They in their turn were to give way after the
Second World War to the models of the bus-shelter, the airport, and the
office-block, the ultimate in bankruptcy of imagination.

The railway industry had a propaganda purpose in the streamlining of outlines and in the new doctrine of modernism in these years.
Streamlining implied speed and, in increasingly acute competition
with road transport, the railways' commitment to superior speed
needed to be stressed constantly. The use of new materials and new
geometric shapes, shorn of 'redundant' decoration, implied a lean, fit,
up-to-date industry, rather than one revelling in a pre-war Victorian
complacency.

There was a self-conscious rejection of the Victorians' lavish
ornamentalism and revivalist eclecticism. But it took the form of an
insufferable élitist arrogance, a blanket rejection of 'Victorian taste',
largely because it was bourgeois, emotional, and—most reprehensible of
all—popular, even with the unenlightened masses. Roger Fry, archetype
of the new breed of self-appointed high priests of modernism, gave voice

to his philosophy in a celebrated essay, published in 1937. Firstly, the masses are dismissed out of hand:

> We must face the fact that the average man has two qualities . . . He has first of all a touching proclivity to awe-struck admiration of whatever is presented to him as noble by a constituted authority; and, secondly, a complete absence of any immediate reaction to a work of art until his judgement has thus been hypnotized by the voice of authority . . . I am speaking . . . of a populace whose emotional life has been drugged by the sugared poison of pseudo-art.

Next, the things ordinary people like are dismissed as vulgar. Fry deliberately wrote the next part of his essay in a railway refreshment room ('One must remember that public places of this kind merely reflect the average citizen's soul, as expressed in his home'). Oozing with contempt, he proceeds to list the room's decoration: the stained-glass windows, patterned lace curtains, Greco-Roman wall mouldings, imitation eighteenth-century satin brocade wallpaper, potted plants, neatly arranged tables.

> This painful catalogue makes up only a small part of the inventory of the 'art' of the restaurant . . . I say their contemplation can give no-one pleasure; they are there because their absence would be resented by the average man who regards a large amount of futile display as in some way inseparable from the conditions of that well-to-do life to which he belongs or aspires to belong. If everything were merely clean and serviceable he would proclaim the place bare and uncomfortable.[22]

Poor average man, cast into outer darkness because he likes what he likes and has the temerity to prefer a little diverting decoration to soulless functionalism. Fry, perhaps consciously, was echoing the views of the foremost artistic panjandrum of a previous age. He wrote in 1849:

> Another of the strange and evil tendencies of the present day is to the decoration of the railroad station. Now, if there be any place in the world in which people are deprived of that portion of temper and discretion which are necessary to the contemplation of beauty, it is there. It is the very temple of discomfort, and the only charity that the builder can extend to us is to show us, plainly as may be, how soonest to escape from it. The whole system of railroad travelling is addressed to people, who, being in a hurry, are therefore, for the time being, miserable. No one would travel in that manner who could help it—who had time to go leisurely over hills and between hedges, instead of through tunnels and between banks; at least those who would, have no sense of beauty so acute that we need to consult it at the station. The railroad is in all its relations a matter of earnest business, to be got through as soon as possible. It transmutes a man from a traveller into a living parcel. For the time he has parted

with the nobler characteristics of his humanity for the sake of a planetary power of locomotion. Do not ask him to admire anything. You might as well ask the wind. Carry him safely, dismiss him soon; he will thank you for nothing else. All attempts to please him in any other way are mere mockery, and insults to the things by which you endeavour to do so. There never was more flagrant nor impertinent folly than the smallest portion of ornament in anything concerned with railroads or near them. Keep them out of the way, take them through the ugliest country you can find, confess them the miserable things they are, and spend nothing on them but for safety and speed ... Better bury gold in the embankments, than put it in ornaments on the stations.[23]

The words are, of course, those of John Ruskin, self-confessed enemy of railways and all their works.

Modern architects were to take a savage and unimaginable revenge on the average man for his rejection of their 'we know best' anti-humanist ethic. For by the 1950s and 1960s, with the connivance of money-grubbing speculators and complacent politicians, their theories had become architectural orthodoxy. As a result monstrous tower blocks, not fit for human souls, were erected to replace the neat streets of individual terraced houses, vast impersonal motorways supplanted the agreeably irregular network of real roads, and as part of the dehumanization process, the great railway stations, the local cinemas, and the corner shops, the familiar landmarks of a lifetime, were swept away. The result was a desolation of the environment and the spirit; identikit Gulag estates, ravaged and abandoned inner cities, stifling individuality, deadening the imagination and provoking in the young an instinctive if unarticulated rage against their surroundings.

The inevitable course of this new aesthetic can be charted in the railway station. There were in France some memorable new stations: a group like Noyon (1929) and Deauville (1930) in a sturdy Norman provincial style with half-timbering, heavy roof-beams, a steep ridge-and-furrow roof and dormer windows; Rouen's Gare de l'Ouest (1928) with an elegant arched frontage, an elaborate clock-tower, and twin statues supporting the central pediment, presenting a stylized refinement of *fin de siècle* forms; the Gare des Bénédictins, Limoges (1923), with its dome, rounded rowers, and half-naked statuary, looking back defiantly to the ornate voluptuousness of the vanished pre-war courtesans. But le Havre and Cherbourg opted for a simple and austere classicism, with the new vogue for geometrical emphasis to the fore. The future lay with Amstel and Muiderpoort in Holland (1939), two stations which created a great stir for their up-to-date functionalism of form and line. The progressive de-stationization of the terminal can be seen in all the eagerly hailed landmarks of twentieth-century station-building: Florence (1936), Finland Tampere (1933), and pre-eminently the Stazioni Termini in Rome, completed in 1951 and proclaimed by Meeks 'the finest modern station to date' and by Pevsner 'the best European station of the last half century'. With its glass and metal screen, protected by floating cantilevered roof, its cold, clinical corridors and public rooms, it is Metropolis or Alphaville, the lifeless, emotionless city of the future. 'C'est magnifique, mais ce n'est pas la gare.' But there have been worse experiences since then, the ultimate loss of identity in the faceless, featureless blocks that have risen to replace individualized and characterful termini: Rotterdam Central (1957), Munich (1963), Leningrad Finland Station (1960), London Euston (1968), Paris Gare Montparnasse (1969), Berne Central (1974), Warsaw Central (1975), and Milton Keynes (1983).

Since the Second World War it has all been downhill. One only has to compare the uniformity of contemporary stations with the richness, profusion, and variety in British nineteenth-century stations: the classical temple of Huddersfield, the Byzantine basilica of Blackfriars, the robust Jacobean manor-house of Stoke-on-Trent, the scholarly Jacobean collegiate buildings of Shrewsbury and Carlisle, the 'Russian dacha' of Petworth, the 'baroque orangery' of Newmarket, the airy French pavilion of Slough, the medieval Gothic abbey of Battle, the Queen Anne town house of Market Harborough and Birkenhead Woodside, so much like the great hall of a medieval house that one expects rushes on the floor, minstrels in the gallery, and foaming tankards of old ale. Since the unforgivable primal sin was to be boring, the Victorians gave us intricate wrought-iron work, sculpted columns, mullioned windows, stained glass, mosaic floors, tiled maps, delicate *portes cochères*, exquisite stone tracery, clock-towers, crenellations, campaniles, wood-panelled booking halls, friezes, glass canopies, triumphal arches, balustrades, gables, chimneys, turrets, spires, drinking-fountains, ornate platform seats, coats of arms, baronial fireplaces, even majestic gentlemen's conveniences in monumental marble or bold ironwork, a constant and unending source of delight in a craftsmanship at its most complex, painstaking, and delicate.

To protect and preserve this unimaginably rich architectural and design heritage is a matter of the utmost urgency. But the devastation already wrought in it is heartrending to contemplate. In Britain alone, Glasgow St Enoch's was torn down in European Architectural Heritage Year (1975); Birmingham Snow Hill was allowed to rot for years and finally demolished on safety grounds, epitomizing a technique in all too frequent use—deliberate and wanton neglect given as a justification for removal. As Marcus Binney and David Pearce put it: 'since its establishment in 1947 British Rail has acquired for itself an all too deserved reputation as the biggest corporate vandal and iconoclast Britain has seen since the Tudor dissolution of the monasteries'.[24]

But even before 1947 there were straws in the wind. Christian Barman, who had written of Britain's country stations 'No country in the world has a collection of minor stations that can begin to compare with ours for sheer quality', prepared for the Great Western Railway just after the war a detailed prospectus for the modernization and transformation of the company's image, operations, and buildings after the lifting of wartime restrictions.[25] He was able with cheerful equanimity to contemplate the removal of Paddington Station:

> That many will miss the old Paddington of Brunel and Wyatt and Paxton with its aisles and transepts, and its slim wrought iron arabesques, is . . . certain. London will be the poorer for its passing; yet London requires that it must go.[26]

Happily, Paddington still stands but a number of other great London stations are under threat and the list of great British stations to have bitten the dust is already too long. There have been some notable conservation conversions, with the Gare d'Orsay in Paris, for instance, becoming an exhibition hall. But for every triumph there are a thousand tragedies.

The Railway Companies' Report on the modernization of station amenities, published in 1944, listed the requirements of the well-designed station:

(i) The highest possible operating convenience and efficiency;
(ii) Easy and direct means of access and egress for passengers and vehicles;
(iii) The standardization of construction and equipment as far as the site and circumstances permit;
(iv) Its immediate recognition as a railway station within the limits of harmony with its surrounding.[27]

Whatever else the planners may have done, they have disastrously lost sight of the last of these objectives.

2

The Station in Architecture (2)
The Americas

United States of America

NO railway system in the world experienced such a spectacular growth, achieved such a startling apogee in the first two decades of this century, followed by such a dramatic decline as that of the United States.[1] Railways somehow symbolized the fact that Americans never did anything by halves, and this was more than borne out by the architecture of American railway stations. Starting from the simplest and most chaste of forms, rooted in a combination of pioneering vernacular and colonial buildings, the American station swiftly moved on to a riot of revivalist and hybrid styles in a complex process of architectural grafting which mirrored the increasingly diverse origins of its immigrant population. Attempts to simplify this, particularly in the vogue for a massive Romanesque style in the 1880s, foundered on the sheer scope of station-building continent-wide, and the range of experimentation which arose from the repeated station renewal of railway companies whose exaggerated energy and corporate conceit were to endanger their own survival. The station represented as much as any other architectural form the megalomania of American capitalism in the first two decades of this century. The dramatic growth of the late nineteenth century, slowed by the depression of the middle years of the 1890s, but renewed between 1900 and 1910, was expected to continue. The railway companies built stations to accommodate passengers who never materialized, to flatter a vanity which was shortly to meet its fall in the face of both economic recession and the rise of alternative modes of transportation. When self-regard is so shatteringly undermined, the symbols of a former shaky greatness become almost an affront. So American railway companies turned on the stations which had impaired their financial health and destroyed many of them in an excess of architectural vandalism.

The nineteenth-century railway history of the United States was dominated by a number of themes which were dramatically reflected in the railway stations. The first was the battles of various railroad companies to enter cities. Each town and city suffered a proliferation of unconnected lines, each with their termini in different quarters. The second was the problem of bridging major rivers, which left the railways almost literally suspended on their banks with temporary terminal stations leading to steamer river crossings. The third was the inevitable period of amalgamation when thrusting American capitalism was to embark on the creation of the railway cartels which were to lead some to cry 'monopoly' by the turn of the century. A vogue for urban planning developed in the early years of this century, and many American cities were the subjects of Civic Plans. In this period, the multiple stations of the various companies were demolished in many cities, and were replaced by large 'Union' stations. Whereas the railways in the past had been an integral part of the cityscape, running down main streets, leaving in their wake a succession of railroad crossings on the classic American street grid plan, by the turn of the century they were already disappearing behind fences, into cuttings, or underground, a process which was to be speeded up in the years leading to the First World War. New types of station were called for.

If in the East the country's development had sometimes run ahead of the railways, as in the great boom decade of the 1850s, in the West the railways *were* the country's development. The railway there brought towns into being, and led to the laying out of and rapid escalation in value of town lots. In securing huge government land grants as an inducement to build, the railways became the prime engine of migration, transporting the migrants, acting as land agents, supplying their machinery, building materials, and seed, and later shipping (a word which developed land-bound connotations) their produce. By the last two or three decades of the nineteenth century the railway stations of the Eastern states were analogous to those of the imperial metropoles in Europe, while those of the West seemed like colonial stations. The difference was, of course, that they shared the same land mass, and were directly connected to each other by transcontinental tracks.

But the western railway dreams encompassed much more than the settling of immigrants or the taming of native peoples (throughout the world railways were credited with this 'pacificatory' role). They were about 'closing the map', creating a great continental empire which the Russians were to seek to emulate in the 1880s and 1890s. And both the American westward and the Russian eastward expansion had, of course, the same destination: the Orient. Americans and Russians sought to outflank the great European shipping routes. European manufacturers could reach the Orient faster by swift crossings of the Atlantic and the

Pacific connected by the American transcontinental lines. And eventually they could be replaced by American products. For Russia the prize was to command railway routes connecting, it was hoped, Calais to Calcutta or Amsterdam to the Amur. But if Russian effort was to be mainly inspired by government and executed by the military, the American was to be quintessentially capitalist. By the end of the century American railways were largely in the hands of ten large companies (although there remained several hundred small ones) commanded by railway versions of merchant princes. Only in the United States and in Britain was there no element of state control by the First World War.

American stations had an almost indeterminate start. Trains often ran down main streets and early stations were sometimes no more than street corners. When this was the case, a small ticket booth might be provided or a ticket office might be established in a shop some distance from the track itself. Old houses were converted, simple single-room frame shacks were built, or inns and hotels were reused as stations. As late as 1866 a hotel at Martinsburg, West Virginia, was turned into a station. In Washington, DC, the first station, of 1835, was no more than a converted house. In the West, early stations, as at Lariat, Colorado, were sometimes old railway 'cars' removed from the tracks or deposited in a siding. In this early period American railway capital and building energies went mainly into track and engineering, and it took some time for the station to catch up with the grandiose schemes of the companies.

The first genuine American station, Mount Clare in Baltimore (1830), was a small octagonal street-corner building not unlike a tollhouse. It was no more than a ticket booth. In the 1830s and 1840s American railway architects turned principally to Greek revivalist and other classical styles. At Lowell, Massachusetts (1835), a small Doric temple carried the track through a colonnade, made up of one of the four bays of the building. Elsewhere, colonial Georgian and early 'Federal' forms provided the inspiration. These elements were incorporated in Richard Upjohn's designs for the Boston and Lowell terminus in Boston (1835) and for Norton, Massachusetts, while a style reminiscent of the Nonconformist chapel in England appeared at Boston Haymarket or New Bedford, Massachusetts.

Many early stations were simply large barn-like structures, a form which was to be used for several decades. These barns could adopt a variety of stylistic detail: there were open-sided 'temple barns' at Relay, Maryland (1850s), and Springfield, Massachusetts (1870s); barns with classical detail like Syracuse (1838); or with Gothic detail, as at Columbus, Ohio (1862), and Meadville, Pennsylvania (1865). American railway architects in this period seem to have been fascinated by the notion of the integration of the station offices with the train-shed, for many of the stations which emerged from the grander developments of the 1850s and 1860s consisted of side buildings with the trains running into the interior through grand portals. Such was the arrangement at Troy, New York, Chicago Great Central, or Cincinnati, all of the 1850s. At Harrisburg, Pennsylvania, dating from the same period, the trains ran through wide twin portals of a double-sided station with a great clock-tower rising between the tracks. When the sheds acquired entirely separate buildings, architects and engineers turned to the 'railroad style', an Italianate villa form with square squat towers. Calvert Station, Baltimore (1848), pioneered this style, and it was adopted in Charleston, South Carolina (1850), Washington, DC (1951), Wheeling, West Virginia (1853), Gettysburg, Pennsylvania (1858), and many other places. The Italianate villa in Washington, DC, which developed many Lincoln associations, was neat, warm, and human in scale, not at all the station of a great capital.

But the Italianate was a relatively 'pure' form. As early as 1848–9 a new and distinctive type of station had appeared. At New Haven, Connecticut, the platforms lay below street level and the buildings were constructed across a cutting. The building, designed by Henry Austin, was remarkable. It combined Italian, Moorish, and, in its central pagoda, Chinese elements. Here was a picturesque exuberance which constituted a dramatic break from earlier styles. And it was in complex hybrid forms that the American station was to develop, particularly after the Civil War. From that time the influences were to be more European than English or colonial. A whole range of styles was to be recycled into a sort of architectural digest of Italianate Gothic, Romanesque, 'Queen Anne', and Venetian. In this era of creative or picturesque eclecticism, the upward element became increasingly emphasized and the squat towers of the Italianate villa became soaring pinnacles, creating dramatic urban landmarks, pin-pointing the positions of the stations to all quarters of rapidly growing American cities and towns. These clock-towers, so powerfully counterpointing the essentially horizontal nature of the railroad, often reached staggering heights.

But in 1869, the year of the completion of the first American transcontinental railway, the greatest examples of the picturesque still lay in the future. Meeks has suggested that in that year the United States still did not possess truly great stations to match the European models.[2] This was to be remedied by Commodore Vanderbilt, the greatest merchant prince of the American railroad companies, president of the New York Central, whose family had started on its route to fortune with a steamboat line. By the late 1860s Vanderbilt required a station in New York which would be, in effect, his grand palace. He turned not to the developing rage for eclecticism, but to the French Renaissance style of the Second Empire. His station was an imitation of the Louvre, backed by the first truly great single-span train-shed built in the United States. French Renaissance and Italian Renaissance styles were taken up by other railway architects —notably at the Michigan, Southern, and Rock Island station at Chicago (1871, and reconstructed after the Great Fire of Chicago in 1872), New Haven (1870s), Chicago Union (1881), and later at Salt Lake City, Utah (1909)—but nothing could halt the headlong growth of the complications of the picturesque. In the 1880s another attempt at simplification was made, when the architect H. H. Richardson and his followers turned to a heavy, neo-Romanesque style. Both small-town stations and large city stations proved amenable to this treatment, and it had some influence in Canada, but still the picturesque could not be stopped in its tracks.

The power of the style lay indeed in its capacity to incorporate so many other forms. The Romanesque was taken over in the last two decades of the nineteenth century, when American railway-station building reached its apogee in masterpieces of creative eclecticism. These stations were multi-faceted structures with complex interrelations of roof lines, varied and dramatic handling of windows, gables, and towers, together with richly ornamented detail. Boston Park Station (1870–4), Washington Baltimore and Potomac (1873–7), and Worcester, Massachusetts (1875–7), were early masterpieces of the eclectic style. Detroit Michigan Central (1882–3), Chicago Dearborn (1883–5), Philadelphia Chestnut Street (1886–8), Louisville Union (1882–91), and, supremely, St Louis, Missouri (1891–5), all reflected the powerful incorporation of the Romanesque into the larger stations. At St Louis the vast Union station of 1891–4 consisted of a variegated range of picturesque buildings with steep pitched roofs and 'Norman revivalist' detail in gables, entrances, and corner elements. The whole was surmounted by a magnificent clock-tower and backed by a massive train-shed of five spans. It made up one of the most satisfying compositions of all American stations.

These were perhaps the finest expressions of American station-building. But Americans had already moved on to another massive and distinctively North American style, the station as office block. Maximum use of valuable real estate here became the crucial factor in station-building. With these stations, extravagance was expressed in scale rather than in exuberance of architecture, although many of them continued to be richly detailed. Philadelphia Broad Street (1892–3), which replaced a station only ten years old, was a block of solid strength picked out with Gothic detail, while the ten-storey Philadelphia Reading of 1891–3 was Italianate with strong central classical elements. At the new Chicago Grand Central of 1888–90, a striking office-block exterior was attached to a massive square corner tower. At Pittsburgh, Daniel Burnham, later to be more famous for his Beaux-Arts work, designed an office-block station which was erected between 1898 and 1901. A magnificent rotunda as carriage concourse projected from the front of the building, and in 1903 a great single-span train-shed, the last to be built in the United States, was added behind.

With the leap to exterior grandeur from the 1870s went a new concentration on the magnificence of the interior arrangements of stations. The highly competitive conditions of American railroad building ensured that every company was determined to display its power, success, and prestige to its patrons. This coincided with their belief that the ordinary person wished to travel from and arrive at great palaces which, with their concourses, restaurants, shops, information centres, medical facilities, theatres, and (later) cinemas constituted virtually civic centres or forums, an impression heightened by the fact that they were often also used for political speeches. For all these reasons, American stations were 'over-built', provided with an external scale and an internal grandeur in the lavishness of their facilities and ornamentation which far exceeded strictly functional requirements.

American stations possessed by now the great train-sheds and large cross-platforms or 'midways' which could compete with their European rivals. In the 'head-building' vast chambers were built which often outmatched anything to be seen in Europe. The change can best be appreciated by comparing Meadville, Pennsylvania, depot of the Atlantic and Great Western (1862), with the interiors of the great stations of the 1880s and 1890s. At Meadville an immense barn-like structure contained long, almost monastic, rooms with exposed rafters. At Indianapolis, the neo-Romanesque station of 1888 contained a vast barrel-vaulted concourse with galleries, rose windows at each end, and elaborate tile-work. Vaulted concourses, matching the form of the train-sheds, became the order of the day, and architects were so enthralled with the power of the vault that they extended its proportions in relation to the side walls. This was done at St Louis where the reduced wall height was pierced by low round-arched portals leading to the various facilities and to the trains. In the 'rotunda' of Chicago Central of 1892–3 the main ribs of the vault were carried down to the floor. In each, a cavernous, but not intimidating, effect was achieved. At St Louis every round-arched open-

Three successive GWR stations occupied the same site at Birmingham's Snow Hill.
The hotel frontage was built in 1863 and demolished in 1969, the rest of the station
in 1977.

Glasgow St Enoch's Station was opened in 1876, the hotel in 1879. The hotel was
demolished in 1977, the station in 1975.

Shughall on the Great Central Line in Cheshire was built in 1892 and closed in 1954.

Hell in Norway, perhaps the ultimate destination, was a typical Scandinavian timber construction.

The Gare de l'Est, Paris (1852).

Copenhagen Central (1911).

Union Station, St Louis, Missouri, built between 1891 and 1894, was the apotheosis of the picturesque Romanesque style.

San Diego, California, built in 1915, was a Spanish colonial revival station with murals illustrating the voyage of Columbus.

ing was made an excuse for a riot of sculptural detail spreading out into a great fan. Female figures with arms outstretched were a recurrent motif. The water fountain became an altar, standing on marble pillars and graced by its own fan design. The ticket office was surmounted by a great mural bearing all the symbols of engineering success, a multi-arched bridge, river steamers, and, of course, the steam engine arriving from the left and dominating all. At Baltimore, Maryland, the Romanesque revivalist style was used to produce an interior divided by arches borne on solid columns giving the appearance of a succession of law courts. In these years the American station came of age.

The final stages of creative eclecticism and the power of the office-block station marked the end of the elaborate experimentation with revivalist styles. Meeks saw the picturesque progression as a rise and fall, from mobile eclecticism in the 1870s to static massy Romanesque, from squat elegant Italianate through soaring Gothic to the squat and stolid approach to the vast stations of the late century. But such a critical cycle does not really work. The final Romanesque phase produced a handling of masses that constituted one of several peaks of station design. Not all buildings with Romanesque detail were squat, as the magnificent St Louis demonstrated. Indeed the soaring clock-tower was an enduring feature through several decades of station-building. It reached staggering heights at Boston Park Square (1872–4), Worcester, Massachusetts (1875–6), Indianapolis Union (1886–9), and supremely at Waterbury, Connecticut (1909), perhaps the last example, where the campanile duplicated the height of the station building some two and a half times. By the beginning of this century, however, the towers had gone as far as they could go. American architects turned to new forms of expressing grandeur.

Many American architectural critics have seen the Beaux-Arts style which developed from the turn of the century as representing a new invigoration in American station styles. There is no doubt at all that this is true in engineering, urban planning, and circulation terms. The Beaux-Arts stations represented the apogee of station design, but scarcely of taste. It is difficult to accept the praises of some American critics for the overblown gigantism of the Beaux-Arts, particularly as none of them has followed Ruskin's injunction to see architecture as mirroring the life of a society in all its facets. The new classical and baroque forms are often said to have arisen from the conscious departure in taste represented in the buildings of the Columbian Exposition in Chicago in 1893. In celebrating the fourth centenary of the voyage of Columbus, the United States was marking, as exhibitions often do, a new phase in its national development. It stood, in fact, on the edge of great-power status. By the turn of the century, the United States of America had become an imperial power and her pre-eminence among Western countries was already confidently predicted. It is true that baroque had long been adopted as the style for state capitols in the United States, but the Beaux-Arts style in all its overblown pomposity was to reflect this new sense of greatness. It was a classic imperial response in every sense, and it is not surprising that it was to feed into Fascist Italian and German canons of architectural taste.

While the Beaux-Arts reflected both this new national conceit and the megalomania of American railroad companies, it also offered American architects a new means to self-assertion through the railway station. The greatest of the picturesque stations had dominated their cities. The great office blocks of the 1890s had taken over that role, and the office-block stations had made some attempt to match them. By the early years of the twentieth century, however, stations could not compete with the upward thrust of American urban architecture. The station could make its statement by spreading, by achieving its grandeur through the vast length of Beaux-Arts façades, the enormous circulation areas within them, and the new approach to land use which the new stations offered.

The temporary terminal for the Chicago World Fair of 1893 pointed the way. Here arch, colonnade, dome, and column were flaunted in a triumphalist manner, with the vault of the great concourse projecting dramatically above the roof line as was to be common in all Beaux-Arts stations. This station was not to survive, but its influence was to be extensively felt. The first manifestation of the influence of Chicago was to be the portal and colonnade style of classical station, as exemplified at Boston North (1893) and at Columbus Ohio (1897). Here the notion of the railway station as city gate was given direct architectural form as at London's Euston half a century earlier. In 1898 Boston South Station was reconstructed in a classical style, with entrance and clock on a curved corner, which was to influence station-building in Australia, notably in Adelaide and Melbourne.

These were different, and in many ways more congenial, responses to the new classicism, but the Beaux-Arts was soon to reign supreme and supplant totally the nineteenth-century eclectic styles. In some places stations built a mere ten or twenty years earlier were swept away to make space for these vast new edifices. These stations represented two important urban developments. Several old stations were now often amalgamated into one great Union station. Building-land in cities was at a premium. Railway lines were being raised on viaducts or sunk into

cuttings and tunnels, and the railway station became the surface reminder of the engineering works below. The new stations became part of
the civic plans for great American cities which inaugurated a new vogue
for city planning. The famous firm of Burnham and Co. became closely
involved with the combination of urban planning and station design,
notably in Washington, DC, and Chicago. In the stations themselves
greater attention was now given to the problems of circulation, the
control, movement, and organization of great numbers of people. In most
cases, the numbers were projected and not actual; the stations were born
of myth for mythic passenger growth.

Obsessed with these circulation problems, architects looked for guidance to the ancient world. In modern times churches and theatres were
the only buildings which were designed to cope with crowds, and they
offered no real clues to the scale of the problem now facing station
architects. But in Rome huge numbers had been controlled at the
Colosseum with its multiple entrances and large ambulatories at each
level. At the greatest of the Roman baths, like those of Caracalla, a large
central concourse led out to the various facilities. A combination of these
principles of assembly and dispersal now appeared in railway stations.

In 1906 Chattanooga acquired a vast brick classical station containing
a huge domed central waiting-room, with service wings lit by floor-to-
ceiling arched windows extending on each side. The façade was decorated with ornamental brickwork and terracotta details. In the following
year the Beaux-Arts style emerged at its most majestic in Washington,
DC, containing some of the most powerful, overpowering indeed, spaces
of any station, and set off in a great park-like setting. The arches,
columns, and huge statuary of the exterior prepared the traveller or
sightseer for the vast vaulted concourse and waiting-room within. The
interior spaces were divided by peristyles bearing classical statuary, while
other statues stood in the round-arched window spaces. All of this was
matched by the immensity of the great train concourse behind, 860 ft.
long, which provided access through gates to the tracks. This station was
consciously designed to match the pretensions of a baroque imperial
capital. Its accommodation was considerably greater than would ever be
needed in normal times, but its nationalistic opulence was intended to
come into its own every four years, at the inauguration of successive
presidents. Washington had come a long way from the converted house
of 1835, the charmingly simple Italianate villa of 1851, or even the
pleasingly revivalist Baltimore and Potomac of 1873–7.

The two most famous stations of this era are the twin Beaux-Arts
stations of New York, the Pennsylvania Central and the Grand Central,

built respectively between 1906 and 1910 and 1903 and 1913. The former contained a remarkable combination of nineteenth-century engineering with the immense columns and stonework of the 'thermal' style. The outer concourse in glass and iron had its architectural roots in the exhibition halls of the nineteenth century. The inner waiting-room re-created the central space of the baths of Caracalla with grand staircases on all four sides, rising through colonnades at each end under immense arches framed by Corinthian columns. All of this was contained within long classical façades, with corner pavilions setting off all four sides.

At Grand Central, New York, the Vanderbilt search for opulence had even outrun the French Empire style of the first Grand Central with its great conventional train-shed behind. The tracks of the New York Central railroad occupied some of the finest land in New York. By sinking them, the Company made available at least a dozen blocks lying between Second and Fifth Avenues. The great train-shed was rendered redundant, with some seventy acres of tracks and yards now provided below street level. Forty-fifth to Fifty-sixth Streets, formerly dead ends at railway yards, became thoroughfares. Yet the temptation to build upwards for the station itself was resisted. A classical palace was created lying athwart Park and Fourth Avenues, surrounded by a raised roadway offering access to the wheeled traffic which would soon pitch the railways into dramatic decline.

Grand Central was in effect two stations, as the contemporary cutaway illustrations were concerned to show, stations with more complex multiple levels below ground than there were above it. The tracks for suburban trains lay below those of the express system, while the suburban concourse and waiting-room in turn lay below the vast apartments in the 'thermal' style for long-distance passengers. Baggage and passengers were separated, and the suburban and express passengers had no need to coincide with each other. It was estimated that no fewer than 30,000 people could congregate at Grand Central without serious crowding. A maximum of 70,000 outward-bound passengers could be carried in an hour. The tunnels, track arrangements, and loop lines were regarded as among the greatest engineering marvels of the age, and more engineers flocked to see them than any other contemporary achievement, even including the Panama Canal. They were, of course, all dependent on one vital technological development, the shift from steam to electricity. All trains approaching New York were to have their steam engines exchanged for electric (in the case of the Pennsylvania Central at a station called Manhattan Transfer), and the vast echoing smoky recesses of the train-shed were dispensed with.

Many contemporaries hailed this development with delight. A writer in the *Town Planning Review* trumpeted that train-sheds were now obsolete: 'modern terminals in great cities must be below street level hereafter'.[3] In 1899, when the New York, New Haven, and Hartford Company had built their magnificent new station at Providence, Rhode Island, they had planned it without a train-shed. The city objected, and after a long controversy one was duly built. But the last shed was that at Pittsburgh of 1903. When John A. Droege came to write his classic work on the American station in 1916, he regarded train-sheds as beyond the pale:

The day of the great awkward arched train shed is long since gone. There was a time when in railroad terminal architecture it was considered as the most necessary adjunct (or evil). It will long remain a problem to the average person that these sheds had such wide popularity and that so little use was made of the cheaper, cleaner, or, in fact, better umbrella sheds. In view of the widespread use of the old style train sheds it is pleasing to our vanity to be reminded how expensive they were to build and how costly to maintain. And what is more, the sheds are dark and dirty, the coldest places in town on cold days, the stuffiest on hot.[4]

With those sentences Droege dismissed decades of dazzling structural and engineering achievements. At a much later date, the Grand Central idea appeared in Britain at Birmingham New Street and London Euston, but without any of the magnificence of the 'thermal' building above. Catching the train had been turned into a furtive, subterranean act, appropriate perhaps to the new status of the railways as a minority and persecuted transport interest.

But the Beaux-Arts was a relatively short-lived fad, and not even its excesses could drive other styles out. Michigan Central Station, Detroit (1913), took the office-block idea a stage further. An arched and columned vestibule block marked out the building as a station, but behind rose a fifteen-storey office block. At Cleveland, an immense skyscraper station, with a central tower and clock fifty-two storeys high, consciously designed as a city gate and as the centre of a great transportation network, was built between 1923 and 1930. Classical ideas were explored further at Chicago Union (1924–5) and Philadelphia Thirtieth Street (1927–34) where the style took on a flashy grandiosity akin to the Fascist classical of contemporary Europe. Carl Condit described this as 'coldly classical monumentalism'.[5]

There were, however, two remarkable late flowerings of the American station. One was revivalist, the Spanish style, and the other was strikingly modern and original, the Art Deco. The Spanish style, favoured by the

Santa Fe and other railroads in the Southern States, can be divided into two streams, the baroque and the mission. The mission style, with its cool Spanish arches, bell-towers, and church-like interior, had strong antecedents in American station architecture. In 1893 the Atchison, Topeka, and Santa Fe opened an extraordinary Byzantine/Moorish station in Los Angeles, called La Grande. The effect was heightened by the pavilions which straddled the track behind the main building. By the end of the century the Santa Fe and the Southern Pacific had built Spanish-style stations throughout the South, as at San Angelo, Texas; Riverside, Santa Barbara, Capistrano, and Burlingame, California. At many of these the mission atmosphere was emphasized by cloisters, gardens, and bell-towers complete with bells. At Atlanta, Georgia, where the old station had played such a key role in the Civil War, three companies, the Southern, Seaboard, and Atlanta and West Point, opened a large Spanish baroque Union station in 1905. Another baroque station appeared at Mobile, Alabama, in 1907. One of the most striking of all the mission stations was opened by the Santa Fe at Albuquerque, New Mexico, in 1910. It was a vast complex of buildings, a mission in the fullest sense with several towers surmounted by triple crowns. The buildings derived their interest from these towers and from the complex interrelationship of the elements. In architectural detail they were austere, with surfaces rendered in adobe and roofed in tiles.

The style was given a powerful fillip by the expositions held at San Francisco and San Diego in 1915 to celebrate the opening of the Panama Canal. As a result, a new interest in the Latin American world led to the Spanish style finding favour until the 1930s. San Diego, San Francisco, Los Angeles, and San Antonio, Texas, all acquired stations in the style, and opulent baroque versions were built at West Palm Beach (1924–5) and Orlando, Florida (1926). At San Diego (1914–15) the cool, dark, chaste interior was lightened by tile-work to a height of eight or nine feet. The church effect was heightened by the Santa Fe's cross symbol and by one or two paintings placed high on the walls. The exterior had a magnificent 'west end'—two fine baroque towers bearing murals illustrative of the early history of California flanking a wide arch protecting stained-glass windows within. The Los Angeles version (1934–9) was much lighter in effect, with full-length windows. There the interior was almost indistinguishable from a church: the nave was the waiting-room complete with seats arranged like pews, memorials on the walls, chandeliers suspended from exposed rafters; the chancel was the booking office, with an information kiosk in the crossing; the apses were the entrance lobby and the route to the tracks. The Southern Pacific depot at

San Francisco (1915) combined both baroque and mission elements, while at Boise, Idaho (1924–5), the mission style achieved its most simplified and exalted form. There the station was perfectly proportioned and almost impossible to identify as a station rather than as a church, both externally and internally.

Art Deco ideas were explored at Omaha Union (1929–30) and, supremely, at Cincinnati Union (1929–33). At the latter the process of incorporating a number of older stations into one arrived late. Since a variety of different routes into the city had to be accommodated and since the planners envisaged a station of massive proportions a central city site proved impossible. It was also to be a station for the motor-car age, situated on ample land with large car-parks. A large number of architects and designers were involved, but none the less the result was stunning. The front consisted of the largest of all station arched façades with tall windows separated by ribs, the whole giving the impression of an enormous speaker of a contemporary radio set. Inside, the semicircular concourse was decorated with remarkable mosaics by Winold Reiss, illustrative of the industries, arts, and people of Cincinnati. Lights and counters followed graceful Art Deco curves and doors in banded woods were surmounted by representations of the exterior of the building. Beyond this great semicircular space was a massive train concourse above the tracks, again decorated by mosaics. The station was consciously designed to be a civic centre with a wide range of rooms including a theatre. Carl Condit's description of the colour schemes and materials used in this sumptuous station cannot be bettered:

Nothing on the exterior, however, prepared one for the stunning exhibition of color, texture, and mural art in the interior, features that constituted a major step in an architectural revolution that was most fully developed in the Century of Progress Exposition in Chicago (1933–34). Only colour photographs, of which too few survive, can do justice to this vivid yet harmonious palette, but a simple catalogue of materials and their distribution may suggest something of its richness. The domed ceiling of the rotunda concourse and certain wall areas were finished in yellow and orange plaster with a trim of Red Verona, Tennessee Fleuri, and Virginia Black marbles, and the lower wall areas over the service facilities were covered with highly colored mosaic murals by the German-born artist Winold Reiss and executed by the Ravenna Mosaic Company. The side-walls of the train concourse were devoted almost entirely to Reiss's murals . . . and the end wall was covered with a world map and clock dials showing the hour differences in various time zones. Elsewhere on the walls there was a trim of Red Verona and various domestic gray and black marbles; the low vault of the ceiling was again done in orange and yellow plaster, and the floor was finished in red and tan terrazzo. Wood veneer finishes with aluminum trim characterised the lounges and offices: zebra wood, holly, and walnut in the men's lounge were arranged in abstract designs derived from railroad locomotives, cars, and signals; panels of zebra and madrone wood covered the women's lounge; and gum, harewood, and holly were used in the offices along with cork flooring. In the restaurant the walls were finished in zebra, birch, red and black marbles, and the floors in terrazzo; in the theater walls of Tennessee Fleuri, black and white marbles stood in subdued contrast to a mulberry carpet; the interior of the ticket offices were finished in Hauteville marble and terrazzo, and the private dining room entirely in Rockwood tile.[6]

Monumental Art Deco and this riot of materials and colours led no-where, however. American station design had found a truly contemporary style which proved to be well suited to station scale. But it was a swan-song. The station opened in 1933, designed for continuing growth in passenger traffic. In the event, that traffic was already spiralling in steep decline and the corresponding losses were to rise dramatically. Cincinnati Union perfectly represented the exaggerated hope of the 1920s and the devastating failure of the 1930s. It also bore alarming signs of the transportation future. Its recognition of the significance of the motor car and its removal to the edge of the main city area was ominous. This was the railway station as airport. Abdication was at hand.

Inevitably, most space in this exploration of the American railway station has been devoted to the large city variety. But station architecture was perhaps expressed in its most vigorous and diversified forms in the countless thousands of small country and medium-sized town stations coast to coast. Some commentators have seen these as representing the true genius of American station architecture. They too were invariably overbuilt, offering by the end of the century a source of small-town and parochial pride. The early country stations had been supplied with small lookout towers rising above the roof of the building to enable railway employees to watch for approaching trains over the horizon. When this utilitarian function was no longer needed, the lookouts became cupolas, lanterns, clock-towers. Spires, corner towers, belfries, even unusually shaped domes soon adorned all but the smaller frame stations. Elaborate wood and iron work, overhanging eaves, *portes cochères*, and all sorts of architectural ornamentation all conveyed a sense of the romance of travel, identified the station as landmark, and offered the various com-panies the opportunity to distinguish themselves by particular 'house' characteristics. On the other hand, internal fitments, like booking counters, benches, and stoves, were usually solid and practical rather than elegant.

Many of these stations pursued a consistent internal design pattern. The ground plan normally consisted of three main rooms, the baggage room and the waiting-room at each end, with the office between, usually with a bay window projecting on to the platform to afford the station agent a view up and down the tracks. Sometimes the agent and his family lived above the station, so that offices and home together formed a rather grander two-storey building. In some the telegraph operator was given an elevated office in the tower. A few were the products of early pre-fabrication techniques, as at Ladson, South Carolina, and many, like American houses, were mobile, capable of being reused in different locations.

The country stations also enjoyed a great range of styles, but they escaped the process of repeated renewal which overwhelmed so many large city and town stations in the nineteenth and early twentieth centuries. Many of the country stations did not enjoy the pedigree of great architects to sire them. They were often designed by engineers, but what they lacked in architectural distinction, they gained in homely practicality and in the opportunities they afforded to local carpenters to display their skills in beautifully carved barge boarding and valances. Even the tiniest of flag stations (where passengers stopped the train by raising a flag or changing a signal) could bear the marks of the expertise of some unsung local craftsman. Appropriately, such stations generally derived their inspiration from vernacular pioneering house styles, in the 'Swiss chalet', the 'cottage orné', the 'stick style', the 'shingle lodge', or, particularly in the West, the frame store or the log cabin.

The medium-sized town stations sometimes reflected the styles in vogue for their grander counterparts. Richardson's Romanesque style appeared at a succession of smaller stations in Massachusetts in the 1880s, at Ashburndale (1881), Framingham (1883), Wellesley (1884), and North Easton (1886). These heavy round-arched stations were to be influential in Ontario, Canada, in the same period, and the Romanesque, rarely among station styles, proved amenable to both small- and large-scale treatment. Cool classical porticoes appeared at Dover, Delaware, and Lexington, Kentucky, early this century and a scaled-down Beaux-Arts style was used at Worcester, Massachusetts, Tacoma, Washington (1910), Montclair, New Jersey (1913), and Broad Street, Richmond, Virginia (1917–19). But the Beaux-Arts was essentially an overblown grandiose manner, ill suited to the smaller station.

Stations frequently expressed the social tone of the areas they served. Glen Ridge, New Jersey, was supplied with an elegant shingle lodge in 1887 to serve its affluent commuters, while Tuxedo Park, a wealthy New

York community, was graced by a pagoda-like structure with steep-pitched roofs and much fine woodwork. Pelham Manor, New York, another wealthy suburban community, had an opulent stone structure with a powerfully squat square tower for ticket lobby and waiting-room. Both Palm Springs, California, and West Palm Beach, Florida, boasted magnificent Spanish stations, built respectively at the beginning of the century and the 1920s. Resort stations and hotels were combined at Cumberland (1871–2) and Relay, Maryland (1870s), and at Susquehanna (1865) and Altoona, Pennsylvania. Many of these stood at junctions where passengers might be expected to stop over before continuing their journeys.

Much more exotic architecture was often used for resort stations. It was as though the railway companies wished to put their excursionists in the mood, remind them of the rather light-hearted, somewhat extravagant outing they were engaged upon, quite different from everyday commuting and business travel. At Bethlehem, New Hampshire, the highest village east of the Rockies, the Boston and Maine created a delightful, half-timbered chalet-style building with a great deal of space for the horse-drawn coaches and carriages which conveyed excursionists from the station. Even more elaborately decorated wooden buildings with long agreeable verandas were built by the Southern Pacific at Shasta Springs, California. The Pennsylvania Central built a holiday pavilion with a high cupola at Cape May, New Jersey, while half-timbering, so often associated with holiday architecture, was the dominant feature of the Southern's Asheville resort in North Carolina. At Ardsley-on-Hudson, New York, a half-timbered, creeper-clad station was connected to a matching hotel by a rustic bridge. The complex also boasted a dock on the Hudson River. But the most astonishing of all these excursion stations was the one provided by the Delaware and Hudson at Lake George, New York, in 1882. It was a multi-storey orientalist, almost pagoda-like confection, sporting elaborately carved verandas, valances, and outside staircases with rustic covered ways leading off from it. It was demolished in 1911 and replaced by a much more utilitarian building. The extravagant resort spirit was already waning.

No other building type secured such a variety of examples. Many were minor masterpieces, from the picturesque cottage and Queen Anne gable porch of the Union Pacific station at Park City, Utah (1886), to the beautiful pavilions with their elegant flights of steps at Haverstraw, New York, and Bryn Mawr, Pennsylvania; from the Norman revivalist Duluth, Minnesota (1892), with its steep-pitched roofs and twin conical towers, to the perfect proportions and beautifully handled materials of Point of

Rocks, Maryland. The American railroad companies boasted their own King Ludwigs and some of their creations succeeded in being both fantastical and architecturally exciting. But their spirit had entirely vanished by the Second World War. New large city stations were built at Toledo (1950) and New Orleans (1954), but in a totally undistinguished style. Otherwise bus shelters were provided when small stations were knocked or burned down. Just such a brave new station was the romantically named 'Route 128' at Boston. By the time that the Educational Facilities Laboratories and the National Endowment for the Arts were producing their two excellent booklets on the reuse of railroad stations in 1974 and 1975, only one per cent of all inter-city travel was by train.[7] The United States which had been supremely the country of the railway at the beginning of the twentieth century had just as dramatically and wholeheartedly become the country of the motor car, the Greyhound bus, and the aeroplane. The thrusting diversity of American capitalist railway operations, which had been its great strength in the nineteenth century, had become its greatest weakness in the twentieth, and not even Amtrak could entirely arrest that decline.

Canada

Canadian station-building styles can be divided up into a number of periods.[8] The early primitive phase of frame shacks and converted buildings was followed by the appearance of rather grander stations in the post-confederation years of the 1870s and 1880s. In these decades the Intercolonial railway was built to connect the eastern provinces, the Grand Trunk and several other railway companies penetrated the country districts of Ontario as well as connecting Canadian cities to each other and to the United States, while Canadian Pacific stretched its metals westwards to Vancouver. As the Canadian railway companies experimented for a distinctive national style, it is perhaps not surprising that they turned to French models, although the styles they adopted were often filtered through the United States. Once the Canadian fears of American invasion had passed, Canadians were happier to accept American influences in their station-building. This ensured that Canadian stations always differed in appearance from the 'Dominion' styles adopted in Australia, New Zealand, and even South Africa. The French Second Empire style found some favour in the 1880s, as did Richardson's neo-Romanesque. The Canadian Pacific developed a French Renaissance château style combined with touches of Scottish baronial, which was both distinctive and neatly combined the main cultural heritages of Canada. But from the early years of the twentieth century to the 1930s classical styles reigned supreme for all larger city stations.

So far as smaller country and town stations were concerned, there was a wave of rebuilding of Grand Trunk stations in the 1880s and 1890s, but the boom years in station-building (though not in profits) were those from the late 1890s to the early 1920s. In this period the 'colonization road', the Canadian Northern, stretched its system east and west from its first line in Manitoba. From 1903, in another effort to break the CPR's monopoly, the Grand Trunk Pacific was chartered by the Canadian government to build another coast-to-coast line. Second and third crossings of the Rockies were effected by the Canadian Northern (to Vancouver) and the Grand Trunk Pacific (to Prince Rupert), while the government-owned Transcontinental set about linking Grand Trunk metals to the east coast. A whole succession of prairie branches was built to develop settlement and to tap the furthest reaches of the grain-growing areas. On the prairie transcontinental and branch lines, stations were required every five to ten miles for the convenience of farmers bringing their grain to the station elevators in horse-drawn vehicles. By the First World War both the Canadian Northern and the GTP, shackled with loss-making mountain railroads, were in deep financial difficulties. In 1918 the Canadian Northern collapsed; in 1920 the GTP followed, bringing down its parent Grand Trunk in 1923. The nationalized Canadian National Railways was constructed out of the wreckage of these lines, and continued the completion of lines and the building of stations. The boom period ensured that every prairie city had two and sometimes three stations, some of them very short-lived indeed. When the Canadian National was formed it inherited no fewer than a thousand stations west of Lake Superior. It is not surprising that one railway executive of the period described this time as one of 'calamitous overbuilding' in Canadian railways.[9]

As the many Ontario lines stretched out in the 1870s and 1880s, dozens of new stations were built. Companies like the Grand Trunk, the Hamilton and North Western, the Toronto, Hamilton, and Buffalo, the Ontario, Huron, and Simcoe, the Toronto, Grey, and Bruce, and the Credit Valley penetrated the furthest corners of the province. Many villages were provided with flag-stop stations—as at Dagmar, Forks of the Credit, Gilford, Crombies, and Hillsburg—just tiny waiting-rooms, with, occasionally, projecting awnings. Elsewhere the stations consisted of the usual combination of waiting-room, baggage room, office, and telegraph-operator's room. In the late 1870s and 1880s a whole succession of attractive stations with complex roof-lines and towers with conical caps were built at towns like Craigleith (1872), Streetsville (1879), Smithville, Grimsby (1882), Whitby, and Don (1899), among many others. Smaller one-storey buildings, often containing attractive woodwork in the gables, were built at Port Hope (1857), St Mary's Junction (1863), Aurora (1900), Kincardine (1903), Maple (1905), and Inglewood (1910). The range of dates indicates the durability of this style. By the 1890s neo-Romanesque had arrived from the United States, and its heavy style with round arches appeared at Brantford (1895), Kitchener (1897), Galt and Brampton. Some of the larger stations aspired to considerable distinction, and Canadian railway architects seem to have favoured rounded features as a dominant element in their stations. At Brantford rounded ends were combined with a square tower. At Petrolia a most attractive station had round waiting-rooms, two end conical towers, and a central square one. At Guelph as late as 1911 a Romanesque effect was combined with an Italianate tower, while at Goderich extensive offices were incorporated in a large round tower.

In a remarkable labour of love Charles Bohi categorized all the Canadian National stations west of Lake Superior and visited all the surviving ones in the early 1970s.[10] Many of the early stations on these lines were portable buildings or baggage cars, but soon both the Canadian Northern and the Grand Trunk Pacific developed standard designs in categories ranging from one to three or four. Despite this standardization the country small-town stations achieved a remarkable diversity, with many individually designed stations for division points and other more important centres. The stations all followed the standard plan with a freight and/or baggage room at one end, the waiting-room at the other, the agent's office with its bay window in the middle, and accommodation for the agent and his family, usually consisting of a kitchen and living-room, downstairs at the back of the station with up to four bedrooms upstairs. The smaller third- or fourth-class stations had only one-roomed living quarters for, presumably, a younger bachelor agent, in a single-storey structure. The larger second-class stations would also have a separate ladies' waiting-room.

The stations were all distinguished by complex roof-lines. Often three different types of roof—pyramid, hip, and gable—were included together with a wide variety of dormers in the upper storey. Most of them had shingled awnings borne on prominent brackets projecting over their simple wooden platforms. On the prairies these stations, with their high steep-pitched roofs and their larger adjacent grain elevators, could be seen from many miles away. With their telegraph and cable facilities, their express freight and post office services, these stations were the most important buildings in their communities. Indeed they often constituted the source of their communities when new villages were laid out by the railway companies beside them. In the Rockies the stations were not expected to secure so much local traffic. There they were more important in train handling and as sectional points. Their accommodation was modified accordingly.

It was only from the 1880s that the larger Canadian cities sprouted stations that would match their rapidly growing civic pride. Both of the great Montreal CPR stations, Windsor (1888) and Place Viger, were designed by the same architect, Bruce Page, in the heavy Richardsonian Romanesque manner. A CPR guidebook of 1897 expressed the company's pride in its Windsor Station:

... Itself one of the sights of the city, which ranks among the most attractive places on the Continent. This is an imposing structure, somewhat resembling in its frontage on two streets the keep of a Norman castle. It is a rare combination of elegance, comfort, and architectural beauty. No expense was spared to ensure its thorough adaptation to the purpose in view, and it is undoubtedly one of the handsomest buildings in the city, and a fitting illustration of the enterprise of the road. Upstairs are the head offices of the Company, where the business of the great artery of travel is arranged, and below are minor offices, the grand general waiting room, with its noble arches and massive polished granite columns; the ladies' waiting room, an illustration of how modern skill can blend luxury and comfort; and last, but not least, the dining-room, the antipodes of those railway dining rooms whose peculiarities afford so many opportunities to the comic journalists of America.[11]

The Grand Trunk's Bonaventure Station in Montreal was built in French Second Empire style with a palatial waiting-room to match. At Quebec the first CPR station was a simple two-storey affair with crow-stepped gables. But the CPR made its distinctive contribution to Canadian station architecture with its French château style, used for both hotels and stations, and its wooden chalets with Scottish baronial touches. An example of the latter was Banff in Alberta, and of the former the great gateway to the Orient which the CPR built in Vancouver. When the first CPR train reached Vancouver on 23 May 1888, the depot on the waterfront was no larger than a wooden shed.[12] This was soon replaced by a large structure in the CPR château/baronial style, with conical towers and steep-pitched roofs. It blocked off the end of Granville Street, Vancouver's main thoroughfare, and was consciously designed to present the city both as the great terminus of the transcontinental railway and as a great Oriental gateway.

But the life of this station was to be short. In the twentieth century, regrettably, Canada abandoned its distinctive combination of French and Scottish elements which so perfectly reflected its cultural heritage. A bastard classical took over and became the dominant form for several decades. This transition is perfectly represented at Thunder Bay on Lake Superior, the great grain trans-shipment centre from the prairies. At Thunder Bay North (then Port Arthur) the Canadian Northern built a distinctive station with pyramidal roofs and battlemented turrets, adorned with its symbolic wheatsheaf motif, in 1905. In Thunder Bay South (formerly Fort William) the CPR built a classical station in 1911. The Canadian Northern continued to build its distinctive style, bearing enlarged features of its smaller stations, at Edmonton and later at Saskatoon (1911). But transcontinental status always brought a classical rush to the head of railroad companies. When the Canadian Northern reached Vancouver in 1915, it reclaimed land at False Creek, one of the many land reclamation schemes which facilitated the building of railway stations as far apart as Bombay and Auckland—and built a massive classical station. The restless CPR, which repeatedly rebuilt the mighty Hotel Vancouver, had already built another, classical station on the Vancouver waterfront. By this time Regina Union (1911), Brandon (1911), and Winnipeg (both CPR and the Union station of the Canadian Northern and the GTP (1911)) were all built in the style. Winnipeg, with its great round ticket lobby, was extolled in Droege's work on the railway station.[13] Suitably updated to twenties and thirties Georgian the style remained dominant in the inter-war years. It was used for new stations at Edmonton (1928) and Saskatoon (1930s). A fine Greek revivalist station, not unlike that at Monkwearmouth in Northumbria, was built in Hamilton, Ontario, in 1930. Sculptures of rail and shipping transportation were inserted above the doors. Even in this period, however, the odd example of eclecticism survived. At Toronto North, a station open only from 1916 to 1930, an Italian Renaissance building was combined with a high clock-tower.

The only Canadian station to vie with the greatest American examples was the remarkable Toronto Union station built between 1915 and 1930 with what one writer called a 'blessed sense of civic excess'.[14] It was opened in 1927, but was not fully completed until 1930. The old Union station had been in a rambling neo-Romanesque style, but the new one was to match the grandest of the American Beaux-Arts school, and in some ways surpass them. The firm of Ross and Macdonald had recently been associated with the building of the Beaux-Arts station in Ottawa. In Toronto an immense frontage 752 ft. long had a central colonnaded entrance-way which led into a great concourse with a slightly curving coffered ceiling. As at Grand Central, New York, care was taken to separate passengers and baggage, as well as incoming and outgoing passengers. The station was conceived in the grandest imperial manner, but although there was much interesting architectural detail, the statuary which was supposed to adorn the entrance and other parts of the exterior was never sculpted as the colder economic winds of the late 1920s began to blow.

The same economic difficulties held up the last great station-building project in Canada. In the 1920s Canadian National Railways planned a new station to replace the old Bonaventure. It was to be on a new site and act as a combined station for suburban and express services. It was started in 1930, but work was stopped by the Depression. It was begun again in 1939 and opened in July 1943.[15] The building was almost unrelievedly functional, although some mural decorations were incorporated into the corners of the concourse and some simple ornamentation appeared above the lifts. The concourse was large, but uninspiring, particularly as the floor area was broken up by stairways down to the tracks. The site made use of the Mount Royal tunnel and of the considerable falling away of the land, so that although the platforms were below the station building, none the less they were above ground. They left the station to the south on a viaduct. Baggage and goods were handled on a sub-track level, and one of the advantages of the new arrangements was that no fewer than fifteen street level-crossings were eliminated. Montreal was catching up with developments which had taken place at many American stations earlier in the century. The *Railway Gazette* reported that it had become an attraction to sightseers, rather like the early days at the first Euston and at the inauguration of the great European and American stations.

Montreal Central eventually served the CPR express lines as well as the CNR, but, compared with Toronto or Cincinnati Union, there was something half-hearted about it, despite the trumpetings with which it was received during the war. Confidence soon ebbed from Canadian railways. The Vancouver stations were run down—and two were demolished—once Vancouver had ceased to be the main portal to the Orient with the ending of the passenger shipping services. In Edmonton the classical station was demolished and replaced by a tower block in 1966. Saskatoon's station was closed in 1969, and replaced by a new one-storeyed, flat-roofed, functional station at the edge of the city. At Ottawa, following a government report, the Gréber Commission, which concluded that stations and railway lines were unsightly in Canadian cities, the Beaux-Arts station, so superbly situated at the base of Parliament Hill, was abandoned and a new station like an airport was built on the edge of the city.[16] The monumental folly of such ideas, produced by planners who have capitulated to the strangulation of the motor car and destroyed city communities from Liverpool to Hong Kong, was to dawn too late. In throwing away the advantages of the nineteenth-century central city site in the nation's capital there could be no surer sign that Canadians were allowing Mammon and the attendant philistines to destroy the heritage that had largely made the country. In Quebec city the same process was set in train, but later reversed. The contrast with the renewed vigour and conservationist sense of Australasian railways in the same period is striking, and says much for the respective cultural health of the Dominions.

Latin America and the Caribbean

Nowhere in the world did the railway station represent so powerfully the combination of an intrusive technical power combined with the search for national identity as in Latin America.[17] Spanish and Portuguese rule had been overthrown before the arrival of the railway, and the building of Latin American lines was to become the classic expression of the informal imperialism of Britain and the United States which penetrated the region from the mid-nineteenth century. The railway none the less became the symbol of progress without which national aspirations had no hope of achievement. In Uruguay the first journal was called *Ferrocarril* ('Railway'), although its content had little or nothing to do with railways. Informal imperialism produced a complex network of companies and lines. A multiplicity of stations would appear in each Latin American capital of importance, some of them among the grandest anywhere. And great engineering heights would be scaled in the whole succession of Andean railways.

There were only modest and tentative beginnings to all of this in the 1850s and 1860s. But during the next few decades, nitrates and minerals in the Andes, wheat and beef in Argentina, and coffee in Brazil were to draw the railways outwards. In the main cities, the early primitive stations were replaced by grandiloquent specimens in the last years of the nineteenth century and in the decade before the First World War. This extraordinary burst of architectural activity has been largely ignored. Even the superb 'All Stations' exhibition contained no examples of Latin American stations, nor were any illustrated in the accompanying, and otherwise excellent, book of the same name. But travellers in Latin

America in the early twentieth century found there stations which led them into rhapsodies of praise.

Nowhere was this more true than in Argentina. W. H. Koebel wrote in *Argentina Past and Present* (1914) that 'In no other branch of Argentine industry is the British capitalist so deeply interested as in that of the railways'.[18] This deep interest was amply reflected in the fact that no fewer than a dozen Argentine railway companies were British-owned. There were, in addition, three French companies, and the Argentine State railways which controlled a number of local lines. Such diversity of ownership was matched by the architectural catholicism of station styles. There was in some cases an extraordinary Englishness about Argentine railways. Station platforms, overbridges, signalling, motive power were all on British lines or British-made, and some country stations even had half-timbered buildings.

In Buenos Aires, however, the great terminal stations of these systems were built in baroque and Renaissance styles. It was a city remarkably endowed with terminal stations. At Retiro, facing on to the Plaza Britannica, there were no fewer than three great head-type stations. In ascending order of grandeur these were the termini of the Buenos Aires and Pacific, the Córdoba Central Railway, and the Central Argentine Railway. The station of the latter, completed in 1915, was described by the *Times Book of Argentina* as 'the finest of its kind south of the Equator and in point of convenience and completeness challenges comparison with any in the world'.[19]

Its dimensions and the details of its decoration indicate that this was no empty boast.[20] Its booking-hall, 200 ft. long and 60 ft. wide, led into an even vaster grand hall, 480 ft. long and 82 ft. wide, challenging comparison with the great halls of New York or Toronto. Both booking and grand halls were decorated in Royal Doulton faience to a height of 7 ft.; each had mosaic floors and balconies ran round the walls at a height of 30 ft. The vaulted dome of the booking-hall stood at a height of 65 ft. from the floor and the outer dome above reached a height of 108 ft. Refreshment and dining halls and train-shed matched these lavish dimensions. Statistics can be tedious, but these demonstrate dramatically the great power and splendour of Argentine railways. Retiro Station offered Paul Theroux a comfortable sense of home-coming after a long rail journey through the continent. It was English-made

with a high curved roof supported by girders forged in a Liverpool ironworks, and marble pillars and floors, ornately carved canopies, shafts of sunlight emphasising its height, and indeed, everything of a cathedral but altars and pews. . . . it was a relief to me, after such a long trip, to arrive at this station . . . I needed to be reassured that I had reached a hospitable culture . . .[21]

These three stations, which from the air offer one of the railway sights of the world, all stood in an area which was closely identified with the British community, significantly close to the docks. That community eventually built on the Plaza Britannica a magnificent clock-tower to complement the stations. It was burned down on the second anniversary of the Falklands War.

For some visitors, the Buenos Aires Great Southern Railway was the greatest of them all. Its station, an imposing structure in the French Second Empire manner with steep mansard roofs, four towers, and an elongated central dome, stood on the Plaza Constitución. Powerful cornices emphasized the horizontality of its façade, and its silhouette was punctuated by large chimneys. The central arched entrance was surmounted by a massive sculptured group. The station was described by Koebel as the Waterloo of the southern hemisphere, handling more passengers than all the Buenos Aires terminals put together. He went on:

There is something very impressive about the Plaza Constitución, the terminus of the Great Southern Railway. Seen from without, the stately building that fronts the open square is sufficiently imposing; viewed from within, the place more than fulfils the promise of its exterior. There is a spaciousness here and a strictly ordered bustle that bespeaks the railway of importance, very sure of itself, its methods, and its officials. The waiting rooms, the ticket office, the refreshment rooms, and the book-stalls all breathe the same atmosphere. In the world of railway companies there are undoubtedly terriers and greyhounds, whose conduct is reflected in their attitude and trains ... The Great Southern is a greyhound.[22]

So great was the growth of passenger traffic in the 1920s that an already vast station was remodelled and enlarged in 1927. There were several more terminals in Buenos Aires, including those of the Buenos Aires Central Railway at Chacarita and the Buenos Aires Western at Once. Together with the freight stations they took up a considerable area of the city.

After the depression of the late nineteenth century Argentina was very much a country on the move in the first three decades of the twentieth. This was well illustrated by station-building and civic pride outside the capital. La Plata, the administrative centre of Buenos Aires province, had undergone economic vicissitudes at the end of the century, but with the upturn in its fortunes in the next few years it acquired a station of striking originality, an overall shed flanked by a staggeringly ornate pentagonal building covered in statuary and surrounded by a dome. The doorway bore 'La Plata' carved above it, and had all the appearance of a city gate.[23] Another La Plata station, quite different, four-square and concrete, belonged to the provincial government's metre-gauge railway. At Rosario the role of the station in civic pride was confirmed in 1925 when the foundation stone for a new station was laid to commemorate the bicentennial of the founding of the city.

At Concordia a fine classical station with twin towers marked the headquarters of the Argentine Northern Railway in the Entre Rios province. From the beautiful brick structure at Alemania, with its over-hanging eves and balconied flat roofs, to the classical façade of the station offices at Tucumán, from the neat brick and stone structure of Puerto Madryn in Welsh Patagonia, with its fine balusters, corner urns, and ironwork, to the white square mass and canopies of Concepción de Uruguay, Argentinian stations explored a remarkable range of styles and materials.

Across the River Plate in Uruguay, the great Central Station in Montevideo, built in 1897 and designed by a Uruguayan architect, Luis Andreoni, virtually marked the coming-of-age of the country. It was the grandest building in Montevideo when it was built, and adopted a style which seems to have been particularly congenial to Latin American nationalism, Second Empire. The complex variegated arcading of its façade was adorned with statues, including those of James Watt and George Stephenson, the whole surmounted by steep mansard roofs and a squat tower with projecting rounded windows. Behind was a magnificent overall train-shed. Throughout Uruguay every station was equipped with a sign announcing the distance from Montevideo station, symbolizing a radiating nationalism well matched by the manner in which all lines led to the capital. Yet Uruguayan stations achieved a diversity almost as great as that as Argentina, from the tin shack at Pan de Azúcar to the heavy, unrelieved, square strength of Paysandú, from the elegant classical Salto to the delightful single-platform country station at Paso de los Toros.

The station at Asunción in Paraguay was one of the most remarkable in Latin America. The tracks were designed to enter the train-shed at a shallow angle to the street and an impressive building with a grand tower was inserted in the triangle formed between the lines and the road. The train-shed arched over the adjacent pavement and a long colonnade carried pedestrians along the side of the station as though rather hoping that they would become passengers. Although the overall effect was classical, the end towers of the shed dominating the street corner had distinctly Gothic elements. It made brilliant use of a difficult site and united station and thoroughfare in a most satisfying way.

A remarkably complex railway system was created in Brazil, with federal, state, and private (largely British) railways. The southern state, São Paulo, was developed by the coffee boom of the late nineteenth century. The railways coped with very difficult terrain there, but none the less enough capital was left, apparently, for some lavish stations. In São Paulo, the Estação da Luz ('Station of Light') was built in an overblown Italianate Renaissance style. In red brick and white stone, it had a façade of great length matched by a high tower which reached up to the light which its name celebrated. It was built as a side station with twin towers flanking the train-shed. Inside, the entrance hall was designed like a grand salon of a Renaissance palace, highly decorated, with Corinthian pilasters rising to a series of cornices surrounding a painted ceiling. The São Paulo railway adopted a range of styles. The station at Santos bore more relation, on a smaller scale, to Montevideo Central, while that at Paranapiacaba was more like an English country station, all wide canopies, with fretted valances on a large island platform surmounted by a fine clock-tower.

At Recife, the capital of Pernambuco province in north-eastern Brazil, the British-owned Great Western of Brazil built an imposing station, grand enough for any capital. Twin towers, each capped by sculptures of four mighty condors, flanked a great semicircular ribbed window. Stepped-down wings extended on each side and the whole was finished off with an elegant domed lantern. The square outside was adorned, a neat British touch, with a bandstand. Only the Brazilian Viação Ferrea do Rio Grande do Sur seemed to adopt a house style, much more Lusitanian in feel, in white stucco with red tiles and large moulded windows. At Rio the old station was replaced by a modern skyscraper which doubles as a clock-tower, but at Belo Horizonte, a provincial capital in central Brazil, a massive station survives from 1922. Its clock-tower, supported on the station's *porte cochère*, and dome were decorated with large female figures on each corner and above the clock itself. Balustraded verandas surmounted each level, and a succession of towers projected from the mass of the building. This was Latin American nationalist classical at its most overblown.

On the other side of the Andes, stations were built in a much more modest style. There, passenger traffic was light, and was generally regarded as a nuisance. The enormous cost of engineering the lines ensured that little money was left for the stations. Nevertheless, stations reflected the same combination of foreign capital and nationalist pride. In

Chile, British railway capital provided Valparaiso with a classical station, while Santiago's Alameida Station was built on the broad Avenida Bernardo O'Higgins, linking the railway to independence heroes in a manner common throughout Latin America. Chilean stations usually had overall roofs in the British manner. At Las Cuevas, on the frontier with Argentina, the cavernous station stands in a vaulted tunnel for protection. The original station in the open was destroyed by an avalanche with the loss of thirty-five lives in 1964.

Lima in Peru at one stage boasted four stations, Monservate, La Palma, Los Desamperados, and Viterbo. Monservate was demolished after an outbreak of bubonic plague, an unusual fate for a station. The original Los Desamperados ('the abandoned ones') was burnt down earlier this century and was replaced by an earthquake-proof Italianate structure clad in cream-coloured stucco. Its name is a curious comment since it is situated beside the back garden of the Presidential palace, and boasts only one train a day. Most of the Andean stations have an abandoned air and see few trains, although those in the capital cities derive a certain faded grandeur from the fact that their buildings often incorporate the headquarters of the railway companies. Cuzco station, the junction for the Santa Ana railways, used by large numbers of tourists to reach the great Incan site of Machu Picchu, was a modest two-storey tin-roofed structure with one platform until the pressure of visitors led to its expansion in recent years. Other principal stations in the Peruvian Andes, like Oroya and Huancayo, are equally modest, although Fawcett described Huancayo as 'the prettiest station I have seen anywhere'.[24] On the southern Peruvian railway

The North American stamp is upon it all, giving the line a flavour completely different to that of the Chilean systems . . . Nowhere on the Southern—not even in Arequipa—is there a train shed. Stations are naked, open to the Andean skies, sometimes divorced from any visible settlement to justify their existence.[25]

The North American flavour was emphasized by the fact that the simple station buildings contained 'the traditional bay window on the low platform, housing the station-agent–operator's office with the usual table in the bay complete with telegraph instruments, sounders, telephones, and so on'.

The station at La Paz, Bolivia, presents a sense of square, muscular, classical power, emphasized by its strong tower, but boasts only one platform behind. In Ecuador, both Quito and Riobamba adopted a modest, charming Spanish style in cream stucco and red tiles, no bigger than large houses. But Bogotá in Colombia was provided with one of the grandest of Andean stations in 1917. Its full-length windows give the appearance, appropriately enough, of a power house, and the quantity of glass gives it a modern, almost Bauhaus feel. Yet the central portion was built with a rusticated lower storey and the entrance canopy supported Corinthian pillars with a sculpture of a mighty condor on the entablature. Elsewhere in Colombia, the stations are like Spanish houses, some of them in wild colour schemes, like the bilious green and pink of Zipaquiva. A multiplicity of railway companies in Venezuela ensured that Caracas had four stations by 1905, but Percy Martin found them dirty, shabby, and comfortless.[26]

Like those of Caracas, the stations of Mexico have generally had a bad press. By the turn of the century Mexican railways were divided into a group which were American-owned, largely connecting Mexico to the United States, and two (the early Mexican Railway started in 1857 and the Mexican Southern of 1889) which were British. Several of these were swept up into the state National Railways of Mexico in the early years of this century. There were at this time few, if any, pretentious stations. The Central Railway's Buenavista terminus in Mexico City did not fulfil the splendid prospect its name implied. It consisted only of a simple two-storey stone block with an overall shed behind covering two platforms. At Puebla, the Inter-Oceanic Station of the National lines was a solid stone range with a squat central tower. But when Mexican stations moved from the era of foreign capital to the period of nationalist fervour, they took on a new self-conscious national grandeur, complete with the acres of frescos which Aldous Huxley noted on his visit to Mexico.[27] Theroux described Potosi station as

a mausoleum of stupefied travellers, which bore on its upper walls frescoes by Fernando Leal. It was very much a Mexican style of interior decoration for public buildings, the preference for mob scenes and battle pieces instead of wall-paper. In this one, a frenzied crowd seemed to be dismantling two locomotives made of rubber. Pandemonium under a thundery sky; muskets, arrows, pickaxes, and symbolic lightning bolts; probably Benito Juarez leading a charge.[28]

The railway stations of the Caribbean, however, deserve close attention. Both Cuba and Jamaica had extensive railway systems, dating from the earliest years of railway construction. In Cuba, where the first line was opened as early as 1837, there were two main systems, British-owned in the west and American-owned in the east, by the end of the century. At the time of the First World War, the United Railways of Havana built a magnificent central terminal. It was in the Spanish Renaissance style, built in American terracotta, and with its waiting-room, concourse, café, and bar finished in Italian marble and Spanish tiles. This was American imperial building on a grand scale. Twin towers bore the arms of the railway companies emblazoned upon them. At San Juan in Puerto Rico, an opulent Spanish-style station was built in 1913. It may well have influenced the Spanish style in the United States and reflected the role of American imperialism in assimilating a Spanish cultural heritage.

No such pomposity was to be found in the British Caribbean islands. Jamaica, where the first railway of 1845 was the first in the British colonial empire, was provided with a diverse group of wonderfully eccentric stations. Many were of wood and featured fine carving, canopies, beautiful lamps, and central towers. At Montego Bay there was an overall shed backed by a long building with an elaborate tower. Montpelier was stone-built with a wooden tower projecting from the top. There, identical buildings stood on each side of the track. But the most beautiful Jamaican station was at Cambridge. The main building had a high pointed roof with a cupola on top. A fine tower with stepped windows stood at one end. Seldom did weather-boarding reach such architectural heights as this, and seldom did one short platform have such a fine building attached.

Railways were also built on Antigua, Barbados, Haiti, and Trinidad, but stations were always rudimentary on these islands. Only in Port of Spain, Trinidad, was there a station of any pretension. This was rebuilt in 1924, with a long, plain, classical two-storey building, three canopied platforms, and an overbridge in the British manner. P. Ransome-Wallis remarked that one platform would have sufficed for the traffic,[29] and indeed it was not long before Trinidad's railways, together with those of all the smaller West Indian islands, were shut down.

The stations of South America and the Caribbean are mainly the products of the great building-boom era between 1890 and the 1920s. They were built in a vital period of political turmoil, growing republican nationalism, and American and British imperialism, formal and informal. Their styles—apart from those of the British West Indies—are generally variations on Renaissance themes, Italianate, Spanish, Second Empire, reflecting national aspirations and the pomposity of civic and national pride of many regimes. British and American capital and technical expertise were dominant almost everywhere, yet seemed anxious to flatter their hosts. But the stations do demonstrate that architectural influences flowed north and south through the Americas, bending styles derived from Europe to new ends.

3

The Station in Architecture (3)
Asia, Australasia, and Africa

IT was the appearance of the railway station in the non-European world
which staked its claim to be not only the distinctive architectural form of
the late nineteenth and early twentieth centuries, but also the first which
was genuinely world-wide.[1] A case might be made for the Christian
church, but there were many more stations than churches, and the railway
penetrated cultures which were resistant to Christianity. The great era of
station-building in Asia, Australasia, and Africa was between the 1860s
and the 1920s, with the boom years from 1890 to 1914. In India, though
the first stations appeared in the 1850s, the finest examples came later and
the building of lines to the deepest recesses of the subcontinent went on
until 1914.[2] Elsewhere in Asia, stations were to emerge as the prime
symbols of European power only at the end of the century. The remarkable
Ceylonese railway network was built largely as a response to the insatiable
demands of tea-planting from the 1880s. Although Central Asia was to fall
to Russian arms—and soon after to the railway station—in the 1870s, it
was not until the turn of the century that Siberia and the Far East bowed to
the onward march of the station, here rigidly classified into a whole range
of categories of importance. Similarly, railways and their stations swiftly
followed the late appearance of imperial rule in upper Burma, Malaya, and
Indo-China. If in Japan the railway symbolized the country's rapid
response to Western power and influence, Chinese resistance to the West
was characterized by an often violent antipathy to railways.

Elsewhere, railways in the last years of the century became an inseparable feature of the ambitions of a self-confident age. The spanning of the
United States in 1869 and of Canada in 1885 led to similar grand designs
being formulated for Australia. In the 1870s the French conceived
extravagant plans which included no less than the conquest of the Sahara,
an impractical design never brought to fruition. The even grander Cape to
Cairo dream came nearer to realization, but only when victorious British
arms took the railway to Khartoum in 1899, and the copper of Northern
Rhodesia (Zambia) and the Belgian Congo (Zaïre) lured it north from the

Zambezi in the early years of this century. If the railways and their stations in Latin America were the classic instance of informal imperialism, economic imperialism without political control, the continental visions of Russia, Australia, and the British and French in Africa were emblematic of the formal control of the world by the European empires.

But grand designs did not necessarily produce great architecture. Indeed some of the grandest designs were based on the weakest economic need. So much capital went into the engineering and the track that little was left for the stations. The French built surprisingly modest stations in North Africa. Very few of the stations on what was built of the Cape to Cairo railway were anything more than small wayside halts. Just as the great majority of stations in the United States and Canada, particularly in the earlier period, were no more than frame sheds, so thousands of stations in Africa and Asia were very simple buildings indeed. In Australia the absence of population in the great central deserts ensured that the stations were built more for the benefit of the trains than for the non-existent passengers and goods. On the other hand, on the Trans-Caspian and Trans-Siberian lines the scale of the enterprise was such that the stations became in effect complete communities dominating their localities as part of the process of conquering those vast outer regions of the Russian Empire. The British built grandly in many places in India, partly to celebrate their own power, but also because the scale of the population, the high degree of urbanization, and the economic potential of the railways demanded it. On smaller-scale railways, in Ceylon, South-East Asia, and West Africa, the richness and diversity of railway architecture was truly striking.

India

Nothing symbolized Britain's power in India so completely as the railway station. Stations were to the British what the motte and bailey and great stone keeps were to the Normans. The difference lay in the fact that there were in India so many of them, exhibiting a hugely diverse range of styles. With significant variations, the architectural progression matched the range of experimentation elsewhere. Some of the early stations were cool classical pavilions. But once the Mutiny had raised the temperature of the relationship between Briton and Indian the fortified station became the norm. After experimentation with Romanesque revivalism, Gothic was introduced with a distinctly Indian flavour. India had its own period of gigantism, symbolized by Calcutta's Howrah, but when the rest of the world reverted to the classical forms, the British in

India set about rediscovering and reinterpreting Indian architectural styles.

Some of the early stations were very primitive affairs. Even in a presidency capital like Bombay, it took some time for the station to catch up with the developing pretension of the city. On the first line out of Bombay, Byculla station was used primarily by Europeans, Bori Bunder by Indians, and both were modest wooden structures. Even when the Prince of Wales visited Bombay in 1875, there was still no adequate station there. He left from a mean wooden structure at Parel, near Government House. The British had reserved their first great station gestures for the interior of the subcontinent. When the first 120 miles of the East India Railway were opened from Calcutta to Raniganj in 1855, the ceremony took place at Burdwan station, a long classical structure 66 miles from Calcutta.[3] The railway seemed to be continuing the classical tradition of the East India Company capital itself.

In the aftermath of the Mutiny, however, the eighteenth-century imperial style was dropped, even as the East India Company was wound up. The symmetry of the classical had symbolized order, regularity, the homogeneity of legal codification, and Macaulay's English education for Indians. The Mutiny of 1857 had disrupted all these, and the British now experimented in social, governmental, and economic practice. Yet 1857 had also demonstrated the full strategic importance of railways and their role in maintaining future order. The railway station would now be seen as a significant strategic point to which Whites could withdraw to be rescued by train-borne troops and from which the forces could fan out into disaffected areas. As a result, a number of fortified stations were built in this period of nervousness. They had strong enclosing walls, round corner towers with firing slits from which defenders could command the outer walls. There were few windows on the exterior, their roofs were supplied with long walkways protected by thick parapets, and high look-out towers flanked the entrance and main concourse. The trains appeared to penetrate the buildings themselves, for shed and offices were conceived in a single mass, and the tracks could be closed off by gates. An *Illustrated London News* illustration of 1864 shows the arrival of the Governor-General at the most famous of these stations, Lahore.[4] Huge crowds have gathered, elephants are drawn up, banners are borne aloft, and pennants and flags fly from the entrance and corner towers. It is like a medieval chivalric scene, and the Governor-General emerges from the fortified station like a king or great lord across the drawbridge of his castle. Here the station was setting the tone for a new British self-image, one more related to the power of medieval romance than classical imperial rule. Later, Lahore was made to look more like a station. The look-out towers were provided with clocks, and the fortified entrance was turned into a long *porte cochère* with projecting canopies. When this happened it was clear that the defensive need was over. Nevertheless, this notion of the station as strong point continued, and was partly the reason for many being built outside the communities they served.

The railway companies soon turned their attention to the presidency cities of Madras, Bombay, and Calcutta. As the complex railway networks fanned out from these nodal points of British power the companies built there stations that would match the railway, civic, and administrative grandeur associated with them. The scale of these stations was dictated not only by the numbers of passengers they had to handle and the imperial power they had to represent, but by the complexity of the Indian railway operation, and the range of facilities that had to be made available to the hierarchic and heterogeneous nature of the passenger traffic. The station buildings had to incorporate a variety of waiting-rooms for the classes, races, and sexes, restaurants and toilets equally diverse, as well as resting-rooms and bathrooms for Europeans.

Madras was the earliest British settlement among these cities, and it was there that a grand station in Romanesque revivalist style was built in 1868. The architect was instructed to keep ornamentation to a minimum, but the Victorian's notion of minimal detail would be considerable elaboration to any other age. The round-arched arcading and windows were capped by variegated coloured voussoirs; there were four corner towers and an imposing central one; and towers and roof ridges were finished in fine iron work. The whole produced a chaste, harmonious, and well-proportioned effect.

Within twenty years the immense complexity of British power had been perfectly represented in the greatest station ever built in India, the remarkable Victoria Terminus in Bombay. The station was built on a site of particular significance in the history of Bombay. It was said to be the site of the shrine of the goddess Mumba Devi or Maha Amba who gave her name to Bombay. The Portuguese had built a public gallows adjacent to the shrine's tank, which itself survived until 1805. Now the British built a steam cathedral on a piece of land which had become a sort of palimpsest of indigenous and alien power. The Great Indian Peninsula Railway, replacing a modest station on the same site, scotched all adverse resonances the place might have possessed by arranging the opening of its new station on Queen Victoria's Jubilee day in 1887. To this day the building has a remarkable power in a modern city of concrete skyscrapers

and oppressive traffic. In 1887 its commanding presence must have
seemed the very epitome of British rule.

It was designed by F. W. Stevens in what is often described as the
Gothic Saracenic style. It cost £300,000 to build, a vast sum for the time,
and Murray's *Handbook for Travellers in India, Burma, and Ceylon*, with
typical travel-guide hyperbole, described it as the finest railway station
in India or any country. It is an extraordinary hybrid, combining domes
with spires, fretted and decorated round-headed arches with lancet
and rose windows all in a warm red colour. Middle English, Venetian,
Romanesque, and Orientalist features jostle with each other in an
architectural epic of commercial and religious power. Marbles and
granites were imported and the building was embellished with appropriate statuary and ornamentation. The apex of the dome was surmounted by a colossal figure, over 16 ft. high, representing 'Progress'.
Sculptural panels illustrating 'Engineering', 'Agriculture', 'Commerce',
'Science', and 'Trade' were set into the gables, and cameo busts of the
directors of the company were placed in the main façade. If Lahore
symbolized military power, Victoria Terminus represented a scientific
and commercial dominance which could suck in and re-process a whole
range of other cultures. To this day, it signifies almost better than any
other building the Victorians' love of spectacle and sentiment and their
confidence that a new world order could be created out of a massive
syncretism.

No other Bombay station could match it, and none tried. The Bombay,
Baroda, and Central India Railway built a grand headquarters building
across the road from their station at Churchgate, but the station was left
to fend for itself. It had been built in 1876 and consisted of a whole
succession of low-roofed, dormer-windowed, gabled buildings. Colaba,
built in 1893, was no more than a pleasant, small, English country town
station, with Gothic windows, a tight upstanding *porte cochère*, and a single
tower.

In Calcutta the railway companies seem almost to have been overawed
by the classical splendour of the Viceroy's palace and the great secretariat
buildings dating from the turn of the eighteenth and nineteenth centuries. The stations were to be vast in size but unexciting in form. The
first Sealdah station of 1862 derived its prime grandeur from its engineering works: a six-mile embankment had to be built to bring the railway
into the centre of Calcutta. The station itself was built with massive
stolidity as though to distance itself from the Georgian grace of the great
imperial buildings near by. This is well illustrated by the photographs of
its construction preserved in the India Office Library in London. The

foundations were in places 45 ft. deep, incorporating great water tanks, and its walls were 10 ft. thick. It was described as Italianate, but it bore little relationship to the contemporary light Italianate villas of the United States and of English country houses. It was later replaced by another station which was said to have features modelled on the Palace of Nineveh. Its 200-foot-long waiting-room was surmounted by an arched gallery and a magnificently arcaded clerestory.

Across the Hooghly, at Howrah, the East India Railway, often described as the premier railway company of India, built another massive terminus, which was opened in 1906. In 1855, when the first railway line was opened from Howrah, there had only been a collection of huts and sheds on the site. Now the architect, Halsey Ricardo, had designed a station in redbrick gigantism, providing a dramatic contrast with the syncretic graces of Bombay's Victoria Terminus. Jan Morris described it as a combination of Tibetan monastic and English penal, with both Moorish and Romanesque detail.[5] But what it lost in architectural refinement, it made up in staggering scale. No fewer than eight towers dominated the façade, six of them capped by shallow-hipped roofs, two of them flat, open, and balustraded, bearing flag-poles, and all arranged in a numbing symmetry. There were several lesser towers, the corner ones with domes. Open balustraded verandas intruded at every level, the frontage being stepped back to incorporate them. Two large *portes cochères* offered ingress to a station which was immediately dubbed the largest in India, perhaps even in all Asia. Only the equally massive Central Station in Tokyo could compare with it.

Outside the presidency cities, the stations can be divided into those of the large provincial cities, those of smaller towns, and those of the princely states. The stations of the presidency cities were all head stations, termini befitting their status as ports and capitals, but those of the provincial cities were generally through stations with side buildings. It was the need to provide so many public areas which produced the enormously long frontages of these stations, the buildings often as long as the platforms themselves. Such was the case at Rawalpindi, a massive stone structure with six powerful crenellated towers, at Mooltan, where a lighter effect was produced by beautiful arcading, stone latticework, long balustrades on three levels, all surmounted by *chatrio*, and at Khargpur, where the central block was surmounted by a tower. At Ahmednagar the massive effect was relieved by a complex division of the building into different projecting, outwards and upwards, separate blocks, whereas at Ambala, Allahabad, and Jullunder the whole was brought together into one single undulating block.

Throughout India there were countless hundreds of smaller stations where simple functionalism reflected a predominantly 'native' passenger business. A covered platform to keep off the worst excesses of the monsoon rain, a ticket office, and a large, bare waiting-room or shed with a stand-pipe outside were all that were provided. By contrast, those places which could be expected to have a predominantly European clientele, particularly at the hill stations, a sort of English country style was adopted to create the right atmosphere for a cool refreshing visit to the hills. Such was the case at Simla, Darjeeling, Solan, Coonoor, and Ootacamund. They were small-scale, comfortable, appropriate to their surroundings. At the other end of the spectrum were the pilgrim stations, expected to be used only by Indians, and in vast numbers. They were given immensely long platforms, like their military counterparts, some of the longest in the world, and huge circulation areas to cope with the great press of travellers at significant pilgrimage periods.

Through the British, the Indian princes acquired armorial bearings, a strict order of precedence, salutes, and much other paraphernalia of an invented tradition. They also acquired the railways and many of them became as proud of their state systems as of the other perquisites of the British connection. Their distinctive stations often tried to adopt local styles. Many in Rajputana, at Jaipur, Jodhpur, Ajmer, Udaipur, incorporated Rajput motifs or were built to match local buildings like forts. The Deccan developed a distinctively four-square stone-built style. Both Secunderabad and Hyderabad presented long arcaded fronts to the platform, back by powerful rectangular blocks containing offices. That at Hyderabad with its wide cornices and balustraded roof detail was somewhat less austere than its more utilitarian neighbour at Secunderabad. Throughout the state of Hyderabad, the smaller stations followed the same pattern in miniature: stone-built, with strongly accented quoins, and heavy arcading often relieved by tubs of flowers and shrubs, and fine iron corner brackets and lamps. At Junagadh in Gujarat a beautiful country-style station with deep-pitched roofs and elaborate wood carving sheltered behind the hugely impressive Reay Gate with its massive clock-tower. Town gate and station were here brought together. The station at Gwalior, a neo-Mughal construction with *chatrio* at every corner, consisted in effect of a series of pavilions connected by verandas in a light and elegant stone. So fascinated was the Maharaja Scindia of Gwalior with railways that his table was adorned with a silver centre-piece, in effect a classical station adorned with statuary and urns, from which there emerged a silver model of a train which circulated liqueurs and cigars.

The tradition of the 'Orientalist' station never died in India through-out the British period. Mughal-style stations had been built in the Lucknow–Agra area, often, as at Nawab, single platform stations with an overall roof framed by minarets—and with a side pavilion capped by domed open towers. Madras Egmore, completed in 1908, was also in a 'Mughal' style, curiously out of place in South India. It was a wildly ornate station in brick trimmed with granite and sandstone. Several towers were capped by domes in the shape the Mughals had brought with them from Persia and Central Asia. There were also *chatrio* and intricate stone carving, particularly in the fantastic stone brackets, the drip stones, and rich friezes. A great range of waiting-rooms, offices, restaurants, baggage rooms, and a post office were supplied within.[6] This tradition was continued in the 1920s with the new stations built at Lucknow in 1926 and Kanpur (Cawnpore) in 1928. The long façades of these redbrick buildings were adorned with Mughal arches; the interiors were provided with airy loggias and wide verandas, from which sprang a whole succession of open towers adorned with lattice-work and capped by domes of varying sizes. This was a splendid late flowering of the 'Orientalist' style, and was to the British in India what the Spanish mission-station style was to the United States.

Elsewhere, however, other styles were taking over. In Bombay the new stations were built in international concrete style. In 1928 a new Churchgate was designed, mainly to cope with suburban traffic. Its totally undistinguished architecture was largely and mercifully obscured by shop-fronts. The old Colaba station was closed in 1930 when the massive Bombay Central was opened. Its façade was dominated by a 65-ft. concrete arch, with a vast concourse beyond flanked by offices and retiring rooms. Its functionalism was at least tempered by a grand conception of space. At the same time the great Victoria Terminus was extended by the addition of another station behind to cope with increased long-distance traffic.

In the same period the new capital of India at New Delhi was being designed by Sir Herbert Baker and Sir Edwin Lutyens. Their original conception involved a great railway station in one of the most important sites in the capital.[7] The Queen's Way, which ran at right angles to the King's Way, was to have a massive terminal station at its head, dominat-ing Connaught Circus and second in importance only to the Viceroy's palace on the Raisina Acropolis at the head of King's Way. The station was never built. The New Delhi station which did appear, somewhat further away, was a functional monstrosity in concrete and steel. Delhi, in fact, despite its status as the Mughal capital and its vital importance as

Cambridge Station, Jamaica.

Puerto Madryn, in the Patagonia region of Argentina, shortly after closure in the early 1960s. The Central Chubut Railway was taken over by the state in the 1920s.

Concordia, Argentina; headquarters of the Argentine North Eastern Railway, and now of the state-owned Urquiza line.

Alemania, terminus of a branch from Salta in north-west Argentina, built in the 1920s for the state-owned FC Central Norte.

Estación Central in Montevideo, Uruguay, designed by Luis Andreoni and built in 1897 for the Central Uruguay Railway.

Belo Horizonte, Brazil, built in 1922 for the Estrada de Ferro Central do Brasil.

Asunción, Paraguay, principal station of the FC Presidente Carlos Antonio Lopez, formerly the Paraguay Central Railway. The station was designed by the Italian architect Alejandro Ravizza and opened in 1862.

Bogotá, Colombia.

a great railway junction, had never had a distinguished station. Delhi Junction had a long, curving, double-arcaded front, in redbrick Eurasian Gothic, with small crenellated towers, the only hint of decoration being supplied by blinds on all the windows. On the other hand, the *Railway Magazine* reported that its internal arrangements were extremely convenient.[8] The only railway building in New Delhi to emerge in the Baker–Lutyens style was in fact the Northern Railway headquarters, Baroda House.

Many of the old imperial stations have now been replaced. The long, low colonial station at Surat was demolished in favour of a modern office-block style station. New stations have been built since independence at Jodhpur, Siliguri, and Baroda, among many others. A station featured as an important part of the design of Le Corbusier for the New Punjabi capital at Chandigarh, but there the station with its ramps, car-parks, and adjacent bus station was mainly designed to benefit the internal combustion engine. None of the new stations conveyed the confident self-assurance or whimsy of their distinguished predecessors. Independent India has been unable to express any distinctive national culture through its new stations. Like Indian airports, which some of them resemble, they are merely poor relations of the international style. Ironically, it was the imperial British who were able to create syncretic styles which became distinctively Indian.

Ceylon, Singapore, and Hong Kong

The British created in Ceylon (Sri Lanka) one of the finest island and mountain networks in the world. The first sections of the Colombo to Kandy railway were opened in 1865, and from that time there was continuous railway-building on the island until the 1920s. Lines extended north and east along the coast, and branch lines were built in the interior to all the main plantation areas, for the cultivation of tea, after coffee had failed, developed dramatically between the 1880s and 1920s. In 1910 a line which was described as being 'of imperial importance' was started to link Ceylon to India. The South India Railway was to be built as far as Ramaswaram and then connected to Ceylon by embankments and bridges.

It was the fact that this was essentially a planters' system which ensured that the stations were built of a standard and elegance which a plantocracy could use with comfort. The photographic archive of the Crown Agents in London contains a magnificent record of these stations in their pristine condition. Many of them were built in a simple, elegant, almost standard form. There was usually a two-storey building, with a cool loggia, surmounted by a veranda at first-floor level, reached by an open staircase. Fine lamps, English rural-style fencing, and lattice-work round the veranda and stairs created a pleasingly English colonial form. Flowers and creepers became almost part of the architecture. In places the platform loggia was formed of a row of Doric columns, as at Negombo. A few were thatched, but most had iron or tile roofs. Henry Cave's *Guide* to the island's railways described the station at Ohiya as being like somewhere in Cornwall,[9] and at the hill stations of Nauwara-Eliya and Nanuoya there were distinct efforts to reproduce English country stations. They were built as country cottages with platform canopies on one side, *portes cochères* on the other, all surrounded by flowers. Handsome stations were built on the line eastwards from Colombo towards Galle because it was along that coast that lawyers and civil servants had their bungalows. At Mount Lavinia, a nineteenth-century Governor, Sir Edward Barnes, had built a marine villa. The expenditure was subsequently repudiated by the Colonial Office and the villa was turned into a fine hotel with a station alongside. The original station in Colombo had twin towers which housed the first- and second-class booking offices at their bases. The platforms had canopies supported by beautiful ironwork, but overall the station fitted no conventional style. There were several stations in Colombo and for many years the principal mode of transport within the city was the train. In 1911 Fort Station was developed as the principal Colombo station. The old terminus was converted into a goods station, a common fate for superannuated passenger stations throughout the world, and Fort was provided with platform canopies and flowers to enhance its attractive position beside the lake in the centre of the city.

Further east, another colonial island was provided with a railway in 1903. The first Singapore station, Cluny Road, was a long brick building on stilts to protect it from flooding. It had a long colonial veranda and a high cupola, while the terminus of the railway, Tank Road Station at the docks, had a tower which made it an aid to ships navigating the harbour. On the other side of the island the terminus was at Woodlands Station, an English country station to match its name, long, low, with overhanging eaves, barge-boarding, and fine lamps. In 1923 Singapore was connected to the state of Johore in Malaya by a causeway and Singapore station, instead of being merely an entrance to a small island system, became a portal to Malaya and ultimately Thailand. Indeed, there had even been plans to connect this area of South-East Asia by railway to India and China. The new Singapore station was built to match these pretensions. Within a plain exterior there was a large booking hall with long slender windows rising to an arched roof and decorated with Italian mosaics depicting aspects of Malayan life.

In the late nineteenth century a succession of small lines had been built to connect the Malayan tin mines to the coast. It was not until 1909 that the spinal railway of Malaya was completed, connecting the rubber plantations to the capital, Kuala Lumpur, north to Ipoh and Penang, and later (after 1931) up the pan-handle to Thailand. The local stations on this system ranged from the simple wooden building at Batu Gajah or Tampin to the large, airy, open-sided barn style at Peluk Amson. Many of them seemed like tiny oases hemmed in by the alien rubber which overran the entire peninsula. Kuala Lumpur acquired at the beginning of the century one of the most spectacular stations in Asia, where building and train-shed were conceived as one architectural whole and the trains entered what seemed like a cross between an extravagant Oriental palace and a mosque. The station was matched by an equally elaborate hotel across the road, and together they owed more to the Mughal style in India than to any local architectural forms. At Ipoh, the capital of the state of Perak, an early station was replaced by a heavy stone structure, quite different from that of Kuala Lumpur, with prominent quoins, powerful arches, and three levels of verandas, surmounted by balustrading and a dome. A clock-towered station in white stone was built at Prai in Butterworth on the other side of the strait from Penang, the earliest British possession in Malaya. In Bangkok the station reflected the origins of the capital that went into Thai railways, with a façade and overall roof that owed much to France. Smaller stations, however, like that at the fashionable resort of Hua Hin, adopted a local multi-roofed pagoda style. If Singapore acquired pretensions as the gateway to a continent in the 1920s and 1930s, Hong Kong had secured similar status earlier in the century. There a 22-mile railway completed in 1911 connected Kowloon to the Canton province and the railway system of China. The first Kowloon station stood opposite the Hong Kong Star Ferries terminal. It was built in an Italianate style with no concessions to the East at all, in red brick with stone columns. The fine clock-tower, together with the famous Peninsula Hotel near by, dominated the Kowloon waterfront, and acted as a powerful Western gateway to China. There the Western merchants and officials of the Chinese treaty ports could entrain for their destinations in China.

The station in Kowloon was demolished in the 1970s and replaced by a soulless concrete and glass structure on reclaimed land at Hung Hom, opened in 1973. The new station is inconvenient to pedestrians, being a considerable walk from the ferries' landing stage. It is enslaved to the

motor car, surrounded by great road ramps, and dominated by an un-
pleasant multi-storey car-park. Now it repels rather than beckons, and
Hong Kong has destroyed another of the fine colonial buildings of the
territory.

Russia

The spreading tentacles of Russian railways into Asia marked the last
great imperial push of the Tsarist empire. It sent alarm bells ringing
throughout the East, and brought Russia into renewed conflict with
China, Britain, and ultimately—more seriously—Japan. The speed and
extravagance (despite all the cheese-parings of the Emperor Alexander
III) of Russian railway-building were remarkable. These were State
enterprises, engineered by the military, and using convict and forced
labour. Revolt between the Aral and Caspian seas occasioned the building of the Trans-Caspian in the 1880s, but the young George Nathaniel
Curzon saw in it a much more sinister imperial plan.[10] Perhaps, he
thought, they hoped to link it up to a Euphrates Valley railway, which
would make Baghdad a Russian southern capital. Otherwise, by securing
railway concessions in Persia, the Russians could reach the Gulf and at
one and the same time create their longed-for warm-water port and turn
the western flank of the British in India. Again they might contemplate
connecting their Central Asian line to Herat and Kandahar and on to
Quetta, thereby creating a through route from Calais to Calcutta. Curzon
had little need to spell out to his contemporaries the commercial and
strategic dangers of such a scheme. Already preparing himself for the
first of his political glittering prizes, the viceroyalty of India, he visited the
Trans-Caspian in 1888 and published a book on it in 1889.

None of the schemes Curzon feared was to be accomplished. But the
Russians had their own grand plan which made even the North American
transcontinental schemes and the Cape to Cairo dream pale into insig-
nificance. That was, of course, the Trans-Siberian railway. Moscow to
Nakhodka, St Petersburg to Vladivostok—however one measured it, that
scheme would be wellnigh 6,000 miles long, compared with a mere 3,420
for New York to Los Angeles or 3,500 miles for the never-completed
Cape to Cairo. The Cossacks had crossed Siberia in the seventeenth
century. It had later become a place of exile and migration. In the second
half of the nineteenth century the population of Siberia had doubled, but
although some short railways had been built to connect river navigations
—as in Canada—conditions of transport remained exceptionally primitive. The forerunners of the railway stations of the Trans-Siberian were
the *étapes*, the stockaded rest stations with barrack-like rooms, and

the post-houses which had been built across Siberia earlier in the century. The railway had advanced across the Urals by 1874. Perm to Ekaterinburg was completed in 1878 and Ekaterinburg to Tyumen in 1885. Proposals for a Trans-Siberian had been made since the 1850s, but it was famine and political disorder in the East at the beginning of the last decade of the century which finally prompted the building of the line. The Tsarevich Nicholas, the future Nicholas II, on a visit to the Far East, cut the first sod and laid the foundation stone of the railway station at Vladivostok on 19 May 1891. He returned to European Russia over-land, leaving a trail of triumphal arches in the towns of Siberia, and in a sense rounding off the old route before the appearance of the railway.

The vast project was pushed forward faster than the spanning of the United States or Canada. Khabarovsk was reached from the direction of the eastern terminus by 1894. The Western Siberia started in 1892 and was opened in 1895. The Central Siberian from Ob to Irkutsk was built between 1893 and 1898. Ice-breaking ferries were launched on Lake Baikal in 1900, the year in which the Trans-Baikal railway to Sretensk was completed. The line round Lake Baikal was finished after the outbreak of the Russo-Japanese war in 1904. The Chinese Eastern railway was completed in 1904, and the Amur railway was developed between 1908 and the First World War. All of this construction took place, of course, in the face of the most severe weather conditions imaginable. Track could be laid only during the brief summer months. Railway stations and associated building works were constructed during the winter.

On such mighty systems as these the stations were clearly to be places of great importance. Their significance was enhanced by the fact that they were often far from the towns whose names they bore. The railways had to be driven by the fastest and most convenient route. Towns had often to be sited in defensive, strategic positions not readily accessible to the railway. The railway stations created new settlements, some of which indeed were ultimately to be more important than the traditional towns they were supposed to serve. In 1888 Curzon found station-building activity going on across the Trans-Caspian route. He noted the classi-fication of these stations, the great variety of styles used, and their relative paucity over vast desert distances compared with European standards —only sixty in a thousand miles—and their distance from the towns and cities they were to serve. At Bukhara the station was ten miles from the old city. Samarkand station, 150 miles from Bukhara with only two stations between, was three miles from the city itself. Many of the stations as Curzon found them were no more than rude shanties, a few planks half-buried in the sands of Central Asia. But the Russians were well aware of the grandeur of their exploit—'mounting the stream of ages into Central Asia', as Curzon called it, taking the 'fire horse' into the very heart of old cultures. At Samarkand, masons were active building a grand terminus (which was to remain so only until the railway was carried through to Tashkent in 1898).[11] Each of the great oases of Central Asia was eventually to be graced with powerfully squat four-square stone-built stations, perfectly symbolizing the implacable toughness of Russian power.

The stations on the Trans-Siberian were classified according to size and amenity into five categories. It was originally decreed that great economies had to be exercised in the provision of stations, which were to be mainly of wood. But all stations of any importance, even category III and IV, soon possessed elaborate churches, hospitals, schools, workshops, engine sheds, living quarters for railway staff, and even theatres. Some had barracks and medical centres for migrants. This was the railway station as town. Merchants and storekeepers flocked to them, building at first only shanties for warehouses and stores, and the nearby towns which they were supposed to serve were seriously damaged. The actual station buildings at the centre of these new railway communities became administrative centres of some importance and this was reflected in their architecture. Fine stone structures, confident in their detail with powerful round arches, were built at Petropavlosk, Zlatoust, and Kurgan (all category III) and at Omsk (II). At Tayga (III)—the junction for Tomsk—Ob, Achinsk, and Olginskaya (III) there were long, low, wooden stations with twin gables fronting on to the platform. Even a simpler station, like that at Vyazemskaya (III), was adorned with high chimneys, dormer windows, and a flag-pole on its front gable. Class III stations could in fact exhibit a great diversity of style and size, while many a class IV, like that at Shumikha, could seem little different in scale. But the class V's showed their lowly status: they were very small and could look lost in their vast and bleak surroundings.

At Vladivostok, the station which rose on Nicholas's foundation stone was a baleful prison-like building with two blocks linked by a single-storey entrance range. The plain, towerless strength of all the stations seemed to be a conscious representation of a powerful and economical practicality. There was nothing of the picturesque or civic excess in these stations. It was left to the adjacent churches to provide elaboration and the upward thrust of towers, domes, and crosses. Tayga, Tatarskaya Isil-Kul, and over one hundred other stations boasted such churches, built from the Alexander III fund and by other donors. Only occasionally was a churchless station built with its own elaboration. At Oyash, 50 miles north-east of Novosibirsk, a small wooden station with a distinctly Orientalist feel to its carved wooden decoration was dominated by a water tower, similarly decorated, which provided the upward thrust so common in Western stations in the nineteenth century and so lacking on the Trans-Siberian.

Many of the old stations were subsequently swept away. Irkutsk acquired a massive station, with two central towers capped by domes and larger corner blocks with connecting wings. Tayga's wooden station was replaced by a much grander structure adorned with elaborate lamps. The American Harmon Tupper found two stations coexisting at Mariinsk in the 1960s.[12] The old wooden structure, in the same style as the original Ob, Achinsk, or Olginskaya, remained in use, but a new stone building with a central booking hall and two wings was completed, ready to take over.

On a journey across the Trans-Siberian in 1977, Eric Newby found many of the old stations still surviving. Near Sverdlovsk (formerly Ekaterinburg) he saw an extravagantly castellated little wooden station in the woods. But everywhere he found a paranoia about photography.[13] Generally, he was not allowed to photograph any of the original wooden stations on the grounds that they were too old, presumably an affront to Soviet progressivism and modernity. At Omsk he was not permitted to photograph the station because its front had been removed. In the Far East, on the route to Nakhodka (Vladivostok is forbidden to visitors), he saw many old-fashioned wooden stations still in use, painted green or blue, each with huge iron stoves in its waiting-room.

The Far East

Nowhere were railway systems begun with such reluctance as in the Far East. And nowhere else did stations suffer such massive mortality. In China there were only 300 miles of railway in 1900, although the figure reached 5,200 miles by 1910. In Japan the first railway line between Yokohama and Tokyo (17 miles) was opened in 1872, and within thirty years there were 3,000 miles of track. The newly restored Japanese Emperor opened the line, and thereby scotched the bitter religious opposition that had been aroused against the building of railways. But whereas Chinese railways became a prey to concession seekers, railway builders, and engineers from Britain, France, Belgium, Germany, Russia, Japan, and the United States, even Portugal, Austria, and Italy, the Japanese tried to keep railway-building, after an initial concessionary period, firmly in their own hands.

The first Chinese station was destroyed in 1876. Another wave of station destruction occurred in the Boxer Rising of 1900. Japanese invasions and wars put paid to hundreds of Chinese stations in the 1930s and 1940s. Others were destroyed in the Cultural Revolution. In Japan, station mortality was caused principally by a combination of earthquakes, the ravages of American bombing in the Second World War, and terminal modernism. In China it took many years for the railway to broach the capital. The railway was brought into the vicinity of Peking only gradually. At one stage the station, not far from the foreign legations, was connected to them by a tram line. But at last, in a gesture symbolic of Western encroachment itself, the railway burst through the city wall of Peking, bridged the great moat, and advanced upon the ancient capital itself. In Japan the new imperial capital of Tokyo became the principal railway centre from the start.

Station architecture reflected the intrusiveness of the new Western technology. At the Chinese treaty ports, the stations used by the inhabitants of the foreign settlements were comfortingly Western. One postcard from Shanghai to Scotland, illustrating the railway station and posted before the First World War, bears the message 'is not the station like that at Fort Matilda?'[14] The latter was a stop on the line between Greenock and Gourock in Renfrewshire. Few truly large stations were built in China until modern times, when the Russians assisted in the building of a vast new station in Peking. Despite all the ravages and destruction wrought on Chinese stations, some still bear a curiously 1930s air. At the border station between Hong Kong and Kuangtung province, Shumchün, the first-class waiting-room still contained in 1980 large 1930s armchairs with antimacassars.[15]

In 1898 there were already several termini in Tokyo. The impression given to one railway traveller in that year contrasts dramatically with that of modern Japan. D. T. Timins thought that Japan and railways constituted a curious incongruity:

What should that placid little people know of the rattle and rush of an express train, typical as it is of the nerve-wasting haste with which we Westerners live our lives? Those shining metals are as the veritable trail of the serpent; they follow inevitably in the wake of civilisations, and give rise to crowded and smoky manufacturing towns, while spreading abroad an unrestful desire for travel, with all its concomitant worries and brain wear. Moreover, the destruction of all peaceful village life comes in their train ... I cannot resist saying that when Japan finally exchanges her peaceful simplicity, her admiration for, and artistic appreciation of, Nature's beauties, and her contented national life, for the storm stress, and hurry of that feverish existence known to the West, she will have given up the substance for the shadow.[16]

Japan's flight from her Eden was to be astonishingly swift. And it was reflected in the growing size of her railway stations. The first Yokohama station consisted of two elegant Georgian houses for the offices with a broad entrance canopy and a waiting-room, lit by a fan-shaped window of stained glass, between. The multiplicity of small early termini in Tokyo was soon replaced in the twentieth century by Tokyo Central, a station so vast as to vie with Howrah in Calcutta. It had an enormous entrance range with squat domes at each end and towers along its façade. There were passenger entrances on each corner and a grand porticoed gateway to the offices between. This was the Far East's contribution to gigantism in station-building, and it reflected the national expansiveness of Japan's imperial and Fascist phase.

Timins found Japanese trains to be leisurely. The Tokyo to Kobe train travelled at an average of 12 m.p.h., because

It makes fifty stops en route, some of them of considerable duration, and, as has been shown, much time must be wasted at stations. As the Japanese are at present constituted, accidents to life and limb would most certainly occur if trains made but a brief halt to entrain passengers.[17]

For Paul Theroux seven decades later one of the great mysteries of Japanese train travel was the manner in which Japanese passengers could safely disembark and entrain at stations where trains stopped merely for seconds. Timins's 'placid little people' had indeed found the 'feverish existence' he had predicted. Nowhere had a traditional culture's response to the Western world been so completely reflected in the life of its railways and stations. Today, few old stations survive. Their architecture has faded into unremarkable modernism, devoted to speed, rush, and disciplined circulation. The railway stations have, like so much of the rest of Japanese life, been subordinated to her economic miracle.

Australasia

The railway stations of Australia and New Zealand exhibit a remarkable muscularity of style. This reflected the nature of the environment, the local pride of the individual Australian colonies, and the awareness of the railway builders and architects that they were building for a grander, though then unrealized, future. Australia and New Zealand illustrate too how rarely British Gothic styles were exported, even to her white dominions. The dominant styles were the cottage and the colonial bungalow for country stations and a variety of appealing Italianate and Renaissance forms for the stations of cities and towns. As in the United States, the large city stations underwent a constant process of renewal, culminating in massive rebuilding in the classical manner between the wars.

Early railway lines in Australia connected coastal points to pioneer settlements inland. This was the pattern of first railways in many parts of the world and it was to produce in Australia great complexities of gauge, rolling stock, and working systems. Six colonies developed their own proud practices. It was not until the 1880s that intercolonial connections were made, and the stations which connected them became important not only as points of break of gauge, and therefore of journey for passengers, but also as customs centres. In 1901 West Australia was enticed into the new Commonwealth with the promise of a transcontinental line, just as British Columbia had been persuaded to join the Canadian Confederation with railway promises. The line from Port Augusta on the South Australian system to Kalgoorlie in Western Australia was begun in 1912 and completed in 1917. As late as 1937 there were no fewer than six breaks of gauge between Sydney and Perth. Three gauges met at Port Pirie. More visionary railway schemes were got up in the inter-war years. A line to connect Port Augusta to Darwin and thence by sea to India and the rest of Asia was begun in the 1920s but got no further than Alice Springs, reached in 1929. It was not until 1966 that the transcontinental standard-gauge line was completed, thereby connecting Sydney to Perth without break of gauge for the first time. It has been suggested by Australian authors that, because of all the gauge problems, Australians have always had an inferiority complex about their railways.[18] But a great deal of energy has gone into the extension of the standard-gauge lines and the building of new stations in the modern period.

It is certainly a brash energy rather than an inferiority complex which is conveyed by Australian stations. They did, however, have very simple beginnings. The first Sydney station, as seen in a print of 1855, was a one-platformed wooden barn. By 1871 a photograph shows it little changed. The first Melbourne station, at Spencer Street, was a somewhat larger three-span shed with a side building. On New South Wales lines simple verandaed stations with short wooden platforms like that at Burwood were the norm. But very soon much grander stations were being produced. When the railway reached Paramatta, its terminus was a fine one-storey classical building with a prominent entrance vestibule. Solid country stations of the 1880s, like Penrith and Picton, had a four-square strength which was to characterize all Australian station-building. At Goulbourne a large brick structure with stone quoins and cornices and a central tower and dome had been built in the 1870s, and when the railway reached Wagga Wagga in 1878, the station provided was a fine, long, stone structure with beautiful ironwork.

But the full glory of the early Australian station appeared at Albury. This was the break-of-gauge frontier station between New South Wales and Victoria. It was by far the finest building in the town. It was an elaborate version of the Italianate station, constructed in white and red bricks from Belgium, roofed in slate, and boasting long platform canopies and beautiful iron and glass verandas fronting on to the street. Its entrance porch was surmounted by a square clock-tower. For a number of years the terminal stations of the two colonies faced each other across the Murray River, and the bridge and track to join them were not completed until 1883. A fierce dispute then broke out as to whether the New South Wales Albury or the Victoria Wodonga station should be the exchange station, and it was not until 1886 that Albury won. The importance of building in a grand manner to enhance colonial pride was now apparent. At Serviceton, the frontier station between Victoria and South Australia stood on disputed territory claimed by both colonies, a problem which was not settled until 1914. Serviceton, another Italianate building, had extensive customs provision and also a jail. But it could not match Albury, perhaps because there was no break of gauge there.

Albury set the standard for Australian stations. It is an interesting comment on the character of the colonies that the more lively and eclectic forms of the picturesque, exuberant Gothic, Orientalism, or Scottish baronial, never found favour there. When the railways of Victoria reached the gold-fields at Ballarat, the terminus (for twelve years until the line was extended) was a robust classical structure with Ionic arcading standing on a rusticated porch, surmounted by a clock-tower. The station seemed to represent the arrival of good government and of law and order at the rip-roaring gold-fields. Railways were developed late in Queensland and Western Australia, but by the end of the century Brisbane had a fine station with a handsome side building in red brick and stone with a classical portico and a clock-tower in the best civic manner, and both Perth and Fremantle had long classical ranges without towers, but with heavily accentuated cornices and balusters running round their roof-lines.

Although this high standard of stolid classicism had been established in the nineteenth century, the great station-building period in Australia was to be the twentieth century. Each state of the new Commonwealth seemed to be as jealous of its prestige as the former colonies had been. When the new Sydney Central Station, which brought the line into the heart of the city for the first time, was opened in 1906, its lengthy structure with powerful round-headed arches and long arcading on two storeys was more reminiscent of Indian stations than of those of Europe or North America. Interior sumptuousness arrived with this station too. The walls of the concourse were finished in New South Wales marble; the ticket office was constructed entirely in Tasmanian blackwood; and a feature of the booking hall was an elaborate gallery in stone and brick. The station was reconstructed in a much grander and more familiar Renaissance manner, complete with clock-tower, at the time of the opening of the Sydney Harbour Bridge in 1932. It now became an important through commuter station as well as a main-line terminus.

If the stations of the Australian capitals did not reach the true gigantism of the last great wave of American stations or of Howrah and Tokyo, they came close to it. The central station at Melbourne, Flinders Street, built in Edwardian times, was reconstructed as a massive classical range with a corner entrance crowned by a dome. Above the doorway was a succession of clocks which indicated the next departures to the principal destinations.[19] At the other end of the long façade was a huge clock-tower, and no fewer than six lesser domes finished the corner and entrance elements of the station. Its form was dictated by the tightness of the site between Flinders Street and the river, which necessitated stringing out the narrow building along the full length of platforms which ran parallel to the river behind. Flinders Street was the commuter station for Melbourne, main-line expresses leaving from the less imposing Spencer Street. It demonstrated the rapidly growing importance of commuters in the Australian cities at this time.

In 1928 Adelaide acquired an even grander classical station, a massive four-square structure with Ionic corner pavilions and a central rusticated *porte cochère* with a powerful portico above. It was a head-building which replaced the earlier station of 1902–3. Its classical central waiting-room had a touch of the first Euston about it, eighty years removed, and South Australian railways were so proud of it that they promptly published a booklet providing statistics of its dimensions, quantities of building materials used, and so on.[20] It was designed, after a competition, by Garlick and Jackman of Adelaide.

Australia makes an interesting case of station-building. There was a robust strength about all Australian stations which seemed to reflect the character of the early colonies, their ambitions, and the part they would play in a successful Commonwealth in the twentieth century. Picturesque eclecticism never found a place there, and a classical tradition emerged which set Australia apart from Canada, India, South Africa, and even to a certain extent neighbouring New Zealand. Australian railways took up and developed the Italianate style which had been so influential in Britain and the United States earlier in the century, and by the time the principal Australian stations were built, classical was in style once more. Just as the classical and baroque triumphed in the design of state capitols and ultimately fed back into railway stations, so did Australia cling to forms which had never entirely been superseded as the official architectural language of imperialism.

Few countries have shown such a remarkable sense of responsibility to their station buildings as New Zealand. From their small and humble beginnings in tiny weather-board stations[21] to the great climaxes of the massive Auckland and Wellington stations of the 1930s, New Zealand Railways have consistently adopted thoughtful and sensitive approaches. When railway confidence was beginning to wane elsewhere in the world in the 1930s, New Zealand not only built two of the greatest stations in the southern hemisphere, but under the Labour Government of 1936–49 continued to invest in railways. While there has been contraction more recently, New Zealand Railways, almost uniquely, use the magnificence of some of their stations as a public relations and marketing feature.

New Zealand stations also demonstrate the manner in which, through repeated renewal, station buildings mirror the development of the country. The earliest stations were no more than collections of weather-board huts, similar to a contemporary group of stores. The next phase of the growth of the New Zealand station was to imitate English country practice. At Invercargill a station with an overall roof and side building was provided. Long platform canopies supported by decorated iron and with wooden valances soon appeared. Later, when Invercargill was extended it adopted a classical form. Soon, however, a much more distinctively New Zealand style emerged. From 1877 trunk lines were begun on both North and South Islands to cement the short, separate, coast-to-interior railways which had developed up to that date. The trunk lines called for stations of all sizes from small lean-to flag stations to large city termini.

At Christchurch the original station was no more than a collection of sheds, but in 1877 it was replaced by a long Gothic structure—a rare example in the southern hemisphere—which looked like a succession of chapels at right angles to the platforms with a connecting range running between them.[22] Later, a remarkable wood and glass conservatory was added to the front.

In 1884 New Zealand was lucky enough to acquire a railway architect and engineer who had been trained in Scotland. This was George

Alexander Troup (later knighted). He swiftly established himself as a dominant influence in New Zealand station architecture and produced many remarkable buildings. At Foxton, Petone, and New Plymouth he created a new and striking wooden style with multiple gables, light verandas, and canopies, often capped by a squat tower with cupola and finial. It was a type that would appear throughout the New Zealand system. At Bluff he designed a charming two-storey half-timbered building with a wide cantilevered canopy. His finishing touch was usually Marseilles tile roofing and ridging. These stations, in providing a large space for parcels, traffic clerks, telegraph offices, and sometimes a post office, reflected the particular needs of rural and small-town communities in New Zealand at that time.

Troup produced his masterpiece in Dunedin in 1907. It replaced three older small stations which had been built there in the 1860s and 1870s. The new station, which was the chief pride of New Zealand railways for a number of years, was in a Flemish Renaissance style. It was constructed in basalt, faced in a white stone, and with polished Aberdeen granite pillars supporting the arched colonnade at the front of the building. A 120-ft. clock-tower with three ornate clock faces dominated one side of the building. The interior of the main foyer boasted mosaics, Royal Doulton surrounds to the ticket offices, and stained-glass windows. At one stage the station was under threat, but it has now been lovingly restored and New Zealand Railways very sensibly issue a tourist booklet to celebrate it. Its façade and finest decorative features appeared in the New Zealand film *Pictures*.

Dunedin was to be overshadowed, but not surpassed in elegance, by the vast new stations at Auckland and Wellington completed in the 1930s. They were built in what has sometimes been called classical bankers' style, more akin to London's Waterloo or Boston South than the Beaux-Arts style. Auckland's first wooden station had been replaced in 1885 by a two-storey classical building with a squat tower. This was replaced in turn by the immense station built on reclaimed land in the late 1920s and opened in 1930. There was a great deal of space on the new site, but the station was less conveniently situated to the city than the old one had been. Wellington station, which was opened in 1937, was even grander, with a massive Doric frontage. It too had space for gardens and car-parks, and both had vast concourses. Wellington also contained the headquarters of New Zealand Railways, and its massive, confident air surmounted by rows of flag-poles represented an extraordinary reaffirmation of support for railways in New Zealand.

New Zealand continued to build stations after the Second World War.

At Christchurch, proposals to replace the Gothic station of 1877 had been made at the time of the First World War and again in the 1930s, but it was not demolished until the 1950s, when it was replaced by a modern station more successful than most. It retained many of the traditional features of stations, including a clock-tower more than 100 ft. high, and large circulation areas adorned with tiles with Maori motifs, and frescos depicting New Zealand scenes. This inaugurated a new wave of station-building. At a time when new stations elsewhere meant bus shelters, fine new stations which retained at least some of the spirit of the old were provided at Taita, Palmerston North, and Rotorua, among others. Nevertheless, small rural stations have been closing throughout New Zealand, often to the accompaniment of vigorous opposition from New Zealand farmers. Despite their rearguard action, however, freight handling has been concentrated at larger stations, destroying the role of the small station in the community.

Africa

In 1870 there were still only short stretches of line in North and South Africa, the only railway of any significance being that between Alexandria and Suez, opened in 1852 and superseded by the Canal in 1869. Diamonds at Kimberley and gold on the Witwatersrand transformed the situation in Southern Africa, and great railway schemes became an inseparable part of the partition of Africa by the European powers in the 1880s and 1890s. By the turn of the century Johannesburg was connected to the coast by no fewer than four lines. The main route north from Kimberley was connected to Bulawayo by 1897 and to Salisbury five years later, thus connecting the Southern African lines to the Indian Ocean at Beira. In 1904 the line was across the Zambezi and crossing Northern Rhodesia (Zambia) for the copper deposits of the Congo. By that time, the French had already built an extensive network in North Africa, the Uganda Railway was under construction, the Germans had begun their railways in both Tanganyika and South West Africa, and the British had driven their railway through the Sudan as part of their reconquest of the upper Nile. French grandiose schemes for the crossing of the Sahara came to nothing, but several lines from the coast to the interior of West Africa were built by the British and the French. These were completed in the inter-war years, by which time the Lobito Bay railway in Angola and the Central African railway from Mozambique to Nyasaland were in operation.

When the British naval officer Captain (later Admiral) Colomb passed through Alexandria to Suez on his way to take up a new command in the anti-slavery squadron in 1868, he wrote of the rudimentary nature of stations in Egypt. In Alexandria he found that the railway meandered down to the beach and passengers had to find their way on to the trains without any benefit of station buildings.[23] But by that time a grand station had already been built in the centre of Alexandria. In 1858 the *Illustrated London News* provided an illustration of it, and described it as 'the most substantially constructed edifice in that city, partaking more of a European or Anglican character than most civil structures in Alexandria'.[24] It was designed by Edwin C. Baines as a side building in a simple classical manner with trains entering an overall shed ventilated by open side arcading. At Cairo Central there were long side and head buildings, with a fine corner tower embellished with Moorish arches. The platforms were again covered by an overall shed in the European style.

Generally, African stations made no concessions to local architecture, but were self-consciously intrusive. The four-volume work on the Cape to Cairo railway, published in the early 1920s, commented on the extraordinary Englishness of Sudanese stations.[25] Even the station-masters' uniforms reminded the traveller of Waterloo or Victoria except that the fez replaced the cap. Stations like those at Atbara, Port Sudan, and El Obeid did indeed have the look of an English country or Scottish Highland station, with the building on an island platform, adorned with travel posters and fine lamps. At Khartoum North there were two platforms in an overall shed affording some protection from a fierce sun.

South of the Sahara, it was only in South Africa that stations were built on a European scale, and only there that stations were replaced by new and larger versions. The first simple station at Cape Town, appropriate to the short lines of the mid-Victorian colony, were soon found to be inadequate when that city became, in effect, the gateway to a subcontinent. A fine Italianate *palazzo* was built in Edwardian times, and by then, as in so many other places, it was in fact two stations that were required, one suburban and one for the main line. This was in turn replaced by a modern station in the 1960s. The early Durban station was superseded at the turn of the century by a large, decorated brick structure with a clock-tower in the civic Renaissance manner, with a fine overall train-shed behind. Pretoria and Bloemfontein acquired large, dour, stone structures which somehow reflected the religion and ethos of the Boer republics which they served. Pretoria acquired a new station, suitable for a capital city and designed by Sir Herbert Baker, after the Union of 1910.

The first station in Johannesburg, called 'Park' because it was situated beside the cricket ground and public park, consisted of an island platform with long elegant buildings, sporting beautifully carved woodwork. This station was purchased from an Amsterdam exhibition and survives as part of a railway training college in the Transvaal. It too was replaced by a larger stone station, part of which still stands beside the modern structure which succeeded it. The new station, consisting of the by then classic steel, concrete, and glass concourse with facilities around its outer flanks and with steps and ramps leading down to the platforms below, gave a new twist to the separation of passengers and baggage regarded as an ideal at so many American stations. Johannesburg station was designed specifically to separate the races as the full-blown policies of apartheid were developed by the Nationalist government in the 1950s and 1960s. It remains to this day one of the most potent monuments to racial segregation.

Elsewhere in South Africa, most stations consisted of plain, stolid, stone structures in keeping with the character of the territories. The larger towns like Kimberley, Mafeking, and Pietermaritzburg provided the full range of facilities in long buildings backed by canopied platforms. At many there were African platforms where tin sheds served as waiting-rooms. On the northern line through Bechuanaland and on to Rhodesia the stations were built in a graceful simple colonial style, usually painted white with columned verandas on the track side. On all of the lines in the interior of Africa the number of trains handled per day was very few, single tracking was the rule, and passenger facilities were slight. The arrival of a train would be a significant event, galvanizing a whole community into action perhaps only once or twice a day. Generally the passengers camped and sat out in the open air. The white passengers would avail themselves of the services of a hotel, in a colonial verandaed style not unlike that of the station itself, just beside the tracks. In consequence no elaborate station architecture was needed.

The only large stations in Southern Rhodesia (Zimbabwe) were in Bulawayo and Salisbury. The Bulawayo station was remodelled in 1913 and the building, a long two-storey range, had outer and inner canopies supported on fine ironwork. In Salisbury the station remained an elongated single-platformed structure throughout its history, with all the passenger and office facilities provided in a building almost as long as the platform itself. Trains from Bulawayo used one end of this platform and trains from Umtali the other. The first station was burnt down in 1917 and the new station was reopened in 1925. Despite the great romance and drama of the building of the East African 'Uganda' railway, none of the stations was particularly grand. Only at Nairobi, where the station created the city, was there a handsome building with a deep, shady, wooden valance along the platform side and a fine tapering clock-tower in the middle. Mombasa, the gateway to East Africa, had an entirely unpretentious station. Later, a large modern station with extensive facilities and a clock-tower was opened at Nakuru, an important junction in eastern Kenya, in the early 1960s on the very eve of decolonization.

The British produced a remarkable variety of stations in West Africa, all faithfully recorded in the photographic collection of the Crown Agents who were closely involved in their building. On the Lagos Government Railway, simple white two-storeyed stations with an upper veranda supported on the columns of the lower, set well back from the tracks, were standard. The style was reminiscent of that of Ceylon, where the Crown Agents had also had a hand in station-building. At Iddo Island a long wooden building with a central gable and flanking verandas dominated the station complex, while on the northern extension the stations were all squat rectangular stone structures with a round-arched loggia on all four sides and with the name of the station sculpted on an entablature rising from the middle. This was the style, not unlike that of the state of Hyderabad in India, at Jebba, Zaria, and Abo, while other towns had quite different multi-gabled wooden structures with long verandas. None of them made any concessions to the local Muslim culture. At all of these stations separate third-class waiting-rooms were supplied further down the tracks.

The manner in which the architecture of these stations reflected colonial racial hierarchies is beautifully illustrated by a Crown Agents photograph showing the proclamation of the First World War at Port Harcourt station in eastern Nigeria. The Europeans all stand on the station veranda, while an African crowd stands outside the station beside the tracks. Variants of the colonial verandaed station, again reminiscent of those in Ceylon, appeared in the Gold Coast, Sierra Leone, and the British Central Africa railway to Nyasaland. Despite the consistent influence of the Crown Agents' technical assistance in all these colonies, a remarkable diversity still prevailed.

The German African stations were noticeably grander than their British counterparts. It was as though the newer imperial power had to assert itself more bombastically through its station architecture. At Kigoma in Tanganyika a multi-storeyed station was constructed just before the First World War. It dominated an otherwise primitive town. At Windhoek in South West Africa a large, white, stuccoed structure was given imposing Dutch gables. Both there and at Keetmanshoep the Germans built headquarters stations which could take on a new strategic role in time of war. The French by contrast seldom built grand stations in North Africa. A few were similar to small stations in southern France, reflecting the control of North African railways by French companies like the Paris–Lyon–Marseille. Rather later, some concessions were made to local architectural styles. At Oran in Algeria the station was built like a mosque, with a minaret for a clock-tower. In French West Africa a few stations, like the fine one at Bobo-Diolassu in Senegal, were built in a recognizably local style.

The railway lines in Portuguese territory were built almost entirely with British capital. At first their station buildings were primitive affairs, no more than clearings in the bush with tin huts. Early travellers to Mozambique described the station at Beira as no more than a muddy, fever-infested street corner. Before the First World War, however, Lourenço Marques had a large baroque station with a central dome. Lourenço Marques was a gateway to both South and Central Africa, and Beira and Lobito Bay were the prime portals of the routes into British Central Africa and the Congo, much used by European settlers and tourists. The Portuguese Empire, which was constantly under threat, had to present a self-confident face to its European neighbours. Large new stations designed to do just that were built in these three cities after the Second World War.

* * *

The railway stations of Asia, Australasia, and Africa reveal to the full the range of styles, many of them of great elegance, which could be encompassed in station architecture world-wide. It is not difficult to find among them ample illustrations of Ruskin's dictum that architecture reflects the life of the society around it. The station had to take account of both the realities and the aspirations of imperial power, the prestige of conquerors and the pride of colonizers, together with class and racial distinctions and economic necessities. Russians in Central Asia, imperialists in India, South-East Asia, and Africa, colonizers in Australasia, and the commercial intruders in China and Japan all expressed themselves with striking forcefulness through this one architectural type.

4

The Station and Society

THE station became at one and the same time one of the principal forces in society for order, regulation, and discipline, and a new focus for violence, crime, and immorality.

Time

Trains had to leave on time for the railway system to make sense in both passenger and goods terms. For the system to work efficiently this had to be standard national time and not solar time. So God's time, or natural time, the time dictated by the sun's progress through the heavens and the countryman's age-old rhythm of life, was superseded by Man's time. The advent of the railways revealed considerable differences in time between different parts of the country. During the 1840s, according to official Great Western and London and North-Western timetables, Reading time was 4 minutes later than London, Bath and Bristol time was 11 minutes later, and Bridgwater 14 minutes later. Birmingham time was 7 minutes later than London, Liverpool 12 minutes later, and Manchester and Preston 10 minutes later.[1]

But it was in that same decade that Greenwich Mean Time (GMT) came to prevail more and more as the dominant and definitive time-scale. It was known colloquially as 'Railway Time', certain testimony to the efficacy of the railways and their inflexible timetables in imposing a single national standard of time-keeping. Some towns, however, held out stubbornly against it, particularly Norwich, Ipswich, Yarmouth, and Cambridge in the east and Bristol, Bath, Exeter, and Portsmouth in the west. It was only in 1880 that GMT was officially adopted as national time.

The time-scale was a different matter in countries which spanned continents. In the United States four standards were fixed: Pacific, Mountain, Central, and Eastern. Each spanned fifteen degrees of longitude. Sometimes stations displayed three clocks carrying Eastern, Western, and local time. It was Sir Sandford Fleming's experience as a railway engineer and his concern for time zones in Canada which led him to organize the international conference in 1884 which set up International Standard Time. In Tsarist Russia, all stations kept St Petersburg time, but stations sometimes displayed local time as well.

The combination of railway and local times was to perplex travellers throughout the world. A hapless British visitor to Portugal in 1900 reported:

Railway time is supposed to be derived from the Lisbon Observatory, but Town time, especially at Oporto, seems to have no defined origin. At any rate, it differs from Railway Time by an amount which may be anything between 8 and 12 minutes, the town being ahead of the railway, which is on the right side of things for lagging travellers.[2]

A traveller on the Rhodesian Railways in the same year pointed out the time complications in that country:

One thing which is most confusing to a stranger is the time of day in Umtali. The postal authorities work to 'Cape' time, which is one and a half hours in front of Greenwich; the railway authorities work to Beira time which is about two and a half hours in front of Greenwich, whilst the local time is about two and a quarter hours in front of Greenwich. However, this is now being altered; negotiations were then proceeding with a view to making one standard time for the whole, which, however, is somewhat difficult in a country extending some 500 miles east and west.[3]

The imposition of British imperial rule in South Africa after the Boer War was symbolized by the introduction of railway standard time throughout the region in 1903. But if imperial rule tended to produce such standardization, railway standard times could create their own complications. In India, as late as 1928, railway time was 24 minutes behind Calcutta time and 39 minutes ahead of Bombay. Indeed, the larger the country, the greater the problem. In Communist Russia all trains and stations maintain Moscow time. All travellers on the Trans-Siberian comment on the extraordinary disorientation this induces, particularly when meals are taken at entirely inappropriate times. Paul Theroux, for instance, found himself taking lunch in the middle of the night.[4]

The clock became a prominent feature of all stations. So prominent that 'meet me under the clock' became a regular phrase in the vocabulary of lovers. In the 1850s and 1860s British railway companies ensured uniform time at stations by arranging for clock manufacturers to send a man once a week from station to station to ensure that the clocks were keeping good time. At every station a porter would be told to have a ladder ready and wait while the clockman ascended, wound the clock, and adjusted the hands. If necessary the train would be kept a minute or two for him so that he could do the journey down the line in one day. If any clock went haywire, he made a special journey to fix it.[5] Once telegraphy was established, however, all railway clocks were synchronized by telegraph each morning at 10 a.m. GMT.

Timetables

Another by-product of the need for time-keeping was the timetable. The veneration in which many Victorians held *Bradshaw's Railway Guide*, the veritable Bible of the nineteenth-century traveller, testifies to the way in which the life of Victorian man had come to be programmed, conditioned, and disciplined by the railway's demand for punctuality in its customers.[6] It was *Bradshaw* for which Sherlock Holmes invariably reached when planning his journeys out of London when 'the game was afoot'. It was the Continental *Bradshaw* that Phileas Fogg tucked under his arm when he left Charing Cross Station to begin his historic journey around the world in eighty days. A 'Bradshaw' became a generic term for a railway timetable. *Punch* declared admiringly in 1865:

Seldom, if ever, has the gigantic intellect of man been employed upon a work of greater utility or upon one of such special application and general comprehensiveness as on the projection, completion, publication and sustentation of the now familiar 'Bradshaw'.[7]

George Bradshaw, a Quaker map-maker in Manchester, was one of a host of publishers who capitalized on the mushroom growth of the network to produce railway-related material. He published railway maps and also turned his hand to a timetable. The earliest surviving copy is from 1839. But dedicated research has suggested that the first timetable was actually issued in 1838.[8] The 1839 issue contained 8 pages of railway matter and cab fares, and 5 pages of maps and plans. By 1840 this had swelled to 32 pages and by 1845 to 89 pages. By the time Bradshaw himself died in 1853, his *Railway Guide* was already a national institution, inspiring jokes in pantomimes and popular ballads. By 1898 the monster volume ran to 946 pages. Throughout the nineteenth century it cost sixpence. But the First World War saw three successive price-rises, so that by 1918 it cost two shillings and by 1937 half a crown.

Already by the end of the nineteenth century its sheer size and massive detail had conferred on *Bradshaw* a reputation for impenetrability. John Pendleton voiced the feelings that this sometimes caused:

When you get into the maze of this huge monthly magazine that scorns fiction and is congested with facts, armed with intricate tables of place-names, dots, figures, warning hands, dark lines, notes, references, indications of trains 'up' and 'down', trains that run on 'week days', trains that run on 'Wednesdays only', and trains that run on 'Saturdays only' and when after striving in vain for half an hour to ascertain really what time you will arrive at your destination, you alight; with your head in a fog and your eyes aching, on the encouraging words in italic 'see above' or 'vice versa' you feel inclined to fling 'Bradshaw' out of the window.[9]

Individual British railway companies issued their own timetables, usually costing a penny each and often with handsome eye-catching covers.[10] But for completeness of information, *Bradshaw* remained the oracle, albeit sometimes opaque.

The counterpart to the national *Bradshaw* was *Bradshaw's Continental Guide*, first issued in June 1847. It grew to more than 1,000 pages, including timetable, guidebook, and hotel directory. Publication was suspended in August 1914. Resumed in a slimmer format after the war, the Continental *Bradshaw* finally vanished in 1939, with the leisured de luxe world it had served.

Bradshaw was the standard against which other countries' timetables were judged. The German timetable, *Hendschels Telegraph*, was four times the price of *Bradshaw* but the same length. It was issued monthly from 1846. France boasted two guides, *Chaix*, the older (1850), running to 400 pages, and *Simplex* (1888), which was twice the size but only half the length of *Bradshaw*. Both cost 75 centimes and adopted the design of printing the names of the stations in the middle of the pages, with the 'up' trains on one side, read from top to bottom, and the 'down' trains on the other, read from bottom to top. The *Railway Magazine* pronounced them 'well arranged and comparing well with our English Bradshaw in everything except price'. It also listed the best of the other Continental timetables, which 'might with advantage be purchased', as Denmark's *Post- og Reisehandbog for Kongeriget Danmark* (1s. 1½d.), Norway's *Norges Communicationer* (2¾d.), Sweden's *Tagtidtabellen* (3½d.), Belgium's *Guide officiel des voyageurs sur tous les chemins de fer belges* (2d.), Italy's *L'indicatore ufficiale delle strade ferrate* (1s. 1d.), Russia's *Amtlicher russischer Eisenbahn- und Dampfschiffsführer* (1s. 4d.), Switzerland's *Schweizer Conducteur* (1d.), Spain and Portugal's *Guía oficial para los Viajeros de los Ferro-carriles* (5d.).[11]

The American *Official Railway Gazette* (1868) was the most comprehensive of timetables, massively detailed because of the long distances involved and the four different time zones. It was physically twice the size of *Bradshaw*, though running to the same number of pages, nearly 1,000. It was issued monthly for 50 cents.

The common characteristic of the trains was that they did not wait and this single fact bred the habit of punctuality in their users. As the London and Birmingham Railway announced as early as 1839, 'Gentlemen's carriage and horses must be at the station at least a quarter of an hour before the time of departure', to facilitate loading on to the flat wagons that carried them. The 'quality' as much as anyone else had to bow to railway rules.

Discipline

The railways were notorious for their tight discipline, long hours, strict hierarchy, and military-style regulations. The staff were usually uniformed, which sometimes caused confusion. The boys of Wellington College, opened in 1856, bore German-style cadet uniforms, designed by Prince Albert. They were rapidly replaced after the Prime Minister, Lord Derby, arrived at Wellington College Station *en route* for the school and handed his ticket to the head boy under the impression that he was an official of the railway company. In the United States the introduction of uniforms was resisted by the staff, though railway porters wore distinguishing headgear which gave them their nickname—'redcaps'. Nevertheless, even in the 'land of the free and the home of the brave', the military analogy dominated the thinking of the great organizers, like Charles Eliot Perkins, President of the Chicago, Burlington and Quincy Railroad, who argued that the army provided the most appropriate model for railroad administration.

Frank McKenna, in his admirable history of the British railway worker, described the military flavour of their lives:

The railwaymen were from the beginning ruled by instructions as detailed as those of the Koran. They were the first 'organization men', stitched firmly into the fabric of their company, noted for punctuality, cleanliness and the smart execution of orders. A railway worker was 'in the service'. He reported for duty and left only after being relieved. Failure to report for duty meant he was absent without leave. He took unpaid leave only after written permission had been granted; unauthorized leave could lead to suspension, fines, dismissal, even prosecution. The military terminology was evident as early as 1830 when on the opening of the Liverpool and Manchester Railway 'orders of the day' were issued to participants.[12]

Discipline even extended to non-railway workers using the station. The South-Eastern and Chatham Company had a notice at Charing Cross Station which read:

Any cabman skylarking or otherwise misconducting himself while on the Managing Committee's premises or smoking whilst his cab is standing alongside the platform will be required to leave the station immediately.

The Cheshire Lines had a notice affixed to their station lavatories announcing:

These closets are intended for the convenience of passengers only. Workmen, cabmen, fish porters and idlers are not permitted to use them.

In this context, it is not surprising to discover that former naval and military officers figured extensively among the superintendents and general managers of the Victorian railway companies of Britain, men such as Captain Huish of the London and North-Western, Captain O'Brien of the North-Eastern, Captain Lawes of the Lancashire and Yorkshire, and Captain Coddington of the Caledonian Railway.

This military connection was even more extensive on the Continent. In both France and Prussia a sizeable proportion of positions on the railway was reserved by law for ex-soldiers. Professor William J. Cunningham of Harvard reported in 1913, after a visit to Germany, on the effect of this military influence:

There is a noticeable orderliness and precision about everything connected with German railways. In respect for authority and strict observance of the rules, the German railway employee has no superior. The traveller will not fail to notice the red-capped station master standing at attention on the station platform as the train passes through each station. He will also find the senior signalman, gatemen and other employees connected with the train service always in evidence, standing like sentries as the train passes. The operating official, while riding over the line, can thus take a census of all employees in a position of responsibility. When he alights at a station his rank is at once recognized. The station master immediately salutes and gives a verbal report of the situation at his station. If the official goes into a signal tower, the signalman in charge salutes and reports. If he goes into an engine station, the foreman salutes and gives a brief report of the work in progress ... The high order of discipline and rigid observance of rules which follows their system of ample and constant supervision bears fruit in their remarkable immunity from train accidents, and in the small number of passengers and employees killed or injured.[13]

The result of such disciplined organization was a corporate loyalty so fierce and lasting that it led successive generations of the same family to serve the company. Adrian Vaughan, in his moving and evocative account of his life as a signalman on the Great Western Railway in the last years of steam, recalled a typical episode illustrating this feeling. There was bitter rivalry between the Great Western and the much smaller Midland and South-Western Junction Railway (M. and S.W.), which crossed GWR territory to link Cheltenham and Southampton:

> The rivalry between the M. and S.W. and G.W.R. only just stopped short of blows as the G.W.R. was openly contemptuous of the small but heroic M. and S.W. . . . Paddington and all right-thinking Great Western men considered the M. and S.W. a crimson intruder on the green and gold heart-land of God's Wonderful Railway.

The GWR men referred to the M. and S.W. as the 'Milk and Soda Water', 'Tiddley Dyke', and the 'Piss 'n Vinegar', the latter a reference to the state of the carriages after the M. and S.W. had carried its regular Saturday-night complement of off-duty soldiers from their night out in Swindon back to their camps on Salisbury Plain.

One of Vaughan's fellow workers, Sid Phillips, had bitter personal experience of the feelings generated by this inter-company rivalry:

> Sid Phillips' background was wholly Great Western; his people were, as near as possible, hereditary employees of the company, his great-grandfather, grandfather and his father had all held the post of Ganger for the Bedwyn–Wolfhall Junction length where the despised M. and S.W. crossed the lordly Great Western on a bridge and had a spur curving down to make the Wolfhall Junction with the G.W.R. Sid's grandfather was seventy before he condescended to retire and Sid's father had arranged a place for his son in the track gang ready for when the boy left school. Unfortunately for family pride Sid had other ideas and in 1915 took a job at Grafton and Burbage station on the Midland South-Western. 'We had a shocking row about it, my Dad and me' said Sid. 'He said that if I was clever enough to find my own work I could find my own lodgings too, so I had to leave home and go into digs.' I made some disbelieving noises but Sid insisted. 'No it's the truth, you wouldn't hardly credit it today, I know, but there was Company loyalty in them days especially if you were a railway family—I'd turned up my nose at the Great Western and that was bad form in our house.'[14]

The central point of command in the railway station was the station-master's office. The station-master, invariably top-hatted, was a figure of substance in the community:

> He is the captain in command of all the human and steam forces that aggregate around that little world-microcosm in the railway cosmos called a station and within his own sphere holds the same place as the commander-in-chief—the general manager—does in the more exalted position.[15]

Writing thus of the station-master in the nineteenth century, F. S. Williams slips naturally into the military mode of expression, indicating just how deeply the service mentality pervaded the railways at every level.

The station-master's duties were carefully defined. Prominent among them was the ensuring of discipline, neatness, and civility among the station staff. But beyond the mere exercise of executive authority, the station-master might well be invested with moral authority, as a local vicar told GWR station-master Hubert Simmons in the mid nineteenth century:

There are very few positions in life where a man has more opportunities for exercising his moral authority, and above all 'charity' than the position of a railway official. You are bound to meet with all classes of society, to deal with all cases of emergency, and it is constantly before you to do this or to do that . . . As you advance in position, you will have more men to command and more opportunities of administering charity; I do not mean by alms, but by deeds. Your example will emulate and stimulate the actions of those under you. Yours will be a sacred trust, for to your care will be entrusted the lives of many thousands; but remember the rich can always command attention; it will be the poor that will need your care. You will be called upon to make great self-sacrifice, as no conscientious stationmaster can ever throw off the burden of his vocation, his mind must necessarily be always prepared to meet and to deal with any emergency, and his children—the trains—are so often out of order that they must not be left to care for themselves. Still you can be very happy if you take pleasure in your business; it will almost become your recreation.[16]

As the railways lost their pre-eminent position in the transportation field, so the position and authority of the station-master was steadily undermined. The substitution of the anodyne 'station manager' for the more authoritarian 'station-master' symbolizes this process.

The morale of dedicated railwaymen was shaken by nationalization and destroyed by Beeching. Len Bedale, who spent his working life on the railways in Yorkshire between 1928 and 1970, latterly as a station-master, sadly recorded the erosion of that life-work after the Beeching axe. He expressed its diminution eloquently in an examination of the changes in the station-master's uniform:

My first uniform, issued to me at Kirk Smeaton in 1943, had a single-breasted jacket, of close texture, navy blue serge and a hard-top cap of the same material, with the words 'Station Master', woven in gold silk, on the band. There is no doubt in my mind that this issue was the smartest and most comfortable uniform that I ever wore, and for many years after that, indeed up to the late sixties, both quality and style steadily deteriorated. Double-breasted jackets were issued at a time when the fashion was on its way out. The original neat cap was changed for a heavier type of headgear, with lavish gold wire and ornate badge, which was a menace in windy weather. I remember the late Walter Baron, Stationmaster at Filey, telling me that he was once at Hunmanby station, supervising the seating of the girls from Hunmanby High School, when a particularly strong gust of wind blew off his uniform hat like a rising kite. Finally it rolled along the platform edge on to the line, to the accompaniment of loud laughter from the waiting females. One can imagine the chagrin of the wearer. In the late sixties the blue uniforms were abandoned in favour of the present grey continental style. From the outset I considered these outfits to be poor, and wearing them only confirmed my suspicions. The old-fashioned double-breasted style was perpetuated, the cloth seeming to gather every speck of grime. It was impossible to retain any crease in the trousers. The pill-box type hat, with soft top and sides, though comfortable to wear, was not much use in wet weather, for when soaked, the water funnelled down the back of one's neck. At least the old mortar boards had the merit of throwing off the wet on to one's mackintosh.[17]

Encapsulated in that testimony is the whole story of the loss of dignity, confidence, and pride in the railway service that has overtaken it since the Second World War.

It was not only the staff who were regimented: so too were the passengers in a form of social discipline. It was a common feature of nineteenth-century writers to compare what they saw as the essentially democratic nature of British society with the more autocratic and authoritarian foreign regimes, epitomized in the procedures at railway stations. F. S. Williams wrote in 1883:

Continental railways have peculiarities unknown in this country which appear strange, and are sometimes annoying, to Mr. Bull. In England, the traveller goes to the station when he pleases; he wanders about the platform and superintends his luggage as he pleases, and, in fact, so long as he does not interfere with the convenience of other people, and does not violate the 'bye-laws' of the company, he may do what he likes. In France, instead of the traveller managing himself, he is managed. On procuring his ticket, he delivers up his luggage, is marched into a waiting room, according to the class of his fare; as if the company were afraid that, having paid his money, he should not have his ride. When the train is ready, the first class passengers are liberated, and everyone scrambles to his seat with as much agility as circumstances will admit; and then the second-class and the third are allowed to follow.[18]

Canon Victor Whitechurch took up the same theme after a visit to Belgium:

I heard it said once that the difference between the English and Continental railway official is that, the one is the servant of the public and the other the master. One realizes this when one travels in Belgium under the control of the state. Railway officials are more like policemen, naturally, and 'red-tapeism' prevails. You are not allowed on the platform on peril of your life without a ticket and this same ticket is everlastingly being scrutinized and clipped.[19]

But this distinction between Britain and the Continent is too sharply drawn. Even if British station arrangements lacked Continental rigour, the very facts of queueing for tickets, waiting on platforms, arriving punctually, presenting and re-presenting tickets, involved submission to the company's discipline and helped to promote obedience. The world of public transport is necessarily a world of discipline for staff and passengers alike and the station symbolizes it.

In nineteenth-century Britain railway regimentation was one of a series of potent factors contributing to a more structured and ordered society. It stands alongside a widespread militarism—the Boys' Brigade, the Salvation Army, sailor suits, school drill; defined and visible social divisions in housing, clothing, education, and transport; the promotion and organization of sport by the middle classes with the ideals of team spirit, rules, and discipline. The photographs of the period stress this with their rows and ranks of sports teams, civic groups, wedding parties, and station staffs, everyone in his place and knowing his place, 'the rich man in his castle, the poor man at the gate. He made them high and lowly and ordered their estate.'

The contribution of railway regimentation to social discipline in the nineteenth century is confirmed by a glance round the world today. Those societies in which private transport is restricted and public transport (particularly the railways) is the norm, societies like Russia, China, and India, remain among the most structured and disciplined. Those like Britain and America, where the private motor car has replaced public transport, are societies which have seen an upsurge of self-centred individualism.

Crime

But just as it was a source of order and discipline in society, the station has also been a haven for social outcasts and a magnet for crime. There is a floating population of station denizens who are not there to travel. Dossers, derelicts, drifters, drug addicts, the homeless and the friendless find in the station, open twenty-four hours a day, warmth, shelter, and light. 'The station lounger' was one of the subjects investigated in *Problems of Boy Life* (1912), edited by J. H. Whitehouse MP, part of a wealth of literature from that period concerned with juvenile life and in particular juvenile crime. T. Norman Chamberlain, basing his account on a study of some 200 station loungers in Birmingham, noted:

The typical lad of this class can be seen any day outside most of our big railway stations ... trying to get a 'carry' from some bag-laden passenger; now and then a traveller for the day brings joy to his heart, but most of the day he is filling up his time in spending pennyworths at the coffee-shop on the corner, gambling with the rest of the boys and dodging the police. Every degree of tidiness and cleanliness, of dirt and disreputability is represented. Their ages vary from fourteen to twenty-three, the most common age being sixteen to nineteen ... Except when cadging off a passer-by they seem a sociable, happy-go-lucky set of lads with many opportunities of seeing life ... They thrive on Royal Visits, Test Matches, local murders and similar excitements.[20]

Chamberlain defended these boys against the common accusation that they were 'born unemployables', suggesting that the majority of them had worked, often for long periods, that they generally came from broken homes and that 'on the whole, I, personally, have found them surprisingly truthful and absolutely honest'. But he agreed that once they appeared at the station, 'they are done for' by a combination of the demoralizing effect of unemployment, the endemic gambling and the effect on their health of the winter weather and continuous ill-nutrition. He noted that they were frequently being fined for sleeping out, obstruction, gaming, jostling, and trespassing on railway property, but unable to pay the fines, they invariably ended up in prison. He therefore advocated a much greater use of probation and the creation of special reform schools to wean them from their station life.

For all its bustle and light, the railway station, particularly the major terminal, has a dark underside, a criminal half-life, coexisting with its more public face. The transient crowds have meant that railway stations have long been a magnet for pickpockets, mingling with the masses to extract purses and wallets from the unsuspecting traveller; for prostitutes, male and female, plying for custom; for pimps and panders who lie in wait for innocent youngsters arriving in the big city in vain hope of fame and fortune. Some seek these youngsters to gratify perverted lusts. Fritz Haarman, the Hanover mass murderer, small-time thief, and police informer in the disturbed years following the First World War, prowled Hanover Station picking up teenage boys. He then sexually abused and murdered them, selling their clothes and disposing of their bodies to butchers short of meat. Eventually caught in 1924, he confessed to forty murders and was beheaded. Peter Kurten, another German mass murderer of the same period, a sadist and pervert who preyed on young women and children in Düsseldorf, was eventually caught and charged with nine murders between 1929 and 1931. He was found guilty and guillotined in Cologne in 1931. He had been tracked down after he permitted to escape a girl he had picked up at Düsseldorf Station and attempted to rape.

The supply of young victims, male and female, for sex is unending. For there have always been and will always be restless, discontented young people, drawn by the glittering lure of the Big City. As often as not they arrive in the metropolis by train. Their plight was examined by Michael Deakin and John Willis in their disturbing television documentary and subsequent book *Johnny Go Home* (1976), where they stressed the role of the station:

Sooner or later most of the kids on the run end up at the London railway stations. Many arrive there, often tired and already more than a little scared after having taken the final decision to run off from the certainties of their birthplace but others simply drift towards the terminals aware that there, at least, there is shelter and some sort of continuing life. The loneliness is often more daunting than hunger or cold. For most of these kids Euston is the favoured station. It stands at the end of the line from Glasgow and on every train a handful of furtive or hesitant children disembark. The resolution of that first impatient flush of their resolve to 'make for the smoke'. As the ordinary passengers hurry off to their homes, and as the night draws on and trains become less frequent, only the dregs of the travellers remain, people who have neither the knowledge of the city nor the will to decide where to go next. In Glasgow they decided simply to come south. Now they are here with the adventure begun, but without the final energy to venture into the unknown city itself . . . Various people clean up the stations at night, often with their own motives in mind. There are the simple old fashioned ponces who whisk away the young girls. There are homosexuals. And people who have some way or another of exploiting the children. The Railway Police come to know these regular nocturnal predators all too well. But they accept them as part of the inevitable life of the station and simply note their comings and goings in the log kept by the duty officer.[21]

In the station lavatories, homosexual pick-ups take place and drug addicts inject themselves with noxious substances. Furtive deals are made with the pedlars of flesh and the pushers of drugs. Squalor, self-abuse, and raw greed intermingle. Combating crime committed on station premises is the work of the railway police. In Britain, the transport police are as old as the railways. The Liverpool and Manchester Railway had a police force as early as 1830 and it became a regular element in the Acts of Parliament establishing railway companies to legislate for the provision of a police force. The separate forces of over a hundred companies were amalgamated into four with the railway grouping of

1923 and finally merged to form British Transport Police after nationalization in 1948. Their organization, uniforms, and powers are similar to
those of the civil police.[22]

In the early days, at some small stations, a policeman was in sole
charge. The 'booking constables' performed all the duties of the station.
Many policemen at larger stations included ticket-collecting among their
duties, the job of ticket-collector not being introduced until later. Signalmen were for many years known as 'bobbies' because policemen had
originally done their duties too.

Theft has always been the most important crime to be dealt with.
There were only seven murders on British railways between 1864 and
1929. Theft from trains and from wagons in sidings constitutes the bulk
of crimes, with food, clothing, wine, spirits, and tobacco the main objects.
As early as 1853 David Stevens, Goods Manager of the LNWR, was
writing:

> Thieves are pilfering the goods from our waggons here to an impudent extent.
> We are at our wits' end to find out the blackguards. Not a night passes without
> wine hampers, silk parcels, drapers' boxes or provisions being robbed; and if the
> articles are not valuable enough they leave them about the station. A roll of chintz
> was found on the station this morning; of course mistaken at first for silk, but on
> tearing the paper the plunderer discovered it to be chintz and threw it away in
> disgust.[23]

Sometimes railway company staff have been involved in these criminal
proceedings. The first great train robbery, the theft of the gold bullion
consignment from the S.E. and C. Railway's train between London
Bridge Station and Folkestone, carried out in 1855 by Edward Agar and
William Pierce, was accomplished with the connivance of the station-
master at London Bridge, William Tester.

The principal larcenies at stations themselves have been by pickpockets and luggage thieves. As J. R. Whitbread, the historian of the
railway police, wrote:

> Night and day, since they were first built, large stations have been hives of
> activity, centres of hustle and bustle, comings and goings, and of people running
> and pushing in every direction ... The platforms are always thronged with
> arriving and departing passengers, their friends and relatives, and many others
> who have come to watch the trains, visit the bookstalls or drink in the refresh-
> ment rooms. Many of the passengers are burdened with suitcases, often contain-
> ing valuables, about which they are surprisingly careless. It is no wonder that a
> station has always been a Mecca of thieves. What could provide better cover,
> with its multitudinous throng? The problem of the thief is not so much what to
> steal, but which of the many articles will prove the most lucrative 'lift' ... Railway

stations must be unique in one respect. Besides providing a rich, albeit risky, hunting ground for the luggage thieves, they also supply, for only a modest charge, the ideally convenient hiding place for the plunder: the station cloakroom.[24]

In 1845 the *Illustrated London News* was reporting 'There is not a railway terminus in or about London which has not been plundered to a very large extent.'[25] In the mid 1870s there was an epidemic of jewel robberies. Among others, within the space of a few days Lady Dudley lost £25,000 worth of jewels at Paddington and Countess Grey £2,000 worth at Waterloo. Theft continues to be a preoccupation of the railway police. H. J. Prytherch of the Great Eastern Railway, writing on the subject in 1900, recorded the fact that

The theft of luggage is not confined to the sterner sex for a record is before the writer in which an educated young lady managed to appropriate some hundreds of pounds worth of property before being detected. The comparatively lenient sentence of 9 months imprisonment to which she was sentenced on her first conviction does not appear, however, to have had the desired deterrent effect, for it is said that on the very day she was liberated from jail, she again succumbed to her predatory instincts by purloining a lady's travelling trunk, valued at 70 pounds, from the identical station at which she had before been arrested.[26]

As railway stations are regular features on the itinerary of the great, so they formed with their crowds and their many avenues of potential escape ideal locations for assassination . . . In March 1882 a lunatic called Roderick McLean fired a pistol at Queen Victoria as she was leaving the Great Western Railway Station at Windsor. In 1900 shots were fired at the Prince and Princess of Wales as their train was halted at the Gare du Nord in Brussels. In both cases, the attempts were unsuccessful.

Although it is generally well known that President Abraham Lincoln was shot at Ford's Theatre, Washington, in 1865, it is perhaps less well known that he survived an earlier plot on his life in 1861. Detectives uncovered a plot to assassinate him at Calvert Street Station, Baltimore, as his inaugural train carried him from his home in Springfield, Illinois, to Washington, DC, to take up the office of President. President James A. Garfield, the second of America's four assassinated presidents, was shot on 2 July 1881 at the Baltimore and Potomac depot, Washington, DC, by a disappointed office-seeker, Charles Julius Guiteau. He died eighty days later of blood-poisoning on 19 September 1881. A star was placed on the station floor to mark the spot where the President fell, and a marble tablet was set into the wall opposite.

It was in fact the Pinkerton agency's success in preventing the assassination attempt upon Lincoln in 1861 which gave a considerable fillip to the employment of such agencies for police work during the Civil War. The railway police in the United States, who were known as 'cinder dicks', had their origins in the lawless times when the railroads were pushing westwards across the continent. For some companies adequate policing became a matter of survival, given the depredations of bands of outlaws and their dynamiting of track and bridges to hold up trains in remote places. But the principal activities of the police soon came to be concentrated at stations, in the protection of freight yards and of passengers. They were charged with preventing the movement of hoboes on freight trains, with reducing the incidence of bag thefts, and with watching for card-sharps, con men, tricksters, and swindlers operating at stations and boarding trains. They rid stations of drunks, disorderly persons, prostitutes, drug pedlars, mashers, gamblers, and pickpockets. They were also concerned with preventing passenger pilfering of railway property, particularly from sleeping and Pullman cars, and with the authenticating of insurance claims.

It took some time, however, for the American railway police to become organized, and when they did so a wide variety of systems and nomenclature appeared. Some employees operated unofficially in a police manner from the earliest days and agencies were employed to protect railway property. As a result, the most common name for the railway police was 'special agents', inherited from the stage-coaches, but they were also organized into protection, investigation, or police departments. In the United States, the situation was a highly complex one, the police securing their commissions from state, county, or municipal authorities. In Canada they were organized on a federal basis under the Railway Act of Canada of 1860. By the 1920s the railway police in North America had become the largest private law-enforcement system in the world, numbering some 10,000 officers. Some companies preferred a uniformed police about their stations, believing the deterrent effect to be important; others considered a plain-clothes force to be more effective. No doubt all would have agreed with the Superintendant of Police of the Pennsylvania Railroad when he said in 1925 that the railroad policeman should be tall to see over the heads of the crowd, 'fit and limber as the athlete', with good feet, eyes, and ears, able to leap on to moving trains, courteous, a good shot, and abstemious, a Sherlock Holmes in powers of observation, and above reproach in his private life. Nevertheless, these paragons remained unpopular figures, with their early reputation clinging to them right up to their swift decline in numbers from the 1950s. In the early days they had been noted more for brawn than brain, for their quick reactions with the gun than with investigative logic. They were hated figures to hoboes, Blacks, station hawkers, and the unemployed, all the disadvantaged of American society.

The Station in Town Planning

The station has played a key role in urban development. Chicago, for instance, owed its growth to its position as the meeting-place of twenty-seven different railway lines, and in Britain the railway and its focus, the station, form the heart of the development of towns like Crewe, Swindon, Middlesbrough, and Carnforth. Station-building decisively redesigned the contours of cities and is still doing so, shifting and promoting the flow of traffic and of population, attracting and repelling different forms of land and building use, commercial and habitational growth.[27]

Ideally railway companies wanted to site their stations as close as possible to the centres of cities. In those British cities where they were initially confined to the periphery of the built-up area, the companies frequently sought to move closer in to the centre, constructing splendid new termini to proclaim their arrival; thus, for instance, the terminus in Liverpool was shifted from Crown Street to Lime Street, in Birmingham from Curzon Street to New Street, in Manchester from Liverpool Road to Hunt's Bank (Victoria), in London from Shoreditch to Liverpool Street, and from Camden to Euston Road. Sometimes in those places where local hostility kept the station on the town outskirts, as in Coventry, Rugby, and Cambridge, the railway itself acted as an irresistible magnet, drawing the town out towards and beyond it.

The siting of a station depended on a number of often interrelated factors: topographical considerations, land-ownership patterns, the strength of vested interests, inter-company rivalry, and whether or not the station was a terminal. In Holland, for instance, the existence of a central canal network dictated the locating of Groningen Station on the edge of the inner-city area. The same consideration dictated the siting of Strasbourg Station on the western side of the city. In Spain topographical considerations were paramount and many local stations were a long way from the places they nominally served. Difficulties of terrain, in particular variations of level, dictated duplication of terminal facilities in such British towns as Halifax, Burnley, and Falkirk.

Company rivalry was also a potent influence in countries where unrestricted free enterprise flourished. Sometimes there was productive co-operation between rivals, as at Carlisle Citadel Station, which housed the trains of seven companies: three Scottish and four English. But more frequently company rivalry dictated the creation of separate stations, often, as in Leeds, Preston, and London, adjacent to each other. In London, three terminals appeared almost side by side. The London and North-Western's Euston Station was first, but at the eastern end of Euston Road the Great Northern constructed their King's Cross terminal. Initially the Midland Railway ran into King's Cross but a quarrel over access led them to construct next door to King's Cross their St Pancras terminal, which was topped by a statue of Britannia, a calculated snook-cocking exercise because Britannia was the company emblem of the Midland's hated rival, the London and North-Western. It may even be that St Pancras's grandiose Gothic style was a calculated response to the severe classical style of Euston.

Considerations of company prestige also dictated the appearance of Marylebone Station, which only just squeezed into the nineteenth century. It was the product of the ambitions of the chairman of the Great Central, Sir Edward Watkin, and according to Sir John Betjeman 'looks like a branch public library in a Manchester suburb'. London did not, in point of fact, need another terminal station, but Marylebone becomes all the more glorious and cherishable for its heroic redundancy. It has become a regular resort for film companies seeking an authentic nineteenth-century station to re-stage the arrivals and departures of that noble age of bustling visionaries. Film companies apart, it remains a genteel and civilized backwater, no longer serving far-away Nottingham and Sheffield but Monks Risborough, Little Kimble, Great Missenden, and Denham Golf Course. Even while the ghastly fate of conversion into a bus station hangs over it, it is still possible at the time of writing to travel from Marylebone via Banbury on a glorious four-hour journey to Birmingham. Try it, before the last great folly of company pride is brought low.

City-planning experts isolate two principal functions for the rail systems of great cities. For the passenger service, the railway must provide the means of transport for suburban dwellers in and out of the city at the two 'rush-hour' periods and it must provide points of access for the principal trunk lines to the other great population centres. This necessitates a radial pattern, with lines fanning out in all directions, but also requires some means of connecting the various terminal points. For freight services there must be adequate unloading, sorting, and transshipment areas and this usually means separate terminal facilities from those provided for passengers. But they similarly require linking to each other by a 'girdle' or 'belt' line and to the networks they serve. S. H. Beaver has written: 'The ideal railway plan for a large city thus somewhat resembles a wheel: the city is the hub, the main lines are the spokes and the circumference is the belt line.'[28] The symmetry of such a system will depend on the historical circumstances of the growth of the lines, the nature of the traffic, and the existing urban topography. But subject to these variations, many of the great cities of Europe have adopted one form or another of this basic ground-plan, with the inevitable consequences for the zoning and partitioning of the central area.

The joints on Beaver's urban wheel are the stations and they dictate the pattern of cross-city linkage. In London, by the end of the nineteenth century there were some fifteen passenger terminals and eleven goods depots. For historical reasons the southern termini which lay closest to the heart of London had no adjacent goods stations because of the shortage and high cost of available land. Their goods depots were further east in the cheaper, humbler Thames-side area of London. The northern termini, built originally on the edge of built-up London, usually located goods and passenger stations adjacent to each other. In London the passenger termini came to be linked by an underground railway, while cross-city belt lines were built to link the various networks for freight purposes: the North London to connect the northern lines with the docks, the West London to link the western and southern systems, and the Northern and South-Western Junction Line to link the north-western and south-western systems.

Paris had a more symmetrical railway plan, with two underground circular systems, one inside the other, the inner circle (the *petite ceinture*) linking the eight central passenger stations and devoted to moving passengers, and the outer circle (the *grande ceinture*) traversing the inner suburbs and carrying freight. The marshalling yards were located on the outer circle but the seven major goods stations close to the central passenger stations.

Berlin had seven terminal stations, initially unconnected and all built on the outer edge of the built-up area of the city in the 1850s. In 1871 they were linked by a belt railway (*Ringbahn*) at a radius of 5 km. from the city centre. In 1882 this was supplemented by a metropolitan railway (*Stadtbahn*) running east to west, much of it on a viaduct. As in Paris, the marshalling yards were on the outer edges of the city but they also got swallowed up as the city expanded.

Warsaw had a particular problem in that two different gauges met there: the standard gauge of the Western lines and the broad gauge of the Russian lines. But after the Great War, the broad gauge was converted to standard and the four terminal stations (Danzig, Vilna, Central, and West) were linked by a double belt line (an inner and outer circle) and a direct line from East to Central. In Moscow the nine terminal stations circling the central area were linked by underground.

The radial pattern with the circular or semicircular girdle was to be found also in Rome, Milan, Brussels, Vienna, Budapest, and Bucharest. Whether overground or underground the linking tracks drew new lines of demarcation for the cities; the areas occupied by passenger and goods stations, underground stations, and marshalling yards had consequences for buses, trams, and cabs, and for those satellite businesses invariably attracted into the station's orbit, which themselves dictated patterns of eating, shopping, and working.

Straightforward logic might dictate a single central terminal—what on the Continent came to be called a *Hauptbahnhof*—and a large number of cities achieved one: Amsterdam, Copenhagen, Dresden, Marseilles, Milan, Frankfurt. But they tended to be cities of the second rank. The major cities all boasted a plethora of terminal stations, London taking the lead with fifteen but Moscow following with nine, Paris with eight, and Berlin with seven. In London there were throughout the nineteenth century persistent advocates for a central London terminus. One was the journalist John Hollingshead, who wrote in 1862:

It seems that we are to be allowed no rest from railway engineering operations until the great idea of a central station in the City of London is made to take material shape. Every railway, at present condemned to have its terminus in the outskirts, is looking wistfully towards that coveted spot within the shadow of St. Paul's and making signs to its brethren to join hands in drawing the circle together.[29]

But the Royal Commission on Railway Termini in the Metropolis (1846) had rejected the idea of one, fearing massive centralized congestion and the practical difficulty of avoiding the disputes involved in joint operation and management of a single station.

A select committee of the House of Lords on metropolitan railway communications took the same line in 1863. In 1855 Sir Joseph Paxton in a glorious flight of fancy proposed an inner-circle railway in a glass arcade to be called 'The Great Victorian Way', but the linkage problem was solved by the London underground lines which between 1863 and 1914 connected all the termini.

In Paris the demands of the rival *arrondissements* for a terminal in their area, with the profitable generation of trade and traffic it entailed, and the desire of the military authorities for a variety of embarkation points for their troops defeated a similar lobby for a central terminal and ensured the continuance of variety and diversity.

In Britain as a whole only three major cities (Newcastle, Aberdeen, and Stoke-on-Trent) succeeded in concentrating their traffic into a single station. Elsewhere, Dublin had five, Manchester and Glasgow four, Leeds, Liverpool, Leicester, Belfast, and Nottingham three, and Birmingham, Sheffield, Edinburgh, and Bradford two central stations. Few of them, however, ever reached the actual city centre, Birmingham New Street, Edinburgh Waverley, and Glasgow Central being notable exceptions.

A practical reason for not pressing on further to a central site once the network was established and the terminals built was the sheer expense, fatigue, and disruption that the necessary linkage would entail. Brussels presents the classic case. As early as 1836 a line to link north and south across the city centre was proposed. For seventy years the proposition was debated. Finally, just before the First World War a viaduct was begun that would link the Nord and Midi stations across the centre. Its destination was to have been a new central station midway between the two. After the war, the plan was reconsidered and an underground link was authorized instead in 1930. Completed eventually after the Second World War, it involved a six-track system between Nord and Midi stations, with three intermediate stations, one of them grandly named Brussels Central. But they were nothing more than glorified underground stations. Midi remained the grand arrival station. The massive demolition programme which this entailed, and the consequent rebuilding with characterless office blocks along the dividing line thus created, tore the heart out of the centre of the city.

Any urban reconstruction needs the most detailed long-term consideration both for the specific objectives and the general environment impact. There have been those who have undertaken just such herculean tasks. One was Baron Haussmann, the architect of modern Paris.

Baron Haussmann, Prefect of the Seine, reconstituted Paris completely during the Second Empire. Between 1858 and 1870 he drove broad avenues through the crowded heart of the city, razing slum areas, producing parks and squares, dramatically siting public buildings, driving radial roads out to the suburbs, and planting circular boulevards to keep the traffic moving around the heart of the city. The central stations were a key element in his vision of a remodelled modern Paris. They were the nodal points of his sweeping new network of roads. The flow of passengers into the stations needed to be distributed speedily and this meant major roads to link up with the termini. So Haussmann extended the boulevard de Sébastopol, the approach road to the Gare de l'Est, to serve the Gare du Nord also. He extended the rue Lafayette south-west from the Gare de l'Est and the Gare du Nord to the business centre of Paris and built the boulevard Magenta south-east towards the Gare de Lyon, the southern terminal. From the Gare de Lyon to the dock and warehouse area of Bercy he constructed the avenue Daumesnil, which also became the main road to the bois de Vincennes. The Gare Saint-Lazare, the north-western terminal, was linked to the centre of Paris by the rue Auber, and the approaches to the Gare de l'Ouest (Montparnasse) were opened up by the rue de Rennes.[30]

Haussmann's grand vision, however, was dwarfed by the dreams of Adolf Hitler, whose architectural plans amounted to megalomania, reflecting his view of himself as the future master of the world. When he was 17 he had drawn up detailed designs for the reconstruction of Linz, among them a plan for a subterranean railway station. Architecture was and had long been an obsession of Hitler's. He decreed that grandiose monumentality and a neo-classical Roman Imperial style were the only forms appropriate to his imperishable Reich.[31] 'Those who enter the Reich Chancellery', he said, 'should feel that they stand before the lords of the world.'[32] There seemed to be no limit to his schemes: massive urban reconstruction, the transmutation of Linz into the cultural centre of the new Europe, new opera houses, war memorials, spas, hotels, airports, etc. Outside Germany entire cities like Warsaw and Leningrad were to disappear. There was to be a network of motorways from Calais to the Crimea, and a new transcontinental railway system.

A massive new central railway station was planned for Munich, which would have dominated the cityscape. It was destined to be the largest steel-framed structure in the world, covering an area six times greater than St Peter's, on which it was modelled, just as the Führer was greater than the successor of St Peter, the Pope. The diameter of the hall was to be 378 m. The dome was to be 136 m. high and 120 m. wide and there would be a massive triumphal roadway on an east–west axis 6.6 km. long, leading at one end to a huge victory column 214.5 m. high. It was planned as the terminal of a major railway link with Rostov-on-the-Don, and a completion date of 1950 was planned. In the event only the foundations were laid.

With his grand design for Berlin, Hitler deliberately set out to surpass Haussmann, creating a new city more beautiful than Vienna and better planned than Paris. With the Champs-Elysées and the Arc de Triomphe as his model, he sought a broad central avenue, 70 ft. wider than the 350 ft. of the Champs-Elysées and two and a half times as long, as the north–south axis for the city. Hitler's architect Albert Speer and

Ministerial Director Leibbrand of the Reich Traffic Ministry saw in Hitler's plans an opportunity for a large-scale reorganization of the Berlin railways. So they planned the city reconstruction around two new central stations, one for the north and the other for the south, these eliminating all other stations and building over them. These stations would stand at each end of the new avenue.

The incurable gigantism of all Hitler's plans had a definite political and ideological role, as Albert Speer recalled:

Our happiest concept, comparatively speaking, was the central railroad station, the southern pole of Hitler's grand boulevard. The station, its steel ribbing showing through sheathings of copper and glass, would have handsomely offset the great blocks of stone dominating the rest of the avenue. It provided for four levels linked to escalators and elevators and was to surpass New York's Grand Central Station in size. State visitors would have descended a large outside staircase. The idea was that as soon as they, as well as ordinary travellers, stepped out of the station they would be overwhelmed, or rather stunned, by the urban scene and thus the power of the Reich. The station plaza, thirty-three hundred feet long, and a thousand feet wide, was to be lined with captured weapons, after the fashion of the Avenue of Rams, which leads from Karnak to Luxor. Hitler conceived this detail after the campaign in France and came back to it again in the late autumn of 1941, after his first defeats in the Soviet Union. The plaza was to be covered by Hitler's great arch or 'Arch of Triumph', as he only occasionally called it. Our triumphal arch, five hundred and fifty feet wide, three hundred and ninety-two feet deep, and three hundred and eighty-six feet high, would have towered over all the other buildings on this southern portion of the avenue and would literally have dwarfed them.[33]

There was to be another great station at the northern end of this axis. 'The avenue between the two central railroad stations was meant to spell out in architecture the political, military and economic power of Germany. In the centre sat the absolute ruler of the Reich.'[34] But this plan too never came to fruition.

Although the careers of Haussmann and Speer suggest the power of an absolutist to alter cityscapes in pursuit of some grand plan of reconstruction, the cityscapes and topographical layouts of many of the big Victorian cities of Britain were dramatically altered by station construction which was the work of commercial companies.

The role of the station in the transformation of the Victorian city has been definitively studied by J. R. Kellett, who concludes:

By 1890 the principal railway companies had expended over £100,000,000, more than one-eighth of all railway capital, on the provision of terminals, had bought thousands of acres of central land, and undertaken the direct work of urban demolition and reconstruction on a large scale. In most cities they had become the owners of up to eight or ten *per cent* of central land, and indirectly influenced the functions of up to twenty *per cent*. The plans of British towns no matter how individual and diverse before 1830, are uniformly super-inscribed within a generation by the gigantic geometrical brush-strokes of the engineers' curving approach lines and cut-offs, and franked with the same bulky and intrusive termini, sidings and marshalling-yards.[35]

Although companies initially planted terminals on the edge of the built-up central area, they were anxious to move closer to the centre. But urban land values in London were so great that the extension of the London and Birmingham Railway from Camden Town to Euston alone, little over a mile, cost £380,000. The expense of the section of line from Mile End to its terminal at Bishopsgate ruined the Eastern Counties Railway financially. When companies tried to avoid expenditure by sharing, as the four south-eastern companies did at London Bridge Station, the result was often constant friction. For as a witness told a parliamentary committee in 1852: 'Joint stations have been a more fruitful source of quarrels, litigation, chancery proceedings and disagreements, than almost anything else connected with the railway system.'[36]

One reason for company mergers was to create the capital aggregations necessary for large-scale land purchase for the provision of central terminals. For example, the three companies who merged to form the LNWR wanted to provide a new central station in Liverpool. The particular need experienced by the major railway companies in the mid 1840s was for improved and more central stations for passengers, who still provided 61 per cent of overall revenues.

The opening of stations in the central business districts of provincial cities, like Exchange in Liverpool and New Street and Snow Hill in Birmingham, produced a redistribution of land use and a realignment and stimulation of internal traffic routes. These often caused massive traffic jams like those across London Bridge and Jamaica Street Bridge, Glasgow. Although residential users were repelled by these termini, retail shopkeepers and transit warehouses were attracted. The central areas were dissected by massive viaducts and the arches of these viaducts provided a further outlet, leased for use as 'smithies, marine stores, stables, mortar mills, the storage of old tubs, casks and lumber, and other low class traders'. By the 1860s these developments were over and the pattern set. Although the creation of vast central termini resulted in the sweeping away of noisome slum and low-life areas, the demarcation caused by lines, bridges, and viaducts had its own social consequences. 'It is noticeable that districts divided and confined by the railways tended to be cast finally and irretrievably into the now familiar mould of coal and timber yards, warehousing, mixed light and heavy industrial uses, and fourth rate residential housing.'[37] Although the business areas already existed and the stations to some extent were built to accommodate that fact, it is clear that in Birmingham and Glasgow there was a tendency for the railway stations and their approach lines to act as outer boundaries of the central bourgeois district. In both Japan and Denmark there is evidence of stations exercising a gravitational pull, attracting businesses, building, and population, and forming significant urban sub-centres.[38] This seems to have happened less in Britain, although both in Britain and on the Continent the stations attracted places of refreshment, accommodation, and entertainment: cafés, restaurants, hotels, lodging-houses, pubs, and brothels.

Railway Towns

The coming of the railways had a direct impact on the social and occupational structure of British towns and cities. Some railway companies set up engineering works in already established industrial towns, such as Derby, Doncaster, and Darlington, which acquired recognizable and definable railway quarters. Others based themselves in small market towns which rapidly expanded into major railway centres, such as Swindon, Peterborough, Carnforth, and Rugby. But perhaps the most dramatic impact was to be seen in those towns that were created virtually from scratch and owed their entire nature and being to the railways, pre-eminently, of course, Crewe. In all these different sorts of railway town, the station became a focal point of their inhabitants' lives, the living heart of the railway interest that eternally pulsed and throbbed with the power of steam. When decline and run-down hit the railways, some of these communities, Carnforth for example, were to have this living heart ripped from them and were to lose with it their distinctive identity and *raison d'être*.[39]

The classic example of the company town was Crewe. In 1840 when the Grand Junction Railway ordered the purchase of land in the parish of Monks Coppenhall as a site for the new repair and construction works, the population of this rural backwater was barely 200. But it lay at the junction of four major trunk lines from Birmingham, Manchester, Liverpool, and Chester, soon to be joined by lines from Stoke, Shrewsbury, and Preston. Its centrality dictated its emergence as a major railway centre. By 1844 the company had built 217 cottages for incoming workers and in 1845 they initiated the transfer of their construction and repair operations from Edgehill to the new location, which, taking its name from the nearby stately home Crewe Hall, became known as Crewe. By 1846 the population had reached 2,000; by 1910 it was 50,000.

The company had to build the houses, since there was nothing there, and the four different types of housing provided, from villa-style lodges for superior officials down to labourers' cottages, faithfully reflected the hierarchical nature of the railway company service. In 1845 a church and a public baths were opened, to provide for those essential Victorian values—godliness and cleanliness. In due course the London and North-Western, successor company to the Grand Junction, built schools and assembly rooms, supplied gas and water, and manned the fire brigade.

It was only in the towns which the railways created that they built the houses, generally solid, well-built, but unadorned terraced dwellings, in row upon serried row. At Swindon, whose population grew from 1,747 in 1831 to over 40,000 in 1900, the Great Western built an estate known as New Swindon, which like Crewe became a total railway town until the end of the nineteenth century. At Ashford in Kent where the South-Eastern Railway built accommodation for the workers in its locomotive works, it did so unusually in the form of tenement flats.

Eastleigh in Hampshire became a thriving railway community almost overnight when the London and South-Western Railway transferred its works there from Nine Elms in 1891. Similarly, Horwich in Lancashire was transformed from a small community of 4,000 in 1887 to a bustling centre of 20,000 in 1900 owing to the decision of the Lancashire and Yorkshire Railway to site its engineering works there. For better or for worse, in good times and in bad, the fate of these communities was bound up with the railways.

Just as the railways created in Britain towns like Crewe and Swindon, devoted to every aspect of railway work, so too did the railways bring into being new technological towns throughout the world. This was particularly the case where the railway had to cross great expanses of almost uninhabited territory, as in western Canada and the United States, the vast wilderness of Siberia, or the deserts of Australia. There, trains rather than people needed stations, and stations became towns. At Homestake Pass in California, a village of sixty people grew up around the station, solely concerned with serving the trains. Across Western Australia, entire townships sprang up in the middle of the desert to serve the trains of the transcontinental line completed in 1917. In both Canada and Australia, the railway companies sent school, cinema, church, and grocery-store coaches to their remote railway communities. At many of these the inhabitants developed the habit of boarding the transcontinental trains to purchase food, confectionery, and drinks from the bars and buffets of the train. News was exchanged in this fashion too. This continued to be a feature of halts on the Trans-Siberian railway until very recently.

At Nairobi in Kenya the station and its associated town became a metropolis, the capital of the country. The railway turned Bulawayo in Zimbabwe into a city which vied with the capital, Salisbury, and at one stage surpassed it in size. In Siberia, stations, often distant from the towns they were supposed to serve, became important communities in their own right. A complete settlement developed at Zlatoust Station, including a theatre. At Ob Station, the school was proudly described in the 1900 Guide to the Siberian railway as having a harmonium and a magic lantern.[40] At Khabarovsk the station buildings included accommodation for employees, engine house, hospital, goods platform, and storehouse. There was a barracks for a company of the Ussuri railway battalion, a feeding-station, bakeries, bath-house, and a technical railway school. Gardens were planted in front of the station, and a church built from the Alexander III fund. At Omsk the population of the station had by 1900 reached 8,000, while the town's own population was 37,470. At Vladivostok there was a large convict settlement which owed its existence to the presence of the station. Strolling players were accustomed to travel on Trans-Siberian trains, performing at stations *en route*.

India, with its vast railway networks, inevitably had its railway towns, proudly dubbed the 'Crewes of India'. Jamalpur, the East India Company's loco works in Bengal, employed no fewer than 250 Europeans and 10,000 Indians at the turn of the century.[41] Kipling, always enthralled by technology, wrote: 'The heart of Jamalpur is the shops, and here a visitor will see more things in an hour than he can understand in a year.' The company had supplied houses for all its employees, and in addition there was a church, a chapel, a club, a Masonic lodge, and several schools. Facilities for hockey, football, and tennis were provided, and there was a large *maidan* for sports. Most of these facilities were, of course, for Europeans, and the Europeans of these stations reproduced all the snobbery and anxiety about precedence so characteristic of the British in India:

That bugbear, precedence, which interferes so much with social enjoyment in India, and which is so often the cause of heated disputes, jealousies, and heart-burnings, is occasionally to be reckoned with in the railway colony. Sometimes, the storekeeper—especially should he be 'chief storekeeper'—is affronted because he has been asked at a dinner-party to take in the assistant engineer's wife instead of the agent's 'lady', contending that his rank is higher than that of the official to whom the coveted partner has been assigned. Or the wife of the general traffic manager may refuse to patronise the club because forsooth! she may meet there the assistant storekeeper's sister—a person whom she considers her social inferior ... the 'upper subordinates' are sometimes a little apt to overrate the importance of their social position; the possession of a five-roomed 'bungalow', a pony and cart, two or three coloured servants, and a seat on the board of the railway co-operative stores may have a tendency to cause what is best described as 'Putting on "side"'. The wife of the recently promoted locomotive foreman has been known to turn up her nose at her former acquaintance, the Eurasian sister of the senior platelayer, and the stationmaster sometimes looks down upon the clerk of work, treating him in a patronising manner.[42]

At Lilloah, formerly merely a small third-class station on the outskirts of Calcutta, the East India Railway built its carriage- and wagon-shops.[43] There a relatively small European Staff supervised 5,000 workers from Bengal, the Punjab, and China. The Europeans had comfortable company quarters 'with electric lights and fans', while the Indian employees lived some distance away and were brought in by special trains. Lilloah built very different types of special train. The royal train to convey the Prince and Princess of Wales on their 1905–6 visit was built there, as were special carriages for the Viceroy and subsequent royal trains. Most of the European mechanical staff were time-expired soldiers who had learned a trade. So far as the employment of Indian mechanics was concerned, the Carriage and Wagon Superintendent noted that

It is to be regretted that some of Indian workmen, whose fathers are among the most skilful and industrious workers in the world, eschew trade and become clerks. A movement, originated in Lilloah, under which the sons of Indian gentlemen who have received a liberal education and sat at the Entrance Examination of the Calcutta University, are taken into the works for a period of seven years, and trained with a view to their subsequently becoming assistants to the European foremen, has met with much favour, and it is encouraging to note the scheme, judging by the number of applications received, is appreciated.[44]

The capacity of the railway to turn unimportant places into significant centres was reflected also at Asansol.[45] This was formerly a small, unknown village, which was put on the map when it became an important junction, marshalling yard, and railway settlement. A district headquarters was positioned there, and an institute, church, market, and schools built. Dozens of trains passed through Asansol daily and large numbers of European drivers and guards lived there. They too had a significant social hierarchy. The drivers were often covenanted from England and were paid much more than the guards who were recruited in India, often from time-expired soldiers. It was from such people that the poorer white communities in India were drawn, and all those recruited from Britain on favourable terms never allowed them to forget their inferior status.

Technology

Many of the railway towns throughout the world were the creation of steam technology. The range of the steam engine is little more than 150–200 miles. Servicing centres were needed roughly at such intervals to re-fuel, re-water engines, as well as act as domiciles for the drivers, firemen, and mechanics. The switch to diesel, and even more so to electricity, reduced the need for such centres. The range of the new locomotives was much greater, and servicing centres could become highly concentrated. Many railway towns became redundant.

The move from conventional goods handling to the container greatly reduced the need for vast marshalling yards where wagons were shunted and trains made up. These developments have often highlighted the widening gap between the Western and the Third worlds. In many developing countries steam—and the railway towns that go with it—still has an important place, and so do marshalling yards and mixed freight-handling techniques. To visit some of these is like taking a railway trip back into nineteenth- and early twentieth-century Britain.

If the yards, engine sheds, and workshops have disappeared from the immediate vicinity of many stations throughout the world, the station itself has undergone dramatic visible change even where the original buildings, train-sheds, and platforms survive. The great goods sheds of larger towns, the goods platforms of country stations have all bowed to the supremacy of the lorry. Water-towers and their attendant pumps, hoses, and employees have disappeared in most places, and in not a few these water-towers contributed notable architectural features to the station. The shift from semaphore signalling and other forms of mechanical signalling to electrical signalling and Centralized Traffic Control (CTC) has removed the great signal gantries and the multiplicity of signal-boxes, formerly such a feature of stations, a source of fascination to many. All of these developments have massively reduced the sense of bustle and noise at the station, and have made it a much less significant centre of employment.

Technical developments in many parts of the world have had another significant effect on country and small-town stations. Trains no longer stop there for the relatively long periods which were formerly the norm. The great multi-volume compendium on the Cape to Cairo railway, published in 1923, listed the stopping times at stations for engines and crews to be changed, carriages to be checked, refreshments to be taken. Stops of seventy or ninety minutes were common, and even at remote stations a stop of ten or twenty minutes would be quite usual. Travellers could stretch their legs on the station platform and in the station buildings on most such stops. Often they could take a walk round town, and visit the hotel or the club before continuing their journey. On a journey lasting several days, such stops seemed less important than on the shorter journeys encountered in Europe. A train journey could genuinely involve seeing the place *en route*. The new technology has reduced the need for such stops. Now all the traveller sees is a brief glimpse of the station, and the opportunities for local vendors and businesses have been much reduced. Leisurely trains with long station stops survive in some places, but even in Africa and India many lines have been dieselized or electrified, and speed has become the most important criterion.

One traveller calculated that no fewer than fourteen hours of the trans-Siberian journey were spent stopped at stations, but ironically those hours could not be used by tourists to see the town or photograph the surroundings. Generally, they are not permitted to leave the stations and photography is strictly forbidden. Even although railway technology is now as a rule hopelessly out of date and railways play a very small role in military matters, some states demonstrate their paranoia through anxieties about station photography. From the Soviet Union to Latin America, from Tanzania to China, stations may not be photographed.

In some places the railway has contributed to its own downfall. The completion in 1965 of the trans-Canada highway—some of the materials for which were carried by train—greatly reduced Canadian dependence on the transcontinental rail routes. In Newfoundland, where the railway disappeared completely, the trains were vital in transporting workers and materials for the building of the new airport which helped to spell its doom.

Victoria Terminus, Bombay, 1878. Watercolour by Axel Hermann Haig. The station was not actually opened until 1887.

Anuradhapura Station, Ceylon.

Kuala Lumpur, an Orientalist palace-mosque, built in Edwardian times as the showpiece of Malayan Railways.

The exterior of Albury Station, New South Wales.

The track side of Albury Station, New South Wales, showing the long platform extension where passengers changed on to the (different gauge) railway system of Victoria.

Petersham Station, New South Wales.

Wallerawang Junction, New South Wales.

5

The Station in Politics

IT is no coincidence that Belgium, which had so recently become an independent state (1831), was the first European country to achieve a fully-fledged railway system. The first line was started in 1835 and by 1848 there were 450 miles in operation, stiffening the state with ribs of iron and powerfully promoting a structure of nationhood. The first line was opened with great ceremony by King Leopold I, who decorated George and Robert Stephenson for advising on the building of the line.

The achievement of unification in Italy in 1861 was followed by a frantic effort on the part of the government to link the existing systems in the peninsula and to provide them where they did not yet exist. The government was willing to spend freely—100 million lire in 1860–1 alone—to achieve a system which would bind the new state together, facilitate the movement of troops, secure the frontiers with Austria, and hold down the hostile South. As Massimo d'Azeglio the Piedmontese novelist and statesman declared, 'Railways will serve to sew up the Italian boot', a view that was shared by Cavour and the other leading proponents of unification.[1] Thus Rome and Naples were linked in 1863, Bologna and Florence in 1864, Florence and Rome in 1866, so that by 1880 the Italian trunk system was complete.

The ease of communication between sometimes widely diverse regions helped in the long run to diminish regional differences and at the same time it advanced the process of urbanization, by breaking down the distinction between town and country. In the second half of the nineteenth century the rural population of Western Europe was in decline. It was not until 1930 in France that more people lived in the towns than in the country, a situation achieved in Britain by 1851. But the railways made the eventual triumph of the city inevitable. In a wider context, they facilitated the emergence of nationhood by establishing a national market, a national taste, a national mood. The circulation of mass-produced clothing helped to diminish regional differences. News, gossip, fashion, political slogans, sports results, financial information circulated along the iron rails, creating a national constituency. The station was the means of tapping this flowing current of life and information, the location of bookstall, telegraph office, and important arrivals. Everywhere, whether in newly established states like Italy and Belgium or old-established ones like Britain and France, national identities were emerging in the wake of the iron horse. The railway stations were almost the chain of outposts signalling the onward march of this nationhood.

Two developments in particular, intimately linked with the railways, focused on the station. One was the development of mass-circulation newspapers which played an important part in raising the level of national consciousness. These had been impossible before the railways. The national newspaper followed on the introduction of the newspaper train. The Liverpool and Manchester Railway in 1831 had agreed to allow newspapers to travel free provided that the printers brought the parcels to the departure platform of the station and the wholesale newsagents collected them at the other end. Such munificence did not last. But in 1866 the railway companies agreed to a standard charge of half the ordinary parcel rate. Already as early as 1848 special trains were bringing London newspapers to Glasgow in ten hours.

From 1843 the railway lines were also accompanied by the telegraph lines and the postal service was becoming more and more effective. The first TPO, rail-borne travelling post office, where letters were sorted *en route* by GPO employees, was introduced between Birmingham and Liverpool in 1838. In 1983 the forty-two British TPOs travelled more than 5 million miles and carried 330 million first-class letters and 2½ million datapost bags. In Italy the dissemination of news by letter and telegram, further cementing the concept of a single state, increased by leaps and bounds as the rail network spread. The number of letters sent increased from 108 million in 1861 to 484 million in 1894 to 1,515 million in 1914, and the number of private telegrams from 100,000 in 1861 to 7.9 million in 1894 to 21 million in 1914.

Politicians were soon to see the advantages that the railway network conferred and in the late nineteenth century both in Britain and America there was developed what came to be called in the United States the 'whistle-stop tour'. In Britain it was popularized by Mr Gladstone, particularly in his Midlothian election campaign of 1879. He succeeded in turning the station into a political meeting-place. John Pendleton described his railway progresses:

There have been some strange scenes at the various stopping-places on the West Coast route during Mr. Gladstone's journeys; and railway officials have not been without anxiety lest some politician or pressman, indiscreet with zeal, should be ground under the carriage wheels. The eager crowds catching sight of the venerable statesman's face, deeply furrowed with thought, and age, never seemed to think of the peril of the platform edge. Everybody desired to gaze upon him, to shake hands with him, to thrust flowers and fruit upon him, and to offer him cigars, though he does not smoke, even while he was speaking to the local deputation in reply to their ardent address; and reporters were clinging to the carriage handles trying desperately to take notes meanwhile.[2]

Mr Gladstone sometimes came a cropper, however, as on one of his speaking stops at Lockerbie Station on the trip to Midlothian in 1892: the speech of welcome was so long that the train left before Gladstone had time to speak. Other politicians disdained Gladstone's demotic approach. The Conservative A. J. Balfour answered demands from a crowd at Huddersfield Station for a speech in 1892:

In other circumstances I should be very pleased indeed to address you, but neither in this nor in any other particular am I anxious to imitate the methods of a very distinguished statesman whose habitual methods of electioneering consist of inconveniencing the officials of the various railways over which he travels and the public who desire to travel in the same train with him.[3]

It is a measure of the decline of American railways that 'whistle-stops' in presidential elections ceased to be a major factor after Harry Truman's election in 1948 when he addressed an audience of thousands at Grand Central Station.

Britain as an island depended on its navy for defence and did not need to build purely strategic railway lines. But on the Continent strategic considerations were often uppermost in the minds of planners and governments. In Russia, Count Witte, the far-sighted and dynamic minister who wanted to mesh Russia in economically productive lines, found his plans frustrated sometimes by the need to build costly unremunerative lines for purely military purposes at the dictates of the Tsar and generals. The lines in Northern Italy between Genoa, Alessandria, Turin, and Novara were developed with a specific strategic purpose, to allow the Italians to concentrate their forces rapidly in the event of war with Austria. France and Austria gave similar prominence to the strategic role of the railways. The 1878 Freycinet Plan, launched by the French Minister of Public Works in the aftermath of the Franco-Prussian war, envisaged 4,500 km. of new lines, primarily in the interests of national security. In the event, it proved much too expensive and in 1883 the government cut its losses and came to terms with the railway companies to take over and complete those projects the State had initiated.

Germany was not yet a nation, but the Prussians were swift to appreciate the strategic and political importance of the iron rails. As early as 1860 the Prussian State operated 55 per cent of the German network. By 1869, 17,330 km. of railway were in operation in Germany, 10,000 of it in Prussia. As L. Girard noted:

> The role of the state in the Germanic world was striking. Railways seemed to be a civilian branch of the army. In a country where capital was sufficient but not overabundant, wastages resulting from speculation, the scourge of Anglo-Saxon countries, were avoided. Moreover lines of public utility, running at a loss but of vital importance, from a national point of view, were undertaken.[4]

In consequence, stations became a regular and familiar point of departure for the troops of all nations whether on manœuvres or on active service and the station gained and retained a continuing military and strategic importance. Where nations were still raw and newly formed, like Italy and later Germany, their role could well be vital in ensuring that the hard-won nationhood was maintained and preserved. But everywhere, whether receiving telegrams and newspapers, providing platforms for politicians, embarkation and disembarkation points for troops, the stations acted as an agent of nationhood.

Countries make statements through their stations, consciously and unconsciously. The station has, for example, invariably been the setting for the personality cults of repressive regimes. Throughout the Soviet Union, though the statues of Stalin have disappeared, those of Lenin are ubiquitous. He stands in a variety of postures, the arm-outstretched 'hailing a taxi' stance, as Eric Newby called it, the most common.[5] Russian stations are also arrayed with posters, celebrating and exhorting workers, calling for united effort. When the Iranian *ancien régime* renewed its northern railway line to the Turkish border, a succession of new stations was built in the glass-and-concrete supermarket style, each dominated by massive posters of the Shah, his wife, and son. They were symptomatic of the many grandiloquent gestures by which the Shah's regime tried to instil confidence in his waning power. Stations in China were adorned with huge portraits of Mao, when he was at the height of his power. Since his death, many of them have been removed.

In India the British had attempted to create a disciplined, ordered hierarchy, and that is reflected in the multiplicity of classes, facilities, and offices at railway stations, each neatly labelled. Indian nationalists recognized the symbolic significance of railway stations, as well as their crucial significance as communications centres. During the 'Quit India' movement of 1941–2, no fewer than 240 stations were attacked. The station lent itself well to passive resistance techniques. The sight of members of the Indian National Congress sitting across railway tracks became one of the familiar images of the Indian nationalist period, firmly imprinted by the film *Bhowani Junction*. Yet the nationalists were themselves assiduous users of the railway, and Gandhi's travels in his fourth-class carriage were as famous as any of his activities. The station was the place to see politicians and hear them speak. And stations continued to have a central role in Indian post-independence culture. When affluent societies moved to road and air transport, countries with large urban and rural under-classes stayed with the railways, although the social prestige of the latter did suffer. It became noticeable that the old railway hotels, formerly as comfortable as any available, rapidly ran down. The new filing-cabinet international hotels, unconnected with railways or stations, became the fashionable hostelries, sharing their soullessness with the aircraft and airports which they served.

Indian stations bear all the hallmarks of a complex, undisciplined society, which none the less contrives to work, if only just. The stations, like India itself, seem constantly on the point of breakdown, in danger of being engulfed by the waves of humanity which break over them with their accompanying detritus. Yet somehow they survive and rise above the social storms which batter them. The visitor to India who avoids railway stations misses a crucial part of India. R. K. Narayan, when embarking on his series of Malgudi novels, chose to use the station as his starting-point.[6] There was the entrance gateway to the town, and the place where a microcosm of its society could be viewed in its greatest immediacy.

It is difficult to imagine anyone cleaning up and disciplining India's stations, but new regimes have attempted just such discipline elsewhere. The marshalling and ordering of porters at Pakistan's stations was at-tempted, with only moderate success, after the introduction of military rule and Islamic law by President Zia ul-Haq. Paul Theroux encountered a transformation in the cleanliness and order of Rangoon Station after the regime of Ne Win came to power in Burma.[7] A functional uniformity, pressures of population, and severe discipline in the circulation of people are all encountered at Japanese stations.

In South Africa, apartheid regulations were never more glaring than at the stations. The station could also reflect cosmetic attempts at 'multi-racialism'. In the 1950s, in the Central African Federation, the 'native' class was renamed fourth class, and the racial signs at stations were replaced by signs indicating the class of travel. This was pure hypocrisy, for everyone knew where the racial lines were still drawn. But in South Africa the station could continue to play a political role long after it had disappeared elsewhere. In 1984 the President of South Africa, P. W.

Botha, met President Samora Machel of Mozambique at a specially constructed station on the South African–Mozambique border. In the attempted *rapprochement* of these two very different regimes, it would have not done for either leader to fly into the capital of the other. The station frontier meeting was the most delicate solution.

'All ritual is fortifying', wrote Rudyard Kipling, and ritual is one of the most substantial forms of cement preserving and sustaining the structure of established order and the status quo, in all forms of society. The railway station is one of architecture's great theatres, purpose-built for splendid ritual occasions, for the fanfares, uniforms, banners, red carpets, and top hats that attend the most solemn and formal events in a nation's history. Photographs and newsreels in abundance testify to the propaganda power of such occasions, the arrival and departure of kings and presidents, State visits and State funerals, the comings and goings of the great and famous: the body of the Unknown Warrior transported with great reverence from the battlefields of Europe to rest overnight at Victoria Station before its conveyance to and interment at Westminster Abbey on 12 November 1920; a triumphant Adolf Hitler arriving at a Berlin station, draped in swastikas and festooned with German eagles, after securing victory over France in 1940 and an armistice signed in the same railway carriage at Compiègne which had witnessed the German surrender in 1918; the last journeys of the bodies of legendary American presidents Abraham Lincoln and Franklin D. Roosevelt, of the beloved British kings George V and George VI, and of the great warriors Churchill and Mountbatten.

President Lincoln's funeral journey from Washington to Springfield, Illinois, lasted twelve days. The train, its engine covered in black crêpe and draped flags and with the carriage decked out in black, stopped at several stations *en route* for the coffin to be removed and funeral services held. The President was finally interred at Oak Ridge Cemetery, Springfield, on 3 May 1865.

The death of Queen Victoria was notable as much for the railways as for the life of the nation and of the Empire. She had been the first British monarch to travel by train and had become an inveterate rail traveller. Her reign had seen the railways grow from fledgeling industry to major national institution, just as it had seen the British Empire spread to embrace a quarter of the globe and British industry to flood the world with its textiles, manufactures, and artefacts. With Victoria both the nineteenth century and the era of Britain's undisputed world eminence passed into history. So it was fitting that the railways should play a central role in the great and sombre occasion of her last journey and the station should function as a forum for funereal ceremonial.

On Saturday, 2 February 1901 the Queen's body was conveyed from the Isle of Wight to the Royal Dockyard Station at Gosport and placed aboard the royal train, which had been brought from Portsmouth Town Station the previous night. Sam Fay, Superintendent of the London and South-Western Railway, took personal charge of the arrangements, as from Gosport to Fareham the train ran over LSWR rails. At Fareham Station the train was handed over to the charge of the London, Brighton and South-Coast Railway. The LBSCR engine *Empress*, decorated with funeral bands, the royal coat of arms, and a gilt crown on a crimson cushion, was attached. Hauled by it, the train made up the nine minutes late it was running and arrived at Victoria Station at 10.58 a.m.—two minutes early. At 1.32 p.m. on the same day, the royal coffin, conveyed in solemn procession across London, left Paddington Station for Windsor in a train hauled by a GWR engine renamed for the occasion *Royal Sovereign*. The *Railway Magazine* was moved to print a poetic tribute to the passing of the Queen:

> Full sixty years a Queen! the well beloved!
> The nation's heart, aye, all the world's, is mov'd;
> And 'mid the courtly cavalcade of woe
> The mingled tears of thronging thousands flow!
> The roll of muffled drum, the minute gun
> Tell forth the tale—the weft of life is spun!
> And hush'd the voice of pleasure thro' the land
> As, mute in sympathy, the mourners stand
> While gilded cars the princely cortege wait
> In all the pomp and pageantry of State;
> Where the great casket, with its blazon'd pall,
> Is borne aloft, the cynosure of all,
> On this last journey; sad, eventful stage,
> A fun'ral bier for queenly equipage!
> A people's grief is echo'd in the sound
> Of wailing music, thro' the gloom profound,
> As Royal Sov'reign, with its priceless load,
> Glides gently forth upon that 'Royal road',
> Whose purpled platform honour oft hath shown
> To noblest Monarch who e'er grac'd a throne!
> But ne'er such regal progress earth had seen,
> As mark'd this passing of an Empress-Queen![8]

The official *Times* account of the obsequies of King George V in 1936 eloquently demonstrates the emotional role of the station in the life of the nation at such solemn moments. The King's body was first transported to Wolferton, the royal station for the Sandringham Estate. A guard of honour at the station was provided by the Sandringham Company of the 5th Battalion, the Norfolk Regiment, Territorial Army. A band played Chopin's Funeral March and 'at five minutes past noon the train glided slowly and almost silently from the station'.⁹

All along the route to London, at level crossings, at stations, in fields, in towns, people gathered bareheaded to pay their last respects to the sovereign who had seen them through a momentous period of change and had stood for the maintenance of duty, decency, and family life as a reassuringly fixed point in an all too rapidly changing world.

The royal train reached King's Cross, London, at a quarter to 3. It came into a silent station, where traffic was still and the hiss of steam had been hushed. Its own arrival made no sound. Its steam added nothing to the faint mistiness in the station. For all the red carpet and purple drapings the bare station could have no beauty, but it had an air of sombre reverence and quiet dignity as the mortal remains of the King came to the end of their longest journey.

. . . A few black-coated officials waited on the platform. The gun-carriage, with its six horses, was ready to move forward to the place where it might receive its Royal burden. The double doors of the saloon in which the body of King George lay were gently opened. . . . No sound yet broke the stillness. For a moment the train was as still as the place was silent. . . . Led by the King and Queen Mary, the little black-garbed party moved forward towards the open doors of the funeral coach. There, at the edge of the red carpet, which had silenced their footsteps too, the mourners halted . . . The King and the Duke of York went quietly forward to the door of the coach while the coffin was being shrouded in the Royal Standard. Then the Imperial Crown, covered with a purple cloth, was carried into the coach and was placed on the coffin . . . The Royal party stood in two rows on the platform facing the path by which the body must be borne to the gun-carriage. For six minutes more the great building and its gloomy arches were emptied of sound and movement. The scene gave a sense of the parting of the ways, as though the little family group had paused before merging its private grief in the great tide of public sorrow waiting to manifest itself in the crowded streets. Here in the unlighted vault of an empty railway station the last act of affection and respect was passing to the husband and the father, before the people of a King should claim the privilege of paying him its own tribute.¹⁰

There were similar scenes amid large crowds at Paddington as the King's body left London after the lying in state for burial at Windsor. Windsor Station, draped in purple and closed to the public, received five special trains containing the royal party, members of the government, and representatives of foreign countries. One hundred and fifty men from the *Excellent*, who were to draw the gun-carriage bearing the King's body, and the guards of honour from the Royal Navy, the Brigade of

Guards, and the Royal Air Force took up their positions in the station courtyard.

A few minutes before one o'clock the last of the special trains arrived. It brought many of the foreign representatives who had taken part in the procession through London, and as they assembled on the platform to await the Royal Train the picture was one of the brilliant colours heightened by the medieval pageantry provided by the Heralds and the Kings of Arms . . . The funeral train . . . glided into the station, to the accompaniment of the minute guns which told the waiting and anxious crowds of the return of King George to the Royal City. The coach containing the coffin was drawn up within a few yards of the Royal waiting room. Under the direction of the Earl Marshal, the bearer party entered the coach and the coffin was borne reverently across the platform to the gun-carriage. In the stillness the command 'Off Caps' rang out, and the men from the *Excellent* stood with bared heads and hands gripping the drag-ropes as the bearers passed. On the coffin lay the Royal Standard and surmounting it the Crown, the Regalia, the Insignia of the Order of the Garter, and the Queen's wreath Then for a moment of unforgettable beauty the stillness was broken by the wailing of the bosun's pipe. The Navy was paying its own tribute to the Monarch whom it regarded as its special possession.[11]

The importance of railways in creating unity and order is attested in the lavish ceremonial attending the inauguration of lines in the British Empire. In 1853, when the first railway in India was opened between Bombay and Thana, the opening ceremony was subjected to a rare and celebrated snub: the Governor of Bombay, the Commander-in-Chief, and the Bishop left for the hills the day before.[12] The occasion was a splendid one none the less, and the opening was performed by the Chief Justice. That rebuff was entirely uncharacteristic in the annals of railway ceremony. From this time onwards, the presence of lieutenant-governors, governors, and governors-general was to be almost obligatory at all such ceremonies. In 1897 a Cassell's illustrated part-book on the British Empire, published for the Jubilee of Queen Victoria, included a photograph of the opening of a Malayan railway.[13] Here was the characteristic expression of British power, with colonial officials, proud railway employees, and bands standing on a station adorned with flags and bunting, with crowds of wondering local people looking on. It was a scene which was repeated in the pages of the *Illustrated London News* and other pictorial journals for more than fifty years. Inevitably, even more space was devoted to such events in the local press, whole issues of papers being turned over to them.

Every colony produced its examples, and the engravings and photographs are legion. In Ceylon a succession of governors were said to be

particularly interested in railways, and there the early companies—
before the colony took over the railways as a State system—spent excessive amounts on ceremony. The ceremony to cut the first sod of the
Colombo to Kandy railway was so lavish that the company could barely
afford to build the line, let alone hold an opening ceremony after it.[14] The
sod-cutting occasion was followed by a splendid tiffin in a specially
constructed 'Banquet Bungalow' which itself resembled a railway station.

The arrival of the first trains in Rhodesia had a particular poignancy,
since the events occurred in the wake of the nearly successful rising of
the Shona and Ndebele people in 1896–7. The first train from the south
entered Bulawayo in 1897, the first from the east arrived in Salisbury in
May 1899. On each occasion elaborate ceremonies were held, and the
trains were decorated with slogans such as 'Advance Rhodesia', 'Now we
shan't be long to Cairo', and 'Pro Bono Publico'. No less than a week of
celebrations was laid on for the opening of the railway to Bulawayo.
At the station, elaborately decorated for the opening, the High Commissioner in South Africa, Sir Alfred Milner, read a message from
Joseph Chamberlain, the Secretary of State for the Colonies, and the
ceremony included the presentation of the Victoria Cross to Trooper
H. S. Henderson for bravery in the Matabele War.

It would, of course, be wrong to imagine that every aspect of these
celebrations was decorous. George Pauling, the great railway contractor
connected with the building of the Central African railway lines, was
famous for the lavishness of his hospitality, not only to distinguished and
invited guests, but also to his work-force, at least the whites among them.
Drunken sprees ensued, which even involved, on one occasion, the
hijacking of a train. At Broken Hill, in Northern Rhodesia, when the
Trans-Zambezi line reached this important station on the way to the
Congo, Pauling dispensed liquor from the balcony of his private saloon.

A more solemn occasion was the funeral of Cecil Rhodes. His body
was taken from the Cape to Bulawayo in March 1902, escorted by two
armoured trains. At Bulawayo Station his coffin was transferred with
great pomp to a gun-carriage to be transported to the grave he had
chosen for himself in the Matopos Hills. Under the terms of his will, a
branch railway line was built to the Matopos, so that the people of
Bulawayo could enjoy weekend excursions to the Matopos and, presumably, visit his grave. It was opened to Matopos terminus station in 1903.
Nothing could be more symbolic of the assertion of white power. The
Matopos had been a prime redoubt of Ndebele resistance in the Revolt
of 1896. Now the African population had been cleared from the hills
which had become instead the playground of white excursionists. The

arrival of the railway in Bulawayo, its progress north of the Zambezi, and the building of branch lines ensured that similar African revolts were unlikely to happen again.

These opening ceremonies continued to be performed until the inter-war years of the twentieth century. In 1929, for example, J. H. Thomas, former Labour Colonial Secretary, opened the new Gold Coast Railway from Takoradi to Kumasi. By then, however, the excitement of such events had lost its edge. Already a new technology was taking over, and the pictorial journals devoted themselves to the new aerial and auto-mobile crazes. It is much more difficult to find illustrations of railway events of this sort in the twentieth century compared with their nineteenth-century counterparts.

In North and South America such ceremonies were performed by mayors, state governors, and even presidents. Ministers met at fron-tiers—for example on the opening of the Argentine–Chile railway in 1915—and the air was heavy with rhetorical metaphor about the bonding power of the rails and the steam locomotion which brought peace, often illusory hopes. No less a personage than the Tsarevich himself inaug-urated the building of the Trans-Siberian line by laying the foundation stone of the railway station at Vladivostok in 1891.

In India, and elsewhere in the British Empire, the station was repeat-edly the setting for elaborate welcomes on gubernatorial, viceregal, and royal visits. Such station pageantry neatly reflects the manner in which the late nineteenth century was an era of invented tradition. Some of the earlier examples of station pomp were halting and chaotic. On the Prince of Wales's tours of Canada in 1863 and India in 1875, ceremonial was often makeshift and imprecise. Towns which had carefully decorated themselves for the occasion were missed, and time-keeping was seldom of the best. By the 1890s the British throughout the world had become past masters of such arrangements: the reviews of troops, the assembling of officials, the quality and precision of bands, the organization of both railway traffic and road conveyances. The Viceroy, Lord Curzon, was a stickler for the effective arrangement of such events: he was well aware of the propaganda value of pomp in providing displays of authority to Indians and in developing the self-confidence and self-regard of the ruling race.

Curzon's Great Delhi Durbar of 1903, the visits of the Prince and Princess of Wales in 1905–6, of King George V and Queen Mary in 1911–12, and of their son Edward, Prince of Wales, in the 1920s put the Indian railway companies on their mettle. Special traffic officers were appointed to control trains, and timings, menus, station arrivals and departures were worked out to the last detail. India offered only more colourful and exotic examples of station events that were duplicated throughout the Empire. Even at stations where viceregal or royal parties were not going to alight, crowds would turn out to see the special white train and hope to catch a glimpse of royal visages behind the curtained windows of the luxurious carriages. The passage of that train could have a dramatic effect on the busiest of railway junctions. The General Manager of the East India Railway, G. Huddleston, described one such royal occasion at Asansol, one of the largest junctions and marshalling yards on the entire Indian railway system:

There is no time of the day or night when things are at rest, no time when quiet reigns. Asansol without train movement, without the ceaseless rumble, bump, and clatter of shunting and marshalling, without the shriek of the engine whistle would be almost unrecognisable, and yet for a few brief minutes on the 29th December, 1905, all was still. On that date practically the whole of the work of the yard was brought to a stand, shunting engines and wagons did not move, the pulse of the busy station ceased to beat. Evidently something very unusual, something very exceptional, something indeed not likely to occur again for a quarter of a century was the cause. The occasion will long be remembered at Asansol; it was nothing more or less than the passing through of the 'Special' conveying their Royal Highnesses the Prince and Princess of Wales, when quiet was essential, when to cease work for a few moments was the greatest compliment the railway could pay the Royal visitors.[15]

Even in this period of exaggerated attention to ceremonial detail, things could go wrong. When Lord Milner arrived in Bulawayo on his visit to Rhodesia in 1897, his train was so late that the crowd which had assembled to meet him at the station dispersed, leaving only a scratch reception committee. Even at Curzon's great Durbar station in Delhi chaos could readily intervene. Dorothy Menpes, the wife of an artist detailed to illustrate the Durbar, described the scene at Delhi when the special train conveying the Viceroy's guests arrived:

When we arrived at Delhi we had to collect our luggage, a feat that required enormous energy and dexterity. It was perhaps one of the most interesting scenes ever witnessed at a railway station and we lingered to watch it. The English valets were paralysed in the confusion. Their masters had to attend to everything. There were officers wheeling trucks, free fights, ladies wringing their hands over lost boxes and quarrelling over the possession of trunks. I was surprised at the very unusual violence of the officers. They kicked the men about them, and swore appallingly. I saw one man tear a trunk away from a railway official, wheel it off, and then spill the contents. It was perhaps the most confused mass you could possibly imagine—such a medley of different nationalities! There among them was our thin black servant, a man who was of a higher caste than the rest, slipping in and out of the people and gathering our luggage without any trouble at all. He was our salvation, and he seemed in an extraordinary way to command respect. Nearly everyone else was desperate. The stationmaster gave up shouting orders which were not heard among the confusion of tongues, and stood still, merely whispering. The man into whose shoes he had stepped, I learned, had gone mad before the arrival of Lord Curzon's guests. Now that they had come, this one was dazed. The strain was too much for him, and he collapsed.[16]

In the 1920s the Prince of Wales made a succession of Empire tours, to Australasia, Canada, India, Burma, the Far East, West Africa, South Africa, and South America. Each of his tours was covered in newsreels, in the pictorial journals, and in a series of illustrated books. The overland parts of these tours were conducted almost entirely by train, and the red carpets and bunting, reviews and receptions at stations along his route continued the tradition begun in the nineteenth century. In India the prince, like previous royal visitors, seemed to spend more time in the Indian princely states than in British India itself. From Udaipur to Hyderabad, from Jammu to Mysore, and from Gwalior to Mandalay the station scenes were repeated, as the prince transferred from imperial steam to pre-colonial conveyance, to State elephants, horse-drawn carriages, State bullock carriages, and the like. These attempts to resuscitate imperial sentiment by the royal progress from station to station may have impressed Indian princes, the citizens of the Dominions, and above all the people at home. But in the Indian case at least, they did not impress the Prince. In a letter to the Secretary of State for India, Edwin Montagu, he wrote:

Let me tell you at once that the newspaper accounts at home of the various visits, ceremonies, and receptions, have almost invariably been hopefully exaggerated. People at home think my tour is a great success, and I must reluctantly tell you that it is no such thing.[17]

It is perhaps not surprising that stations, just as they were forums for dispensing positive political propaganda, should become targets for the darker propaganda of political terrorists. The blowing-up of the railway station in the Communist city of Bologna by right-wing Italian terrorists in 1980 with the loss of eighty-five lives is the most horrific recent example of such actions. But Corsican separatists blew up Villepinte station near Paris in 1977 and railway stations in Britain have been regular targets for the IRA in both the nineteenth and twentieth centuries. Between 1880 and 1887, for instance, fanatical Fenians waged a bombing campaign in Britain in pursuit of independence for Ireland.

During the course of this, as well as attacking the London underground, they left portmanteaus containing bombs at four London Railway stations, Charing Cross, Paddington, Victoria, and Ludgate Hill, in 1884. The one at Victoria went off without loss of life: the others failed to explode. But in 1939 there were further IRA outrages against stations in mainland Britain. As part of a nationwide campaign of arson in 1913–14 in pursuit of votes for women, British suffragettes burned down five stations, including Leuchars Junction, the local station of Prime Minister Asquith. As recently as New Year's Eve 1983, two people were killed and thirty-five injured when bombs exploded at Marseilles Railway Station. Islamic fundamentalists were believed responsible but the terrorist 'Carlos the Jackal' claimed responsibility. In 1984 Sikh terrorists blew up track at Karuebeghu and Khaimpheuki stations a week after Sikh extremists set fire to forty railway stations all over the Punjab in an attempt to paralyse communications. It is certain that as long as there are stations they will be used for political statements of one kind or another, grand or futile, joyous or murderous, rhetorical or explosive.

6

Class, Race, and Sex

THE station was an extraordinary agent of social mixing. Its position at
the centre of cities and in most suburban, country-town, and rural
communities meant that it was accessible to all classes. They met there as
fellow travellers, as masters and servants, as patrons and employees. For
the very poorest the station was one of the few places where they could
encounter the better-off, and attempt some income redistribution by the
provision of services like newspaper-selling, boot-blacking, hawking, or
simply begging. Outside Europe, class hierarchies were further complicated by those of race. Where class was underpinned by race, the
economic and cultural gulf was even greater. Again, it was at stations that
the classes were most likely to encounter each other, and be provided with
brief windows into each other's lives. But the stations were in many
respects designed to avoid these encounters across class and racial
boundaries as much as possible. The provision of waiting-rooms for the
different travelling classes effectively separated social class and racial
group. The railway ticket was an indication of social standing, and, in the
case of first class, a passport to protection. The first-class passenger could
move from wheeled conveyance to first-class waiting-room to first-class
compartment with only the briefest rubbing of shoulders with other classes
in between.

European railways not only reflected but also played their part in
institutionalizing the stratified class system which had emerged in the
wake of the Industrial Revolution. Britain set the pattern with three classes
of travel and the concomitant gradation of station facilities. The rest of
Europe followed. In Imperial Russia the carriages were painted different
colours for ease of recognition: blue for first class, brown for second class,
and green for third.[1] The earliest big city terminals, like London Euston
(1839) and Naples Porta Nolana (1839), had separate station entrances
and separate booking-halls for different classes of travellers.

But as the century proceeded, these rigid differences were to some
extent eroded. In Britain the Midland Railway Company announced its
intention in 1872 to admit third-class passengers to all of its trains at a
penny-a-mile fare and in 1874 to abolish second class and reduce all

first-class fares to second-class rates.[2] Other companies reluctantly followed suit, though it was not until 1910 that the Great Western Railway phased out the last of its second-class carriages. This marked a major transformation in railway-company thinking. The companies had initially encouraged the 'quality' and lavished their attention on first-class passengers. When compelled by Gladstone's 1844 Act to introduce cheap workmen's trains every weekday the companies complied only with reluctance and their 'parliamentary trains' became a byword for slowness, dirtiness, and discomfort. The Midland, however, cannily saw the profit to be made from exploiting the potential mass market and led the way. The figures speak for themselves. In 1845, 40.51 per cent of all passengers carried in Britain were first class, 42.34 per cent second, and 17.15 per cent third. By 1922, 1.72 per cent were first, 0.37 per cent second, and 97.91 per cent third. It is no coincidence that the Midland's liberalization policy follows closely on the passing of the second Reform Act (1867), which extended the franchise, and Forster's Education Act (1870), which extended educational provision. They can all be seen as part of a gradual but progressive process in the spreading of democracy. But it was an extension that in the first instance was of greatest benefit to the middle classes, who were, in both a social and a transportation sense, the mobile classes. The working classes rarely travelled far, and if they did it was on foot or, in the later years of the century, by tram, 'the gondola of the working classes'.

A similar process of levelling can be seen on the Continent. In Denmark, for instance, there were technically three classes of train travel, but first class came to be restricted to the sleeping-car stock on international trains.[3] So, effectively, there were only two classes, and by 1931 an estimated 96 per cent of all Danish train travellers went third class.

For all this, class divisions remained, particularly in the station facilities of the larger terminals. John Pendleton reported in 1896:

The class 'barrier' is still strong and sturdy in the railway refreshment room. The bishop and the blacksmith may travel third class together, and chat by the way; but they will not be permitted to take luncheon side by side in the first-class refreshment room, if the blacksmith, like the bishop, wears the apron of his calling. 'You must go to the other room, sir' says the graceful girl behind the counter firmly to the blacksmith; and the great robust worker, blushing through the grime that streaks his face, awkwardly protests, perhaps, but withdraws. The first-class refreshment is sacred to the well-dressed and those free from toil stain.[4]

This class division is further reflected, as profound truths so often are, in humour. Refreshment-room manageress to waitress: 'These tarts are quite stale. They've been on the counter a fortnight. Would you mind taking them through into the third-class refreshment room?'[5]

Such distinctions continued even after the Great War. At the rebuilt Waterloo Station, opened in 1922, there were first- and third-class ladies' lavatories. But there was no class distinction for the men, who had access to a subterranean 'gentlemen's court' 800 ft. long and 40 ft. wide, with marble floors, white-tiled walls, bathrooms, boot-cleaning, and a hairdressing salon, as well as the actual lavatories. *Railway Magazine* in 1910 described this convenience as 'perhaps the finest in England'.[6] It was after the Second World War that the class distinction in station facilities disappeared, although it remained on the trains.

No such levelling process took place in Asia and Africa. In the non-European world it was the requirement to provide separate facilities for a complex hierarchy of class and race which made many railway stations larger affairs than they need otherwise have been. In India the situation was further complicated by dietary requirements. At stations where catering facilities were available, there would be provision for first-class, European, passengers and for both vegetarian and non-vegetarian diets. At many stations in India, and particularly in Africa, the third- and fourth-class waiting-rooms were often physically removed from the main range of station buildings. However grand the latter might be, those who bought the lower order of tickets were condemned to tin huts at the end of the platforms where the sole facility might be a single stand-pipe tap. Although the imperial and colonial railway companies discovered that Indians and Africans desired to travel in large numbers and contributed the bulk of passenger earnings, little money was spent on their comforts. The rudimentary nature of sanitary provision both justified and necessitated the separation of the races. Stations jealous of their disciplines maintained a class and racial division on specific parts of the platform and between platforms. The provision of trains that were solely first and second class, and therefore expected to be used only by the imperial race, helped this arrangement. This was the case on the main routes in India and in southern and eastern Africa. These disciplines were to prove an index of the strength of imperial rule. With decline, such distinctions broke down, and the ruling race was forced to come into closer contact with the ruled. The imperial guides offered advice on such problems. Murray's *Handbook* advised that Europeans should allow their servants to tip coolies and not do so themselves.[7] It also warned against thieves at stations and advised that possessions should not be left near carriage windows. When passengers went to station refreshment rooms, servants should be left in charge of their property.

In India the railways never made any attempt to distinguish among the castes. Indeed, the manner in which the railways forced the mixing of the castes was said to have been a contributory cause of the Mutiny in 1857, although it must be said that the revolt broke out in an area still far from the early Indian railway projects. The British persisted in this, and all their economic and social policies were directed towards the substitution of class for caste. The effect of the separate dietary arrangements was to separate Hindu from Muslim in station buffets rather than caste from caste. But even without the sanction of separate waiting-rooms or toilets, caste continued to condition the reaction of Indians to each other. The higher castes often attempted, though not always successfully, to create their own *cordon sanitaire* about them when travelling. It was always said that water-sellers at Indian stations had to be of a high caste.

At one time the classes of passenger vehicles on Indian railways were painted in different colours, as in Russia. On the Madras railway the first-class carriages were white, the second-class dark green, and the third-class were dark red.[8] The choice of colours is instructive. The Great Indian Peninsula Railway soon abandoned this system, and up-graded some third-class trains by upholstering the seats and providing Venetian shutters. Some Indian railways attempted to cope with the great pressure of third-class passengers by installing them in double-decker carriages, but these had soon to be abandoned because they proved to be unsafe and top-heavy.

The 1919 Murray's *Handbook* asked in a revealing suggestion that travellers should watch out for instances when third-class passengers were not treated considerately and should report them to the management.[9] It was, of course, at stations that acts of gross racial prejudice were indeed committed. The brutal ejection of Gandhi on to a station platform in South Africa has been made famous by Sir Richard Attenborough's film. But such scenes could also be witnessed in his native India. One visitor to India reported on just such an event which occurred in the Bombay presidency at the end of Victoria's reign:

One day a subaltern got into a first-class railway carriage and found sitting there a 'coloured gentleman'. In a fit of rage, he seized the poor man by the shoulders, and, shouting to him 'Out you go, you black beast!' pitched him and his portmanteaus on to the platform. This, to his great astonishment, caused a considerable disturbance; and when he inquired what the people meant by putting themselves out over a black man, an Englishman who was passing answered: 'Well, perhaps you don't know it, but you have just thrown one of Her Majesty's judges out of the train.'[10]

The terms of this account make it sound like a common occurrence; only the rank of the victim was uncommon.

One of the strongest indications of class throughout the world came to be the length of time the travellers were prepared to spend at the station and the quantity of baggage which they had with them when they passed through it. Members of upper class or ruling race were always able to send servants to the station to book tickets and to check baggage. The higher order of passenger was able to arrive at the station shortly before the departure of the train and proceed directly to accommodation on it. If the train were late, then these passengers could repair to the hotel which would almost certainly have been provided near by to eat, drink, or rest. It is ironical, then, that the superior accommodation of the station was perhaps the accommodation least used. The passage of the European through the Indian station, his dependence on servants, and the quantity of baggage carried were all well described by Sir Sidney Low, writing in 1911. Low commented that the British in India spent much of their time on long journeys by rail, and their journeys were 'elaborate proceedings, not to be transacted in the casual fashion' customary in Europe:

It is no case of packing a portmanteau, whistling at the door for a hansom, arriving at the station ten minutes before the train starts, giving a sixpence to the civil porter, and finding yourself under way with an open magazine on your knees. There are no hansoms; and if there were, a file of them would be needed to transport a very ordinary Sahib's effects. The amount of luggage which people take with them, even on comparatively short journeys, would amaze those austere travellers who believe that the trunk and a handbag should be enough to carry them anywhere. [In India] every white traveller . . . must move rather like a snail, and sometimes at a snail's pace, with his house, or a good part of it, on his back. When he arrives at his destination he cannot rely upon finding effective substitutes, not merely for the luxuries, but for the common necessaries, which he may have left behind. Thus, like an army in campaigning order, or a ship on the high seas, he must have sufficient in his own stores to be equal to all emergencies.[11]

It was scarcely on his own back, however, that the Sahib's impedimenta were borne:

The servants manage it. Some hours before the train is due to leave, a bullock-cart, or camel-cart, or perhaps even an elephant-lorry, arrives at the bungalow, and takes the whole of the load to the station, in charge of the head 'boy'. Round it on arrival a disorderly crowd of ragged coolies collects, and amid squabbling and objurgations about their female relatives, the various parcels are distributed among them. The number of these bearers is large. My own not immoderate personal effects have furnished employment for eleven persons . . . Long after all this excitement has subsided, the owner of the property drives down comfortably in a carriage or pony-cart, having sent the indispensable chit to the station-master, asking that official to allow his servants to stow his hand-baggage in the compartment reserved for him.[12]

Quantity of baggage was everywhere a sign of class and status. On the Ceylon railways, first-class passengers were allowed 84 lb., second-class 56 lb., and third-class a mere 28 lb.[13] The *General Regulations and Information for Passengers* of the railways of that colony had elaborate provisions for the conveyance of horses, dogcarts, carriages, and palanquins, together with their servants.

The railway station seems to have symbolized the reliance of Europeans upon their servants throughout Asia and Africa. In Egypt, Lord Edward Cecil was incapable of buying so much as his ticket on his own. When going to leave, Cecil sent his servant with all his baggage to the station, but the servant forgot his master's railway pass (the servant forgot it, note), so

I am obliged to take a ticket. The ticket clerk, who is a villainous-looking Copt, is apparently adding up the monetary results of his last night's murders, and dislikes being interrupted. To mark his disapproval of my doing so he gives me the wrong ticket and some change, of which the amount, as far as I can see, bears no relation to any previous transaction between us. Just as I am drawing his attention to the point and beginning what I know will be a long and wearying discussion, Mirsal, who has been fighting the cabman about his fare outside, appears and lets loose such a torrent of thumbnail word portraits of the clerk's family that, used as I am to his powers in this respect, I am struck dumb with admiration. The clerk, realising from Mirsal's uniform that I belong to the sacred official class, merely bows his head to the storm, pays up and looks pleasant.[14]

On finding his carriage on the train, Cecil is

greeted by my secretary and the man with the feather brush, no one else having arrived as it is so early. However, the man with the feather brush is there. The man with the feather brush is indispensable in the highest ceremonials, and is present on the most ordinary occasions. When you enter a railway compartment, the seats are dusted by him. The operation itself is usually purely formal, and only just stirs up enough dust to make you cough a little, but it is a sign that you belong to the higher or fit-to-be-dusted classes.[15]

The man with the feather brush seems to have been a station functionary unique to Egypt.

At the lower end of the social scale, the dusty rather than the 'fit-to-be-dusted' classes, people were prepared to encamp at the station for days. With less reliable means of reaching the station, with perhaps less requirement for haste, and less opportunity to understand the timetables or gauge time by any other means than the sun, these passengers used all the patience of the peasant to wait for their appropriate train. And they normally used the 'mixed' trains, which, since they stopped at every station and carried all manner of freight as well as third- and fourth-class carriages, were the ones which were most likely to be inordinately late. It was regarded as a great advance when third-class passenger expresses were introduced on the East India Railway.[16] The distinction between the punctual 'mail' train for first- and second-class passengers and the unpunctual 'mixed' for the others persists in Southern Africa to this day.

On his 'Big Red Train Ride' in 1977, Eric Newby found these class approaches to the catching of and waiting for the trains, which have been such a characteristic of colonial societies in India and Africa, still very much the norm in the communist countries.[17] The waiting room at the Moscow station where Newby caught the Trans-Siberian was like waiting-rooms in all communist countries, the 'preserve of the lumpen proletariat, the hoi polloi', with not a member of the administrative or managerial class to be seen. The latter would arrive by taxi or office car, and proximity to the time of departure of the train would be a sign of status. In the waiting-room itself, the poorer people encamped for days, eating, sleeping, occupying every available area of seating and floor space. And, Newby went on, the superior class would have their baggage wheeled to and installed on the train, tipping the porters in the process, much as in the time of the last of the Tsars.

Just as the Revolution in Russia made little difference, so has the departure of imperial rule from most Afro-Asian countries. The lower classes still wait, as in Russia, days for the train. If there is any difference, it is that they have now taken over all the station and the upper classes have generally disappeared. The latter now choose to use what they regard as the more salubrious transportation of the motor car or the aeroplane. But for the rest the similarity in the descriptions of station encampments shows a remarkable continuity between the nineteenth and twentieth centuries. No such continuity can be found, however, in the case of Japan. In 1898 a visitor noted that the poorest among early Japanese rail travellers were prepared to make long waits for the train:

For hurry and the Oriental are two. Though the Japanese are by no means a lazy or an idle race, and though they possess none of that apathetic indolence common to those Eastern races who dwell beneath a tropical sun, still all notions of speed, haste or flurry are utterly foreign to their nature. Centuries of Western training will be necessary before a Japanese will be able to appreciate the significance of such a phrase as 'catching a train by the skin of one's teeth!' The native of Japan arrives at the station two or three hours before the train is due. If he be a rustic, or unused to travelling, and he intends to take a morning train, he will probably make a point of taking up a strong position at the station the night before his prospective journey and camping on the platform.[18]

The contrast with modern Japanese rail travel can well be imagined.

But not all station encampments have been of rail travellers. Others —pilgrims, itinerants, beggars, hawkers—used the station because they could find there light, water, security from robbers, as well as the opportunity to earn some money. The station thus harboured a community of people who slept, ate, cooked, suckled infants, and tried to earn a living there. It was divided into its own hierarchies, the commercial sector of small-scale business men and women at the top, the beggars at the bottom. European stations showed signs of developing such communities in the nineteenth century, but they were usually swept away. In Africa and Asia such encampments were tolerated because of the sheer scale of the problem. But beggars everywhere have found the station a prime pitch. When leaving on his epic journey around the world, Phileas Fogg encountered a begging woman with her child at Charing Cross Station and gave her the proceeds of his recent success at whist.[19] In the early 1950s an English visitor to Russia observed that beggars were still to be found around the terminals of Moscow, 'often young men with one or more limbs missing'.[20] They were probably war veterans. But although they had vanished by the late 1950s, together with beggars from most European stations, the importunate begging hand thrust through the window of the railway carriage remains common throughout much of the Third World. In these parts of the world, the genuine passenger still picks his way through the station encampment, with a sense almost of intruding upon the privacy of a village community.

The presence or absence of station dwellers was part of the social tone of stations throughout the world. In Europe and the United States, stations reflected the tone of the areas they served, in their style of architecture, in the services they provided. But this was even more striking in the colonial empires. Murray's *Handbook* repeatedly warned white passengers that particular stations were only used by Indians. The railway buildings at the hill stations, on the other hand, only expected a European clientele (together with servants) and were organized accordingly. All the large cities had at least two stations, the town and the cantonment. A town station, like Agra Fort, lying beneath the great

Mughal palace itself, adjacent to the densely packed old city, would mainly be used by Indians. Agra Cantonment, on the other hand, had space and air, waiting-rooms and restaurants, and a hotel near by. It was the European station. That pattern was duplicated all over the subcontinent. In some cities there was an additional pilgrim station where special pilgrim trains could be brought directly to the pilgrimage area without having to cause alarm or inconvenience to European residents. In others, there were stations near barracks for the convenience of moving troops. Some of the Indian princes had private stations, and in China special stations were even built so that the Emperor could visit the western tombs at the appropriate time of the year.[21]

In Ceylon, stations ranged from those which served the elegant bungalow coastal suburbs of Colombo and those used by Europeans seeking refreshment at the hill stations or at Mount Lavinia to special 'coolie' stations, where the Tamil labour migrants introduced from South India to the tea plantations could be detrained and kept in quarantine until health requirements could be met. These were analogous to the special migrant stations in the United States and Russia with the exception that most of the Tamils were expected to be only temporary migrants.

A station's status in Africa would depend upon its proximity to a European community or a white plantation area. In South Africa the social and racial tone of stations was institutionalized through apartheid, although systems of racial segregation had, of course, existed long before they were systematized by the Nationalists. Certain stations in black rural areas or town locations were expected to be used exclusively by Africans. Throughout the Johannesburg commuter system, all station platforms were divided in half, for Whites and non-Whites respectively, and the trains were similarly divided so that the appropriate part stopped at the relevant stretch of platform. At Johannesburg Central Station, Africans used separate entrances and exits together with their own small concourse and facilities. The main concourse with its waiting-rooms, restaurants, and shops would only be penetrated by Africans in their capacities as porters or cleaners. For many visitors to the country the stations might present the main opportunity to see apartheid in action. In the 1950s one of the authors of this book, as a boy, was first confronted with the racial realities of South Africa at Mafeking Station. There, sitting in his plush first-class compartment on the mail train, he saw the overcrowding, squalor, and discomfort of a wooden-seated African train on an adjacent platform. When Ransome-Wallis visited South Africa during the war, he allowed his desire to get close to the steam engine to overwhelm his awareness of South African racial niceties.[22] At one station he entered the coach directly behind the engine, only to be summarily ejected by the guard. Since the front of the train was more likely to be affected by coal and smuts, that was the section reserved for Blacks.

Boer nationalism merely erected a massive legislative panoply for racial discrimination. It was just as apparent elsewhere in Africa, if more insidiously so. When the station arrangements at Bulawayo in Southern Rhodesia were reorganized in 1960, a special African station was built near the African locations, ostensibly for the convenience of African travellers but, one suspects, rather for the comfort of the Whites, who secured more exclusive use of the main Bulawayo station with its important connections to Salisbury, the Victoria Falls, and through Bechuanaland to Kimberley and the Cape.[23] Throughout colonial Africa there were often unwritten regulations about who could use which accommodation and facilities both on the trains and in the stations. Such racial discrimination was also apparent at all stations in the Southern States of the United States. Blacks had separate waiting-rooms, toilets, and sometimes lunch-rooms. At most of these stations the accommodation for coloured people was directly accessible from street and tracks, so that there was no need for the races to mix. This was the case at Memphis, Tennessee, New Orleans, Louisiana, and Savannah, Georgia.[24] Even small country stations had separate waiting-rooms. An examination of the plans of these Southern stations reveals an interesting sanitary discrimination. Whereas the men's and women's toilets in large American stations usually led off the separate men's and women's waiting-rooms, no such delicacy prevailed for the Blacks. Given the lavishness of accommodation provided for white and upper-class passengers on railway systems everywhere, it is ironic that they were the first to desert the railways. In Southern Rhodesia after the Second World War, Whites abandoned the trains for the motor car, while black rail passengers increased in numbers. It happened too in the United States and in many other places.

American stations in fact illustrated better than anywhere the great dichotomy between social theory and practice in the United States. American trains were classless, but none the less they had a wide range of different styles of accommodation, and the passengers paid for the luxury appropriate to their standing. This was made possible by the fact that long American journeys involved overnight sleeping accommodation. Instead of booking a class, the passenger booked different forms of sleeping arrangement rather like booking a hotel room. But it was perhaps in the great days of immigration that the station acted as a centre of awareness for the existing population viewing their new fellow citizens, and for the immigrants discovering the no less real inequalities of their adopted country.

These migrants were pushed from station pillar to post from the moment they left their homes in Europe to the time they settled in the western United States. In the nineteenth century, Italians and Alsatians heading for the New World arrived and departed via the great Paris terminals. In Britain, for the Irish entering in search of a new life, Liverpool and London stations were their gateways to the streets more often paved with misery than with gold. But more exotic figures than the ubiquitous Irish thronged the platforms of Liverpool's stations, as John Pendleton described in 1896:

[Liverpool's] great stations—Lime Street, the Central and the Exchange —are centres of bustling life, of passengers coming and going; and scarcely a day passes without the reminder that the city by the Mersey is not only English but the Continental portal to the New World. On the platforms may be found groups of Germans, Swedes, Poles, of men, women and children of nearly every European nationality, surrounding curious luggage, and, in railway porters' opinion, 'jabbering a lot of nice lingo'.[25]

For those who reached the New World, a special station was built at the Castle Garden immigrant centre in New York where they entrained for the West. The rough wooden immigrant cars supplied for their use were often segregated by both sex and race, in order that discipline could be maintained. Western railway companies like the Union Pacific built immigrant lodging-houses and segregated eating-places at stations throughout the West, and attempted to keep immigrant and normal trains separate, but this proved to be impossible at the larger stations. Cheap fares were available only for the westward journey, so that the disincentive to return to the East was considerable.

Most of the larger stations in the United States had separate immigrants' waiting-rooms. Often these were actually designated 'second-class', as at Spokane, Washington, neatly reflecting the American attitude to recently arrived immigrants. At the new Grand Central in New York there was a separate waiting-room for gangs of labourers and immigrants, with its own attendants, so designed that these groups need not encounter other passengers. Droege recommended that the immigrants' waiting-room should be

in an out of the way place, and may even be a separate building. It should be furnished with complete sanitary equipment, and, if possible, tubs for washing clothes and dryers. A lunch room for immigrants where food can be served at a low price is desirable. Immigrant rooms should be well ventilated and the interior of them so designed that they may be easily cleaned.[26]

The image of the immigrant as not yet integrated into American society, poor, and not fulfilling American standards of cleanliness was complete. Some stations also had immigrants' or colonization agents, some of whom were expected to speak a variety of languages. The new Fort Garry Station at Winnipeg of 1911 contained elaborate provision for the offices of the agents.[27] As was so often the case with railway stations, these facilities were reaching their highest point at just the time when immigration—like the passenger statistics themselves—was about to take a steep downturn.

For travellers to the United States in the last few decades of the nineteenth century the immigrants to be seen at stations in the West, particularly in Omaha, were one of the most striking images of their visits. R. L. Stevenson encountered immigrants from China as well as from Europe and reflected upon the irony of immigrants from hungry Europe and hungry China meeting face to face in the American West. Sometimes migrant trains were seen travelling eastward, despite the higher fares, just as packed as those going west. Their occupants had failed to find land or position and stood on station platforms calling on their westbound fellows to give up and turn back. Languages from all over Europe as well as the Orient could be heard on all stations west, where the platforms often overflowed with migrants. Better-heeled passengers penned a succession of sad descriptions of the flotsam and jetsam of Europe they encountered beached on many an American station. The women were often contrasted with the men and the children, the first representing the cares of the past and the present, while the husbands and little ones looked to the future, full of hope. One traveller wrote of 'swarthy men with bare arms splashing about in buckets', who seemed 'energetic and strong, confident and assured, with a bright never-say-die look upon their faces', while the women looked 'faded, wan, and anxious'. Another thought the women looked 'tired and sad ... dressed in gowns that must have been old on their grandmothers', while the children were dressed in 'garments of nondescript purpose and size, but were generally chubby, and gay, as they frolicked in and out among the baskets, bundles, bedding, babies' chairs etc, piled waist-high on various parts of the platform'. A poor German woman presented a pathetic sight kneeling before her chest, which had burst open. The contents, the observer thought, could not have been worth five dollars. But 'it was evidently all she owned; it was the home she had brought with her from the Fatherland, and would be the home she would set up on the prairie'. Rudyard Kipling wrote of a train-load of 'Scotch crofters' which arrived at Winnipeg on a Sunday:

They wanted to stop then and there for the Sabbath—they and all the little stock they had brought with them. It was the Winnipeg agent who had to go among them arguing (he was Scotch too, and they could not quite understand it) on the impropriety of dislocating the company's traffic. So their own minister held a service at the station, and the agent gave them a good dinner cheering them on in Gaelic, at which they wept, and they went on to settle at Moosomin, where they lived happily ever afterwards.[28]

The migrants in other parts of the world were often internal. Like the American western railroads, the Russian Trans-Siberian had been built with an eye to migration and settlement. Almost five million rail-borne settlers entered Siberia between 1894 and 1914. To gauge the extent to which the railway transformed migration patterns we need only note that whereas 40,000 migrants per annum travelled east between 1887 and 1892, 250,000 per annum migrated after the Russo-Japanese War. Some of them travelled in fifth class, which consisted of boxcars totally bereft of comfort. They too were segregated into wagons for families and those for single men. Like the western stations of the United States, the eastern stations of Russia had special facilities for them. Spur lines led from principal stations into vast spartan dormitory accommodation where they could be quarantined and prepared for settlement. The emigrants were just as strikingly a part of any Russian railway journey as they were in America.

There were times when Russian and American migration overlapped, and British stations became stopping-off points for Russian migrants. Pendleton described some at Liverpool's Central Station in the 1890s:

Railway travel develops many interesting situations; but it has created few more bewildering than those occasionally to be seen during the Russian famine, when a number of peasantry, weary of the Czar's despotic rule and black bread, or no bread at all, came through England on their way to America, and clustered, apparently hopeless, on the platform at the Central Station. They were in costumes that, in spite of their crumpled shabbiness, recalled the garb of Count Arnheim in the opera of 'The Bohemian Girl', and looked like fugitive kings and emperors beside the thick-set railway porter, in capacious velveteens, whose duty it was to put them on the right track towards the 'free land'. What the Russians thought of their rough but kindly guide it is impossible to say; but he grinned, and exclaimed in amazement as he tried in vain, with a stumpy pencil to get a list of their names, and then sympathetically remarked, as he looked at their wan faces, 'There is no wonder at the chaps being ill; even their names is all coughs and sneezes'.[29]

But the vast majority of Russian migrants travelled east on their own railway lines. In 1902 the Trans-Siberian railway carried well over one million passengers, and the statistics of their class breakdown are fascinating:[30]

First	8,000
Second	140,000
Third	370,000
Fourth	420,000
Fifth	140,000
Soldiers	55,000
	1,133,000

Thus only a tiny fraction of passengers (0.71 per cent) travelled in the luxurious first class. It is clear that large numbers of migrants avoided the boxcars of emigrant fifth and travelled fourth. The Trans-Caspian line in Central Asia similarly sucked in migrants to dominate the local Islamic population. But the local population was soon assembling at the stations to use the train for its own purposes. Curzon reported that as early as 1887, with the line barely completed, 6,000 Central Asian pilgrims used the Trans-Caspian westwards on the first leg of their journey to Mecca.[31] Railways throughout the East were to contribute to that greatest religious migration of all.

It was not just in Russia that lower-class passengers were transported on freight wagons. It happened in many parts of Africa and Asia, particularly in the early days of railways. The third-class passengers on the Beira and Mashonaland railway travelled in this way in 1900 and for many years afterwards. Photographs in the Crown Agents' collection indicate that excursion trains laid on to celebrate the opening of West African lines carried their African passengers in 'flat cars'. Pilgrims in India were often conveyed in boxcars into the twentieth century.[32] African labour migrants were invariably transported in this way. They were temporary, not permanent, migrants: not for them the single journey to a new land. It was an experience which normally they would repeat many times in their lives, for they were expected to return to their home territories at the end of a year-long contract. As the mines of Central and Southern Africa set up their insatiable demand for cheap black labour, labour-recruiting agents and organizations scoured African areas for labourers. Once recruited they were marched to the nearest railway station, entrained on a variety of wagons, and transported to recruiting reception centres and on to the mines. It was at stations that other travellers were made aware of these human shipments and their minimal comforts. Throughout the black 'homelands' and adjacent African territories of modern Southern Africa the station continues to bear its reputation as the beginning of the migrant trail to labour in the 'white' economy. Stations throughout these areas invariably have their quota of migrants lying on the platforms waiting for trains to take them to another instalment of toil.

Native peoples throughout the world were also turned into a source of picturesque ethnic entertainment on railway stations. In the western United States travellers encountered the native Americans, the Indians who had so often been dispossessed of their lands and livelihoods by the railway companies. The first train of excursionists west on the Union Pacific was treated to a war dance performed by Pawnees on the station at Columbus, Nebraska. Next day they provided a mock battle. But they were well aware of the dangers of trusting white men. They had demanded to be paid first. Such entertainments by Indians at stations which not so long earlier they had attacked became commonplace. Chief Black Moon and a thousand braves attacked the station at Huntly, Montana, only a few years before they were appearing in a more peaceable guise there.

The numbers of Indians at stations did indeed become an index of the distance the American traveller had journeyed westwards. In Russia the same effect was produced by Buryats, Tatars, and other eastern peoples encountered on the Trans-Siberian. In Australia and New Zealand travel into remoter parts produced station encounters with Aborigines and Maoris. In East Africa, travellers were advised to watch out for the variety of indigenous 'types' to be seen at railway stations, from the Islamic, partly Arabized, Swahili of the coast, to the Kamba and Kikuyu of the interior, and then, a special treat, the magnificent Masai, bearing their shields and spears in a sadly peaceable demonstration of subjection, before reaching the Nilotic peoples of the shore of Lake Victoria.

Many of these peoples were soon producing 'station art'. For most of them the railway symbolized dispossession and in some cases the collapse of their traditional economies. In entertaining, begging, or hawking at stations they were making shift to use the railway as an inadequate substitute. Soon villages by railway lines became centres of new craft industries, in wood-carving and other allegedly traditional bric-à-brac. In fact, of course, much of this material bore only a tenuous similarity to its genuinely customary counterparts. Styles changed to suit the visitors' demands, and with volume and speed of production becoming the prime considerations, standards of craftsmanship steadily declined. So did prices, as hard-nosed passengers haggling on railway platforms and through carriage windows clinched on their lowest offer as the engine hooted a warning of the train's imminent departure. It was a form of bargaining in which the enforced departure of the customer placed all power in his hands. Indian women in the Western states discovered that they could charge travellers to peep at their papooses. When the novelty wore off, the female beggar's gesture to the baby on her back and to her mouth became a standard plea throughout the world.

The Indians in America soon took to travelling on the trains. In some cases their treaty rights specifically gave them access to them, but as passengers they underwent a steady process of rejection. In Nevada, Shoshani and Paiute Indians made frequent use of their treaty rights to ride on the trains. But this was desert country and the Indians were usually dusty and unwashed. They were soon relegated to the emigrants' cars, and when even the emigrants complained they were forced to travel on baggage wagons or on the boarding steps. In Canada, a train frequently used by Mohawk Indians came to be known as 'The Moccasin'.

Famous people also became a source of station spectacle. Rudyard Kipling (who once was forced to travel on a migrant train in the United States and found it a 'nightmare') encountered a peculiarly American hazard for the famous traveller. Conductors could make some money for themselves by selling lists of well-known passengers on their trains to representatives of the Associated Press. Such passengers would then be met by reception committees and crowds at stations along the route, as well as at their destinations. Worse, there would be the still-familiar posse of jostling journalists.

Railway stations not only illuminated the full social and racial hierarchy of the railway traveller, they also reflected the great range of employment offered by the railways themselves. For railway employment was notably hierarchical, with as finely graded a sense of status as any group of below-stairs servants in a great Victorian country house. As a result a form of class and, most notably, racial job reservation grew up in railway employment. In Andean Latin America the racial gradations were particularly complex, as Brian Fawcett described.[33] Railway employment was divided into *obreros* and *empleados*, 'workers' and 'employees', that is those paid respectively by the day and by the month. The lowliest of railway jobs were carried out by the mountain Indians or the men of slightly mixed blood, the cholos. On the coast, the middling types of position were held by the mestizos, the people of mixed race which could include African, European, and Chinese. The clerks and station officials were normally people of pure Spanish descent, while the managers and engineers at the top were usually British or American. At times this racial mixture could be modified. In 1909 the Hispanic station-master at Antofagasta in Chile was discovered to have been embezzling. The problem went right up to the London board of the company, and it decreed that, in future, sums of money of any size should be handled only by European expatriate employees of the company.[34] On the Mexican Central Railway, the higher officials, engine-drivers, and conductors were all American at the turn of the century (on the British-financed lines, many of these would have been British); the brakesmen and station-masters were Mexican; while all catering was in the hands of Chinese.[35]

In India a similar hierarchy established itself. There the middling positions, engine-drivers and mechanics, clerks, station-masters at the medium-sized stations, were all held by Anglo-Indian people of mixed race. A Eurasian engine-driver would invariably be accompanied by both a trainee of his own race and a fireman, much inferior, who would be an Indian. The porters, labourers, and cleansing menials would be low-caste Indians, while the engineers and senior officials were all British. The Goanese from the Portuguese territory in western India traditionally dominated the catering trades. Even among the whites in a single grade there was a strict sense of hierarchy. Engine-drivers recruited from Britain earned a great deal more than and regarded themselves as distinctly superior to those white employees who were recruited in India. These social distinctions were reflected in the residential patterns of workers associated with the stations. At the bottom end of the scale, some small 'third-class' stations, which were expected to be used only by Indian travellers, were staffed entirely by Indians. The Anglo-Indians, for whom railway employment became a special preserve, were always accommodated in their own railway settlements not far from the larger stations. Just such a community is graphically described in John Masters's *Bhowani Junction*.

The role of people of mixed race in the railways spilled out of India into Malaya and East Africa. As late as the 1940s, Ransome-Wallis discovered that engine-driving in Malaya remained the preserve of Scottish Eurasians.[36] There racial employment hierarchies were complicated by the presence of both indigenous Malays and immigrant Chinese on railway staffs. The Kuala Lumpur railway workshops employed 1,000 Chinese. The Chinese, despite their own alleged antipathy to railways, had a world-wide connection with them. As well as providing the catering in Mexico, they had provided much of the labour for the construction of the Canadian Pacific through the Rockies. It was their absence from the building of the later Grand Trunk line which was alleged to have made its construction much less speedy. To complicate matters further, the railway police in South-East Asia, Hong Kong, and East Africa were invariably Indians, usually Sikhs.

When the East African railways were built, Anglo-Indians, Goanese, and Sikhs arrived to perform their usual tasks. In Africa the racial proportions depended on the nature of the territory. In settler colonies, a higher proportion of railway workers was white. The capital of Kenya, Nairobi, can truly be said to have been made by its station.[37] The divisional point was established there only because it marked a significant change in grade, and the station buildings, tracks, and settlements always dominated the city. The European employees had superior bungalows closer to the station, the special quarters for the people of mixed race lay in an intermediate position, and the African workers were accommodated in a 'location' further out. It was a pattern to be found in many other railway cities. Bulawayo was another such, and there the large white railway population voted *en masse* not to join the Union of South Africa in the referendum of 1922 because they considered that conditions of railway employment were poorer there. Their votes played no small part in ensuring that Southern Rhodesia remained a British colony. Later, one of the dominant figures of Central African white politics was an ex-engine-driver, Sir Roy Welensky. In West Africa, as in all aspects of life there, Africans played a much larger part on railway staffs. Engine-drivers on the Gold Coast, Sierra Leone, and the Lagos Government Railway were always white, assisted by African firemen and stokers, but guards, conductors, and even station-masters were usually Africans. Ernest Protheroe in his *Railways of the World*, published in 1914, reported that this led to considerable language difficulties:

> The [Gold Coast] line is equipped with Webb and Thompson's instruments, and to explain the electric staff regulations, in a temperature somewhere around 90 degrees, to a native stationmaster who understands about as much of English as the average English railway official does of French, is a task which white officials feelingly affirm requires a considerable amount of patience, to say nothing of linguistic gymnastics.[38]

Very similar racial hierarchies, involving a mix of Europeans, people of mixed race, Arabs, and Africans, occurred in the French North and West African territories.

In China and Japan it was an article of faith to replace European railway workers by local employees as soon as possible. A fascinating insight is provided into those two cultures by the fact that Western writers disapproved in the case of China, but greatly approved in the case of Japan. In 1900 a writer in the *Railway Magazine* commented disapprovingly on Chinese efforts to man the newly opened Sung-Wu Railway:

The line had not been run a week before all Europeans connected with it were discharged, and the whole thing was controlled by the Chinese, who had carefully watched the progress of the work, and had stored up a vast mass of data for future use. The engine drivers are Chinese, and the repairers are Chinese. Not one person now connected with the line has had experience of railways in Europe or America. In these circumstances it is not difficult to predict speedy failure, unless, as has been proposed, the line is taken over by a British firm which has secured the concession for the building of a line from Shanghai to Peking.[39]

On the other hand, Ernest Protheroe noted approvingly the speed with which the Japanese had taken over their railways:

It did not take long for the Japanese to recognise the value of railways, and their natural imitativeness served them well in grasping the salient features of railway work. In 1877 there were 120 British engineers, drivers, foremen etc. employed by the Railway Administration, but by 1880 only three foreign advisers remained.[40]

In colonial territories, railways were often the largest employers of labour. A vast number of local people performed the menial tasks; people of mixed race found jobs most appropriate to their status as buffers between the white managerial class and the mass of indigenous employees. These jobs also enabled the mixed-race people to band together into tightly knit communities, where they could keep their existence constantly before the white masters whose earlier sexual peccadillos had brought them into being.

Such hierarchies produced, as they always do, an intense jealousy of status. In the United States the first 'engineers' or drivers and their firemen performed other tasks, such as selling tickets and moving baggage and freight. Demarcation soon reigned, however, and the 'engineers', particularly those in the West, aspired to a high status. Station-masters and conductors were also anxious to emphasize their exalted positions. This was done by uniform, demeanour, and voice. The conductor prided himself on being the 'captain' of the train, a sort of superior butler with a whole range of footmen, menials, and tweenies under his command. These lower orders also had racial dimensions. Sleeping-car and Pullman attendants were invariably black. All Pullman-car attendants were traditionally called 'George', presumably after the name of the founder of the company. Even in Canada, sleeping-car attendants were usually black Canadians. Their community was largely made up of American slaves who had fled across the border to freedom in a British territory. Now the railways levelled them with their black cousins on the other side of the 49th parallel.

The Civil War was a significant turning-point in the history of American Black employment on the railways. In the ante-bellum period, remarkably few Blacks were employed on Northern railways, but in the South they played a key role. Almost all locomotive firemen were slaves, either hired from slave masters or owned directly by the railroad companies. The companies often preferred slaves to white skilled labour and as a result slaves aspired to skilled positions which were later denied to them as freedmen. Many other tasks were performed by Blacks, and female slaves could be found on the trains carrying water, attending lady travellers, and selling fruit. After the war, Blacks formed the backbone of the unskilled labour force in both North and South, laying the tracks and building the stations, working as firemen, switch-tenders, and brakemen in freight yards, as cleaners, station porters, or redcaps, cooks, waiters, kitchen helpers, and sleeping-car attendants. They could be found in low-grade clerical jobs, but positions like drivers, conductors, clerks in contact with the public, telegraphers, station agents, and train dispatchers were all closed to them.[41]

White unionization led to the increasing exclusion of Blacks from the better-paid jobs. Railway employers often used Blacks as strike-breakers or as a means of fighting unions by employing them to depress wages. Thus Blacks became a prime source of hostility for white unionists who set about erecting discriminatory barriers. In the twentieth century the position of Blacks on the railways steadily deteriorated. As railway employment declined (there were two million railway workers in 1920 and only one million in 1930) it was Blacks in unskilled work who were the most vulnerable. In the 1940s fourteen railway unions excluded Blacks. When station redcaps were self-employed, there were many of them, but when the federal authorities insisted that they should be employed by their companies their numbers rapidly dwindled. The formal elimination of colour bars made little difference. Black employment at stations continued to decline until working on the railway was seen as detracting from black dignity. The poor record of black conditions on American railways is well illustrated in the manner in which several civil rights leaders emerged from railway employment.

In Russia, station positions were as rigidly hierarchical as the classification of both stations and passenger accommodation into five categories might indicate. Station-masters in all but the meanest stations aspired to high status, although they were subjected to great physical dangers during times of civil disturbance, the Revolution, and the Civil War. They wore white uniforms in summer to distinguish them from the crowds that might throng their stations. But they also had an unenviable reputation for drunkenness, particularly on the Trans-Siberian, no doubt as a result of the privations of climate and loneliness they had to endure there. In Tsarist times the official positions on all Russian railway lines were occupied by European Russians but the menial tasks were more likely to be performed by the lowest order of migrant or by members of the local population. By the time Eric Newby and Paul Theroux travelled on the Trans-Siberian, many of the station-masters were women, who seemed to establish their authority by dispatching trains in the traditional manner. This was done by standing to attention outside the station building with the station-master's staff of office held out in front of the body.

The appearance of women at Russian stations has to some extent been matched by a growth in women's employment in railways elsewhere. However complex the racial and social hierarchies of station employment in the nineteenth and early twentieth centuries, generally they were exclusively male. Women first appeared as station employees in Europe on tasks such as carriage-cleaning or waiting in refreshment rooms. In small country stations, a husband and wife team might run the station together. Gradually women secured employment on larger stations in clerical positions, at information counters, or as station announcers. In 1900 Edinburgh Waverley Station boasted forty lady operators working in the telegraph department, sending out 4,000 messages a day.[42] But it was of course the First World War which suddenly gave a tremendous fillip to women's employment in stations. In 1914, 13,046 women were employed by British railway companies, mainly on jobs at stations.[43] By 1918 the figure had reached nearly 60,000. Women had come to take over men's jobs as platform, goods, and parcel-porters, ticket-collectors, and engine cleaners. So that women porters could cope, the weight of luggage allowed to passengers was restricted and three women were employed in the place of two men. Early in the war a postcard was issued at Crewe Station showing women railway workers holding out their hands to indicate that it was clean work.[44]. The same growth in women's employment at stations took place in France and Germany.[45] In 1915 the Prussian State Railways employed 35,000 women; by 1918 this had risen to 89,000. In the United States many of the jobs performed by women in

Europe continued to be done by men, as John Droege indicated in his instructions for station operation in his *Passenger Terminals* of 1916, although black women often performed cleaning tasks.

The wartime surge in women's employment in Europe was, however, largely temporary. In 1919 most of their jobs reverted to the men returning from the war. Women had to wait until the Second World War before invading station employment once more. A painting by W. Roberts, *Women Railway Porters in Wartime*, depicts them shapelessly dressed in grey and brown, hauling cases, milk churns, and pigeon crates, almost unidentifiable as women. The presence of women working at stations was by then a clearer indication of the changes in their status taking place throughout society.

Stations reflected most powerfully, however, the desire of their male designers and operators to protect women. The provision of separate waiting facilities for women was almost universal. Where three waiting-rooms were provided, general, men's, and women's, the men's was usually designated, particularly in the United States, the 'smoking-room'. In the larger American stations the women's waiting-room sometimes had a 'matron' available to help women with their children or those fatigued by their journey. The status of a small-town or country station would be marked by whether it had a women's waiting-room or not. In Canada, second-class stations invariably had them, but third- and fourth-class did not. On the other hand, neither coloured nor immigrant waiting-rooms were separated by sex. All sorts of additional class niceties were well known to travellers, even if they were not hallowed by sign-posts. Lower-class women who did not come into the black or immigrant categories would be expected to use the general waiting-room, rather than the ladies', which was largely the preserve of the well-dressed middle class. In India and in the colonial environment generally the women of the ruling race were especially cosseted at stations. In India there was an additional need for female protection among the Muslims. Some stations had purdah rooms, and many trains carried a special carriage for third-class women Muslims. There was a bell at the end, which was rung by the ticket-collector or guard to warn the women of his approach so that they could cover themselves appropriately.

Stations were invariably seen as places of danger for women. In Canada and the United States representatives of the Travellers' Aid society were to be found at most large stations to advise women.[46] Posters were displayed at stations large and small across the continent bearing the following message:

Young Women Travelling Alone. Do not start for a strange city or town, even for a night, without previous information of a safe place to stay. Do not ask for or accept information, advice, or direction except from railway officials or the Travellers' Aid. On arrival in a strange city, if you are alone, if your friends fail to meet you, if you wish the address of a reliable hotel or boarding house, look for the woman at the station wearing the Travellers' Aid badge.

In modern times the careful protection of women at stations has declined, and the complex hierarchies of race and class have been simplified. In Southern Rhodesia so many Whites were withdrawn for war service, particularly in the Second World War, that Africans and mixed-race 'coloureds' had to be trained to do some of their jobs. Expatriates have disappeared from the official positions in Latin America, much of Africa, and Asia. In Latin America this occurred during the great wave of nationalizations which took place after the Second World War and involved dislocation from which some of the railways have never recovered. In the ex-French territories of North Africa the sudden removal of Frenchmen from all senior and technical posts caused severe problems for the railways for a period after independence. Elsewhere, people of mixed race lost their monopoly of the middling-rank jobs, as they found themselves jostled from below. The class disciplines of stations broke down, although in many places the wealthiest took themselves off to other forms of transport. And with the declining status of railways and of railway employment, station-masters, clerks, guards, and the like no longer possessed the prestige which had been theirs when the railway was the vital source of communication with the outside world for entire communities.

With the end of empires, Europeans found a curious reversal taking place. Black and Asian guards began to appear in Britain and in many places menial station tasks, catering employment, and the like were taken over by immigrants or by guest workers. As racial distinctions were ironed out and replaced by class in the Third World, a certain amount of the reverse process was taking place in the old imperial metropoles.

7

Some Station Types

STATIONS came in all shapes and sizes, and served a multiplicity of functions. They ranged in size from towering architectural master-works like London St Pancras and the Victoria Terminus, Bombay, to undistinguished single-platform halts like Borrobol and Salzcraggie, re-quest stops on the Highland Line for the shooting gentry. Some stations stood in the heart of thriving capital cities and teemed with life day and night; others in desolate fastnesses, where as Dickens remarked of the remote New England depots, 'the wild impossibility of anybody having the smallest reason to get out is only equalled by the apparently desperate hopelessness of there being anybody to get in'.[1]

There are passenger stations and goods stations. There are public stations and there are private stations. Private stations often resulted from deals done by railway companies with landlords as part of the purchase of land for railway development. The most famous is probably the delightful half-timbered Dunrobin, on the Highland line to Wick. It is the prime example of the station as lodge to the great house, in this case the Duke of Sutherland's home, Dunrobin Castle. There were a number of such privileged gatehouse stations to the aristocracy.[2]

There have been racecourse stations, such as Newbury Racecourse and Aintree. There have been port stations, waterfront interchanges between the railways and the water-borne transport of river, lake, and sea: in the United States, New Bedford, New Haven, and East Boston; in Canada, Prince Rupert, Vancouver, Montreal; in Britain, Holyhead, Folkestone Harbour, and Portsmouth Harbour. There have been stations for service establishments, such as RAF Cranwell and Cosford Aerodrome. There have been stations for factories. In Britain there were the Daimler Halt for the motor-car works, Singer for the sewing-machine factory, Irlam Halt for the Co-op soap works. In the USA there was the Boeing Aircraft Factory Station at Seattle. In Australia there was a spur line, known locally as 'The Chocolate Box Line', from Hobart, Tasmania, to Cadbury's Factory Station. There have been stations for hospitals (Cheddleton Asylum, Whittingham Hospital) and stations for schools (Wellington College, Christ's Hospital). There have been coal stations and milk stations. The Société l'Anthracine had its own Paris station, the Gare des Mines, in the boulevard Victor Hugo to receive exclusive coal supplies. Also in Paris, each network had its own centralized milk station from the 1930s on: Nord at La Chapelle-Charbons, Etat at the Gare de Vouillé, Paris–Orléans at the Gare de Chevaleret, and PLM at the Gare de Bercy. There has even been a hotel station. Just after the turn of the century, Leland Stanford, President of the Southern Pacific Railroad, built the luxurious Delmonte Hotel two miles from Monterey in California. Southern Pacific ran a spur line from Monterey to a Delmonte Hotel station one mile from the actual hotel. At weekends a special train was kept with steam up in the hotel station yard, so that Mr Stanford could leave at a moment's notice if his business affairs called. Each of these station types had its own distinctive character and ambience. Let us linger a while at some of them.

Royal Stations

Where better to begin than at the top? The heyday of the railways coincided with the last great age of monarchy. Kings and queens travelled regularly by train and all the big city stations in monarchies boasted lavishly appointed suites reserved for the sovereign. The king of Italy was able to retire from the gaping gaze of the public into his royal waiting-rooms at Milan and Rome stations; at Hanover Station there was a special royal dining-room for the use of the Kaiser.

Queen Victoria too had her own royal stations. The most notable was at Windsor and Eton, where it is possible to see it now in its pristine state, for in 1983 Madame Tussaud's opened the fully restored and refurbished royal station, adjoining the main Windsor terminal and unused for thirty years. Tussaud's spent two million pounds re-creating the scene on Jubilee Day 1897, with Queen Victoria receiving her royal guests in the elegant waiting-room, with its marble fireplace, crimson upholstery, and glass-domed Renaissance cupola. The fact that she actually arrived a week after the Jubilee is a trifling historical detail unlikely to mar the magnificence of the concept.

The royal station was specifically built by the Great Western Railway for the Jubilee. Now standing at the platform is a reconstruction of the royal train, hauled by the GWR locomotive *The Queen*. Behind it is the royal day saloon, a stunning creation in plush and velvet, green, gold, and white, superbly wood-panelled and wonderfully comfortable. Inside stand the figures of Grand Duke Serge of Russia and his wife, Grand Duchess Elizabeth. The visitor crosses the maroon red carpet into the royal waiting-room of Bath stone, complete with original fireplace. In the ante-room the Queen's Indian servant, the Munshi, sits beside the royal tea service, preparing to dispense refreshment to the royal party. Beyond it are the royal conveniences.

The Queen-Empress herself, attended by the Prince and Princess of Wales, sits beside the fireplace. From the sitting-room the royal party proceeds to the concourse, where an Ascot landau waits, its postilion in highland dress. Seventy men of the 2nd Battalion, Coldstream Guards, parade in full review as the Guard of Honour, resplendent in scarlet and gold. Overhead, the canopy gleams, decorated with festive flags and garlanded in green. The Queen, attended by the Prime Minister Lord Salisbury, the Lord-Lieutenant of Berkshire, the Mayor of Windsor, and the Chairman of the Great Western Railway, prepares to board the landau. Behind her Princess Henry of Battenberg is trying to control a sailor-suited Prince Maurice and Princess Ena of Battenberg, while Prince Henry chats with the Prince of Wales. Watching the scene is a cross-section of British society—barefoot crossing-sweeper, prosperous bourgeois party, child in baby-carriage with attendant nursemaid, and a single lady with one of the new-fangled bicycles. This splendid succession of tableaux of life-size figures, enhanced by patriotic music and natural sounds of the period, is further complemented by a panoramic exhibition of highlights of the Queen's sixty glorious years, a remarkable example of modern technology being put to use to re-create the sights and sounds of the past.

The Jubilee Day display demonstrates all the meticulous organization and mastery of pageantry for which the British have become renowned. But they only started to perfect it at the end of the nineteenth century. Earlier, an almost surrealistic comic chaos attended royal occasions. In 1863 the special train bringing royal visitors to the Prince of Wales's wedding at Windsor had too few carriages. So when the wedding was over, the special train pulled out amidst a rainstorm, and there was an undignified scramble for seats in the first ordinary scheduled train into Windsor Station. The Archbishop of Canterbury grabbed a seat in third class and the Chancellor of the Exchequer ended up sitting on Mrs Disraeli's lap.[3]

The London and South-Western Company had a royal station, the Royal Dockyard Station at Gosport. It had a single curved platform and a handsome waiting-room, and provided access from the railway to the royal yacht. Every August the Queen travelled from her house at Osborne on the Isle of Wight to Gosport and thence to Balmoral by train. It was at this royal station that the body of the Queen arrived on its final journey on 1 February 1901. She had died at Osborne and the royal yacht *Alberta*, with an escort of eight torpedo-boat destroyers, carried her to the mainland where she was reverently placed aboard the royal train for London.[4]

Although Nine Elms Station was closed to passenger traffic in 1848 and converted to goods traffic when Waterloo opened, Queen Victoria continued to use it. She liked it for its privacy and its proximity to Buckingham Palace. So her royal saloons were kept there permanently. Eventually, however, the London and South-Western accommodated the imperial will by building her a private station at Wandsworth Road in 1854. This was not used after her death, as Edward VII and his successors were perfectly happy to use Waterloo.

After the purchase of the Sandringham Estate in 1862 by the Prince of Wales, Wolferton Station on the Great Eastern Railway became a royal station. In 1876 a handsome suite of royal waiting-rooms was erected and often used for luncheon parties when the royal party was on a shoot. The station was damaged in a curious fashion during the coming of age celebrations of the Prince of Wales's eldest son, Albert Victor, Duke of Clarence and Avondale. Sanger's Circus arrived to give a command performance for the estate workers, and an elephant escaped and demolished the station gates.

Queen Victoria had first used the railway in 1842 to travel from Slough to Paddington and thereafter she became a regular railway traveller. Royal patronage put the seal of approval on the new form and the companies went to particular pains to arrange the Queen's journeys. George P. Neele, line superintendent of the London and North-Western Railway, devoted three long and detailed chapters of his memoirs to describing the organization of the royal progresses. Special timetables and special trains, cleared lines and cleared platforms, official receptions, all had to be readied and accommodated. Neele took extraordinary pride in the smooth operation of the Queen's journeys. The Queen's own saloon was always kept in special care at an equable temperature. The electricians were apprised so that all electrical appliances could be in perfect order. The Locomotive Department and the District Superintendent were advised, in order to ensure the clear road required not only for the train but for the pilot engine running fifteen minutes in advance. The Engineering Department received notice, so that the whole length of the line could be watched and patrolled, because of constant fears of a Fenian outrage. The hotel proprietors and refreshment rooms who were to furnish meals were advised of the Palace's requirements. Most of all the Queen insisted on privacy and quiet during her journey. 'Almost a funereal silence was observed', commented Neele.

Neele was ultra-sensitive to the proprieties and was particularly pre-occupied with keeping undesirables away from the Queen, even though these sometimes included notabilities. When the Queen called at Perth General Station for breakfast, which was taken in the company offices, she invariably encountered, much to Neele's distaste, the Chairman of the North British Railway, Mr Stirling, known locally as 'Kippen Davie',

a very able man in business matters, but unfortunately lame; he had to support himself on a crutch, in addition to which the dark glasses he wore to hide some defect in his eyes, did not improve his appearance; altogether it always struck me that the prominence of position he seemed to claim was undesirable.[5]

At whatever cost, royal orders had to be adhered to. This led to an unfortunate incident at Leamington Station in 1874. Special instructions were issued to keep the station completely private. Lord Aylesford, however, in his Volunteer uniform, determined to be on the platform to greet the Queen. The railway staff on duty refused him admission and he demanded to see Mr Burlinson, Birmingham District Superintendent of the Great Western Railway:

Mr. Burlinson ... went down to the gateway and told his lordship that the orders were stringent, and he was bound to refuse admission. 'And, pray, who are you?' said his lordship. 'I am the Superintendent of this division of the Great Western Railway', 'And where do you come from?' 'Birmingham', 'Oh' (with supreme contempt), 'Birmingham! I thought so.' However little his lordship might think of Birmingham or a Birmingham man, he failed to get admission that night to the platform and was 'left swearing'.[6]

There were, none the less, sometimes unforeseen station encounters. One such occurred at Dunbar Station when the Queen was *en route* for Balmoral in 1858. The *Illustrated London News* reported it:

On the 7th of September a monster train of excursionists, under the guidance of Mr. Cook of Leicester, were returning from their wanderings in the land of the mountain and the flood, and nearing the ancient town of Dunbar ... when the exclamation was suddenly heard, 'The Queen is coming!' The train stopped, and instantly passenger after passenger mounted the roofs, and thence saluted the Royal company with a united shout of welcome. The next moment, as the Royal train stopped, hundreds of men, women and children left their carriages, resolved to see the Queen; and their wish was gratified; there were no officials to interfere. All ranks joined in hearty cheer after cheer for every member of the Royal family: the young Princess gained laurels by her quick apprehension of the wishes of the people. The carriage window was quickly let down, and the Queen and Prince Consort ... turned with smiling faces to the multitude who thought only of expressing their loyalty to the utmost. After five minutes spent in this familiar manner the excursionists withdrew, greatly delighted at this unexpected meeting with their Queen; and her Majesty, equally pleased, no doubt, with such an impromptu outburst of genuine loyalty, proceeded towards her Highland home.[7]

Other crowned heads enjoyed less smooth organization on their travels than did Queen Victoria. Count Witte, Head of the Russian Department of Railway Affairs and later Prime Minister, recalled a number of highly eventful railway journeys to the Crimea by Tsar Alexander II. On one occasion, the Tsar got out of the Imperial train for a stroll at Birzul Station and the train left without him. On another occasion, the train left the rails near Zhmerinka Station and the Tsar had to make his way to the station on foot. On a third occasion, Alexander II was returning from the front during the Russo-Turkish War and recognized on a station plat-form an officer who had deserted from the army. The Tsar ordered his immediate arrest. But the man stabbed himself to death. Witte ordered the body hustled out of sight and dispatched the train at once, so that the Tsar should not be distressed by the sight. It was all so unlike the train life of our own dear Queen.[8]

Commuter Stations

The words 'commuter' and 'suburbia' are nineteenth-century coin-ings, potent by-products of the railway age. The nineteenth century was also the era of the Great City, sucking in population from the countryside to staff factories, shops, and homes. The 1851 census revealed that in Britain for the first time more people lived in towns than in the country and that trend continued. Between 1871 and 1901 alone the number of towns with populations over 50,000 doubled. But at the same time, a reverse movement was taking place which was to accelerate in the last decades of the century—the flight from the city centres to the suburbs.[9]

The association in the popular mind of the city with crime, squalor, and the physical deterioration of the population was a recurrent theme in nineteenth-century literature and thought. It gave a boost to the exalta-tion of the countryside, the idealization of a lost, golden, pre-industrial Arcadia. Total remove from the city was impossible. But a half-way house was possible—suburbia—which combined the fresh air, green fields, and floral delights of the countryside with easy and speedy access to the place of work in the city.

So an integral element in the life of the great city became the daily weekday ingress and exodus of commuters. Arnold Bennett described the grim scene in his novel *Hilda Lessways*:

A dark torrent of human beings, chiefly men, gathered out of all the streets of the vicinity, had dashed unceasingly into the enclosure and covered the long platform with tramping feet. Every few minutes a train rolled in, as if from some inexhaustible magazine of trains beyond the horizon, and, sucking into itself a multitude and departing again, left one platform for one moment emptying—and the next moment the platform was once more filled by the quenchless stream . . . It was like the flight of some enormous and excited population from a country menaced with disaster.[10]

He was writing of the London suburb of Hornsey but the same phenomenon was observable in Paris, New York, Tokyo, and Moscow.

The railways in Britain did not take the lead in developing the suburbs. Indeed the earliest suburban development preceded railway expansion by a decade or so in the big cities. But the existence of the railways made continued suburban development a real possibility. Land availability, the activities of speculative builders, and rapid association of suburban living with status and respectability, combined with the growing railway network, contrived to ensure that during the second half of the nineteenth century the population of London's outer suburban ring grew by approximately 50 per cent in each of the ten years between 1861 and 1891 and by 45 per cent between 1891 and 1901. Simultaneously the residential population of the City itself fell from 128,000 in 1851 to 75,000 in 1871. For most of the new suburbanites the railways and the railway station became an integral part of their lives. As one child remembered it before 1914: 'Suburbia was a railway state . . . a state of existence within a few minutes walk of the railway station, a few minutes walk of the shops, a few minutes walk of the fields.'[11]

The inhabitants of the new suburbs were in the main middle class. They were drawn from that army of white-collar workers, managers, administrators, lawyers, technicians, and clerks which had been called into existence by Britain's commercial and financial pre-eminence. It was these men who travelled into London each day by train from Clapham, Wimbledon, Richmond, Putney, and Barnes.

It was not long before such people became the butt of the intellectuals. The suburbans were seen as the epitome of clerkly conformism, complacency, and conservatism. In the course of a comprehensive attack on English suburbia, its inhabitants, manners, and mores, T. W. H. Crosland distilled the view that the essence of 'suburbanism' was 'shallowness and cheapness and mediocrity and dullness and stupidity and snobbishness'. Most seriously, their lack of taste was encapsulated in 'a sublime appreciation of red-brick villas, seven-guinea saddle-bag suites, ceraceous fruit in glass shades, pampas grass, hire-system gramophones, anecdotal oleographs, tinned soup, music in the parks and kindred horrors'.[12] The poor suburbans were thus condemned as a race of unregenerate Pooters.

The working classes were not by and large users of trains in the nineteenth century. Indeed the railway companies resisted the idea of workmen's trains, for which from the middle of the nineteenth century there had been a vocal lobby. Charles Booth wrote in the 1890s: 'It is only the man whose position is assured who can treat railway and tram fares as a regular item of his daily budget.'[13] The 1883 Cheap Trains Act made concessionary fares for workers general and compulsory. But the London and North-Western and the Great Western Railway companies were criticized for their poor provision of workmen's trains in 1892 and a parliamentary select committee was still pressing for the provision of cheap trains for workers in 1905. The railway companies' resistance had both social and economic roots. On the one hand, they did not want working-class hooligans swarming all over the country causing mayhem. They were only too aware of complaints from some seaside resorts about the descent of *hoi polloi* on them at bank holidays. They also feared that the workers, inclined to swearing, smelling, and spitting and given to assorted vandalism, would deter better-class passengers. On the other hand, there was no profit in short journeys and irregular runnings of trains at peak times. There was also the fear that clerks and shop assistants who could afford the more expensive fares would use the cheap trains for preference. An exception to this general attitude was the Great Eastern Railway, which, as the price for getting parliamentary permission for the extension of Liverpool Street Station, introduced workmen's trains in 1872, with two-penny return tickets for a journey of up to ten miles. Under the stimulus of this concession, large working-class suburbs developed in north-east London at Ilford, Leytonstone, Walthamstow, and Tottenham.

In the provinces, commuting was smaller in scale, but no less significant. Buses, trams, and particularly suburban railways began to segregate the classes into precisely defined, socially distinct areas, a process which sharpened the awareness of class differences and fuelled resentment in the increasingly active and vocal working-class movements. Manchester and Salford provided the classic example of suburbanization. By the 1860s high-class suburbs had developed at Alderley Edge on the Manchester to Crewe main line and at Bowden and Altrincham on the Manchester to Chester line. The intervening stations along both the main lines became the focuses for the growth of prosperous, if not quite so grand, suburbs: Heaton Moor, Cheadle Hulme, Bramhall, Wilmslow, Sale, and Stretford. Urmston and Flixton developed on the Manchester to Warrington line, and Heaton Park, Crumpsall, and Prestwich on the Bury line. The opening in 1880 of the Midland Railways' London connection across South Manchester to Central Station initiated suburban development in Heaton Mersey and Cheadle Heath. This left the profile of the city as an inner core of offices, factories, shops, railway yards, and slums; an outer ring of lower middle-class and middle-class estates for clerks and small professional people; then the railway suburbs, strung out along the lines, each of them a self-contained village within walking distance of the station.

Elsewhere the private carriage and the omnibus dominated early suburban traffic. But in both Liverpool and Birmingham in the 1870s there was suburban railway development. In Liverpool from the 1870s on, the stations on the Southport line to the north (Waterloo, Crosby, Formby) and on the Wirral line to the south became the focuses of respectable residential development. There was railway development too in Birmingham to link Selly Oak, Bournville, King's Norton, Harborne, Yardley, and Acocks Green to the centre. But in Birmingham the railways were never the principal means of transport for the urban commuter. It was London where the railway suburbs were numerically the largest and most populous with regular commuters.

The predominantly middle-class character of the suburbs and the commuting population was to have important social consequences. Since mid century, philanthropists and social reformers had been urging the removal of the population of the inner-city slums to the more salubrious outskirts of the city. John Blundell Maple, the furniture magnate, declared in 1891, for instance: 'It must be infinitely more wholesome for the workers of London to reside in their own suburban homes than to be congregated together . . . Our working population would be reared in a more healthy atmosphere, becoming thereby in every respect better citizens and keener for the welfare and future of their Empire.'[14] But it did not happen. It was the fault not so much of the railways as of the suburban landowners who deliberately kept land prices beyond the pockets of the working class and thus preserved social exclusivity.

But in the 1880s and 1890s there was a sharpening of class antagonism with the rise of militant trade-unionism and the expansion of popular socialist organizations like the Social Democratic Federation and the infant Labour Party. Surveys revealed that a third of the population lived below the poverty line. As a result, the urban masses turned to the Labour Party and the suburbanites in self-defence to the Tories. Harold Perkin has concluded that 'The ground was thus laid in the Victorian commuter age, and to a large extent by the social consequences of commuting itself, for the class politics of the twentieth century, with a predominantly working-class Labour party on the one side and the middle-class led Conservative party on the other.'[15]

Nevertheless suburban development proceeded apace. The Great Western, London and North-Western, and Midland railways had refused point-blank to make any concessions to suburban travellers or workmen in fares or services throughout the nineteenth century. The Great Northern, however, enterprisingly inaugurated a policy of half-rate fares to attract the lower-middle classes moving into the northern suburbs, with the result that passenger traffic increased from 12.9 million in 1880 to 30 million in 1900. In the Edwardian era, with company revenues falling, the companies began to cultivate the suburban commuter. The Great Western began actively to promote its Thames Valley services, the Great Eastern Broxbourne and Bishop's Stortford, and the London and South-Western Epsom. The Great Northern opened an enquiry bureau, giving information on houses in 'The Northern Heights'. Thirty-four new stations were opened in the period 1900 to 1914.

Although few new railways were opened in the London area after 1919, almost seventy new stations were provided. The railways remained vital to suburban development. When choosing estate sites, many developers gave priority to their convenience in relation to the railway. 'Station on the estate' was a favourite phrase in housing promotion and the promise of new railway facilities usually caused a rapid rise in land values.

The railway companies were debarred from acquiring land for themselves in excess of their need for lines. But there was one exception, the Metropolitan Railway. It had the power to grant building leases and fix ground rents. In 1919 the Metropolitan Railway set up its own company to promote select housing estates in Buckinghamshire, Hertfordshire, and Middlesex. Posters, magazines, even songs, held out the prospect of Arcadia within travelling distance of the metropolis—a detached house in leafy seclusion, but close enough to golf club, tennis club, and railway station. It was Metroland, the inter-war middle-class paradise so lovingly celebrated by Sir John Betjeman.[16]

Almost all the new stations opened in the London suburban area after 1920 had some form of subsidy from the developers. Their names are somehow redolent of inter-war suburban values: West Weybridge and Sunnymeads (1927), Pett's Wood (1928), Woodmansterne and Belmont Halt (1932), Berrylands and Northwood Hills (1933). By 1937 Pett's Wood alone was issuing 320,000 tickets a year. A number of older stations, particularly on the Southern Railway, were modernized and enlarged, often with shops added, to accommodate extra passenger traffic. Over a third of the additional stations opened in the London area after 1919 were on Southern Region. This company actively promoted commuter traffic, completing its electrification programme by 1931. The traffic figures at Charing Cross Station reflect this development. A 1926 survey showed 13,446 passengers arriving at Charing Cross Station between 7 and 10 a.m. on a typical day. By 1935 the figure had grown to 31,723 and by 1938 to 37,095.

The availability of cheap and regular transport by train and tram promoted suburbanization in the United States too, though a generation or so later than in Britain. It was not until the 1920s that suburbanization became a common feature of American cities. But between 1850 and 1920 some 15 per cent of the total population of the United States moved to the suburbs. The highest rate of suburban development was in the cities of the North-East. The trend for suburban dwelling was set by the wealthy, and planned suburbs appeared in order to meet their needs in the 1860s. By the end of the century the middle classes were emulating them.

Out along the railway lines between 1880 and 1930 there developed 'a metropolitan corridor', whose history J. R. Stilgoe has traced in his absorbing book of the same title. It was the matrix of an American suburbia, with a population of commuters and a distinctive architecture, environment, and life-style. Its appearance symbolized the transition of the United States from a rural to an urban nation, a transition reflected in a wealth of literature featuring the railways as *the* system of transportation and in the development of an industrial aesthetic which found beauty in factories, chimneys, freight yards, and machinery.

In France, where between 1801 and 1881 the population grew by 40 per cent, the population of Paris grew by 134 per cent. The second half of the nineteenth century saw suburban development along the railway lines stretching out of Paris. But there was a difference in the social composition of the Paris suburbs. The very rich in Paris preferred to live in high-class areas within the city, and the suburbs tended to attract the lower-middle classes and skilled working class. As a result of this suburban development, the annual movement of travellers in Paris rose from 16 million to 400 million between 1900 and 1930. By 1930, from 400,000 to 450,000 people were travelling in from the suburbs to work in Paris: 180,000 into the Gares Saint-Lazare, Montparnasse, and des Invalides, 90,000 into the Gare du Nord, 85,000 into the Gares de l'Est and de la Bastille, and 45,00 into the Gares d'Austerlitz, d'Orsay, and de Lyon.[17] In 1916 the Gare Saint-Lazare was declared by the American

railwayman John A. Droege to be 'the busiest station in the world', with
1,200 daily train arrivals and a maximum traffic of 250,000 passengers a
day. London Liverpool Street, with 200,000 a day, was thought to be
the next busiest. Today, Europe's busiest station, handling 180,000
passengers a day, is London Waterloo.

The station etiquette of the suburban commuter was quite distinctive.
Alan A. Jackson, the perceptive and meticulous historian of surburban
London, described it:

> Arrived at the station, the daily travellers, dressed to a man in dark suits, white,
> stiff-collared shirts, and bowler or trilby hats, with their tightly furled umbrellas
> held as elegantly as they were able, would quickly assemble in their respective
> and habitual positions along the platform, for they knew exactly where 'their'
> compartment would come to rest. As advanced amateur gardeners, they would,
> whilst they waited, offer unsolicited advice on the station gardens, tended
> lovingly by an abundant uniformed staff with little to do between the rush hours.
> By unspoken arrangement, those who preferred to travel in silence were left
> alone when they had received and returned a nod of acknowledgement from
> their closest neighbours ... If he cared to make use of it, station and train
> fulfilled the role of a social centre for the suburban male, a forum for the
> exchange of news, the making of new acquaintances and contacts, the publi-
> cation of requirements, even the collection of money for charities. Station staff
> knew everyone worth knowing in the suburb apart from the few tradesmen who
> made no use of the railway for carriage of goods.[18]

The suburban commuter station was emphatically a male preserve at
certain times of day. Katherine Chorley recalled the commuting habits in
Edwardian Alderley Edge:

> Every morning in my childhood the businessmen caught the 8.25 or the 8.50
> or the 9.18 trains in Manchester. The times are graven on my memory. Anyone
> out early would see them hurrying to the station ... The businessmen travelled,
> of course, in the first-class carriages, dividing easily into groups so that compart-
> ments were made up between more or less particular cronies ... any wife or
> daughter who had to go to Manchester by one of those trains always travelled
> third; to share a compartment with the 'gentlemen' (we were taught never to call
> them just plainly 'men') would have been unthinkable. Indeed the ladies always
> avoided the business trains if they possibly could. It was highly embarrassing, a
> sort of indelicacy, to stand on the platform surrounded by a crowd of males who
> had to be polite but were obviously not in the mood for feminine society.[19]

In the film *The Rebel* (1960) Tony Hancock memorably demonstrated
how to get the corner seat in a commuter train. As the film opens, one
platform of a suburban station is crowded with bowler-hatted, umbrella-
wielding, *Times*-reading city gents. The other platform is empty but for

Hancock. Two trains come in simultaneously and Hancock simply scampers through one and into the corner seat of the other, while the commuters are struggling to enter.

Pilgrim Stations

The religious metaphor is never very far from the pen of the writer on railways and stations. But railways have also had a powerful literal effect upon religious movements around the world. Stations everywhere took on the role of the Tabard Inn at Southwark, where Chaucer's pilgrims assembled for their journey to Canterbury. Muslims flocked to the stations of Russian Central Asia, up-country India, Malaya, and North Africa to commence their long journeys to Mecca. The leaders of Eastern religions which had resisted the appearance of the railway, as in China and Japan, soon found that their co-religionists swiftly took to the rails to visit temples and shrines. The stations of the South African Boer Republics, themselves huge concessions to the modern world which the Boers would originally much rather have done without, took on some of the dour, flinty character of Dutch Reformed Calvinism.

But it was in India that the railways produced their most dramatic religious effect. Hinduism is one of the most mobile of all religions and Hindus found in the railways a hitherto unimaginable opportunity to travel to shrines, pilgrim centres, and important ceremonies. The Murray's *Handbooks to India* are punctuated with references to stations much used by pilgrims. In 1906 the Chief Superintendent of the East India Railway provided readers of the *Railway Magazine* with a graphic description of a pilgrimage to Allahabad.[20] Every twelve years, a ceremony known as the *Kumbh mela* took place at the confluence of the Jumna (Yamuna) and Ganges rivers just outside Allahabad. The ceremonies lasted for a month and millions attended, many coming only for a few days.

For the duration of the *mela* as many as twenty pilgrim trains a day, each carrying a thousand passengers, might be brought into Allahabad in addition to the normal traffic. It was necessary to use all the Allahabad stations, Naini, Kotaparcha, Kyogunge, Allengunge, as well as the Main and Fort stations to distribute the tremendous pressure of passengers. Temporary booking-offices, thatched and constructed of railway sleepers, were built near the site of the *mela* itself to sell tickets to returning pilgrims. At the station barriers, barricades and pens had to be constructed to separate 'up' from 'down' passengers and avoid crushing and injury. Most of the special pilgrim 'rakes' were made of goods wagons with a mat on the floor to sit on, and an oil lamp hung from the roof for illumination. Superintendent Huddleston assured his readers that pilgrims found this accommodation perfectly comfortable and never made any complaints. Pilgrims, he went on, were the most patient of passengers. But even they had been known to take direct action when driven to desperation. Some years earlier a train carrying pilgrims had been so seriously held up that its journey had taken twenty-four hours rather than seven or eight. Towards the end of the journey the pilgrims discovered that their train had been shunted into a siding at a station in order to give precedence to the mail train:

They thought it time to take action on their own account. Several of them thereupon left their carriages and placed their heads on the rails vowing that, rather than allow another train to pass by they would sacrifice their lives. After this demonstration it is needless to say which train got away first, but, of course, there was an outcry because the Mail ran late![21]

Sometimes the lack of co-ordination among the different Indian railway companies made things difficult for pilgrims. There were, for example, no through trains from the East India Railway to the Oudh and Rohilkan railway, and pilgrims together with other travellers had all to change trains at Moghalsarai junction, a mere ten miles from the great pilgrim city of Benares (now Varanasi). Huddleston described the scene:

During pilgrim rushes, surging, struggling crowds filled the platforms and the waiting halls, and while the masses changed from one train to another the station was a Babel. The delays between connecting trains often being considerable, it is needless to remark that the position was one of intolerable discomfort, though it was accepted by both passengers and railway staff as part of the day's work.[22]

Through trains were eventually provided, and 'the convenience to pilgrims and relief to Moghalsarai station is immense'.

The complexities of the arrangements made for pilgrimages is borne out in a number of ways. The Government Health Department sent men to examine pilgrims alighting from trains. Their job was to watch out for cases of smallpox and cholera. The railway also had its own medical department, which attempted to take action when cases of plague, smallpox, or cholera were reported:

During the *mela* a slight outbreak of cholera occurred at a small station called Manickpore on the Jubbulpore line. The company's doctor was on the spot in no time, attended the patients, examined the sanitary arrangements, disinfected and closed the station well, and arranged for tanks of pure water to be conveyed from 62 miles away.[23]

The traffic arrangements for the *Kumbh mela* in 1906 were entrusted to the same officer who had made all the arrangements for the Great Delhi Durbar organized by the Viceroy Curzon in 1904. He was provided with 450 employees to help. The earnings from the pilgrims, who travelled at very low fares, amounted to £53,500 in 27 days. Superintendent Huddleston noted with evident self-satisfaction that 'everything worked without a hitch, and there was not a single accident of any kind'.

Seaside Stations

By the end of the eighteenth century, the seaside resorts were undergoing the first stages of the process that was to transform the seaside holiday from an exclusive upper-class recreation into a national institution. The Industrial Revolution gave birth to a large and well-to-do middle class and they were not slow to emulate their betters in travelling to the seaside to enjoy the air and the water. The last three decades of the nineteenth century in Britain were to see a similar move on the part of the working class, desirous of experiencing the benefit of sea air and sea water, the chance of amusement and relaxation from their work, or just a change of scene from the grim tenements and back-to-back houses in which they lived, and the mills and factories in which they toiled.[24]

To bring the new holiday-makers to the sea, however, a transport revolution was required. Steam was the great liberator. The railways carried middle-class visitors to the seaside in their thousands for a week's holiday and the urban proletariat on the increasingly popular day trips. The upper classes rapidly gave up the struggle to maintain social exclusivity at the seaside resorts and fled to the Highlands, the Lakes, and eventually the Continent, to pursue their particular pleasures, unhampered by the proximity of their inferiors. By the 1860s, middle-class holiday-makers had effectively taken over the resorts. They brought with them their families, particularly the young children, and under this stimulus the seaside holiday became something which it had not been in its aristocratic heyday—a family affair. This accurately reflects the dominance of the family concept in Victorian society. For both middle and working classes, where the sexes tended to undertake their leisure activities in strict segregation, it provided an outward and visible sign of the family's cohesiveness. For the children, the long railway journey to the seaside became one of the year's great adventures and the station a place of mystery, anxiety, excitement, and unending interest.

Molly Hughes in her touching memoir of a London childhood in the 1870s recalled the excitement of the family's annual holiday trip to Cornwall:

We used to go to bed earlier the day before, not so much to please mother as to bring to-morrow a bit sooner. We got up long before it was necessary, impeding all the sandwich-making and hard-boiling of eggs that was going on. But eat a good breakfast we could not, being 'journey-proud', as our old cook used to express our excited state . . . The next crisis was the fetching of a cab. At 7 o'clock in the morning there was no certainty of getting one quickly and we kept rushing to the window until someone shouted 'Here it comes' . . . To us children, no Cinderella's fairy-carriage could have been handsomer than the cab actually at the door. If we were all going my father and the elder boys had to follow in a second cab. Luggage was piled on top and we were packed in among rugs, umbrellas and hand-bags. At last the cabby climbed up to his seat and whipped up the horse. It took an hour or more to jog along from Canonbury to Paddington, but we did reach the enchanted spot at last.

The 'enchanted spot' presented its own set of problems:

In order to travel all together in one compartment, we had to arrive more than half an hour before the train was to start. There was then the suspense of waiting for it to come in, and my fear that we might not be on the right platform or that the Great Western had forgotten about it. My father meanwhile was taking the tickets and having the luggage labelled. Never did he hasten his steps or hurry, no matter what the emergency, so that there was the additional fear that he would miss the train. When at last we were all safely in a carriage, he would saunter off to buy a paper, and other people were coming in. In time everything was settled and we were gliding out, 'with our faces towards Cornwall', as mother used to say.

Thereafter the stations passed *en route* provided a never-failing source of fascination:

Reading, the first stop, was great fun for those on the near side. What more cheering than to see distracted people looking for seats when we were definitely full up? . . . Didcot had one definite pleasure. We knew that little boys would be going up and down the platform singing out 'Banbury cakes! Banbury cakes!' And mother would crane out and buy some, just to encourage the crew. Next came Swindon—name of sweet assurance. How often Mother used to say 'They *can't* leave Swindon under ten minutes, no matter how late we are'. Considering our early breakfast, or lack of it, the refreshment-room at Swindon was a land of Canaan, and the hot soup all round is still a joyful memory . . . The charm of Bristol was its appearance of being a half-way house. Not that it was so by any means, but it was the elbow-joint in the journey. The muddle and rush were greater even than at Reading, and we were often kept there for some twenty minutes. Yet we dared not leave the carriage for more than a mere leg-stretch just outside the door . . . We used to hail Exeter as almost being 'almost there', for it was Devon, actually the next county to Cornwall, and definitely 'west'. A quiet dignity pervaded its saintly stations but we could never stay long because of course we were late . . .

Finally they reached Cornwall:

We greeted the tiny whitewashed cottages of the 'natives' with far greater fervour than we had shown over Windsor Castle. We vied with one another in trying to remember the order in which the stations came. We stopped at all of them. And when I say stopped I mean stopped. There was none of the hurry of Reading or Bristol. We leant out to catch the accents of the porter, proclaiming his piece in the soft west-country drawl. We watched all the greetings and partings and wavings of hands of the travellers . . . Then would descend that peculiar silence of a country station that signifies that every one is settled, and the guard feels that it is safe to let the train start again.[25]

Eventually, if the train was on time, their journey which began at Paddington at 9 a.m. ended at Camborne Station at 9 p.m.

The railway companies did not initially appreciate their potential as a means of mass cheap travel and concentrated on providing for the better-off. But when enterprising individuals like Thomas Cook began chartering trains and organizing cheap day excursions, the working classes seized upon the opportunity to get away. In Whit Week 1850 over 200,000 day-trippers left Manchester for the countryside and the sea. The 1850s became the heyday of the excursion, particularly on Sundays, for most people their only free day. Despite the fact that excursion trains were often extremely uncomfortable, slow, and dirty, the volume of travellers they carried eventually convinced the railway companies of the value of the mass travel market.

A railway link came to be essential for a seaside resort. The relatively cheap and rapid transportation it provided and the elasticity of capacity the companies boasted gave a powerful boost to the mass holiday-making industry. The railway revived the flagging fortunes of Brighton. When the railway reached Torquay in 1848 a public holiday was declared. It was the opening of a direct rail link between Morecambe and the West Riding which created the strong tradition of Yorkshire holidays in that resort. The coming of the railways literally made possible resorts like Skegness and Rhyl; conversely, the lack of a rail link retarded Eastbourne's development. But the role of the railways must not be overstressed.

The Furness Railway invested heavily in the promotion of the seaside resorts of Grange and Seascale. But this was to increase utilization of that Cumbrian coast line which had originally been conceived for the movement of iron ore and coke and this symbolized the extent to which the railway companies, as distinct from the resorts, long regarded the holiday traffic. The Lancashire and Yorkshire Company's service to Blackpool and Southport was regularly criticized as slow, uncomfortable, and dilatory. It only improved in the last years of the nineteenth century with the company's realization of a profitable traffic in middle-class commuters living at the seaside while working in Manchester and Liverpool.

John K. Walton, the premier historian of the British seaside resort, concludes:

The seaside resorts in the North-West of England, as elsewhere, could not have grown very far without the railways . . . In general, however, and especially in south Lancashire, the major growth area, their role was passive and their attitude lukewarm for most of the period under discussion [i.e. 1830–1914]. The demand for working class seaside visits in Lancashire predated the railways and they were a convenience for, rather than a cause of, its subsequent growth . . . The railways were necessary to the rise of the North-Western holiday industry, but they did little actively to promote it, and the real cause of its growth, and of the pattern of its development, lay in rising living standards and changing attitudes to the use of leisure time among the potential visiting public.[26]

Nevertheless for many industrial workers the station was their gateway to one week's or two weeks' escape from mill and factory, and they rejoiced at its sight. Just as they came late in the century to promote travel facilities actively, so the railway companies were slow to issue promotional travel literature. Nevertheless the promotion of tourism was as old as the railway itself. For others were quick to see the advantages of swift and economical access to the beauty spots of Britain.[27] As early as 1835 there was a *Tourist Companion to the Leeds, Selby and Hull Railway* and in 1836 *The Scenery of the Whitby and Pickering Railway* was published. By the 1880s guides to all the railways of England had been published by Cassell's. It was not until the 1890s that the railway companies themselves entered the promotional market. In 1887 the Great Eastern Railway produced lists of seaside and country lodgings for tourists using their services. By 1900 twenty other companies had followed suit. The North-Eastern Railway produced a series of pocket guides to various beauty spots in their area. The Great Eastern then pioneered a new development, annotated timetables designed for tourist use and pamphlets detailing local trips with train times and fares for each of the Great Eastern seaside resorts. The Glasgow and South-Western catered for a more specialist interest with *The Golfing Resorts of The*

Glasgow and South-Western. Rather less of this tourist literature was available on the Continent, though Swiss and Belgian Railways produced similar material on tourist trips and resorts. In the United States, the New York Central Railway issued a 532-page book entitled *Health and Pleasure on America's Greatest Railway*, while the Northern Pacific issued a very detailed guide to its natural beauties and resorts enticingly entitled *Wonderland*. So the eager tourist, arriving at the station, could arm himself with all the necessary guidance and advice to make the most of his visit and of the railway routes connected with his destination.

For those who could not afford a seaside holiday—and they were still many—excursions provided the escape. As late as 1934 the *New Survey of London Life and Labour* was opining that 'a large proportion, perhaps a majority, of London working class families are still unable to reach this very modest standard [a week's holiday] and have to be content with day outings on Bank Holidays or Sundays'. Excursions were regularly organized by churches and chapels, firms, clubs, street committees, and this for many would be the great occasion of their encounter with the railway station.[28]

With so many people pouring into the stations on these occasions, there was always concern about keeping the excursionists disciplined and organized. There are instances of people being crushed to death or pushed under trains by the crush of excursionists on station platforms. In 1847, for instance, excursionists at Hadleigh Station, awaiting the train to Ipswich, were buried under bricks when a newly built 300-ft. wall was blown down on them. Fortunately there were no fatalities.

The smooth and successful handling of excursionists came only with experience. Its Nine Elms terminal had only been open a week when in 1838 the London and South-Western announced the running of eight special trains on Derby Day to Kingston, the nearest station to Epsom. Five thousand people gathered early in the morning, but the trains were not sufficient to accommodate them. An impatient mob broke down the doors, took possession of the station, and commandeered the trains without paying their fares. The police were called in and no further trains were dispatched that day.

It was not just the seaside or the countryside that drew excursionists. Exhibitions, cup finals, race meetings, and great royal occasions drew the excursionists to their local station. For Diamond Jubilee Day, 1897, Lever Brothers chartered six special trains to take 2,300 employees from Port Sunlight to Euston. Ten years earlier, on the Saturday afternoon of the Golden Jubilee Review, seventy-two special trains had been run into Aldershot without interrupting the usual flow of traffic.

But for many people, the Sunday-school outing remained the fondest memory of day-tripping and the station a vivid part of that memory. A. J. Taylor recalled his annual Sunday-school outing from Sutton Bridge to Hunstanton in 1936:

For at least an hour previously the straggling, laden families would have walked along the Main Road towards the station . . . Entire families too had travelled to the station on bicycles . . . bicycles that were now parked untidily by the diamond woodwork of the station-yard fence. The sun always seemed to shine on that crowded platform. It smelled of shellfish, newsprint, disinfectant —and the lime-encrusted urinal at the far end. It was too late in the year for daffodils and tulips but there were a few cardboard boxes of cut flowers stacked on a trolley waiting for the Peterborough train. And a few early punnets of strawberries. There was a marvellous happy sort of chaos—trippings over push-chairs, bucket and spades; a faded last-year's Union Jack, baskets and string bags holding sandwiches and towels and costumes for bathing and pad-dling . . . As the time approached the late arrivals would join the jostling to get a good seat. Families manœuvred and mothers shepherded in the hope of corner-ing a compartment to themselves. The train would be too long for the platform; as it approached there would be frantic snatchings and shrieks . . . When one half of the train had been filled to bursting point it would 'draw up' . . . The stragglers took their seats in the second half of the train. They joined those who had deliberately held back . . . the wise ones knew that the train turned round at Lynn. The rear end would get into Hunstanton first—a precious six coach-lengths nearer to the ticket barrier.

But the eagerness to get to Sutton Bridge Station to start the trip was matched by the reluctance to get to Hunstanton Station at the end of the day for it meant the excursion was over:

Getting to the station early was surely an adult ploy, and we were never first . . . The train of carriages was already in the station. The western sun would scorch and dazzle and we would pull down the blinds in the compartment. There would be sticky fingers everywhere, the result of handling rock, candy floss, oranges. Last drops of lemonade would be squeezed from near-empty bottles. Bananas and apples helped to stave off the effect of raging thirst . . . At Sutton Bridge there were fathers and relatives waiting on the platform to greet us . . . Home again.[29]

Country Stations

The country station was literally a lifeline, a vital and potent source of contact with the outside world. It was also a community centre. In the Highlands of Scotland, for instance, stations like Rannoch and Kyle of Lochalsh doubled as village halls, where church services could be performed, council meetings convened, school classes given, and dances held. At Garsdale Station (formerly Hawes Junction) on the Settle–Carlisle line, there was a library, whose nucleus was 150 books presented at the turn of the century by two elderly ladies from Wensleydale who travelled regularly from the station. It was kept in the ladies' waiting-room and was used by staff and their families, and by stranded passengers. On a celebrated occasion in Wales a county court judge sitting in a civil case in Bridgend had not completed the case when the train was due to leave, so he continued it on the train and gave his final judgement in the station-master's office at Llantrisant.[30]

David St John Thomas, celebrant of the English country station, has summed up eloquently the multiplicity of functions the country station performed:

The station was the place where the railway greeted its local customers and took their money, the doorway through which important people right up to royalty would pass on visits to the district, the storeplace for every kind of commodity, precious and bulky in transit from town to country and vice versa. It was also the place where news came from the outside world either by telegraph —provided on the railways long before post offices began transmitting telegrams —or by newspaper or word of mouth. It was the place where every piece of invention of the Victorian age could first be seen—from the railway's own telegraph instrument and signalling system, newest engine or crane, to threshing machines, mangles, toilet cisterns and bicycles. And here troops would arrive to quell local disturbances and uprisings, while local organizers of the Anti-Corn-Law League and early unions went off to national gatherings. Here, too, came Gladstone and other politicians to whip up support. Just how important the station was to the life of the community can be gauged from the numerous stretches of approach road and land that were improved at the ratepayers' expense—widened, often given pavements which look particularly incongruous leading from nowhere today, and lit with gas lamps. In many cases, the gas came from new works with their own coal sidings beside the station.[31]

The massacre of country stations which accompanied the dismembering of the British railway network in the 1960s permanently diminished the lives of the villages these stations had served. Nothing equivalent took their place. The bus services which replaced the train service did not long survive. Instead the planners condemned many villages to long, slow, lingering decline. Like so many of the decisions of sixties planners, this cruel decision has brought both spiritual and physical desolation in its wake.

Quite apart from anything else, the country station was a thing of beauty, and was encouraged to be so by the railway companies. Several companies offered prizes annually for the best-kept country station, promoting keen rivalry among stations. The North-Eastern Railway set aside 200 guineas annually to be divided among the 60 best-kept stations, divided into four groups. Each of the groups had five first-class prizes of £6 each, five second-class prizes of £3 each, and five third-class prizes of £1.10s. each. No station was allowed to take a prize in the same class for more than two successive years, but if a station which had done so was deemed worthy of being placed in the same class in a third year, it received a special first-class certificate but no money. Judging was done by directors and heads of staff each August. The money was divided amongst the station staff, with the station-master taking the largest share. Castle Howard, Clifton, Coxwold, Middleton-in-Teesdale, Brough, and Snainton all won first-class certificates for three successive wins in 1897-9. Brough in the East Riding of Yorkshire not only won several first prizes in the North-Eastern Railway's own competition, but it also won a prize of £10 offered by a London weekly paper for the prettiest station in Britain. It was lovingly tended by its station-master, Mr James, who retired in 1899 after fifty years of service there, during which time he had installed not only flower-beds but a fountain complete with goldfish. Sleights, also on the North-Eastern Railway, won the award for photographs of the prettiest station at the National Co-operative Show at the Crystal Palace. Among town stations, Tynemouth was long notable for its wealth of flowers and plants. Across the Pennines, the Lancashire and Yorkshire Railway's Fleetwood Station, with its hanging baskets, potted plants, foliage and greenery was described by the *Railway Magazine* in 1898 as a 'floricultural paradise'.

The Great Western Railway set aside £250 annually to be divided among the winners of twelve sections, with a first prize of £5 in each section. No prize was given unless the offices, waiting-rooms, and lavatories were also spotless. Torquay was a frequent winner, with its carefully designed beds of petunias, zinnias, and brilliant pink geraniums, designed to show off the colour harmonies. The Midland Railway's competition was often won by Matlock Bath Station. Such competitions kept the country stations on their toes, provided the service with valuable publicity, and gave to the travelling public a pleasing and uplifting sight to welcome them to their rural destination, the ideal blending of technology and nature.[32]

The garden competitions in England had a direct effect on the maintenance of stations in Britain's greatest dependency, India. In 1926 the *Railway Gazette* published the awards made to London and North-Eastern stations for garden upkeep. Later that year the *Great Indian*

Peninsula Railway Magazine quoted these results in full and announced its own competition:

> Anyone who is acquainted with the many beautiful station gardens at home must be impressed painfully by the apparent absolute lack of interest shown in the appearance of railway stations, particularly in connection with gardens, in India. True, there are some enterprising station staffs who take a pride in beautifying their charges, but these are few and far between. The Agent has, therefore, decided to encourage Great Indian Peninsula railwaymen to take a greater interest in such matters by the institution of a competition under the rules of which first, second and third prizes of Rs. 150, Rs. 100 and Rs. 50 respectively will be awarded annually for the best station platform gardens and premises.[33]

The great complexities of Indian railway employment were recognized: the prizes were to be shared among the permanent way inspectors, the station-masters, and the *malis* (Indian gardeners). It must be presumed too that much of this effort would be concentrated on those stations used by Europeans, where they could expect to find every facility, including even letter-racks for their mail.

In the United States, as early as 1867 a Connecticut landscape architect, Donald G. Mitchell, was arguing the case for the railroad companies to plant station gardens to advertise both the train service and the town it served. The companies took the point and began beautifying the environs of their stations in the manner suggested by Mitchell, designing their station gardens to be seen to best advantage by both those arriving on the train and those waiting on the station. The Boston and Albany Railroad appointed one of its suburban station-masters who had achieved considerable success with his gardens as the company's superintendent of station gardens. The Michigan Central Railroad Company built greenhouses to provide flowers for its dining-car tables and station gardens. The Boston and Maine Railroad Company established an annual prize for the best station gardens. By 1905 learning to design station grounds had become an accepted part of landscape architectural education.

But a dispute grew up in the always cost-conscious companies between those who wanted to beautify the trackside to delight the approaching train travellers and those who wanted more spacious station gardens as an urban amenity. By the 1920s the former had won the day and landscape architects turned their talents to municipal projects. The companies dispensed with their services and left it to their employees to provide the beautification. Those gardens which survived were in the main bulldozed and concreted over to provide station car-parking in the 1950s, another victory for functionalism over aesthetics.

In the United States and Canada the country station, with or without garden, was much more than a stopping-place for passing trains. It was invariably a community centre, where the pot-bellied stove, the wooden benches, and the convivial sense of being in touch with the rest of the world drew local inhabitants to hear the news, discuss problems, and entertain each other. Farmers collected to discuss livestock prices. People went to buy newspapers and get the weather forecast. At least one railway company regularized this by posting weather symbols on the side of trains for the benefit of local farming communities. People brought their musical instruments and had impromptu—or sometimes organized —concerts and sing-songs there. On election nights members of the locality would collect in a state of great excitement to hear the results coming in on the station telegraph. All of these uses of the railway station survive in the oral evidence of many North American villages and townships that have long since lost their rail service.[34] Appropriately enough, one station in Canada, Harriston, Ontario, has been reused as a senior citizens' recreation centre.

Necropolis Stations

The station—so vital and bustling and alive—also played a part in man's last journey—to 'the undiscovered country from whose bourn no traveller returns'. The London Necropolis Company had its own station, first opened in 1854 as part of the Waterloo Station complex.[35] Funeral parties left with the deceased from the Company's platform and ran over London and South-Western lines to the Company's cemetery at Brookwood, near Woking. The London terminal was moved and rebuilt with two new platforms in 1902 during the reconstruction of Waterloo and the Company was provided with its own suitable ornate and monumental private entrance at 121 Westminster Bridge Rd. It was destroyed by enemy bombing in 1941. At the Brookwood end there were two cheap wooden and cast-iron structures to serve as receiving stations, one for Anglicans and the other for dissenters, Roman Catholics, Parsees, and others.

In 1861 another private company founded the Great Northern Cemetery at Colney Hatch and served it by rail from King's Cross. Australia followed the lead of Britain with an ornate cemetery receiving-station at Haslam's Creek for Rookwood Cemetery, Sydney.[36] It was built in 1868 and connected by rail to a dispatching station, Redfern, at Regent's St., Sydney. The Rookwood branch fell into disuse in 1939 with the advent of the motor car. But for the receiving-station there was to be life after death. The design, roof beams, decorated columns, and funerary angels so much resembled a chapel that, after the station was closed, it was demolished in 1958 and removed to Canberra to be re-erected as a church. Thus the often-employed religious metaphor applied to the railway station became a reality.

8

The Station in the Economy (1)
Britain and Europe

THE station's prime economic function was as a reception and distribution point for goods of all kinds. The magic castle that is London's St Pancras Station rests upon a forest of unseen arches, forming a vault which in the railways' heydays, from the 1870s to the 1920s, housed the thousands of barrels of beer that arrived daily from Burton-on-Trent. Nothing could more eloquently express the nature of the Victorian railway system—a towering, splendid, multi-faceted edifice built four-square on a foundation of industry and trade.[1]

It was the economic imperative—the energy demands of an industrializing North-East of England—that prompted the building of the world's first railway line, the Stockton and Darlington Railway (1825), which was essentially a coal-carrying line. Coal-carrying was thus from the first, and has remained both in Britain and on the Continent, one of the basic economic functions of the railway. Indeed George Stephenson originally envisaged the railway system as an extension of the colliery system. Once the success of the Liverpool and Manchester Railway (1830) in transporting both passengers and freight was demonstrated, industrial and commercial Britain began vociferously to demand this vital new mode of transport, which would link centres of production, distribution, and raw material and would progressively quicken the pace of economic life. By 1837 the railway had linked Birmingham with Liverpool and Manchester, by 1838 Birmingham with London, by 1840 London with Southampton, by 1841 London with Bristol.

The railway spread outwards from Britain to continental Europe, initially often with British capital, technology, and expertise. Belgium was the first European country to possess a fully fledged rail network. The first line (Brussels to Malines) was opened in 1835. By 1842 Brussels was linked to Antwerp, Ostend, and the French frontier. Germany's first line opened in 1835, Austria's in 1837, Italy's and Holland's in 1839, Switzerland's in 1847, Spain's in 1848.

The pace of development varied. Holland, with its extensive waterways, had only 211 miles by 1860. Scandinavia, equally well served by rivers and coastal sea traffic, was also slow to develop national networks after initial line foundations—Denmark in 1847, Norway in 1854, and Sweden in 1856. Although France had a railway line from the coalfield of Saint Etienne to Lyons in 1832, it too was slow to develop a national network, partly because of governmental reluctance to embrace the new form of transportation and also because the economy remained predominantly agricultural and the road system was more efficient and extensive than Britain's. By 1842 France had only 350 route miles and by 1850 only 1,870, compared with Germany's 3,735 miles and Britain's 6,621. But Napoleon III's Second Empire changed all this, decisively and enthusiastically embracing railway-building so that by 1870 11,000 miles had been built by a partnership between the State and the six great companies that emerged from the initial burst of railway fever.

On the whole, railway development on the Continent was a generation behind Britain. Between 1850 and 1870, 50,000 miles of new line were laid in Europe, as against 15,000 in all the years before. By 1870 the major European trunk lines had been established and it was a matter of filling in the network, a process that continued until the end of the century.

The story of the railways is intimately tied up with the wider saga of the industrialization of Europe, and it proceeded at a different rate in each country. Britain set the pace in the first half of the nineteenth century. In the 1850s and 1860s France and Germany, particularly Germany, followed suit; they caught up with, and by 1914 had overtaken, Britain in the field of industry. Italy, Russia, and Austria lagged further behind, their major period of industrialization being concentrated in the last three decades before the First World War. But their industrialization remained partial because of an entrenched semi-feudal agrarian system and large peasant populations. Spain and Hungary, despite the presence of the railways, remained industrially backward, with comparatively little development by 1914. Clearly, then, the provision of railways does not lead inevitably to industrialization. There is an interlocking complex of reasons for industrial take-off. But the presence of railways is one of them and when industrialization occurs, the railways speed the process.

In recent years there had been considerable debate about the nature of the railways' contribution to economic growth. This was initiated by the practitioners of the so-called New Economic History. These scholars, with their narrow reliance on sometimes incomplete statistics and a hypothetical input for 'social saving', argue that the railways were much less important than is usually assumed, because if they had not existed, something else would have emerged to take their place. But this is like suggesting that pigs might fly. They might, but they don't. Far too much scholarly energy has been wasted in trying to assess what would have happened to industrialization without the railways. The railways were a fact and the economy responded directly to that fact.

The arrival of the railways made an important and lasting impact on many sectors of the economy. The building and then the operation of the railways created a vast new industry, which provided work across the whole range of employment grades. In Britain, on average 60,000 men were employed annually in building the railways between the 1830s and the 1870s. The number of permanent employees of the companies grew from 56,000 in 1850 to 350,000 in 1890 to 600,000 in 1910. In France the number of railway workers increased from 27,900 in 1851 to 113,000 in 1866, 222,800 in 1881, 308,000 in 1907, 355,600 in 1913. These figures take no account of the numbers employed in ancillary activities, such as delivery-men, cab-drivers, and employees of businesses like shops, cafés, and hotels, which regularly sprang up in the environs of the great railway termini. Neither can they measure the stimulus the railways provided to the growth and maturation of the professions—law, engineering, accounting, surveying—all of whose services were in demand by the railway companies.

The railways stimulated capital investment, entrepreneurial adventure, and the money market. As *The Economist* noted in 1845: 'Railway property is a new feature in England's social economy which has introduced commercial feelings to the firesides of thousands.'[2] Britain had a large stake in the early overseas railway-building. Robert Stephenson and Co. had by 1840 supplied locomotives to Austria, Belgium, France, Germany, Italy, Russia, and North America. Thomas Brassey built the Paris to Rouen Railway in the early 1840s and held contracts in fifteen other countries. Later in the nineteenth century the British Empire and South America became potent fields of railway investment activity. Belgian industry and capital played an important part in developing the railways of France and Russia. France itself, once it moved into the railway field, carved out lucrative areas of railway-building in, for instance, Spain. An estimated 5,250 million francs was invested in foreign transportation between 1852 and 1881.

The railways stimulated demand for coal, iron, engineering, and from the 1870s steel. The cheapening delivery costs of coal extended its use in manufacturing and in domestic consumption. Between 1844 and 1851 British railways probably took one-fifth of the total output of the engineering industry. The industrial stimulus and technological acceleration which the railways caused in the metallurgical and engineering industries has been traced in Belgium, Russia, and Germany. For Germany, one scholar has demonstrated that 'both the growth and modernization of the German iron industry and to a lesser extent the engineering sector, may be regarded as a consequence of the railroad'.[3] Figures for locomotive manufacture in Prussia show that up to 1842 the bulk of Prussian locomotives were imported from Britain. The proportion dropped steadily until 1851 when all fifty-four locomotives brought into use were made in Prussia. Similarly, until 1845 most rails were imported. By the 1850s most rails were produced in Germany.

But the rise of the railways had much more general effects. The railways provided a cheap, efficient method of bulk transportation which dramatically lowered costs. In Britain in the 1860s coal was carried by British railways at one-twentieth the cost by road. In France it was three or four times as expensive for French farmers to send merchandise by road as by rail. By 1914, 70 per cent of total freight transport in France was by rail, 77 per cent in Belgium. Falling freight costs led directly to easier marketing, cheaper raw materials, reduced prices, greater demand, and increased productivity.

The railway linked up manufacturing areas with raw material sources and centres of distribution and consumption, providing a major stimulus to further growth in coalfields like the Ruhr in Germany, the Pas-de-Calais in France, and those in Central Spain, in the iron ore works of South Wales, and in the new industrial centres of the developing European economies, like the Ukraine in Russia and the upper Po valley in Italy. In all these areas, stations played a vital role as the staging posts of industrial supply and demand.

Industrialization and its concomitant—urbanization—had a direct effect on agriculture. The increased demand for food to feed the growing populations of the great cities was met by speedy rail communication with the countryside, which allowed the transportation of perishable goods over long distances and promoted commercialization, specialization, and modernization in the agriculture of many countries. In France, for instance, the railways became the suppliers of Paris. In 1889 the railways supplied half the 44,969 tonnes of dead meat and half the 8,013 tonnes of cheese imported into the capital, almost all the 20,899 tonnes of poultry and game and the 15,694 tonnes of fruit and vegetables, and all the 25,215 tonnes of fish, the 12,076 tonnes of eggs, and the 5,790 tonnes of mussels. In all, 122,243 tonnes out of a total of 149,990 tonnes of foodstuffs of all kinds was carried into Paris by rail.

Roger Price, in his masterly account of the modernization of rural

France, has demonstrated the pivotal role of the railways in transforming the *ancien régime* economy of the countryside in the middle of the nineteenth century. Up to that time, the rural economy was characterized by slow and expensive modes of communication, over-population, subsistence agriculture, and compartmentalized markets. Rural society was isolated, localized, and subject to recurrent food crises which bred an atmosphere of apprehension and insecurity and led to periodic outbreaks of disorder. There had been some reduction in transport costs and a degree of commercialization in the early part of the century, but not enough to break the recurrent cycle of harvest failure, food shortage, price increase, misery, and unrest. The basic cause was low productivity, exacerbated by distribution difficulties and the inefficient transmission of information. The coming of the railways and their ally, the telegraph system, put an end to this situation. Subsistence crises ceased after the 1850s and their disappearance can be linked directly with the rise of the railways. In their wake, French economic life came to be characterized by market integration, specialization and commercialization in farming methods instead of subsistence polyculture, and intensified competition between the regions. For the people, this meant stable price levels, rising living standards, and increased employment opportunities. Price notes that one potent expression of this transformation was the physical change that took place in bakers' shops. They ceased to be fortresses protected by strong doors and iron bars and became elegant shops with windows in place of grilles.

The change did not, of course, take place uniformly. There were variations between areas, classes, and products. There were periods of advance and of stagnation. Urbanization, for instance, proceeded much more slowly in France than in England. By 1901 only 41 per cent of the French population lived in towns. In England the figure had passed 50 per cent as early as 1851. Nevertheless the coming of the railways had permanently transformed the structure and nature of French agriculture and rural life.

The role of the station was, as ever, crucial in this process, as Roger Price reminds us:

An initial distinction might be made between communes with and those without a railway station. In general, the latter tended to experience economic (and demographic) decline and to place all hope of arresting this in the improvement of their communications. The former did not invariably experience substantial development as commercial centres—some railway centres were better located than others—but were better placed to market their own products and to develop economically, even though Le Mans developed at the expense of

Alençon, for example, and Orléans, Besançon and Montpellier all lost some of their traditional importance in the wine trade, the last losing out to Béziers and Nîmes which were at junctions in the railway network. Position on main rather than on secondary rail routes and especially at crossroads in the network (nodal points) was an important factor for growth.[4]

It was in the mid 1840s that the full implications of the potential for the new transport system sank in. Britain's railway companies laid increasing emphasis on freight, in pursuit of the dictum of Captain Mark Huish of the London and North-Western Railway: 'Quantity is the essential element of Railway success.'[5] It was 1852 before freight receipts exceeded passenger receipts and it was around the same time that the railways overtook the canals to become the principal freight carriers. By 1856 the canals were carrying half as much freight as the railways. British railways carried an estimated 38 million tons of freight in 1850. By 1875 the total was 199.6 million tons. In France, the railway companies underestimated the demand for their services. The Compagnie de l'Est admitted in 1853 that goods traffic had 'increased . . . with such rapidity that our material has been found to be insufficient. We have found it necessary to refuse traffic.'[6] In 1850, 64.74 per cent of total receipts on French railways came from passengers and only 35.26 per cent from goods. But by 1860 the proportion was almost exactly opposite: 33.96 per cent of receipts came from passengers and 66.04 per cent from goods.

What were the goods carried by the railways in such bulk? Everywhere from Spain and Russia to Italy and Britain, the principal freight cargo was coal, the key to industrialization. For more than a century after 1850 the movement of coal was the life-blood of British railways. The tonnage carried was always well over half the total volume of freight traffic. In 1856 the quantity of coal carried by rail was 50 million tons, compared with 13 million tons of other minerals and 32 million tons of general merchandise. The Midland Railway Company, which linked eight major coalfields, transported one-tenth of all British coal.

In Germany the average rate per ton-kilometre declined by 74 per cent between 1840 and 1880. The initially high freight charges encouraged the import of cheap British coal. But establishment of a special rate for domestic coal in the 1850s enabled German mines to undercut British coal, and regular coal traffic from Upper Silesia and the Ruhr to Berlin and other big cities was established.

In countries like Spain and Italy, where coal was imported in bulk, it was the railways which transported it and distributed it. For much of the period 1860 to 1900 Spain was a net importer of foreign, mainly British, coal, which dramatically undercut the price of home-produced coal. In

Italy in 1911, coal formed 55 per cent of total rail-borne imports. In Russia in the 1960s, which with only a tenth of the world's railway mileage carried almost half the amount of freight moved by the rest of the world, coal and coke constituted a quarter of total freight, with other goods like petrol, oil, ore, and timber comprising only one-fifteenth each. Coal-sidings came to be a feature of stations large and small right across Europe.

After coal, building materials figured importantly among bulk cargoes. In Italy in the later nineteenth century high-grade building materials formed one of the principal bulk cargoes for internal rail distribution. In Russia in the 1960s building materials formed a fifth of all freight. In Britain the railways not only transported but considerably stimulated the making of bricks. In 1845 an estimated 740 million bricks were used in stations, bridges, aqueducts, and embankments under construction. In 1847, the record year of rail-building, a third of all the bricks produced in Britain were used in the railways. But as urbanization proceeded apace, bricks remained in demand for house-building. Brick-making was expanded in country market towns to provide employment at a time of decline in the need for farm labourers. The brick-making operations were often directly linked with the railway, as for instance at Whittlesea, near Peterborough. At Whittlesea Station in 1898 a staff of twelve dispatched 108,000 tons of bricks during the year, a total which represented a spectacular increase over 1891, which had seen the dispatch of 7,130 tons. The increase meant more and more work for the staff. From thirty to sixty trucks were loaded with bricks daily for dispatch to London and its surrounding area. Work began at seven in the morning and went on until the time, as the station-master put it, 'when the work is finished', usually seven in the evening. The station also supplied the nearby brickworks with its coal, 23,000 tons in 1898, chiefly from Yorkshire.[7]

Among foodstuffs, grain was the principal bulk freight. The possibility of widespread internal and, indeed, export distribution by rail caused a major transformation in Hungarian agriculture from pastoral to cereal production. The reduction in cost of transportation in Spain due to railways stimulated the integration of the home market there, with domestic consumption of grain increasing dramatically. In 1882 only 25 per cent of Spanish grain was transported by rail. This had almost doubled by 1913.

Railways made a particularly dramatic impact on the grain trade in Russia, where it supplanted the use of waterways and short-haul wagons. In 1870 grain constituted 27.5 per cent of total freight. By 1875 this figure had reached 42.1 per cent. On some railroads, however, it was far and away the most important single item of freight. On the Tambov–Kozlov railway 73.1 per cent of total freight was grain, on the Oryol–Gryazi railway 83.6 per cent, and on the Ryazhsk–Morshansk 88.9 per cent.

The net result of this activity was to create a national grain market, with trade no longer centred on a few major points of collection, transit, and marketing.[8] The Ryazan–Uralsk railway succeeded in linking the grain producing regions along the Volga with the major consuming area around Moscow, and the Trans-Caucasus Railway linked the southern port cities of Odessa, Rostov, and Novorossiysk with the grain areas of the Middle Volga. This facilitated not only internal grain trade but also export. By the 1880s half the wheat harvest was being exported. Regional price variations equalized, agriculture was commercialized and a new breed of entrepreneurs was brought into being, dependent upon the railway and the station. As Peter Lyaschenko wrote:

In place of the great Moscow or Kolomna merchant, the Nizhny Novogorod miller, the Moscow flax or hemp-factory owner, the large export wholesaler, and the old 'flour dealers', the railroad stations now swarmed with a mass of small traders, exporters, and commission merchants, all buying grain, hemp, hides, lard, sheepskin, down and bristles—in a word, everything bound for either the domestic or the foreign market. Operating with relatively little capital, aided by credit, with a small mark-up in prices but with rapid turnover of capital, these petty commercial middlemen penetrated deep into the village, constantly drawing the rural area into the orbit of cash turnover, increasing the role of the market in the economy of the village, and augmenting the volume of goods available both for domestic and foreign commerce.[9]

The most immediate effect upon the lives of the people, however, came in the railways' ability to transport perishable foodstuffs very long distances, not just within but between countries. For this had revolutionary effects on agriculture, on food manufacture, on retailing, and on diet. The railways carried right across Europe Danish eggs and dairy produce, Russian grain and poultry, Italian and French fruit, and Dutch vegetables. In most countries, the railways were responsible for the speedy and cheap distribution from countryside to town of slaughtered meat, fresh fruit and vegetables, and fresh milk, and from the coast to the town of fresh fish. This was particularly important in a country like Britain whose population grew from 17,900,000 in 1851 to 36,000,000 in 1911, the majority living in towns and cities.

But no country was immune from railway developments in any other

The opening up of North America by the railways made American wheat available to Europe. It was so cheap that it could be sold at half the price of the home-grown grain. So in Britain in the 1870s many wheat farmers went over to meat production. But in the 1880s a successful means of refrigerating meat cargoes was found, and within a few years Australian and Argentine beef, New Zealand lamb, and American pork were flooding into the country. By 1900, imports had halved the cost of meat and bread, greatly assisting the diet of the working classes.

The response of British farmers to this development was to turn increasingly to specialization—dairy farming, market gardening, poultry and fruit farming. The acreage under small fruit increased from 15,949 in 1871 to 76,331 in 1914. This, of course, stimulated the jam-making industry considerably.[10]

Indeed food manufacture as a whole underwent a transformation. In 1850 the food industries were generally small-scale and localized. But improved communications, technological change, and increased demand led to concentration of food production in fewer and greater units. Jam, chocolate, and biscuits began to be produced under factory conditions and shipped out by rail, thus introducing household names in food-production like Huntley and Palmer at Reading and Cadbury at Bournville. Similarly, brewing came increasingly to be concentrated in major provincial centres like Burton and Norwich, which utilized the rail network to the full to distribute their product. The result of all this was that, although at the end of the century a third of the population still lived below the poverty line and the diet of the poorest included items such as white bread, condensed milk, and vegetable oil margarine, the earnings of a Lancashire cotton operative in 1913 permitted him 'a breakfast of coffee or tea, bread, bacon and eggs—when eggs are cheap—a dinner of potatoes and beef, an evening meal of tea, bread and butter, cheap vegetables or fish, and a slight supper at moderate price'.[11]

In the transport of all these different perishables, the station was intimately concerned. It was the hub of activity in milk delivery and milk churns were a feature of every station. Philip Unwin recalled: 'The clatter of these milk churns was inseparable from railway stations, suggestive of cheerful bustle by day but strangely mournful in the small hours of a night journey.'[12] It was not called 'railway milk' for nothing.

The railways were to transform dairying. Before the railways, most of the milk produced in the country went for butter and cheese. The demand for milk in the cities was met mainly by cow-keepers operating in the city itself or in the suburbs. Milk was brought to Manchester by train as early as 1844 and to London by 1845. But the volume of 'railway milk' traffic grew only slowly in the first decades of railway transport. By the mid 1850s, for instance, only 5 per cent of London's milk arrived by train, and the bulk of that carried by the Eastern Counties Railway. By 1914, however, the situation was totally transformed: 96 per cent of London's milk came by train. The amount of milk carried by train had risen steadily, from 1.4 million gallons in 1861 to 10 million gallons in 1871, 26 million gallons in 1881, 42 million gallons in 1891, 93 million gallons in 1914. There was at the same time a dramatic decline in the amount of milk produced by urban cattle-keepers and supplied by road.[13]

'Railway milk' had received its first boost with an outbreak of cattle plague in the mid 1860s which had seriously restricted urban milk production. But its real take-off period was the 1870s when the introduction of a new cooling apparatus and the addition of chemical preservatives to the milk enabled it to be transported very long distances while remaining fresh. By the 1870s London was drawing on Berkshire and Wiltshire for its milk, by the 1880s on Somerset, and by the 1900s on Devon and Cornwall. In 1910 St Erth, 300 miles from London, sent nearly 30,000 gallons of milk to Paddington Station. So much milk came into Waterloo that it was renowned for smelling of sour milk all day.

At the outset, the railways adopted a negative attitude to the trade, failing to provide special terminal facilities, refusing to grant concessionary freight rates, and making no special timetable provision for milk trains. But as the value and importance of the trade became clear, some companies moved to meet the milk importers' requirements. The Great Western, whose rich agricultural heartland was providing an increasing volume of the capital's milk, opened a special milk halt at Wootton Bassett in Wiltshire and constructed special milk platforms at Paddington, the first in 1881. But as late as 1890, only the Great Western and the Great Northern, with its London milk depot at Finsbury Park, had provided special terminal facilities.

Milk was generally carried by passenger trains, but increasingly milk rather than passengers became their *raison d'être*. In 1890 the Great Western inaugurated two daily express milk specials from Swindon Junction. Already from the 1860s they had introduced a reduced long-distance freight rate for milk to encourage the trade. The Midland Company also increased its share of the London milk trade by offering special freight concessions to Derbyshire farmers. The London, Brighton and South Coast Company introduced special rates for milk sent from particular stations. So it was that the companies gradually came to terms with the increasing traffic and provided it with a further impetus.

Other factors converged in the 1870s. There was increased urban demand, with a fast-growing population and with a rise in real wages, competition from cheap imported foodstuffs encouraged farmers to switch to milk production, and the wholesale and retail end of the business became more efficient and organized. But it could not have taken place without the railways, which once again proved to be the vital enabling factor. The milk train became an essential fact of rural life, altering its rhythms by demanding the co-ordination of milking times with train departures.

Fruit, flowers, and vegetables, of course, had their seasons. The railways had to accommodate a wide variety of produce under different conditions and at different times of the year. In June and July there were the 'strawberry specials', 30 tonnes of strawberries being carried daily by the Midland Railway from the Vale of Evesham to London. The London and South-Western carried in a whole season one million baskets of strawberries from ten stations in Hampshire: Swanwick, Dotley, Romsey, Eastleigh, Wickham, Fareham, Bursledon, Netley, Sholing, and Bitterne.[14]

Both the Great Western and the Midland were involved in the carriage of produce from the Vale of Evesham virtually all the year round, but the actual cargoes varied according to the time of year. The transportation of early vegetables such as cabbages, Brussels sprouts, and young onions began in March, with asparagus following until June, and after the strawberry harvest, the plum season in August and September, which had the Midland conveying a thousand tons of plums a week. In autumn and winter the cargoes were damsons, tomatoes, marrows, cucumbers, apples, and pears. West Cornwall was a centre of broccoli- and potato-growing. In 1898 the Great Western Railway conveyed 5,978 tons of broccoli from Cornwall, much of it going north via Didcot, Birmingham, and Crewe. Similarly, in 1898, 12,395 tons of potatoes were distributed by the GWR network, mainly to the North and Midlands. At the end of July the Great Eastern Railways conveyed 500 tons of green peas on a single day from the area around Maldon in Essex. Perhaps most romantic of all were the 'flower specials'. Flowers from the Isles of Scilly were picked in the morning, packed in light, non-returnable boxes, made up into packets of five, and conveyed by steamer to Penzance. They left for London on the 4.50 p.m. GWR mail train from Penzance, arriving at Paddington by 4 a.m. next morning. But at the height of the season, there were so many extra loads of flowers that 'flower specials' were laid on. Coaches containing flowers for Manchester were detached at Bristol and for Birmingham at Didcot. In 1896, 514 tons of flowers left Penzance Station for various parts of the country.[15]

But the railways were also involved in the next stage of the life of some of the fruit harvested round the country. At the Great Eastern Station of Histon near Cambridge, 90 per cent of the goods traffic was involved in the local jam-making industry. The jam factory was next to the station and had its own sidings. Six goods trains arrived at Histon every day, bringing in the necessaries for jam-making: sugar from Amsterdam, Hamburg, and other Continental ports, earthenware jars from St Helens, Newcastle, and Chesterfield. The trucks were shunted on to the company's sidings, unloaded by the company's employees, and loaded with the jam, made from fruit harvested locally and brought direct to the factory. The station-master and his staff of twelve dealt with 20,099 tons of goods traffic incoming and outgoing in 1898. Furthermore, many of the women and girls working at fruit-picking and jam-making were related to railway workers at nearby Cambridge Station and were brought to work by the 8.20 train from Cambridge in the morning and taken back home by the 6.34 in the evening.[16]

Before the railways came, livestock was usually driven 'on the hoof' to the market, which not only took time but resulted inevitably in the animals losing weight and hence value. Cattle trucks made the transport of meat both faster and easier. They also facilitated the movement of perishable dead meat quite long distances. Indeed it was at one time believed that the advent of the railways had signalled the end of the movement of live meat. But this never occurred, as the railways charged high rates for the carriage of dead meat, which required greater handling, than they did for livestock.[17]

The central role played by the railways in transporting meat dictated the location of the meat markets. In 1855 the new Metropolitan Meat Market at Islington was opened. It was provided with a direct link to the London and North-Western's Camden Station and so animals were driven direct to it from the trains. Wolverhampton, Bristol, Shrewsbury, and Liverpool also built new cattle markets close to railway stations.

The dead-meat trade increased in the 1860s as a result of restrictions on the movement of live cattle in order to control the spread of cattle plague. It was a vital part of the railway freight business. Seymour Clarke, General Manager of the Great Northern Railway, told the 1869 Parliamentary Select Committee on the transit of animals that his company sent meat from almost all the 197 stations on its lines.

In the 1850s and 1860s, before cold storage was introduced, the dead-meat trade was seasonal, the heaviest burden falling in the coldest months of the year, between September and May. Different meat-market centres tended to specialize in different forms of meat, Aberdeen,

Edinburgh, and Leeds dispatching mainly dead meat and Leicester and Norwich livestock. The great stations in these cities thus became massive meat railheads.

The existence of the railways also opened up the Continent, and Hamburg and Rotterdam served as terminal stations on a network of lines running to Austria, Hungary, and Poland, along which livestock was carried for export. During the 1880s the Scandinavian countries sent an average 106,244 head of cattle to Britain every year. But after 1892 animal disease legislation put an end to the importation of European livestock.

By that time, however, refrigeration techniques had ensured that meat could be brought from much further afield: beef from North and South America, mutton from Australia and New Zealand. By 1910 the inhabitants of Britain consumed a million tons of meat over and above home produce. Much of the beef from the United States in fact arrived in cattle ships on the hoof. Typical was the American meat traffic to Birkenhead. The cattle arrived at the landing-stage at Woodside, spent 10–14 days in pens ('lairages') recovering from the crossing, and were then slaughtered. At the Woodside and Wallasey abattoirs 2,600 cattle a day could be killed. The meat was then skinned, dressed, cut into 'sides', sewn into canvas, and placed in refrigerator vans for distribution throughout Britain by the London and North-Western Railway. Seventeen trains a day, mostly filled with such meat, left Birkenhead Station.

Every part of the animal was used and nothing went to waste. The entrails, blood, and skulls were used for manure on the farms of Cheshire. The kidneys, liver, heart, tail, tripe, and heels were packed into hampers and sent to the Lancashire manufacturing towns like Bury, Wigan, and Oldham where the factory workers prized them as cheap and nourishing food.[18]

Game and poultry were also imported in this way, to Fishguard from Ireland, to Liverpool from Canada, and to the East Coast ports from the Continent. Two forms of livestock in particular are worth singling out. The railways were vital in facilitating pigeon-racing. National competitions entailed special trains to carry the birds to the agreed starting-points. Where there were only a few birds they were carried in the guard's van and released at the time and place stated on the label. But the traffic was so heavy in the North-East that the North-Eastern Railway from 1905 on ran a 'pigeon special' every weekend from Newcastle to the South. At the height of the season, they ran two a day. The runs became longer in successive weeks, with the destinations moving from Selby to Doncaster to Nottingham and ultimately as far south as Southampton. At the named destination, all the baskets would be unloaded and the birds liberated simultaneously. At a number of North-Eastern stations a porter would spend half an hour every Saturday or Sunday releasing pigeons from individual baskets, according to the instructions on the label.[19]

No such freedom awaited another exotic cargo, the quails from Alexandria and Algiers, which arrived at King's Cross Goods Station for dispatch to Leadenhall Market. They were conveyed in crates with a hundred live birds in each, fed *en route* by attendants; 200,000 a month reached London in the season. Their destination was the tables of the well-to-do.[20]

But the poor had cause to be grateful to the railways too, in particular for their supplies of fresh fish. Until the mid nineteenth century, pickled or salted herring was the only form of fish available to the working classes. But in the 1860s and 1870s the development of the steam trawler, the use of ice for preservation, and the exploitation of the rail network signalled the arrival of cheap cod and made possible the fish-and-chip shops which multiplied at the end of the century to furnish an important source of protein to the working class. Between 4.30 and 9 a.m. every day a dozen fish trains left Grimsby for all parts of the country. By 1861, 100,000 tons of fish was being carried by rail in England and Wales. This development had a marked effect on the structure and nature of the fishing industry. Small-scale and localized in the early nineteenth century, it became large-scale and increasingly concentrated in several main trawler ports as the century wore on.[21]

There were few stations without their coal sidings or their milk churns. Many had livestock pens and some had specialized functions connected with a local firm or factory. But the principal focus for freight traffic was the goods station. Goods traffic comprised three general categories —minerals (coal, metal ore, stone), livestock, and general merchandise (everything from raw cotton and spun silk to shovels and bicycles). Into the goods stations would come fish trains, milk trains, coal trains, meat trains. But the greater proportion of goods traffic was not carried in specials but in ordinary merchandise trains, made up of all kinds of vehicles containing an assortment of commodities, raw and manufactured.

The term 'goods station' conjures up an impression of a grim, functional building, a sort of glorified warehouse wholly lacking the glamour of the great passenger terminal. But some goods stations were by an accident of history very grand. As the railways penetrated deeper into the heart of the great cities, many large terminals were superseded. Instead of being demolished, they were turned into goods stations. The earliest purpose-built station, Manchester Liverpool Road, closed to passengers in 1844, continued as a goods station until 1975. The London and Southampton Railway's terminal at Nine Elms, with its fine classical portico designed by Sir William Tite, closed to passenger traffic in 1848 when Waterloo opened. But it remained in service as a goods station. The Eastern Counties Railways' terminus at Shoreditch, opened in 1840 and renamed Bishopsgate in 1846, boasted an impressive façade in the Italianate style by Sancton Wood. It closed to passengers when Liverpool Street Station opened in 1875. But it was converted to a goods station and reopened in 1881. Birmingham's Curzon Street, with its Ionic portico, the Midlands' equivalent of the triumphal arch at Euston, was replaced as passenger terminal in 1854 by New Street Station but continued as a goods station. Elsewhere Southport Central, Sheffield Wicker, Leicester West Bridge, and Bradford Adolphus Street went over from passenger to goods traffic, when supplanted by more extensive terminals.

The picture of life in a goods station was painted by Ernest Protheroe:

All through the day the collecting vans and lorries bring consignments of every description to the goods station proper, which consists of lines of rails and long platforms under cover. As fast as the packages are unloaded they are checked with the consignment notes, trundled off to weighing machines for their weight to be recorded, and are then conveyed to the decks or platforms convenient to the spot where they will be loaded later in the day. By eight o'clock at night the platforms of a London goods station are congested with great stacks of goods, every imaginable commodity and every conceivable shape. When the work of loading the vans and trucks commences, one is persuaded that the chaotic array will never be reduced to order. Men, busy as ants, wheel the packages to the waiting vehicles; there is bustle and noise, but no confusion, since each man knows what to do—and does it. The loaders are skilled in fitting in packages of the most awkward shapes; and as each article is placed in a van it is entered upon a slip for later reference. As soon as a truck is loaded it is removed by a 'traverser' on to a clear inner set of metals, and is then drawn out into the outer goods yard. Upon a network of metals, lighted by great arc lamps, the workers here deal not with packages but with trucks. They are shunted from one set of rails to another; turn-tables spin them round until they can be run upon any particular line; by means of capstans and ropes the loaded trucks are warped this way or that; and tank engines push them hither and thither. Most of the movements are directed by voice or a waving lantern. To the uninitiated it might seem that the shunters are engaged in a game of hide-and-seek with the trucks; they appear to scatter them all over the yard, as if their object were to separate many of them as completely as possible. But when a goods engine makes its appearance from the outer darkness, it is possible to realize that the shunters' apparent madness is nothing but the acme of method. The engine backs down upon a few trucks, perhaps a single one; there is a quick manipulation of a coupling stick, and the engine draws off with its insignificant load. Shortly it reappears upon another set of metals, and bears down upon more trucks. Backwards and forwards the engine passes, increasing its load at each operation, until behind its tender it may have a string of vehicles more than two hundred yards in length with a brake van in the rear. As far as possible the trucks are in the order in which they will be disconnected from the train at the various stopping-places. There is then a pause of perhaps only a few seconds, a semaphore drops, a gleaming red light changes to green, and the long goods train moves out on its journey.[22]

Goods stations had their *aficionados*, every bit as keen as the devotees of passenger stations. One of them, D. T. Timins, wrote:

The great goods depots of London possess an importance superior even to that of the passenger termini themselves and furnish to the keen observer fields of study every whit as interesting as those afforded by the heterogeneous masses of humanity which daily pack themselves into express and local trains.[23]

In pursuit of this philosophy, the *Railway Magazine* in 1900 ran a series of articles on the notable British goods station, preserving for us a picture of these hives of economic activity at the height of the railway age. D. T. Timins was one of their eager reporters, and he began with a visit to the London and South-Western's Nine Elms Station. Covering 37 acres and employing a staff of 1,170, it was a vital centre not only for the arrival and departure of merchandise and foodstuffs to and from the South and South-West of England but also France, the Channel Islands, and the Americas. The New Shed dealt with manufactured goods (toys, groceries, hardware, etc.), the Old Down Shed with bulk traffic (flour, grain, fresh fruit), and two special sheds were set aside for American and French imported goods.[24]

S. E. Marsh, assistant goods superintendent, described the rich variety of produce the station handled:

On this side we handle the up-goods from the American and Cape line ships. It is nothing for 50 trucks of Canadian pea-fed bacon to arrive in one day, or as many as 2,000 barrels of apples. Oysters and American bicycles, together with large consignments of hops, are among some of the principal items of a very varied and numerous assortment of commodities which we receive in quantities from the United States. From the Cape comes wool, skins, fruit etc. etc., while from France we often get 3,000 sacks of chestnuts at a time. During last autumn 20,000 packets of English hops, grown at Farnham, Bentley and Alton, were unloaded in this shed.[25]

There was seasonal trade too. Five hundred truck-loads of holly and mistletoe arrived from the New Forest for Christmas 1899, and in May and June 'we are flooded with potatoes and also with strawberries'. Several special trains of American frozen meat arrived every week, leaving Southampton at 6 p.m., arriving at Nine Elms at 10 p.m., and being at the market by midnight. In one month at Nine Elms the clerks invoiced 35,874 tons of general goods, 5,933 tons of minerals, and 7,753 tons of coal and coke inwards, and 50,311 tons of general goods, 9,426 tons of minerals, and 2,849 tons of coal and coke outwards. The steady increase in goods traffic which had taken place over the century can be demonstrated by the fact that during twenty-six weeks in 1847 the London and South-Western took in £38,906. 19s. 11d. as a result of their freight traffic. The equivalent period in 1899 brought them in £637,515. 11s. 11d.

The Forth Goods Station, Newcastle upon Tyne, was living proof of the comprehensive functionality of the goods station. Built on the banks of the Tyne and opened in 1873, it had been extended in 1893 until it stood three storeys high, 609 ft. long and 330 ft. wide. A complex of cellars, warehouses, and offices, it was bounded on the north by the seventeen arches of the bridge carrying the Newcastle–Carlisle line into Central Station. These arches were used for storage. To the west was the junction, where a thousand or more trucks were marshalled daily and where the cattle docks lay, and the machinery supplying the motive power for the hydraulic cranes, capstans, and traversers. To the east lay the entrances to the warehouse for road vehicles and the entrance yard, around which were the carting, time, weigh, telegraph, and enquiry offices. The station had twelve platforms ('benches') in constant use, while attached to the station were farriers', joiners', plumbers', and saddlers' departments, and stables for the 250 horses used in carting.[26]

A staff of 1,400 employees of the North-Eastern Railway worked there, not to mention men of the North British and Caledonian railways who also had of part of the station. During the course of a year, 1.1 million tons of merchandise and 800,000 head of livestock were dealt with.

Paddington Goods Depot, built in 1838, covered 22 acres and employed a staff of 2,000, which included 255 clerks, 711 porters, 893 carters, and 30 policemen. Its eleven platforms were capable of accommodating 300 trucks under cover at the same time. Each platform dealt with thirty-six trains outwards and thirty-eight inwards each day. Paddington was essentially a station for mixed general traffic, but foodstuffs of various kinds formed a large proportion of incoming merchandise.

In season, 1,100 tons of vegetables arrived daily from Worcester and Evesham. This included 69,000 packages of asparagus alone. Four hundred tons of potatoes arrived daily from the Channel Islands. Three hundred tons of fish arrived daily from the western fishing ports. Major recurrent items were bacon from Ireland and meat from Birkenhead. Three days a week the Irish cross-channel boats brought over between 600 and 700 bales of bacon, requiring fourteen trucks to convey them to London. The bacon was stored under the station arches on arrival at Paddington but the meat was conveyed to Smithfield. There was traffic too in the opposite direction. Fresh-killed meat from Deptford, nineteen wagon-loads of it, arrived every evening to be loaded into 800 special refrigerator vans waiting to receive it. In the prepared food line, 30 tons of Cadbury's chocolate and 30 tons of Fry's cocoa arrived at Paddington every day. South Wales, the principal supplier of paper for London newspapers and magazines, was part of the GWR empire and so Paddington was the destination for that bulk cargo, an average of 623 reels of paper arriving daily.[27]

Perhaps the classic London Goods Station was King's Cross, the product of the entrepreneurial acumen of the Great Northern Railway. Hemmed in by a board school, a gasworks, a depot for Bass ale, and the neighbouring St Pancras Station, King's Cross Goods Station was proclaimed by its retired outdoor Goods Manager to be in appearance 'prosaic enough—you can't go into ecstasies over the beauty of its situation or the classic lines of its architecture'. Its clerks had for many years to work in 'dark, stuffy offices, with smoke-grimed ceilings and an atmosphere compounded of overnight gas-burning and the indefinable mouldiness of adjacent "bookrooms" '. Yet the Great Northern was the first company to establish a large potato depot in London, fed by bulk cargoes from Lincolnshire and Yorkshire. It was the first company to set up a coal depot to supply the capital, displacing with railway coal the hitherto pre-eminent 'sea coal'. It also secured its own connection with the Islington Cattle Market by means of Holloway unloading pens and a private road. At King's Cross itself there was a granary covering an area of 9,000 square yards, sheds for the storage of bricks from Hertfordshire, Lincolnshire, Staffordshire, and Yorkshire, and accommodation for the other regular bulk cargoes of stone, timber, hay, and straw.[28]

The growth of goods traffic as a proportion of railway activity can be traced in the story of the Paris goods stations of the Nord network. In

Christchurch Station, New Zealand, a Victorian Gothic structure, opened in 1877. It was demolished between 1957 and 1960.

Que Que (now Kwekwe), typical small-town station on the main line between Bulawayo and Harare, Zimbabwe.

The opening of Goderich Station on the Buffalo and Lake Huron Railway in Canada, 185?

Artillery salute during the funeral procession of Count Moltke at Lehrter Station, Berlin, 1891.

Arrival of the workmen's 'penny' train, Victoria Station, 1865.

A mob wrecking Motherwell Station after the Caledonian Railway Company had brought in strike-breaking labour and ejected strikers from their company houses, 1891.

France, as in many Continental countries, there was a two-tier freight system, parcel (*grande vitesse*), carried in passenger trains, and goods (*petite vitesse*), carried on special freight trains. Parcels thus came into the Gare du Nord, the splendid Paris terminal of the network opened in 1846 and rebuilt and extended in 1864. So much of the station was given over to the passengers, who by 1863 numbered 2.1 million annually, that a special parcels depot was built next to the station proper in 1889. But in 1899 the principle of transporting all parcels by passenger train was abandoned and a new parcels station (Paris-Messageries) was established at the rue du Faubourg-Saint-Denis. Even this proved insufficient for both receipt and dispatch of parcels, so domestic parcel dispatch was moved in 1903 to La Chapelle.[29]

The original Nord goods station was opened at La Chapelle-Saint-Denis in 1842. Over the years, the traffic swelled to such an extent that La Chapelle eventually expanded to form four separate stations: La Chapelle-Intérieure, La Chapelle-Charbons, La Chapelle-Triage, and La Chapelle-Annexe. In 1856 a special coal station was established (La Chapelle-Charbons) and in 1864, as a result of Baron Haussmann's building boom, a station was set up to receive building materials, particularly finished stone. But in 1878 the building goods station was merged with the coal station and La Chapelle-Annexe was built to receive all bulk goods, including building materials. In 1873 the Nord network purchased the Saint-Ouen Docks and turned the reception centre for water-borne goods there into a major goods station, linked to La Chapelle by rail. Finally in 1886 La Chapelle-Triage, a marshalling station, was created to co-ordinate traffic for all the Nord goods stations and was linked to the Gare du Bourget (1884), a regulating station for ensuring transit between Nord and the other networks. By 1886 La Chapelle covered 60 hectares of land, and it was lit by electric light from 1877. A further major goods station had been opened in 1876 at La Plaine Saint-Denis to supplement the activities of the others and by 1904 still another was required at Gennevilliers. By the peak year of 1913, these stations between them were receiving 5,791,700 tonnes of goods.

This grand total included 1,837,500 tonnes of combustibles, 925,600 tonnes of building materials, 809,800 tonnes of foodstuffs, 525,100 tonnes of metallurgical products, 340,400 tonnes of chemicals and industrial products, 280,600 tonnes of papers and textiles, and 108,100 tonnes of ceramics and glass. As everywhere else, coal formed the principal bulk freight, a quarter of all the tonnage of the Nord stations in Paris; its destinations were industrial, domestic, and public utility use. It was a sixfold increase in coal traffic between 1850 and 1855 that had prompted the building of La Chapelle-Charbons. By 1862, La Chapelle was receiving 565,000 tonnes of coal, 364,000 tonnes from Belgium, dispatched principally from Erquelines and Quévy Stations, and 194,000 tonnes from the North French coalfields, dispatched chiefly from Somain and Lens stations. By 1896 La Chapelle was receiving more than a million tonnes, but by now the bulk of it was French and only a small proportion Belgian, testimony to the industrialization that had taken place in the wake of the railways.

Building materials—stone, wood, bricks, sand, and gravel—were next in importance and were the principal traffic from certain stations, notably Gennevilliers, Saint-Ouen-les-Docks, and La Chapelle-Annexe. There was, as in England, the usual wide variety of foodstuffs and produce. In 1913, 150,000 tons of unrefined sugar arrived at the Nord stations, 85 per cent of it at La Chapelle-Charbons. This was seasonal traffic, between October and December, and was largely a Nord monopoly, dispatched from Valois, Soissonnais, and Santerre. The three great grain stations were La Chapelle-Intérieure, La Plaine-Saint-Denis, and Saint-Ouen-les-Docks, which between them received a quarter of all the grain and a fifth of all the flour brought into Paris by train. It came in the form of imports from the ports of Dunkirk, Le Tréport, Dieppe, and Rouen, or from home-grown stocks dispatched from stations in the Vexin, Valois, and Picardy.

Fruit and vegetable production was localized and seasonal. Thus May–June saw the arrival of new potatoes from Algeria, June–August peas and August–October beans from the Soissons region, July–October cauliflowers from Saint-Omer, October–December potatoes from Flanders, and all the year round mushrooms from Chantilly and Villers-Cotterêts and watercress from Duvy, Clermont, Senlis, and Nanteuil. Wine arrived usually at Saint-Ouen and La Plaine Saint-Denis. Only a sixth of Paris's milk came in on the Nord network, the biggest importer being Etat. The total for 1913 was around 60 million litres. There was a special Paris station (Paris-Bestiaux) for the meat market at La Villette, where 2,476,149 head of livestock arrived in 1913. Only 34,690 head were handled by La Chapelle. The First World War represented a major turning-point. Thereafter, with the rise of road transport, there was a slow, steady, and continuing decline in the amount of freight carried by rail. But the Nord goods stations went through one more transformation in 1937 when, in pursuit of efficiency and stream-lining, all the goods depots were merged into a single, centralized complex with a single controlling authority, a *chef de gare principal*. It was typical of moves that were to take place on other systems. But nothing was to stem the loss of traffic to the road. The reign of King Steam was moving peacefully to its close.

The Station in the Economy (2)
The Non-European World

IN Britain the development of the railways followed the Industrial Revolution, accelerated its impact, and pressed it forward into a new phase. But almost everywhere else in the world, railways were the necessary engine of the nineteenth-century world economic integration which followed that revolution. It is true that oceanic, river, lake, and only rudimentary land transport had been responsible for the extension of Christendom and the transfer of Iberian culture to Latin America and elsewhere, for the establishment of Dutch power in the East, British hegemony in India, French authority in North Africa, and the carving out of the great territories of white settlement. But it was the railway which pressed forward the industrialization of the United States and of parts of Europe and which confirmed the continental power of Europeans in North America, Asia, Australasia, and Africa. The railway acted as a great consolidator, confirming strategic power and opening up new areas for settlement, industrial markets, mineral extraction, and the production of raw materials and foodstuffs.

The railway station lay at the heart of all these developments. In the late nineteenth and early twentieth centuries the railways were like a great international grid, and the railway stations, freight yards, and depots were like power stations, sub-stations, and power-points on that grid. But this was a system which was slow to develop. In Britain, Europe, and the eastern United States it is perhaps customary to think of the decades from the 1830s to the 1880s as the great era of railway-building. But in much of the rest of the world, the extension of the railways was to be a characteristic of the period from 1890 to the 1920s. In Latin America, in North and South Africa, in some parts of Asia, and in the Australasian colonies, there had been tentative beginnings to railway-building in the middle of the century, but the great explosion of lines was not to come until its last decade. Even in India, where railway-building developed rapidly between the 1860s and 1880s, the crucial feeder lines most important to the exploitation of India's resources were only built in the twenty years before the First World War. In Canada, Siberia, and the Far East, in the trans-Andean regions of Latin America and in Africa, the heroic building period was to come in the years when the railways stood on the threshold of being overtaken by new transportation developments, the internal-combustion engine and later the aeroplane. In the Canadian prairies and in some parts of Africa the last branch lines constructed in the 1920s were obsolete almost as soon as they were built. The lorry, with its greater flexibility and convenience to farmers and country shippers, was about to take over. What the lorry did for goods, the omnipresent omnibus soon did for passengers. Transportation systems have a habit of being overtaken by new technology even as they reach their apogee. The railways had done it to the canals and now it was to happen in turn to the railways.

It is this speed of development of alternative means of land transport which helped to produce the 'new' economic history's approach to railways in the 1960s. By then railways were no longer fashionable, and the financial shenanigans of the nineteenth-century railway-builders were all too open to exposure. So the role of railways in the late nineteenth-century economic order was decried.[1] The old vision of the centrality of the railways was replaced by a set of counterfactual conditionals, estimations of the extent to which development could have taken place without the railway. However true this may be for the economic development of the United States—and even there such contentious hypotheticals are highly dubious—it certainly cannot hold good for European expansion and supremacy in the later nineteenth century. Railways were crucial to the erection of the new specialized and integrated economic order. So far as white settlement is concerned, the rapid peopling of the Canadian prairies and north country, of southern, central, and eastern Africa could not have taken place at such a speed without the railway. Such settlement, indeed, took place just in time, before the First World War created a whole new set of conditions.

When the great wave of railway-building took place at the end of the nineteenth century, the old industrial commodities of iron, coal, and cotton were still important, but they were now joined by many others. There was a renewed interest in gold and other precious metals, but base metals like copper, lead, and zinc took on a new significance, together with a whole range of new raw materials and foodstuffs. What amounted to a second phase in the Industrial Revolution accelerated world integration and specialization, confirming the division of the world's peoples into industrial workers in Europe and the eastern United States and producers of raw materials and foodstuffs elsewhere. And these two blocks of people would be united by railway lines and steamships, inseparably associated with each other through the railway station and the port.

Few railway lines were built for non-economic reasons. A few branches were constructed for 'refreshment' and tourism, like the hill-station lines in India. The Hejaz line in the Middle East was primarily designed to take pilgrims to Mecca and Medina. In one or two places railways were said to have been built to alleviate famine. In India some lines were laid down to expedite famine relief. In Japan the stimulus for the building of the first railway line came from a famine in 1869. The British emissary, Sir Harry Parkes, urged that a railway line should be built to ensure that it would not happen again, and the first line, connecting Tokyo to Yokohama, was duly opened in 1872. Many railway lines were dubbed strategic, but strategy and economics are so inseparably intertwined that it is a meaningless exercise to attempt to separate them. Thus, for example, the 'strategic' lines of India were ultimately concerned with the protection of Britain's vital economic interests in the Subcontinent.

For the rest, all railways had economic origins, even if some were based on known resources, while others were planned in the hope of creating new economic opportunity. The few short railway lines of southern Africa were galvanized into rapid growth by the discovery of diamonds and gold between 1869 and 1885. Gold was the propelling force in New South Wales and Western Australia, British Columbia, and the Yukon. (The Whitehorse and Yukon railway did, however, eventually carry many more tourists than prospectors or miners.) Coal in India, copper in Central Africa, tin in Malaysia, silver in Mexico, and nitrates and copper in the Andes all drew railways to them like lightning to its earth. Elsewhere, railway lines tapped more effectively crops which had formerly been transported on water, by animals, or by porters. This was the case with ground-nuts, cocoa, and palm-oil in West Africa, cotton and gums in Egypt and the Sudan, sugar in the West Indies, Natal, Queensland, and elsewhere, cotton, jute, and tea in India. Finally, the railway was the vital engine of settlement and of the opening of vast regions to new crops, in the prairies of Canada and the plains of the United States, the interior of East Africa, the tea-growing mountain areas of Ceylon, the Argentine pampas, the stock-rearing and fruit-growing areas of Australia and New Zealand, and the rubber plantations of Malaya. Although there had been considerable Russian settlement in Asia before the railway age, it was not until the building of the Central Asian and Trans-Siberian lines that settlement, and with it the exploitation of minerals and other natural resources, really took off.

There has been no greater continuity in the economic power of railways than in tapping minerals. The first railway line in Bengal, the forerunner of the entire East India Railway network, was built to exploit the coal of Raniganj. The line to the Zambezi in Central Africa was diverted to run through the Wankie coalfields, while one of the largest projects in the inter-war years in Africa was designed to tap the coal of the Tete province of Mozambique. The particular suitability of railways to carry bulk minerals like coal cheaply has ensured that the connection between the railways and such minerals has been maintained to the present day. New railway lines have been built in British Columbia, Australia, Siberia, and elsewhere to exploit coal and other minerals. These recent ones are, however, often specialized railways without passengers or conventional stations. In the late nineteenth century, minerals acted as lead sectors for other aspects of economic growth, encouraging migration, urbanization, and cash-cropping in large regions of the world. Moreover, geopolitics have played a role in duplicating lines to land-locked deposits. The copper of Central Africa has struggled to find outlets south, west, east, and north, creating vital junction stations and new communites in the process.

Although imperial lines, like the Canadian Pacific and the Grand Trunk Pacific in Canada or the Uganda and Cape to Cairo railways in Africa, stole the British headlines since they enhanced so many colonial myths, British investment and railway-building were more considerable and in many respects more potent in the Anglo-American 'informal Empire' of Latin America. The journalist and geographer Percy F. Martin visited Latin America just as this process was reaching a great peak in the early years of this century. On his journey 'through five republics' (Argentina, Brazil, Chile, Uruguay, and Venezuela) in 1905 he devoted more attention to railways than to any other single development.[2] British companies had to build their lines between revolutions and had to be prepared to accept the damage to bridges, track, and stations caused by civil war and insurgency, but the opportunities presented in the wheat-growing and stock-rearing of Argentina, the coffee, rubber, and minerals of Brazil, the gold, silver, copper, nitrates, and sheep-farming of Chile, the cattle of Uruguay, and the sugar, coffee, cocoa, tobacco, cotton, and cattle of Venezuela seemed at that time limitless. Even Caracas in Venezuela, a small capital as South American cities went, could boast four railway stations. But although there was a multiplicity of (short) railway systems in Venezuela, its relative lack of railway development matched its comparative economic backwardness.

In his two-volume *Mexico of the Twentieth Century* (1907) Martin moved on to examine British investment and influence in that country. 'Five and twenty years ago', he wrote, 'who in all the earth would have invested his money in a Mexican bank; have trusted his savings in a Mexican mine; or have considered it a safe and prudent thing to go to Mexico at all?'[3] Part of the answer for the change by 1907 lay in the fact that by then Mexico had 20,000 miles of telegraph lines and 17,000 miles of railways. To make the country even more civilized the railways were embarking on building great hotels by their stations for the first time. Stations, hotels, and all other railway works were capitalized on the mineral riches which had first attracted the Spanish. Mexico produced no less than one-third of all the world's silver, together with copper, lead, gold, and many agricultural products. In his survey of each of the states of Mexico, Martin linked the extent of their prosperity and economic integration directly to railway-building. It was these mineral riches which enabled so many Latin American railway companies to build grandiose stations for a passenger traffic which formed an insignificant part of their revenues, to flatter a national vanity which demanded a new 'civic excess' in the period.

Coal was, of course, always central to the railways. Not only were lines built to tap it, not only did almost every station become a distribution centre in all those areas where the fossil fuel was vital for domestic and industrial use, but trains themselves in many countries ran on it. Divisional stations stockpiled coal. Its dust penetrated to all corners of such stations and lumps of coal, as well as cinders, littered the tracks. Coal was labour-intensive and the need to move it around the station and load it into engine tenders required large numbers of labourers. In Europe and in North America automatic coal hoists were introduced and became yet another stark element in the silhouette of many stations, but where labour was cheap, loading was done by the most primitive of methods, by men running up ramps with baskets on their heads.

But coal was not universal as engine fuel. In Russian Central Asia the engines were designed to burn the naphtha left over after the refining of the petroleum from the Central Asian oilfields. This was a process which fascinated George Curzon, the future Viceroy of India, when he travelled on the line in 1888 soon after its opening. 'The tenders for the year 1889', he wrote, 'specified the total amount required as 6 million gallons. Large reservoirs of this naphtha are kept at the superior stations, the tank at Askabad containing 80,000 gallons, and it is transported along the line in cistern cars, holding 2,400 gallons each.'[4] Here was a striking portent of things to come.

But wood was a much more common fuel for engines, and the appearance of railways and the provision of stations had the power to change the appearance of vast regions. The building of the Trans-Siberian, it was noted in 1900, had led to the systematic extermination of the forests of Siberia, for the construction of the line and its stations and for fuel for the workers and engines. Similar deforestation took place in Canada and in Africa. In Canada, so profligate were railway-builders and settlers of the country's timber resources that huge fires were started to clear areas. Where coal was used as engine fuel, the divisional stations became overshadowed by their enormous woodpiles. On the Lobito Bay line through Angola, so dependent were the engines on wood that re-afforestation had to be undertaken to keep the engines supplied. The fast-growing, drought-resistant eucalyptus was imported for this purpose and the appearance of an entire region was transformed by the importation of an alien tree.

As well as the flora, railways had a devastating effect on the fauna of the regions they penetrated. The hunting of game meat, particularly in Africa, was a vital support system for the builders of the lines and, for a few years at least, for those who ran them. Hunting was a common pursuit of station-masters in game-rich areas in Canada and the United States, above all in Mozambique, Rhodesia, Kenya, and elsewhere in Africa. But apart from hunting for the pot, there was often a requirement to hunt dangerous predators to protect railway employees. The most famous such incident was the case of 'the man-eaters of Tsavo' in the building of the East Africa line.[5] Both there and in the lion-infested flats of Mozambique, the water-towers of stations became redoubts against the marauders. It was at stations that the carcasses, horns, and tusks of successful hunts were often displayed. Soon the hunters who travelled by rail hunted not for food or protection, but for trophies and sport. Armed to the teeth, they were to be seen in North America, Africa, and Asia and many stations became notable as jumping-off points for hunting expeditions. When Winston Churchill visited East Africa in 1906 as Under-Secretary of State for the colonies, his private coach was frequently detached at station sidings along the line so that the distinguished Nimrod could go hunting near by.[6] In the early days, both in the United States and in Africa, some even hunted from the railway carriages themselves, but very soon the game was being driven further and further from the railway lines. The retreat and disappearance of game was lamented in countless travel- and guide-books.

Many lines were designed to tap peasant production: for example, ground-nuts, cocoa, palm-oil in West Africa, cotton, jute, and rice in India, rice in Burma, cotton in Egypt, and so on. In all these areas the country stations and the great freight yards of the main cities represented the concentration of the staple crop. India was perhaps the classic case. In Bombay, cotton was king; in Calcutta and Dacca jute supreme. In such areas station design had to take account of the nature of the main crop and of the manner in which that crop was fed into the station by the producers. The produce was brought to the station by a multiplicity of carts and wagons drawn by oxen, ponies, mules, camels, or even on the backs of elephants. The station had to have yards large enough for hundreds of such vehicles to be marshalled, areas where the animals could be tethered or grazed, perhaps for days. Sir Bartle Frere, the Governor of Bombay in the 1860s and a great enthusiast for railways, pointed out to his London masters that for these reasons the Indian station required three or four times more space than its British counterpart. Moreover, the large city or freight terminals had to have massive capacity to cope with intense seasonal pressures. In the country districts, so great was the pressure of traffic to the stations that the approach roads were so worn as to be impassable, and in wet weather were impossible quagmires. One of Frere's subordinates, the Collector of Dharwar, wrote to him:

I write from here while the senses of smell and sight are still suffering acutely from the dreadful state of the approaches to the stations at Kandalia and Campoolie . . . About two or three hundred yards of road approaching either of these stations is absolutely half knee-deep in the most offensive and malarious black mud. It is disgraceful to our Public Works Department, most unhealthy to the wretched people, European and native, who have to live in the neighbourhood, and most offensive to all railway passengers.[7]

There could be no more vivid illustration of the manner in which the railway station acted as a magnet for all the vehicles of its locality. Similar concentrations of peasant products could be encountered at stations on other continents. In Brazil, hundreds of ponies brought bales of cotton to stations. There is a photograph of just such a scene at Vicosa Station on the Alagoas section of the Great Western Railway of Brazil.[8]

Elsewhere in India and in Central Asia, the railway station became the new setting for an ancient trade. Central Asian merchants bringing raw materials to the carpet-making, silk, gold, silver-thread, and ribbon manufactories of Amritsar took to the train. In turn, Amritsar became the depot for piece goods, copper, and brass which were destined for the Central Asian markets. At the other end of the Central Asian connection, the economic changes wrought by the great Russian Asian railways were particularly striking. In 1873 there was only one Russian merchant in Bukhara. As late as 1885, the agents of the Russian Commercial Company lived there almost as prisoners of the Amir. By 1888, however, when the trans-Caspian railway had been opened to Bukhara, the situation had been transformed. A whole range of Russian banks and commercial agencies had opened there, and the stations themselves reflected the quickening of the commercial tempo. As a contemporary German writer, Dr Heyfelder, wrote:

In the summer of 1888 landowners from Poltawa came to the Amir's dominion and bought up live sheep in Kara Kul, which they took home by the railway. From Moscow came buyers of lambskins; from Asia Minor, French dealers for the export of walnut-trees; from the Caucasus, Armenians and Jews, who bought huge quantities of carpets, so that the price was almost doubled. Not a single foreigner who attended the opening ceremonies, not one of the travellers from France, England, Italy, and Russia, who have journeyed over the half-finished line, went away without purchasing some silks, embroideries, metal-work, arms, or knives. But they also brought with them European innovations; and already, in the winter of 1888, the bazaars were stocked with articles never before seen: porcelain, lamps, glasses, mirrors, brushes, writing materials, coffee, preserves, biscuits. At the railway stations appeared cards, cigars, beer, wine, brandy (the sale of which on their own soil the Bokhariots have prohibited by agreement) . . . Moreover, some engineers have constructed the station-buildings in beautifully hewn freestone and marble from the neighbouring rocks, as an example to the Sarmatians for the use of their rich mountain stones and marbles.[9]

Even in Central Asia, the railway and its stations were helping to make the world one. Nowhere was the process of imperial specialization more apparent than on the Trans-Siberian railway. The manganese and iron ores of the Urals were linked to great coalfields 1,250 miles further east. The vast grain production of Western Siberia could now be distributed throughout the Russian Empire, and the Chinese Eastern Railway (built by the Russians) hoped to tap the riches of Manchuria in gold, iron, coal, soda, cattle, silkworms, rice, tobacco, ginseng, and the opium poppy. The 1900 *Guide to the Great Siberian Railway* marked out for travellers the important stations in these new trading networks. Belebey, Aksakovo, and Develekanovo were important stations for grain exports; Osharovka and Kryazh for cattle and animal products; Samara for grain, cattle, and tallow. Further east, Yurganysh had a settlement of corn merchants near the station; Kurgan was important for butter and grain; Omsk for meat, hides, and grain; while timber came from any number of sources. Travellers on Indian railways similarly had their attention drawn to the important products shipped through the stations *en route*: Bangalore for grain and cotton, Dacca for jute, and so on.

Subsequent extensions to the Siberian system continued this process of creating complementary economies. The Turkistan–Siberian (or Turksib) line was built between 1928 and 1931 so that the grain of Western Siberia could be exchanged for the cotton of Central Asia, releasing the Central Asian cotton-growers from the need for food production. This complementarity was, of course, developed through the massive emigration which the Trans-Siberian made possible from European Russia. That was but one of the great waves of migration which took Europeans to the New World, Africa, and Asia in the period.

While a great deal has been written about railways in migration, little notice has been taken of the role of the railway station. Throughout western Canada and the United States, in the interior of Latin America, in Australasia and the settler territories of Africa, the provision of railway stations was the vital adjunct of settlement. Although railway-building in North America has been described above as 'quintessentially capitalist', in fact railway companies were prepared to build to the West only in return for massive inducements. The American western railroads received no fewer than 155 million acres of land as subsidies and guarantees. Not all of the conditions of these land grants were fulfilled, but the companies still secured almost 140 million acres. At a time when vast tracts were unsettled, it was all too easy for governments to be profligate. Most western towns were created by the railroad land grant companies. They had, according to Dee Brown, a 'drab uniformity', with the station painted a sombre colour, a water tank, a grain elevator, and a bleak main street.[10] In Canada, the Canadian Pacific Railway was provided with a subsidy of 25 million dollars and land grants amounting to 25 million acres.[11] Such liberal financing added to the wealth and power of the railway magnates, and turned the railway into an immigrant and land agency on a grand scale. The CPR created no fewer than 600 new communities with villages, towns, and farming settlements growing out from the railway stations.

This process was to gain momentum in the last three decades of the nineteenth century, reaching a peak in the years before the First World War. This was truly the boom era in western Canada. In the early 1870s there were only 23,000 people west of Lake Superior. In 1875 there were 5,800 miles of railway line in Canada; by 1935 there were 45,000 miles. At first Canadian settlement had been largely along the border with the United States, south of the 50th parallel, and American railway companies had taken Canadian grain to the world market. The Canadian

Pacific, in both its western and its eastern guises, had been designed to alleviate this dependence, to keep Canadian grain on Canadian metals and shipped through Canadian ports. It therefore took a southerly route across the prairie provinces of the Dominion. It had indeed been thought that the climate was too severe for wheat to grow further north, but the richness of the soil there, the abundance of river and lake water, and the intensity of the short summer soon exploded this theory. The Grand Trunk Pacific Railway, chartered by a Canadian Liberal government in 1904, was designed to exploit these vast northern regions. It was suggested that no fewer than 300 million acres of grain-growing land were opened up by this railway.[12] Moreover, it transformed the fortunes of the northern prairie cities. In 1903 there were only 113 people in Saskatoon; in 1910 there were 14,000. Edmonton in 1901 had a population of 2,626; by 1910 there were 30,000. Within ten years, the GTP had created between Winnipeg and Edson 120 new towns with a total population of 50,000. Many more were created in British Columbia and in northern Ontario in the same period.

But although the GTP produced a massive land boom, it was not given the vast land grants of its predecessor, the CPR. The Liberals chartered the GTP specifically as an act of defiance to the Canadian Conservative party and its allies on the CPR. Different, liberal, techniques had to be used. An election was fought and massively won on the issue in 1904. The GTP was given land grants only for its line from Lake Superior Junction on the main line to Fort William on Lake Superior (a distance of 188 miles). It received a subsidy of 6,000 acres per mile. Together with the Temiskamming and Northern Ontario Railway it also opened up northern Ontario, which was discovered not only to be good for settlement, but also to possess staggering mineral resources in copper, gold, silver, zinc, and cobalt.[13] In addition to opening up the northern prairies, it produced a land boom in northern British Columbia, where land values rose from 50 cents an acre to 30–60 dollars an acre in the space of a few years, and created a new Pacific port at Prince Rupert, 500 miles north of Vancouver, a new town where the population reached 5,000 in the space of two years. All this was happening at a time when the Canadian Northern Railway was creating, in effect, a *third* transcontinental railway, built on much more economical lines than the exceptionally expensive and high-quality GTP. There can be no doubt that all this constituted, as D. B. Hanna put it, 'calamitous overbuilding', and trapped many investors still enthralled by nineteenth-century railway booms. Many would lose a great deal as a result.

Wherever railway lines were to go, settlers eager to secure land bargains just preceded them. When the GTP was built, settlers had begun to develop the land along its route to such an extent that construction trains had to bring back wheat despite the unfinished nature of the track. Town 'boomers' also preceded the railway builders, hoping to secure land where new towns would grow up. Such an atmosphere inevitably produced intense speculation as to the route of the line, the positioning of small towns and of the more important divisional points. But the speculators were not always successful. Even although stations were established every four to nine miles along this immense line of rail, the boomers often chose the wrong spots. As F. A. Talbot put it:

Commercial interests always flocked around the point where the train stopped to take up and set down passengers and merchandise. The railway station became the hub of the community within a certain surrounding radius.[14]

And he went on to describe the manner in which the station made and broke settlements:

The speculating element had pushed far ahead of the line into Alberta along the location, and a place called Denwood sprang up. True, it was but a small village, but the fact was maintained that the railway would have to establish their station at that point. The speculators tolerated a rough-and-ready existence for several months, dwelling in rude shacks and tents, and subsisting as best they could. The future of Denwood was their sole topic of conversation, and many a pioneer built a magnificent castle in the air. The outlook was considered all the more rosy from their point of view, since Denwood would have to be made what is known as a divisional point, that is to say, a station of more than ordinary importance, inasmuch as it would indicate the end of a running section—the point where the train would have to change engines. Consequently round houses, extensive sidings, and various buildings essential to the railway's purpose would have to spring up, and these in their turn would require labour, which would have to live in the vicinity. From the flamboyant tone in which the speculators discussed the prospects for Denwood, a stranger within its precincts might have come to the conclusion that he was standing upon ground which was destined to become the Winnipeg of the Middle West.

Any scrap of intelligence regarding the approach of the steel, as the rail-head is called, was devoured and discussed with keen delight. As the line crawled gradually closer and closer excitement and enthusiasm rose to fever pitch. On July 25th, 1908, the rails forced their way into Denwood, and those who had been waiting so long and patiently considered that the prizes were theirs at last. Many a 'boomer' saw his pocket bulging with dollars accruing from the result of his determination and success in being first on the spot. The next day their feelings of joy gave way to dismay. The line continued its progress as if Denwood were at the North Pole. The speculators rubbed their eyes. What! Was Denwood going to be overlooked? The engineers did not know; they could give no intelligible reply. Ah, well, perhaps the steel was pushing ahead with renewed vigour to meet some condition beyond which was not conspicuous to the 'boomers', so they sat down to another period of waiting. Suddenly they learned the truth. Denwood, 'the coming metropolis of the Middle West', despite its attractive situation, was useless to the railway. Their point was 2½ miles farther west, and they had named the station Wainwright. This was to be the divisional point. Then ensued a mad stampede from Denwood. The 'boomers' packed their tents hurriedly, the log buildings were emptied of their contents and demolished, and one and all hurried to Wainwright as best they could, and with what vehicles they could command. Within a few hours Denwood was stripped of everything; there was not a soul or a vestige of its recent occupation to be seen in the place. In a month it was forgotten; it was but a dream, and to-day you might search in vain for the place which enthusiastic optimists averred was the cradle of a second Winnipeg.[15]

Once the railway company and the engineers had decreed where the station was in fact to be located, particularly the larger divisional points, 120–140 miles apart, towns were laid out on the traditional grid-plan. The towns were generally laid out on the northern side of the tracks. The street leading from the station was usually dubbed 'Main Street', with lateral thoroughfares crossing it. Auctions were held to sell off the town lots, those nearest the station being the most expensive. Moreover, restrictions were placed upon these to ensure that they would be developed and not simply held by speculators. Otherwise, 'a stranger detraining and observing the vacant appearance of a town around the station where there should be bustle would think naturally that something serious was the matter'.[16]

Once the several grades of station were built (see Chapter 2), the distinctive economic elements of the prairie station, the grain elevator and (sometimes) the stock pens, would reflect the whole life of the community and its local region. Although the GTP has been used as a late and well-documented model, the same developments could be found wherever the 'colonizing roads' went in North America. As the local elevators filled with grain, laden trains conveyed it to the lake-head shipping points, where the world's largest elevators dominated the stations at Port Arthur and Fort William in Canada and, of course, at Chicago in the United States. The growth in this traffic was staggering. The CPR carried 3.9 million bushels of grain in 1882; 7.8 million bushels in 1885; 29.3 million bushels in 1892; 42.8 million at the end of the century; and 175.5 million in 1921.[17] The growth between the latter two dates was achieved at a time when the GTP and the Canadian

Northern were themselves turning into grain-carrying lines. The passenger traffic through the hundreds of stations created by the CPR and its rivals exhibited a similar expansion. In 1882 the CPR carried only 317,841 passengers. By 1886, the first year after the completion of the transcontinental line, the figure was 1,665,960. In 1890, 4.6 million passengers were carried; 8.3 million in 1902; 22.3 million in 1913 (the peak year), falling back to 20.5 million in 1920 after the lean war years when immigration largely fell away.[18] Such a dramatic movement of peoples could not have been undertaken by any other contemporary transportation method, and must reflect remarkable activity at the hundreds of newly built stations throughout the system.

In northern Ontario, railways that had originally been designed as 'colonization roads' to link tiny pioneering agricultural communities and to increase settlement in the 'clay belt' had become instead 'prospecting roads' in the remarkable scramble for the mineral riches of the area which developed in Edwardian times. In 1904 the Ontario Provincial Geologist, impressed by the quantities of the rare mineral cobalt he had detected in the ores of one locality, Long Lake, put up a post with a board attached bearing the legend 'Cobalt Station, Temiskamming and Northern Ontario Railway'. As S. A. Pain put it, 'The idea caught on at once, the station was built, and received its famous name'.[19] Soon afterwards a gold rush developed to an area known as the Porcupine goldfields. The prospectors, unlike their predecessors in many parts of the world, were able to go by train:

Clad in their khaki-coloured canvas, with slouch hat, high, thick-soled boots, with a tin mug strapped to their belt, and their gunny-sack crammed to bursting point with gold-pan, pick, axe, and other impedimenta, they left the railway at Kelso, the railway point nearest the gold fields. Even this station was in embryo. There was no platform, not a building to indicate its whereabouts, nothing but a small board nailed to a decapitated tree trunk with the name inscribed thereon in white letters upon a black background. A magnificent station replete with various buildings will rise there some day, but its time is not yet.[20]

The railways in Russian Asia also had the power to make and break cities. The Trans-Siberian railway bypassed Tomsk some sixty miles to the south. Until that time Tomsk, with Irkutsk, had been the most important city in Siberia. The wealth and power of Tomsk were irreparably damaged, and supremacy passed to Novosibirsk, the 'Chicago of the Soviet Union', a small settlement which became a great city simply because it was on the main line. There is a story, probably apocryphal, that the surveyors had demanded a bribe of the merchants of Tomsk to take the railway there. They had refused, convinced that their city was so important it could not be avoided.[21] In Central Asia, the train was known as the 'Devil's Wagon' and the rulers of Bukhara stipulated that the line should pass the old city at a distance of ten miles. The Russians proceeded to lay out a new town. Plots of land were taken up by commercial companies near the imposing station, the Russian Agent moved there, and Bukharan merchants and others from the old city flocked there. As Curzon noted:

In another decade the new Bokhara will have attracted to itself much of the importance of the ancient city, and with its rise and growth the prestige of the latter must inevitably decline. Thus, by a seeming concession to native sentiment, the Russians are in reality playing their own game.[22]

In the United States, the various railway companies were known by the products which supplied the freight profits which underpinned the passenger business and therefore the stations. Fifty per cent of the traffic of the Vanderbilt lines in the late nineteenth century was in grain; the Pennsylvania was dependent on iron and coal; the Hill lines on cotton and lumber; the Rock Island, more diversified, on corn and cotton, timber and iron, precious metals and fruit; the Atchison on corn and cattle; the Chicago and North-Western on iron ore.[23] The installations of the great freight yards and stations of these systems reflected these concerns and Chicago represented them most profoundly of all.

Chicago was made by the railway. Its 1½ square miles of business district were completely surrounded by railway tracks and terminals. Twenty-five trunk lines went into Chicago and most of them had attendant freight and passenger depots. As one writer put it, all trains went to Chicago and none passed through. In 1912 it was said that the rail freight yards of the city handled 112,000 tons of freight per day.[24] 307 million bushels of grain passed through the city's elevators in 1907, representing an 88 per cent increase over 1887. Her eighty-seven elevators could store almost 60 million bushels, more than the entire annual load of the Canadian Pacific. Three and a half million head of cattle were moved to the great stock yards by rail each year, together with 8 million hogs and 5 million sheep. These stock yards covered 500 acres and could accommodate at any one time 75,000 cattle, 125,000 sheep, 300,000 hogs, and 6,000 horses. Chicago had to be supplied by a mass of smaller stations where grain and stock were loaded. There were 800 grain elevators at stations on the Northern Pacific alone.

Chicago was, of course, a massive centre of collection and distribution, a key point in America's export system. A host of smaller cities and towns were supplied with the foodstuffs and manufacturing goods essential for the rapidly developing American living standards of the day. Every American city had its multiplicity of freight stations, with more sidings, land, and staff lavished upon them than the greatest of the passenger terminals. In many places the freight yards were more carefully and conveniently located, as in Carl Condit's Cincinnati, than the passenger stations themselves.[25]

These freight stations, like their European counterparts, were febrile centres of activity, collecting and distributing all manner of goods. They had transformed what some writers saw as being the traditional American way of life. The Americans, wrote Frank Spearman in 1905, had become a 'hand-to-mouth' people:

> The last generation laid in its supplies in the fall for the winter; this generation buys from day to day. The country merchant bought then twice a year; he now buys twice a week. Why carry stock when trains run so often and it has been made so easy to get goods? The travelling man no longer makes a sixty-day trip. He sees his trade once a week or once in two weeks, and covers three or four towns in a day.[26]

Railways, Spearman went on, had the power to break local strikes, as they had done in a recent coal strike in the United States, and the operating officers and freight-yard superintendents took on a military-style power. They moved battalions, controlled division staffs, and were, in effect, 'the field marshals of our daily bread'.[27] John Droege, in his *Freight Terminals and Trains* of 1912, also wrote of freight-station masters in heroic terms, 'men of the hour, men of initiative and resourcefulness', constantly in 'action—consistent, insistent, persistent'.[28] They were like generals in command of armies, receiving, sorting, dispatching thousands of vehicles in an irregular flow, fighting their great enemy, blockade.

This massive power was to last only three or four decades, but as late as 1916, 77 per cent of all inter-city freight traffic in the United States went by rail (much of the balance was water-borne), and 98 per cent of all passengers took the train. Railway revenues constituted 8 per cent of the gross national product, and 4 per cent of all those employed in the United States—about 1.7 million people—worked for the railways.[29] After the depression of the 1890s and the dilapidation of many of the lines, the companies were able to make a remarkable resurgence in the early decades of the twentieth century before their terminal decline.

In 1923, on the eve of that decline, American railways passed 2,200 million tons of freight and 1,250 million passengers through their stations. But by 1925, when Droege published the second edition of his

Freight Terminals, the truck was making its ominous presence felt. In the years since the First World War, trucks had come to transport 100 million tons of farm produce per annum directly to the cities.[30]

North America provides, of course, the most striking instance of European settlement on a grand scale. But wherever Whites went to settle they clamoured for railway stations. The presence of a nearby station obviously greatly enhanced the value of land. The building of branch lines could transform a previously struggling region. Not surprisingly, the building of branch lines and the provision of freight sidings never failed to create controversy. In Ceylon each new highland railway project was attended by public meetings, agitations, and petitions by white plantation owners hoping to secure the most favourable route and the most convenient placing of stations. In eastern and central Africa the value of 'white' land was often directly related to its proximity to the railway station. The cost of human or animal-borne transport was so great that the economic viability of white farming rapidly declined as the distance from the station increased. White settlers on the line of rail from Umtali (Mtare) to Salisbury (Harare) demanded that stations should be established at suitably frequent intervals near them. Branch lines were arranged to tap either mineral resources or new areas of settlement. Africans were moved further and further from the line of rail, reflecting the fact that in settler territories their main economic contribution was to be labour for the Whites. For them stations would act principally as a means of access to the labour market in mines, farms, and towns, not as a route to the world market for their produce. In the 1920s and 1930s such distinctions in land and station use were given even more precise legislative sanctions. Norman Leys, a doctor critical of white settlement in Kenya, noted that the branch lines there were designed to support white areas, particularly the vast estates of Kenyan settlers like Lord Delamere and E. S. Grogan.[31] They carefully avoided the black peasant producing regions which would probably have been more beneficial to the Kenyan economy.

As well as playing a role in grand economic affairs, world-wide integration no less, the station was vital in small-scale local economic relations. In Ceylon it was discovered that mountain areas could produce fresh vegetables which could be conveyed from local stations to Colombo to provision passing ocean liners. The extension of the Ceylon railways southwards enabled the fishermen of the Galle coast to send their fish to Colombo. Stations became associated with certain products: Dehiwala for fish, Dodanduwa for plumbago and coir rope, Ambawela for vegetables.[32]

Although the railways were crucial to tea-growing and marketing from Ceylon—because of the absence of other suitable forms of transportation—tea was successfully brought out from Assam by elephant, 'country boat', and steamer for several decades before the arrival of the railway. But in the Darjeeling districts and in Assam a complex railway network soon became a vital part of the supply system and comforts of the white tea planters. The railways brought coal to fuel the tea factories, and above all transported labour to work the plantations. Recruitment took place in Bengal as well as in South India, and the remarkably comprehensive Murray's *Handbook* pointed out to European travellers the stations where the migrants might be seen entraining for the tea plantations.

Throughout North America, farmers' wives in country districts could be seen boarding local trains, often known as 'butter and egg specials', bearing a basket of eggs and some home-churned butter for the market at the local town. A once-weekly trip gave them the opportunity to earn some 'pin money' and secure a change of scene from their relatively monotonous round. In Latin America, Africa, and Asia, peasants might make a similar journey to market with a few chickens or other stock and produce if the fare were low enough to leave some profit. As in Britain and Europe, milk churns became a characteristic of stations everywhere that cows could be kept and a town market found. One example will suffice. The tiny 'Cordwood Ltd.' line on British Columbia's Vancouver Island, opened in 1894, became the principal supplier of milk to the provincial capital, Victoria. Trains had to wait upon the cows and were frequently late in consequence:

The morning train from Sidney picked up milk from various farms for shipment to Victoria and on at least one occasion it was held up for two hours while cows, that had been turned into the bush the previous night to pick up what nourishment they could were searched for, rounded up, milked and the milk loaded for the trip to town.[33]

The line was a mere eighteen miles long, and there were no fewer than seven stations on its route. The trains which handled the local traffic took ninety minutes for the journey. As the name implied, the line carried timber, but it also conveyed the rather more exotic salmon and clams.

The railway station, then, acted as the collection and distribution point for local, regional, and international economic systems. The local and regional networks were based on the railways with animal power feeding to and distributing from the stations. The international network, at least for the Western imperial system, added a long ocean voyage between two rail journeys. Through the great Asian railways, Russia created a system that was entirely rail-borne. Commodities like fish, milk, and vegetables might be transferred locally; labourers—as in India and Southern Africa —regionally, together with grain, rice, coal, and perhaps some manufactured goods; while the great international transfers included human migrants, cotton from India, Egypt, the United States, and some parts of Africa and Latin America, tea from India and Ceylon, coffee from Latin America, wheat from Canada and the United States, gold from South Africa, silver from Mexico, copper from Central Africa and South America, cattle from the Argentine and the United States, lamb, wool, and dairy products from Australasia. In the other direction countless stations throughout the world were the distribution points for manufactured goods. Cotton piece-goods, pots and pans, hoes and ploughs, all manner of tools, and a host of other commodities arrived by train. It is in this respect that the role of the railway station has been most dramatically transformed. In very few places does this economic function survive. With the exception of bulk traffic like coal and other minerals, the world's collection and distribution systems are now largely operated by road. Great imperial systems propelled by steam have broken down into a myriad nationalities propelled by the internal-combustion engine and oil. Where a great imperial system survives, as in the Soviet Union, the railways retain some semblance of their former power.

10

The Station as Place of Work

MOST railway passengers are oblivious to the fact that where for them the station is a place of arrival, departure, and transition, for many thousands the station is a permanent feature in their lives—their place of work. The coming of the railways called into being a major industry. It grew more rapidly than any other employment in the early and mid-Victorian period. The number of people employed by British railway companies rose from 59,974 in 1850 to 621,340 in 1910. In 1850 railway work was the thirty-third largest occupation in Britain. By 1870 it was sixth largest and involved over 3 per cent of the national work-force. In the United States the total number of railwaymen employed rose from an estimated 7,000 in 1840 to 1,018,00 in 1900.[1]

In the United States, the total work force in 1880 had reached 416,000. Fifteen per cent of them (63,380) were station-men. In Britain in 1910, at the peak of the railways' heyday, 169,572 people worked in stations. This figure comprised 8,688 station-masters, 4,163 ticket-collectors and examiners, 51,707 porters, 4,695 lad porters, 28,658 signalmen, 13,158 shunters, and 58,503 clerks, male and female.

A complex and subtle hierarchy emerged within the industry. Rowland Kenney, who worked in a goods yard in the north of England at the end of the nineteenth century, observed it in action:

> The man in one of the higher grades was regarded as socially superior to the lower grade man. The goods porter was looked upon as an inferior animal by the shunter. The shunter was tolerated as a necessary evil by the goods guard, who had wild hopes that some day he would be able to look a passenger guard squarely in the eyes as a man and brother of equal rank. The nippers, being wiser than we and too young to be snobs, gave us all an equal amount of 'cheek'.[2]

This sort of thing tended to happen everywhere in the railway world. But there were important differences between the old world and the new which reflect the different national histories and cultures.

Agricultural labourers formed the pool from which rural station staff were recruited in Britain and Europe. Their urban counterparts came from the ranks of general labourers very often. But discharged soldiers and sailors, former policemen, and ex-domestic servants, all of them working under discipline, were encouraged. In France and Prussia the law required that a large proportion of railway positions be reserved for ex-soldiers. In the United States the emerging railway industry drew on the rival transport enterprises it was overtaking for staff—shipping, stage-coach, and freight wagon companies.

Everywhere strong family links developed and railway dynasties, spanning the generations, became a regular feature of the pattern of employment. In France the children of employees of the Est network were put to good use assisting the drivers of delivery wagons. They were left on the seat of the wagon while the driver delivered the goods, a practice which, according to F. Jacqmin, the traffic manager of the Est company, put an end to thefts from such wagons. In 1877, ten of these children were serving their apprenticeship at La Villette Station. The Est company also encouraged the widows and womenfolk of employees to serve the company. In country stations, the wives of the station-masters often sold tickets. But at the large stations at Paris, Metz, Nancy, and Strasbourg, almost all the ticket-sellers were female. In 1877 there were ninety-one women running bookstalls, while the widows of employees without means were put in charge of the water-closets and permitted to receive gratuities.[3]

In Britain, staff selection methods were stringent. At least as early as the 1850s there were medical examinations to attest general health, physical strength, and eyesight. Most companies also demanded the ability to read and write from an early date. The General Railway Regulations in Britain in 1877 required that a candidate for porter should be 5 feet 7 inches tall at least, aged between 21 and 35, intelligent, fit, strong, able to read and write, and provided with three character references, one of them from his previous employer. In Britain, France, and the United States financial sureties were required from all grades handling cash: station-masters, ticket-sellers, chief clerks, etc. In Britain the sureties were on a sliding scale from £50 to £1,000 and in the United States from $1,000 to $5,000.

The companies had a clear idea of the sort of employees they wanted. Sir George Findlay, General Manager of the London and North-Western from 1880 to 1893, declared: 'The railway service is pre-eminently one requiring for its efficient conduct a high degree of smartness, alacrity, energy and zeal on the part of every individual engaged in it.'[4] Benjamin C. Burt in his handbook on station service defines the required qualities as 'physical energy, quick powers of observation, fair mathematical ability, good judgement, a certain breadth of information and facility in conversation and in writing, affability of manner, energy of will and loyalty of disposition'.[5]

Railway staff were expected to display encyclopedic knowledge. Writing of the British and American systems in 1878, Marshall M. Kirkman declared: 'One of the tests of an employé's fitness is the extent and accuracy of the information he possesses in reference to train and station service.'[6] American station agents were expected to have at their fingertips the company's rules and regulations, the train schedules, the classification of trains, dining-car and sleeping-car facilities, details of connections with other lines and with steamships. In Britain, the Great Northern Railway required all clerks in charge, inspectors, and foremen porters to master the use of the electric telegraph for emergencies.

Courtesy was a prerequisite and was expected to be maintained heroically even in the most difficult of circumstances. Burt drew attention to

the little trials which the agent at a smaller station undergoes in dealing with people, who, unlike the city folk, do not ride every day, travel only occasionally, and are lacking somewhat in the intelligence which is acquired by an experienced traveller. At such a station many grown people manifest a childish simplicity which is at once annoying and amusing. Often the would-be traveller knows merely the name of the state and county in which his destination may be located; he has never thought to make a little study as to how to get there. And the agent, when he should be taking care of a dozen other passengers, finds himself totally engrossed by the necessity of having to do for the seemingly witless passenger the thinking and investigating which said passenger should have tried to do for himself.[7]

Time has not rectified that situation and the same scene can still be seen being played out daily in stations large and small. Recently British Rail have been sending their staff to courtesy lessons. But it is still not unknown for a polite request for information to be met with the reply: 'Don't ask me, mate. I only work here.'

Discipline was strict. D. B. Hanna, who obtained a clerkship at the Caledonian goods station at Buchanan Street, Glasgow, in 1875, recalled:

The first thing I learned there was that Presbyterian strictness was nothing compared to one brand of railway rigidity. The office was six miles from home, and a few minutes' walk from the South Side passenger station. The first morning train arrived there at nine o'clock. Wishing still to live at home, I asked my immediate superior to excuse me from beginning work until shortly after nine, if I made up the time at noon, or in the evening. He refused; and so, for a year I walked the six miles from Thornliebank six mornings a week.[8]

In Britain the enforcement of discipline was institutionalized in a system of cautions, fines, and ultimately dismissals for misdemeanours, ranging from neglect of duties and unauthorized absence to theft, drunkenness, and damage of railway property. An 1872 circular from the London, Brighton and South Coast Railway to its staff listed the offences recorded in the previous month. They included a booking-clerk dismissed for not accounting for excess fares, a booking-clerk cautioned for erroneously booking a passenger through ignorance of the train service, a telegraph clerk fined for violently using his instrument, a ticket-collector cautioned for incivility, a parcels porter dismissed for being absent without leave, and a porter fined for damaging a passenger's box. In the United States, by contrast, there is little evidence of fining. Walter Licht suggests that 'it went against the democratic grain of the society. American workers, also, possessed of the vote and political power and less constrained by strict class barriers, may have been more defiant and less willing to accept fining practices.'[9] But there were reprimands, warnings, demotions, suspensions, and dismissals for misdemeanours. Unofficially, black lists were operated by the companies to prevent the re-employment in the industry of dismissed workers.

The code of conduct in Britain, Europe, and the United States invariably included bans on smoking, drinking, and swearing while on duty. Drunkenness was a continual worry to the authorities. It was the most common cause of dismissal on the American railways in the nineteenth century. It was one of the problems that station-masters in Britain were expected to encounter and E. B. Ivatts of the Midland Great Western advised station-masters faced with drunken employees to enlist the help of the wife, who, 'fearing the husband's dismissal, watches him at home, and thus the united action of the agent and the wife often proves a check upon the offender, and strengthens his weakness of character'.[10] More practically, he suggests that every large station should have a comfortable, furnished porters' room with a hotplate to enable them to warm food and coffee:

If a comfortable room is not provided, the natural consequence is, the men during meal times go to the nearest public house ... We do not object to a working man going to a respectable public house of an evening when he has done his work, but we do strongly object to public houses that are so frequently found opposite to railway stations being frequented three or four times a day by porters supposed to be on duty.[11]

In France there was concern about the ex-soldiers. Jacqmin of the Est Company noted:

They bring precious habits of discipline and regularity in service, but also they often have not sufficient courtesy towards the public; and finally they sometimes have an unfortunate tendency to pass a part of their time at the café or the dram shop.[12]

In fairness to the railway companies, however, it should be pointed out that they expected the same standard of conduct from their passengers as they did from their staff, as witness this Great Western Railway regulation:

Any passenger found in a carriage or elsewhere upon the Company's premises, in a state of intoxication, or using obscene or abusive language or writing obscene or offensive words on any part of the company's stations or carriages, or committing any nuisance or otherwise wilfully interfering with the comfort of other passengers is hereby subjected to a penalty not exceeding 40 shillings and shall immediately . . . be removed from the company's premises.[13]

In Britain, wages were not lavish but they were supplemented officially by company provision of domestic fuel, uniforms, and later free railway travel and sometimes unofficially by pilferage ('the workman's perk'). Tips were initially banned by most lines but in 1857 the London and North-Western Company permitted them and other companies followed suit. Railwaymen in the United States enjoyed relatively high wages, being paid twice the rate of their British counterparts. There were regional variations, and differentials as, for instance, between the aristocrats of the engine cab and the lowly station hands. In both Britain and America stations were graded according to size and importance and their staff's pay varied accordingly.

The hours worked were often scandalously long. In the 1840s porters on the Eastern Counties' Railway Company's London stations worked 14–16 hours a day. It became the prime objective of the early railway trade unions to obtain a six-day week and a ten-hour day. But in 1902 the Board of Trade reported that 216,219 cases of men working longer than 12 hours had been discovered during a check on a single day, 31 December 1901; 8,087 men were actually working more than 18 hours on the day in question. This puts into grim perspective the statistics of 5,508 railwaymen killed and 238,798 injured between 1901 and 1911. Not only were hours long but railwaymen often worked what would now be called 'unsocial hours' but which were then part of the job. The work itself was often hard, tiring, dirty, and demanding. But it bred pride, loyalty, *esprit de corps*, and self-discipline. For in the last resort railway-men knew that upon their efficiency human lives depended.

The prospect of promotion was a very real incentive when working for companies whose operations were so ramified and variegated. In America it was said to be gained by merit. Similarly in Britain Sir George Findlay wrote that promotion was usually by merit, adding: 'Thus it is no unusual thing for a station-master, by reason of special aptitude, to rise to the position of divisional superintendent, and even of General Manager.'[14] But specific factors—local conditions and family connections—could well come into play.

The London, Brighton and South Coast records show that for the period 1856 to 1861 the great majority of station-masters began in the lower grades and worked their way up. Of 60 station-masters appointed during these years, 18 had been porters, 14 policemen, 12 clerks, and 5 gatekeepers. Promotion was quite rapid, the average wait being three years. In the United States a similar route to promotion was followed, with a man entering the service as a station labourer in his late teens or a clerk in his early twenties and working up to station agent or depot-master. The average age at which Illinois Central station-masters gained their positions was 35. But if you wanted promotion, you had to be prepared to move. Mobility was perhaps the key characteristic of railway promotion.

By the end of the century, there was no shortage of handbooks to guide the station-master through his job. The most compendious of them was by E. B. Ivatts, Goods Manager of the Irish company the Midland Great Western, a man who had seen service with the Great Indian Peninsula Railway, the London and North-Western, the Buffalo and Lake Huron, and the Lancashire and Yorkshire railways. His *Railway Management at Stations* (1885) ran to 600 pages and covered every conceivable aspect of the job.

Ivatts applied in effect the principle of social Darwinism to railway management, laying great stress on leadership:

Obedience is necessary to carry out discipline, and discipline is necessary to maintain obedience. Obedience is gained by fear and respect, and lost by a deficiency of firmness and moral courage—by a want of detail knowledge of the business—by undue familiarity—by disreputable conduct or anything that by lowering the superior officer in the estimation of his staff creates disrespect. Submission to a leader is given tacitly upon the belief that the leader is able to lead, and on that account is a superior kind of man.[15]

He believed that the ideal station-master should know the job inside out, work hard, and 'develop a kind of cultivated instinct, an intuitive and momentary impulse as to what is the right thing to do under nearly every given circumstance'.[16] He favoured reward and the hope of advancement as an incentive, with promotion going 'to the most willing, most regular and well conducted ... Length of service speaks for little, unless accompanied by the traits above mentioned.'[17] He believed in promoting a spirit of competition among the men ('a great lever in keeping up the spirit of emulation among the men').[18] Punishment, he thought, should be used sparingly and sensibly ('There is no punishment so effective as extra duty without pay, or the infliction of some dirty, disagreeable work for a few days').[19] He believed that the best knowledge of system and organization was to be learned at a large station and the best knowledge of goods detail at a small station. The whole book is a massive testament to the scientific desire of the Victorians to systematize, tabulate, and docket everything. For order was the bulwark against a turbulent universe. Dickens would have loved Mr Ivatts.

The duties of the station-master were carefully defined by the company and scarcely varied between countries. He was primarily charged with receiving and dispatching the trains on time, but he was also responsible for the care of all forms of company property, the state of the company buildings, the appearance and efficiency of the staff, the security of all valuables, and the maintenance of complete and up-to-date records.[20] According to Burt, he was also expected 'to be able and ready to answer inquiries in regard to agricultural and industrial conditions, municipal matters, political affairs, the temperance situation; in regard to prominent personalities and to employees of the company; in regard to the business of competing lines, new enterprises in the community etc. etc.'[21]

There were some situations, however, which the rule-book did not cover. Dealing with difficult customers was one of them, as Mr Watkins, station-master at Stonehouse on the Midland Railway's main Birmingham to Bristol line, recalled in 1898. People travelling without tickets was one problem. He had encountered people travelling under seats, on the roof of carriages, on the buffers, and one man stretched at full length along the footboard. Another problem was drunks:

Often we get several in one compartment on one of our night trains—a rowdy football team perhaps—who have broken half the glass in the place. Yet what can you do? They swear the windows were smashed when they got in, although you can see the freshly-splintered fragments lying about; but you can't father the affair upon any one of them in particular, and if you try to take their names and addresses, they are pretty sure to show fight and give you no end of trouble; meanwhile you are naturally all anxiety to get the train away to time, and taking it altogether, you scarcely know what to do for the best. Bank holidays are our special *bêtes noires*. We can deal with any amount of extra traffic in reason, and get on tolerably comfortably, so long as we have a fairly decent class to deal with; but when it comes to a noisy, drunken, swearing mob—no uncommon element in a Bank Holiday excursion—it makes our work very hard and irksome indeed.[22]

Hubert Simmons, station-master at various Great Western stations in the 1860s, published his sardonic account of his service in the heyday of the railways under the title *Ernest Struggles* in 1879. It was banned from sale at the GWR station bookstalls, but Simmons had advertising boards put up in fields adjoining the railway line, which invited the public to write to him for copies.[23] He painted a careful picture of the responsibilities, power, and perks of a station-master.

The standing of the station-master in the community and the role of the station in preserving and defining social distinctions emerge clearly from his account:

There is a considerable amount of importance attached to this public place of meeting—the railway station. The Jones's who don't associate with the Robinsons, meet there. Mr. Jones would not like the station master to touch his cap to the Robinsons, and pass him without notice, so he sends the station master a hare. The Rev. Mr. Silvertongue is always wanting to take a party somewhere at single fare for the double journey, or some other concession, so he honours the station master by conversing with him, as an equivalent for concessions. The old lady, with her dog, would not, on any account, have the little dear put into that dreadful dungeon of a dog box when she travels, so she sends the station master a basket of plums once in the year. The farmer would not like his teams of horses to be sent back without his oil cake or seed corn, for which he is waiting, in case he is not at home to write out a cheque for the carriage when he sends for the goods, so he sends a couple of rabbits about once in two years. The grocer and other tradesmen want their claims for delay and damage (by which they hope to extort an additional profit) attended to, so they encourage the station master by standing treat whenever they meet him at the inn; or send a little box of French plums. The doctor hopes to be sent for in case of a railway accident, so he is polite. 'My Lord' knows that he has no right to bully at the railway station, so he brings a brace of pheasants and thus adds Mr. Station Master to the train of his servants. The old egg woman, who goes to market, and takes a huge market basket with her, which takes up the room of one passenger, ties up a few primroses and daffodils in a cabbage leaf, and hands them through the pigeon hole when she takes her ticket. The fish dealer, who is continually making claims for delay to his fish, drops a pair of soles, and when the station master says 'How much?' he replies, 'We will settle for them when you pays me that claim, sir!' The stockbroker hands his cigar case. In fact all but magistrates and the shareholders pay homage to the station master.[24]

At a tiny British station, the station-master might be signalman, porter, and booking-clerk as well. The smallest American stations had a station agent who took care of everything—selling tickets, handling baggage, pumping water, chopping wood, drumming up business, operating the telegraph, and keeping the stove going. At many small British stations, the station-master, who generally lived 'over the shop', might be responsible also for coal sidings, a goods yard, a signal-box, and a livestock pen as well as the actual station. All this would be run with a staff of about half a dozen.

In the largest stations, on the other hand, the station master would often command a staff running into hundreds, if not thousands. In 1904–5 Frankfurt Station had a staff of 1,000, London Paddington 720, Turin 620, and Dresden 580.[25] A typical breakdown of the staff at a British station in the railways' heyday is furnished by Newcastle Central, a station which dealt with an average of 700 trains a day. There in 1901 Mr S. Holliday, the station-master, had 11 assistant station-masters, 300 porters, 96 signalmen, 16 clerks, 22 booking-clerks, and 34 parcels clerks.[26]

The amount of paperwork generated by the railways was phenomenal. Benjamin Burt recorded that the American station-master's monthly report, itself compiled from the daily and weekly reports covering the various activities of the station, included: (i) a combined tonnage and revenue statement for freight and a revenue statement for passenger business; (ii) a statement of the total tonnage handled, regardless of revenue; (iii) copy of station payroll; (iv) statement of car-loads forwarded and received, showing kinds of commodities; (v) statement of amount paid out for handling of freight; (vi) statement of causes of increase or decrease in business. The statement was throughout comparative, giving the previous year's totals. The freight tonnage and revenue statement were also expected to include, with comparative figures: (i) freight forwarded to local points, tonnage and revenue; (ii) freight forwarded to points on other companies' systems; (iii) freight received from local points, tonnage and revenue; (iv) freight received from points on other railroads on the system; (v) freight received from other systems, and so forth.[27]

Each item of freight had to be checked, booked, invoiced, and dispatched. The Parcels Office at Newcastle Central with thirty-four parcels clerks dealt in 1899 with 922,038 packages and parcels, 8,469 horses, 1,534 carriages, 8,969 dogs, 93,376 cans of milk, and 5,899 tons of perishable foodstuffs. The conditions under which such parcels clerks worked was graphically described by F. S. Williams:

We enter a parcels office just before a train is starting. Men and boys, porters and clerks, are shouting to one another at the top of their voices. A parcel porter seizes a parcel, calls out the name and destination written thereon, and the clerk replies by assigning the route along which it is to travel. 'Tomlinson, Falmouth' exclaims the parcel porter; 'Bristol and West' replies the clerk. 'Aberdeen' bawls another porter; 'Edinburgh' answers the clerk. Meanwhile, while the porter shouts the address to the clerk, and he replies, the clerk, with the aid of a 'manifold writer', makes out a way-bill in duplicate, with name, address and amount to be charged. One way-bill is sent with the parcel, the other is filed. At the end of the day the duplicates are placed together, the amounts entered thereon are checked with the cash book; and they are then passed to the 'abstract clerk', who abstracts the amounts that will be due from each station to which the parcels have been sent. At the end of the month these abstracts are balanced, summarized, and sent to the audit office, where they are checked with the foreign stations, and then despatched to the Clearing House for the division of receipts among the different companies over whose lines the parcels have travelled . . . The work is all done in a noise and a bustle, but the clerks become so used to it that, with two or three sets at work at the same time, they will despatch or receive two or three hundred parcels in half an hour.[28]

The procedure for dealing with 'inwards' parcels was merely the reverse. They were received, called off, checked with the way-bills, sorted, and distributed by the vans. The freight activity of the railway, though less glamorous than passenger work, was none the less important. Benjamin Burt devotes seven chapters of his *Railway Station Service* to freight classification, freight tariffs, freight weights, the receipt and delivery of freight, the accepting and forwarding of freight, and the report procedures. He even gives a comprehensive list of unacceptable freight, which includes uncrated billiard tables, uncaged live birds, loose cheese, and opium.[29] Ivatts devotes 100 pages to how to deal with correspondence on such matters as goods damaged in transit, goods arriving in different wagons from those in which they had been invoiced, goods received different from the invoice, goods received with consignee unknown, consignee refusing to pay charges and overcharging.

Rather more solitary but no less onerous was the work of the booking-clerks. The twenty-two at Newcastle Central issued 3,159,480 tickets in 1899, an average of 8,656 per day, including Sundays. They also booked a total of 20,989 bicycles. The booking-clerk did not just issue tickets. He had to record the number, class, destination, and value of every ticket issued, first in a 'train' book and then in a 'proof' book. At the end of the month, a summary was prepared of every transaction that had taken place and forwarded to head office. But every day the ticket clerk had to balance up the cash before going off duty.

People complain today about the wide variety of British Rail tickets and concessions but it is nothing compared with the situation when there were 100 companies, each with its own tickets and concessions. Apart from ordinary passenger tickets, there were season tickets, market tickets, workman's tickets, excursion tickets (day trips, half-day trips, short period excursions, long period excursions, circular tours, road–rail–sea trips, picnic tickets, angler's tickets), and tickets for bicycles, tricycles, motor bicycles, sewing-machines, perambulators, hand-carts, typewriters, bath-chairs, dogs, and cellos.

The work of a clerk, although it guaranteed a certain status and continuity of employment, was hard, long, and poorly paid. 'Every servant must devote himself exclusively to the service of the company, attend during the appointed hours, reside and do duty where and when required, Sundays included' was the company regulation quoted by one disgruntled clerk in 1872.[30] In the second half of the nineteenth century, a clerk might work from 9 a.m. to 6 p.m. with a half-day off on Saturday for no more than a pound a week. Discontent at the situation led to the foundation of the Railway Clerks Association in 1887 to obtain better conditions. But railway companies penalized clerks who joined in an effort to discourage them.

The person the general public probably had most dealings with was the platform porter, 'ever at the beck and call of passengers generally and upon the top of it all answering hosts of unnecessary questions'.[31] Porters' cries were among the railway arcana studied by zealous observers of the iron road in all its aspects. W. J. Gordon recalled:

Passing through Newton Abbot we once overheard a discussion on porters' cries. It seems they are fairly divisible into three groups. There are the mere grunts, as at Havant and Yeovil; the abbreviations, as at 'Snks' (otherwise Sevenoaks) and 'Drm', 'S'num', 'St'rum' and 'Bl'um' (as at Durham, Sydenham, Streatham and Balham); and the jubilantly rhythmical, as the 'Woodleywood-leywoodley Junc.' of the M.S. and L., and that glorious crescendo of the Midland, 'Mangots*field*! Mangots*field*! Change here—for Glaster and Chalte-nam, Woster and Barmingham, Darby and the Narth!'[32]

But in large stations there were many different kinds of porter: passenger porters, goods porters, office porters, clock-room porters, lamp porters, and letter porters. There were also outside or badge porters, who

Leaving Home. Engraving by Eugene Edmond Ramus after Frank Holl.

Waiting-room vignettes captured in Frederick Bacon Barwell's painting, *Parting Words, Fenchurch Street Station*, 1859.

European soldiers board a troop train at Tientsin, China, during the Boxer Rebellion.

Women Railway Porters in Wartime. Painting by William Roberts.

York, Station Staff, 1909.

The Governor of Northern Nigeria, Sir Hesketh Bell, and his staff at Jebba South
Station, c. 1910.

The exquisite detail of Victorian ironwork is illustrated in the Grecian-style gentlemen's convenience at Melrose Station.

The distinctive terracotta booking-hall at Nottingham Midland Station, 1904.

attended to the needs of passengers with a short distance to go from the station and no need for a cab. Ivatts suggested that they should be 'men or youths of good character and cleanly appearance'.[33] At country stations the sons of regular porters often did this work. The main aim of the companies in employing such portering staff was to cut out the men and boys who hung about the station exits hoping to pick up a few coppers by transporting luggage for passengers.

At big stations the porters were controlled by a head porter and worked a shift system: early shift (6 a.m. to 2 p.m.), middle shift (2 p.m. to 10 p.m.), and night shift (10 p.m. to 6 a.m.). Although the porters' duties were usually confined to portering, the night porters were often required to undertake cleaning duties. In small stations the station-master controlled the porters and they often combined portering duties with shunting, ticket-collecting, and lamp-lighting. Whoever controlled the porters had to keep their eyes open for two particular abuses. Sometimes porters confined their activities to the first-class carriages in the hope of picking up rich tips and ignored the second- and third-class passengers. As Ivatts noted: 'It is a grievance with the public that second- and third-class passengers do not get adequate attention equal to that given to the first-class passengers, and it is a grievance that should be remedied and may be remedied, if the porters are closely supervised.'[34] There were also sometimes alliances between porters and cabmen where porters touted for particular cabmen and brought them the good fares, i.e. long journeys, extensive luggage, numerous persons in the party.

The lamp porters had under them the lowest form of station life, the 'lamp lads', known as 'lampies', who were employed in cleaning, trimming, and lighting the lamps. They started work at the age of fourteen on this, the bottom grade of the hierarchy. Their hours varied according to the seasons, but the work was hard because a lot of lamps were required, not just for the station buildings, but for all the trains, which had side-lamps and tail-lamps. They were kept in the lamp room, which was run by a lamp foreman who had several lamp porters to collect and distribute the heavy roof lamps. The 'lamp lads' did the rest. The work lessened somewhat as stations went over to gaslight. But trains and signal-boxes continued to be lit by oil lamps. Eventually the general adoption of electricity put an end to the job.

Several railway porters have left accounts of their careers, which help to illuminate the nature and range of their jobs. Harry Aland, who joined the London and North-Western in 1921 as a porter at Rugby, put in forty-four years' service as porter and signalman in the Rugby area. The discipline remained strict. One Saturday morning when he turned up at work in a non-regulation tie, he was summoned by the station-master and told: 'The next time I catch you without your black tie, you will go home and probably stay there for good.'[35] The work was hard and the hours were long. In 1926 he was transferred to Ullesthorpe, eight miles north of Rugby. The station boasted only two platform porters and they did all the passenger and goods work between them:

> Early turn was 6 a.m. to 3.30 p.m., with 12 noon to 1 p.m. for a meal; late turn was 11 a.m. to 8.30 p.m. with a meal break from 1 to 2 p.m. So that the hour from 2 till 3 p.m. spent together, was the lap-over for jobs needing two people. A typical morning's work was to book the first two passenger trains, which carried numerous passengers, then fetch in the six signal lamps . . . to be cleaned and trimmed by the signalman. Then, a round of the goods yard getting sheets off empty wagons, putting up wagon doors, and so on, before the first local goods arrived at 7.45 a.m. We had to do the shunting of all local goods trains, the checking of Coltman's timber, labelling, sheeting and roping where required. Among the inwards traffic, we had many wagons of cake . . . for the various local farmers. There could be as many as twenty-two transfer orders in one truck, all to be checked, entered and given out . . . Every Tuesday, there was a cattle market at Ullesthorpe, from which we loaded from five to seven trucks of animals for despatch. There were cattle arriving every day off nearly every train from Leicester, as well as horse-boxes. The latter had to be cleaned out, labelled and returned to the respective companies . . . In addition, as soon as the late turn man booked on at 11 a.m., the early turn started on the 'Mary-Anning', or domestic roster, which was strictly adhered to. All the scrubbing was done properly on hands and knees. Monday was the Station Master's office; Tuesday, the general waiting room, which was huge; Wednesday, the Ladies waiting-room; Thursday, lavatories and pumps; Friday, window cleaning and Saturday, the weighbridge.[36]

Arthur Randell worked for forty-two years at Coldham Station on the Great Eastern Railway, first as a goods porter and later as a signalman. But he began work just after the First World War as a platform porter at Magdalen Road Station, where he worked eight-hour shifts. He lit fires, loaded milk on to the London train, shifted goods and mail, cleaned and filled lamps, sorted parcels, drove livestock, operated level-crossing gates: 'In fact there always seemed another job to be done as soon as one was finished.'[37]

Coldham Station, four miles from March, saw a busy agricultural trade in potatoes, beans, corn, hay, mangels, and, after shearing, great bales of wool. But the busiest time of the year was the summer, when the station was inundated with fruit. Extra staff were taken on in the fruit season at all the stations in the area, while clerks were drafted in from other areas for three months to help with the booking. The entire station staff at

Coldham, including three plate-layers, three clerks, and the station-master, leant a hand. Representatives of the fruit-buying firms attended to help with loading and checking. But by 1930 only half the fruit that used to go by rail still did so. Road transport was making great inroads into the traffic, a process that was to continue with tragic inexorability.

For all the aching weariness that this manual labour induced, there was, as these men and others like them testify, considerable pride taken in the work done. Harry Aland noted:

There was a pride in the railway for which one was working and an especial pride in the cleanliness of the station. Rugby Station was like a palace with a glass roof and sides to the platforms. Each of us had our allocated portion of cleaning and sweeping, which had to be done, whatever the circumstances.[38]

Attached to many a station was a signal-box. These signal-boxes were the 'lighthouses of the iron road'. Their denizens literally had the power of life and death in their hands, as they manipulated the levers which switched trains on to their tracks. Signalman's error, often induced by overwork and constant strain, was a frequent cause of accidents in the nineteenth century. It was not until 1919 that British signalmen achieved an eight-hour day and a six-day week.

In the early days of the railway, the railway policemen operated the points and for many years thereafter signalmen were known as 'bobbies'. They were required to have perfect hearing and eyesight, and to be in good physical health. They were subjected to stiff examinations in the theory and practice of signalling. Station signalmen had a particularly onerous job, 'for in addition to the trains that run through the station without stopping, there are the local trains, the rail motors etc., that bring in traffic, horse-boxes, cattle-trucks, milk-trucks, carriage trucks—all sorts of trucks, loaded or empty, for the station itself, or for transfer to other trains going to different parts.'[39]

Contact between signal-boxes was maintained by an electric telegraph key, on which the signalmen tapped out a code. Every beat or combination of beats, activating a bell or gong in the next box, conveyed a message: 'Is line clear for branch passenger?'—1 beat, pause, 3 beats; 'Is line clear for express cattle or goods?'—1 beat, pause, 4 beats; 'Vehicles running away on a wrong line'—2 beats, pause, 5 beats, pause, 5 beats. Any number of beats in rapid succession was the emergency signal for attention. Every signal received was recorded.

Like all aspects of railway life, the signal-box was susceptible of a romantic evocation. It prompted Henry Chappell to launch into poetic prose:

At night in the box of a busy junction or station, where the roar of traffic never ceases and the iron steeds snort and puff and whistle and clank the whole night long, there is no time to think about anything but work in hand. The bells and gongs keep up their more or less musical chorus, the tapping of the keys is like a whole colony of wood-peckers very busy indeed, the rasping call of the telephone is heard about every other second and the voice of the operator 'Hello, hello' . . . Far otherwise is it in some of the little boxes out in the wilds, maybe a mile or two from the nearest human habitation, by the side of a deep cutting, or in the shadow of a wood . . . The only sound that breaks the numbing silence being the tick of the clock on the wall, the occasional clatter of a single needle against the bone pegs as a message goes through or the hooting of an owl at intervals from the black wood that lies above and behind the box.[40]

The working of modern industrial capitalism required total order and absolute discipline to produce and deliver the goods and to generate the maximum profit. The railways in both the Old World and the New spearheaded the bureaucratization and systematization of industrial management which became a keynote of developed industrialism. With railway company operations so wide-ranging and multifarious, a precise, carefully defined, and strictly maintained structure was vital. This explains both the military-style regimentation and the proliferation of rule-books which delineated the chain of command, laid down standards of conduct, and expounded in minute details the duties of every grade in the service. This had a knock-on effect with the emergence of the unions, as in Britain the National Union of Railwaymen developed exactly the same kind of corporate loyalty, intricately detailed regulations, and strict hierarchy as the industry they served.

The last decades of the nineteenth century witnessed what one historian has succinctly called 'the awakening of Caliban': the forces of labour organized themselves, flexed their muscles, and went into battle for better pay, hours, and conditions of work. This happened almost simultaneously in Britain and America. There were no railway trade unions in Britain before 1870, though there had been strikes, usually provoked by company attempts to cut wages at times of economic recession. It was agitation about excessive hours, which had been held responsible for a spate of accidents, that led to the birth of the first railway trade union, the Amalgamated Society of Railway Servants (ASR) in 1871. Its aim was a ten-hour day for all, except for signalmen and watchmen, who were to have eight. Their activities were hampered by the jealousy and mistrust that existed within the union between London and the provinces. But the companies remained for the most part intransigent, endorsing Sir George Findlay's comment 'That you might as well have trades unions in Her Majesty's Army as have it in the railway service. The thing is totally incompatible.'[41]

Nevertheless there was an upsurge of trade union militancy in the 1890s as part of a general rise in labour activism, and there were several strikes aimed at reducing hours. But it was not until after the First World War that railwaymen's hours were to be comparable with those of other workers. One of these railway strikes—the Taff Vale strike of 1900 —was to have a historic by-product, the passing of the Trades Disputes Act of 1906 which exempted trade unions from legal actions and legalized peaceful picketing.

The rising discontent within the railways culminated in the first national railway strike in 1911; its object—shorter hours and higher wages. Stations played a crucial part in the struggle, as focal points of activity. The companies offered loyalty bonuses and, in some cases, free beer to railmen who continued to work. The Great Northern and Midland companies actually fed and housed non-strikers in their stations so that they could avoid the pickets. Nevertheless stations became scenes of violence in Liverpool, where police and troops attempted to move goods from the central stations, and Manchester, where the positioning of armed soldiers at the central stations acted as a provocation to the strikers. Despite the serious effects of the strike on industry and the sympathy of sections of the press and public with the strikers' demands, the companies remained intransigent and compelled the intervention of the government. Lloyd George, President of the Board of Trade, brought the two sides together and got them to agree to a commission of inquiry, which led to an increase in wages but no improvement in hours.

But following the co-operation of the ASR and other railway unions in the conduct of the strike, they merged to form the National Union of Railwaymen (NUR). The NUR established the triple alliance with the miners and the transport workers to pursue mutual aims. It was an attempt to cut wages as part of post-war retrenchment which led to the next national railway strike in 1919, when troops were again ordered in to protect all stations, signal-boxes, and bridges. There was also the novel sight of aristocrats volunteering to do manual labour in order to keep the trains running. So during the nine days of the strike it was possible to see Lord Cholmondeley acting as a porter at Paddington, Lady Meux collecting tickets on the Great Eastern Railway, and Lord Grimthorpe 'doing the work of two ordinary men in the provinder department' of King's Cross. Once again Lloyd George, now Prime Minister, intervened and the wage cuts were dropped.

In pursuit of the triple alliance, the railwaymen came out on strike in support of the miners in 1926 and once again middle- and upper-class volunteers attempted, in vain, to fill the gap and keep the trains running. But after the failure of the General Strike, the unions retreated from confrontation and an era of trade union activity came to an end.

The pattern of events in Britain was followed almost exactly in America. In the first decades of the railways, there were no unions. But by 1877 there were three and by 1890 ten unions, brotherhoods as they were called, of skilled men. By 1901 there were fifteen, including those for signalmen, clerks, and telegraphers. As Walter Licht has observed: 'Hardly a year went by in the late 19th and early 20th century without at least one significant and easily documented strike of railwaymen.'[42] In 1887 there was a major strike when most of the Eastern lines cut wages as a response to economic depression. There was rioting, killing, and the destruction of railroad property in such notable railroad centres as Baltimore and Pittsburgh.

After the failure of the Buffalo switchmen's strike in 1892, in pursuit of a ten-hour day, pressure for united action led to the foundation of the American Railway Union (ARU) in 1893. Its aims were a living wage and an eight-hour day. It received a great boost to its membership following the Great Northern Railroad Strike in 1894 when all 9,000 employees of the railroad struck over wage cuts. This included all the station staff, and even the station agents. After eighteen days the company gave way and agreed to wage rises. But then, when in 1894 the Pullman Company employees struck for better conditions and the ARU organized a boycott of all Pullman cars in support of the strikers, the companies called in the Federal Government, who sent in the troops. The strike was broken and the ARU collapsed. But the brotherhoods continued to press for shorter hours and in 1916 the four train-operating brotherhoods demanded an eight-hour day and threatened a national strike. The companies refused to listen. So President Woodrow Wilson, emulating Lloyd George, intervened and persuaded the union leaders to agree to a special commission on railroad labour and the implementation of the eight-hour day and to drop demands for extra overtime pay. The company executives flatly refused. So Wilson arranged for the rapid passing of the Adamson Act, introducing a statutory eight-hour day, and signed it in his private railroad car at Washington Union Station the day before the deadline for the strike. During the war the government took control of the railroads but returned them to private ownership in 1920. Wage cuts provoked a strike in 1922 lasting seventy-five days, marked by considerable bitterness and violence, and it ended in unconditional surrender. As in Britain after the General Strike, the unions were not to recover in membership, strength, or morale until the 1930s. In 1926 the Railway Labour Act was passed, which laid down careful procedures for avoiding strikes, including arbitration by government-sponsored conciliation boards, a thirty-day cooling-off period, and, in the last resort, emergency powers for the President to settle disputes. The act still remains in force.

What is notable about the American railroad strikes is the ferocity of the violence that accompanied them, and this seems to have been particularly marked in those places, such as Chicago, Martinsburg, and Pittsburgh, where the railroads dominated the local economy, where individual companies had monopolistic control, where the railwaymen formed cohesive communities, and where there was a sizeable proportion of younger men. In the outbreaks accompanying work stoppages in these places, stations, marshalling yards, and other company property often suffered considerable damage.

But if the First World War marked the peak of union activity, the Second World War marked the beginning of a rapid period of railroad decline, intensifying trends already apparent in the inter-war period. The railways were being overtaken by other forms of transportation, in carrying both passengers and freight. In Britain it was road transport and in America, air. But either way, it meant a dramatic reduction in the railway industry in both countries. In the United States, by 1966 the work-force had fallen to 630,000. In Britain, by 1980 it stood at around 170,000. Not only did men disappear, but so too did specialized jobs as technological change overtook the industry along with reduction.

In Britain the 1960s were the vital decade. Until then, despite nationalization in 1947 and despite its mounting losses, the structure of the railways and the nature of railway work had remained recognizably what it had been in its heyday. But the appointment of Dr Richard Beeching as Chairman changed all that. He initiated changes which altered the face and nature of the railways for ever. He wielded the most celebrated axe since Lizzie Borden, dramatically reducing the size of the network and abolishing rural branch-lines wholesale, together with their stations. Many of those which survived became in course of time unmanned halts, with staff, activities, and life altogether removed. The freight service was geared to concentrate on the bulk traffic, further reducing the already diminishing parcels service, which had once required so many clerks and delivery men. New techniques such as containerization further diminished the work-force. Computerized control centres rendered many signal-boxes and signalmen redundant. Steam trains, with all their grime and mystique, were finally phased out and replaced completely by diesels and electrics, which required new and different skills. At the surviving stations, porters, the mainstay and symbol of the old labour-intensive railways, disappeared. The old men with forty and fifty years' service and the accumulated lore of the days of steam and of the old companies retired. The work practices, ethos, and attitudes forged in the white heat of the Victorian industrial world faded away.

It is still possible to recapture them, however, in Adrian Vaughan's two volumes *Signalman's Morning* (1981) and *Signalman's Twilight* (1983). No better account of the day-to-day life of a small country station is to be found. These volumes are the work of a man whose enthusiasm for steam railways and their world burns like a sacred flame and who has reached inside his memories to draw forth and distil the pure poetry of the railways. He served as porter and signalman at Challow and later Uffington between 1960 and 1968 and recalls every minute and every detail with crystal clarity. Together these volumes constitute a moving and eloquent lament for the lost age of steam by one who lived during and for it.

He lovingly chronicles, explains, and reanimates the porter's work, loading and unloading all kinds of freight, collecting and issuing tickets, tending the station garden, lighting lamps, shunting engines, winding the clock, cleaning the waiting-room, whitewashing the platform. He is equally good on work in the signal-box: the solitude, the shifts, the responsibility, the pride, the closeness to nature, to the elements, to the primal force of railways. Here was a man who loved his work, even porter's duty on a wet night when others might shiver and curse and dream of warm fires and hot toddies. But not Adrian Vaughan:

> The solitude of the evening porter's position made a blank sheet for indelible impressions. I loved the rainy, windswept, winter evenings when the wet plat-forms gleamed under the harsh lights of the Tilleys, their garishness accentuat-ing the surrounding, inky, blackness. And out of the dark would thunder the 'Kings' and 'Castles', showering fire, their brasswork catching momentarily the station lights, their long trains of yellow lit coaches blurring past to the sound of the rail joints' rhythm—till, suddenly, there was only steam and smoke, swirling and rolling under the platform canopy and the sound of the wind in the telephone wires.[43]

But others loved the work too, less poetic souls perhaps, but still men who developed their own rituals, their special language, the emblems of 'the day's work' so beloved by Kipling, and who warmed to the camarad-erie, to the comforting familiarity of an unchanging routine, to the shared experiences told and retold with undiminishing relish.

II

The Station in Wartime (1)
The Nineteenth Century

ALMOST from the first, the strategic importance of railways was perceived—in the transportation of troops and supplies to the front and the removal of the wounded and prisoners to the rear. In these operations, the station functioned as an embarkation point and a reception area, and as a centre for the concentration and distribution of men and supplies. The military transportation implications of the railways became clear as early as the opening of the Liverpool and Manchester Railway in 1830 when a British regiment was conveyed the 34 miles between the two cities in two hours, a journey which would have taken two days on foot. In this case the regiment was required for ceremonial purposes. But in 1831 in the United States of America, a military detachment of 100 volunteers travelled 14 miles on the Baltimore and Ohio Railroad from the B. and O. station at Mount Clare Street, Baltimore, to Ellicott's Mills to put down a riot of striking railway workers. The first example of large-scale troop transportation came in 1846 when 12,000 men of the Prussian Sixth Army Corps were transported together with guns, ammunition, and road vehicles to Cracow to suppress a revolt by the Poles.[1]

It was only a matter of time and organization before the full-scale utilization of the railways as an integral part in modern warfare. It came in 1859 in the conflict between France and Austria in Italy. Working to a pre-arranged plan, the French mounted a speedy and efficient invasion of Italy by rail, transporting 640,000 men and 129,000 horses to the battle-front. They were rather less efficient in the matter of supply, leaving both men and horses without food for sometimes up to twenty-four hours. But as a result of this rail-borne activity, the railway itself became a military objective. A contemporary British commentator, Major Miller, reported:

The railway cuttings, embankments and bridges presented features of import-ance equal or superior to the ordinary accidents of the ground and the possession of which was hotly contested. If you go to Magenta you will see, close to the railway platform on which you alight, an excavation full of rough mounds and simple black crosses, erected to mark the resting places of many hundred men who fell in the great fight.[2]

The poignant linkage of the station, the soldiery, and death was thus early on established.

It was, however, the American Civil War which was to demonstrate the central importance of the railways to modern warfare. There was a foreshadowing of this role in October 1859 when a station-master and porter were killed in the abolitionist John Brown's attempt to hold up the Baltimore and Ohio Railway's Wheeling to Baltimore express. News of the outrage, telegraphed to the company's head office in Baltimore, brought a detachment of United States marines to the scene. John Brown and his followers were besieged in a locomotive roundhouse, captured, and hanged.

By 1861 the American railroad consisted of 30,635 miles of track, much of it single track, imperfectly ballasted. But only 9,000 miles of this was in the Confederacy and much of this was not linked up. There was therefore little through traffic, many bottle-necks, and large areas poorly served. The Confederacy compounded its railroad weakness by not acting sensibly over it. It was not until 1865 that the Confederate President Jefferson Davis took direct control of the Southern railways or that the Confederate Congress voted substantial sums to extend and adapt the network. President Abraham Lincoln, on the other hand, took over the key railway and telegraph lines in the flourishing Northern network by Act of Congress in 1862 and the war was to demonstrate decisively the need for central and unified control of the railways in wartime.

Railway communications were to be vital to the war effort of both sides. The Baltimore and Ohio was the main artery of communication between North and South and so in 1861 Southern forces attacked the Martinsburg Yards of the B. and O., burned them to the ground, wrecked 386 passenger and freight vehicles, and destroyed 42 locomotives. The yards were rebuilt, restocked, and redestroyed in 1862. The destruction and rebuilding of the lines, bridges, stations, and rolling stock by ever more efficient means runs as a recurrent theme through the grim story of the war. As the Confederates devised ever more spectacular and permanent means of destruction, so the Unionists invented better and swifter methods of reconstruction. The North had the advantage of the services of an engineering genius, Herman Haupt, appointed chief of construction and transport. With speed, efficiency, and innovative technique, he and his construction corps worked to replace damaged lines. In 1864 the Nashville and Chattanooga Railroad, a vital route for General

Sherman's advance on Atlanta, was systematically destroyed by Confederates and systematically rebuilt by the Construction Corps for 196 days. By the end of the war the Federal Construction Corps had laid or relaid 641 miles of track.

In all of this, stations found themselves in the front line, regarded as legitimate targets by both sides. Being wooden in many cases, they burned all too easily. Unionist General William Tecumseh Sherman stated his policy with chilling succinctness: 'The railroad station as the heart of the modern artery of business was second only in importance to the buildings and institutions of the Confederate government itself as a subject for elimination.' As good as his word, Sherman began his march to the sea in November 1864 by levelling the great railroad terminus at Atlanta. *En route* the fine railroad station at Millen was destroyed on his orders. It is still a matter of dispute as to whether it was Sherman's men or retreating Confederate forces who fired the railroad depot and warehouses at Columbia, but whoever started it, the ensuing fire spread to engulf the entire centre of the city.

Stations also fell victim to notable and daring raids. General John H. Morgan, one of the boldest and most brilliant Confederate guerrilla leaders, made a speciality of attacking Northern railroad installations, destroying stations, tearing up lines, cutting telegraph wires, capturing stores, and disrupting lines of communication. Perhaps his most celebrated exploit began on Christmas Day 1862, which saw the beginning of the Louisville and Nashville raid. Morgan seized the station at Upton, telegraphed the Unionist General Boyle at Louisville for information about the disposition of Unionist troops, and, on the basis of that, proceeded north-east from Upton to Shepherdsville knocking out dozens of garrisons, blowing up bridges, and effectively destroying the Union troops' route into Georgia. It took General Haupt six months to rebuild it.

But taking a leaf out of the Confederate book, General Grant in 1863 dispatched Colonel B. H. Grierson on a raid deep into Confederate territory. He left Lagrange with 17,000 men, swept west and south, destroying the Jackson and New Orleans Railroad, cutting the east–west trunk line, serving Mobile and Ohio, at three places, destroying the rolling stock, track, marshalling yards, and stations on the line into Louisiana. Sixteen days later he reached Baton Rouge safely. John Ford was later to immortalize the raid in his film *The Horse Soldiers* (1959).

As a result of their superior communications, the Union troops were better supplied than the Confederates. When in 1862 Confederate troops under General 'Stonewall' Jackson captured the vital communications centre of Manasses Junction, the ragged, hungry Southerners found stored there an Aladdin's Cave:

Warehouses crammed with such staples as meat, flour, sugar, and good coffee stood beside others filled with clothing, which ranged from shoes and overcoats to linen handkerchiefs. There were barrels of whisky, cases of cigars and luxuries, which many of the soldiers had never hoped to see. Cakes and canned lobster, candy and soap, French mustard and Rhine wine drew their attention away from fine saddles and fancy underwear. In addition to the warehouses the railroad yard was crowded with loaded cars . . . There were two miles of them.[3]

The Confederates took what they could carry and burned the rest.

Railwaymen and station staff found themselves regularly in the midst of mass evacuations, mass movements of reinforcements, even of pitched battles. They had to cope with wartime shortages and restrictions, with military authorities whose idea of transport priorities was invariably different from those of the professional railwaymen and often led to bitter clashes. They had to deal with a dramatic upsurge in passenger traffic, not just of servicemen but of civilians travelling to visit relatives in the armed forces. They had to survive and overcome enemy attack and sabotage. The war also produced an authentic railway hero, W. R. Fuller, a conductor on the Georgia State Railway who, when his train was hijacked in 1862 by Unionist raiders aiming to destroy the railway bridges, pursued the enemy on foot, by handcar, and by commandeered engine until he caught up with them and helped recapture his train.

In the post-bellum United States attention was directed towards the West, and the railway lines which stretched out there had their own military significance. It was soon recognized that settlers on the great western plains and mountains would only be safe from Indian attack once they could be supported by cavalry reinforcements from their local stations. The Indian population in their turn recognized the importance of stations. Stations on the Central and Union Pacific lines, as well as on the Santa Fe, were being attacked by Indian bands until the 1880s. Railway survey and construction parties were frequently attacked and many were killed. In Wyoming a small station bears the name of Percy after an engineer, Percy T. Brown, who was killed in just such an Indian raid.

Indeed railways were constantly extolled in the late nineteenth century as the 'pacificator' of warring and resistant peoples in the non-European world. Contemporary writers wrote both of their economic virtues and of their 'moral effects'. But if railways provided opportunities for dominance they also presented threats from rival powers. Depending on the observer's standpoint, they could be depicted either as an imperial panacea or as a source of national paranoia. The Russian lines in Central Asia seemed to be directed against Afghanistan and India; the Siberian against China and Japan. German lines in Africa were seen to pose serious dangers to adjacent British colonies. And the mighty United States threatened the very existence of neighbouring Canada.

Canadian early railway history beautifully expressed this extraordinary combination of hope and fear. The first Canadian railways were built to standard guage, but in 1851 legislation was passed decreeing that a 5' 6" gauge should be adopted. This was consciously designed to prevent direct crossings of the Canadian–American border, lest the Americans should be tempted to invade via the railway lines. As on the borders of Australian states, frontier stations would have been required. But the Canadian legislation was repealed in 1870, when, apparently, fear of American invasion had passed. Canadian railway lines like the Grand Trunk and the Canadian Northern were indeed to invade the United States as much as the other way round. On the other hand, the railway to western Canada was conceived partly with pacification in mind, after the Louis Riel (Red River) rebellion of 1870. In 1885 a second rebellion in Manitoba was swiftly put down using the railway. And as in the United States, it was only with the building of the railway that the Canadian Indian tribes could be fully brought to heel.

In Asia, too, the apologists for railway-building could find no better argument for the extension of railway lines than the need to suppress insurrection. In 1857 in India the first short railways played only a small part in the movement of troops to put down the revolt of that year, but in its aftermath the building of the East India and Delhi railways was greatly speeded up. As we have seen in Chapter 3, some stations were built as forts, though the Government expressed some anxieties about the commitment to garrison them. Nevertheless, instructions were issued that stations should be built in such positions that they could readily be reached by troops in time of trouble. Many stations, particularly in the South, were built outside towns to protect them from civil disorder, to render them safe points to which Europeans might withdraw and where troops could detrain. Important stations, particularly those with workshops and engine sheds, were expected to be compactly built, with walls, gates, and towers, all to facilitate defence. The station at Lahore was provided with massive sliding doors to shut off the track entrances to the train-sheds.

On the North-West Frontier, where stations had a very specific strategic objective, they were built in a solid stone style close to the barracks. Tunnel mouths, like the famous Khojak Tunnel, had fortified entrances, and often a station just a few hundred yards down the line. At

Landi Khotal on the North-West Frontier and at military points throughout India, long platforms were provided for the entrainment of troops and cavalry mounts. The same lengthy platforms were equally convenient for the large numbers and diversity of Indian passengers, particularly at pilgrimage centres. The longest station platform in India was also one of the longest in the world, at Sonepur on the Bengal and North-Western Railway, where the platform was 2,418 ft.—nearly half a mile—long. It became a standard gibe of Indian nationalists at the end of the century that railways and their installations had been built more for strategic than for economic reasons. But Hinduism is a mobile religion, and so are nationalist politics. What had been built for imperial strategy was to serve Indian religion and political agitation just as well.

It was also insurrection or the threat of it which prompted Russian railway-building into Central Asia and Siberia. Not for nothing was Tsar Alexander III, the progenitor of these lines, known as the 'Tsar Pacificator'. There railway-building was in the hands of the military, and it was inevitable that stations should be seen as key strategic points. Barracks were close to the principal stations so that troops could protect the new settlements of Russian migrants and overawe Siberian tribes like the Kirghiz, Tatars, and Yakuts, Ostyaks, Buryats, and Tungus. In Central Asia the stations often created rival towns to existing cities, as at Bukhara and Samarkand, separate from the great Central Asian oases, yet able to dominate them. Noting the military character of the Trans-Caspian railway, George Curzon, future Viceroy of India, wrote:

. . . the railway has been in its execution and is in its immediate object a military railway; . . . all the labour which we associate at home with co-operative industry or private effort has here been undertaken by an official department, under the control of the War Minister at St. Petersburg. Not only was the construction of the line entrusted to a lieutenant-general (General Annenkoff having since been appointed for two years director-in-chief of the railway), but the technical and, to a large extent, the manual labour was in military hands. . . . the bulk of the staff is composed of soldiers of the line. The engines are in many cases driven by soldiers; the station-masters are officers, or veterans who have been wounded in battle; and the guards, conductors, ticket-collectors, and pointsmen, as well as the telegraph and post-office clerks attached to the stations, are soldiers also.[4]

In Africa the railways were seen to have a vital role in conquest. In the Abyssinian campaign of 1867–8 a short railway line was built from the Red Sea coast. Its main role was in facilitating the withdrawal of British troops and its stations were never any more than rudimentary. In 1885 the expedition to rescue General Gordon in Khartoum began the laborious process of building a railway south from Wadi Halfa. It was abandoned after the débâcle of Gordon's death and the British withdrawal. When G. W. Steevens, the young war correspondent, reached Wadi Halfa in 1898 he found it to be a railway town where 'every street is also a railway' and where 'one of the largest, solidest structures', the Egyptian military hospital, had originally had a quite different intended function:

In shape and style, you will notice, it is not unlike a railway station—and that was just what it was meant to be. That was the northern terminus of Ismail Pasha's great railway to Khartum, which was to have run up-river to Dongola and Debbeh, and thence across the Bayuda, by Jakdul and Abu Klea to Metemmeh. The scheme fell short, like all Ismail Pasha's grandiose ambitions.[5]

With General Kitchener's new campaign to take the Sudan, which began in 1896, Halfa was forging 'the deadliest weapon that Britain has ever used against Mahdism—the Sudan Military Railway'. It reached Abu Hamed, 234 miles from Wadi Halfa, by the end of 1897. Within a few months it had reached Atbara, and was poised to continue southwards. Steevens, eager to cover the closing stages of the campaign, pursued Kitchener down the line from Wadi Halfa to Abu Hamed. In the desert he found a whole succession of stations which had been given only numbers for names because there were no habitations near them. Deep wells had been dug to secure the water necessary for the engines. The fifth of these stations was merely a wayside station bearing a board with the inscription 'No. 5', but No. 6, Steevens went on,

is a Swindon of the desert. Every train stops there half-an-hour or more to fill up with water, for there is a great trifoliate well there. Also the train changes drivers. And here, a hundred miles into the heart of the Nubian desert, two years ago a sanctuary of inviolate silence, where no blade of grass ever sprang, where, possibly, no foot trod since the birth of the world, here is a little colony of British engine drivers. They have a little rest-house shanty of board and galvanised iron; there are pictures from the illustrated papers on the walls, and a pup at the door. There they swelter and smoke and spit and look out at the winking rails and the red-hot sand, and wait till their turn comes to take the train. They don't love the life—who would?—but they stick to it like Britons, and take the trains out and home. They, too, are not the meanest of the conquerors of the Sudan.[6]

In the year after Omdurman, the railway was at Khartoum North, where the station symbolized the new alien power. By 1910 the railway had crossed the Blue Nile into the very heart of Khartoum to Khartoum Central, an important part of the British rebuilding of the city.[7] By that time the railway had advanced deep into the southern Sudan. Barely a decade after the conquest of the Khalifa, the Mahdi's successor, tourist brochures were being published describing the joys of railway and steamer travel on the upper Nile, and the civilized facilities of the main railway stations there.[8]

Further south, revolt in Southern Rhodesia in 1896–7 acted as a similar spur to the railway builder. When the revolt broke out the railway had reached no further than Mafeking, 900 miles from Cape Town. Mafeking became the supremely important railhead for Rhodesia, even although 587 miles of road separated the town from Bulawayo. R. S. S. Baden-Powell, later a national hero for his conduct of the defence of Mafeking and founder of the Boy Scouts, arrived there to join the staff of Sir Frederick Carrington, who commanded the imperial troops dispatched to suppress the revolt. Baden-Powell described the great gap between the appearance and the importance of the place which was to make his name three years later:

22nd May—At last, after three nights and two days jogging along in the train, we rattle into Mafeking at 6 a.m. 'Into Mafeking?' Well, there's a little tin (corrugated iron) house and a goods shed to form the station; hundreds of waggons and mounds of stores covered with tarpaulins, and on beyond a street and market square of low-roofed tin houses. Mafeking is at present the railway terminus . . . Next to the station is the camp of the 7th Hussars and mounted infantry of the West Riding and the York and Lancaster regiments. These troops are waiting here in case they may be wanted in Matabeleland. Thus Mafeking is crowded.[9]

A second column approached Southern Rhodesia from the east, led by Lt.-Col. E. A. H. Alderson. He too published his reminiscences of the campaign, but his disquisition on the importance of railway stations came in a later work, *Pink and Scarlet, or Hunting as a School for Soldiering*, published in 1900. In it, in a passage of which Baden-Powell would have approved, Alderson described the exercise of observation while riding to join a hunt in the early morning. He passed a village station and it prompted logistical speculation:

Now we go under the line, and there is the station. Can we entrain or detrain horses there? If so, how many at a time? What about the capacity of the station for the entraining and detraining of troops, and is there room to improve this? What would be the quickest and best way to render the station useless? Let's see. Two-thirds of a pound of gun-cotton will break the best iron rail—won't it?

Rolling stock? Not much; four passenger coaches in that siding there quite fill it, therefore it cannot be more than one hundred and twenty feet long. A poor station for troops, but lots of room to improve it, and lots of room for forming troops up outside too etc. etc.[10]

The year *Pink and Scarlet* was published, 1900, was a year when these very techniques were being put into practice in the South African War, a war in which stations were crucial in a variety of ways. In Britain, large numbers of troops had to be sent to Southampton for shipping to the Cape. Railway transport officers were stationed by the War Office at all important railway stations throughout the country to facilitate the forwarding of troops. In South Africa a military railway controlling staff was formed and railway staff officers were appointed to all the leading stations. It was their job to act as a channel of communication between the military and the station-masters. This system was established and commanded by Percy Girouard, a Canadian who possessed a wide range of imperial railway experience. He had been involved in building part of the Canadian Pacific Railway, had been in charge of the Sudan Military Railway, and went to South Africa from his prestigious post as Director-General of the Egyptian Railways. Steevens had enthused upon a career which he described as a 'triumph of youth': 'But just reflect again on the crowning wonder of British Egypt—a subaltern with all but Cabinet rank and £2,000 a year.'[11] Now Girouard ('Bimbashi' as he had been known in the Sudan and Egypt) had the key position in the transport arrangements of the South African War. He wrote a history of his experiences there, and his ideas about station commandants and the organization of railway departments were to influence railway arrangements in future wars.[12] He went on to become a colonial governor.

Both sides in South Africa soon recognized that railway stations were key points in the campaign. As well as ripping up track, the Boers attacked and wrecked stations, smashed their instruments and batteries, and burned any trucks and fuel which might be lying in their sidings. At times the war became a race between the Boer destroyers of track and the British engineers relaying it. Construction trains were kept in readiness at key stations and groups of men, white and African, varying from 300 to 1,000, camped by the station sidings. When war broke out there were six armoured trains in the two British colonies of the Cape and Natal, but two were trapped in the Siege of Ladysmith. For a considerable period important stretches of railway line in Natal were under Boer control, and they were able to make use of the fact that

At various stations in northern Natal long platforms had been specially constructed by the British, and other arrangements made, to permit large movements of troops and especially the detraining of cavalry. They came in very handy for the Boers.[13]

In the Natal campaigns and sieges on the borders of the Orange Free State, stations frequently played an important part. At Estcourt on the

Bushman's River, British imperial troops were shut up for some time. The station became the centre of all operations and a battle was fought near by. At Ladysmith the railways had large workshops close to the station, and these soon acquired a vital military role. In the siege, the goods sheds were soon full of military stores and commissariat, while the station buildings themselves became an important headquarters. At Elandsfontein in the Transvaal an event took place which reflected the key and vulnerable role of stations and their staffs. Boer station staff who had been unwillingly working for the British eventually absconded, leaving behind only one assistant station-master and one engine-driver, who elected to throw in their lot with the imperial power.

The British capture of Bloemfontein in the Orange Free State marked a most important railway development in the war. There were extensive railway workshops there, and it now became possible to build another fourteen armoured trains. Girouard described it as the most important military railway centre in the country. There was an army of 35,000 men there, and this was to build up to 100,000 once the capacity of the station had been massively increased. The armoured trains were to prove vital in the concluding stages of the war.

An armoured train had already shown its worth in the Siege of Mafeking. It was the stores of railway material and the workshops at the station which had made that town a potentially valuable prize for the Boers. Just before the siege was laid the platforms at Mafeking Station were packed with evacuees attempting to board the evacuation trains. The first one out, however, was forced to return, and the station became, instead of an escape hatch, a key point in the defence of the town. Railway workers formed the Railway Volunteers and makeshift armoured trains were built. The station was connected by newly laid track to the hospital, the convent, and the racecourse, which was being used as a camping ground. A large quantity of goods intended for Rhodesia was requisitioned and proved vital in sustaining the defence. The Boers attempted to shell the station, but without success. An engine was constantly in steam there, ready to haul one of the armoured trains, and it not only played a vital role in moving men and materials around the town, but also had a powerfully symbolic effect on morale.

Soon after the end of the Boer War, South African stations began to play a new part. They became the centres of battlefield tourism. The *Natal Province Descriptive Guide and Official Handbook* of 1911 described the many excursions which could be made from Ladysmith and neighbouring stations to scenes of the war. Graves could be seen by many of the stations, and visitors on this macabre search could hire conveyances, saddle-ponies, and the services of well-informed guides from the stations and their hotels. The *Handbook* went on, 'Tourists and military representatives of various nations throng from all parts of the world to visit this historical town and its neighbouring battlefields'.[14] Meanwhile, stations in other parts of the British Empire continued to carry echoes of the Boer War. Boer prisoners of war had been moved to Ceylon, where they had occupied camps near Ragama and Diyatawala stations. In 1900, 5,000 Boers were imprisoned at the latter. Ragama later became an observation camp for Tamil 'coolie' labour migrants and Diyatawala a convalescent camp for soldiers.

In that critical year of 1900, serious disturbances in northern China also had considerable significance for railways and their stations. Nothing had symbolized the dangerous encroachments of the West upon China more powerfully than railways. They had become a prime bone of contention between the 'modernizing' and 'reactionary' factions which struggled for ascendancy at the Chinese court. Western concessionaires fought to secure railway rights that would have pushed the Chinese door dramatically open. The first railway line was opened between Shanghai and Woosung in 1876, but under the Chefoo Convention of that year the Chinese secured the right to acquire it. They bought it at cost price, and in 1877 all the rails were torn up. Track, engines, and rolling stock were dumped on the island of Formosa. Shanghai Station was demolished, and a temple was raised in its place. Thus Western technological magic was to be exorcised by a return to the old Chinese values.

The pressure for concessions continued, however, and by the 1890s lines were being built throughout northern China. The great Chinese reformist Viceroy Li Hung Chang tried to maintain these developments under Chinese control, but with little success. That remarkable traveller Curzon visited the Far East on two journeys around the world in 1887–8 and 1892–3. On his first visit to China in 1887 not a mile of railway existed in the Celestial Empire, but by 1892 'the stranger can travel in an English-built carriage upon English steel rails from the station at Tongku near the Taku forts at the mouth of the Peho River, over the 27 miles that separate him from Tientsin'.[15] By 1900 the line had been built on to Peking.

The rapid development of railways was one of the principal reasons for the Boxer Rising. Wherever foreigners went their arrival seemed to be accompanied by disastrous harvests and acute distress. The building of railways disturbed Chinese residences and their venerated tombs, and forcibly removed land from the peasantry. The purchase price for such land became a source of corruption and was more likely to find its way into the hands of officials than of the landholders themselves. Everywhere the Boxers wreaked their wrath upon railway stations. According to H. C. Thomson, whose account of the Rising was published in 1902, when the Boxers destroyed the Peking line, 'the first thing they did was to tear up the tickets; for, said they, if there are no tickets, people will no longer be able to travel.'[16] Generally, however, their destruction took more monumental forms. Stations were wrecked on the Russian Chinese Eastern Railway, and on several other lines in the affected region.

At Tientsin, the last train left for Tongku with women and children on 16 June. That night the Taku forts were attacked, and on the following day the foreign settlements at Tientsin were laid under siege. The railway station was so positioned that, if the Chinese had been able to mount their guns upon the station platforms, shells could have been poured into the settlements at short range. The station was held by a joint force of British, French, and Japanese troops, the Japanese and French occupying the platforms and station buildings, the British the engine house, which they defended with a Maxim gun. The station was under attack for several days, and at one stage the French in the station and the British in the engine house were cut off from each other by Boxers who had been able to use the cover of wagons in the sidings. Some Sikhs of the Hong Kong Regiment drove the Boxers off, but only after a fierce battle lasting three hours.

The siege was relieved on 25 June; the Chinese quarter of Tientsin was taken on 14 July; and on 4 August a relief force of 20,000 men from all the foreign powers invading China set out for Peking. A fierce battle ensued at the ruins of the railway station at Yangtsun, and the relieving force continued to fight its way up the railway line past the burnt out railway stations to Peking. The stations had been the eyes of the storms set up by the Western encroachments on China.

No war was such a test of communications as the Russo-Japanese War. The recently completed Trans-Siberian railway proved to be entirely inadequate in the transmission of troops and supplies to the Far East. Kuropatkin, the Russian general, argued that it was these inadequacies which lost the war for Russia. On a single-track railway, the stations and passing-places take on an entirely new significance. On the Trans-Siberian they were so far apart that on some sections only three trains a day could be run. The pressure to run trains was so great, however, that some sections could become completely clogged, requiring a complex unsnarling process which had to be accomplished by station-masters who were often ill-trained and invariably drunk.

Two stations of crucial importance in the early part of the war were Baikal and Tankhoy at opposite sides of Lake Baikal. The ice-breaking steamer *Baikal*, built in Newcastle, had been brought up in sections, reconstructed, and launched on the lake in 1900. All troops, armament, and supplies had to be trans-shipped at each side of the lake. When steamer operations became impossible in winter, troops had to walk and supplies were dragged across the ice. When it was 4½ ft. thick an ice railway was built between the two stations. The crisis of the war caused the swift remedying of these defects. The circum-Baikal link was completed by September 1904 and additional stations were built in order to increase the frequency of the trains. Without the line and its crucial stations the Russians could not have fought the war at all. As it turned out, its inadequacies ensured that they could not win. On his journey on the Trans-Siberian line in 1977, Eric Newby made a side trip to Port Baikal. He found it to be 'a ghostly place . . . decaying gently'.[17]

On the Japanese side, the railways and their stations also played a vital part in the war. The main trunk system, with its branches, had been completed by 1890, in time to be used to send troops out to Korea and China for the Sino-Japanese war of 1894, the first demonstration of potential Japanese power and an indication of the weakness of China. In the Russo-Japanese war of 1904, the railways were strained to their utmost in transporting troops to the seaports for the front. Already the Japanese had developed their reputation for precision and order. A writer in the *Railway Magazine* in 1904 described the manner in which a Japanese regiment was entrained:

. . . this one manœuvre demonstrates the perfection of discipline to which the army has been brought. The iron gates at the entrance of a railway station are thrown open, and the head of the regiment appears. The column advances along the platform until the leading men have reached the engine, when, on the word of command, the men halt, turn sharply to the right or left, and enter the carriages. There is no hurry or confusion, and in two minutes every man is seated and the train started.[18]

Confusion was the watchword of Latin American politics, and the railway station was often a key point in their revolutions. When Percy Martin wrote about his journey 'through five republics' in 1905, he listed all the revolts, civil wars, revolutions, and cross-border wars which had taken place in Latin America between 1840 and 1905. 'It is to be observed with much regret', he went on, 'that for a period of fifty years there has not been one year of undisturbed peace in South America.'[19] British railway companies repeatedly faced not only damage from insurrections, but also new governments defaulting on the guarantees and subsidies negotiated by the old. Building had to proceed 'in the brief interval between revolutions'. In 1896 the Central Railway of Uruguay had its Central Station and offices in Montevideo burnt down. Further serious damage was done to its system in the Revolution of 1904.

In February 1905 Martin found himself caught up in an attempted military coup in Argentina. Revolts broke out among several regiments in Bahía Blanca, Rosario, Mendoza, and close to Buenos Aires itself. At Mendoza

the most damage had been done, the Revolutionists having turned their cannon upon the Governor's official residence, reducing it almost to ruins, and finally taking possession of the premises and the inmates. . . . Nothing of this, however, was known publicly in the Capital, and in all ignorance of what awaited them, the passengers by the usual morning train of the Buenos Aires and Pacific Railway, Chile-bound via Mercedes and Mendoza left the Retiro Station at the appointed hour . . . News of a disquieting character commenced to reach us as we came to each succeeding station on the line, until arriving at about 1 a.m. the following morning at Villa Mercedes . . . our train was completely stopped by orders of the Revolutionists and the Government troops alike. The locomotive was removed and run some miles down the line, while the train itself, consisting of some eight saloon and sleeping cars, was ignominiously run into a siding and left there. The passengers were left to kick their heels to their hearts' content, not a vestige of information being vouchsafed them as to how long they were to remain practically prisoners—a day, a week, or a month.[20]

As the dining-car of the train had only been provisioned for the twenty-four hours' journey from Buenos Aires to Mendoza the passengers were soon out of food, and as they waited,

snatches of news from the Revolutionary quarters continued to arrive, and from this it seemed that things were rapidly becoming worse. Government troops to the number of several thousand had gone forth to meet the rebels; much firing and many deaths had occurred; the reactionaries had torn up many yards of rails over which our train would have had to pass; and both sides of the contestants were playing havoc with the railway rolling-stock. It also seemed that while the Revolutionists would not permit the train to go forward, the Government objected to it going back to Buenos Aires, so, like Mahomet's coffin, there we were 'suspended between heaven and earth', or, perhaps to use a more suitable simile, we were cast from the Scylla of Villa Mercedes to the Charybdis of Buenos Aires, and our weary feet knew no abiding-place. Travelling in South American Republics, where revolutions have in the past been as plentiful as blackberries in September, has few pleasures, if some startling surprises.[21]

Plus ça change . . . In 1979, when making one of the BBC television series *Great Railway Journeys of the World*, Miles Kington found himself trapped by a military coup at Viacha, a station in Bolivia, twenty miles from La Paz, unable to finish either his journey or his programme.[22]

But the delay and destruction experienced at Latin American stations was to be as nothing compared with the devastation wrought by the great European wars of the twentieth century. While revolt, insurrection, and acts of conquest were taking place around the world, European military theorists were speculating on the role of railways in European wars. In many ways it was all to be a preparation for 1914. The example of the American railways in the Civil War was not lost on expansionist Prussia. The Prussian Chief of Staff, General von Möltke, had written as long ago as 1843, 'Every new railway development is a military benefit, and for national defence it is far more profitable to spend a few million on completing our railways than on new fortresses'. In 1864 a railway section was formed by the Prussian General Staff and in 1866 the Prussians set up a Field Railway Section, partly civil and partly military in personnel, to fulfil the same repair and construction functions as the United States Construction Corps. Valuable experience was gained and lessons learned in Prussia's wars with Denmark in 1864 and Austria in 1866.

The result of these lessons was a set of new regulations for the military control of the railways in wartime, approved in 1867. Under them, there was to be a central supervising commission, but each army corps was to have its own line of communication, separate and distinct from that of others. Each of these lines started from a designated station, which was to act as a concentration point. There supplies for each corps would be collected and dispatched and so would the troops. At a distance of 100–125 miles along each line selected stations would serve as halting-places for the feeding of troops, watering of horses, reception of sick and wounded, repair of rolling stock, etc. The furthest point reached by rail from day to day would constitute a railhead. All this would take place under an Inspector-General of communications. Upon the declaration of war, the Inspector-General was to designate the railhead stations and organize the intermediate stations for feeding men and horses. The station thus fulfilled a crucial role at every stage.

In 1870 the German troops mobilized effectively along nine lines of concentration. But supplies proved problematical, with train-loads of supplies dispatched to stations inadequately provided with sidings to house them and staff to unload them. The French proved even more inefficient. Plans to create a similar organization to that of the Germans had not been implemented. So when war with Prussia broke out, France was caught unprepared. The French railway companies were ordered to put themselves at the disposal of the War Ministry on 15 July 1870. The first troop trains left Paris next day.

Their point of departure was the Gare de l'Est, a station which came to occupy a particular place in the emotional memories of the French, for in France's three great modern wars (1870, 1914–18, 1939–40), it was the Est Railway that carried French troops to the front. The Gare de l'Est might well be the last place that many soldiers would see their loved ones.

It was farce rather than tragedy, however, which marked the first day of the Franco-Prussian War. The first troop train was due to start at 5.45 a.m., but such was the lack of liaison that the troops waited for four hours at the station. By the time they left they were too drunk to notice that their ammunition had been purloined by friends and relatives as souvenirs. During the next nineteen days nearly a thousand trains left the capital with 300,000 men, 65,000 horses, and 5,000 wagon-loads of supplies. But incompetent organization meant that some trains were full and others empty; troops lost contact with their officers; soldiers did not know their destinations. Within a few days, thousands of 'lost' soldiers were eating and sleeping in station restaurants on the railway to the front. No transfer stations had been designated and no one nominated to control the unloading of supplies. So stations near the frontier became blocked by unloaded wagons. Some had no platforms free and troops were forced to descend some distance from the station and walk along the track because their trains could not get any closer. Most of the traffic went to Metz where the station facilities were inadequate, and soon the platforms were blocked. Wagons were backed up for miles and could not be unloaded because many were unlabelled. Indeed shortages were reported in Metz because no one knew what was in the wagons and there were not enough staff to unload them. Eventually the whole lot fell into the hands of the Germans. During the siege of Paris, with railway communications cut, the great terminal stations were put to other more unusual uses, as hospitals, flour mills, and manufactories of observation balloons.

After the débâcle of the Franco-Prussian War the French made urgent arrangements for railway regulation in wartime. A series of laws was passed to cover every aspect of potential future hostilities. A railway regiment was formed, and a railway school set up to train it. The railway companies were obliged to send an annual contingent of their employees to the War Ministry for training. In December 1913 the French military rail transport organization was made more effective by the provision of a line commission attached to each of the large railway systems, each commission controlling a combined railway technical and military staff. Under the line commissions and sub-line commissions were station commissions. Their job was the superintending of entrainment and detrainment of troops, loading and unloading of materials, provision of trains, prevention of congestion, and ensuring the protection of station and lines. Finally France was divided into two railway zones: interior zone and army zone, with transition stations at the points where the railways passed from one zone to another. There were also organized mobilization stations, meals stations, detraining stations, base, supply, evacuation, and hospital stations, infirmary stations, and distribution stations, a very comprehensive scheme aimed at preventing the recurrence of the terrible defeats which had characterized the Franco-Prussian War.

But the Germans were far from idle. After the war, they revised their arrangements, developing a more complex and sophisticated system for railway control in wartime. Comprehensive instructions were issued in 1899 carefully defining the duties and responsibilities of all the authorities, civil and military, connected with the military use of the railways. Once again the regulations involved designated base stations for each army corps, and dispatch of supplies and troops to stations acting as collection points near the front line. The Germans continued actively to extend their network, building many lines for purely military purposes in their frontier region. By 1911 they had no fewer than nineteen rail crossings of the Rhine. Their military lines tended to be provided with large sidings and long-platformed stations for the accommodation of troop trains. From the railway point of view, both sides were clearly gearing themselves up for a return bout. It would be called the Great War.

The Station in Wartime (2)
The Twentieth Century

THE First World War decisively demonstrated the truth of General von Schlieffen's confident assertion:

The railways have become an instrument of war without which the great modern armies are not able to be assembled or moved forward. Today you no longer ask how many battalions your enemy has but how many railway lines: you no longer compare only the valour and armaments of opposing forces, but the capacity for action of their railways. Since 1866, and especially since 1870, we have entered through this a new phase in the conduct of war.[1]

The war called forth prodigious feats of achievement, particularly from the railways of Britain, France, and Germany. The tracks, the rolling stock, the personnel equally bore the brunt of the insatiable demand of this all-devouring Armageddon for transportation of men, munitions, and supplies.[2]

The young men of all three nations flocked to the colours in 1914, exhilarated by the prospect of martial glory. They had drunk deep of the myths of chivalry and heroism which had permeated the literature, poetry, and history of the nineteenth century. But there was little of swords and sagas in the mud of the trenches and the scarred, nightmarish terrain of no man's land. The carnage was unimaginably high. Amidst it all, the trains ran inexorably on—to the front and back from the front, on leave and back from leave, into Hell and sometimes back again from the abyss.

The station figured on a greater scale than ever before in the emotional memories of individuals and of nations. Leave-taking and reunion took on a heightened intensity. Vera Brittain, in her deeply moving *Testament of Youth* (1933), spoke for all the lovers parted by war. She highlighted the role railway stations played in the course of many an all too brief wartime romance. She recalled how she realized that the brilliant young officer Roland Leighton returned her love when, after a night at the theatre, they repaired to Charing Cross Station:

At Charing Cross, with half an hour to wait for the last train to Purley, we walked together up and down the platform. It was New Year's Eve, a bright night with infinities of stars and a cold, brilliant moon; the station was crowded with soldiers and their friends who had gathered there to greet the New Year. What would it bring, that menacing 1915?

Neither Roland nor I was able to continue the ardent conversation that had been so easy in the theatre. After two unforgettable days which seemed to relegate the whole of our previous experience into a dim and entirely insignificant past, we had to leave one another just as everything was beginning, and we did not know—as in those days no one for whom France loomed in the distance ever could know—when or even whether we should meet again. Just before the train was due to leave, I got into the carriage, but it did not actually go for another ten minutes, and we gazed at each other submerged in complete, melancholy silence.

My aunt, intending, I suppose, to relieve the strain—which must have made the atmosphere uncomfortable for a third party—asked us jokingly: 'Why don't you say something? Is it too deep for words?' We laughed rather constrainedly and said that we hoped it wasn't as bad as all that, but in our hearts we knew that it was just as bad and a great deal worse. The previous night I had become ecstatically conscious that I loved him; on the New Year's Eve I realized that he, too, loved me, and the knowledge that had been an unutterable joy so long as any part of the evening remained became an anguish that no words could describe as soon as we had to say goodbye.[3]

Soon Roland was off to the front and they met again when he was given leave. He wired Vera to meet him at St Pancras and she came up from Buxton by train:

During the few minutes that I had to wait at St. Pancras for him to arrive from Liverpool Street, I shivered with cold in spite of the hot August noon. When at last I saw him come into the station and speak to a porter, his air of maturity and sophistication turned me stiff with alarm. At that stage of the War it was fashionable for officers who had been at the front to look as disreputable and war-worn as possible in order to distinguish them from the brand-new subalterns of Kitchener's Army ... Modishly shabby, noticeably thinner and looking at least thirty, Roland on leave seemed Active Service personified. In another moment we were standing face to face, tense with that anxiety to find one another unchanged which only lovers know at its worst. Just as we had parted we shook hands without any sign of emotion, except for his usual pallor in moments of excitement. For quite a minute we looked at each other without speaking, and then broke awkwardly into polite conversation.[4]

But the leave comes to an end and she returns to St Pancras to catch the train back to Buxton:

At St. Pancras there was no empty carriage in which we could talk for the few minutes left to us, so we had perforce to walk up and down the noisy platform, saying nothing of importance and ferociously detesting the cheerful, chattering group round my carriage door.

'I wish to God there weren't other people in the world!' he exclaimed irritably.

'I agree', I said, and remarked wearily that I should have to put up with their pleasant company in a lighted dining-car all the way to Buxton.

'Oh, damn!' he responded.

But when, suddenly, the shriek of the whistle cut sharply through the tumult of sound, our resolution not to kiss on a crowded platform vanished with our consciousness of the crowd's exasperating presence. Too angry and miserable to be shy any more, we clung together and kissed in forlorn desperation.

'I shan't look out of the window and wave to you', I told him, and he replied incoherently: 'No—don't; I can't!'

To my amazement, taut and tearless as I was, I saw him hastily mop his eyes with his handkerchief, and in that moment, when it was too late to respond or to show that I understood, I realized how much more he cared for me than I had supposed or he had ever shown. I felt, too, so bitterly sorry for him because he had to fight against his tears while I had no wish to cry at all, and the intolerable longing to comfort him when there was no more time in which to do it made me furious with the frantic pain of impotent desire. And then, all at once, the whistle sounded again, and the train started. As the noisy group moved away from the door he sprang on to the footboard, clung to my hand, and, drawing my face down to his, kissed my lips with a sudden vehemence of despair. And I kissed his, and just managed to whisper 'Good-bye!' The next moment he was walking rapidly down the platform, with his head bent and his face very pale. Although I had said that I would not, I stood by the door as the train left the station and watched him moving through the crowd. But he never turned again.[5]

Roland Leighton died of wounds received in action in France on 23 December 1915.

The previous year, when the outbreak of war was becoming inevitable, it was announced in Germany that a military timetable would come into operation on the railways from 4 August. This was the signal for civilian travellers, wherever they were, to take to the rails while it was still possible. Stations became choked with civilians heading home. The number of civilian trains on the Prussian network doubled and trebled in the days leading up to 4 August. On 31 July, 61 normal trains left the Berlin stations; on 1 August, 157; on 2 August, 106; and on 3 August, 65. From Munich Station the number of trains doubled and trebled on 31 July and 1 August. The Prussian Minister of Railways declared: 'Such an avalanche of travellers has never been seen since the beginning of the railways.'[6] There was so much luggage that the trains simply could not carry it. Berlin stations announced a delay of up to two weeks in dispatching luggage to its destinations. More than 120,000 items of luggage were heaped up at Berlin stations, 45,000 in the Stettiner Bahnhof alone. The left-luggage deposits were swamped completely and much luggage was simply abandoned on the platforms, seriously impeding traffic.

Army mobilization was actually ordered on 1 August 1914 and between 4 August, when military timetables came into force on the railways, and 18 August, 18,000 trains conveyed 3,834,000 men to the front. A train crossed the Hohenzollern Bridge near Cologne every ten minutes. The designation of stations for assembly, supply, detrainment, and so on, as required under detailed plans for the use of the railways in wartime, came into effect. Work began at once on lengthening platforms, installing ramps, and erecting additional sheds and warehouses at important strategic stations and junctions.

In France, army mobilization was declared for Sunday, 2 August 1914. At midnight French railways passed under military authority and all their resources were placed at the disposal of the army. Military timetables came into operation and commercial transportation was suspended. During the first four days (2–6 August) 10,000 train-loads of troops were dispatched. They arrived at the designated regulating stations and the troops aboard were then directed to their individual destinations. At some of the regulating stations, a train passed through every eight minutes. The greatest burden fell on the Est network, which had to borrow 316 train crews from other networks and as many reserve locomotives as the other networks could spare. Etat handed over ninety-seven of its most powerful engines. Crews worked 40–45 hours without leaving their machines. By 19 August, 1,296,000 French soldiers with 449,000 horses and large quantities of munitions and supplies had been assembled in their concentration points by rail.

On 4 August the British government took control of the British railway system. It was put under the control of a management committee formed of the General Managers of the twelve big companies under the chairmanship of the President of the Board of Trade. Special timetables were rapidly drawn up and on 9 August the grand operation began to mobilize the British Expeditionary Force. Servicemen were collected from railway stations all over Britain, and during the next eight days 334 trains arrived at Southampton, bringing nearly 70,000 personnel, 22,000 horses, 2,400 guns, 1,200 bicycles, 97 motorcycles, and 2,550 tons of stores. By the end of August, 670 troop trains had reached Southampton and over 118,000 troops had embarked for overseas.

Once the British Expeditionary Force arrived in France, it had to be transported to the front. Beginning on 15 August and continuing in the following days, with a frequency attaining a total of forty-five trains every twenty-four hours, the Nord network transported 120,000 British soldiers, plus horses, guns, vehicles, and bicycles to the northern frontier. As the Germans swept across Belgium, many Belgians fled. Between 11 and 20 August, Belgian and northern French stations were filled to bursting point with fugitives. Between 20 and 22 August, fourteen trains of Belgian refugees crossed the frontier into France. In ten days, more than 100,000 people passed through Laon Station. They descended on Paris, their number swelled by fleeing Frenchmen. In all, 1,500,000 people crossed Paris from the Gare du Nord to the stations for the south and west. On a single day (3 September) 50,000 people left the Gare d'Orléans. On 2 September, with the victorious German advance still unchecked, the government decided to move to Bordeaux and to evacuate Paris's art treasures and financial reserves. The PLM, Paris–Orléans, and Etat networks organized special trains to remove these vital cargoes.

So rapid was the German advance that parts of the French railway network were swallowed up by the enemy, complete with staff, stations, and locomotives. The Nord network lost seventy-two engines and 1,200 men. All available trains and rolling stock were pressed into service to evacuate key staff, supplies, and reserves from endangered regulating stations. Fifty-seven trains removed everything and everyone movable from the regulating station of Châlons to its fall-back position at Montereau. Eighty-four trains took everything movable from Reims Regulating Station to Noisy-le-Sec, thirty-nine of them detailed to remove the entire operations of the Army Bakery. By 4 September the major part of the Nord network and much of Est was in German hands.

The Battle of the Marne stemmed the German tide and Nord and Est regained control of large numbers of lines, many of them damaged or destroyed. They set to work repairing them at once in order to convey forces forward for the counter-attack. The stations at Compiègne, Amiens, Lille, then Calais, successively disembarked 800 trains of fresh troops. While Est and Nord poured reinforcements into the fray, the PLM network was sending north from Marseilles forty-five trains a day, filled with French colonial and British Indian troops who were arriving in the South of France by ship. In August and September the Paris–Orléans network forwarded thirty trains loaded with Moroccan troops who had arrived at Bordeaux and fifty trains full of territorials from Bordeaux and Nantes. The P.–O. was also supplying provisions in bulk for the reserve troops kept in camp at Paris: between the end of August and the end of September, 11,700 tonnes of foodstuffs, 66,000 tonnes of fodder, 117,000 cattle, and 211,000 lambs and pigs.

Once the front had stabilized and the two sides had settled down to slog it out, both sides turned their attention to strengthening and improving the railway facilities. The Allied regulating stations became so overloaded with the amounts of ammunition and supplies going forward and wounded men being transported to the rear that massive building and engineering programmes were initiated to provide extra track, larger marshalling yards, more depots for arms, pens for livestock, and reception points for the injured. The initial regulating stations for the French forces were Gray, Is-sur-Tille, Saint-Dizier, Troyes, Noisy-le-Sec, Le Bourget, and Creil. Not only were the facilities at these stations considerably enlarged during the next few years, but as the war ebbed and flowed, additional regulating stations were designated. A major new regulating station for British troops was set up at Romescamps before the Battle of the Somme, to join the existing ones at Abbeville, Calais, and Outreau. At Boulogne Station, 23,000 m. of earthworks were built to protect the revictualling of British forces. To cater for the ever pressing ammunition needs, three great ammo dumps were established at Vaivre, Brienne, and Formerie, which could supply at once the needs of forces in any sector of the front line. Equipped with immense sheds, platforms, and marshalling yards, each of the three depots allowed simultaneous loading of 2,400 wagons. During the siege of Verdun in 1916, French engineers built an entirely new railway line 60 km. long, as well as branch lines, two hospitals, and seven stations, in order to supply the Verdun defenders. Towards the end of 1916, 100 stations near the front line were extended and 700 km. of extra track laid in preparation for the next big push.

The Germans were engaged in similar operations. The fleeing Belgians had ripped up railway lines, blown up bridges, blocked tunnels, destroyed telegraph and telephone lines, and sabotaged station installations. The Prussian Railway Regiment took charge of restoring them to use. After one year of the war, the Germans had in the occupied territories rebuilt 164 bridges and eight tunnels, reopened fourteen damaged lines and greatly extended 160 stations in order to cope with the embarkation and disembarkation of their troops. Throughout the war vast sums were expended on railway and station expansion for the war effort. As late as 1918, the Germans were allocating 3 million marks for the extension of Mülheim Station in the Ruhr, 6 million for the extension of Duisburg Station, and 1.8 million for extensions to the two stations of

Essen. The aim was to open up still further access to the metallurgical and munitions areas around Essen.

In order to clear existing stations and to free rolling stock from non-military commitments, civilian travellers in Germany were subjected to greater and greater restrictions as the war progressed. From 1916 onwards, speeds were reduced, services cut back, special reduced-price tickets withdrawn, and restaurant cars taken out of service. There were further reductions in 1917, when 1,000 or more services were cancelled. Some State railway authorities withdrew first- and second-class facilities, others withdrew third-class. In order to prevent the railways being clogged by refugees, as the war began to go against Germany, restrictions on foreign travel were tightened. From October 1917 no German station was allowed to sell tickets to Switzerland and in 1918 the weekly Berlin–Constantinople service was withdrawn. Restrictions on the movement of non-essential freight were equally severe. The government introduced a policy of transferring as much of this freight as possible to river transport, and merchandise intended for stations on the Elbe, Oder, or any navigable river in the Mark was not allowed to be carried on the railways.

By 1916 French railways had reached breaking-point. It was estimated that in order to meet French needs 200–300 locomotives, 10,000–20,000 wagons, and 1,000 miles of new track were needed. The British Prime Minister Lloyd George took action at once and on 1 January 1917 introduced restrictions on British railways, which involved the curtailment, alteration, and deceleration of passenger services, the discontinuing of seat reservations, a great reduction in the number of sleeping-cars, dining-cars, and through carriages, and the cancellation of all cheap fares. On top of all this, passenger fares were increased by 50 per cent. This resulted in the release of 370 locomotives for service in France. But in addition a number of branch lines were closed and their tracks taken up for use in France. In all, this resulted in the closure of 225 stations for the duration of the war.

The American entry into the war in 1917 put an even greater strain on the railway facilities of France. The Americans arrived at the ports of Brest, Saint-Nazaire, and Bordeaux where great base camps were established. Their addition to the conflict raised a whole new demand for troop trains, provisions trains, munitions trains, leave trains, and hospital trains. Nevertheless, by November 1918 the railways had carried 2 million American soldiers to the battle-front. But this was by no means the last great railway effort of the war. The German Spring offensive of 1918 meant the evacuation of the civil population of Picardy, 40–45 trains a day conveying 100,000 people to the west and the south. At the same time the P.–O. network removed 103,000 Parisians to safety in the countryside. The threat to the railway workshops at Amiens and Epernay caused the removal of all vital equipment and material to replacement depots at La Garenne-Bezons and Saint-Etienne-du-Rouvray. The regulating stations of Creil and Le Bourget were evacuated to Mantes and Aubrais.

When the Armistice finally came on 11 November 1918, the work of railways still did not end. There were Allied troops to demobilize, prisoners to repatriate, refugees to return to their homes, devastated areas to reprovision. The work was made more difficult by the depredations wrought by the defeated Germans. When the guns were finally stilled, the Germans were found to have destroyed on the Nord and Est networks 5,600 km. of track, 1,510 bridges and other works, 12 tunnels, and 590 stations, 338 of them belonging to Nord and the remainder to Est.

Apart from the obvious and continuing need to provide troop trains —6,591 troop and artillery trains sent to the German Fourth Army in Flanders between June and November 1916 alone—the railways of both sides served a number of other vital continuing military needs. First, there were supply trains. Colonel Henaff and Captain Bornecque in their account of the French railways at war estimated that in normal periods during the war an average of 200 trains a day was needed to convey essential foodstuffs, munitions, engineering materials, and so forth.[7] In all, more than 400,000 supply trains were dispatched during the war.

Then there were leave trains. Initially these created considerable difficulties. In 1915, during a lull in the war, the French High Command granted extensive leave to their soldiers. In theory, the men were expected to leave by ordinary trains or empty supply trains returning from the front. They were to alight at the regulating stations, be forwarded to military assembly stations in their regions, and then proceed on to their home station by ordinary passenger train. But the leave-taking soldiers simply ignored all this and poured on to the civilian trains, creating havoc and sometimes violence in their anxiety to get home. The authorities acted to set up special train-change stations which served as termini for all trains to and from the front and as starting-points for special leave trains running to all the major population centres. Facilities such as cinemas and canteens were installed at the stations to induce the soldiers to wait for their designated trains. But although the worst of the chaos was stemmed, there continued to be a problem with eager leave-takers simply circumventing the carefully prescribed arrangements.

A vital lifeline for the serving soldier was the postal train. During the course of the war an estimated 9 million parcels were sent to the front, and between March 1915 and the Armistice the Central Military Post Office in Paris dealt with an average of 3.5 million letters a day, three times the pre-war daily average.

Lastly, there were the hospital trains. Initially there were seven permanent French hospital trains, each capable of carrying 128 wounded men. But these were continually supplemented throughout the conflict until by the end there were 200 hospital trains in service. In all, Est network ran 32,894 hospital train services during the war and Nord ran 66,213. Inevitably they were at their most numerous during the great battles. During the Battle of the Marne, for instance, fifty-six hospital trains arrived at Troyes Station and sixty-five at Noisy-le-Sec alone. In Britain, twelve special ambulance trains were built as soon as the war began. But more were soon needed to cope with the tragic flood of injured crossing the Channel. Fourteen ambulance trains were stationed at Southampton Station and six at Dover Town, both of which became designated ambulance depots. All in all 2,680,000 wounded were transported to hospitals up and down the country by ambulance trains. Between 2 January 1915 and 28 February 1919 no fewer than 1,260,000 wounded were brought across the Channel and dispatched in 7,781 ambulance trains from Dover alone.

But the war stretched its tentacles far beyond Western Europe into Africa, the Middle East, and Central Asia. Soon after the war began, Edwin A. Pratt published his *The Rise of Rail Power in War and Conquest, 1833–1914*, in which he was concerned to show the absolute necessity of efficient railway operations in the fighting of modern wars. He also sought to reveal the great German railway plot which had caused them to drive lines towards the most vulnerable parts of the British Empire. For Pratt, the railway plot involved not just the Baghdad Railway, which had been such a vital part of railway paranoia before the war, but the African railways in East Africa, the Cameroon, and South-West Africa, threatening British interests in Central, West, and Southern Africa respectively.

The plot was reflected in the German approach to station-building. At Keetmanshoop in South-West Africa, the terminus of a line of little economic significance, but a relatively short distance from the South African frontier, a large headquarters building had been constructed which could be readily fortified and converted for use as a supply base in a campaign. To this day, the impressive German station survives at Kigoma on Lake Tanganyika. It was by far the most notable building in the town, and was to play a crucial role in the East African campaigns, including the extraordinary miniature naval battles that took place on the lake. This was the station as Menace. The East African campaign did indeed become a battle for the German line and its crucial stations. In Dar es Salaam the retreating Germans destroyed the harbour works and the railway station, leaving the rest of the town relatively undamaged. The war in the Middle East centred on the destruction of existing railway lines and the building of new ones, particularly in Mesopotamia. But there, in the exigencies of war, stations were usually only of the most rudimentary sort.

The Trans-Siberian line was overwhelmed by war once again after the Bolshevik Revolution, and particularly during the Russian Civil War. When the Bolsheviks withdrew from the war, the Allied Czechoslovak corps of 40,000–50,000 Czech troops was stranded in Russia. The corps was stationed in the Ukraine and the French government, together with the Czech nationalist leader Masaryk, negotiated for it to be moved to Vladivostok for repatriation to Europe and deployment on the western front. The Czechs were soon strung out along the line. Contrary to the agreement they had kept their arms and ammunition. In May 1918 they seized Chelyabinsk station after a fracas and found themselves, in effect, at war with the Bolsheviks.

Those who had reached Vladivostok turned back to participate and the corps was soon swept up into the Civil War. Later in the year, General William Graves landed with the American Expeditionary Force (Siberia) at Vladivostok to aid the Czechs. The most important part of Graves's brief was to keep the railway open. And indeed much of the war that followed was fought along the line. In such conditions the stations became crucial strategic points, and their staffs found themselves in the dangerous situation of having to satisfy different parties in the movement of trains. Few of them survived.

The wooden churches which had been built at many stations from the Alexander III fund were destroyed, often broken up and used for fuel. At Irkutsk Station, Admiral Alexander Kolchak, head of the White Russian force, was captured while travelling in a six-train convoy with large stores of Russian treasure to Vladivostok. He was shot. In Trans-Baikalia, the anti-Bolshevik Cossack war-lord Grigory Semyonov and his deputy Kalymokov with their Cossack and Mongolian band travelled the line in armoured trains, looting and murdering as they went. Many station-masters and staff were executed for alleged Red sympathies.

As Harmon Tupper put it, graft and venality had plagued Kolchak's supply lines on the Trans-Siberian.[8] Merchants everywhere bribed station-masters to attach shipments to westbound trains. When the

White defeat was recognized as inevitable in 1919 the White generals requisitioned a train each for themselves, their suites, and their baggage. Station-masters were forced to supply them with fuel and to halt and side-track other trains to allow them to get through. Soon they and the Czechs were vying for control of the line to make their respective escapes. Huge numbers of refugees were on the move too, in the depths of a bitter winter. Famine and typhus struck, and it was said that every station became a graveyard, each one surrounded by hundreds and sometimes thousands of unburied bodies.

Although Britain was not immediately threatened by invasion, the country was at risk from air raids, and the massive conflict being fought out in France and beyond had its repercussions on the British railway system. Britain was divided into seven operational, or forward, sectors, and two rearward sectors, with a troop-regulating station in each sector. Standard routes and specially integrated timetables were drawn up to promote maximum flexibility and efficiency. The focal points of all the railway activities in transporting men and materials were the systems of the South-Eastern and Chatham, the London, Brighton and South Coast, and the London and South-Western railways, because these included all the ports nearest to the western front. Troop trains and supply trains thundered over these systems day and night without cease.

There were special services too. One of the most celebrated was the Euston–Thurso 'Naval Special' which ran every day from London to the bases of the Grand Fleet in the north of Scotland. During the two years in which the service ran (15 February 1917 to 30 April 1919) it carried half a million passengers. The journey was 717 miles and took 21 hours 30 minutes going north and 22 hours 20 minutes coming south. Stations played a key role in the operation of the Naval Special. Naval personnel from Harwich, Dover, Chatham, Brighton, Portsmouth, and Southampton were conveyed by special trains to rendezvous in Euston; men from Plymouth, Devonport, Exeter, Bristol, Cardiff, Barry, Pembroke, and Milford Haven, and also Birkenhead, joined the Special at Crewe; men from Liverpool at Preston; from Hull, Newcastle, and Berwick at Edinburgh; and from Kyle of Lochalsh at Dingwall. There were no feeding arrangements on the train and so refreshments were served by voluntary workers at the stations where stops were made: Crewe, Preston, Carlisle, Hawick, Edinburgh, Inverkeithing, Perth, Inverness, Alness, and Invergordon.

The war transformed the appearance of some stations and the functions of others for the duration. Track and sidings were added to many stations which the war imbued with strategic significance. Halts were created and spur-lines run out to army camps and factories. Platforms were lengthened and provided with ramps to give troops, horses, and vehicles speedier and more efficient access to trains. New junctions with other companies' lines were effected for government use. A new station with platforms 400 ft. long was erected by the London and South-Western Railway for the Naval Cordite Factory at Holton Heath and the Midland Railway erected special stations for munitions workers at Quedgeley, Longbridge, Torrisholme, Cardington, and Halesowen Junction.

Specific stations became known for specific war materials. London and North-Western freight trains carried a million tons of salt from Middlewich, 56 million yards of Service uniform cloth from Huddersfield, 1½ million tons of TNT and gun-cotton from Queensferry, 5,000 tons of government stationery from Wolverton, over a million cylinders of poison gas, tear-gas, hydrogen gas, and sulphur chloride from Runcorn, 55,000 tons of motor tyres to and from the RASC tyre depot at Camden Station, and 10¾ million filled hand-grenades from the little West Yorkshire station of Fenay Bridge and Lepton. Newhaven and Littlehampton stations received literally millions of tons of munitions and war stores for dispatch to the Continent.

In London, each of the South-Eastern Railway's terminal stations was given a specific function. Ambulance-train traffic from Dover came into Charing Cross. All dead officers' kit was forwarded to Holborn Viaduct. Most of the petrol and aeroplane parts for Dover and the South Coast went from Cannon Street. Leave services in both directions and outward mail for the front went from Victoria.

The war also transformed the rail traffic of Scotland, where Aberdeen became the railhead for the Grand Fleet. The new joint station, completed in 1915, with thirteen platforms and massive sidings, saw the arrival of many train-loads of provisions, naval stores, ordnance, and medical stores. Every week 6,000 bags of potatoes were forwarded to Aberdeen from stations in all parts of Scotland and 2,000–3,000 packages of fresh fruit from all over Britain. The tiny wayside station of Invergordon became one of the most important railway stations in Britain. For it was not only serving the naval base and the fleet but was the artery for communication with Russia. From Invergordon Station, special trains carried refugees, mail, and bullion from Eastern Europe during 1918 and 1919. To Invergordon came special bullion trains from London carrying funds from the Bank of England for dispatch to Russia.

Another of the linchpins of naval operations in Scotland was Inverness Station, centre for the distribution of mail and personnel to the Grand

Fleet. A permanent naval staff of 70 officers, 300–400 men, and 120 Wrens were based at Inverness to co-ordinate these operations. It was often at Inverness that officer and rating learned to which ship they had been assigned. Mail arrived and was housed in a specially built shed on station premises, and part of the laundry of the Station Hotel was also commandeered for this purpose. Ammunition was distributed from Inverness Station and the harbour. Naval Ambulance Train No. 4 was based at Inverness. Additional sidings were provided at the station for the trains of ammunition and naval materials. The Station Hotel accommodated late-arriving service personnel; passengers on the Naval Special were fed there; and seven enemy spies were caught there.

But stations had to get used to many new functions during the war. One was as air-raid warning centre. There were 108 German air raids on Britain in the First World War. Twenty-four railwaymen in all were killed in air raids, eight in a single raid on St Pancras on 17 February 1918. Twenty people sheltering under the roadway entrance arch were also killed and the station hotel was badly damaged, but rail traffic was not affected. There were a number of spectacular narrow escapes, with bombs on Cannon Street Station and Waterloo in 1917 resulting only in broken glass in the canopy. The provinces on the whole escaped lightly, though Nottingham Victoria and Hull Paragon stations received direct hits.

Although it was obvious that the enemy would attempt to destroy and disorganize strategic railway stations, tracks, piers, and harbours, no arrangements were made by the government to direct the railway companies as to precautionary measures until three months after the outbreak of war. But the Great Eastern Company, expecting enemy operations over its territory, acted at once, instructing station staff to watch out for hostile aircraft and to telegraph the Company's head office at Liverpool Street Station. The information was then passed by telephone to Home Forces' GHQ. Once air raids began in earnest, a military office was set up at Liverpool Street Station to co-ordinate the information coming in and to act upon it. In May 1917 the Germans began daylight raids and in June 1917 sent an armada of ten Zeppelins, which crossed the Yorkshire coast near Flamborough Head. It was the GER's Walsingham Station which gave the first warning of its approach. In the event, although many bombs were dropped, little damage was done. The three railways which suffered most during the war were the Great Eastern, the North London, and the London, Tilbury and Southend section of the Midland, the greatest damage occurring in the Stratford–Poplar–Dalston–Blackwell–Liverpool Street area.

Railway stations were particularly vulnerable and there could have been considerably greater casualties at them than there were. As E. A. Pratt pointed out:

On the occasion, for instance, of the raid on the Midland counties on January 31, 1916, the stoppage of traffic in London for periods of up to two hours or more led to the principal railway stations there being packed with dense masses of belated passengers, who, in most cases, had only a glass roof over their heads as protection against any bomb dropped among them—and there were times when the raiders seemed to be making special efforts to destroy certain of the railway termini in London. Such was the state of congestion that at the Victoria Station of the London, Brighton and South Coast Company—without taking into account the Victoria Station of the South-Eastern and Chatham alongside —there were from 3,000 to 4,000 persons waiting for the trains to resume their running. Under such conditions as these there were possibilities of an appalling loss of life had bombs actually been dropped in the midst of so great a crowd of people.[9]

Precautions against such a tragedy were improved with the adoption in 1916 of a nationwide air-raid warning scheme, which involved dividing Scotland into ten districts and England and Wales into forty-three. In England and Wales the forty-three districts were further divided up between six District Warning Controls, centred in Newcastle, Hull, Liverpool, Birmingham, London, and Portsmouth, all of them responsible to a Central Control. GHQ Home Forces communicated air-raid warnings to Central Control, who then circulated them through the system as appropriate. Four kinds of message were sent out: Warning Only, Take Air Raid Action, Resume Normal Conditions, All Clear. These arrangements generally had the effect of giving adequate warning of approaching danger.

Stations became regular fixtures on the itineraries of servicemen, in particular when going on or returning from leave. With the co-operation of the railway companies, who provided free accommodation and facilities, voluntary organizations sprang up to provide comforts for the troops at the stations. E. A. Pratt pronounced this 'Free Buffet' movement

one of the best and most successful of the schemes of practical beneficence in the interests of our fighting men to which the war gave rise . . . Well supported by the British public, it conferred incalculable benefits on untold millions of men; it diminished the strain of their long journeys; it showed them the genuine sympathy of those on whose behalf they were fighting, and it helped them to retain their fighting strength and to return to their duties overseas in better spirits and in greater vigour than, humanly speaking, would otherwise have been possible, the nation thus obtaining a substantial advantage no less than the men themselves.[10]

It began spontaneously at Perth General Station on 7 August 1914, three days after the outbreak of war. Perth, a joint railway station of the Caledonian, North British, and Highland Railway companies, became a major distribution centre for soldiers travelling north and south and changes of train frequently necessitated long waits there. Some of the ladies of Perth, seeing the waiting soldiers, took it upon themselves to distribute to them baskets of fruit, and soon extended this to the provision of tea and cakes. The need became ever greater, and an organization 'Perthshire Women's Patriotic Committee' was set up to raise funds, procure supplies, and organize. Schoolmasters volunteered to serve men waiting cold and hungry in the early hours of the morning for Highland trains and the ladies took over later. Before long, forty volunteers were working in relays between 5 a.m. and 1 a.m. The station authorities gave them a waiting room for conversion into a rest and recreation centre, open from 8 p.m. to 1 a.m. for soldiers and sailors waiting for night trains.

This organization did not service troop trains. They were provided for by the Perth Churches' Association, working closely with the military and railway authorities. Knowing of the train movements, they were able to lay on tea and sandwiches in the Perth Station Hotel for the occupants of troop trains. The ladies' committee dealt with men on leave passing through Perth, the sick and wounded in ambulance trains, and the passengers on the Naval Special from Euston to Thurso. In all, between its inauguration and its closure on 28 June 1919, the organization, which eventually comprised 200 voluntary workers, served an estimated 1,449,000 servicemen.

The earliest date for such operations in England is 16 August 1914, when the Red Cross organized a Station Refreshment Fund for troops passing through the GWR's Banbury Station. Distribution of refreshments by relays of Red Cross nurses and volunteers took place between 7 a.m. and 10 p.m. In 1915 the ladies of York formed a committee to supply refreshments at very low charges to men in uniform passing through the city. The North-Eastern Railway Company supplied two railway vehicles to serve as stationary buffets, and barrows were wheeled along the more distant platforms. Eighteen thousand men a week were thus served, and in the first twelve months of its operation £7,630 was spent on food, tea, and coffee.

In London, the first railway buffet, free to soldiers and sailors, was opened at Euston on 4 February 1915. The inspiration came from the example offered by the Gare du Nord in Paris, where an excellent buffet, capable of providing dinners for fifty guests at a time and affording sleeping accommodation for forty, had been opened for the benefit of British and Belgian troops passing through. Lord Esher suggested something similar in London and the London and North-Western placed a room at the disposal of a team of volunteer women workers. The buffet, which offered not just a refreshment room but also a rest room, catered for 1,029,000 men in 1918 alone and by the time it closed on 9 July 1919 had served 6 million free meals.

A buffet was opened at Victoria on 15 February 1915. Since the flow of men through that station was continuous, it had to be kept open day and night. A corps of eighty voluntary workers ensured that it was. By the end of 1915 the buffet was supplying tea, coffee, cocoa, cakes, sandwiches, biscuits, soup, new-laid eggs, etc., to between 3,000 and 4,000 during the course of each twenty-four hours. The weekly bill included such items as 1,700 loaves, 2,800 pounds of cake, 210 gallons of milk, 350 pounds of tea, 280 pounds of cocoa, 500 pounds of sugar, and 420 pounds of butter. The buffet remained open until 30 June 1919, and by that time the number of men supplied with free refreshment was over 12 million.

Similar free buffets followed at Liverpool Street, Paddington, and Waterloo. But these were not the only facilities provided. The YMCA provided 'station huts' adjoining the main stations, where there was sleeping accommodation provided to supplement the comforts on offer in the buffets. By 1918 there were buffets, hutments, or hostels catering for the needs of travelling servicemen in almost every important station connected with military or naval traffic. At Victoria, the principal leave station, other organizations were established to provide for service personnel on leave. The Motor Transport Volunteers conveyed soldiers across London to stations for the North and West. The Green Cross Women's Guard met all trains with female service personnel and the National Guard met all leave trains and looked after the welfare of the men. The Salvation Army, the Church Army, the YMCA, the District Rest Houses, the Overseas Reception Committee, the Ladies' Vigilance Society, the St Columba Society (devoted to looking after Scottish soldiers on leave), and the Knights of St Columbus (American soldiers) all had offices at Victoria. Also at Victoria, eight money-exchange offices, later increased to fourteen, were set up in 1915 to change the French money of returning troops into English.

As the echoes of the war died away, the stations gradually returned to normal, but a permanent reminder of those days was to be found in the memorials to railwaymen who died serving their country at home and overseas. At Euston the names of 3,719 employees of the London and North-Western Railway who fell were listed and at Victoria the names of the 556 men lost by the South-Eastern and Chatham. At Paddington the memorial took the form of a bronze statue of a heroic British infantry-man, holding in his hands not a gun but a letter from home. But perhaps the most spectacular memorial was the Victory Arch erected at Waterloo and inscribed with the names of the 585 employees of the London and South-Western Railway who had been killed. The architect James Robb Scott described the decoration that he had added to the arch:

The sculptural decorations are three groups, two of which are semi-circular in composition, placed on the pylons either side of the arch. The one on the left, representing War 1914, has a central figure of Bellona, Goddess of War, wild and distraught, clad in scaled armour, astride the world, with flaming torch and naked sword dealing death and destruction. The other, on the right, represent-ing Peace, 1919, has for its motive a figure of Peace seated and enthroned upon the earth, and holding a palm branch and a small figure of winged victory, symbolical of Peace with Victory, bringing abundance and contentment whilst commerce and liberal arts flourish. The panel round the Arch is decorated with war trophies and discs giving the names of the different countries where our men have fought. The whole is surmounted and finished by the central group of Britannia, seated and triumphant holding aloft the sacred torch of Liberty to her own greatness and glory, and for the guidance of her children and children's children and the benefit of mankind in general.[11]

The Great Eastern's memorial at Liverpool Street Station had, however, its own tragic aftermath. Returning from unveiling it in 1922, Field Marshal Sir Henry Wilson was murdered on his own doorstep by two I R A gunmen. Horrified, the Great Eastern installed a memorial to Sir Henry next to the laurel-wreathed columns and solemn plaques of the war memorial.

   The experience of the First World War stood the railways in good stead for the outbreak of the second global conflict. The railways came under the control of the Railway Executive Committee, appointed by the Minister of Transport. It consisted of the General Managers of the four big companies and of the London Passenger Transport Board. They were to run in all 538,559 special trains during the war. Among their earliest tasks was providing 261 trains to transport 102,000 men of the British Expeditionary Force to Southampton. Bank of England bullion and national art treasures were moved by special trains to safety in Wales. But most spectacular of all was the evacuation of schoolchildren and selected categories of adults from London. Six hundred thousand were transported in the first four days of September 1939.

George C. Nash, official historian of the L M S war effort, described the company's part in the operation and the role of the stations in it:

A railway station sees life from a peculiar angle—beginnings and ends, arrivals and departures, happy home-comings and sad goodbyes. The vast exodus of children which took place from many of the largest cities of Great Britain in the first four days of September, 1939, was unique among such scenes. Known as the Evacuation, it was probably the greatest controlled mass movement of human beings within so short a time that the world had ever seen. A page in the nation's history, and at the same time a page in the intimate diary of millions of British homes up and down the land ... The L.M.S. handled much of this traffic. It came in a steady flow to 15 of the Company's stations. 1,450 special trains were run, and on the evening of the fourth day the total number of passengers dealt with was returned as approximately half a million. And all without a single casualty, and all interwoven with the extensive ordinary summer services then still running. Even the Company's electric service was hard at it (one train every eight minutes) taking passengers out of the city to where steam trains waited to move them farther afield. The children, some accompanied by their mothers, but generally by school officials, ranged from 3 to 13 years of age. Each child carried a gas mask, food, a change of clothing and wore three labels. As they entered the railway stations they marched with a good step, but many of their little faces were hard set trying to be brave. . . . During those four days the railway staff on duty in the stations acted as guide, philosopher and friend to many bewildered little people . . . As train after train pulled out to the safe areas some of the staff must have looked wistfully after them, perhaps especially remembering a little girl of ten, who in parting from her mother, had said: 'Will I ever see you again, Mummy, here or anywhere else?' No one knew.[12]

The same scene was repeated at many times in many places during the war. In all, after the first great evacuations of 1939, the railways of Britain handled another million evacuees in nearly 2,000 special trains during the six years of the war. Patients from hospitals in danger areas were cleared by thirty-four specially equipped casualty evacuation trains. For the Dunkirk Evacuation, 186 special trains were readied and shuttled back and forth to the Channel ports to collect the returning survivors. Over 200,000 men were transported in this operation, with Southern Railway's drivers and firemen on the footplate continuously for anything from 18 to 28 hours. The returnees had to be taken to military depots for reorganization and re-equipment, and then almost immediately sent on leave, necessitating a further massive movement of travelling servicemen from already congested stations.

For the families of servicemen, the station had become again a place pregnant with emotion. Barrow housewife Nella Last recorded her feelings when seeing her soldier son Cliff off on 10 March 1940:

We took Cliff to the station at 7.45 and found a huge crowd waiting. There must have been at least 200 soldiers, airmen and sailors going off leave, and a lot had come to see them off. We heard by conversation that one group were on draft leave, and there was one young fellow, who looked about twenty-four, parting from his wife of twenty-two to twenty-four. She was such a pretty, frail-looking girl, who would be having her baby soon, and my heart ached as I saw her poor little brave face with its fixed grin as she waved goodbye. Stations to me are always rather sad-making, but tonight, with the mist wreathing and steaming under the roof and the blue lights half-obscured by smoke and mist, I thought it was the most hopeless, deadening place on earth.[13]

The Second World War, like the First, saw temporary celebrity conferred on what were usually sleepy wayside stations. Stations which were situated near army camps, air bases, and factories became hives of activity. At the tiny village station of Dinton near Salisbury, the 5,000 passengers using the station in 1938 had increased to 32,000 in 1943, and the number of wagons handled increased from 1,318 to nearly 10,000. At the quiet Wiltshire town of Tisbury, passenger traffic rose from 16,300 in 1938 to 73,000 in 1943, while wagons handled increased from 5,000 to 24,500. The number of passengers using Honiton Station in Devon rose from 48,000 in 1938 to over a quarter of a million in 1943. As E. F. Carter put it: 'To achieve such fantastic figures, station staffs often had to work right round the clock but the spirit of the Men of the West was as strong and true during World War Two as ever it was in the days of the Spanish Armada. This was the railways' greatest hour.'[14]

The preparations for D-Day involved another massive railway effort, with 25,000 special trains run in the two months leading up to the invasion and 18,000 in the thirty days after it. Quite apart from such landmarks as Dunkirk and D-Day, stations handled regular troop trains, leave trains, prisoner-of-war trains, hospital trains, vital freight trains, evacuation trains, repatriation trains, and, when the Americans entered the war, train after train of US servicemen. In 1942, 167,000 US Air Force personnel were carried to the East Anglian airfields by the London and North-Eastern Railway.

The distribution of post and parcels for the forces was in the hands of the railways. The Army Post Office, Nottingham, dealt with mails for British Overseas Forces. In the early months of 1944, mail was conveyed by special trains from Nottingham to army camps in southern England, as forces gathered for D-Day. After the invasion, a special ran daily to Dover or Tilbury with mail for the forces on the Continent. There was also a good deal of traffic in parcels sent home by forces abroad. These were sent to a central depot at Bournemouth for customs examination. During December 1944 alone, no fewer than 74,570 items were handled at Bournemouth. Overseas troops in England had their own mail stations. Canadian forces' mail was handled initially at Manchester Mayfield Station and subsequently at Kensington Addison Road Station. The US Army Post Office was assigned the LMS goods station at Sutton Park near Walsall as its central sorting depot. From July 1942 until the end of 1944 nearly 1,200 special mail trains carried US forces mail from Sutton Park to various distribution points.

Far more than in the First World War, however, the railways suffered from enemy bombing. Too many stations were hit for them to be listed. But there were some notable casualties. St Pancras was hit three times during the Blitz in October 1940 and was closed for five days. The roof of the Great Hall at Euston was set on fire and platforms 2 and 3 wrecked. At one time in early May 1941 seven London termini were out of action owing to bomb damage: Waterloo, Victoria, Charing Cross, Cannon Street, London Bridge, King's Cross, and St Pancras. The most bombed section of railway in London was the line between Waterloo and Queen's Road Station, on which ninety-two 'incidents' occurred between September 1940 and May 1941. The low-level terminus side of London Bridge Station was partially destroyed by bombing. Waterloo was hit by sixty-six bombs during the war. Birmingham New Street and Coventry stations were hit repeatedly, forty-two bombs being dropped on one Coventry track alone. For all this, traffic on the main lines was restored within four days. Liverpool Exchange Station was blocked for over three months when three arches and two bridge-piers fell on to the lines. Manchester Exchange Station was closed to passengers for two weeks after bomb damage sustained in the first air raid on the city on 22 December 1940. The Divisional Control Office at Salford received a direct hit and the Emergency Control Office at Victoria was flooded. But by brilliant improvisation the traffic was got moving again. Over one-third of the bomb damage suffered by British railways in the war was on the Southern Railway. Stations were among the regular and specific targets of enemy bombers. The first of the V1 flying bombs was dropped in 1944 near Cuckfield Station, smashing the signal-box windows. Forest Hill Station received a direct hit from a V1. The most bombed station in Britain was Poplar in East London, which suffered 1,200 high-explosive bombs, over 50,000 incendiary bombs, 43 flying bombs, and 9 rocket-bombs.

All in all, the railways of Britain reported 9,239 bombing incidents, about a third of which interfered only slightly, the rest seriously with the running of trains; 395 railwaymen were killed and 2,444 injured, the heaviest toll again being on the Southern Railway. In total, 893 railwaymen and civilians were killed on railway property during the war. But the railways escaped any major station disaster, just as they had in the First World War.

The Second World War saw the railway buffet enjoying its finest hour. O. S. Nock, doyen of railway historians, recalled:

When travelling to training camps, medical boards, depots and on leave, members of His Majesty's forces were provided with railway warrants which were exchanged at the railway stations for railway tickets. When a long journey had to be made, they were also issued with warrants that enabled them to obtain meals at special prices in railway refreshment rooms. In this connection the work of the refreshment room staffs at the larger stations was beyond praise. Trains of gargantuan length, packed from end to end, would arrive at all hours of the day and night; there would be a concerted dash for the refreshment rooms, and the speed, efficiency and good humour, with which those stalwart women of all ages coped with successions of such crowds was inspiring to watch.[15]

There were some epic feeding episodes at stations. When 330,000 men arrived back exhausted from Dunkirk to be transported in special trains from the coast, a marathon feeding operation was organized by the RASC, reinforced by civilian volunteers. Various stations were designated as feeding stations. The first stopping-place was either Paddock's Wood or Headcorn. Bernard Darwin, official historian of the Southern Railway at war, painted a vivid picture of the scene at Headcorn, where a staff of station-master and two porters was faced with the prospect of feeding 145,000 troops:

The R.A.S.C. provided the food and forty soldiers to hand it out, but these forty were helped by forty to fifty ladies of the neighbourhood. For nine days and nights they worked in shifts of eight hours each; but eight hours were often not enough to satisfy their enthusiasm, and one of them stayed on duty for twenty-four hours. Their headquarters was a large barn where the food was made ready and then carried across some fields and across the line to the Up platform. One lady cut so many sandwiches that she declared she never wanted to eat a sandwich or anything else again. And yet sandwiches were but one choice in that stupendous bill of fare. For the mere sensual pleasure of writing them down let me record jellied veal, sardines, cheese, oranges and apples and that culminating romance of every railway lunch, the hard boiled egg. Hard boiled eggs were reckoned in thousands; so were meat pies and rolls and sausages. Five thousand of each of these last three delicacies appeared at Headcorn one evening . . . Such noble viands were washed down by oceans of tea and coffee, in the making of which nineteen stoves were unresting night and day. The whole of Kent could hardly have produced cups enough and the drinks were handed into the trains in tin cans. When time was up the R.A.S.C. on the platform shouted to the B.E.F. in the train 'Sling them out'; a shower of tin cans clattered on to the platform, the train passed away and the staff, amateur and professional, at Headcorn fell to washing the cans and preparing for the next train.[16]

Similar scenes were reported at the other feeding stations, at Tonbridge, Faversham, Redhill, Guildford, and at Penge East, where the Salvation Army band serenaded the returning Dunkirk veterans.

The normal demand on railway refreshment facilities was so intense —at Rugby, St Pancras, and Euston in 1943 nearly one transaction per minute per unit of staff—that facilities were given to voluntary organizations such as the YMCA to establish service canteens in all big stations. Nevertheless, the railway companies did as much as they were able, establishing, for instance, nineteen rail bars at Euston in 1943. The LMS estimated that they served 60 million people with meals, drinks, and light refreshments in 1944 alone.

During the war, civilians were discouraged from travelling by slogans like 'Is your journey really necessary?' and 'Stay at Home. You may be stranded if you travel.' For those who did travel, the experience was often extremely uncomfortable. Stations and trains were invariably packed, as it seemed that the whole nation was constantly in transit. If there were delays and crowds built up, trains would be stormed. There was a chronic shortage of porters. The difficulty of travelling was compounded after June 1940 when the name-signs of all but the smallest stations were taken down. At night it was almost impossible for people to tell where they were and many passengers ended up miles from where they wanted to be. With maintenance and painting deferred, stations became shabby and run-down. Queues at the buffets were often endless and sometimes food and crockery ran out. By August 1942 the shortage of cups in refreshment rooms was becoming so acute that notices appeared urging the public to bring their own. But, on the whole, people seem to have put up with it. There was, after all, a war on, a fact which you could not escape, if for no other reason that in the place of posters proclaiming the delights of bracing Bridlington and elegant Eastbourne, 24,000 separate railway sites were plastered with posters proclaiming stirring messages such as 'Freedom is in peril—defend it with all your might'.

With the rise of air power, airstrips and their aircraft became the most important strategic points of the Second World War. But in the Japanese invasions of the Far East and South-East Asia the control of the railways remained a vital consideration. In the Sino-Japanese war, railway lines and stations were bombed mercilessly. In Malaya and Burma the battles took place at strategic points along the railway lines which constituted the spinal cords of those territories. And the Allied campaigns for their recapture took a similar form. One of the most famous of the actions in Burma in 1944 occurred around the railway station at Myitkyina, the terminus of the northern line from Rangoon. There the action, through the station buildings and sidings, was reminiscent of that which had occurred over forty years earlier at Tientsin. But the capture of Myitkyina and its station was only achieved after its airstrip had been secured.

In Canada, the United States, South Africa, Australia, and New Zealand, it was the stations which provided, for those societies remote from the war, the main evidence that a war was happening. For the stations became troop marshalling points. The great cross-platforms, or 'midways' as they were called in the United States, at the large stations had been designed with this purpose in view. In 1943 when the new Montreal Central was opened, it was provided with a special room for servicemen, and the new tracks and signalling associated with it greatly facilitated the movement of troops towards Halifax and their Atlantic crossings.

Troops were landed in the great ports of India for the eastern theatre of war. In several of those ports the berthing facilities and the harbour-side stations had been greatly improved in the inter-war years. Troops were entrained there for long journeys towards Assam, where a relatively light railway originally designed purely to transport tea suddenly found itself as a vital strategic railway feeding the Burmese front. The ideas of Baden-Powell and Alderson on station logistics and the need for military liaison at stations, as organized by Girouard, still held true.

During the German occupation of France, members of the State railway system, SNCF, played a prominent part in the Resistance. In 1943 they undertook an intensive campaign of railway sabotage following a prolonged programme in 1942 of Allied bombing of key railway installations. By 1944 the railway system had been broken up into isolated fragments and some cities, such as Grenoble, Troyes, Rouen and Strasburg, had no rail link left at all. By the time France was liberated, 100 large and nearly 1,000 smaller stations had been destroyed; 8,750 miles of track was useless owing to the wrecking of bridges and viaducts, and only 300 locomotives were in working order. Elsewhere the war had taken a fearful toll on the railways and on their stations. The retreating Germans had destroyed most of the stations in European Russia, an estimated 2,460.[17] In Italy a quarter of all lines and 40 per cent of railway facilities were destroyed during the war. Stations and railway installations in Austria, Holland, and Germany were the regular targets of Allied bombing. Greek railways were largely destroyed by the Allies, the Resistance, and the departing Germans. In Yugoslavia, half the track and half the stations were obliterated. In occupied Europe, it seems to have been the case that if the Germans did not destroy a station, the Allies did. In Holland, for instance, Rotterdam Station was destroyed by German bombing in 1940, while Nijmegen Station was destroyed in the fighting following the Allied landings at Arnhem in 1944.

All of this allowed the post-war planners and architects a free hand to impose modern forms on the rebuilt stations. In Russia, replacement big city stations were initially built in what has been called 'Stalin's Doric Revival', massive monoliths with high ceilings and heavy monumental staircases. It is not perhaps surprising that totalitarian regimes such as Nazi Germany and Stalinist Russia should have tended to build 'totalitarian' stations—huge, blank blocks. The Nazi 'House of German Art' in Munich was in fact derisively known as Athens Railway Station, indicating the heavy, debased pseudo-classical style that dictators have seen as reflections of their imperial ambitions. It should, however, give modern architects in democratic countries pause for thought that they are perpetrating their own form of artistic totalitarianism in the concrete and glass blocks they have foisted on the world. For these too have all the hallmarks of those regimes that suppress individuality, dissent, eccentricity, heroic irrelevance—the predominant characteristics of the picturesque eclectic stations—and exalt the mindless uniformity of the faceless mass, the social ideal of all totalitarian states.

In recent times, the station has lost its significance in war and in *coups d'état*. Troops are no longer moved by rail but by air and road. In very few countries now is it possible to see trains at stations packed with uniformed men. They are both too obvious and too vulnerable there. Whereas in the Russian Revolution the seizure of the railway stations in Moscow was a top priority, now the stations secured are of the radio variety. Today it is the airport which is regarded as the critical transportation point.

Even so, some countries remain highly paranoid about their railway stations. In many countries in Asia, Africa, and Latin America, taking photographs of railway stations is likely to brand the railway enthusiast as a dangerous spy. Yet occasionally stations have come back into their own during periods of conflict. Ian Smith's UDI in Southern Rhodesia could not have been sustained but for the railway lines which connected that country to South Africa and the then Portuguese colony of Mozambique. Even more fortunately for the Whites, the southern line through Botswana was actually controlled by Rhodesian Railways from Mafeking, that town of so much railway lore, northwards. Again Mafeking became a crucial railhead, and at stations in Botswana like Lobatse and Gaberone it was possible to see sidings filled with freight and fuel trains which kept the Rhodesian rebellion alive. Once again stations, with their telegraphs and telephones, their water, fuel, and workshops, became the vital power points on a system which retained many of its late nineteenth-century characteristics. In consequence they, and the lines which they served, became targets for guerrillas. It is likely, therefore, that in much of the world, particularly the Third World, stations will continue to occupy an important strategic position for the foreseeable future.

13

The Usual Offices

THE station itself was made up of a number of different units or areas, each serving a specific function. They ranged from the ticket office to the left-luggage deposit, from the lost-property department to the public conveniences. The most notable of them carried a connotation beyond the merely specific function. For instance, the waiting-rooms with their divisions by class and race reflected the wider structure of the society which was the setting for the system. The bookstall and the telegraph office underlined the role of the station as an information source, and the refreshment rooms the role of the station as a source of sustenance and revival.

The extent of the facilities varied according to the size of the station. At one extreme there was the Gare de Lyon in Paris. In 1931 this station boasted the following: in the left wing, a booking-hall (seventy ticket and baggage windows), left-luggage cloakroom (departure), information and telegraph office, exchange and sleeping-car company offices, twelve automatic luggage-weighing machines, five automatic distributors of plat-form tickets, several telephone boxes, two waiting-rooms, and lavatories (including baths, hairdressing, and shoe-cleaning rooms); in the central block, the buffet and restaurant, left-luggage office (arrival), ticket-collectors' and other offices, entrance to the Underground; in the right wing, luggage arrival hall, omnibus order office, customs hall, lost-property office, station-master's and police offices, and medical rooms.[1]

At the other extreme was Wanstrow, the smallest station on the Great Western Railway. It consisted of a platform about 24 yards long and a small waiting-room. In the waiting-room was a fire-grate and on the platform one lamp. Wanstrow had neither station-master nor staff. But it was under the supervision of the nearby Witham station-master, who was required to visit it to check its condition periodically. During the winter a plate-layer would light the fire in the waiting-room and light the lamp in the evening. Five trains a day in each direction called there in the Edwardian era.[2]

The range of facilities was just as great in North America. The tiny flag-halts, where passengers had to wave a flag or change a signal to stop the train, usually consisted of a wooden shack no bigger than a garden shed to afford some protection from the elements. John Droege wrote in his *Passenger Terminals and Trains* of 1916 that, of 85,000 stations then in use in the United States, no fewer than 80,000 cost less than $25,000 to build.[3] Most of these simple stations contained no more than waiting-room, baggage room, and office. The slightly larger ones added a women's waiting-room, or in the South—as in the standard combination station in Virginia—a coloured waiting-room.

On the other hand, the external elaboration of the larger American stations reflected the increasingly diverse provision of public rooms within. The news-stand, lunch counter, and dining-room were standard, and tobacco shops, barbers, drugstores, gifts, and furnishing outlets became increasingly common at large stations as the companies set about maximizing their income from lessees by providing shopping arcades. Through these shops the railway companies encouraged non-travellers to use the railway facilities, emphasizing the role of the station as civic and shopping centre. The dining-rooms, theatres, and later cinemas performed the same function. Through all of these the companies emphasized the importance of their stations, as well as raising income and advertising their services.

If a distinction can be made between the facilities offered solely to travellers and those which could also be used for visitors to the station, another can be drawn between those provided for the ordinary passengers and those for the extraordinary. Many stations had unusual offices. Windsor had a special waiting-room for Queen Victoria, New Delhi one for the Viceroy—occupied for several years more recently by a slighted Indian aristocratic lady.[4] At Ottawa there were special rooms laid aside for government officials and politicians. Washington Union had a special retiring-room and reception-room for the President. There were also mortuary chambers, perhaps anticipating assassinations—remembering the fate of President Garfield at an earlier Washington station. A few had special rooms for funeral parties. At Glasgow St Enoch there was a room in which commercial travellers could show off their sample cases in comfort and privacy, and showrooms for salesmen were provided at several American stations, containing tables and other equipment appropriate to the exhibition of goods.

Some large stations in Tsarist Russia provided libraries. Moscow Leningrad Station, when reconstructed in 1931, introduced a crèche.[5] Milan Station had a special waiting-room for invalids, and an umbrella-hire service, which the *Railway Magazine* described as a 'touch of true Italian inventiveness'.[6] Until the modern system of heating trains by means of pipes, supplied by steam from the locomotives, was introduced in 1884, barrow-loads of footwarmers were available for passengers at some British stations. In the United States, some stations, like New York Grand Central, had well-equipped hospitals. Several contained police stations, and some, like Penn Central in New York, had a room for the detention of prisoners and suspected persons. Washington Union had offices for a resident physician, dressing-rooms and baths (often provided for those wishing to change for evening functions), a Turkish bath, and a swimming-pool. At Detroit there was a men's reading-room with, according to Droege, 'an abundance of good reading matter'. Women were not, apparently, expected to read. Worcester, Massachusetts, on the other hand, had a women's café. At Chicago Union the men's facilities were designed with a club-like atmosphere, and the women had separate tea-rooms, and rooms for a nurse and a matron. In this chapter, however, some of the more usual offices will be surveyed.

Booking-Office

The booking-office was a major point of contact with the public. The French called the booking-hall 'la salle des pas perdus'—the place of lost footsteps, a wonderfully resonant concept. The booking-clerk was for many the face of the railway company. He had to keep careful records, meet deficits out of his own pocket, and put up uncomplainingly with the foibles of the passengers. One clerk told F. S. Williams:

> Yes, some passengers are odd. They ask for tickets for places they are thinking of, but not going to, and are very angry when we give them one they don't want. Others sometimes come short of money, and they wish us to trust them for the balance. We don't turn them away if we can help it. If they have luggage, we send them and it to our station master's office. He perhaps takes what money they have and issues a way-bill.[7]

In countries where journeys are considerably longer than in Britain and other parts of Europe, the importance of the booking-office and the complexity of its procedures are greatly enhanced. In the Americas, in Africa, Asia, or Australasia many journeys include at least one night on the train. Booking therefore becomes a much more complex business than simply buying a ticket. The options of seat, berth, coupé, or other form of compartment have to be considered, together with the hiring of bedding, perhaps additional items of comfort, and maybe the pre-ordering of meals. A number of different offices have to be visited, and it is essential to do so in the right order.

But the complexities for the passenger are as nothing compared with the complications of the booking procedures for the station booking-staffs. Train plans of every train have to be maintained, perhaps for months in advance. Requirements as to baggage, bedding, and food have to be recorded. Numbers and names have to be telegraphed or telephoned from station to station along with food orders and other messages. The system largely survives in India, and the very appearance of the Indian booking-offices, with their ledgers, train plans, cupboards, pigeon-holes, desks, and manifold functionaries bespeaks this complexity and gives an indication of the way things were in many parts of the world in the nineteenth century. As each train is prepared for departure, the names of all the passengers in berths have to be posted on boards on station platforms or perhaps on the doors of coaches. Copies have to be in the hands of the conductor, and it is he who has the power to allocate accommodation to passengers wishing to join unbooked at intermediate stops. The train conductor becomes all-powerful at such stops. He can be found with a throng of anxious passengers courting him, or alternatively being pursued and harried along the platform if he refuses to stop to consider the needs of importunate travellers. At country stations throughout Africa and Asia, he becomes the vital booking-point, and the dividing line between the tip and the bribe becomes a fine one. It is a system which marks out the superior class of traveller, for only they need make such complicated arrangements. For the poorer carriages the passengers merely indulge in a free-for-all.

As in so many other respects, it was in the United States that booking procedures and ticket offices were developed to their highest point. In the great era of railway-building, advice was proferred to architects and designers on everything from the height of the ticket counters to the nature of the grille, from the positioning of the ticket rack to the types of material that would prevent the tickets from sticking.[8] In the late twentieth century, some railways in advanced countries have followed the airlines in making the computer the vital accessory to booking. Whereas railway technology, in booking as in other respects, was relatively uniform in the nineteenth century, now a large gap has opened up between the advanced and the less advanced systems. In Ceylon one hundred years ago, more primitive booking techniques made overbooking common. The railway regulations decreed that when this occurred those with tickets for further destinations would be given priority.[9] The platform heartaches when such a crude system was implemented can well be imagined.

With the increasing complexity of railway operations the booking-office spawned other offices in the early twentieth century. In the early decades of railway operation, booking-offices had always doubled as information bureaux. This continued to be the case in the smaller stations, but large city stations acquired separate information offices. When the vast 'thermal' stations were built in the United States these were often positioned in the middle of the concourse, where they became striking landmarks. In Europe, but not in the United States, they swiftly became a preserve of women's employment.

If the information bureau was for long-range information, the train indicators offered the signposts and news of immediate interest to passengers. Indicators came in a wide variety of shapes and sizes. At their simplest, common in small stations throughout the world, they were merely blackboards on which was chalked the news of arrivals and departures. At large stations a wide variety of methods developed, wooden boards with destinations painted on them slotting into display cabinets, rollers of cloth with successive departures printed on them, metal plates which could be hoisted into position. Revolving slats with names of destinations, hand or mechanically operated, were the prototypes of the modern indicators so common at airports and stations today. By the First World War the Siemens Company of Berlin had already produced an early remote-controlled electrical indicator. Here was the object of constant and ingenious experimentation by the station operator. In his survey of these systems Droege noted with approval the indicator office in Glasgow Central.[10] Thirteen windows had been provided in a long, slim building on the station concourse, one for each of the station's platforms. Into these windows the operators placed placards indicating the destinations of departing trains. It was striking, simple, and unique. It continued in use until 1985.

When railways were at the peak of their influence, these station indicators were used by the companies to create a self-conciously romantic aura to travel. The casual watcher of the station scene was filled with a desire to catch the named trains and visit the exotic places displayed. At Blackfriars in London, destinations were carved in stone on the façade, with Sevenoaks and Bromley rubbing shoulders with Istanbul, Budapest, and Cairo. Manchester Victoria proclaimed Southport, Leeds, and many others in stained glass around its street canopies. The destination indicators orientated passengers at all stations. Like Muslims facing the mihrab of the mosque, all turn their attention in one direction. Named trains have always provided a special tone. The 'Royal Scot', the 'Clansman', the 'Thames–Clyde Express', the 'Brighton Belle', the 'Cheltenham Flyer', the 'Cornish Riviera' in Britain, the 'Edelweiss Express', the 'North Star', the 'Blue Bird', the 'Rheingold Express', the 'Golden Arrow', and the 'Orient Express' in Europe, the last two starting in

London. In Egypt there was the 'Sunshine' and 'Star of Egypt' expresses, while the 'Taurus Express' embraced, incredibly, Ostend, Istanbul, Aleppo, Baghdad, and Cairo. Canada had the 'Trans-Canada Limited' and 'The Dominion', while the United States boasted the 'Redwing', the 'Mohawk', the 'Empire Builder', the 'Twin Cities Zephyr', the 'Olympian Hiawatha', the 'Golden State' and 'Oriental' limiteds. In India there were the 'Imperial Indian Mail', the 'Deccan Queen', the 'Frontier Mail', the 'Rajdhani Express'; in New Zealand the 'Blue Streak'; and in Australia the 'Spirit of Progress', the 'Southern Aurora', the 'Sunlander', the 'Fish', and the 'Chips'.

The destinations and the stops *en route* had their own resonances. In Europe and the United States, stations generally took the names of existing cities and towns, naturally enough, although station naming could give a new aura of importance to previously insignificant streets or localities. Sometimes stations were given saints' names, like St Enoch or St Pancras, reflecting the mystical associations of the railway. Elsewhere, stations created places and the names could be transferred the other way round. In doing so they often reflected the ethnic and cultural history of whole areas through which they passed. In colonies of settlement local indigenous names might alternate with familiar English or Scots names on long stretches of railway: Maori in New Zealand, Aborigine in Australia, Zulu in Natal, Ndebele and Shona in Southern Rhodesia (Zimbabwe), less commonly Red Indian in Canada and the United States. It was as though the railway companies and settlers wished to be reminded where they were while none the less enjoying the familiarity of names from home. In Canada, hundreds of stations—and the communities near them—were named by railway executives. On some lines they might choose a succession of names each starting with a different letter of the alphabet from A to Z. The names of the company's executives and senior employees, their wives, daughters, and even pets would be used in this way. In some places names had historical connections. In the United States there was a Custer Station and a Big Horn Station. In Australia the transcontinental line reflected the period in which it was built, the First World War, by having important stations named Kitchener, Haig, and Fisher. Others were named after geographical features, Summit, Escarpment, Forks of the Credit (where the River Credit did just that), Falls of Cruachan, while some had merely numbers, as in the Sudan. Some had a curious incongruity, like Waterloo in Sierra Leone, while others fitted perfectly, like Log Cabin in the Yukon, which was one.

The Refreshment Room

Like mothers-in-law and seaside landladies, railway food is one of the staples of British humour:

Customer. Excuse me, miss, but this cup of coffee has a distinct taste of cocoa.
Waitress. I'm very sorry, sir, I must have given you tea.

Customer. Are the sandwiches fresh?
Waitress. I don't know, sir, I've only been on the job a fortnight.[11]

Many a great writer has left us his reflections on the state of railway buffet food. Dickens, who disliked the railways, expatiated with relish upon

The pork and veal pies, with their bumps of delusive promise and their little cubes of gristle and bad fat; the scalding infusion satirically called tea, the stale bath buns with their veneering of furniture polish, the sawdusty sandwiches, so frequently and energetically condemned.[12]

Anthony Trollope, who travelled frequently by train and wrote some of his novels in railway carriages, found that the railway sandwich in particular left much to be desired. He wrote of it in 1869:

We are often told in our newspapers that England is disgraced by this and by that; by the wretchedness of our army, by the unfitness of our navy, by the irrationality of our laws, by the immobility of our prejudices, and what not; but the real disgrace of England is the railway sandwich—that whited sepulchre, fair enough outside but so meagre, poor and spiritless within, such a thing of shreds and parings, with a dab of food, telling us that the poor bone whence it was scraped had been made utterly bare before it was sent into the kitchen for the soup pot.[13]

It was not until the 1880s that the dining-car became a regular feature of railway travel, and since the main trunk routes from London to Scotland, Wales, and the West County usually involved eight- to ten-hour journeys, there were designated refreshment stops with timetables showing halts for dining purposes. On the East Coast route from King's Cross, the dining stop was York. On the Midland Railway's service from St Pancras to Carlisle and Glasgow, it was Normanton. On the West Coast route, from Euston to Glasgow, it was Preston. On the GWR, all trains between London and the West stopped at Swindon.

The GWR let the management of the Swindon refreshment rooms on long-term contract and agreed that all trains passing through the station should stop for 'a reasonable period of about 10 minutes' for refreshment. Successive proprietors, however, used the contract to profiteer at the expense of their captive customers, so much so that long after the arrangement had been terminated, Swindon was sometimes referred to in the railway community as 'Swindleum'.

The first and possibly the worst of the abusers of the contract was S. Y. Griffiths, who provoked from the GWR's founding father, Isambard Kingdom Brunel, a memorable letter of rebuke:

Dear sir, I assure you Mr. Player is wrong in supposing that I thought you purchased inferior coffee. I thought I said to him I was surprised that you should buy such bad roasted corn. I did not believe you had any such thing as coffee in the place; I am certain I never tasted any. I have long ceased to make complaints about Swindon. I avoid taking anything there when I can help it.[14]

The GWR tried to avoid Swindon by starting the trains before the ten minutes was up. But they were restrained by an injunction. They finally got out of it by threatening to build a branch line via Newbury and Westbury to bypass Swindon and the lessee sold out for £60,000.

But ten minutes was hardly long enough to dispense refreshments to a train-load of passengers and an undignified scramble invariably resulted. Thomas Burke reported that coffee which was too hot to drink during a five-minute refreshment stop was regularly poured back into the urn for the next train. *The Railway Traveller's Handy Book of Hints, Suggestions and Advice* (1862) gave some salutary advice:

On a long journey refreshment will be needed, and this can be either obtained on the road, or the traveller may be his own purveyor, and take it with him. The rule generally is for the train to stop five or ten minutes, for the purpose of taking refreshment; in such cases, especially with anything like a heavy train, a rush of passengers is made simultaneously towards the refreshment-room, and the counter is besieged by hungry and thirsty applicants, urging their various re-quests for sandwiches, buns, biscuits, wine, brandy, ale etc. But inasmuch as there are usually some two or three hundred persons requiring refreshments, and only about a dozen hands to supply them, it stands to reason that the task of serving out the viands is no easy one, and many are the disappointments accordingly. Let the traveller remember that he has only the short space of five or ten minutes to gain the refreshment counter, to obtain the refreshment, to pay and perhaps receive change, to perform the operation of eating and drinking, and regain the seat in the carriage. It is obvious therefore that a person must exercise his utmost ingenuity and energy in order to accomplish this edible feast. Now, in this, as in everything else, a certain amount of tact is necessary to insure the desired end. When the train is on the point of stopping, mark well the place where the words 'Refreshment-Room' are written up, so that directly the train stops, you may make at once for this place without wasting your time in looking about for it. Walk straight to that part of the counter where one of the attendants is stationed, and having, in parliamentary phraseology, 'caught her eye', declare your wants. But in doing this, be quick and concise. If you desire a basin of soup, never minds the words 'a basin of', but simply utter the monosyllable 'soup'; so with a cup of tea, content yourself with calling out the latter word; a bottle of ale, 'ale' etc. Call out distinctly and in a loud voice, have the precise sum ready, if you know what it will be, or at any rate tender a small coin. Beware of taking hot refreshments; whether it be by accident or design we know not, but certainly the fluids supplied are so excessively hot, and so long in forthcoming, that it is utterly impossible for a person to swallow them, unless his throat be sheathed with iron. Observe also, that you should repair to the refreshment-room either immediately the train stops, or just before it starts again, for during the mid-interval the counter is literally besieged with a crowd of eager applicants, and a person standing behind these and endeavouring to make his wants known through the din of voices and the clatter of plates and cups and saucers has but an indifferent chance. On the whole, we should advise the railway traveller to take his refreshment with him; a few ham and beef sandwiches, together with a little cold wine or brandy and water will answer every purpose.[15]

For travellers who did not want to risk the buffet or bother with self-catering, the railway companies issued luncheon baskets from 1873 on. As late as the 1930s the Great Western Railway was offering breakfast and luncheon baskets at main stations: for breakfast, eggs and bacon, bread, butter, preserves, and tea, coffee, or cocoa, at three shillings and sixpence; for luncheon, meat, bread and butter, cheese, salad, etc., at three shillings, with steak, chop, or chicken and ham provided with the same trimmings, for sixpence extra. Sir William Acworth tactfully but vainly suggested that English railway companies experiment with the German idea of trays with legs instead of baskets: 'it is not given to everyone to balance a mutton-chop and potatoes gracefully on his knees the while he pours himself out a glass of claret with his hands'.[16]

The most celebrated satire on refreshment rooms came from the fertile pen of Charles Dickens in his tale 'Mugby Junction', a thinly disguised version of Rugby. It includes a lengthy monologue by the refreshment-room boy:

I am the boy at what is called the Refreshment Room at Mugby Junction, and what's proudest boast is that it never yet refreshed a mortal being . . . You should hear Our Misses give the word 'Here Comes the Beast to be Fed!' and then you should see 'em indignantly skipping across the line, from the Up to the Down, or Wicer Warsaw, and begin to pitch the stale pastry into the plates and chuck the sawdust sangwiches under the glass covers, and get out the—ha, ha, ha—the sherry—oh, my eye, my eye!—for your refreshment. It's only in the Isle of the Brave and the Land of the Free (by which, of course, I mean to say Britannia) that refreshmenting is so effective, so 'olesome, so constitutional a check upon the public.[17]

Things were little better at the GWR's Didcot Station in the 1860s. Hubert Simmons recalled it:

It was a mystery to me how Mrs. Jones could pay £200 *per annum* as rent, and something heavy as rates and taxes, for so small a room; but she did, and has since retired. It was however no mystery to the 'British public', for everything was assessed at double the price charged at public-houses—a cup of tea cost sixpence; and oh, if they only looked at the sandwiches, such a charge. The people who needed refreshment walked in and enquired the price and came out again.[18]

Neither Dickens nor Simmons would have recognized the idyllic picture of the refreshment rooms at Wolverton painted by Sir Francis Head:

As these youthful handmaidens stand in a row behind bright silver urns, silver coffee-pots, silver tea-pots, cups, saucers, cakes, sugar, milk, with other delicacies over which they preside, the confused crowd of passengers simultaneously liberated from the train hurry towards them with a velocity exactly proportionate to their appetite ... Considering that the row of young persons have among them all only seven right hands, it is really astonishing how, with such slender assistance, they can in the short space of a few minutes manage to extend and withdraw them so often—sometimes to give a cup of tea—sometimes to receive half-a-crown, of which they have to return two shillings—then to give an old gentleman a plate of warm soup—then to drop another lump of sugar into his nephew's coffee-cup—then to receive a penny for a bun and then again threepence for four 'lady's fingers'. It is their rule as well as their desire never, if they can possibly prevent it, to speak to any one; and although sometimes, when thunder has turned the milk, or the kitchen-maid over-peppered the soup, it may occasionally be necessary to smooth the fastidious complaints of some beardless ensign by an infinitesimal appeal to the generous feelings of his nature—we mean by the hundred-thousandth part of a smile—yet they endeavour on no account ever to exceed that harmless dose.[19]

Sir Francis recorded that Wolverton refreshment rooms annually got through 182,500 Banbury cakes, 1,277 pounds of tea, 8,088 bottles of lemonade, and 2,392 bottles of brandy.

The introduction and spread of the dining-car in the last decades of the nineteenth century eventually eliminated the need for refreshment stops. But the railway buffet continued to be an integral part of station life. For all the humour it has provoked over the years, it remains true that it was the railway buffet which pioneered the emergence of the restaurant in the Victorian city in the second half of the nineteenth century. Mid-nineteenth-century London, for instance, was very badly provided with decent eating-houses where it was possible to obtain a meal at a reasonable price. It was in the 1860s that a major transformation in the situation began, spearheaded by the partners Felix Spiers and Christopher Pond, who saw in the railway-station buffet trade their point of departure. They established their first two restaurants at Victoria and Ludgate Hill stations in 1865–6. From there they launched themselves into the West End. In 1879 *The Architect* was drawing attention to the excellence of the restaurants at St Pancras Station and at Holborn Viaduct Station.[30]

Food was a matter of primary concern to the English traveller abroad, and writers regularly included assessments of restaurant facilities in their accounts of foreign travel. G. F. Chambers, for instance, writing in 1901 of a recent trip to Portugal, reported:

Though I cannot speak very highly of the railway buffets, yet it is a matter of satisfaction that during the spring months, which are chiefly the months when tourists are to be found in Portugal, fruit of all sorts, and cold water (*acqua fria*) can be purchased at many of the railway stations, from girls with baskets and jugs who promenade up and down the platforms.[21]

Continental Guides were sure to include some comment on railway food. Baedeker's 1912 Guide to Southern Italy reported that 'Italian restaurants are few in number and leave much to be desired in quality'.[22] The 1912 Guide to Norway, Denmark, and Sweden declared: 'There are good restaurants at the larger stations only. Passengers help themselves, and pay on entering or on leaving.'[23] But it was British India that came off best in culinary arrangements. A contemporary account of dining on the journey from Calcutta to Bombay opined:

The refreshment-rooms at the several places along the line were very good. For *chota-hazri* (little breakfast), which we took just after daybreak, we would have a cup of tea and some toast or bread-and-butter. Breakfast proper followed this at 9 or 10 o'clock, then tiffin at 1, and dinner about 6 in the evening. All the meals were exceptionally good. For dinner there would be, besides soup and fish, beef, mutton, snipe, duck, partridge, quail, pastry, four or five different kinds of fruits, and the universal curry and rice. The tables were laid more in the style of a first-class club than a railway refreshment room; and there was a native servant to every two passengers who partook of meals. The guard or some other official of the train came to our carriage and asked what wine or beer we wished to have, and he would then send a wire for it to be put on ice. The charges were for breakfast and tiffin about one shilling and for dinner half-a-crown.[24]

Famous though the Indian arrangements were, the Ceylon Government Railway thought otherwise. It was proud of its refreshment cars, as was made clear in a Guide of 1910 which commented on their advantages compared with 'the inconvenience and loss of time involved by the Indian system of "refreshment stops" '.[25]

In the United States, all trains stopped at mealtimes in the early years of rail travel. Meals were taken at monastic-like refectories at first, but standards of both food and décor soon improved in the East. Nevertheless, railway refreshment rooms remained a constant butt of American commentators on transport conditions in the country. In the West, meals were taken in large frame buildings with long tables where meals were laid out on platters for the descending passengers to help themselves. These developed varied reputations. One, in Wyoming, was unusual in being very highly regarded. Elsewhere, tough beefstakes were often describes as 'antelope steak' to disguise their inadequacies with the charm of novelty, as Dee Brown put it.[26] Often insufficient time was allowed for meals, as in Britain, and undignified scrambles ensued. One vivid account of such a stop in Canada as late as 1907 is provided by Harriet Black, a seventeen-year-old Toronto girl, on a journey from Muskoka:

> Oh! I wish I was a man. When we got to Allandale, the train stopped and all the passengers got off and rushed to the restaurant. There were hundreds of people and only four men to serve them, and only ten minutes to do it in. Consequently, many people came away hungry. We at last got a plate of sandwiches and two cups of coffee which was too hot to drink. Before it had time to cool off, the gong rang for us to go back to the train. I burned my tongue trying to swallow a mouthful of coffee, then ran out on to the platform and jumped on the train just a few seconds before it started.[27]

John Droege had many strictures to make on station refreshment facilities:

> In the lunch rooms on many roads the prices are too high, the food too stale or tasteless and the service too poor to gain the railroad any friends. There is room in this respect for all kinds of criticism and a great field for improvement.[28]

One man became closely associated with station dining-rooms and established a high reputation for them. This was Fred Harvey, who secured the concession for the entire Santa Fe system in the 1870s. His operations eventually spread to other lines, and by the First World War his system employed 4,800 people and had 1,000 outlets, large and small.[29] In 1911 the appropriately named Edward Hungerford published an article on Harvey in the *Saturday Evening Post*. Fred Harvey, Hungerford suggested, had established himself 'by cutting a pie into four pieces instead of six and by his infinite attention to the vast details of feeding a travelling army so that each wanderer in that army might think that the meal had been cooked for his own single delight'.[30] Harvey seemed to elicit universal praise and it was even suggested that he had made the Santa Fe system.

Although dining, buffet, lunch-counter, café, bar, and club cars became standard on trains in many parts of the world, meal stops survived as a feature of railway operation not only in India, but in some parts of Africa, on the White Horse and Yukon Railway, and in one or two journeys in Australia. The use of crockery, cutlery, tables, and table-cloths rapidly declined, however, in the twentieth century, as the 'fast' and 'junk' food revolutions took place. The railway station reflected this earlier, and perhaps more potently, than any other public building, excepting only the airport.

Dining-room, lunch-counters, Fred Harvey systems, and the like do, however, reflect only the upper end of station catering. Almost everywhere, the station has presented economic opportunities to vast numbers of people to provide food and liquid of one sort or another to rail passengers. In the poorer parts of Latin America, in Africa, India, even on the Trans-Siberian in Russia, station platforms are thronged with vendors of all sorts. A train journey in such countries seems to be a constant process of eating and drinking between stations. In India the arrival of the train at a station platform immediately makes the traveller the subject of vigorous importuning to buy a staggering range of consumables. All travellers on the Trans-Siberian have noted that basic capitalist enterprise operates at most stations. Peasant women sell potatoes and boiled onions, fruit and other foodstuffs. At most stations in the hotter parts of the world, it was not only the engine which had to be watered. Water-carriers and sellers offered water to the passengers too.[31] The water vendor was a ubiquitous figure at all Indian stations, and generally he had to be of high caste to make his water acceptable. Boiling water (*kipyatok*) was available at Russian stations. The incidence of hawkers and vendors at European and North American stations has of course declined in the twentieth century, but they were familiar figures in the nineteenth. As in many other aspects of railway travel, the Third World offers today impressions of what nineteenth-century travel was like throughout the world.

The Bookstall

An indispensable element at any decent railway station was a bookstall. The Victorians went regularly to their local station to buy the newspaper and to change their library books. Just as the railways promoted the use of standard time ('railway time') and the distribution of fresh milk ('railway milk'), they also fostered the habit of reading. Richard Altick has written of the railways: 'Perhaps no other single element in the evolving pattern of Victorian life was so responsible for the spread of reading.'[32] Indeed the measurable upsurge in the sales of books and periodicals accompanied the almost manic expansion of the railways in the 1850s. Whether for business trips, family visits, seaside holidays, or, later, regular suburban commuting, reading matter was essential. This was not just a British habit. A French observer noted in 1860: 'Practically everybody passes the time reading while travelling on the train. This is so common that one rarely sees members of a certain social class embark on a journey without first purchasing the means by which they can enjoy this pastime.'[33]

Reading was thus the universal habit of the bourgeois traveller and was put within the means even of the lower middle class by the appearance of 'cheap railway libraries'. During the earliest years of the railways, the companies tended to lease their bookstall concessions to injured employees or their widows, who supplied newspapers, magazines, beer, and sandwiches, later adding novels to their stock. These were generally cheap, reprehensible, and insalubrious, often translated French novels of the kind that respectable citizens would be ashamed to be seen buying at their local bookstall.

The term 'railway literature' became one of abuse and disapprobation, and there was a mounting outcry against its pernicious influence. Charles Manby Smith, in a comment typical of the critics, observed in 1857:

There can be but little doubt that the railroad has been the means of at least doubling the number of books printed and published; not that by any means half the books sold are sold at railway stations, but there are few railway stations without their book-stall; but the habit of reading on railways has created new classes of readers, and spread the taste for reading, and awakened so general a desire for the accumulation of books, that myriads of volumes are now sold elsewhere, which, but for railway reading, would not have been sold at all. Looking at this new fact in a moral light, its aspect is not so pleasant as it might be, inasmuch as no small amount of literary rubbish travels by the rail, and a considerable quantity besides which might be designated as something much worse. But we are mending in this respect of late; works of the very best class are now to be found on the railway stalls; and there one hopes that the grand means of intercommunication may one day become the channel also of an uncorrupted literature.[34]

The railway companies took note of the criticism. Bibles chained to lecterns appeared at the principal London termini. But rather more far-reaching was the decision to let the bookstalls to respectable concerns. In 1848 W. H. Smith was granted the exclusive right to sell books and papers on the London to Birmingham railway. His first stall was at Euston and by 1851 he had gained a monopoly of the stalls on the London and North-Western. Smith, later First Lord of the Admiralty and the prototype of Gilbert and Sullivan's Sir Joseph Porter, KCB, was extremely high-minded and took such care in selecting the books for his stalls that he earned the nickname 'The North-Western Missionary'. By 1863 he had gained control of the bookstall concessions on all the principal railway lines, a control that his firm exercised until 1905, when the companies raised the rental so high that Smith's surrendered the concessions on both the LNWR and the GWR to Wyman's. In response to losing the railway concessions, Smith's opened bookstalls in the centre of the towns they had previously served from the station and retained much of their custom, thus curtailing the primacy of the station as purveyor of books and papers. Smith was emulated in France by Louis Hachette who opened his first station bookstall in 1852 and within two years had sixty station bookstalls. By 1864 he was earning an annual income in excess of one million francs from them.

In 1851 Samuel Phillips toured station bookstalls for *The Times* and noted that 'with few exceptions unmitigated rubbish encumbered the bookshelves of almost every bookstall we visited'. But an exception was made in the case of W. H. Smith, who had cleaned up the bookstalls at the LNWR stations:

At one fell swoop the injurious heap was removed. At first the result was most discouraging. An evident check had been given to demand; but as the new proprietor was gradually able to obtain the assistance of young men who had been educated as booksellers, and as public attention was drawn to the improvement in the character of the books exposed for sale, the returns perceptibly improved, and have maintained a steady progressive increase greatly in excess of the proportion to be expected from the increase of travelling up to the present time . . . Cheap literature is a paying literature, if judiciously managed.[35]

The *Times* article also noted regional variations in taste in reading:

Stations have their idiosyncracies. Yorkshire is not partial to poetry. It is difficult to sell a valuable book at any of the stations between Derby, Leeds and Manchester. Religious books hardly find a purchaser at Liverpool, while at Manchester, at the other end of the line, they are in high demand.[36]

As a direct response to this article, the publisher John Murray launched a
series of books specifically designed for reading on the railway. His
prospectus ringingly proclaimed:

> The principle which will guide him in the selection of these works will be to
> disperse sound and entertaining information and innocent amusement, by which
> he hopes to counteract and supersede the trivial, and often immoral, publications
> at present destroying the taste, and corrupting the morals of Railway Readers,
> more especially of the young.[37]

The initial titles included *Specimens of the Table-talk of Samuel Taylor
Coleridge, A Popular Account of Layard's Discoveries at Nineveh*, and *Jesse's
Gleanings in Natural History*.

Despite the steady improvement in overall tone pioneered by W. H.
Smith, the term 'railway novel' continued to carry a connotation of
disapproval, as did its synonym 'yellowback', from the colour of the
books' covers. The commentators, with that fierce and earnest Victorian
commitment to uplift, educate, and improve, berated the frivolity implied
by the reading of mere novels. But the issue by the publishing house of
Simms and Macintyre of their 'Parlour Library' in 1847, a series of 279
titles issued monthly at a shilling, was such a roaring success that it was
immediately imitated by Routledge with their 'Railway Library', deliberately designed to tap the lucrative railway trade. By 1898 they had
published 1,300 titles, mainly popular novelists reprinted in bulk—
W. Harrison Ainsworth, G. P. R. James, Bulwer-Lytton, Captain Mar-
ryat, Charles Lever, Miss M. E. Braddon. There was some non-fiction in
the form of narratives of the Crimean War and the Indian Mutiny.
Nevertheless, this flood of novels did not please *The Times*, which noted
of the 'Parlour Library' that 'every addition to the stock was positively
made on the assumption that persons of the better class who constitute
the larger portion of railway readers lose their accustomed taste the
moment they enter the station'.[38]

W. H. Smith's bookstalls were generally well managed, neatly
arranged, and plastered with posters advertising the news headlines and
details of the stories in current issues of the magazines. They dealt in
magazines, newspapers, and books. Many also ran circulating libraries
with stock exchanged by train with headquarters. The nature and scope
of the bookstall manager's duties can be gleaned from the memoirs of
William Vincent, published in 1919. Beginning in 1859, he spent fifty
years in the service of Smith's, managing bookstalls at Neath, Tiverton,
Didcot, Taunton, Swansea, Reading, and London Euston stations,
ending his career as District Superintendent for the whole of

Wales. Vincent combined deference and total devotion to his work. His book is dedicated to Lord Rothschild and is filled with admiring references to all the gracious and good-natured royal and aristocratic persons he has encountered in the course of his duties. They included Empress Eugénie of France, Lord Roberts of Kandahar, Lord Palmerston, the Duke of Grafton, and the Queen of Madagascar. When he was at Reading in the 1880s, Vincent made it a rule that every member of staff, himself included, should come on duty by 6.15 a.m. and anyone who was late would be fined a penny and the total at the end of the quarter could be divided among those who had never missed the time. If no one claimed it, it would go to a hospital. The hospital never received the money because of the punctuality of the staff, encouraged by Vincent, who set them an example by regularly arriving early.

On Thursday, Friday, and Saturday, Vincent breakfasted at 5 a.m. in order to be at the bookstall at 6 to receive the weeklies arriving on the night mail. On Thursdays there would be over a thousand copies of *The Weekly Budget* and a similar quantity of the *Family Herald*. On Fridays there was *Lloyd's News* and *Reynolds' News*, about 1,800 copies each, *Christian World*, a thousand copies, plus a dozen other titles. All had to be folded, as did dailies like *The Times* and the *Telegraph*. Some of Vincent's assistants became so expert that they could fold fifteen copies of the *Telegraph* in a minute.

They were required to work on Christmas Day and Good Friday to receive the London daily papers, which, since the trains ran on Sunday schedules, were not due to arrive until 7.40 in the evening:

This meant leaving the family circle and gathering of friends at 6.30, and not being able to return again until close on 10 o'clock or later. The non-publication of daily newspapers on these days in the present first quarter of this twentieth century is a boon that was undreamed of in the mid-Victorian period. Added to this, we had to be on duty at 6 o'clock on the mornings of Christmas Day and Good Friday, just as on the other days of the week, to meet the huge consignment ... of parcels by the night mail, for, being two hundred miles from London, the weeklies and monthlies despatched on the two previous days —some by relief parcels trains, often delayed—would not reach us until early morning, so that frequently, a double quantity had to be dealt with. This meant hard work from 6 o'clock till 10 or 11 o'clock in the morning. In those days customers were very exacting, especially the trade booksellers and newsagents, who would often refuse goods if delayed, complaining that the market was lost.[39]

The hours were long, the working conditions difficult. Often the stations were freezing and wind-swept. The lengths to which the bookstall staff were prepared to go to oblige their customers were simply staggering.

Newspapers were dispatched from the main-line stations by 'travelling youths', 'at considerable trouble and expense, chiefly to accommodate county families and save them having to wait till the next day for the London morning papers'. Vincent himself sometimes undertook special deliveries:

Owing to the delay of parcels containing library-books from London, I was unable one day to send books to a twelve-volume subscriber some miles out of Taunton by a weekly carrier, so after business in the evening I took the 7.40 train to Wellington (Somerset) station . . . and walked the remaining five miles with the books. In returning to Wellington I found the last train back had been gone some time, therefore I put up at the 'White Horse Inn' but thinking the bed damp, I slept in my overcoat and was up early the next morning for the first train. This was much better than keeping a client waiting a whole week until the carrier's next journey. Indeed I didn't mind a journey like this now and then, even, as in the present case, at my own expense.[40]

It is small wonder, with this kind of assiduity, that people seeking the latest number of a magazine or the latest issue of a newspaper at a time of crisis turned invariably to the station, which thus furnished a vital channel of news, information, and entertainment. Writing of the addiction of working-class youngsters in Edwardian Salford to the school stories of Frank Richards, Robert Roberts observed: 'I knew boys so avid for current numbers of the *Magnet* and *Gem* that they would trek on a weekday to the City Railway Station to catch the bulk arrival from London and buy the first copies from the bookstall.'[41] Public schoolboys too sought out the station for their periodical reading, as P. G. Wodehouse recalled in a letter to his friend Bill Townend: 'Do you remember when we used to stand outside the bookstall at Dulwich station on the first of the month, waiting for Stanhope to open it so that we could get the new *Strand* with the latest instalment of *Rodney Stone*?'[42] One of George Orwell's most vivid memories of the outbreak of the First World War was of 'a mob of young men at the railway station, scrambling for the evening papers that had just arrived on the London train'.[43] The authors of the present study have themselves joined the queue at Mallaig Station to collect the morning papers, newly arrived at midday.

The news-stand and bookstall have been a feature of stations worldwide, turning the station into a distributor of written as well as spoken news, providing for writers a wider distribution of their works. In India the franchise for railway bookstalls was won by a firm called A. H. Wheeler and Co. Their bookstalls could be found at every major Indian station, and, like some of their British counterparts, Wheeler's went into publishing themselves. They produced a cheap railway library, priced at one rupee, and in 1888 published six volumes of short stories by the virtually unknown Rudyard Kipling, then a young journalist on the *Pioneer* newspaper. The covers of these paperback editions were designed by Lockwood Kipling, Rudyard's father, and tales like *Soldiers Three*, *Wee Willie Winkie*, and *The Phantom Rickshaw* (published with 'Other Eerie Tales') soon became best-sellers among railway travellers in India.[44] Though few can lay claims to the popularization of an author of such distinction, bookstalls have remained a feature of Indian stations, selling magazines and illustrated romantic materials.

The Telegraph Office

The Victorians, to whom industry, invention, engineering, and commerce were tinged with a romance which their twentieth-century heirs have never shared, saw in the electric telegraph something marvellous and magical. John Pendleton captured this mood when he wrote in 1896:

Now the electric telegraph has become a necessity to our political, commercial and social life. It tells England, by means of submarine cable and code, of ministerial crises abroad, and how the pulse of commerce beats; and along a thousand home wires, by day and night, it flashes myriads of words that speak of work achieved or in prospect, of trade enterprise, of buying and selling, of joyous pastime or grim endeavour, of disaster or noble exploit, of the million incidents that make up our national life.[45]

The telegraph was inextricably involved with the railway almost from the start. The first practical telegraph was patented in England by William Fothergill Cooke and Professor Charles Wheatstone in 1837. Cooke convinced the Great Western Railway of the value of electrical communication in its operations, and in 1839 the GWR opened its first telegraph line from Paddington to West Drayton. Cooke had argued that 'with a telegraph the manager in his office at Paddington would live like a spider along the line'. But the company was unwilling to undertake the expense of extending the telegraph line. Instead, they agreed to Cooke taking it over and maintaining it at his own expense, as long as he sent railway messages free of charge, and extended it to Slough. It was extended beyond Slough to Windsor, and the twin crowd-pullers, royalty and crime, ensured that it rapidly caught on with the public as a means of transmitting information. For it was by telegraph that the news of the birth of Queen Victoria's second son, Prince Alfred, was transmitted to London in 1844 and it was the telegraph that ensured that the murderer

John Tawell was arrested in London for a crime committed in Slough. By 1850 Scotland Yard had a private telegraph line running from Charing Cross Station.[46]

The year 1844 saw the first telegraph line laid in the United States, along the Baltimore and Ohio Railway, and in 1845 the telegraph came to France. On the Continent, almost from the start, the telegraph was considered a military and political asset and was run as a State monopoly. In Britain, however, it was developed by private enterprise, with Cooke's Electric Telegraph Company leading the field. It derived its principal revenue from contracts with the railway companies for the construction and maintenance of railway telegraphs. By 1848, telegraphs covered 1,800 miles of railway. But in 1849 after a telegraph was established at the Central Post Office, the system spread out beyond the railway network to cover the whole country. In 1851 the laying of a submarine cable from Dover to Calais linked the British telegraph system to the Continent, and by the end of 1852 London was in direct telegraphic communication with all the chief cities of the Continent.

It was the telegraph which so greatly facilitated the railways' adoption of Greenwich Mean Time as standard national time. For in 1852 arrangements were introduced between the Electric Telegraph Company, the Astronomer Royal, and the South-Eastern Railway Company to transmit GMT to London and the provinces. The time signals sent out by the hour from Greenwich were instantly telegraphed throughout the land.

By 1868 the public telegraph network in the United Kingdom had grown to 21,751 miles of line. Public facilities were provided by railway companies at 1,226 railway stations, 36 per cent of the total number of telegraph offices in existence. At a further 738 stations there were telegraph facilities exclusively for railway use. At the big stations, the telegraph companies had their own staff operating the machines. But at country stations, railway staff undertook the work, not only sending and receiving messages but also delivering them. In 1870 the General Post Office took over the telegraphic service and the private companies were bought out. But railway messages continued to be carried free.

During its heyday, the telegraph came to be essential for the smooth running of the railway. In 1884 the Midland Railway Company alone sent 5 million telegraphic messages. John Pendleton declared:

The telegraph, though it occasionally blunders, is the swiftest and most zealous of all railway servants. It gives a word of warning to the signalman, a hint of danger to the driver, a peremptory instruction to the station-master in emergency; it speaks even to the shunter amid the maze of waggons, and to the platelayer busy with his gang on the creosoted sleepers and the rusty rails in the lonely cutting. It marshals goods trains, stops expresses, orders special trains, helps every official on the line; and is helped in its turn by the telephone, which in many a crowded depôt forwards and supplements the telegraph message. The railway is an interminable whispering gallery. Along its wires, on which the wind makes strange music, flash a thousand instructions relating to the working of the line, and sometimes a purely personal message is slipped in—a robust curse to an ill-tempered clerk at the next station, a phrase of endearment to a female operator miles away, or a staggering answer to an innocent question such as that put by the signalman, who, hearing his bell whirring, asked, 'What is it?', the reply coming in desperate spasmodic rings: 'It's twins.'[47]

But it was not just for the use of the railway company. It became, for good or ill, part of the life of the rail passenger:

Its winged words tell your friend to meet you at some station two hundred miles north, or inform your agent in town that you will be at Euston or King's Cross or St. Pancras in time for luncheon and talk on some big contract. The message just sent in cipher to the bank manager in the country is to apprise him that a large amount of bullion, in charge of two trusty clerks, armed with revolvers, is coming by train; and the cramped writing on the telegraph form that nearly touches corners with it on the smooth counter, is the calligraphy of Detective Fudgit, who is going down the line too, and has wired Mark Flint, the railway detective, to saunter to the station and watch the arrival of the mail, for Jim Moody's gang have tired of coining and intend to make a rush for real gold, so there may be 'a bit of stiff work'. The telegraph is a friend to all honest people travelling by rail, and now and then assists the swindler and the rogue in his schemes. Nevertheless it is generally on the side of right and justice, and it has checked many a forger in his flight from his dupes and the Assize court, and more than one murderer trying to travel beyond the memory of his victim, and the uncomfortable sensation that is inseparable from the hangman's touch.[48]

It was the presence of the telegraph and cable offices at stations which made the railway station such a vital centre of communications throughout the world. The telegraph was vital to the railways' operations everywhere, and for that reason the telegraph wires usually marched in step with the railway lines. In large cities the station telegraph office was but one of many, but in small communities it was usually the only one. In the multitude of stations across the Canadian prairies it was the sign of the telegraph and cable office which was usually the most prominent at the station. In all remote communities throughout Asia, Africa, Latin America, and Australasia the telegraph symbolized the miracle of rapid communication with the outside world, the vital adjunct of all economic activity in an integrated world system. In New Zealand the smaller stations were often also post offices, marking them out not only as the very centre of all communications but also as the symbol of the national government presence. In Canada, the United States, and elsewhere, the status of stations was often distinguished by the presence or absence of a separate telegraph operator. At the very smallest, the Morse-code key would be in the hands of the station agent—or whatever other title he held—himself. In some Canadian stations, where there was a separate telegraph operator, he was given an office in a tower, conveniently positioned at the very level at which the telegraph lines entered the building, and providing him with views along the line and over the community.

Left-Luggage Deposit

Cloakroom or left-luggage facilities were first introduced on British railways in 1840. Since then left-luggage deposits have sometimes revealed bizarre items. Michael Bond's Paddington Bear was left at that London terminal from which he derived his name. Even more notably, in Oscar Wilde's *The Importance of Being Earnest*, Jack Worthing confessed to having been found in a handbag in the cloakroom at Victoria Station, earning the magisterial reproof from Lady Bracknell:

A cloak room at a railway station might serve to conceal a social indiscretion —has probably, indeed, been used for that purpose before now—but it could hardly be regarded as an assured basis for a recognized position in good society.[49]

Certainly, unwanted babies have regularly turned up in waiting-rooms, cloakrooms, and other station offices. But a more eccentric use of left luggage was resorted to by the film star George Arliss at Charing Cross Station:

On Saturday afternoon when I went to catch my train my autograph collectors collected in alarming numbers and bore down upon me with that spirit of determination that makes England what it is. I had about ten minutes to wait. I couldn't retreat and leave the station, because I should have lost my train. I couldn't seek refuge in the refreshment rooms, because my attackers would have no compunction in following me. So with presence of mind worthy of a great general, I thought of the Left Luggage Office. It was just behind me and close to the platform from which I was to start. I turned to the man in charge and demanded the right to book myself in as a parcel. I paid my twopence and the man took me over the counter and I was saved. This method of retreat I confidently recommend to other picture stars in railway stations.[50]

In some cases, the left luggage became a permanent resting-place. For in that office, along with the parcels, packages, suitcases, and trunks, would sometimes be found more gruesome and odoriferous objects —dismembered corpses. There was something of a vogue for depositing corpses, usually in trunks, at the major London terminals in the inter-war years. George Orwell went so far as to include 'trunk murders' along with 'astrology, the Oxford groupers, the rector of Stiffkey . . . spiritualism, the Modern Girl, nudism, dogracing, Shirley Temple, B.O., halitosis, night-starvation and Should a Doctor tell?' in a list of the distinctive phenomena of the age.

In May 1927 the left-luggage attendant at Charing Cross Station noticed a noxious smell coming from a large black trunk deposited five days earlier. Opened, the trunk was found to contain a dismembered female body. She had been asphyxiated. The taxi-driver who had delivered the trunk was traced and the trail led to John Robinson, who admitted to killing the woman in a struggle over money and cutting her up with a knife. He was hanged at Pentonville Prison on 12 August 1927. Patrick Mahon, a philandering sales manager, had killed and dismembered his pregnant mistress. But his suspicious wife, going through his pockets, found a cloakroom ticket for Waterloo Station. She presented the ticket and received a Gladstone bag full of blood-stained female clothing. The police found the dismembered body hidden in a bungalow at the Crumbles, the Sussex 'love nest' of the guilty pair. Mahon was hanged on 3 September 1924. Neville Heath, the sadistic RAF officer and double murderer, was incriminated by a blood-stained scarf left with other belongings at Bournemouth West Station left luggage. He was hanged on 16 October 1946. On 17 June 1933 a headless torso was discovered at Brighton Station in a trunk deposited eleven years earlier. But the Brighton Trunk Murderer was never apprehended.

The Baggage Room

On a visit to India, Sir Sidney Low commented on the different baggage conventions between India and the United States.

Hand-baggage is an elastic term. The two extreme interpretations are to be met with in the United States and in India. On a train in the West you have about room enough in the parlour car for a minute satchel, in which you can keep a razor and a toothbrush. In a first-class carriage on an Indian railway, the voyager expects to find space for at least a leather portmanteau, a suit-case, a dressing-bag, a hat-box, a helmet-case, a lunch-basket, and a huge roll of bedding. The rest of his modest belongings will have been deposited in the brake van.[51]

The reason for the tiny quantity of baggage permitted on American trains was that they had developed an elaborate system for checking baggage. It was a distinctive part of all train travel in North America. In the early years of this century, one-tenth of all American passengers checked their baggage, which was presumably a high proportion of all express passengers, given that most of the remaining nine-tenths would have been commuters. Passengers with baggage had to arrive at the station twenty minutes to half an hour before the departure of the train. At some stations, ticket office and baggage counter were far apart, necessitating a considerable amount of walking in order to go through the various operations preparatory to departure. From the turn of the century, station designers spent more time considering baggage-handling than almost any other aspect of these stations. The connection between ticket and baggage offices, facilities for depositing from outside vehicles, the baggage store, the use of elevators, ramps, baggage trolleys, the separation of passenger and baggage movement all came in for close attention. Baggage cars had, of course, to be correctly positioned on the trains, although there was never any guarantee that a passenger's baggage would travel on the same train as himself. American railroad companies stored baggage free of charge as a public service until collected, and up to a certain weight all checked baggage was handled free of charge. By the First World War, the companies were beginning to be aware of the great cost of the system, and the considerable drain on their profits which it represented. Moreover, the storage of baggage had come to be so abused that the companies could no longer cope.

The system had existed in a modified form in other countries, but significantly it was in colonial territories that the largest quantity of baggage was moved about by the ruling race. Quantity of baggage was often an indicator of social class and prestige; it was also symptomatic of an expansive age with cheap labour. In the twentieth century, travellers travel light compared with their nineteenth-century counterparts. Complex baggage arrangements at stations have disappeared, transmigrating to airports, where they are essential for entirely different reasons.

The Lost-Property Office

That Aladdin's cave of wonders, the lost-property office, was a feature of all big stations. In Britain in the nineteenth century a standard procedure was followed with regard to lost property. When handed in at the office, it would be recorded in a book which stated on what date and in what train it was found and by whom. If it bore an address, it would be kept for forty-eight hours and then forwarded to the address. If it had no address, it would be opened after a month, and if it contained any clue to an address, a letter would be sent to that address. If no clue to its ownership emerged and it was not claimed, it would be kept for two years, and then sold by public auction. A second ledger, the Luggage Enquiry Book, was also kept, recording enquiries about missing items that had not been handed in, and for which queries were addressed to all the stations on the line until it could be ascertained that the lost property was not on the railway.

Sir Francis Head described in Dickensian detail a visit to the lost-property office at Euston in 1849:

It would be infinitely easier to say what there is not than what there is, in the forty compartments like great wine-bins in which all this lost property is arranged. One is choke-full of men's hats, another of parasols, umbrellas and sticks of every possible description. One would think that all the ladies' reticules on earth were deposited in a third. How many little smelling-bottles—how many little embroidered pocket-handkerchiefs—how many little musty eatables and comfortable drinkables—how many little bills, important little notes, and other very small secrets each may have contained, we felt that we would not for all the world have ascertained; but when we gazed at the enormous quantity of red cloaks, red shawls, red tartan-plaids and red scarfs piled up in one corner, it was, we own, impossible to help reflecting that surely English ladies of all ages, who wear red cloaks etc. must in some mysterious way be powerfully affected by the whine of compressed air, by the sudden ringing of a bell, by the sight of their friends—in short by the various conflicting emotions that disturb the human heart on arriving at the up-terminus of the Euston Station.

Sometimes discoveries of considerable value could be made:

Some little time ago the superintendent, on breaking open previous to a general sale, a locked leather hat-box, which had lain in this dungeon two years, found in it, under the hat 65 pounds in Bank of England notes, with one or two private letters, which enabled him to restore the money to the owner, who, it turned out, had been so positive that he had left his hat-box at an hotel in Birmingham that he had made no enquiry for it at the railway-office.[52]

Unclaimed items over the years included feather beds, casks of cement, oil paintings, galvanized iron coppers, crutches, bagpipes, spades, sewing-machines, bicycles, deck-chairs, fishing-rods, birdcages, spinning-wheels, coffins, parrots, a stone Irish giant, and an early edition of Chaucer.

But in 1883 F. S. Williams reported that there had been a general diminution in lost property, due to greater care either on the part of the passengers or on the part of the railway companies, perhaps both. But it did mean a decline in the *outré* and bizarre items left on trains. A lost-property attendant told Williams:

We've only very common-place things here . . . umbrellas, sticks, wrappers and such sort of things. Whatever is found in the carriages at Euston, and whatever the other stations can't find an owner for, they are all sent up here. Everything we have is entered in this register . . . Last year we had 18,000 [items] . . . Do we ever have anything strange? Once I had. I opened a square box sent from Preston, lifted up some straw, and found a dead child. When I touched it, it sent a cold thrill through me. It was naked—a little child with golden curls. Yes, we sent to it the coroner. The mother had poisoned it with laudanum; mother was found out and convicted.[53]

Out of 27,000 items registered at the Great Eastern's central deposit at Liverpool Street in 1897, only one-third were returned to their owners. The rest would be sold at auction in lots: trousers by the dozen, walking-sticks and umbrellas by the hundred, gloves by the thousand, and the rest in groups, for example 'a pair of braces, a clock, a lamp, a china figure, a box of collars, and a length of lace trimmings' or 'a knife, a thermometer, a pencil, a glazier's diamond, a scent bottle, a whistle, a pair of scissors, a seal and five pieces of jewellery'.

During twelve months' auction sales by a firm acting for the Great Eastern Railway, the Company disposed of 3,350 gloves, 2,280 umbrellas, 1,150 sticks, 1,000 hats, 770 collars and cuffs, 510 pipes, 320 socks and stockings, 300 boots, 260 handkerchiefs, 150 aprons, 120 boas and muffs, 110 coats and jackets, 64 vests, 38 trousers, 9 chains, 8 rings, and 3 revolvers.[54]

Lavatories

Public conveniences have existed since Roman times. But it was the Victorians who turned them into what Lucinda Lambton calls 'temples of convenience'. It was George Jennings who, in the middle of the nineteenth century, applied the new technology (penny in the slot, flushing lavatories, wash-out urinals) to public conveniences. He began with the Great Exhibition of 1851, a turning-point in sanitary engineering as in so much else. There was a general onslaught on insanitary conditions in the mid nineteenth century. In London the Metropolitan Board of Works began laying new sewerage in 1859 and by 1865 had completed 1,000 miles of sewers.

The railways sought to provide the most up-to-date sanitary organizations, particularly in their top stations. By 1895 Jennings could boast of supplying thirty railway companies with his new conveniences. In the best station conveniences, marbled slate urinals, decorated columns, faience tiles, and ceramic arches testified to the ubiquity of the Victorian taste for the grandiose. Many of these were underground. But above-ground urinals on platforms provided a challenge for cast-iron workers and they rose to the challenge at, for instance, Melrose Station, to provide elaborate and delicately worked cast-iron masterworks.[55]

Washing, shaving, and hairdressing facilities were often installed to accompany new conveniences and they frequently earned praise, as for instance those at Glasgow St Enoch's:

A special word of praise is due to the toilet rooms adjoining the lavatories on No. 1 platform. These are 'run' by Mr. Taynton, and the accommodation comprises two handsomely fitted-up rooms, in which palms and ferns make a very attractive show against the white-glazed tiles. In these two rooms no less than 11 unshorn and unkempt passengers can be operated on at once, there being a staff of 13 in all. The dozen or so circular brushes which go to make this department complete are revolved by an electric motor.[56]

But it was extent rather than quality of facilities that was demanded at the major seaside resorts, especially in the days of non-corridor trains, when hordes of working-class day-trippers, who had been swigging beer on the journey and had been subjected to the delays notorious in the excursion traffic of, for instance, the Lancashire and Yorkshire Railway, disembarked. The conveniences at Blackpool Central, therefore, were vast in extent. They had to be when you realize that on Saturday, 13 August 1910, for instance, 200 ordinary and special trains ran into Blackpool North and Blackpool Central stations, disgorging 92,000 passengers, many of whose first destination would be the 'gents'.

Cab-stand

The railways had not, as some had expected, displaced the horse. They provided more work than ever for horses. In the early 1830s there were 1,265 cabs in London. By 1863 the number was 6,800 and by 1888, 11,000. The two-and-a-half-fold increase in cabs between 1840 and 1870 coincided with the twentyfold increase in railway passengers, suggesting a direct link. In Glasgow, similarly, the number of cab-stands increased fivefold in the two decades after the passenger terminals opened. More than half of them were at the stations.

At most stations, arrangements were made to accommodate the cabs and to allow them to set down near the booking-office and pick up at the arrival platforms. Most companies licensed cabs to pick up at their termini. But in 1897 all the companies except the London and South-

Western agreed to an interchange system by which any cab licensed by one company could work any other company's station without extra payment. At Waterloo, the exception to the scheme, any cab could use the station on payment of one penny. The system of company licensing of cabs was ended by Act of Parliament in 1907, but cab-drivers were still expected to abide by company regulations when using their premises.[57]

It was the internal-combustion engine rather than the railways which killed the horse-vehicle. The change-over came in the Edwardian era. In 1903 there were 11,000 hansom and hackney coaches and one motor taxi. By 1913 there were more than 8,000 motor taxi-cabs and only 1,900 horse-drawn vehicles. The age of the horse-drawn cab was coming to an end. The change of vehicle, though, did not mean a diminution of work at the station. Station work continued for the cabby, and there were still rich pickings at certain times of the year: Christmas, bank holidays, and the end of term at the public schools. Of the latter period, one writer noted in 1904:

> These are golden days for 'cabby'; but the Eton boy is perhaps more generous when returning to school 'flush' with money than when breaking up for the holidays. Visit the cab rank and you will see scrawled in chalk on the walls warnings not to forget the 'Eton boys' special'.[58]

The Railway Arches

The arches provided shelter, in peacetime for the homeless and the vagrant, in wartime for travellers seeking protection from bombs. Derelicts today still cluster beneath the arches at Waterloo and Charing Cross, continuing the tradition celebrated by Flanagan and Allen in their sentimental song: 'Underneath the arches, I dream my dreams away'.

The arches also provided valuable storage space and were often let to merchants and traders. Leeds Joint Station was built on arches, for under the station flowed the Leeds–Liverpool Canal and the River Aire. The arches, known locally as 'the dark arches', were notorious 'both for the effluvia arising from the somewhat noisome river and as a resort of bad characters'. In 1892, however, the arches were tenanted by a firm of soap-makers and stocked with tallow, resin, palm-oil, etc. A fire broke out in them which raged for two days, caused portions of the platforms to collapse, and cost the life of one fireman. The station itself was saved.[59]

Station Pets

If anything surpasses the Englishman's love of steam trains, it is his love of dogs. One feature of stations in the nineteenth century that caught the fancy of contemporary writers was the phenomenon of station pets. On the Great Western station at Slough there is still to be seen today the stuffed carcass of a mongrel dog called Station Jim, who died in 1869. He wandered the platform in harness, collecting for GWR widows and orphans, and he raised in all £40. He rarely left Slough, but on one occasion he did board a train for Leamington and was promptly sent back. At GWR's Birmingham Snow Hill Station, Dash, the station dog, also collected for widows and orphans, raising an estimated 12s. 6d. to 15s. a week.

At the Great Eastern's Lowestoft Station a black and tan collie acted as effective deputy station-master. He knew when the trains were due to leave and would appear, bark to start them, and disappear until the next train was due to depart. A fox-terrier called Pincher at Hawkesbury Station on the Coventry and Nuneaton Railway was famous for ringing the station bell at the approach of stopping trains. One day after performing this act he ran from the signal box on to the line and was cut in two.[60]

The Station in Painting and Poetry, Postcard and Poster

'THERE is nothing romantic about the railways', said Sir Richard Marsh sourly when he retired as Chairman of British Rail. He thus contrived to range himself metaphorically with that grumbling gaggle of commuters captured for all time by Kipling in his poem 'The King'. They stood on that station platform long ago lamenting the absence from the railways of romance and earning Kipling's reproof:

> . . . And all unseen,
> Romance brought up the nine-fifteen.[1]

There is romance enough even today for those with hearts to feel and imaginations to see—in the organization, in the technology, in the sheer experience of train travel. There is poetry too, a fact lost on as many now as it was on their blinkered Victorian forebears, for whom Charles MacKay wrote *Railways 1846*:

> 'No poetry in railways!' foolish thought
> Of a dull brain, to no fine music wrought.
> By mammon dazzled, though the people prize
> The gold alone, yet shall we not despise
> The triumphs of our time, or fail to see
> Of pregnant mind the fruitful progeny
> Ushering the daylight of the world's new morn.[8]

Over the years the railways have inspired a wealth of artistic expression, at its purest perhaps in poetry and painting, which have contrived to capture the essence of railways in all their manifestations. There have been poems and paintings about speed and power, engines and carriages, expresses and locals, working and travelling, wrecks and disasters, journeys and arrivals, landscapes and destinations. Stations have shared fully in this artistic celebration.[3]

The mystique of the station was captured to perfection by Thomas Wolfe's prose poem 'The Railroad Station', in which he describes un-

forgettably 'the immense and distant sound of time' compounded of the
voices and the movements of the people swarming beneath its capacious
carapace;

>The station, as he entered it, was murmurous
>With the immense and distant sound of time.
>Great slant beams of moted light
>Fell ponderously athwart the station's floor,
>And the calm voice of time
>Hovered along the walls and ceiling
>Of that mighty room,
>Distilled out of the voices and movements
>Of the people who swarmed beneath.
>
>It had the murmur of a distant sea,
>The languorous lapse and flow
>Of waters on a beach.
>It was elemental, detached,
>Indifferent to the lives of men.
>They contributed to it
>As drops of rain contribute to a river
>That draws its flood and movement
>Majestically from great depths,
>Out of purple hills at evening.
>
>Few buildings are vast enough
>To hold the sound of time
>And now it seemed to him
>That there was a superb fitness in the fact
>That the one which held it better than all others
>Should be a railroad station.
>For here, as nowhere else on earth,
>Men were brought together for a moment
>At the beginning or end
>Of their innumerable journeys,
>Here one saw their greetings and farewells,
>Here, in a single instant,
>One got the entire picture of the human destiny.
>
>Men came and went, they passed and vanished,
>And all were moving through the moments of their lives
>To death,
>All made small tickings in the sound of time—
>But the voice of time remained aloof and unperturbed
>A drowsy and eternal murmur
>Below the immense and distant roof.[4]

Broadly speaking, artistic interpretations of the station fall into two groups. The first group is representational and narrative, and is concerned with the station as a stage upon which drama is encountered. This is essentially the Victorian image. The second group is symbolic and atmospheric, concerned with the nature, essence, and effect of the station. In many cases, this is a post-Victorian view, the product of a twentieth-century compulsion to get beneath the surface to the inner meaning.

Initially the illustration of the railways was dominated by the work of print-makers, sketchers, and engravers rather than painters. It is estimated that some 2,000 different railway prints were published in the twenty years after 1830, mainly in the form of lithographs. Over 200 of them came in book form, accompanied by commentaries.[5] Many of these prints were commissioned directly by the railway companies to promote a positive and attractive image of train travel and dispel the many fears that people entertained about the new form of locomotion. Without exception these prints stress the engineering miracles achieved by the railway builders and highlight the grace, symmetry, and formal order of the railway system. The railway becomes comfortingly part of the landscape without brutalizing it, and is itself seen as an object of beauty.

Station facilities were included almost from the outset. I. Shaw's series includes a drawing of Manchester's Liverpool Road Station, where beneath a barn-like roof, cheerful and excited passengers, clutching their luggage, mill about the track awaiting the arrival of the train. But the lack of distinction in the buildings shown here is soon compensated for in the grandeur of both station frontages and train-sheds which are depicted. Classical elegance is the keynote of the buildings in T. T. Bury's print of London Euston (1837), S. Kelper's Liverpool Lime Street (1836), and J. C. Bourne's Tunbridge Wells Station (1845). The sheer dominating dynamism of the train-shed is highlighted in Tait's Manchester Victoria (1845), and in Bourne's GWR Station, Bath (1846) and his superb lithograph of the GWR Goods Station, Bristol Templemeads, where in a richly autumnal colour scheme of browns, creams, and russets, he stresses the form and line of the train-shed roof which frames the scene, in a composition that was to become standard for paintings and photographs over the years. The symmetry of an engineering construct is hymned by the artist who celebrates its sheer visual beauty. The Railway Guides, like Osborne's *London and Birmingham Railway Guide* (1840) and George Measom's *Illustrated Guide to the Great Western Railway* (1852), contain a wealth of station engravings, enabling the observer to follow the gradually evolving style of station architecture.[6]

By the middle of the century it is not so much the simplicity of form and line as the complexity of the life under the platform awnings that is starting to catch the eye, and this parallels the development under way in painting. The relatively little-known series of fifteen lithographs of the London and North-Western Railway by A. F. Tait (1848) includes bustling scenes of activity at Crewe and Edgehill stations, and the anonymous print of the interior of Chester General (1864) is full of marvellously observed detail.

In the United States the railways were greeted as the symbol of progress, financial and industrial power, and national expansion. They were seen in Walt Whitman's words as 'type of the modern—emblem of motion and power—pulse of the continent'. But in America, unlike Europe, the railway tended to find its artistic expression not in serious novels and plays but in the wider field of popular culture—the dime novel, melodrama, and juvenile fiction. In art, it was in prints and magazine illustrations rather than painting that the railway and the station became familiar landmarks. Painters, using the European masters as models, concentrated on landscape and nature, rarely on the institutions of the modern world. The vivid prints of Currier and Ives, with their primary colours and bold lines, are what celebrate the exuberance of the railway age. One exception to the general avoidance of the railway by serious painters is Edward Lamson Henry's *The 9.45 Accommodation, Stanford, Connecticut* (1867), with the trim, cottage-style station dominating the centre of the scene, a gaggle of wagons, carriages, coaches, and buckboards clustered around it, disgorging passengers to board the waiting train, eloquent testimony to the centrality of the station to the community and its symbolic role as local outpost in a long-distance communication system.

The railway in general and the station in particular entered the mainstream of Victorian painting with the rise of narrative realism in the middle years of the century. Spurred on by the example of literature, by the panoramic effect of Charles Dickens's novels pulsating with life, colour, and variety, and by Henry Mayhew's in-depth investigations of the life of the London poor, a group of young British artists in mid century turned from the then fashionable historical and classical themes to explore modern life. W. P. Frith's *Ramsgate Sands* was the standard-bearer of the new movement—an encapsulation of life in a panoramic microcosm.

There is more than a fortuitous connection between the Victorian novel and Victorian painting. As Peter Conrad has written: 'Paintings and novels and even poems have a chaotic fullness, a superabundance, which [Henry] James thought to be their weakness, but which is perhaps their glory . . . They succeed by daring, by energetic idiosyncrasy, by force of will, rather than by artistic scruple.'' Just as the three-decker, multi-plot Victorian novels were grand canvases, teeming with life, so Victorian narrative paintings, rich in detail, set out to tell a variety of stories, and were valued in proportion to their 'readability'.

Dickens's *Sketches by Boz* were praised for presenting 'the romance of real life'. This phrase sums up the fascinating paradox at the heart of Victorian art. It sought a meticulous factual exactness in its settings, but within those settings gloried in drama and spectacle. It was an era in which romance and reality ran side by side and often intermingled. The extremes were delineated by Dickens and Kipling. Dickens's Mr Gradgrind, grim archetype of the nineteenth-century industrialist, declares: 'You are to be in all things regulated and governed by fact. We hope to have before long, a board of fact, composed of commissioners of fact, who will force the people to be a people of fact and of nothing but fact.' Kipling, however, hymns a nation of dreamers:

> We were dreamers, dreaming greatly, in the man stifled town;
> We yearned beyond the sky-line where the strange roads go down.
> Came the Whisper, came the Vision, came the Power with the Need,
> Till the soul that is not man's soul was lent us to lead.

There was bound to be tension between fact and dreams. But it was a creative tension and it gave birth to a world-wide empire based on the hard reality of technology and trade and the high-flown concepts of destiny and duty. It can be seen at work in that most eminent Victorian, Mr Sherlock Holmes of Baker Street, 'pure thinking-machine', hawk-eyed observer of detail, and at the same time chivalrous, patriotic, and intense romantic, not beyond recourse to drugs to stimulate a jaded imagination.

Narrative painting similarly dealt both in reality and in romance, in spectacle and in detail. But it also took care to impose order on the tumult, to give meaning to the confusion, and thus to impart to the spectator the reassurance that the 'great god of order' was in his heaven and was controlling the destinies of the nation.

It was W. P. Frith, capturing for all time the bustle of Paddington Station in *The Railroad Station* (1860), who produced the definitive narrative painting. On his canvas, and framed by Brunel's columns and arches, a representative cross-section of mid Victorian society prepares to board a GWR express. Porters are struggling with luggage, a bridal party are seeing off a newly wedded couple, a mother is seeing her sons off to school, the police are arresting an absconding criminal, a soldier lifts and kisses his baby son as he leaves to bear arms for Queen and country. Many of the figures, such as the detectives, were painted from life, and great care was taken to achieve authenticity in every aspect. The painting was an instant success, earning a fortune for the London picture-dealer Louis Victor Flatow, who had commissioned it. During the spring and summer of 1862, 80,000 people paid to see it on exhibition. It was reproduced in print form and recreated in stage tableaux, and such was the continuing fascination it held for people that in 1865 the dramatist Tom Taylor wrote a thirty-two-page booklet explaining the life histories of the various characters. He sought also to explain its appeal:

> Somebody has said that life is made up of meetings and partings.
> Mr. Frith has chosen as the scene of his picture one of the places in which life, thus conceived, is best epitomised—the platform of a Railway Station ... The same eternal elements of human joy and sorrow are mingling on the railway-platform which have furnished material to all the poets who have dealt with humanity from Homer downwards. Only the tragedy is *bourgeois*; the interest for the most part domestic; the joy and the suffering, generally, on the scale suited to the world-wide stages peopled by great epic or dramatic creators. It is the function of the painter to intensify and point his subject by selection and combination of incidents, just as he gives unity and harmony to his composition by studied arrangement of forms, colours and lines. No such juxtaposition, perhaps, as Mr. Frith has here painted, of the joys and sorrows, the fun and fuss, the littleness and misery, the tenderness and terror of life, was ever found gathered about the doors of any particular train that ever started from the Great Western Station. But joys and sorrows of this kind are to be found in contrast and combination at every railway platform. There is nothing here that does not come within the round of common experiences. We are all of us competent to understand these troubles or pleasures, anxieties or annoyances ... The painter, in choosing such a subject, makes every spectator his critic.[8]

Thus painting is democratized and made accessible. Frithian bustle, drama, and variety became the hallmarks of many station interiors, including such meticulously detailed and executed canvases as Karl Karger's *Arrival of a Train at the North-West Station, Vienna* (1875), Angelo Morbelli's *La Stazione Centrale di Milano* (1889), N. Van der Waay's *Amsterdam Central* (1891), and J. Enders's *In the Gare Saint-Lazare* (1900). All of these painters used the arch of the train-shed to frame the action, almost as a proscenium arch, containing and defining the life of the station.

It is this sense of overriding order and bourgeois certainty of the structured crowd in an age of equipoise that marks another group of station interiors from the mid nineteenth century. George Elgar Hicks, Frith's principal rival in the field of narrative realism, painted a detailed canvas of the notorious refreshment room at Swindon Station (1863). It is crowded but there is no sign of the rush, discomfort, or discontent that attended these refreshment rooms according to popular report. A bridal couple hold the centre of the stage, with a group of young women in mourning, a couple of old soldiers, and a cadet bidding farewell to his parents representing other aspects of the human interest so fascinating to Victorians.

But it is a human interest that is predominantly middle-class, as is the tone of other indoor station scenes of the period. Lefevre J. Cranstone's *Waiting at the Station* (1850) depicts a placid, almost rustic, scene in a station waiting-room. It is littered with heaps of luggage and features a sleeping dog, a yawning man, an old man resting on his cane, and three family groups of mothers with their preternaturally well-behaved children.

Frederick Bacon Barwell's *Parting Words* (1859) is set in the waiting-room at Fenchurch Street Station. In the background can be seen porters, railway officials, and travellers snatching a cup of tea or coffee at the refreshment counter. But in the foreground are two bourgeois groups speaking their parting words. A father, his hands on the shoulders of his son, is bidding him farewell as he leaves, no doubt for school, with the sorts of words of instruction that Kipling later framed in 'If'. Near by, a young woman with downcast eyes gently touches the sleeve of an equally lovesick young man: a newly married couple, perhaps, parting for the first time.

Bourgeois certainty is one of the links between the prosperous heyday of the nineteenth century and the interwar years of the twentieth. In James Fraser's *Perth Station Entrance, St Leonard's St.* (1883), cabs and brakes move briskly to and fro, a couple of red-coated soldiers march smartly away, a mother and child ask directions of a stately policeman. The only sign of haste is a diminutive proletarian with a bundle on his shoulders racing hell-for-leather for his train. A similar sense of certitude, placidity, and timeless order radiates from Lilian Gladys Tickell's *Cheltenham* (1930), in which sweating porters strain to haul cases, while one passenger buries himself in his newspaper, a well-dressed mother with her daughter and her dog looks complacently on, and a prosperous golfer in plus-fours questions the guard.

There is no sense of separation or of loss in J. J. Tissot's *Waiting for the Train* (1874). His prosperous bourgeoise stands serenely on the platform

at Willesden Junction, surrounded by trunks, boxes labelled and in-
itialled, an island of organization and order amidst the hurly-burly of
life, a confident symbol of a confident age. With her richly hued plaid
travelling rug, tasselled parasol, her railway novel to while away the
hours, a bunch of freshly picked flowers, she has everything necessary for
a comfortable and trouble-free journey.

Towards the end of the century, however, there was a shift in interest
from the first class to the third, part of a trend towards social realism that
was an artistic reflection of the rise of socialism, the increase in trade-
union activity, and the in-depth studies into poverty and deprivation. In
the 1870s in Britain a group of young painters with a social conscience
went to work for the illustrated weekly paper *The Graphic*. One of the
most notable of them, Frank Holl, converted one of his *Graphic* drawings
into a painting, initially called *Leaving Home* but later rechristened *A Seat
in a Railway Station—Third Class*. There is an air of melancholy and
introspection about the scene in a drab third-class waiting-room, where
on a bench are ranged an old man sunk in reverie, a working-class wife
taking leave of her soldier husband, and a young, respectably dressed
single woman with downcast eyes, perhaps leaving home to take up a
position. Holl's *Gone* (1877) centres on a cluster of shabby women, some
clutching babies, watching a train disappear into the smoky darkness,
bearing their menfolk away, who knows where.

Continental painters began to take up the same theme. The Spaniard
Joaquín Sorolla y Bastida's *The Railway Waiting Room* (1895) shows four
young women asleep in the corner of a bare and cheerless room, watched
over by a gaunt, worn-out, black-clad old woman, with luggage ranged
along the bench beside her. It captures the bone-weary fatigue of travel
experienced by the working class on the move in the never-ending search
for work. Another gloomy waiting-room features in Luigi Selvatico's
Morning Departure (1899). It contains two figures, separated from each
other and isolated in the emptiness: a woman burying her face in a
handkerchief and a man with his back to the spectator, his shoulders
hunched in eloquent despair.

Station exteriors tended to be more stylized. The romantic architectural styles of the great nineteenth-century stations lent themselves
ideally to visual dramatization. The anonymous mid-century paintings of
King's Cross Station in London, with its sturdy brick façade, double
window, and central clock-tower, and the Gare de l'Est in Paris, with its
frontal colonnade, showed both as the imposing focus of a flurry of cabs,
luggage, and passengers. Axel Hermann Haig's watercolour of the Victoria Terminus, Bombay, dating from 1878, displays less evidence of

agitation and a more appropriately reverential stateliness in the approach of passengers to the magnificently ornate station, the station as Oriental temple, a fittingly decorative setting for the worship of the god Steam, the latest addition to the subcontinent's pantheon and one who was to transform the face of British India.

But the most memorable exterior painting is John O'Connor's crimson and gold fantasy *St. Pancras Station, seen from Pentonville Road* (1884), a fitting tribute to the most exuberant expression of Victorian architectural imagination. The canvas somehow encapsulates the ethos of the Victorian age. In the foreground occupying the bottom half of the canvas are the busy streets of the great metropolis, hub of the mightiest empire the world has ever seen: a tangled complex of open-top, horse-drawn omnibuses and hackney carriages, sandwich-board men, children, dogs, workers, the mundane, bustling, energetic, everyday reality. Towering above it, and seeming to float in a golden mist, the romance, a fairy-tale castle of turrets and spires, symbol of Victorian aspirations, of a reaching out to the stars, onwards and upwards, excelsior. It is a permanent monument to the soaring imagination, boundless confidence, and sheer gusto of the Victorian age. Looking at it with sympathetic eyes, it is easy to see what inspired the wonderment of the age that produced such architectural eloquence and caused G. K. Chesterton to write of the King's Cross train-shed: 'What poet race shot such cyclopean arches to the stars?' O'Connor's painting, like Frith's, has become deservedly well known through frequent reproduction in the form of postcards, posters, and dust-jackets.

Romance and reality interweave in John Davidson's 'Liverpool Street Station'. At one level it is a place holding a promise of golden delights:

> Through crystal roofs the sunlight fell,
> And pencilled beams the gloss renewed
> On iron rafters balanced well
> On iron struts; though dimly hued,
> With some o'erlaid, with dust endued,
> The walls and beams like beryl shone;
> And dappled light the platforms strewed
> With yellow foliage of the dawn
> That withered by the porch of day's divan.

But at another level, the station is the haunt of hopeless derelicts:

> But orchards lit with golden lamps,
> Or purple moor, or nutbrown stream,
> Or mountains where the morn encamps

Frequent no station-loafer's dream:
A breed of folk forlorn that seem
The heirs of disappointment, cast
By fate to be the preacher's theme,
To hunger daily and to fast,
And sink to helpless indigence at last.

From early morn they hang about
The bookstall, the refreshment room;
They pause and think, as if in doubt
Which train to go by; now assume
A jaunty air, and now in gloom
They take the platform for a stage
And pace it, meditating doom—
Their own, the world's; in baffled rage
Condemning still the imperceptive age.[9]

Davidson was quite prepared to criticize the inadequate station, and many a hapless Victorian traveller will have warmed to his strictures on 'London Bridge Station':

Much tolerance and genial strength of mind
Unbiased witnesses who wish to find
This railway-station possible at all
Must cheerfully expend. Artistical
Ideas wither here; a magic power
Alone can pardon and in pity dower
With fictive charm a structure so immane.
How then may fancy, to begin with, feign
An origin for such a roundabout
Approach—so intricate, yet so without
Intention, and so spanned by tenebrous
And thundering viaducts? Grotesquely, thus:—
One night the disposition of the ward
Was shifted; for the streets with one accord,
Enfranchised by a landslip, danced the hay
And innocently jumbled up the way.
And so we enter. Here, without perhaps,
Except the automatic money-traps,
Inside the station, everything's so old,
So inconvenient, of such manifold
Perplexity, and, as a mole might see,
So strictly what a station shouldn't be,
That no idea minifies its crude
And yet elaborate ineptitude,[10]

The main business is, of course, the arrival and departure of the trains, and the kaleidoscopic effect created, the bustle, noise, and sheer variety, was to provide a potent source of inspiration. Siegfried Sassoon caught the departure of the 'Morning Express' with vivid photographic immediacy:

> Along the wind-swept platform, pinched and white,
> The travellers stand in pools of wintry light,
> Offering themselves to morn's long, slanting arrows.
> The train's due; porters trundle laden barrows.
> The train steams in, volleying resplendent clouds
> Of sun-blown vapour. Hither and about,
> Scared people hurry, storming the doors in crowds.
> The officials seem to waken with a shout,
> Resolved to hoist and plunder; some to the vans
> Leap; others rumble the milk in gleaming cans.
> Boys, indolent-eyed, from baskets leaning back,
> Questioning each face; a man with a hammer steals
> Stooping from coach to coach; with clang and clack
> Touches and tests, and listens to the wheels.
> Guard sounds a warning whistle, points to the clock
> With brandished flag, and on his folded flock
> Claps the last door; the monster grunts: 'Enough!'
> Tightening his load of links with pant and puff.
> Under the arch, then forth into blue day,
> Glide the processional windows on their way,
> And glimpse the stately folk who sit at ease
> To view the world like kings taking the seas
> In prosperous weather: drifting banners tell
> Their progress to the counties; with them goes
> The clamour of their journeying; while those
> Who sped them stand to wave a last farewell.[11]

J. Ashby Sterry passed rather more sardonic observations on the denizens of the Continental mail express in 'At Charing Cross':

> They take up their tickets, pay their fare
> They're booked right through to everywhere
> To lead a life of hopeless worry
> With Bradshaw, Baedecker and Murray.[12]

But it is parting, especially parting from a loved one, which imbues the station with so much of its emotional resonance. Thomas Hardy captured this in 'On the Departure Platform':

> We kissed at the barrier; and passing through
> She left me, and moment by moment got
> Smaller and smaller, until to my view
> She was but a spot.[13]

He evoked a feeling powerfully echoed in Coventry Patmore's 'Leave-Taking at Salisbury' and Philip Henderson's 'Night Express'. In Henderson's poem the narrator sees his sweetheart off on the Aberdeen express:

> And I saw the smoke under the roof at the end of the platform,
> And the long train with all its blinds drawn down,
> And I knew she would have to go by that train, so I told her
> To get into the carriage and I would go away. But she
> Stood behind the glass window looking like a little girl.
> She said, I love you, and the whistle blew and I wondered
> If that would be the last time I would see her.
> The carriages slid away up the platform and everyone waved,
> But I walked back into the street by myself.
> If I should die to-night,
> If all our love and life together should suddenly end
> In a wreckage of steam and shattered lights and tangled iron,
> If she should be left lying (I can't think how)
> With some wheel gradually ceasing to spin near her face,
> And all my regrets for our misunderstandings, for my impatience with her,
> Be suddenly left with me unsolved because of a mistake in a box,
> What should I do?[14]

But departure had an even greater emotional resonance for the individual in wartime. The time-honoured and potentially tragic separation that attends war and makes the station so poignant a part of the memories of those who have lived through this century's world wars is a universal experience, its timelessness evoked by Frances Cornford in 'Parting in Wartime':

> How long ago Hector took off his plume
> Not wanting his little son should cry
> Then kissed his sad Andromache goodbye—
> And now we three in Euston Waiting Room.[15]

The unexpressed fear underlying all these partings is that they may be permanent. Jean Cocteau's 'Farewell to a Marine Fusilier' (1918) expresses the feelings of a woman who has seen her sweetheart off:

> When the train leaves, it empties
> Her heart, the beloved dies.
> Dead, she must go away
> From the station, from the empty world.[16]

Thomas Hardy caught a similar moment 'In a Waiting Room':

> A soldier and his wife, with haggard look
> Subdued to stone by strong endeavour;
> And then I heard
> From a casual word
> They were parting as they believed for ever.[17]

The station and the train were inexorably intertwined with death, which is why the faces of the soldiers marching to the siding-shed in Wilfred Owen's 'The Send-Off' are so 'grimly gay'. They may have a song on their lips, but there is anxiety in their hearts, anxiety about their ultimate destination. Karl Shapiro's 'Troop Train' eloquently makes the link between wartime transportation and that destination.

> Trains lead to ships and ships to death or trains
> And trains to death or trucks and trucks to death
> Or trucks lead to the march, the march to death
> Or that survival which is all our hope;
> And death leads back to trucks and trains and ships.[18]

Every war has produced its station-painting, a visual expression of the emotions at the centre of poetic evocations of parting. James Collinson's *Return to the Front* (1855) shows a splendidly uniformed soldier leaning out of a railway carriage to take leave of his wife as he returns to the Crimea. The guard behind them waves a green flag. It was a pose and scene much repeated. George Harcourt's *Goodbye* (1900) depicted the 3rd Battalion, the Grenadier Guards, leaving Waterloo for the Boer War. Against a background of soldiers waving, several vignettes are highlighted. Centre-stage are a pair of sweethearts kissing, but there is also an old man looking on, clearly seeing off a son, and a shawled mother carrying a baby and attended by a daughter, bidding a husband farewell. In R. Jack's *Return to the Front* (1917) Scots and English soldiers mill about the platform, making their farewells, lighting up cigarettes, or just looking dejected. William Roberts's *Soldiers At Train* depicts a similar scene from the Second World War, a crowded platform awash with soldiers and sailors, smoking, drinking cups of tea, eating sandwiches, all but swamping the occasional anxious female, the wife carrying a child or the daughter gazing up at a departing father. The faces and the uniforms change but the venue and the emotions remain the same. The corollary of these scenes is the tragic return, nowhere more poignant than in J. Hodgson Lobley's *Ambulances leaving Charing Cross Station* (1916), a seemingly endless procession of Red Cross vehicles leaving the station precincts and carrying injured soldiers through anxiously waiting crowds. A comprehensive summation of the role of the station in war is to be found in one of the two panoramic paintings by Helen McKie commissioned to celebrate the centenary of Waterloo Station in 1948. The canvases depict Waterloo in wartime and peacetime from the same high angle, at the same time, 6.42 p.m. The wartime painting, in which the station roof is blacked out and the green of the Southern Railway locomotives painted over, shows soldiers and sailors, male and female, on duty and on leave, arriving and departing in various groupings and combinations. Henry Marvell Carr's *A Railway Terminus* (1941) gives a more impressionistic picture of the wartime station interior, the black out broken here and there by flaring lights which reveal knots of passengers huddled around departure boards, timetables, and bookstall.

In France the station made a considerable appeal to the Impressionists. They were part of a modernist movement in the arts, committed to capturing the atmosphere of the present day, scenes from everyday life. By the 1870s, stations had become an acceptable subject for high art. Indeed Théophile Gautier suggested that artists should find inspiration in the railways and railway stations. When the poet Paul Bourget asserted the ugliness of the station and of the train in a poem of 1878, Emile Zola reproved him: 'You, modern poet, you detest modern life. You go against your gods, you don't really accept your age. Why do you find a railway station ugly? A station is beautiful.'[19]

The Impressionists prized the station not so much for the drama and the incident that fascinated British painters but as a source of objective visual effects and atmospheric observation. Camille Pissarro, having fled from France to England to escape the Franco-Prussian War, painted in 1871 a train leaving what was long thought to be Penge Station but is now believed to be the Lordship Lane Station on the London, Chatham and Dover line. The long-distance view, dominated by the green banks of a cutting, creates the effect of train, station, and surrounding buildings being dwarfed and swallowed up by the landscape. Edouard Manet's *Gare Saint-Lazare* (1873) depicted a mother and child in the foreground before some railings, with smoke billowing up from behind and below them where the station lies unseen. But Claude Monet tackled the station more directly, producing in 1877 a celebrated series of seven paintings in which he depicted the station as a vehicle for the study of light and shade, smoke and shape: a hazy evocation of station atmosphere.

The Impressionists influenced painters abroad, such as 'The Camden Town Group', who, inspired by Walter Sickert, believed that 'magic and poetry were to be found in the everyday urban surroundings of the artist'. Their technique resembled that of their French counterparts, with whom they were linked by Camille Pissarro's son Lucien, who settled in England in 1890 and painted the Railway Cuttings, Acton in 1908. Stations figure prominently in the 'Camden Town' repertoire of themes, as evidenced by Malcolm Drummond's *Paddington Station* (1911, now lost), Spencer Gore's *Letchworth Station* (1912) and *Mornington Crescent Tube Station* (1911), and Charles Ginner's *Victoria Station. The Sunlit Square* (1913). In Gore's *The Nursery Window, Rowlandson House* (1911), the view from the window is of Euston Station, seen across the railway tracks.

Impressionism also influenced the Glasgow School, which flourished in the 1880s and 1890s. William Kennedy, recently returned from Paris, evoked atmosphere and ambience in his painting of *Stirling Station at Evening* (1888). He faithfully reproduced the respectable bourgeois, kilted highlanders and errand boy heading a stream of passengers pouring from a recently arrived train. But there are distinct echoes of Monet in the effect of gleaming station lights and opalescent clouds of steam.

The same kind of feeling for the atmosphere, particularly of country stations, inspired French poets. One of them was Léon-Paul Fargue. He evoked the ambience of the station in the morning in 'The Deserted Station':

I long to see again the great farm lamp which lit up at the arrival of the first morning train. I'll reach there by the narrow track drenched in dew . . . It is the hour when the scent from the avenue of lime trees makes the lamp flicker. But the carriage steams and grumbles. One must take to the rails when the post arrives by the 10 o'clock train and the first of Vulcan's butterflies leave a trail along the ditches. Before then I'll have plenty of time to stop at the first villages blue with anvils and see some of my cousins in the houses behind the fir-trees and the fences.[20]

He expanded on it in a later poem:

The little station with short shadows is tired of it being 5 o'clock.—Like a reflection of the sky skipping along on tall grasses, the rails, to which blue eyes flee, are off to fetch the eyes reddened by travel: the short, dull rumble of a train comes from low on the horizon . . . A sunbeam gilds the exit-gate, and this great flower, on the left, like the hand of a sleeping infant. The gig of the Little-Hell

Hotel attends—the passenger coach waits nearby in the blue avenue under the limes. A dying machine emits a dark, hollow cough—then is silent. Everything stops and falls to dreaming. Just as in time gone by. The old folk give a yawn, check the time and return to sleep.[21]

These are the sort of fleeting fragments, frozen in the memory, that feed the poetic imagination. An unexpected halt at a slumbering country station one day at the height of summer in 1915 inspired Edward Thomas to confer instant immortality on an obscure Gloucestershire village. He paints a picture of sounds and smells and sensations that remains recognizable, capturing a moment of Arcadian peace in the midst of the madness of world conflict. It is a picture that Fargue would have recognized:

> Yes, I remember Adlestrop—
> The name, because one afternoon
> Of heat the express-train drew up there
> Unwontedly. It was late June.
> The steam hissed. Someone cleared his throat.
> No one left and no one came
> On the bare platform. What I saw
> Was Adlestrop—only the name,
> And willows, willow-herb, and grass,
> And meadowsweet and haycocks dry,
> No whit less still and lonely fair
> Than the high cloudlets in the sky.
> And for that minute a blackbird sang
> Close by, and round him, mistier,
> Farther and farther, all the birds
> Of Oxfordshire and Gloucestershire.[22]

There is perhaps no more melancholy sight than a deserted railway station at night. The emptiness, the half-light, the distant echoes, all contrive to make almost palpable that metaphysical concept 'the dark night of the soul'. The sight of forlorn passengers on a platform at night ('Figures on a Platform') evoked in Frances Cornford the feeling of being lost in a hostile universe ('Travelling at night no man has any home, beyond the station's melancholy dome'). Henry Maxwell in his 'Dusk on a Branch' sought to capture the unique feel of the gloaming:

> The lamps are lit, the gas-lamps and the oil,
> And shed their lemon and their yellow light,
> Pallid and calm, while overhead the night
> Draws up its wings and settles on the soil.

> In little worlds the larger world dissolves:
> An overbridge, a parcels room, a board—
> Arrivals and Departures—while abroad
> In space and darkness lost, a wheel revolves.
>
> Both 'Up and 'Down' the signal lamps show red,
> The semaphores have faded in the dark:
> The gaslight falls upon the booking clerk,
> Glimpsed through his grille, intent, with tilted head.
>
> Along the platform, where the awning ends,
> Some milk-churns glow, and by the exit door
> A pile of newspapers lies on the floor—
> And over all the lemon light extends.[23]

The French were more prone than the British to use the station as what Gordon Inkster has called 'a metaphorical vehicle for metaphysical reflection'. Jules Laforgue, finding himself at Korsør Station on the Danish coast on New Year's Day 1886, was prompted to reflect on life, death, and the cosmos by the sight of the station, the fog, and the stormy sea:

> Yet the Infinite is there, end of the line for all missed trains,
> Where, blinded by the signals, folk commiserate with the sob
> Of the goods trains, and are about to hurry along in a moment
> And die, stretched out across the tracks . . .
> For life is everywhere the same. We know naught.
> But *it* is the Station, and we have to get up steam; some for
> Future rejoicing, some for the so-called days of yore.
> Come on. Spin your wheel, and pray and try to be good.[24]

In the twentieth century, European artists saw the station more in terms of symbolism and abstraction. For Futurists, as for the Impressionists before them, stations were part of the new and the now. Futurism, which began in Italy, sought to reflect the modern world, to dramatize science and technology. It was bold, febrile, adventurous, violently innovative, self-consciously opposed to the concepts of 'good taste' and 'harmony'. F. T. Marinetti declared in the 1909 Futurist Manifesto:

We intend to exalt aggressive action, a feverish insomnia, the racer's stride, the mortal leap, the punch and the slap . . . We will sing of great crowds excited by work, by pleasure and by riot; we will sing of the multi-coloured, polyphonic tides of revolution in the modern capitals; we will sing of the vibrant nightly fervour of arsenals and shipyards blazing with violent electric moons; greedy railway stations that devour smoke-plumed serpents; factories hung on clouds by the crooked lines of their smoke; bridges that stride the rivers like giant gymnasts, flashing in the sun with a glitter of knives; adventurous steamers that sniff the horizon; deep-chested locomotives whose wheels paw the tracks like the hooves of enormous steel horses bridled by tubing; and the sleek flight of planes whose propellers chatter in the wind like banners and seem to cheer like an enthusiastic crowd.[25]

They saw the station as one of the primary sources of the din of modern life, a symbol of the acceleration of life, of their hatred of quiet, their dread of slowness, their love of the new, of greater freedom, increased travel, energy, motion, and mechanical power. Gino Severini's *Suburban Train Arriving at Paris* seeks to capture the nature of speed, a dizzying whirl of smoke, buildings, billboards, telegraph poles, a helter-skelter turmoil of glimpsed shapes. His *Nord-Sud* (1912) is a phantasmagoria of station signs, 'Métro', 'Sortie', 'First Class', 'Direction Saint-Lazare', a confusion of overlapping images, the feel of rapid transit. Carlo Carra's *La Stazione di Milano* (1910–11) is a whirling maelstrom of shapes and colours, vaguely recalling tracks, roof, buildings, embodiment of the Futurist idea of the station.

The Cubists aimed at dissecting objects and depicting their essential nature and constitution rather than their superficial appearance. Fernand Léger's *The Station* (1923) thus celebrated the station as geometrical construct, an amalgam of blocks, lines, and shapes. Nicolas de Staël's *La Gare de Vaugirard* (1945), a dark-hued, abstract, expressionist canvas influenced by Léger, similarly conveys the geometric shapes of the station, combining the lines, squares, and curves into an overall phantasmagoria suggesting a scene of perpetual motion.

There are elements of this approach too in the work of the Surrealists, but they sought to utilize the station to convey inner feelings. Perhaps the most Surrealist celebrant of the station was Giorgio de Chirico. His *Gare Montparnasse*, also known as *The Melancholy of Departure*, was painted in Paris in 1914 at a time when he was homesick for Italy. It depicts a massive columned structure, empty, shadowed, and with the station clock prominent overhead. Two tiny figures are dwarfed on an approach-ramp and a tiny train seems stalled in the distance. It captures the vastness and emptiness of the station when the train has gone, the feeling of being left behind, of being stranded in a place from which others have departed but from which you cannot. It is the antithesis of the bustle and excitement of the Futurists' stations.

Chirico's *The Anxious Journey* (1913) also has a distant train, but on the edge of a labyrinth of arches, winding in and out, leading nowhere. James Thrall Soby has written of this painting that it is 'clearly a dream-image expressing the terror of being lost in a railroad station before an important journey, of trying desperately to locate a train, only to discover it finally at the far end of an inaccessible corridor'.[26] The influence of Chirico on British artist Paul Nash can clearly be seen in his *Northern Adventure* (1929), the exterior of St Pancras as seen from the window of his nearby flat, which has been called 'an allegory of progress towards a spiritual goal'.

It has often been said that the arts do not so much mirror the mood of the age as prefigure the era to come. Thus Jacobean Revenge Tragedy is seen in its violence and bloodshed to presage the English Civil War. Siegfried Kracauer, in a celebrated book *From Caligari to Hitler*, argued that the films of Weimar Germany demonstrated a psychological preparedness for the rise of the Nazis. This view is now critically discounted. But it is hard not to see in German painting of the 1920s a vision of the totalitarian society that was to be imposed in the following decade. Josef Wedewer's *Railway Crossing* (1927) shows the end of a platform, empty but for two milk churns and a discarded newspaper. Beyond it is a level crossing and the crossing-keeper's house. The railway lines stretch into the distance. The whole scene is empty, desolate, and forbidding. Friedrich Busack's *Railway Crossing* (1928) features railway lines, telegraph poles, wires, the sharp outlines of a building, a street lamp, a notice on a post, and a railway official with a stick. All is harsh, geometric, stern, and ordered. The feeling is similar in Gustav Wunderwald's paintings. The setting of *Railway Embankment Berlin N.* (1926) is dominated by the huge system of telegraph poles and wires, dwarfing a small station in the distance and a train, with a long plume of smoke, passing beneath. It is a metaphor for the irresistible forces of power crushing humanity. *S-Bahn Station Spandau* (1928) similarly shows the corner of a platform, gloomy and overhung, and containing a single railway official. But the prevailing mood is conveyed by the railway lines, the fencing beyond, the solid oblong mass of the building beyond that. One is irresistibly reminded of the Nuremberg Rallies, at which masses of people were organized into solid, de-humanized, geometrical shapes, the visual expression of their loss of individuality, liberty, and conscience.

Latterly the station has come to stand for polar opposites. But both derive from dissatisfaction with the present and with the state of the world. One attitude is to see the station as a symbol of alienation, a feeling profoundly present in Fabio Rieti's *Wall in Dijon* (1973), a station name-plate starkly lit by a back-light on a brick wall, and in Friedrich Gerlach's *Train Station* (1965), where the straight lines of track and platform, the stiff figures, and the harsh light catching them in its beam powerfully suggest a hostile universe. It is a feeling that pervades the work of the twentieth-century American artists of the 'ash can school', who regularly use deserted stations as a symbol of the monotony, emptiness, and anonymity of modern existence, as for instance Edward Hopper's deserted and silent railway halt, *North Truro Station*.

The other reaction is one of escape into the past, where steam is for ever King. Nostalgia is the dominant element in the appeal of the meticulous recreations of powerful locomotives in major stations in the golden age of steam, such as the canvases of Hamilton Ellis and Alan Fearnley, and in the intricate narrative paintings of Helen Bradley in the *Miss Carter* series, where family trips to the seaside in the long-lost Indian summer of Edwardian England are lovingly recalled. The same remembered bustle and colour inform *Sunday Visitors* by Helen Bradley's American counterpart, Melvin Bolstad.

Visual representations of railway stations began in the latter years of the nineteenth century to drop through people's letter-boxes as the new visual art of photography was pressed into service by the postcard. The first postcards were issued in Austria in 1869 and within a year they were in use in Britain. By the time Edward VII ascended the throne, picture postcards were an accepted part of national life. They were given a final boost by the Boer War and the decision of the Postmaster-General in January 1902 to authorize the divided-back postcard permitting both message and address on the back, instead of the address alone, which was all that had been legally allowed before. In fact, messages had long been written on the cards and the Postmaster-General was simply legalizing an existing practice. They began to be sold everywhere and by 1903 some 600 million postcards were being sent annually. By 1914, 880 million cards were posted. During the Boer War and later during the First World War postcards were invaluable in maintaining links between families and in the dissemination of propaganda. After 1918, with the cost of sending the postcard doubled and with the increasing use of the telephone, the postcard declined from its peak and by 1930 its golden age was over. But in its heyday the picture postcard charted and celebrated every aspect of national life. Prominent among the topics featured in the photographs were the railways. In Britain most of the major railway companies issued their own cards, depicting the scenic beauties of their routes. But stations also figured on cards in Britain and the Empire, in the United States and on the Continent. It is a good bet that there is a picture postcard photograph of every station in Britain, however small. Large and small, full and empty, city and country, stations of every description adorn postcards, their recurrence inscribing stations into the nation's collective visual memory. The messages on the back, arranging meetings, deliveries, departures, and rendezvous, confirm their centrality to everyday life.[27]

But the station has not just served as an inspiration for artists and photographers. It has functioned as a gallery of sorts. Gustave Courbet talked of

... the railway stations that are already churches of progress and will soon become temples of Art. Enter the waiting halls and look at those admirable vast sites, airy and full of light; you'll agree that we need only to hang pictures there to make without any expense, the most matchless of museums, the only ones where art can really live. From where the crowd betakes itself there is life.[28]

It did not turn out quite as he had anticipated. But those station walls did not stay empty. In some cases, railway companies commissioned friezes, frescos, and murals. At Lens, in Northern France, the work of local miners was celebrated in a mural; at Bienne in Switzerland, the family was idealized; in the booking-office of the Gare de Lyon were scenes from the route from Paris to Marseilles of the Paris–Lyon–Marseille Railway; in Milan Central, bas-reliefs of episodes from Ancient Roman history testified to the revived Roman imperialism of the twentieth century. At Hastings Station, the Southern Railway installed Cubist murals of beach scenes. In Portugal many stations large and small, rural and urban, boasted scenes in ceramic tiles (*azulejos*) glorifying local themes and traditions. Oporto's São Bento Station was decorated with scenes of peasant life and of the building of the railway, for instance. In the departure hall of the Gare de l'Est the painter Albert Herter painted in 1926 a magnificent tableau depicting the departure of the troops on mobilization in August 1914. It was in memory of his son Everit-Albert Herter, who had fallen in action in 1918. A platform is seen, with the troops boarding a train, and elderly parents seeing off their sons, young children their fathers, and grieving wives their husbands. There are tears, sadness, and downcast looks. The prevailing mood is sombre. There is none of the jubilation and euphoria that really attended the outbreak of war. For this is 1914 seen in tragic retrospect. Form, style, and content varied greatly but the whole tradition of station murals is one which would repay detailed study. What might have been the most memorable of all station paintings, however, was never carried out. G. F. Watts offered to decorate the ceiling of the great hall at Euston Station with scenes from the history of the world, making it thereby a sort of Sistine Chapel of the Railway Age. He asked only for the price of his materials. The London and North-Western Railway politely refused his offer.

Statuary formed part of the decoration of many of the stations erected in the golden age of station-building. The French characteristically filled their stations with voluptuous female statues. On the façade of the Gare de l'Est, two naked female figures, representing the Rhine and the Seine, the rivers linked by the network, reclined above the station clock. An armed and helmeted female warrior with sword and shield, the spirit of Verdun, crowns the pediment. On top of the Gare du Nord, a female statue symbolizing the city of Paris is flanked by four others on each side, representing the cities reached via the Nord network: London, Vienna, Berlin, Cologne, Frankfurt, Amsterdam, Brussels, and St Petersburg. On the columns of the capitals at Metz, however, are engraved two men embracing, to symbolize the friendship of nations. The corbels of St Pancras Station booking-hall are decorated with the handsome figures of railwaymen—an engine-driver, a guard, an engineer, and a signal boy.

In the United States, the repeated process of station renewal in the twentieth century produced a powerful and heavy classicism which included much statuary as part of its ornamentation. One of the great façades of Grand Central Station, New York, was surmounted by a winged Mercury, attended by a sculptured group of figures and symbols including the globe of the world. Washington Union Station, opened not long before Grand Central, was conceived in the Beaux-Arts style. Massive draped statues surmounted the capitals of the enormous columns of the classical frontage. Similar statues stood on the peristyle which divided the vaulted booking-hall from the vast concourse, where the arched window openings were also graced by classical figures.

In the British dominions and colonies the twentieth century saw an increasingly confident elaboration of station architecture. With that elaboration went a growing concern for artistic detail. In 1907 New Zealand Railways opened their magnificent new Dunedin Station. Its Flemish Renaissance style was matched internally by a booking-hall with classical friezes of cherubs and foliage in Royal Doulton China and a floor of fifty-seven panels made up of 725,760 Royal Doulton porcelain squares specially ordered from England. Above the balcony were stained-glass windows, each depicting an approaching train. The glass was assembled in such a way that the engines appeared to be approaching with headlights burning. The station, including the magnificent mosaic, has recently been restored by a conservation-conscious New Zealand Railways. The new Singapore Station was opened to celebrate the completion of the Johore causeway, thereby linking the island colony to

Malaya by railway lines leading to Kuala Lumpur and Penang, and ultimately to Thailand. Around the walls of an otherwise austere building were placed mosaics symbolic of the life of the Malaysian peninsula. The striking thing about the artistic detail of almost all colonial railway stations is, however, the fact that the arts incorporated were nearly all European and imported. The technology of the railways required a Western art to glorify it. There were occasionally attempts to match the local architectural styles in railway stations, but at most of the large city stations the adornments were a statuary with friezes and mosaics that were entirely European in inspiration.

But the station became not just a location for murals and statuary, it became, in direct reflection of the station's key role in the economic life of the nineteenth- and twentieth-century worlds, a vast hoarding, an advertising man's dream, acres of blank wall to be filled with enticing materials. With the development of new techniques of mass printing, mass production of advertising posters meant an all-out assault on the senses of the consumers. The station also became a major location for the brightly coloured and eye-catching enamel signs that flourished between the 1880s and the 1930s and are now collector's items themselves. Station after station could be found proclaiming the virtues of Fry's Chocolate and Pears' Soap, Sutton's Seeds and Mazawattee Tea, Van Houten's Cocoa and Camp Coffee, Wills' Gold Flake and Stone's Ginger Wine, Vim and Virol. W. H. Lever, the founder of Unilever, who manufactured Sunlight Soap, set great store by railway station advertising. He said: 'We ourselves chose the positions for our advertising plates on the railways and the advantage of right hand or left hand side of a booking office were matters that received personal and weighty consideration.'[29] Virol acquired sites on the station approach, lining entrance and exit routes with their blue, white, and orange signs. The advertisers' influence extended even to the Continent. A visitor to Holland reported in 1899:

The Dutch are famous for their cleanliness, and this is forcibly brought home to the traveller by the extensive way a large firm of English soap makers advertize their wares all along the line; every station, and seemingly, every signal cabin and every cottage, beside the level crossings, bear one or more of these familiar enamelled iron plates.[30]

By the turn of the century stations were so smothered that one District Railway traveller complained that it was difficult to 'decide whether one was at Victoria, Virol or Vinolia'.[31]

Pride of place at the station was inevitably taken by the railway companies' own posters. Railway posters provide important testimony to the 'pride the company felt in its service, the image which it felt itself to have (or wished to have), the type of traffic it was anxious to capture'. They provided colour, diversion, and fantasy for the waiting traveller and might well plant the seed of plans for future travel from which the company might benefit.[32]

Railway advertising was as old as the railway itself. The opening of the Stockton and Darlington line in 1825 was advertised by printed handbills in the style of eighteenth-century broadsheets. The earliest railway posters from the 1830s aimed at the clear and uncomplicated transmission of information about trips, times, and rates. By the 1840s there was an increasing use of woodcuts to provide visual decoration, usually engines and carriages. The railways, confident of their hold on the travelling public, made little effort to promote their activities or co-ordinate advertising. It was not until 1886 that the Great Western Railway set up a specific advertising department to co-ordinate publicity. But thereafter development was rapid and by 1900 the Lancashire and Yorkshire were allocating £7,000 a year for publicity work.

The advent of the lithographic poster provided the ideal stimulus for railway advertising. It developed in France in the 1870s and 1880s where Jules Chéret took the lead in producing posters that integrated pictures and text, utilized bold colours, and often deployed the female form to catch the eye of the passer-by. The railway companies in both France and England tended to utilize eye-catching coloured posters to promote traffic which they hoped would be regular and recurrent, particularly seaside travel, which the railways had done much to facilitate.

The French tended to concentrate in their posters on stylized representations of the hills, the coast, or an elegant seaside resort, often with an attractive nymph taking advantage of the clear mountain air or the health-giving ozone. For the French, sex appeal was from the first an integral element in their posters. The British companies, moving into coloured posters in a big way in the Edwardian period, went in for more staid and less *risqué* images. They often worked in conjunction with the local authorities, who invariably sought a responsible and respectable promotion of their amenities. It was, as so often in England, a matter of taking one's pleasures soberly, gravely, and seriously. Emphasis was laid not on the promise of 'Ooh-la-la' but on health and healthy activities such as golf, fishing, and hiking. This approach is epitomized by John Hassall's classic 1908 poster for the Great Northern Railway—'Skegness is so bracing'—with its jolly, red-faced, rotund fishermen skipping along the beach. It was to continue in use for decades.

Destinations tended to be the principal theme of railway posters—and the more romantic the better. All companies were anxious to publicize the scenic beauties of the areas to which they could transport customers, hence many and handsome were the representations of the Lake District, the Scottish Highlands, the Yorkshire Dales, and the Cambrian Coast. In an ingenious device, the Great Western Railway had a poster created which compared the shape of Cornwall and Italy, drawing a comparison between the climate and beauty of the two areas, and with two girls in national peasant costume in the centre. 'See your own country first' was the caption, an indication that the railways were aiming in this instance at prosperous middle-class traffic. The working classes could hardly afford to go abroad. In some cases, they couldn't even afford to go to the seaside in their own country. This desire to counter the attractions of 'abroad' continued to exercise the Great Western Railway, with their deliberate promotion of the concept of the Cornish Riviera.

In the 1920s the actual trains and their engines began to figure much more and the posters drew attention to the speed, comfort, and punctuality of their services, as the railways began to feel the effect of competition from road transport. It was the era of the luxury trains, and on both sides of the Channel and the Atlantic posters celebrated in elegant designs the delights of 'Le Train Bleu' and 'L'Etoile du Nord', 'The Flying Scotsman' and 'The Silver Jubilee', 'The Golden Arrow' and 'The Blue Bird', 'The Twentieth Century Limited' and 'The Empire State Express'.

During the First World War, travel posters were replaced by more urgent national matters, and for five years after it the railway system was exhausted and could afford little for posters. When they returned, they reflected the disappearance of the Edwardian bourgeois world, with greater use of bathing beauties to entice travellers to the seaside.

A major impetus was given to advertising in Britain by the grouping of the companies into four in 1923. Prestige and distinction were sought by these huge new undertakings. At the suggestion of Norman Wilkinson of the Royal Academy, the London, Midland, and Scottish Company commissioned members of the Academy to design a memorable series of posters for them, which stressed orthodoxy and respectability, in stark contrast to the London Underground where, under the imaginative direction of Frank Pick, younger and more avant-garde artists like McKnight Kauffer were stamping their distinctive image on the tube stations. The nine original RA canvases exhibited in London in January

1924 included both the romantic and the realistic. Sir Bertram Macken-
nal's *Speed* was a bas-relief of a winged man in flight outlined against the
rays of the sun, while Maurice Grieffenhagen's *Carlisle: the Gateway to
Scotland* featured St George in full medieval armour, mounted on a
magnificently caparisoned white charger, flourishing the red and white
banner of England and leaving by the gateway of a border castle for the
distant beckoning hills of Scotland.

The dignity of labour, however, formed the central idea of Stanhope
Forbes's *The Permanent Way*, which showed gangers at work on the track,
and George Clausen's *Coal*, with its cloth-capped miners trudging home
from the pit at dusk. Although the rail-men were part of the General
Strike, crushed in 1926, the sympathetic and sometimes heroic depiction
of the proletariat was a theme dear to the heart of artists and intellectuals
in the inter-war years.

By contrast with the orthodoxy of style to be seen in the LMS posters,
the London and North-Eastern Railway's advertising manager, W. M.
Teasdale, following the precedent set by Frank Pick, chose a more
avant-garde approach, involving Art Deco, Cubist, and Modernist styles.
In one bold gesture they promoted a poster by A. P. Thompson sending
up the celebrated Southern Railways poster of a small curly-haired boy
on the end of the platform at Waterloo, thanking the driver of an express
train for his journey ('I'm taking an early holiday cos I know summer
comes soonest in the South'). The LNER version had a tiny boy
dwarfed by a vast stylized 'Flying Scotsman' and being hailed through a
megaphone by the driver.

In France there was considerably greater innovation, experimentation,
and adventurousness. Although the subjects were the same as in Britain
(luxury expresses, seaside holidays, and so forth), Cubism, Bauhaus, and
montage techniques all figured in their depiction. The inter-war years
saw a golden age of railway posters with prime examples of the art to be
seen at many a station. But just as the First World War ended the first
boom, so the Second World War ended the second, and 'Is your journey
really necessary?' and 'Careless talk costs lives' replaced the odes to the
beauties of Devon and paeans to the luxury of Pullman expresses. After
the war, railways everywhere were in decline, photography took over
from graphic design, and, although the SNCF in France imaginatively
commissioned posters from Dali and Utrillo, the great age of the railway
poster, like the great age of the railway, was at an end.

15

The Station in Literature and Film

EMILE ZOLA triumphantly fulfilled his own demand that the artists of
his day should find poetry in railway stations.[1] His novel *La Bête
humaine* (1890), arguably the greatest of all railway novels, contains several
strongly impressionistic station descriptions, which are the verbal equivalents of Monet's station paintings. They can be directly compared because
both chose to depict the Gare Saint-Lazare. They capture better than
anything else the changing moods of the station:

> The train was about to move. The fine drizzle had begun again, filling the huge,
> dark space through which trains were continually passing, but all that could be
> seen of them was the square glass lights, rows of little moving windows. Green
> lights had appeared, and some lamps were dancing about at ground level. That was
> all, nothing but an immense blackness in which the only thing to be made out was
> the roof over the mainline platforms showing dim in the gaslight. Everything else
> was lost in the shadows, and even the noises were dying down, except the roar of
> the engine when it opened its steam-cocks and emitted whirling masses of white
> vapour. A cloud went up and spread like a ghostly shroud, streaked with black
> smoke from some unknown source. The sky was obscured again, and a cloud of
> soot moved off over the blazing furnace of the night life of Paris.[2]

One can almost feel the cold and hear the train sounds in his description
of the Le Havre train preparing to depart:

> Because of extra traffic it had not been possible to put this train under the
> mainline roof. It was waiting in the open air at the platform extension which ran
> out like a long jetty under a pitch-black sky and on which the few gas jets along
> the platform did no more than string a line of smoky stars. A downpour of rain
> had just stopped, but it had left behind a damp, icy air spreading a mist through
> this vast open space as far as the little dim lights in the windows of the rue de
> Rome. It was immense, dreary, drenched with rain, pierced here and there by a
> blood-red light, vaguely peopled by opaque masses, isolated engines or carriages,
> bits of trains slumbering on side lines; and out of the depths of this sea of
> darkness came noises, the breathing of giants feverishly gasping, whistle-blasts
> like piercing shrieks of women being violated, distant horns sounding dismally
> amid the roar of neighbouring streets. Somebody shouted orders for an extra
> carriage to be put on. The express engine stood motionless, letting off from its

safety valve a great jet of steam up into all this blackness, and there it flaked off in little wisps, bedewing with white tears the limitless funereal hangings of the heavens.[3]

Inspired in part by the unsolved murder of Prefect Barrême, killed in a railway carriage and thrown from the window in 1886, Zola wove together two themes which he had originally contemplated for separate novels. One was a murder, the judicial investigation, and an analysis of the French legal process, and the other was the life, work, and symbolic significance of the railways and railwaymen. The resulting story of jealousy, madness, and murder unfolded his belief that 'love, death, possessing, and killing are the dark foundations of the human soul'.

The train became on the personal level a symbol of fate, power, and uncontrollable passion, with trains flashing past Jacques Lantier as he has his murderous fits, and on the general level, in the unforgettable final image of a driverless train running away down the line, a symbol of a mechanized society hurtling out of control towards the unknown. But the book also contains a detailed account of the life and works of railwaymen in nineteenth-century France and much of the action takes place on the Paris Saint-Lazare–Rouen–Normandy route which Zola knew well and used regularly. The train journeys that punctuate the action of the book are the subject of powerfully evocative descriptions, the prose snorting, pulsating, and racing like the steam engines it describes.

The central thread is a murderous triangle, which begins when the jealous Roubaud, deputy station-master at Le Havre, with the complicity of his young wife Séverine, murders the elderly railway company president Grandmorin, who has been having an affair with Séverine. The engine-driver Lantier, suspecting their guilt, is led into an affair with Séverine. Together they plot to kill Roubaud, but Lantier is unable to go through with it and instead kills Séverine and throws himself from his train.

Roubaud's duties at Le Havre inevitably involve Zola in descriptions of station life and the duties of the sub-station-master at the end of the nineteenth century:

When Roubaud was left alone on the platform he went slowly back towards the Montvilliers train standing ready. The doors of the waiting-room had been opened and some passengers were appearing—a few men off hunting with their dogs, two or three shopkeepers and their families taking advantage of a Sunday, not many people really. But when that train had gone, the first of the day, he had no time to waste, having at once to see the 5.45 made up, a stopping train for Rouen and Paris. At that early hour there were not many staff on duty, and the deputy-station-master's job was complicated by all sorts of responsibilities. Having given an eye to the marshalling of the vehicles, taken one by one from the shed, put on a transporter and then pushed under the station roof by a gang of men, he then had to hurry to the booking-hall and give an eye to the sale of tickets and registering of luggage. A dispute broke out between some soldiers and a railwayman in which he had to intervene. For another half-hour, what with freezing draughts, shivering passengers, and eyes heavy with sleep, and his own irritability through fussing about in the dark, he never had a moment to think of himself. Then, when the departure of the slow train had cleared the station, he hurried off to the pointsman's box to make sure that everything was all right in that quarter because another train was due in, the semi-fast from Paris which was running late. Back he went to see the people off that, and waited until the stream of passengers had given up their tickets and piled into hotel buses, which in those days came in and stood under the roof with only a low fence between them and the line. And it was only then that he had a minute to breathe in the now deserted and silent station.[4]

The importance of this daily routine is that it has a calming effect after the turmoil of the murder and the constant fear of discovery. The station itself, one of the earliest on the line, is deemed by Roubaud inadequate and quite unworthy of Le Havre, 'what with its old timber carriage sheds, station roof of wood and zinc with small skylights and bare, dreary buildings with cracks everywhere'. It is nevertheless a positive maelstrom of gossip. Quite apart from the murder, there is the continuing scandal of the fireman Pecqueux who has a woman at each end of the run, a wife in Paris and a mistress in Le Havre. Then there is the running theme of the quarrel over the accommodation above the waiting-room. This takes the form of flats assigned to station employees. Not only do the flats at the front have the best view, they signal a defined place in the hierarchy. Roubaud believes that as deputy station-master he should have the front flat and so there is a feud between him and the actual occupants of the front flat, a feud in which everyone at the station takes sides.

One of the greatest of railway novels became in 1938 one of the greatest of railway films. Adapted and up-dated by director Jean Renoir, the film *La Bête humaine* largely omitted the examination of the judicial system to concentrate on the railway aspect, and made a number of changes in that. But Renoir declared:

I was as faithful as possible to the spirit of the book. I didn't follow the plot of the book exactly but I have always thought it was better to be faithful to the spirit of the work than to its exterior form . . . I did nothing that I wasn't sure would have pleased Zola.[5]

It remains a work of tremendous dramatic and visual power, broodingly atmospheric and graced by some memorable acting from Jean Gabin as the haunted driver and Simone Simon as his fluffily sensuous nemesis, Séverine. The opening sequence of a train journey from Paris to Le Havre, shot from the train itself and involving almost no cutting, is exhilaratingly dramatic and fascinating historically. The ending, however, eschews Zola's social metaphor for a more personal resolution, as Gabin admits to the murder and throws himself from the train, leaving it to proceed without him. Renoir's film was unsuccessfully remade as *Human Desire* in Hollywood in 1954. But with the action transposed to America, the driver (Glenn Ford) stripped of his dementia, and the whole thing set on the infinitely less charismatic diesel engines, even veteran director Fritz Lang could make little of it.

There have been comparatively few masterworks of the rail like *La Bête humaine*. On the whole it has been popular culture rather than serious literature which has most enthusiastically taken up the railways, responding to the immediacy of the sensations they provoke, to the bold iconographic power, strength, and modernity of the steam engine, to the kaleidoscopic nature of train travel, to the whirl and bustle and breathlessness of transience. Stage melodramas, dime novels, thrillers, prints, boys' books, these are the forms that pulsate with the rhythm of the rails and most notably, because unconsciously, reflect the tremendous social impact of the railways.

Even in these forms, comparatively few works have been set wholly in railway stations. 'Light fiction' is perhaps the best description of them. W. Pett Ridge, best known for his novel *Mord Em'ly*, was a cockney writer, an acute observer and collector of cockneyana. His *On Company's Service* (1905) is a collection of atmospheric pieces, character sketches and short stories, often with a twist ending, which evoke the lives and loves of station-masters, porters, ticket-collectors, and guards in the employ of an unnamed railway company. They encompass the story of a young station-master harassed by his retired predecessor; the grumbles of a night inspector; the doomed rivalry of two shunters for the hand of the snooty refreshment-room manageress; the trials and tribulations of a new parcels clerk.

The French writer Franc-Nohain took the station waiting-room as the setting for a series of short stories detailing a variety of encounters, both comic and dramatic, in his *Les Salles d'attente* (1925). A fractious theatrical touring company, trapped at a country station by a line blockage, rehearses its next play in the waiting-room and is arrested for disturbing the peace. A man poses as a masked bandit in order to obtain the key to a small-station waiting-room where he can tryst with his inamorata. An embezzling bank clerk, planning a last wild weekend at the casino and then suicide, meets his employer and family in a station waiting-room and changes his mind. The petty jealousies, drama, and activity attending preparations for a stop-over by the President of France on his special train culminate in the cancellation of the stop-over.

Most revealingly Franc-Nohain proclaims the Gare d'Austerlitz 'adultery's birthplace' in the story of an elopement by a married woman and her lover, foiled by an omniscient stranger who indicates separately to each of them that he knows their plans, and the station regularly plays the same role in the lives of others:

This station's only importance is for irregular couples, for lovers. Think, it is so convenient . . . The one arrives at the Gare d'Orsay; the other at the Gare d'Austerlitz. Like you, monsieur, one comes to wait at Austerlitz for the person who got on the train and who has said their tearful farewells five minutes earlier at the Gare d'Orsay. And they continue the journey together from the Gare de Lyon which is very close; it is the birthplace of adultery.[6]

There is a sharper satirical edge in the picture of life at Chalk Farm Goods Station painted by R. D. Blackmore in his little-known novel *Cradock Nowell* (1866). His hero gets a job as clerk with the Grand Junction Wasting and Screwing Company, a name Blackmore considers generally applicable to railway companies. He is interviewed at the railway terminus 'miserably lighted, a disgrace to any style of architecture, teeming with insolence, pretence, dirt, discomfort, fuss and confusion'. He is taken on without references because the Company have just lost another worker in an accident and is assigned to Cramjam Goods Station ('No man comes here, unless he be tired of his life, or be druv to it by the little ones'). He works from eight in the morning till eight in the evening with five minutes break for lunch. Daily he dices with death in the hellish confines of the goods yard:

Trucks, and vans and boxes on wheels were gliding past in every direction, thick as the carts on London Bridge, creaking, groaning, ricketing, lurching; thumping up against one another, and then recoiling with a heavy kick, straining upon coupling-chains, butting against bulkheads, staggering and jerking into grooves and out of them, crushing flints into a shower of sparks, doing anything and everything except standing still for a moment. And among them rushed about, like dragons—ramping, and routing, and swearing fearfully, gargling their throats with a boiling riot, and then goring the ground with tusks of steam, whisking and flicking their tails, and themselves, in and out as the countless cross-webs, screaming and leaping, and rattling and booming—the great ponderous giant goods-engines. Every man was out-swearing his neighbour, every truck browbeating its fellow, every engine out-yelling its rival. There is nothing on earth to compare with this scene, unless it be the jostling and churning of ice-packs in Davis's Straits, when the tide runs hard, and a gale of wind is blowing, and the floes have broken up suddenly. And even that comparison fails, because, though the monsters grind and crash, and labour and leap with agony, they do not roar, and vomit steam, and swear at one another.[7]

The decline of the railways provided a context for comic novels about the struggle to survive. The elegiac Ealing comedy *The Titfield Thunderbolt* (1952), in which a country branch line axed by British Railways goes it alone with the aid of a relic of the early steam age, removed from the local museum, can be said to have set the tone for these novels. None of the novels, however, has thus far equalled the charm or poignancy of the film, qualities which seem to be heightened as each year goes by and its one-time realistic setting retreats further and further into the realm of myth.

Two novels in particular centre on stations. Ernest Corbyn's *All Along the Line* (1958) is set at Exmer Junction, a seaside railway station scheduled for closure. The book stresses the strict hierarchy and class divisions on the railway as it follows the progress of Albert Jackson, a new booking-clerk. The station-master, Jordan, is a martinet, downgraded from a London terminus after reprimanding a Cabinet Minister for dropping ash on the platform. The station staff engage in a running battle with a local bus company for passengers and freight. Eventually the rail enthusiasts win, by hijacking the buses and hiding them in a railway tunnel.

Connery Chappell's *Trouble on the Line* (1963) hinges on an administrative mistake whereby booking-clerk Percy Smithers is appointed station-master at Silverton Junction. He introduces a drastic programme of modernization, efficiency, and reform, becoming such a disciplinarian that the workers combine to sabotage his plans. Although the workers are initially thwarted, the opening of a new station is successfully disrupted. Percy resigns but is appointed general manager of a Canadian railway.

However, while few serious novels have devoted themselves to station life, many have seen the symbolic role of the station at crucial points in the lives of the characters and highlight the shifting moods and emotions induced by the station. The role of the station in relation to the journey was best observed by Marcel Proust:

The specific attraction of a journey lies not in our being able to alight at places on the way and to stop altogether as soon as we grow tired, but in its making the difference between departure and arrival not as imperceptible but as intense as possible, so that we are conscious of it in its totality, intact, as it existed in us when our imagination bore us from the place in which we were living right to the very heart of a place we longed to see, in a single sweep which seemed miraculous to us not so much because it covered a certain distance as because it united two distinct individualities of the world, took us from one name to another name, and which is schematised ... by the mysterious operation performed in those peculiar places, railway stations, which scarcely form part of the surrounding town but contain the essence of its personality just as upon their sign-boards they bear its painted name ... Unhappily those marvellous places, railway stations, from which one sets out for a remote destination, are tragic places, for in them the miracle is accomplished whereby scenes which hitherto have no existence save in our minds are about to become the scenes among which we shall be living; for that very reason we must as we emerge from the waiting-room, abandon any thoughts of presently finding ourselves once more in the familiar room which but a moment ago housed us. We must lay aside all hope of going home to sleep in our own bed, once we have decided to penetrate into the pestiferous cavern through which we gain access to the mystery, into one of those vast, glass-roofed sheds, like that of Saint-Lazare into which I went to find the train for Balbec.[8]

For some the station is associated with pain, the pain of separation and loss. This feeling is perfectly captured by Lawrence Durrell in *Justine*. His setting is Alexandria Main Station at midnight:

A deathly heavy dew. The noise of wheels cracking the slime-slithering pavements. Yellow pools of phosphorous light, and corridors of darkness like tears in the dull brick façade of a stage set. Policemen in the shadows. Standing against an insanitary brick wall to kiss her goodbye. She is going for a week, but in the panic, half-asleep, I can see that she may never come back. The soft resolute kiss and the bright eyes fill me with emptiness. From the dark platform comes the crunch of rifle-butts and the clicking of Bengali. A detail of Indian troops on some routine transfer to Cairo. It is only as the train begins to move, and as the figure at the window, dark against the darkness, lets go of my hand, that I feel Melissa is really leaving; feel everything that is inexorably denied—the long pull of the train into the silver light reminds me of the sudden long pull of the vertebrae of her white back turning in bed. 'Melissa', I call out but the giant sniffing of the engine blots out all sound. She begins to tilt, to curve and slide; and quick as a scene-shifter the station packs away advertisement after advertisement, stacking them in the darkness. I stand as if marooned on an iceberg. Beside me a tall Sikh shoulders the rifle he has stopped with a rose. The shadowy figure is sliding away down the steel rails into the darkness; a final lurch and the train pours away down a tunnel, as if turned to liquid.[9]

For Aschenbach in Thomas Mann's *Death in Venice* the station at Venice·represents the point of no return. Once he enters it and boards

A plethora of 'usual offices' at Victoria Station, London, 1916: the bookstall, post and telegraph office, and departure boards.

The private station of the Duke of Sutherland, reopened 1985. This serves nearby Dunrobin Castle. It is the station as gatehouse.

Waiting at the Station, 1850. Painting by Lefevre J. Cranstone.

Cheltenham: War Decoration for Railway Office, 1930. Painting by Lilian Gladys Tickell.

The buffet as romantic venue: *Brief Encounter* with Celia Johnson and Trevor Howard.

The station as musical stage: *Shipyard Sally* with Gracie Fields.

The station in politics, dramatized in *Bhowani Junction*.

The station as background to mystery and suspense: *The Ghost Train* with Jack Hulbert and Cicely Courtneidge.

the train, he will be swept away for ever from Tadzio, the vision of beauty that has entranced him on his stay in the city. But he is to be spared this separation by an act of fate which turns him back to the plague-haunted city and his own eventual death:

Meanwhile the steamer neared the station landing; his anguish of irresolution amounted almost to panic. To leave seemed to the sufferer impossible, to remain no less so. Torn thus between two alternatives, he entered the station. It was very late, he had not a moment to lose. Time pressed, it scourged him onward. He hastened to buy his ticket and looked round in the crowd to find the hotel porter. The man appeared and said that the trunk had already gone off. 'Gone already?', 'Yes, it has gone to Como', 'To Como?' A hasty exchange of words—angry questions from Aschenbach, and puzzled replies from the porter—at length made it clear that the trunk had been put with the wrong luggage even before leaving the hotel, and in company with other trunks was now well on its way in precisely the wrong direction. Aschenbach found it hard to wear the right expression when he heard the news. A reckless joy, a deep incredible mirthful-ness shook him almost as with a spasm. The porter dashed off after the lost trunk, returning very soon, of course, to announce that his efforts were unavail-ing. Aschenbach said he would not travel without his luggage; that he would go back and wait at the Hôtel des Bains until it turned up . . . And the unbelievable thing came to pass; the traveller, twenty minutes after he had reached the station, found himself once more on the Grand Canal on his way back to the Lido.[10]

For Aschenbach, anguish turned to joy at the station, thanks to an error by the hotel. But stations could sometimes be scenes of unalloyed joy, as at dramatic reunions. E. Nesbit compressed a wealth of station-based emotion into two pregnant paragraphs in her children's classic *The Railway Children*:

Only three people got out of the 11.54. The first was a countrywoman with two baskety boxes full of live chickens who stuck their russet heads out anxiously through the wicker bars; the second was Miss Peckitt, the grocer's wife's cousin, with a tin box and three brown-paper parcels; and the third—'Oh! My Daddy, my Daddy!' That scream went like a knife into the heart of everyone in the train, and people put their heads out of the window to see a tall pale man with lips set in a thin close line, and a little girl clinging to him with arms and legs, while his arms went tightly round her.[11]

A wrongfully imprisoned father released and reunited with his eldest daughter at a small country station is just one of the many literary vignettes of joy evoked by the station.

For nineteenth-century travellers, stations are the fixed points on their itineraries. Jules Verne's quintessential Englishman Phileas Fogg sets out on his journey around the world in eighty days from Charing Cross Station, London, where he boards a train, armed with a copy of *Bradshaw's*

Continental Railway, Steam Transit and General Guide and a carpet-bag containing £20,000 in Bank of England notes. Arriving in Bombay, Fogg repairs to the Bombay terminus of the Great Indian Peninsula Railway. He is served a 'rabbit' dish, which causes him to call the steward and remind him that 'cats used to be sacred in India'. Fogg's servant, Passepartout, having violated a Hindu temple in shoes, is chased to the station by irate worshippers but manages to scramble aboard the departing train on which his master awaits him. Crossing India by train, Fogg takes time out to rescue Princess Aouda from a funeral pyre. At Calcutta Station they are all arrested because of Passepartout's exploits in Bombay. Once released, they proceed across the Pacific to San Francisco. They cross America by transcontinental express, surviving an Indian attack. Reaching Liverpool, Fogg is arrested, mistaken for a bank robber, and thus misses the London train. Released, he charters a special train and arrives in London, to complete his journey in the nick of time to win his bet. No story more potently illustrates the extent to which steam trains and steam boats girdled the world in the nineteenth century.

For other travellers too the station was the starting-point for adventure. The major London railway terminals were the invariable embarkation points for Sherlock Holmes and Dr Watson as they set out on their cases. The cry 'the game's afoot' was almost always followed by a reference to *Bradshaw* to check on the time of the first convenient train. They always travelled first class and in their time departed from every London terminal except Marylebone.

For some, like those inter-war literati and *jeunesse dorée* so aptly characterized by Martin Green as 'the children of the sun', the station represented escape from a restricting, parochial, philistine, and puritanical England. For them Victoria Station was the glorious antechamber to a wider, freer world. Henry Green, in his novel *Partygoing*, traced the fortunes of one such group, when fog descended on Victoria to cut off their escape route.

In English fiction escape from the provinces to the glittering, beckoning world of the great metropolis has been as important a theme as escape from London to the wider world. In Arnold Bennett's *A Man from the North* (1898) and *Whom God Hath Joined* (1906), the railway route to London is a source of magic and excitement for the denizens of the Potteries and the key to this route is the station.

A Man from the North opens with an evocation of London-yearning:

There grows in the North Country a certain kind of youth of whom it may be said that he is born to be a Londoner. The metropolis, and everything that appertains to it, that comes down from it, that goes up into it, has for him an imperious fascination. Long before schooldays are over he learns to take a doleful pleasure in watching the exit of the London train from the railway station. He stands by the hot engine and envies the very stoker. Gazing curiously into the carriages, he wonders that men and women who in a few hours will be treading streets called Piccadilly and the Strand can contemplate the immediate future with so much apparent calmness; some of them even have the audacity to look bored. He finds it difficult to keep from throwing himself in the guard's van as it glides past him; and not until the last coach is a speck upon the distance does he turn away and, nodding absently to the ticket clerk who knows him well, go home to nurse a vague ambition and dream of Town.[12]

In *Whom God Hath Joined*, it is the emotions of the London-bound that are probed:

Now the lordly up-platform of Knype is at its best between nine-twenty and nine-forty in the morning, for at the latter instant of time the Manchester to London corridor express, having paused five minutes alongside, steams out while porters cry proudly: 'Next stop Euston!' The worlds of pleasure and of business meet on that platform to await the great train with its two engines. The spacious pavement is crowded with the correctness of travelling suits and suit-cases; it is alive with the spurious calm of those who are about to travel and to whom travelling is an everyday trifle. 'Going up to the village?' the wits ask, and are answered by nods in a fashion to indicate that going up to the village is a supreme bore. And yet beneath all this weary satiety there lurks in each demeanour a suppressed anticipatory eagerness, a consciousness of vast enterprise, that would not be unsuitable if the London train were a caravan setting forth to Bagdad.[13]

Bennett in fact devoted the whole of a short story to the fraught business of 'Catching the Train'. It detailed with an accuracy universally recognizable to the regular traveller the anxieties, miseries, and frustrations attendant upon being in a certain place at a certain time. Here a Potteries bachelor has to be in London by 2.00 p.m. for his marriage. After a saga of mounting crises involving lost luggage, inability to get a porter, and boarding the wrong train, he ends up in Birmingham, with 55 minutes to wait for the Birmingham–London express:

At another time New Street, as the largest single station in the British Empire, might have interested him. But now it was no more interesting than Purgatory when you know where you are ultimately going to. He sought out the telegraph-office, and telegraphed to London—a despairing, yet a manly telegram. Then he sought out the refreshment-room, and ordered a whisky. He was just putting the whisky to his lips when he remembered that if, after all, he did arrive in time, the whisky would amount to a serious breach of manners. So he put the glass down untasted and the barmaid justifiably felt herself to have been insulted. He watched the slow formation of the Birmingham–London express. He also watched the various clocks. For whole hours the fingers of the clocks never budged, and even then they would show an advance of only a minute or two. 'Is this the train for London?' he asked an inspector at 11.35. 'Can't you see?' said the inspector brightly. As a fact, Euston was written all over the train. But Arthur wanted to be sure this time. The express departed from Birmingham with the nicest exactitude and covered itself with glory as far as Watford, when it ran into a mist, and lost more than a quarter of an hour, besides ruining Arthur's career. Arthur arrived in London at one minute past two. He got out of the train with no plan. The one feasible enterprise seemed to be that of suicide.[14]

Escape from the provinces via the station continued to be a theme of the new post-war generation of provincial writers, treading the realist path in Bennett's footsteps. Keith Waterhouse's novel *Billy Liar* (1959), which was adapted successively into a stage play, a film, a musical, and a television series, centres on Billy Fisher, the day-dreaming, discontented undertaker's assistant in the Yorkshire town of Stradhoughton longing to go to London to become a comedy script-writer. Waterhouse sympathetically and amusingly charts his life, building up to his arrival at the station, as he prepares to turn his back on Yorkshire. Waterhouse expertly captures the numbing sense of desolation that can be conveyed by a deserted city station at night:

The station was ablaze with cold, white light. The booking hall was deserted except for a fleet of electric trollies piled high with newspaper parcels. The last Harrogate diesel was just pulling sleekly away from platform two. The inquiry office was closed ... There were no other trains to London that night. All the windows but one at the ticket office were boarded up. I waited under A–G until a tired man in his shirt-sleeves appeared and I bought a single second-class to St. Pancras. It cost thirty-five shillings. I looked up at the big station clock. It was ten minutes to one. Below the ticket office was the buffet and main waiting-room. The buffet end was closed, its counter still lined with crusts of bread, but there were about a dozen people still in the waiting room, most of them asleep with their feet up on the scratched tubular chairs or their heads down on the rockety tables, among the flattened straws and empty lemon-squash cartons. I went in and stood by the door, under one of the large, empty-looking pictures of fields and hills that lined the walls. A few people were awake; half a dozen soldiers, all in civvies, going home on leave, three old prostitutes, a man in a large black coat. I was sleepy, recognizing everything about five seconds after it happened.[15]

In the end, Billy cannot go through with his departure and retreats into the fantasy world he has created for himself. But his girl-friend Liz does go without him. Departure created different, but equally recognizable, problems for Jerome K. Jerome's three men in a boat:

We got to Waterloo at eleven and asked where the eleven-five started from. Of course nobody knew; nobody at Waterloo ever does know where a train is going to start from, or where a train when it does start is going to, or anything about it. The porter who took our things thought it would go from number two platform, while another porter, with whom he discussed the question, had heard a rumour that it would go from number one. The station master, on the other hand, was convinced it would start from the local. To put an end to the matter we went upstairs and asked the traffic superintendent, and he told us that he had just met a man who said he had seen it at number three platform. We went to number three platform, but the authorities there said that they rather thought that train was the Southampton express, or else the Windsor loop. But they were sure it wasn't the Kingston train, though why they were sure it wasn't they couldn't say.[16]

In the end, they slip half a crown to the driver of a stationary train to take them to Kingston. Since he is not sure where he is supposed to be going, he obliges them. It transpires later that the train they had commandeered was the Exeter Mail and that the railway authorities had spent hours at Waterloo looking for it. Not only is the story amusing, but it is also based on a measure of truth. For in 1898 N. Wilson of the London and South-Western Railway admitted to readers of the *Railway Magazine* that the confusion at Waterloo portrayed by Jerome was 'not too farfetched'.[17] But it had all been changed by the introduction of an elaborate and complex system of train indicators.

The very turmoil and bustle of the station made it the perfect place for lovers to tryst. They can kiss and embrace unnoticed among the many doing the same as they see people off. The agony and ecstasy of lovers' meetings in terminal stations is captured by Alphonse Daudet in *Fromont Junior and Risler Senior* (1874). Sidonie Risler agrees to meet and run away with her brother-in-law Franz, but she fails to keep the assignation:

Two hours before the opening of the wicket for the issue of tickets for the appointed train Franz was already at the Lyons Station, that melancholy terminus, which, situated in a remote part of Paris, seems the first stage into the country. He seated himself in the darkest corner, and remained there without moving, as if giddy. At that moment his brain was as agitated and busy as the station itself. He felt invaded by a host of inconsequent reflections, vague memories, strange comparisons. Within the space of a minute he made such remote mental excursions that he asked himself two or three times why he was there and what he was waiting for. But the idea of Sidonie sprang out from these incoherent thoughts, and illuminated them with a bright light. She was coming. And, without reflecting that the hour of meeting was still far off, he looked among the people who crowded in calling out to each other, searching for that elegant outline, which he expected to see emerge suddenly from the throng and scatter it at every step by the radiance of beauty. After many departures and arrivals, accompanied by shrill whistles, which, confined under the arched roof, seemed like cries of anguish, the station suddenly became as deserted as a church on weekdays. At last the time for the departure of the ten o'clock train drew near. There were no others before it. Franz rose. Now it was no longer a dream, a chimera, lost in the vast and uncertain limits of time. In a quarter of an hour, half an hour at the most, she would be there. Then began the horrible torment of waiting, that suspension of one's whole being, that singular state of body and mind when the heart stops beating, when breath and thought fail, when motion and speech are incomplete, when all is in suspense, when everything waits. Poets have a hundred times described the grievous anguish of the lover, listening for the rumble of the carriage in the deserted street, a furtive step ascending the stairs. But waiting for your mistress at a railway station is a much more mournful affair. The dim lamps, throwing no reflex on a dusty floor, the great glazed bays, the incessant noise of feet and doors resounding in anxious ears, the bare, high walls with their posters announcing an 'Excursion to Mona-co', a 'Tour of Switzerland', the atmosphere of travel, change, indifference, inconstancy—all is well calculated to oppress the heart and increase the agony. Franz walked up and down, watching the carriages that arrived. They stopped at the long stone steps. The doors opened and closed noisily, the countenances of the new arrivals, suddenly emerging from outer darkness, appeared in the light on the threshold—faces serene or troubled, happy or heart-broken, hats with feathers and tightly drawn, light-coloured veils, country folks' caps, sleepy children being dragged along by the hand. Every new-comer made him start. He thought he saw her—hesitating, veiled, slightly embarrassed.[18]

But he is mistaken. He goes outside, runs from one entrance to another, nervously watches all the women and all the arriving carriages. But she never comes.

The station could also be the place for the ultimate rendezvous—with death. In *Dombey and Son* Dickens charted with horrified fascination the impact of the railways on Victorian London. Appropriately, then, the villainous James Carker, confronted by the employer he had wronged, fell to his death beneath the wheels of an oncoming train. The unnamed station where he met this fate has been identified by a zealous researcher as the Paddock's Wood Station of the South-Eastern and Chatham Railway.[19]

In *The Prime Minister* (1876) Trollope's stylish but unscrupulous adventurer, Ferdinand Lopez, his schemes in ruins, chooses to end his life. He proceeds to Euston Station, breakfasts there heartily on a mutton chop and some tea, and then buys a first-class return ticket to what Trollope calls the Tenway Junction but is in fact Willesden. There

Lopez throws himself beneath the wheels of the Euston to Inverness express.

Trollope paints a vivid picture of Willesden Junction, which reflects not only the turbulence but also his belief in an ultimate order:

It is a marvellous place, quite unintelligible to the uninitiated, and yet daily used by thousands who only know that when they get there, they are to do what some one tells them. The space occupied by the convergent rails seems to be sufficient for a large farm. And these rails always run one into another with sloping points, and cross passages, and mysterious meandering sidings, till it seems to the thoughtful stranger to be impossible that the best trained engine should know its own line. Here and there and around there is ever a wilderness of wagons, some loaded, some empty, some smoking with close-packed oxen, and others furlongs in length black with coals, which look as though they had been stranded there by chance, and were never destined to get again into the right path of traffic. Not a minute passes without a train going here or there, some rushing by without noticing Tenway in the least, crashing through like flashes of substantial lightning, and others stopping, disgorging and taking up passengers by the hundreds. Men and women—especially the men, for the women knowing their ignorance are generally willing to trust to the pundits of the place—look doubtful, uneasy and bewildered. But they all do get properly placed and unplaced, so that the spectator at last acknowledges that over all this apparent chaos there is presiding a great genius of order.[20]

Even more famously the life of Tolstoy's tragic heroine Anna Karenina comes full circle at a station. It was at Moscow station that Anna first met Count Vronsky, with whom she embarked upon her tragic love affair. When it is over, she finds herself at another station:

Two servant girls strolling up and down the platform turned their heads to stare at her and made some audible remarks about her dress. 'Real', they said, referring to the lace she was wearing. The young men would not leave her in peace. They passed by again, peering into her face and talking and laughing in loud, unnatural voices. The station-master as he walked by asked her if she was going in the train. A boy selling kvas never took his eyes off her. 'Oh, God, where am I to go?' she thought, continuing farther and farther along the platform. At the end she stopped. Some ladies and children, who had come to meet a gentleman in spectacles and who were laughing and talking noisily, fell silent and scanned her as she drew even with them. She hastened her step and walked away to the edge of the platform. A goods train was approaching. The platform began to shake and she fancied she was in the train again. In a flash she remembered the man who had been run down by the train the day she first met Vronsky, and knew what she had to do. Quickly and lightly she descended the steps that led from the water-tank to the rails, and stopped close to the passing train. She looked at the lower part of the trucks, at the bolts and chains and the tall iron wheels of the first truck slowly moving up, and tried to measure the point midway between the front and back wheels, and the exact moment when it would be opposite her. 'There' she said to herself, looking in the shadow of the truck at the mixture of sand and coal dust which covered the sleepers 'There, in the very middle, and I shall punish him and escape from them all and from myself.'[21]

So Anna throws herself to her death, a station drama re-created in the memorable film versions of the book with Greta Garbo (1935) and Vivien Leigh (1948), ending under the wheels of a steam train at that lonely wayside station.

The station has great potential, however, not just for encapsulating the dramatic cruces in the lives of individuals, but as a microcosm of a political situation. The best example of this is John Masters's *Bhowani Junction* (1954). Dedicated to 'Number One Down Mail, which was to many a prideful train, to them an absolute ideal of service', it is a vivid and compelling drama of three people from different backgrounds caught up in the ferment of British India on the eve of Independence. It is entirely fitting that a vital railway junction should be the location chosen to mirror the tensions and traumas of the time, as the railways and the Raj were inseparably intertwined and had been part of the landscape of British life since before Kipling incorporated them into his panoramic novel of Indian life, *Kim* (1901). It is at Marwar Junction that the narrator of Kipling's *The Man who Would be King* (1888) passes a mysterious message to a red-bearded giant that sends two ex-soldiers off on a madcap adventure to carve out a kingdom beyond the Khyber Pass. It is at Chandrapore Station that the unfortunate Dr Aziz is arrested after the incident at the Marabar Caves which leads to a sensational trial and the exposure of the strains and stresses of Raj society in E. M. Forster's *A Passage to India* (1924). In Paul Scott's monumental four-volume saga of the last years of British India, *The Raj Quartet* (1966–75), people are constantly on the move, frequently by train, and stations figure in a number of key political scenes. At Mirat Cantonment Station the repressive role of the sinister Captain Merrick is highlighted when the aunt of his victim Hari Kumar falls at his feet, begging for mercy, in front of the mystified Layton family wedding party. At Ranpur Station Sarah Layton is entertained to a champagne supper by Count Bronowsky in his private carriage and begins to penetrate the complex mystery in which her family has become enmeshed. Almost the last scene of the novels is at Premanagar Station, where the horrific results of the sectarian violence which accompanied independence are confronted by the departing British. All these works have been filmed, complete with railway station scenes: *Kim* in 1950, *The Man who Would be King* in 1975, *A Passage to*

India in 1984, and *The Raj Quartet* as a Granada Television series *The Jewel in the Crown* in 1983–4.

The central character of *Bhowani Junction* is the beautiful half-caste Victoria Jones, daughter of a Welsh engine-driver and an Indian mother. She epitomizes the tragic dilemma of the Anglo-Indians who are neither truly English nor truly Indian. She is loved by three different men, each of whom offers her a place in a different world and each of whom comes to her from the railway. Lt.-Col. Rodney Savage is the British officer commanding the military garrison of the station. Victoria becomes his liaison officer and eventually his mistress. But she is in fact engaged to Patrick Taylor, District Traffic Superintendent at Bhowani Junction, another prickly Anglo-Indian, painfully conscious of his superiority to the Indians, who refuses to anticipate the end of the Raj. The third man is Ranjit Kasel, a gentle and idealistic Sikh, who works as a railway clerk but is hoping after Independence to move into education, which he sees as the key to India's future. Victoria tries to solve her problem of identity by becoming an Indian, adopting Indian dress and marrying Ranjit. But at the last moment she cannot go through with it. In the end she settles for life with Patrick and the acknowledgement that she is an Anglo-Indian and must seek her future in India as such.

On the wider level, Bhowani Junction epitomizes India at large. The Congress Party is doing everything in its power to hasten the departure of the British (strikes, passive resistance, disruption of communications). The Communists have infiltrated the movement and turn every peaceful demonstration into a riot as well as blowing up trains and fomenting intercommunal Hindu–Muslim strife. The British do what they can to keep the peace and maintain order and normality, symbolized by determination to keep the trains running.

In 1956 George Cukor made a stunning film version of the novel, creating on Pakistani locations and with the aid of an excellent cast (Ava Gardner as Victoria, Stewart Granger as Rodney, Bill Travers as Patrick, Francis Matthews as Ranjit) a memorable picture of a teeming and turbulent society in transition. The railway system and the station in particular are central to both film and book. The film opens with Colonel Savage's departure from Bhowani, seen off by his Gurkhas from the station. It is Savage who tells the story in flashback. Victoria arrives at Bhowani Junction on the day that the Congress Party seek to bring the railways to a halt by filling the station with people and paralysing communications. Later their passive resistance takes the form of lying on the track in front of the trains. But in a powerful scene in the book Savage orders his men to urinate on the protesters, in consequence of which the

Hindus will be obliged to undergo six months' purification. In the film, he rather more tastefully orders buckets of urine to be thrown over them. Later there is a train strike, a train blown up, and, in the exciting finale, Taylor and Savage race to prevent the Communists from blowing up a train carrying Gandhi. By the logic of the Hollywood star system, the book's ending is altered. Bill Travers's Patrick is killed, saving the life of Gandhi, leader of the despised Indians, a not inappropriately ironic comment on his stance. Victoria thereupon settles for Colonel Savage, who is, after all, played by Stewart Granger. But they will remain in India and make their lives there.

The successful filming of both *La Bête humaine* and *Bhowani Junction* confirms the cinema's appreciation of the dramatic possibilities of the railways. The cinema's utilization of the railway station is as old as the medium itself. On 28 December 1895 the Lumière brothers opened what was in effect the world's first public cinema in Paris. They included in their first programme a short film entitled 'Arrival of a train at La Ciotat Station'. This event had been photographed by the Lumières on their family holiday in July 1895. It was the prototype of many such shorts taken by many different film-makers in many different countries. It was simply a matter of setting the camera up on the platform and letting the train steam towards it out of the distance, to obtain a striking image of movement and action. The disgorging of the passengers on to the platform provided further interest and activity for the camera to capture.

Trains and stations already had an established visual image and impact, thanks to their regular appearances in paintings, engravings, and still photographs. But the cinema, first silent and then sound, enhanced their dramatic potential, with the deployment of the visual and aural imagery of fire-breathing engines, billowing smoke, bustling termini, chattering rails, and melancholy train-whistles. In the nineteenth century the train was more than just a means of transportation, it was a symbol of power, speed, progress, civilization, destiny. The station as the gateway to these sensations shared in this symbolism. Train and station were instantly dramatic, mysterious, and exciting.

It is no coincidence that the most celebrated, if not quite the earliest, feature film to tell a story is *The Great Train Robbery* (1903), since when every aspect of train travel has been utilized by the cinema. The most popular train theme is the thriller, which treats the train as a microcosm, an enclosed world in which a mixed group of passengers on a particular journey are tried and tested by the drama of murder, theft, abduction, or assault. This usually takes place on an express in some appropriately romantic location. The station as point of arrival and departure frames the action, and station-stops, at which something dramatic may occur and frequently does, punctuate it. Thus, for instance, *Shanghai Express* (1932), *Rome Express* (1932), *Orient Express* (1934) (based on Graham Greene's *Stamboul Train*), *Kongo Express* (1936), *Berlin Express* (1948), *Peking Express* (1951), *Istanbul Express* (1968), *Avalanche Express* (1979). When film-makers ran out of expresses, they turned to night trains: *Night Train to Munich* (1940), *Night Train to Inverness* (1959), *Night Train to Paris* (1964), *Night Train to Milan* (1965). Expresses and night trains went in on the whole for high drama. Rather more light-hearted and comedic episodes took place in other films named after specific trains, such as *Twentieth Century* (1934), *The Golden Arrow* (1951), and *The Silver Streak* (1976), the eponymous hero of which, running away out of control, succeeded in demolishing Chicago Union Station.

Mysterious murders are apt to take place on trains and to necessitate calling on famous detectives: thus, for instance, Peter Haddon's Lord Peter Wimsey in *The Silent Passenger* (1935), Basil Rathbone's Sherlock Holmes in *Terror by Night* (1946), John Howard's Hugh Drummond in *Bulldog Drummond's Revenge* (1937), and Albert Finney's Hercule Poirot in *Murder on the Orient Express* (1974). Latterly cinematic train journeys have become ever more hazardous, with, in the engaging *Horror Express* (1972), a fossilized 'missing link' coming to life and causing mayhem on the Trans-Siberian Express and bubonic plague breaking out on the Trans-European Express in *The Cassandra Crossing* (1976).

Every aspect of the railway experience can serve a symbolic purpose. The engine can be seen as the image of technological might, as in John Ford's *The Iron Horse* (1924), where the Indians of the Great Plains are initially terrified by its appearance. It can be seen as a symbol of uncontrollable passion, as in *La Bête humaine* (1938). The railway lines, straight, hard, inexorable, carrying you to your ultimate destination, indeed to your destiny, serve as a metaphor for that destiny in *Train of Events* (1949) or *The Man Who Watched Trains Go By* (1952). The climactic train crash serves as a dramatic resolution to the personal, national, even cosmic, problems a film has been exploring: thus, for instance, *Seven Sinners* (1936), *Hatter's Castle* (1940), *Interrupted Journey* (1949), *The Greatest Show on Earth* (1952), *Lawrence of Arabia* (1962), *Crack in the World* (1964).

Railway stations have generally figured in all these films, if only in passing. But the film companies often went to great lengths to ensure authenticity. When Gaumont–British produced *Rome Express* at their Shepherd's Bush studio, they recreated a French railway station:

The whole of the largest studio, covering 900 square feet, was converted into the likeness of the interior of a large P.L.M. station, including *bureau de change*, tobacco kiosk, train departure indicators and late arrival and duplicated train indicators, the notices on these being written up by one of the French Railway officials who came over to advise the producers. Advertisements were obtained from the P.L.M. publicity department at Lyons, and all railway officials who take part in the story are Frenchmen. Gaumont–British also enlisted the services of a wagon-lits attendant who served for many years on the Rome Express.[22]

But the station in its own right has figured strongly in films. There have been a handful of films in which much of the action takes place in and around a station. Asked to think of a station film, most people will first of all mention *Brief Encounter*. It began life as a play, and demonstrated perfectly the theatrical potential of the station as a place where the dramatic unities of time, place, and action could be preserved, an enclosed location where friends and strangers could meet, mingle, interact, and separate.

In the nineteenth century it was the spectacular potential of the station that appealed. In the second half of the century, melodrama became more elaborate and lavish, and there was a simultaneous move towards realism in settings. This was particularly true of the popular metropolitan dramas, which depicted the dangers and temptations of life in the big city. Railway stations were regularly re-created as dramatic and bustling focuses for such dramas, representing as they did the gateways to the metropolis. As stage technology was pushed to its utmost limits in the creation of train crashes, shipwrecks, steamboat collisions, avalanches, and fires, so producers strained to create perfect facsimiles of the settings for the action. In W. T. Moncrieff's *The Scamps of London* (1843), the curtain rises on 'The London terminus of the Birmingham Railway', and calls for cabmen, potato-sellers, match-sellers, fish vendors, and miscellaneous vagabonds, creating the flavour of the mid-Victorian station with a babel of cries, such as 'baked taters, all hot', 'fried fish, a penny a slice', 'lucifer matches', etc. Dion Boucicault's *London by Night* (1868) opens with a scene of the villains hatching their plot at a 'London railway terminus, exterior. The stage filled with passengers, newspaper boys calling out the names of their papers, shoeblacks following their occupation, vendors of fruit and cigar-lights, porters with luggage. Railway and engine heard without; the scene, in fact, to realize the arrival of a train.' In *The Silver King* (1882) by Henry Arthur Jones and Henry Herman, the hero Wilfred Denver, believing he has committed a murder, flees north by train from a realistically re-created Euston Station, minutes ahead of pursuing detectives. The authors included a nice cameo of a railway inspector courteously showing a lady to a first-class carriage, carrying her rugs and umbrella. He then deals peremptorily with a drunken third-class passenger who also demands an escort, seizing him by the scruff of the neck and running him off. Andrew Halliday's *Great City* (1867) acknowledged the inspiration of many of these station sequences by culminating in an officially advertised stage re-creation of Frith's *The Railway Station*, with the villain arrested as he attempts to board a train.

Station scenes were accorded similar prominence on the French stage. Since the Second Empire was the great age of French railroad expansion, it was not inappropriate that Offenbach should set the first act of *La Vie parisienne* (1866), his satirical panorama of high and low life in Napoleon III's Paris, in a great Paris terminal, the Gare de l'Ouest. There the amorous meetings, misunderstandings, and impostures that are to provide the plot strands are all hatched. The master *farceur* Eugène Labiche similarly set the first act of *Le Voyage de Monsieur Perrichon* (1860) in the Gare de Lyon.

In the twentieth century the theatre tended to surrender spectacle to the cinema and move to more intimate dramas, where the single set of the railway station proved ideal for character interplay, whether in the form of comedy, thriller, drama, or romance. William Dean Howells's *The Albany Depot* (1892), which was set in the B. and A. depot in Boston, used a comic imbroglio to make a comment on the American class system. Boston Brahmin Mr Edward Roberts, asked to meet the new cook in the station waiting-room while his wife is out shopping, accosts by mistake the wife of a drunken Irish bruiser, Mrs Michael McIlhenny. An altercation between Roberts and McIlhenny, who claims that his wife has been insulted by being mistaken for the cook, is resolved by the arrival of the real cook, who lays into McIlhenny for disparaging her profession.

By contrast, novelist R. C. Hutchinson's first play, *Last Train South* (1937), was a sombre drama set in a Russian railway station during the Revolution. A former White Russian general is lured there with his wife and daughter while attempting to leave the country. They are detained by the station-master's Bolshevik son Fyodor to avenge the sufferings of a young man who was made a mental and physical wreck through being flogged while wounded for desertion during the war. Flora Robson played the wife of the wrecked man and had her big scene towards the end, explaining how her child had been stillborn as a result of the horror induced by her witnessing her husband's punishment.

Alexander Afinogenov in his play *Distant Point* (1934) used the station setting to celebrate the heroic spirit and party comradeship of the

Russian people. Distant Point is 'an infinitesimally small wayside Railway station on the Trans-Siberian Railway about 7,000 kilometres from Moscow and 2,000 from Vladivostok'. The lives of the station staff are transformed by the twenty-four-hour stay of General Malko, Commander of the Far Eastern Front, who is on his way back to Moscow. Malko's own life is at crisis point. For, as his wife Vera reveals to the women at the station, he is dying of cancer. It transpires, however, that although Vera thinks he is ignorant of the fact, he knows. He upbraids her for trying to deceive him and tells her that together they will fight the illness. Vlas, the second linesman, a drunken ex-priest who has lost his faith, finds a new faith in the prospect of a brave man facing death. Lavrenti, the first linesman, discontented with provincial life and pining in true Chekhovian fashion for Moscow, begs the General to take him, even though it means leaving his wife and child behind. However, when the general agrees and he is on the point of leaving, he realizes what he is losing and decides to stay. The tension in the marriage of station-master Koriushko, caused by his wife's refusal to disclose her discovery of gold in a nearby river for fear of provoking a gold rush and destroying their peace, is resolved by the General's blessing their silence. The station-master's teenage daughter Zhenia, thrown into an ecstasy of commitment to the Party, wants to go to Moscow too, to give her blood to the General for use in transfusions, but is gently refused. When General Malko leaves, the staff he has encountered are all better and happier people.

The Orpheus legend has inspired many diverse talents, Gluck, Cocteau, and Offenbach amongst them. When Jean Anouilh reworked the story of Orpheus in a modern setting, he used a railway station as the entrance-hall to the underworld. In *Eurydice* (1941), rechristened *Point of Departure* in its English translation, the first act and the first scene of the third act take place in the refreshment room of a French provincial station. Orpheus, a street musician, meets and falls in love with a touring actress, Eurydice. Her rejected lover, Mathias, in consequence throws himself under a train. After a brief but ecstatic affair, Eurydice is killed in a bus crash. A mysterious stranger takes Orpheus to the station where they first met, to reunite them at the gates of death. If he looks at her, however, she will be lost to him. He cannot resist looking and she is lost. The stranger, with true Gallic philosophicality, consoles him by saying that life would not have matched up to their ideals, but that they can be united in eternity. So Orpheus too goes joyfully to his death.

But whatever the merits of these and other station plays, one stands out from the rest, just as its film version remains a landmark in British film history—*Brief Encounter*. It was based on Noël Coward's 1936 one-act play *Still Life*, one of a sequence of nine one-act plays which he had written as vehicles for himself and Gertrude Lawrence. When it was first performed, George W. Bishop wrote in *The Sunday Times* that it was 'a tiny masterpiece of economical writing'.[23] Ten years later it formed the basis of the film *Brief Encounter*, which, despite changed times and altered mores, remains for many people a special memory, a film, as C. A. Lejeune said in her review in *The Observer*, 'to be taken out and relished to one's heart's content; to be familiarized and loved; to be seen, and savoured, in quietness, over and over again'.[24]

The play is set entirely in the refreshment room at Milford Junction, but when Coward, the director David Lean, and Anthony Havelock-Allan adapted it for the screen, they opened it out without losing any of the dramatic coherence or dissipating the tension. The film, narrated by Laura Jesson, tells in flashback the story of a rapturous but doomed love affair. Two middle-aged, middle-class people, housewife Laura Jesson and local GP Alec Harvey, meet one day at Milford Junction Station, when he takes some grit out of her eye. They fall in love but eventually part for the sake of their families.

David Lean's direction is brilliant, reworking the play in totally and compellingly cinematic terms. The use of Rachmaninov's Second Piano Concerto as sound-track was so appropriate that many people ever after associated it with the film. This very gentle, very understated, very English love affair is conducted against the beautifully observed background of the town, where they tryst at the Kardomah with its comical female orchestral trio, the Grand Hotel with its potted palms, the luxurious super-cinema, the botanical gardens. But their chief meeting-place remains the refreshment room at the station.

The film begins with the buffet staff at work, and the camera pans across to the couple sitting sadly and quietly in a corner—as we learn later, at a crisis point in their lives. It encapsulates the romance of the refreshment room, the possibility of crimes and tragedies occurring in the nooks and crannies of a public room, while everyday life eddies and swirls around them.

The working-class buffet staff counterpoint the adulterous middle-class couple, with their whispers, glances, and unstated emotions. Mrs Bagot, the self-important manageress with the 'refained' accent who once ran a tea-room in Hythe, conducts a flirtation with Albert Godby, the down-to-earth, robust ticket-collector. The cheerful banter with its overtly sexual overtones contrasts sharply with the demeanour of Alec and Laura. Godby slaps Mrs Bagot's bottom as she bends over and another railman declares cheerfully: 'Just in time or born in the vestry.' Mrs Bagot mockingly reproves Godby but clearly enjoys his attentions. Beryl, her assistant, also has a boy-friend, Stan, whom she arranges to meet in the yard and with whom, giggling, she runs past the tragic couple. She is preoccupied with closing-time, feeding the cat, and her boy-friend. In both staff relationships, the keynote is a cheerful, overt, and uncomplicated sexuality.

The poignancy of Alec and Laura's situation is enhanced by the station setting, in particular the prosaic buffet, with its polished tea urns, Bath buns under glass domes, and coal-fired stove. The station itself, plastered with posters for Sunlight Soap, Virol, Gold Flake, Capstan Full Strength, and Mazawattee Tea, with its subway, clock, and regular announcements, is a fixed point in a changing world. The express racing through is their passion. She plans to throw herself under it but pulls back to resume her life. The stopping trains going in opposite directions, taking her to Ketchworth and him to Churley, represent the humdrum reality of their normal lives. Although Milford Junction appears to be in the Home Counties, the actual filming took place at Carnforth in Lancashire. If you look closely, you can see station signs pointing to the platforms for Lancaster, Morecambe, Skipton, Hellifield, and Leeds. The subway, the clock, and some of the platforms are still in use. But the famous buffet is long since closed.

The understated realism and genuine tenderness of the relationship between Alec and Laura is emphasized by two counterpointing elements of deliberate unreality. The first is that of the romantic films she attends. We see a trailer to one of them, *Flames of Passion*, billed as 'stupendous —colossal—gigantic'. It is the Hollywood view of love as a Technicolor extravaganza. Significantly, Laura and Alec walk out of the film the next week when they go to the cinema. The second is the schoolgirl visions Laura has of what life with Alec might have been like—picturing them in a gondola in Venice, in a box at the Paris Opéra, waltzing in evening dress in a ballroom, on a tropical beach beneath the palms, on the deck of a ship at sea. But the reality of their love is snatched meetings in a station buffet.

Nevertheless, for Laura it constitutes a major emotional crisis. Her life revolves around her family and her home at Ketchworth, where she lives with her steady, reliable husband Fred with his nightly *Times* crossword puzzle, children Bobby and Margaret, and Ethel the maid. She is preoccupied with domestic arrangements, raising the children, and her weekly Thursday trip to Milford to do the shopping, change her library book at Boots, have lunch at the Kardomah, and go to the pictures.

There in sum is a picture of life for the average middle-class English woman of the 1930s and 1940s. It is why it touched so many film-goers so personally. Middle-class women undoubtedly saw something of themselves in Laura.

'I've fallen in love. I'm an ordinary woman. I didn't think such things could happen to ordinary people', she says. It happens in—of all placcs—a buffet. Alec is talking about his work. She tells him he suddenly looks like a little boy and as the camera moves in on her face, we see her in that instant falling in love. But it is in the end doomed, unreal. Fred, doing his crossword, asks for a word that links 'delirium' and 'Baluchistan', i.e. madness and dreamy far-off lands. The answer is 'romance'. It is eschewed by Laura. The recurrent refrain throughout the affair is 'one has one's roots'; 'we must be sensible'; 'I'm a happily married woman'; 'we are neither of us free to love each other. There is too much in the way'. In the end, the pull of home, respectability, and common decency is too much. Guilt triumphs over sex. 'Whatever your dream was', says Fred at the end of her reverie, 'it wasn't a very happy one, was it.' She agrees, sadder but wiser. For a nation seeking to return to normality at the end of a war, it struck all the right notes.

With its dialogue in a clipped, upper middle-class idiom, its well-bred suffering, its exaltation of restraint, *Brief Encounter* is sometimes mocked today. But for all that, it is heartbreakingly true to the reality of emotion and of responsibility as recognized and experienced by a stratum of British society. There is a whole unspoken world-view in the pressure of Alec's hand on Laura's shoulder, which is his only parting gesture— a system of values, a way of life, decency, restraint, self-sacrifice, which characterized the lives of many people in Britain for several generations.

This was recognized fully at the time of its release in the almost uniformly excellent reviews it received from the critics, who sprang from the same background in many cases as the film's chief characters. C. A. Lejeune called it 'One of the most emotionally honest and deeply satisfying films that has ever been made in this country'.[25] Richard Winnington in *The New Chronicle* called it 'uncomfortably true and fascinating'.[26] The two central performances were also widely praised. Roger Manvell was quite right when he wrote in 1955: 'I do not remember a moment when Celia Johnson's performance falters in a part where emotional overplaying or false intonations would have turned the film from a study of life itself into another piece of cinema fiction. It is a uniquely beautiful portrait.'[27] That remains true, and is beautifully complemented by the sensitivity and thoughtfulness of Trevor Howard and the neatly etched supporting performances (Stanley Holloway, Joyce Carey, Cyril Raymond).

Brief Encounter has several times been imitated but never equalled. David Lean's own later film *The Passionate Friends* (1948), though based on an H. G. Wells novel, emerged as a rather more melodramatic variant on the Coward story, what with Trevor Howard playing the understanding lover, the heroine (Ann Todd) contemplating throwing herself under a train, and the eventual triumph of marriage over adultery. The film included a planned and long-awaited reunion at Victoria Station. But the returning lover is met by his wife and served with a writ by Ann Todd's banker husband citing him as co-respondent. Ann Todd shrinks into the shadows of the station and the reunion never takes place.

Despite the sense of *déjà vu*, *The Passionate Friends* was at least a stylish piece of cinema, which is more than can be said for the disastrous remake of *Brief Encounter* written by John Bowen and directed by Alan Bridges in 1975. Shot in colour and utilizing Winchester Station, it was an abject failure in every department. Gone was the Carnforth buffet and the steam trains. Gone was the comic by-play of the refreshment room, patronizing, perhaps, but a necessary counterpoint to the tragedy. Gone was the flashback structure, which added so much depth and poignancy. Gone was the Rachmaninov. As if this was not bad enough, there was an absurd attempt to update it, the heroine Ann Jesson being a part-time social worker, one of whose charges attempts suicide while she is off with Alec. The buffet manageress is black but reduced to a bit-part. The casting compounded the catastrophe, with Sophia Loren too glamorous and too foreign in the quintessentially English role of the heroine and Richard Burton too mature and worldly-wise as Alec. Most destructively, it was no longer rooted in the middle-class accents, mores, and rituals that made *Brief Encounter* so telling a comment on England. There was no sense of life going on around the couple as they went through their private tragedy. In the end only bathos can result from setting a doomed love affair in the plastic and neon buffet of a station through which diesels complacently chug, lacking both the visual and the symbological power of the steam trains of Milford Junction.

Brief Encounter did, however, confer on the railway refreshment room a unique romantic resonance. It became *the* place for lovers to meet. So in Daniel Birt's *The Interrupted Journey* (1949) another couple of married lovers planning to run away together, played this time by Richard Todd and Christine Norden, meet in the buffet at Paddington Station, to be served rock-cakes by waitress Dora Bryan. The same director used the buffet at Waterloo for the last meeting of a divorcing middle-class couple, Valerie Hobson and Philip Friend, in *Background* (1953).

Echoes of *Brief Encounter* too were to be found in *Indiscretion of an American Wife* (1953). This was the ill-fated product of a foredoomed alliance. It began as a joint project of one of Italy's foremost neo-realist directors, Vittorio da Sica, whose documentary-style accounts of the ordinary life of real people had earned international acclaim in the post-war cinema, and of producer David O. Selznick, the flamboyant impresario of *Gone With the Wind* and *Duel in the Sun*, the apotheosis of Hollywood romanticism. Working from a screen story with his regular writer Cesare Zavattini under the title *Terminal Station*, Da Sica set his film entirely in Rome's newly completed Stazioni Termini. It fulfilled the dramatic unities of time, place, and action, the action of the story running for an hour and a half and never leaving the station and its precincts after an opening shot. It was filmed at the station between 2 a.m. and dawn, when it was closed to the public, and it was the first film to be shot entirely in the main station of a capital city. But the film was built around a romantic story, featuring two screen idols, Jennifer Jones and Montgomery Clift, enjoying a brief encounter in Rome, and was equipped with a surging romantic score.

The film charts the end of the holiday affair of a married middle-class Philadelphian matron, Mary Forbes, and a young Italian professor, Giovanni Doria. Unwilling to destroy the happiness of her husband and daughter, Mary flees to the station to take the train to Paris. Giovanni pursues her there to try to persuade her to stay and Da Sica uses all the principal areas of the station for their various meetings.

They repair to the buffet and there discuss their holiday idyll. But the sight of her nephew Paul recalls her to her determination to return home. She rejects Giovanni, who strikes her and leaves. Paul takes her to sit in the third-class waiting-room—first-class is full. There the pregnant wife of an unemployed coal-miner is taken ill. The husband tells Mary that his wife has been denying herself food and rest in order to save for the baby. She is thus reminded of family loyalty and is moved to tears. She sends Paul home and wanders the platform. But Giovanni, returning, spots her, runs across the tracks, narrowly missing an express and they fall into each other's arms. They seek privacy in a carriage in a siding but are caught by the railway police and taken to the Commissioner's office. The shame of detection, the sly looks, winks, and coarse jokes of the police, passers-by, and other criminals in the office bring home to her the impossibility of the situation. The Commissioner hears their story and tells her that if she stays, it will mean a court case; if she leaves, he will tear up the complaint. She agrees to go, and Giovanni escorts her to the train, Da Sica cutting to close-ups of the station clock as their time together runs out. Finally as the train pulls out, he jumps off and wanders away, the idyll over.

Da Sica sketches in the life of the station, skilfully establishing the texture of existence going on around the lovers: a gaggle of priests buying their tickets, a school party being kept in order, singing sports fans. There is much activity by *carabinieri* and top-hatted officials connected with a red carpet for the arrival of the President, who comes and goes during the film. Unlike *Brief Encounter*, where it is the homely formality of the surroundings that points up the grand tragedy in their midst, here it is the spacious, glittering, echoing modernity of the new station, angular, cold, and unfriendly, heightening the sense of alienation in Mary, already induced by the foreign language of the announcements and of the people who talk to her.

But when the film was finished at 85 minutes and handed over to Selznick, he hated it, complaining that he had been given more of a documentary than the romantic drama he expected. So he cut it to 63 minutes, pruning much of the footage of the terminal exterior and some of the vignettes of station life. He changed the title from *Terminal Station*, which had its own resonance, to the catchpenny *Indiscretion of an American Wife* and tacked on an introductory sequence in which pop singer Patti Page sang a song entitled 'Autumn in Rome'. The film opened and closed to general public indifference. The serious British critics pronounced it 'an interesting failure' and it has since been seen as an aberration in Da Sica's career. In retrospect, with Jennifer Jones and Montgomery Clift both looking rather uncomfortable and Truman Capote's dialogue rarely rising above the level of banality, its interest remains the station atmosphere and Da Sica's evocation of its life.

A great London terminal, Waterloo, and its environs was central to the action of Robert Sherwood's play *Waterloo Bridge* (1930). It was the tender story of a First World War love affair between a shy, lonely nineteen-year-old soldier and a hard-bitten, worldly prostitute whose beat is Waterloo Bridge, where she can pick up the soldiers arriving at the station. It inspired three successive film versions. James Whale's 1931 film elicited beautiful performances from Douglass Montgomery (then called Kent Douglass) as the gentle, trusting, innocent boy and Mae Clarke as the prostitute. Whale sensitively traced the progress of the love affair, as she picks him up and finds him falling in love with her. When he insists on taking her to meet his family, she tries to give him up. But eventually she agrees to marry him. He is recalled to the front and she is killed in an air raid. We do not actually see the station, only its environs, in this version. But that omission is rectified in Mervyn Leroy's 1940 remake. Much expanded and embellished, it became a lavishly upholstered four-handkerchief movie in the grand MGM tradition. The out-of-work chorus girl turned prostitute of the 1931 film became a ballerina (Vivien Leigh) and the simple private soldier an officer (Robert Taylor), the heir to a ducal estate. Waterloo Station, as recreated in Hollywood, played a central role in the film in order to draw on the accumulated emotional associations of the station and the Great War. The idyll between the ballerina and her officer is interrupted by his recall to the front. He asks her to meet him at the station. The camera pans down from the station clock to Taylor waiting, then tracks him through the station as he hurries to board his train. She rushes into the station, just as the train pulls away into the distance. Sacked from the ballet and believing that her lover is dead, she becomes a prostitute. Her beat is the station and she is there greeting the troops one day when her lover returns. The reunion leads inevitably to tragedy, as he takes her to his family's Scottish home, introduces her to society and announces his intention of marrying her. But fearful of her past coming out, she flees back to London and throws herself under a lorry on Waterloo Bridge.

A third version of the story appeared in 1956, retitled *Gaby*, updated to the Second World War, and reworked so that the protagonists are now a French Ballerina (Leslie Caron) and an American paratrooper (John Kerr). Uniquely it was given a happy ending, with the lover finding the ballerina alive under the debris of bomb damage. Critics generally disparaged it. C. A. Lejeune in *The Observer* found it 'embarrassing'.[28] *The Daily Worker* summed up best what most people found wrong with it:

Everything is painstakingly wrong in *Gaby* . . . This is a wartime London in which the buses are not London buses and only run every half-hour. All the taxis seem to be battered veterans of the late 20's. Nearly all the Londoners talk off-beat cockney and discuss the buzz-bombs exclusively in 'typical' cockney wisecracks. The typical London railway station doesn't quite manage to look like a London railway station and the trains don't quite look like British trains.[29]

The most notable celebrant of the station as a setting for a thriller is Arnold Ridley, author of a brace of cleverly contrived and popular stage plays, *The Ghost Train* and *The Wrecker*. *The Ghost Train* is set entirely in the small general waiting-room of Fal Vale, a wayside station on the South Cornwall Joint Railway, and the action takes place during the course of four hours. Ridley uses the familiar device of stranding an oddly assorted group of passengers in a remote place: a honeymoon couple, a dotty spinster with a parrot, a monocled man about town among them. The place is a station, which they discover is haunted by a spectral train-driver who appears singing 'Rock of Ages'. This is the result of a disaster in 1897 when the station-master dropped dead, having failed to close the swing bridge, and an express train plunged into the river, killing all the passengers. Amid a raging storm, the stranded travellers are locked into the waiting-room, the current station-master drops dead, and a ghost train thunders through the station. It all turns out to be a plot contrived by Bolshevik agitators, who are smuggling guns into England to start a revolution. But the plot is uncovered and foiled by the 'silly ass' hero, who turns out to be a secret service agent. The play was first produced in 1925 and ran for 655 performances. The play was turned into a novel by Ruth Alexander and formed the basis of three successive film versions. The 1927 version, directed by Geza von Bolvary and starring Guy Newall, was silent. The 1931 version, directed by Walter Forde, was a sound film. It starred Jack Hulbert and Cicely Courtneidge, and was filmed in part on the GWR's Limpley Stoke–Camerton branch line, subsequently also used for *The Titfield Thunderbolt*. It earned from *The Bioscope* the comment: 'One of the most gripping British films ever produced.'[30] Walter Forde also directed the 1941 remake, this time featuring Arthur Askey, Richard Murdoch, and Kathleen Harrison, using much of the train footage from the 1931 effort and turning the villains, not surprisingly, into Nazis. All three films were popular with audiences and faithfully translated Ridley's sure-fire combination of thrills and suspense to the screen.

The success of *The Ghost Train* prompted Ridley to write in collaboration with Bernard Merivale *The Wrecker*. This was a rather more ambitious and less successful thriller. It centred on a series of spectacular train crashes contrived by an individual calling himself 'Jack the Wrecker'. Sir Gervaise Bartlett, Chairman of the Great Trunk Railway, is on the verge of unmasking 'Jack', when he is shot dead. His nephew, rugby international Roger 'Lucky' Doyle, investigates the murder and the wrecks. He saves the prestigious 'Rainbow Express' and on New Year's Eve identifies the wrecker as the company's timetabler Barney, who breaks down:

Noise, engines, steam! How could a man work—every damned thing went against me. My time-table would have been great—great! But the engines—lost time to spite me—noise—late—engines—noise—late—kill them. Kill the trains that lose time! Kill them! Kill them!

So saying he throws himself out of the window and under a passing train

Acts 1 and 3 of the play take place in the general manager's office at the London terminus of the Great Trunk Railway, and the second act in the signal box at Pagham Junction.

The play ran for 165 performances after its opening in December 1927 and was also novelized by Ruth Alexander. It was filmed silent in 1928 by Geza von Bolvary with Joseph Striker as 'Lucky' Doyle, who becomes in this version England's finest amateur cricketer. Script-writer Angus MacPhail, considering the play's denouement too far-fetched, sensibly substituted as villain a suave criminal master-mind Ambrose Barney (Carlyle Blackwell), anxious to discredit the railway company (rechristened the United Coast Lines) in favour of the rival bus company. The result was exciting, fast-moving, and replete with spectacular train crashes. An alleged remake, *Seven Sinners* (1936), bore no relation to Ridley's play. It was a polished and witty sub-Hitchcockian adventure, with two detectives hunting down a gang of international gun-runners. But it did utilize several of the train wrecks, staged for the 1928 film on the Basingstoke–Alton line.[31]

The station as a source of comedy was the mainspring of Michael McHugh's play *A Minute's Wait*. This formed the basis of one of the three episodes comprising *The Rising of the Moon* (1957), another of John Ford's cinematic celebrations of his beloved Ireland. It was also the pick of the bunch. It took a simple idea—a local Irish train which stops at Dunfaill for a minute's wait and ends up waiting two hours—and turned it into a gloriously and cumulatively funny comic masterpiece. After the original minute's wait a succession of waits are proclaimed: so that a prize goat can arrive, so that the local hurling team who have just won the all-Ireland championship can arrive, so that the lobsters for the bishop's jubilee dinner can arrive, so that the engine-driver can finish telling a ghost story and downing a pint. The officious station-master, who is concerned by the mounting delay, is persuaded each time to extend the wait by the threat of the exposure of some dark secret in his family's past.

At each announcement of a further wait, the passengers pile off the train and tear into the station bar for a drink. And the diminutive barmaid, Miss Molloy (Maureen Potter) has a field day, leaping over the bar at each fresh invasion of customers, delightedly dancing to the strains of 'Slattery's Mounted Foot', and when the telephone rings, timorously enquiring of it 'What'll ye have?' During the wait Mrs Folsey and Mr Dunnigan arrange the marriage of her niece and his son. Morrissey the porter, having courted Miss Molloy for eleven years, at long last proposes: 'How would you like to be buried with my people?' Finally, when the hurling team arrives with flags waving and pipes playing, the passengers start singing, everyone gets aboard, and the train finally departs.

Behind all the comical toing and froing lies an affirmation of all the old values that Ford holds dear and which are seen encapsulated in this wayside station. The strength of the community feeling is as usual manifested in scenes of drinking together and singing together, in respect for the Church (the bishop's lobsters), sport (the hurling team), and the past (the ghost story). The arranged marriage, though treated with amusement, is a part of the ritual which is the community's cement. Ford stresses that the older generation know what is best for the younger. These values are pointed up by the presence of outsiders, but they are English outsiders, and for them, Ford has no sympathy. One of the film's themes is their progressive humiliation, and their characteristics are seen as the antithesis of the 'real' values of the Irish. When they arrive, they are in a first-class carriage, separate from, and in their own eyes superior to, the rest. But they are moved out of there to make way for the goat, and placed in a third-class carriage, where they are joined by the bishop's lobsters. When they alight, they take no part in the communal festivities, and instead of drinking beer, they have tea served at a little table at the back of the station. When the train leaves, they are left behind, standing disconsolately on the platform, watching the train vanish into the distance. Ford clearly believes that this is no more than they deserve.

The cinema, when devising station stories *de novo*, fully exploited the potential of the station as a setting for thriller, comedy, romance, and drama. Rudolph Maté's *Union Station* (1950) was one of the post-war cycle of location-shot semi-documentary films which placed their emphasis on the meticulous recreation of detailed police work and kept characterization to a minimum. In *Union Station*, which was set in the central station of an unnamed town and partly filmed at Los Angeles Union Station, we see the station as focus of crime. William Holden stars as the dedicated young cop Lt. Bill Calhoun ('I'm a cop twenty-four hours a day. All I care about is my railroad station.') Barry Fitzgerald plays his folksy old Irish Inspector. We see Calhoun in action on his station—warning off a prostitute, catching a bag thief. But the main action of the film comes with the kidnapping on the train of the blind daughter of a wealthy industrialist. She is held for ransom and the station is designated as the dropping-point for the money. The station is staked out but the kidnappers fail to show. Later the father is ordered to leave the money at the left-luggage office where the chief kidnapper is holding the staff at gunpoint. There is a final chase and shoot-out in the Post

Office's underground narrow-gauge railway. Calhoun rescues the girl. Effective use is made of the Moorish-style station interior, where the information desk, the baggage deposit, and the main concourse serve as focuses of the action. The tension created by criminals using the station while its ordinary life goes on is well built up and maintained.

Gun-runners figured as the villains in Arnold Ridley's *The Ghost Train* and this was almost certainly the inspiration for the funniest station film and one of the best British comedies ever made, *Oh, Mr Porter* (1937). The eponymous hero, William Porter, was the great Will Hay, who at the start of the film, working very incompetently as a wheel-tapper, contrives to tip water over a group of VIP's launching a new train. As a penance, he is banished as station-master to the tumbledown station of Buggleskelly on the Northern Irish border, operated by the fictional SRNI—the Southern Railway of Northern Ireland. From the first he is engaged in comic. conflict with his staff, Albert (Graham Moffat) and Harbottle (Moore Marriott), who run the station for their own benefit, regarding passengers as an intrusion. They grow marrows on the track, stretch washing across the lines and utilize Farmer Murphy's consignment of pigs to provide their breakfast bacon. Mr Porter determines to shake things up. He stops the express in order to introduce himself and is very rudely received. He tries to put a special together and shunts the trucks over a cliff and the carriage into the path of the express which reduces it to matchwood. When finally he gets a special off with the local football team, Buggleskelly Wednesday, aboard, it vanishes. It is in fact being used by IRA gun-runners who conceal it in a disused tunnel, deterring snoopers by spreading tales of a haunted mill and its environs. But Porter and his cohorts couple an elderly engine *Gladstone* to the gunmen's train, and in a magnificent chase sequence they drive the train to Belfast and hand over the gunmen, just as the old engine blows up.

The fun comes fast and furious, inventive and often inspired. It was filmed on the abandoned Basingstoke–Alton line of the Southern Railway, with the derelict halt of Cliddesden turned into a spectacularly ramshackle and tumbledown folly by art director Alex Vetchinsky. The film marked the acme of the work of the comic team of Will Hay, Moore Marriott, and Graham Moffat, and their director Marcel Varnel. Hay's screen persona, whether as public-school master or prison governor or station-master, was a quintessentially English archetype—the sly, shabby-genteel, pompous, blustering, fundamentally fraudulent professional man, claiming an education but forever revealing his abysmal ignorance, aspiring to authority but seeing this constantly subverted by his underlings. The secret of both his appeal and his success lies in the split-level response of the British audience, blended of a love of seeing petty authority exposed and deflated, the national mistrust of the intellectual, and the affection for the genial incompetent who always muddles through. The presence of Marriott and Moffat gave a rich and subtle extra dimension to Hay's comedy: Marriott is the cranky, toothless old man who embodies an anarchy with its own relentless logic that Hay can never tame. It is summed up by his immortal one-liner: 'Next train's gone.' Moffat, on the other hand, is the deliberately level-headed down-to-earth boy who sees through all Hay's posturing pretences and is often responsible for saving him from the disastrous consequences of them.

During the Second World War, the British cinema for the first time began to get to grips with the reality of ordinary people's lives and away from the artificiality, backstage and Ruritanian settings that had dominated 1930s cinema. Frank Launder and Sidney Gilliat were in the forefront of the development, particularly with their film about women war-workers, *Millions Like Us* (1943). Gilliat followed this in 1944 with *Waterloo Road*. It tells the story of an ordinary soldier, Jim Colter (John Mills), who goes absent without leave when he hears that his wife Tillie (Joy Shelton) is carrying on with a local spiv, Ted Purvis (Stewart Granger). The story is set against a convincingly evoked panorama of wartime life to which Waterloo Station is central.

The railway impinges in many ways on the lives of the characters. Jim Colter is an ex-locomotive repairman and his sister Ruby works at the travel enquiry office. Her husband Fred is also a railwayman. The arrival and departure of trains at Waterloo can be seen behind the credits and the station itself figures in several crucial sequences. Ted and Tillie meet under the clock in the station concourse. Jim, being taken back to the army camp under guard, escapes from the train and flees across the tracks. The public take refuge in Waterloo underground station during air raids. Jim also encounters and gains help from a cheerful Canadian deserter who haunts the station, enjoying himself dodging the military police. But he is a fugitive not from action but from 'bull' and gives himself up as soon as there is a prospect of action. Art director Alex Vetchinsky, one of the best British designers, skilfully recreates Waterloo and its environs, and the film perfectly demonstrates the station's centrality to wartime life.

Gilliat had originally intended to produce a portmanteau picture, covering the lives of half a dozen different characters all revolving around the station. This device, sometimes called the 'Grand Hotel' format after the successful MGM film adopting this structure, had already been used by Hollywood in the film *Union Depot* (1932), known in Britain as

Gentleman for a Day. Based on a play by Gene Fowler and directed by Alfred E. Green, it mingled the lives and fortunes of various serious and comic characters at a single railroad terminal. The film was set entirely in the terminal and involved a massive and intricate studio set. The central characters are two station loafers, Chick (Douglas Fairbanks, Jr.) and 'Scrap Iron' (Guy Kibbee). When a drunk leaves his case with Chick, Chick puts on the suit he finds inside and is able to use the refreshment room as a gentleman. There he befriends a stranded actress Ruth (Joan Blondell), who cannot afford a ticket to join her company. 'Scrap Iron' finds a cloakroom ticket and, when he presents it, retrieves a violin case full of money. Chick gives Ruth some of the money to buy a new dress but the shopkeeper reports the money as counterfeit. Chick and Ruth are arrested. But the counterfeiter turns up to reclaim his money. Chick chases him through the station and catches him. He is vindicated and sees Ruth off on the train. *Picturegoer* pronounced the film 'fascinating' and *The Bioscope* called it 'a decidedly original entertainment'.[32]

In lighter vein, Lionel Jeffries's delightful film adaptation of E. Nesbit's *The Railway Children* (1970) created on celluloid an Edwardian idyll which captured much of the magical appeal of steam trains and railway lines for children. Bobbie, Phyllis, and Peter, three middle-class children living in genteel poverty in Yorkshire, find excitement and adventure both at their local station and on their local line. They are to be found lending aid to the deserving poor, to political refugees, and to injured waifs. Eventually a fairy godfather in the person of a director of the Grand Northern and Southern Railway is instrumental in securing the release of their wrongfully imprisoned father. The film was shot on the photogenic Keighley and Worth Valley Line, where steam trains still run, with Oakhurst Station, where Bernard Cribbins plays the sturdy station-master, as the focus of all the comings and goings, dramas and reunions.

Jiří Menzel's *Closely Observed Trains* (1966) is the sympathetic, quirky, and closely observed study of a youth seeking sexual initiation in a sleepy country station in Czechoslovakia during the Second World War. Trains pass through, soldiers straggle past, the local Nazi supervisor turns up accompanied by blasts of Wagner. But the war rarely impinges until the end, when the young hero Miloš Hrma (Václav Neckar) is killed trying to blow up a Nazi ammunition train on behalf of the resistance, one of whose female members has performed the much-sought initiation.

The status that working for the railways conferred in Eastern Europe is splendidly conveyed in the early sequence in which Miloš, preparing to go to work at the station for the first time, is solemnly arrayed in full uniform and cape, and topped off with a ceremonial crowning with a peaked cap, reverently placed on his head by his mother. Regularly throughout the film the station staff turn out to salute passing trains. The deferential, status-conscious station-master, who is seen bowing and scraping to the local aristocrat, is also obsessed with and constantly denouncing immorality, even though it is going on around him all the time. For *Closely Observed Trains* is also concerned with the rather improbable and decidedly un-English idea of the station as hotbed of sex, stimulating the fevered adolescent imagination of Miloš. The cynical Hubícka carries on with a succession of willing young women in the office and in fact stamps the buttocks of one of them with the official rubber stamp of the railroad. A hospital train full of nurses dispenses their sexual favours to sex-starved soldiers while the train is halted in the station. Even Miloš chats up a female train guard on a passing train, in search of sexual initiation.

It is not difficult to recognize the emotional resonance created by a station where individual lives are blighted or brightened as all around them the world bustles on. Stations figure indelibly in a mosaic of memories culled from a thousand and one nights amid the plush seats of the local Odeon and Roxy. Quite apart from the main station films, stations have figured notably in many other films, too many to attempt a comprehensive listing. But they tend to fulfil different functions in different genres.

Many films open and close in stations, stressing the Proustian image of the fixed points of arrival and departure, with an intervening course of events which ensures that you are never the same at the end of the journey. In this category come *Son of Frankenstein* (1939), *Bad Day at Black Rock* (1956), and *Cabaret* (1972). The film versions of *Anna Karenina* (1935, 1948), unlike the novel, open and close at stations. In *Doctor Terror's House of Horrors* (1964) the lonely and deserted station at the end of the train journey is the ultimate destination—death.

One of the most common uses of the station is in romantic films, where separations, departures, arrivals, and reunions, the dramatic cruces of such films, are enhanced by the setting. *A Streetcar named Desire* (1951) begins with the arrival of faded Southern belle Blanche Dubois (Vivien Leigh) in steamy New Orleans by train. She emerges from the station, amid clouds of smoke, to ask for a streetcar named Desire, which will convey her to humiliation and madness. This is the station as gateway to tragedy.

That most perfect of costume dramas, *The Prisoner of Zenda* (1937), opens with the arrival at Zenda of the Orient Express, bearing the

Ruritanian King's English double Rudolph Rassendyll (Ronald Colman) on a fishing holiday. Here the station is the gateway to adventure.

In *Flesh and the Devil* (1926) army officer John Gilbert, arriving at his local station on leave, retrieves Greta Garbo's fallen bouquet and plucks from it a rose, the token of love at first sight. This is the station as gateway to passion. *Last Train from Madrid* (1937), set during the Spanish Civil War, traces the attempts of an assortment of characters to reach Madrid Station by midnight, in order to catch the last train out before the city falls. Similarly *Daniel Takes a Train* (1983), set during the Soviet invasion of Hungary in 1956, opens at Budapest East Station with refugees pouring on to trains to escape to Austria. This is the station as gateway to freedom.

The station occupied a particular place in the lives of those permanently in transit, like touring theatrical companies, particularly before the Second World War. For them Crewe on Sunday, piles of luggage being transferred from one train to another, and fleeting encounters with the No. 3 or No. 4 company of the touring version of *East Lynne* or *A Royal Divorce* were recurrent events. Such scenes were re-created in the British musicals *Raise the Roof* (1930), *The Good Companions* (1933), and *The Show Goes On* (1937). In *The Dresser* (1984) Albert Finney as an ageing actor-manager at the head of a wartime company of 'old men, cripples, and nancy boys' strides majestically across York Station to demand in a stentorian voice that echoes round the arching vault of the roof 'stop that train'. The departing connection obediently grinds to a halt. The film's author, Ronald Harwood, apparently based this vignette on an authentic incident involving Sir Donald Wolfit.

Most poignant are station partings, particularly when they are for ever, whether between obscure Viennese shopgirl Joan Fontaine and her amoral concert pianist lover Louis Jourdan in *Letter from an Unknown Woman* (1948) or between an old couple married for fifty years (Victor Moore and Beulah Bondi) who know they will never see each other again, in *Make Way for Tomorrow* (1936).

Wartime partings give the station an even deeper emotional resonance. A studio reconstruction of the Gare de Lyon figures in perhaps the most celebrated of romantic dramas, *Casablanca* (1942). With the Germans advancing on Paris in 1940, crowds board the last train heading south amidst pouring rain. Humphrey Bogart learns from the faithful Sam that Ingrid Bergman has left him. He boards the train numbly, as steam from the engine clouds over the scene. In *Since You Went Away* (1944), young lovers Jennifer Jones and Robert Walker part for the last time at a crowded Grand Central Station. As his train moves off, she runs alongside it in tears. Later she will learn that he has been killed at Salerno. It is the paradigm of all Second World War station farewells.

Robert Walker was involved in a happier parting in *The Clock* (1945) (UK title: *Under the Clock*), in which he plays a shy, lonely young soldier on a weekend pass, who literally bumps into bright-eyed secretary Judy Garland in Pennsylvania Station, New York. Romance blossoms as she shows him round the town. They are accidentally separated, but reunited at the station. By the end of the film, they are married and she is seeing him off from the station at the end of his leave. Ironically the clock of the title is not the station clock, a regular rendezvous for lovers, but the clock at the Astor Hotel where they first arrange to meet.

But it was not only the Second World War that conferred poignancy on station partings. In *Khartoum* (1968) and *The Four Feathers* (1978) Sudanese expeditionary forces in the late nineteenth century leave from a London terminal, complete with military bands, tearful farewells, and clouds of steam. In fact both departures were filmed at Marylebone Station, which would actually have taken the troops to Princes Risborough rather than Khartoum. First World War sequences were very common. *The Black Watch* (1929) is typical. As the train waits, a piper plays, the troops march into the station, and there are various vignettes of individual farewells before the soldiers board the train, and the train moves off with everyone singing 'Annie Laurie'. The station was as significant in wartime returns as departures. In both *Smilin' Through* (1932) and *The Dark Angel* (1935) Fredrick March as a wounded First World War soldier arrives back at his local station, anxious to spare his sweetheart the sight of his injuries. But perhaps the most moving of station returns came in *Oh, What a Lovely War* (1968), in which a line of blinded soldiers, each with a hand on the shoulder of the man in front, march through the station, singing 'There's a long, long trail a-winding'.

The station as point of return figures in *The Marriage of Maria Braun* (1978), in which the eponymous heroine (Hanna Schygulla) haunts the local station with the other wives of returning German POW's holding up photographs of their menfolk, something that actually happened in post-war Germany. Her husband does not appear but the gift of a package of cigarettes from one of the US soldiers at the station starts her off on her rise via the black market to affluence and success.

A variation on separation is the parting which becomes a reunion. In both *Intermezzo* (1939) and *Back Street* (1941) the female star (Ingrid Bergman, Margaret Sullavan) flees her married lover (Leslie Howard, Charles Boyer), but he pursues her to the station (Stockholm, Cincinnati) and persuades her to change her mind. In *Ariane* (1931) at a

Paris station an older man (Rudolph Forster), leaving his younger lover (Elizabeth Bergner), changes his mind just as the train is pulling out. In *Goodbye Mr Chips* (1939) the older man (Robert Donat), parting from the younger woman (Greer Garson) he has met on holiday, plucks up courage to propose just as the train is leaving the Austrian station. In *Knight Without Armour* (1937) British agent Robert Donat and Tsarist countess Marlene Dietrich, escaping from Russia during the Revolution, arrive at a country station, to find the station-master marching up and down announcing the imminent arrival of the next train. But it turns out that the station-master has gone mad, unable to accept the collapse of the system and the failure of the trains to run. Although separated, Donat and Dietrich are later reunited on a train after he escapes his Bolshevik captors at a station.

Although it is probably romantic films that have made the most use of the station as a locale, all other genres have used it too. In thrillers, stations often figure as places of mystery and menace. Alfred Hitchcock made frequent use of railways in his films and contrived sequences of great tension in stations. An attempt is made on the life of English governess Miss Froy in the little Alpine station in *The Lady Vanishes* (1938). In both *Spellbound* (1945) and *North by Northwest* (1959) the hero (Gregory Peck, Cary Grant), suspected of murder, evades the police at Grand Central Station.

In the 1978 remake of John Buchan's *The Thirty-Nine Steps*, a British agent is knifed in the back and falls dead in the arms of Richard Hannay (Robert Powell), in full view of the horrified passengers at St Pancras Station booking-office. Similarly in *The Four Just Men* (1939), one of Edgar Wallace's heroes (Frank Lawton) is stabbed in the arm by a poisoned suitcase as he arrives back from the Continent at Victoria Station with news of a plot to destroy the British Empire. In the classic train thriller *Berlin Express* (1948) a gang of Nazi fanatics kidnap a prominent anti-Nazi German statesman at Frankfurt Station, where the crowd of ill-dressed and hapless Germans frequenting the concourse scramble for dropped cigarette butts or hawk their precious possessions, encapsulating the plight of post-war Germany.

The First Great Train Robbery (1978) reconstructed the theft of the Crimean gold shipment from the London to Folkestone express in 1855. It included the breath-taking theft of the vital safe keys from the office of the station-master at London Bridge Station. It was actually filmed at Dublin's majestic Heuston Station, and the Harbour Station, Cork, doubled for Folkestone, with the actual train robbery filmed on the Castletown to Athlone line in County Meath.

In westerns, the station figures most frequently as a setting for conflict. It is one of the most dramatic centres of action in the classic *High Noon* (1952), where a gang await their leader, newly released from prison and heading for Hadleyville to kill marshal Gary Cooper. As Cooper desperately and unavailingly tries to raise a posse to oppose the gang, the director Fred Zinnemann cuts back constantly to the station, as the clock ticks away towards high noon. Eventually the train arrives and the inevitable gunfight ensues. The station is itself the scene of classic shoot-outs in such films as *3.10 to Yuma* (1957), *Last Train from Gun Hill* (1959), and *Once Upon a Time in the West* (1968).

In the American Civil War, stations were a prime strategic target and this was magnificently demonstrated in *The Horse Soldiers* (1959), in which ex-railroad engineer John Wayne leads a Union Army expedition to destroy the key Confederate railhead at Newton Station. A pitched battle is fought in the streets of the railway town between Unionists and Confederates before the Unionists destroy the engines, tracks, and railroad equipment at the station. The station serves a different function in perhaps the most celebrated of all Civil War tales, *Gone With the Wind* (1939), in the memorable sequence at Atlanta Station, where a crane shot shows the entire station area to be littered with the dead and wounded of the Confederate Army, awaiting the ministrations of the handful of doctors and nurses who can be mustered to help.

In musicals, the station provides the perfect backdrop for singing and dancing on a large scale, as in *Shipyard Sally* (1939), *You'll Never Get Rich* (1940), *The Student Prince* (1954), and *Oklahoma* (1956). In quieter vein, Fred Astaire as a fading Hollywood film star arrives in New York at the start of *The Bandwagon* (1953) and strolls along the platform, singing 'I'll go my way by myself'.

In comedies, the station provides with its bustle of comings and goings an ideal venue for comic contretemps, as in *I See Ice* (1938), *The Palm Beach Story* (1942), and *The Ladykillers* (1955). The Marx Brothers comedy *Go West* (1940) has a notable station booking-hall opening, in which Groucho dismisses a line of porters with the classic: 'Any of you boys got change of ten cents? Well, keep the baggage.'

Censorship restrictions have until recently tended to restrict the cinema's opportunities to show the station's role in politics. However, in *Gandhi* (1982) stations were seen to play a crucial role in the career of the Mahatma. He begins his long struggle against the British Empire after being thrown off a segregated South African train at Pietermaritzburg Station. Later, as Gandhi travels India by train, a young British subaltern is nonplussed by the sight of a station overflowing with Indians awaiting his arrival, a palpable symbol of his hold over his people. In earlier films, a crucial though unhistorical meeting between General Gordon and Mr Gladstone takes place in a station waiting-room on the eve of Gordon's departure for the Sudan in *Khartoum* (1966), and American presidents arrive regularly at stations to address the faithful from the observation platforms of trains, for instance Abraham Lincoln (Raymond Massey) in *Abe Lincoln in Illinois* (1940) and Theodore Roosevelt (Brian Keith) in *The Wind and the Lion* (1975). Horrific massacres are discovered at stations in India (*Northwest Frontier*) and the Belgian Congo (*The Mercenaries*), where the passengers on refugee trains have been slaughtered and the eyes of the films' characters are opened to the possibility of such atrocities. Iconographic arrivals of a different kind are to be seen in the re-creations of Lenin's arrival at the Finland Station in April 1917, one of the key symbolic moments in the Russian Revolution and a paradigm of the role of the station as political theatre. It was dramatized in Eisenstein's *October* (1927), Romm's *Lenin in October* (1937), and Yutkevich's *The Man with a Gun* (1938).

A single bravura sequence in the political thriller *Mission to Moscow* (1943) demonstrates the power of the Nazis. A long shot of Hamburg Station, decorated with swastika banners, is followed by closer shots of the arrival of the American ambassador Walter Huston and his party *en route* for Russia on the eve of the war. Storm-troopers stamp through the station, a group of forlorn, labelled Jews await transportation to the death camps, copies of *Mein Kampf* fill the bookstalls, and a patrol of the Hitler Youth marches round the station singing. It is a comprehensive picture of order, cruelty, and fear. The contrast with the Russian border station could not be more pointed. There the Americans are welcomed by friendly Russians, given breakfast, and are able to chat freely with soldiers and railway workers.

Nazi panoply at railway stations provides a ready source of humour for Charlie Chaplin in *The Great Dictator* (1940), when Benzino Napaloni, dictator of Bacteria, arrives to visit Adenoid Hynkel, dictator of Tomania, and his train has to be backed up and down the platform several times in order to get level with the red carpet. The station provided a more abstract but none the less powerful symbol of repression in Orson Welles's haunting film version of Kafka's *The Trial* (1962). Part of the film was shot in the echoing, shadowy, decaying remains of the abandoned Gare d'Orsay in Paris, a powerful metaphor for the crushing, labyrinthine reality of a totalitarian legal system.

Although in the several versions of *Waterloo Bridge* Waterloo Station is depicted as a haunt of prostitutes, only recently has a greater degree of realism in depicting the dark underside of terminal life been permitted. *Runners* (1982) charts the heart-breaking search of parents for children who have gone missing. James Fox and Jane Asher, seeking a son and daughter respectively, scour London, constantly returning to the great terminals, and in particular Victoria, St Pancras, and Paddington, where director Charles Sturridge deftly evokes a half-life of loafers, drug addicts, prostitutes, and cranks drifting aimlessly around the concourse day and night. The film captures the role of the station as a limbo wherein the flotsam and jetsam of society exist as permanent transients. *Christiane F* (1981) is an unsparing account of life among Berlin's teenage drug addicts. Its German title, *Christiane F. Wir Kinder von Bahnhof Zoo*, stresses the centrality of the station to their existence. Drifting through boredom from soft to hard drugs, Christiane and her friends become heroin addicts and join the legion of the living dead who haunt the Zoo Station, boys and girls resorting to prostitution to get money for drugs, dealers, addicts, clients, and whores, endlessly circling the station and its environs. Amid kiosks and doorways and under arches they lurk, half-closed eyes, corpse-like pallor, lank hair, locked into a descending spiral of degradation and self-destruction. For many of them this will indeed be a terminal station.

The atmosphere of alienation that a station can convey, of life going on around people whose own lives are in crisis, makes it a potent scene for nervous breakdowns: Massimo Girotti's occurring in the vast concourse of Milan Station in Pasolini's *Theorem* (1969) and Merle Oberon's in a small Louisiana country station in *Dark Waters* (1944). Alan Bates in *A Kind of Loving* (1962) is not having a nervous breakdown but his life is at its lowest ebb, his marriage in trouble, his future bleak and empty, when we see him sitting cold, huddled, and desolate on a lonely station platform at night, aimlessly smoking a cigarette. It is the image of the station at night, drained of life, haunted, empty, that serves as a resonant setting for such a moment of ultimate despair.

One of the most famous of British documentaries was *Night Mail* (1936), directed by Harry Watt for the celebrated GPO Film Unit. It followed the journey of a mail train from London Euston to Glasgow Central, while on the sound-track the rhythmic rhyme of W. H. Auden kept time with the train ('This is the Night Mail crossing the border / Bringing the cheque and the postal order'). The only stop on the journey was 13 minutes at Crewe around midnight, when the English postal sorters changed over with a new team of Scots and great quantities of mail were exchanged. A week's filming at Crewe produced the change-over sequence, though one or two night shots were subsequently filmed at London Broad Street Station and edited in.

These were the scenes of station life at midnight that the ordinary traveller never saw: mails loaded and unloaded, Crewe control room sanctioning 4 minutes' delay to await the late-running Holyhead Mail, the change-over of crews. Producer Basil Wright took a stenographer along to take down the dialogue of railmen and sorters, faithfully recording the jokes and the chat about holidays and football for dubbing in later. The whole film celebrated the romance of the railway and its role as the essential link between people and communities.[33]

But perhaps the best purely cinematic evocation of the station in all its aspects is John Schlesinger's documentary *Terminus* (1961), a poetic evocation of a day in the life of Waterloo in the last days of steam. It relates directly to the greatest of station paintings, focusing on many of the same elements in station life that had caught the attention of W P. Frith in his panorama of Paddington. It is a total encapsulation of the life and the mystique of the station, with the added bonus of steam.

It opens with dawn breaking over the great train-shed of Waterloo, and on the station roof a railwayman tends beehives, a nice contrast of nature and culture, natural life continuing in the heart of a great city, and on top of one of the finest productions of man's creative genius, one of nature's most intricate constructs—the honeycomb. The idea of the station, teeming with life and activity, is thus subtly paralleled by the hive and its industrious denizens.

The gates to the platforms open and the early morning commuters pour through, some moving slowly and reflectively, others frantically and bustlingly, one of them Schlesinger himself. From then on the film cuts between the work and life of the station: the ticket-office, the enquiry office, the left-luggage office, the station announcer's office, the station-master's office, the signal box, the buffet, and the bar, where always homely details humanize the impersonal proceedings: the station announcer knits between announcements, the signalmen brew up their tea and feed the station cat. There is an eager train-spotter, who gets grit in his eye and has it removed by the station nurse.

The key functions of the station in everyday life are all covered. There is a sequence of partings: a voluble and tear-stained Jewish party are seeing someone off, a hushed and reverential group of nuns performing their farewells less histrionically. An invalid is helped slowly aboard a train, honeymooners are jovially dispatched, and a horde of holiday-makers queue with characteristic British phlegm, clutching cases, buckets, and spades, waiting to be allowed on to the platform. There is an eloquent sequence of waiting—a long succession of close-ups of anxious faces scouring the departure and arrival boards, all ages and sorts and conditions of men, a visual expression of *angoisse des gares*. A woman waits with a bunch of flowers for a loved one to arrive on the Boat Train. He does not come and the bunch of flowers is left forlornly on a bench. Elsewhere lovers kiss, oblivious of their surroundings.

Then there are departures: a group of handcuffed prisoners arrive by coach and are herded into carriages euphemistically labelled 'Home Office Party'; newly-weds are seen off and the camera lingers on the confetti as the breeze disperses it. But the film then cuts to the arrival of a coffin reverentially loaded on to the luggage van, a potent reminder of the transience of life. The station becomes literally a station on the road of life. A troop train arrives and the soldiers are reunited with waiting wives and children. An immigrant train arrives and the station is awash with Jamaicans clutching luggage, as they greet with some apprehension the beginning of a new life in a new land. The social contrast is made by cutting to the wealthy, dripping in furs and diamonds, departing in first-class Pullmans for the Continent.

In one memorable sequence a small boy wanders about lost. We get his point of view of pushing crowds and terrifying babble. Finally his face crumples into tears. A kindly bobby finds him and takes him to the office where an announcement is put out for his mother, and mother and child are reunited. A cacophony of voices and destinations, a succession of faces and stories, punctuate the daytime sequences. But then the gates close behind the returning commuters and night falls. The bustle and brightness give way to the melancholy of the station after dark. An elderly female derelict scavenges in the bins. People slumber in the waiting-room. The life of the station goes on, as wheel-tappers and shunters wheel-tap and shunt, the night mail is loaded, parcels are shifted. Finally dawn breaks over the station roof. Another day begins.

But by 1961 the contemporary station was already ceasing to be *the* symbol of glamour and excitement in travel and was taking on an air of seediness, decay, despair, and irrelevance. It had been overtaken by the airport, with all its 'with-it' implications: 'the jet set', intercontinental travel, supersonic speed, the prospect of instant transportation to Acapulco or Bali in the time it took a clapped-out and endlessly refur-bished DMU to travel from the desecrated hulk of London Broad Street to a vandalized bus shelter in the suburbs. Increasingly those makers of myths and artificers of dreams, the film industry, celebrated airports and aeroplanes where before they had exalted stations and trains. There were still to be nostalgic evocations of the great age of steam and its Victorian citadels. But they were self-conscious historical re-creations. Aeroplanes were the 'now' means of travel. It was Heathrow where the glamorous international figures in Anthony Asquith's *The VIP's* (1963) were stranded by fog, whereas a generation earlier it would have been Victoria Station. It was now the airport where variegated lives overlapped and drama ensued. No one would ever make films called *Euston*, *Euston 1975*, *Euston 1977*, and *Euston 1980*. But Hollywood has made millions with *Airport*, *Airport 1975*, *Airport 1977*, and *Airport 1980*.

Epilogue

FEW building types can have had as many examples constructed in as short a period as the railway station. It is almost impossible to estimate the numbers which were built in the nineteenth and twentieth centuries. In the United States almost 140,000 stations (including flag halts and station renewals) were built in the period 1830–1950. New Zealand, a much smaller country, had at least 2,000. The Indian railway system accounted for several thousand more, and even an island like Sri Lanka had almost 200 when its railways reached their fullest extent. No other type of building was given such a world-wide incidence so rapidly. It was the railway station, alone of all nineteenth-century architecture, which truly united the world through the unstoppable force of the imperialism of steam. From China to the high Andes, from the Rockies to the heart of Africa, it was the station which was the most immediately recognizable intrusion of the modern world. It acted as a magnet for travellers and produce, a centre of information and communications, a strategic and administrative point capable of creating new towns and destroying old ones. Despite the vast numbers of stations built in so many different environments, they were all united by function, and it is this unity which has made it possible to write in general terms of their architecture and their role in society and the arts.

The railway set in motion new national unities and the appearance of a first world-wide culture. Track and trains have always been seen as the vital element in this, but it was stations which gave it human scale, which linked the railway system to localities, and provided the principal point of contact for their inhabitants. At stations trains were controlled, ordered, loaded, and unloaded, and performed a host of social and economic functions. In Europe, the United States, Latin America, and the British dominions, a new nationalism arrived with the passengers and manufactured goods at railway stations throughout the country, while in the big cities and towns a newly integrated economic system was symbolized by the unloading of milk churns and market produce. Everywhere in Asia and Africa the most potent unloading of all was of the agents and artifacts of a new dominant culture.

The most striking thing about the railway station, however, is its remarkable diversity. A great multiplicity of companies and architects in a period of experimentation in styles ensured such diversity in Europe and the Americas. But one might have expected that imperial railway powers, marching masterfully across their colonial territories, might have laid down, at least within specific countries or along particular routes, a series of uniform stations, rather like the Romans' forts and marching camps. Very rarely was this the case. Different communities, varieties of terrain, and diversity in traffic demanded a striking range of station styles.

Architectural historians have tended to be obsessed with the big city stations, so often triumphs of architecture, engineering, and design, but architectural joys are also to be found in smaller stations, and it is usually these which have influenced communities most markedly. The large urban stations have been studied within their cityscapes: they were a striking combination of the great mass of the station building itself, circulation areas, offices, hotel, with the enclosed space of the shed acting as a funnel through which passengers are sucked into an escape from the inner city. The country station, on the other hand, represents the linking of a specific community or region to a transport network which not only tamed an infinity of open space, but also linked the localities to a world-wide economic system. If the city station represented escape (and it was perhaps departure which was always the most potent image), the country station offered a route to the centre of things. Whereas on the great city railway networks passenger and freight functions were usually widely separated, the country station constituted a complete system in itself. It was not only a stopping-place for trains, a place for booking, embarking, and disembarking passengers, but also an export assembly point and a distribution centre for information, fuel, imported goods, and civil and military power. Through the telegraph office it was a vital and often strategic communications centre. It was a fuel dump, sometimes a technical support centre, and a residence for railway workers. The country station was a station in the widest sense, a collection of buildings which often attracted other services and additional population to its vicinity.

Large city stations were concentrated in their immensity; country ones were small and dispersed. The city station enclosed; the country one opened out. If the first were the cathedrals of steam, the second were like the mission stations performing a wide variety of economic and social functions as well as ministering to the central technological faith. And just as cathedrals, churches, chapels, and mission stations represented an intrusive religion in the world-wide expansion of Christendom from 1500 to 1900, stations represented, in an infinitely more extensive and faster gathering-in of the flock, an intrusive economic order. The religious analogy is not a fanciful one. When the Chinese tore up the first railway line built on their territory, they destroyed the railway station and built a temple in its place. The station represented a more potent threat to Chinese culture than even the Christian missionaries.

Generally, the insidious power of railway architecture, though highly derivative, was not as alien as the religious. Christianity could not dabble with local religious styles. To do so would be to compromise its very identity as well as its theology. But the great strength of railway architecture was its striking eclecticism. In Europe and the Americas it acted as a remarkable digest of all past architectural styles here summed up and developed through the power of Victorian technology. In the wider world, it often was intrusive and made dramatic gestures to its European origins, but not infrequently it disguised itself in local garb. Stations could be made to look like mosques, oriental palaces, fortifications, Spanish missions, or even smaller-scale vernacular architecture. Its form could also be dictated by the locally available building materials. Yet whatever disguise it took upon itself, its function was always clear. The technology and the economic power it represented were never compromised. Like the cathedral or the church the station also seemed to demand a strong upward element to represent this power, but whereas church tower or spire could only take a relatively limited number of forms, the clock, look-out, or signal tower at the railway station could ape church, mosque, pagoda, palace, or fort. In the simplest of all a flag-pole might suffice, providing a neat counterpart to the marching of telegraph poles, for stations were connected not just by railway tracks, but also by the laying-on of wires.

The historian of the railway station does well to remember that passengers have invariably been regarded as a necessary evil to railway companies. It was natural resources which teased railways out from their early local beginnings, and it was natural resources which generally kept them alive. Passengers were profitable in Europe and the Americas in the nineteenth century, but they soon ceased to be so as the demands for their comforts—including the ever more opulent railway stations—increased. In some cases in the rest of the world passengers were carried only because governments insisted. Passenger receipts on the Andean railways, for example, constituted only a tiny fraction of total income. They had been built entirely to tap mineral resources. Even in densely populated India, freight income was more important than passenger. The grandeur of many stations, then, reflected not the economic importance of passengers, but the significance of the railway in national, civic, imperial, and colonial pride and self-respect.

But however much the station sometimes masked the realities of transport economics, its powerful presence in every community ensured its central role in art, literature, and film. Human dramas of arrival and departure in personal relations and in global human affairs, in love, politics, and war, could not be depicted without the station. It was the essential backdrop for the arrival of the famous, the departure of the notorious, the comings and goings of the unknown, a striking combination of the extraordinary—royal visits, political speeches, ceremonial—and the very ordinary.

The railway station has lost this central role. Before the First World War neither motor cars nor omnibuses posed much threat, although tramway systems did make inroads on suburban networks. In the interwar years decline began. Henry Ford and the Model T, with mass production and the vision of cheap motoring for all, spelled doom for the railways in the industrialized world. Bus services soon replaced country lines, and trucks took over in the delivery of agricultural produce and freight. The first closures of British country lines took place in the 1930s and John Droege was already noting the power of the truck in the second edition of his *Freight Terminals* in 1925.[1] In the post-Second World War period the aeroplane completed the process. The great and the famous were photographed at airports, not stations. As hordes of tourists were packaged into coaches and planes, the airports became the setting for arrivals and departures of ordinary people too.

Films were made of aeroplane and airport dramas, though few poets or artists seemed to derive much inspiration there. The airport was not of the city, but beyond it. It was not a place for the pedestrian, somewhere to linger to watch the passing scene, but a utilitarian necessity, to be passed through as rapidly as possible, from escalator to travellator to car or coach. Whereas in Western countries the airport has become an experience for almost all classes, in the Third World there is now a pronounced class distinction between the users of the airport and the users of the station. No longer is the station the mixing-point of all classes. The lower classes in Russia and in many Afro-Asian countries still wait days for the train, but the upper classes have generally disappeared to the car and the plane. In some Latin American countries the railways have lost so much social cachet that no one uses the stations at all. Paul Theroux found this to be the case in El Salvador, where the station in Santa Ana was in a part of the town that was crumbling into the surrounding countryside, deserted apart from one man behind an empty desk—the station-master.[2] In Colombia none of the locals seemed to know where a station was, and when he found it the ticket-seller was surprised to see him, 'a little incredulous, as if I had penetrated his secret by some devious stratagem'.[3] A few years later, when Miles Kington wanted to see the railway station in Lima, Peru, the taxi-driver regarded him as a madman and tried desperately to convince him of its unimportance and of his desire to show Kington fine ruins.[4] The remains of far-distant cultures were more worthy of notice than one only recently superseded.

The reaction in most countries has not been quite so extreme, but none the less there are few where railways do not seem to be an old and declining transportation system. For many observers of this decline the destruction of railways and of their stations has come about because of an entirely unfair competition. John Droege noted this in 1925. In 1923 the Report of the Joint New England Railroad Committees to the governors of the six north-eastern states of the United States complained of the 'state-subsidised truck competition'.[5] Both the railroads and the tax-payers were forced to subsidize the trucking lines by maintaining highways for them free of charge, while the railroads had to pay for all their own track maintenance from their earnings. Trucks, Droege went on, operate only in good weather. A survey of the Connecticut highways department had shown that a third of them were grossly and dangerously overloaded, while in California trucks caused such damage that roads failed only four years after construction. Sixty years on, all the arguments are very familiar. But in that time roads and trucks have caused environmental damage such as Droege could never have imagined. Thousands of acres of countryside have been concreted over to make track-beds for trucks; historic villages and buildings have been shaken to their foundations by roaring juggernauts; and deaths from coach, truck, and other road accidents have cumulatively produced a carnage of wartime proportions. Venal politicians have played the vital part in this, accepting extensive funds from trucking interests. It is hard indeed to imagine a future work celebrating the architectural and social significance of coach and truck parks.

In England, beautiful valleys, like the Lune Gorge in Cumbria, where the railway line hugged the contours as an almost invisible and sympathetic feature, have been raped by six-lane motorways. The planners of the sixties destroyed whole areas of cities for ring roads, expressways, and tower blocks. People were expected to live like ants, and if they did not have access to the all-conquering internal-combustion engine they were abandoned and lost. The isolation of inner-city communities contributed to riots and disorders from Watts County, Los Angeles, to Toxteth, Liverpool. The demolition of stations and their surrounding environments created new and unfamiliar wastelands. In both urban localities and country towns and villages it was often like the removal of a beating heart, a community centre soon weed-overgrown and vermin-infested. In Ontario, Canada, one small station, Forks of the Credit, was destroyed when vandals pushed it into a gorge. Elsewhere, the vandals have been of the official variety.

It is true that to some extent the railways' very success in the nineteenth century brought this destruction upon their works in the twentieth. The rivalries of nineteenth-century companies led to over-building in many cities and towns. Tracks and passenger and freight terminals took up too much land, created too many obstacles to city growth and to urban communications. The civic plans of many American cities were the first recognitions of this problem. The Holt Commission of 1913–15 on Canada's capital, Ottawa, noted the particular conditions prevailing in North America. Towns and cities competed for railway facilities, recognizing that they could be put on the map if successful. The railways could therefore get almost any concession they asked for:

> It was not to be expected that men would look ahead fifty or seventy-five years to see whether or not a certain location would hurt the city at a time far in the future. The cities needed the railways and took the line of least resistance to obtain them. So we find areas, occupied by railways, in what has become the most valuable business districts of a city. When these areas were acquired for freight and passenger terminals, they were on the outskirts of the city or town as it then existed.[6]

The conclusion was, of course, that railway facilities would have to be closed and relocated. The Gréber Master Plan for Ottawa of 1950 went further and proposed the creation of a railway station as an airport outside the city connected to it by wide boulevards. It was not long before the 'multi-modal concept' came into vogue in Canada and the United States, that is, the station as car park, coach park, bus centre, travel agency, airport bus terminal, with perhaps a few trains as an afterthought. This jargon was a passing fad, however, which soon became unpopular when passengers discovered that it was merely a code for the destruction of down-town facilities.

In the rebuilding and relocation of so many stations, from the first 'Union' Beaux-Arts schemes in the United States, through the Art Deco Cincinnati Union of the 1930s, to Kowloon and one or two Canadian prairie cities in recent times the role of the station as a community centre and as an essentially pedestrian facility has been forgotten. In con-sequence many of these new schemes failed to make their mark, becom-ing merely grand milestones on the route of railway decline. Mercifully, European city stations have been largely free of this relocation effect, having been subjected rather to consolidation and amalgamation into existing buildings.

While the large city stations were consolidated, relocated, and demolished, thousands of suburban, country, and small-town stations throughout the world have been closed, though seldom without the fierce resistance of local communities. Generally they have been overridden by the official vandals who do so much to create the small-scale vandalism which they hypocritically deplore. In Britain, the British Rail Board has often held out for such an inflated price for closed station buildings that no one would buy and the stations rapidly deteriorated through neglect, climate, and hooliganism. As Marcus Binney put it, valuable assets swiftly became expensive liabilities.[7] Meanwhile, small-scale vandals get probation and the large-scale peerages. The architectural conservation group SAVE (Save Britain's Heritage) became closely concerned with the destruction of railway stations, helped local communities to fight demolition and find possible reuse, and issued a great deal of publicity on buildings under threat.

It was perhaps inevitable that American railroads which had been so profligate in station-building should have been the most destructive in the era of railway decline. In a calamitous demolition period in the 1960s, the remarkable Pennsylvania Central in New York crashed to the ground to make way for the misnamed Madison Square Garden. It had survived barely more than half a century, and left not even a noble ruin like the Baths of Caracalla on which it had been based. Memphis, Tennessee, Spokane, Washington, Cumberland, Maryland, Pawtucket, Rhode Island, and more than one of Chicago's many terminals were similarly reduced to rubble. In 1961 the *Portland Press Herald* reported the demolition of the Union Station in Portland, Maine:

An historic Portland landmark passed from sight in a matter of seconds Thursday afternoon. While hundreds of persons watched, workmen razing Union Station toppled the clock tower with a swinging steel ball. The station, built in 1888, is being razed to make way for a shopping centre.[8]

It is difficult to establish whether the monumental bathos was intentional and whether the crowds were there to see a spectacle or mourn the loss of a friendly landmark. These were just a few of the large stations which disappeared. The removal of local services and the concentration of American railroads upon a few inter-city services meant that the small-town and country variety became, in the words of the American Educational Facilities Laboratories and the National Endowment for the Arts, 'an endangered species'.[9]

In Canada considerable public and legal disputes have developed around the closure of railway stations. When Canadian Pacific demolished without permission their West Toronto railway station, their action was described by the Canadian Transportation Commission as a serious breach of the law. CPR had imported workers from outside Toronto to flatten the station without notice in the early hours of the morning. The City of Toronto's buildings commissioner issued an order to stop the demolition, but it was ignored by both CPR and the demolition workers. CPR fought on and, amid public consternation and mutual recriminations, the accusation was reversed in the courts. The station was judged to be federal land, not under either city or provincial jurisdiction. CPR had won a legal victory but suffered a massive moral defeat. Such controversies rumbled on in local and provincial papers throughout Canada, with headlines to articles and editorials like 'CP Rail Fight Looms', 'Protecting Historic Sites', and 'Contempt for History'.[10] Like Britain's SAVE, the Heritage Canada Foundation took up the cause of station buildings. Jacques Dalibard, its executive director, wrote in *Canadian Heritage*:

In the wake of the public outcry which followed the November 1982 demolition of Canadian Pacific's West Toronto station, I asked myself a question: Would people's outrage have been as great if the building had been, say, a hospital or a hotel? The answer, clearly, is that it would not. The reason, I think, is that a railway station, more than any other building in the country, touches something deep in us. The stations are more than mere buildings, they are symbolic of our nationhood; and it is for this reason that they deserve our best efforts to save them.[11]

When the CPR station was demolished in Calgary, a journalist on the *Calgary Herald* extolled its former glory, its extensive public rooms, the beautiful model of a CPR ocean liner and other embellishments, a place which symbolized the city, a great transportation system, and 'the spirit, friendliness, and hospitality of the prairies'. The original station had been replaced by what he described as a 'hole underground':

It looks and feels like a morgue, with no life in it. All that is in the hole is a ticket-selling counter, a few dozen plastic chairs, and two small ever-locked toilets. The passengers have been brutally robbed of comfort and convenience. The people of Calgary have suffered an enormous loss. The originators and builders of the great Canadian Pacific Railway system must be turning in their graves.[12]

Similar controversies raged in far-off New Zealand. In 1980 the *Auckland Star* reported 'The Railways to close many stations'.[13] The closures, numbering as many as 200, were to be scattered 'over the entire rail system'. The destruction of the 81-year-old Dannevirks Station, one of the creations of Sir George Troup (see above, Chapter 3), caused the Historic Places Trust of New Zealand to become concerned about the loss of her railway heritage, and to demand that more money should be made available to preserve railway history. A few local communities succeeded in their own preservation attempts. The residents of the small community of Hakanui saved their station by petitioning and lobbying. They argued that the passenger service was vital to the community, together with the many tons of fertilizer which were delivered there for the local farmers.

In New Zealand, however, some of the larger stations have been well cared for by New Zealand Railways, and a few fine stations have been built there in recent times. In Australia the extension of the standard gauge routes, obliterating the problems of break of gauge between the states, has maintained railway vigour and has led to the building of new stations. Westrail, for example, built in recent years a new transcontinental terminus worthy of such a grand railway project.[14] Nor is the situation one of unrelieved gloom elsewhere. The various pressure groups have done sterling work in publicizing and agitating. The range of possible reuses of railway stations is immense and when the stations are caught in time, such schemes can be profitable both to the community and to the developer.

The most common reuse of small and medium-sized stations is, of course, as private houses, and as many nineteenth-century stations were built as cottages and villas conversion was not difficult. A survey by the Countryside Commission in Britain indicated that 38 per cent of planning permissions for the conversion of old stations were as private residences (21 per cent were for warehousing, 14 per cent for educational purposes, and 12 per cent for manufacturing industry). Some of the residences were given such heartfelt names as Booking Hall, Beeching's Way, and Beeching's Folly. In Canada and the United States the wooden construction of many stations meant they could sometimes be moved to become residences on more convenient sites.

Many other reuse schemes have been imaginative and encouraging. Several stations, like Darlington North Road and Monkwearmouth in Britain, Mount Clare, Baltimore, and Maliebaan in Holland have become railway museums.[15] Some in Canada have been moved to museums of pioneer history. Others have found a new lease of life in several countries as the stations of privately run steam lines. Richmond, Yorkshire, has become a garden centre, Pocklington, Humberside, a sports centre, Halton, Lancashire, a University boathouse, Bath, Avon and Windermere, Cumbria, supermarkets, Maldon, Essex, a pub, Kelvinside, Glasgow, a restaurant (appropriately called Carriages). Petrolia, Ontario, became the local library as early as the 1930s. Chattanooga, made so famous in railway lore by the song, became both museum and restaurant, Pittsburgh became a very grand restaurant indeed, while Washington Union continued to symbolize American patriotic pride as the National Visitor Center. Lincoln, Nebraska, became a bank, Yuma, Arizona, a performing arts centre, Duluth, Minnesota, an area cultural centre, Baltimore, Maryland, a college of art, and many others, like Indianapolis, Indiana, Hartford, Connecticut, Los Angeles, California, and Fargo, North Dakota, have been converted for multiple use. In New London, Connecticut, a non-profit-making organization, the Union Station Trust Inc., was formed to negotiate a mortgage and save the station for commercial reuse. In Australia, Adelaide Station has become a casino, the magnificent marble hall acting as the casino foyer.

The fact that this activity is going on in so many diverse places, at least in those countries where conservation has become an issue, is proof enough, if any further proof were needed, of the essential place of the railway station in the history, the social life, the arts, and the affections of so many communities, large and small. The station was not only the vital linking-point of each town and village to its wider locality, region, and state, it was also a meeting-place, a community centre, and shopping area. It was the telegraph office, post office, newsagent, and vital news and intelligence-gathering centre in countless places around the globe. The products of the community were sent off from it, and necessities and luxuries were received in return. With the fragmentation of transport facilities and opportunities, the containerization of freight, and the rise of the mass media, no other building will ever have the same all-embracing role. In that sense, the original significance of railway stations can never be resurrected.

A few countries, like Libya and some of the West Indian islands, have given up their railways for good. Others, like Oman, never had any. But in many parts of the Third World, the station retains its central role, and even in the industrial world there are signs that railways may have a new lease of life. Environmental and conservation groups are growing in power. A new generation is rising which finds no novelty or romance in the motor car. For some time its technology has been relatively static while that of the railway is seeking and achieving new advances. The next generation may recognize the environmental destruction, the pollution, and the human carnage wrought by the internal-combustion engine, and force politicians hooked on their Cadillacs, Mercedes, and Jaguars to return to a more communal and ecologically sympathetic transportation system, one through which they can more satisfactorily restore their contacts with the people, the towns, and the countryside which they presume to rule. The truly damaging period of contraction in the 1960s and 1970s at least led to stations being more highly valued again. Many have gone, but others survive to provide pleasure and instruction to people in the twenty-first century.

Notes

INTRODUCTION

1. Bryan Morgan (ed.), *The Railway Lover's Companion* (London, 1963), 523.
2. E. Foxwell and T. C. Farrer, *Express Trains English and Foreign* (London, 1889), 70–2.
3. Charles Dickens, *Dombey and Son* (London, 1848; repr. Oxford, 1974), 218.
4. Jean Dethier (ed.), *All Stations* (London, 1981), 6.
5. Robert Lynd, *In Defence of Pink* (London, 1937), 71, 74–5.
6. *Time with Betjeman*, BBC 2, 13 March 1983.
7. David St John Thomas, *The Country Station* (Newton Abbot, 1976), 9.
8. Hilaire Belloc, *On Nothing and Kindred Subjects* (London, 1908), 71–2.
9. James Scott, *Railway Romance and Other Essays* (London, 1913), 71, 89–90.
10. Eric Treacy, *Steam Up!* (London, 1950), 39–40.
11. Henry James, *English Hours* (Oxford, 1981), 22.
12. *Railway Magazine*, 15 (1904), 330–3.
13. This period is studied in detail in Paul Fussell's *Abroad: British Literary Travelling between the Wars* (Oxford, 1980).
14. T. S. Eliot, *Collected Poems 1909–1962* (London, 1963), 210.
15. *Railway Magazine*, 69 (1931), 383.
16. Roger Lloyd, *The Fascination of Railways* (London, 1951), 91.
17. G. K. Chesterton, *Tremendous Trifles* (London, 1909), 219–24.
18. Karel Čapek, *Intimate Things* (London, 1935), 99–101.
19. Roger Lloyd, op. cit. 99.
20. Jean Dethier, op. cit. 9.
21. 'Palinurus', *The Unquiet Grave* (Harmondsworth, 1984), 66.
22. Samuel Carr (ed.), *The Poetry of Railways* (London, 1978), 69.

CHAPTER 1

1. The outstanding work on both British and European Stations is Carroll Meeks, *The Railroad Station* (New Haven and London, 1956). On Britain alone, Gordon Biddle, *Victorian Stations* (Newton Abbot, 1973) and Marcus Binney and David Pearce (eds.), *Railway Architecture* (London, 1979) are notable studies. On Europe, see in particular Mihaly Kubinszky, *Bahnhöfe Europas* (Stuttgart, 1969), Nikolaus Pevsner, *A History of Building Types* (London, 1979), 225–34, and Jean Dethier (ed.), *All Stations* (London, 1981). For a wide range of illustrations of British stations see Gordon Biddle and O. S. Nock (eds.), *The Railway Heritage of Britain* (London, 1983) and Gordon Biddle and Jeoffrey Spence, *The British Railway Station* (Newton Abbot, 1977). The architectural style of Britain's best-loved company is covered in A. Vaughan, *Great Western Architecture* (Oxford, 1977). London is well covered by Alan A. Jackson, *London's Termini* (Newton Abbot, 1969) and John Betjeman and John Gay, *London's Historic Railway Stations* (London, 1972). There is also now a good book on Glasgow, *Glasgow Stations* by Colin Johnston and John R. Hume (Newton Abbot, 1979). There are a number of

individual station biographies, the most notable being Jack Simmons, *St. Pancras Station* (London, 1968). But see also Derek Harrison, *Salute to Snow Hill* (Birmingham, 1978), G. R. Smith, *Old Euston* (London, 1938), R. S. Fitzgerald, *Liverpool Road Station, Manchester* (Manchester, 1980), Robert Thorne, *Liverpool Street Station* (London, 1978), René Clozier, *La Gare du Nord* (Paris, 1940), Compagnie des Chemins de Fer de l'Est, *La Gare de l'Est* (Paris, 1931).

2. E. F. Carter, *Famous Railway Stations of the World* (London, 1958), 9–13.
3. R. S. Fitzgerald, *Liverpool Road Station, Manchester: an Historical and Architectural Survey* (Manchester, 1980).
4. *Building News*, 29 (1875), 133.
5. Meeks, op. cit. 40–1.
6. Michael Booth, *Victorian Spectacular Theatre* (London, 1981), 2.
7. Henry-Russell Hitchcock, *Early Victorian Architecture in Britain* (London, 1972), vol. i, pp. 492–571.
8. John Ruskin, *The Seven Lamps of Architecture* (London, 1907), 40.
9. Christian Barman, *An Introduction to Railway Architecture* (London, 1950), 35.
10. *Railway Magazine*, 16 (1905), 483, 383, 379.
11. Dionysius Lardner, *Railway Economy* (1850; repr. New York, 1968), 119–20.
12. Biddle, *Victorian Stations*, 23.
13. Ibid. 34.
14. Meeks, op. cit. 90.
15. F. S. Williams, *The Midland Railway: its Rise and Progress* (1888; repr. Newton Abbot, 1968), 257.
16. Alan A. Jackson, op. cit. 67.
17. Donald J. Olsen, *The Growth of Victorian London* (Harmondsworth, 1979), 98.
18. Derek Taylor and David Bush, *The Golden Age of British Hotels* (London, 1974); Christopher Monkhouse, 'Railway Hotels', in Binney and Pearce (eds.), *Railway Architecture*, 118–38.
19. See Biddle, *Victorian Stations*, 163–76, which has sketches of the standard station types.
20. Jack Simmons, *The Railways of Britain* (London, 1968), 103.
21. There is a detailed description of the station in *Railway Magazine*, 69 (1931), 331–6.
22. Roger Fry, *Vision and Design* (London, 1937), 60–4.
23. John Ruskin, op. cit. 122–3.
24. Binney and Pearce, op. cit. 12.
25. Quoted in David St John Thomas, *The Country Station* (Newton Abbot, 1976), 49.
26. Christian Barman, *Next Station* (London, 1947), 62.
27. Railway Companies Report on the Modernization of Stations (April 1944), 2.

CHAPTER 2

1. Carroll Meeks, *The Railroad Station* (New Haven and London, 1956), is the starting-point for all studies of American station architecture. Extensive illustrations of stations can be found in Lawrence Grow, *Waiting for the 5.05* (New York, 1977), Edwin P. Alexander, *Down at the Depot* (New York, 1970), and the two volumes entitled *Reusing Railway Stations*, produced by the Educational Facilities Laboratories and National Endowment for the Arts (New York, 1974 and 1975). John A. Droege, *Passenger Terminals and Trains* (New York, 1916), also has many illustrations as well as descriptions of building materials and internal fitments of

stations. Carl W. Condit's *The Railroad and the City* (Columbus, 1977) surveys the development of the station in one city, Cincinnati.

2. Meeks, op. cit. 49.
3. Robert Anderson Pope, 'Grand Central Terminal Station, New York', *Town Planning Review*, 2 (1911), 55–64.
4. Droege, op. cit. 10.
5. Condit, op. cit. 268.
6. Ibid. 248–9.
7. *Reusing Railroad Stations*, vol. 1, p. 10.
8. There has been little serious architectural discussion of Canadian railway stations, but there are many illustrations in Elizabeth A. Wilmot, *Meet Me at the Station* (Toronto, 1977), and Charles Bohi, *Canadian National's Western Depots* (Toronto, 1977). Richard Bébout's *The Open Gate, Toronto Union Station* (Toronto, n.d.) provides an excellent survey of one station.
9. D. B. Hanna, *Trains of Recollection* (Toronto, 1924), 235.
10. Bohi's book offers not only a large number of illustrations of Canada's western stations and lists all of them in categories, but also attempts some architectural classification related to the nature of the traffic and the community each served.
11. Canadian Pacific Railway, *Summer Tours* (Montreal, 1897), 18.
12. Raymond Hull et al., *Vancouver's Past* (Vancouver, 1974), 40–1.
13. Droege, op. cit. 85.
14. Douglas Richardson, 'The Architecture of Union Station', in Bébout, op. cit. 67–96.
15. *Railway Gazette*, 80 (1944), 571–3, 594–8, 620–1.
16. Plan for the National Capital: General Report (J. Gréber, Ottawa, 1950).
17. The Latin American station has never received its due share of attention. There is some information in Brian Fawcett, *Railways of the Andes* (London, 1963), and in earlier works like Percy F. Martin, *Through Five Republics* (London, 1905), and the same author's *Mexico of the Twentieth Century*, 2 vols. (London, 1907); W. H. Koebel, *Argentina, Past and Present* (London, 1914); *The Times Book of Argentina* (London, 1927); Adolphus Augusto Pinto, *História da Viação Pública de São Paulo* (São Paulo, 1903). The collection of photographs of Henry Finch was a valuable source for Latin American stations, and the extensive photographic collections of the Crown Agents were vital for the Caribbean. As always, the pages of the *Railway Magazine* and the *Railway Gazette* were rich in references to stations throughout the hemisphere.
18. Koebel, op. cit. 443.
19. *Times Book*, 82.
20. *Railway Magazine*, 63 (1928), 171–83.
21. Paul Theroux, *The Old Patagonian Express* (Harmondsworth, 1980), 378.
22. Koebel, op. cit. 244–5.
23. La Plata station was renamed 'Eva Perón' when the name of the city was similarly changed in 1952. Tucumán station was renamed '26 de Julio', the date of the death of Señora Perón. *Railway Gazette*, 19 September 1952.
24. Fawcett, op. cit. 225.
25. Ibid. 155.
26. Martin, *Five Republics*, 448.
27. Aldous Huxley, *Beyond the Mexique Bay* (London, 1950), 303.
28. Theroux, op. cit. 67.
29. P. Ransome-Wallis, *On Railways* (London, 1951), 193.

CHAPTER 3

1. The railway architecture of Asia, Australasia, and Africa is virtually uncharted territory. Most works on railways have little to say on stations and there is little architectural criticism. General works include O. S. Nock, *Railways of Asia and the Far East* (London, 1978) and J. N. Westwood, *Railways of India* (Newton Abbot, 1974). The Indian Railways Board published *Indian Railways, One Hundred Years* (New Delhi, 1953), with a section on Indian stations. Other information on Indian stations can be found in M. Satow and R. Desmond, *Railways of the Raj* (London, 1980), Jan Morris with Simon Winchester, *Stones of Empire* (Oxford, 1983), and the various editions of Murray's *Handbook*. On Ceylon, see Henry W. Cave, *The Ceylon Government Railway* (London, 1910), G. F. Perera, *The Ceylon Railway* (Colombo, 1925), and John Falconer, 'Nineteenth-Century Photography in Ceylon', *The Photographic Collector*, 2 (1981), 39–53. There are many illustrations of Siberian stations in A. I. Dmitriev-Mamonov and A. F. Zdziarski, *Guide to the Great Siberian Railway* (1900; repr. Newton Abbot, 1971), and comments in Harmon Tupper, *To the Great Ocean* (London, 1965), Eric Newby, *The Big Red Train Ride* (London, 1978), J. N. Westwood, *A History of Russian Railways* (London, 1964), and G. N. Curzon, *Russia in Central Asia* (London, 1889). Illustrations of and information about Australian stations can be found in Anon., *The Railways of New South Wales, 1855–1955* (Sydney, 1955), O. S. Nock, *Railways of Australia* (London, 1971), C. C. Singleton and David Burke, *Railways of Australia* (Sydney, 1963). New Zealand is well served. As well as David B. Leitch, *Railways of New Zealand* (Newton Abbot, 1972), there are local studies like those of W. A. Pierre, *Canterbury Provincial Railways* (Wellington, 1964), and J. O. P. Watt, *Southland's Pioneer Railways* (Wellington, 1965). New Zealand Railways issue booklets on Dunedin and Auckland stations; there are articles on stations in the New Zealand Railways Staff Bulletin, and there is a major study, L. C. Staffan, *Railway Station Buildings, an Historical Survey* (New Zealand Institute of Architects, 1965). The four-volume *The Story of the Cape to Cairo Railway*, ed. Leo Weinthal (London, 1923), has many illustrations and descriptions of African stations, as do John R. Day, *Railways of Southern Africa* (London, 1963), the *Natal Province Descriptive Guide* (Durban, 1911), and various editions of the *Union-Castle Line Guide to South and East Africa*. M. F. Hill, *Permanent Way*, 2 vols. (Nairobi, 1957) and Ronald Hardy, *The Iron Snake* (London, 1965) deal with the East African railways, and other regions are covered in Anthony H. Croxton, *Railways of Rhodesia* (Newton Abbot, 1973), John R. Day, *Railways of Northern Africa* (London, 1964), and E. D. Brant, *Railways of North Africa* (Newton Abbot, 1971). The photographic collections of the India Office Library, the Royal Commonwealth Society, and the Crown Agents have proved invaluable; Zimbabwean Railways sent a set of photographs of their stations; and postcards of stations in the authors' collections filled many gaps.
2. Daniel Thorner, 'Great Britain and the Development of Indian Railways', *Journal of Economic History* 11 (1951), 389–402.
3. *Illustrated London News*, 14 April 1855, p. 341.
4. Ibid., 24 December 1864, p. 625.
5. Morris, op. cit. 128.
6. John A. Droege, *Passenger Terminals and Trains* (New York, 1916), 296–8.
7. Robert Grant Irving, *Indian Summer* (New Haven and London, 1981), 73–9.
8. *Railway Magazine*, 19 (1906), 44. The Delhi 'waiting halls' were described as 'capacious', the 'two largest in India'.

9. Cave, op. cit. 151.
10. Curzon, op. cit. 10–14. Merv, Curzon wrote, which 'less than a decade ago was pronounced to be the key of the Indian Empire is now an inferior wayside station on a Russian line of rail'.
11. Ibid. 212.
12. Tupper, op. cit. 436.
13. Newby, op. cit. 43, 114, 124.
14. This postcard is in the author's collection.
15. Personal observation by the author.
16. *Railway Magazine*, 2 (1898), 230–6.
17. Ibid. 236.
18. Singleton and Burke, op. cit. 5.
19. *Railway Magazine*, 71 (1932), 1–9.
20. The State Railways Commission of South Australia kindly sent the authors a copy.
21. 'Out of the Weatherboard Era', *New Zealand Railways Staff Bulletin* (1963), 74–5.
22. 'Historic Christchurch Station', *New Zealand Railways Staff Bulletin* (1959), 86–7; 'New Railway Station for Christchurch', *New Zealand Railways Staff Bulletin* (1960), 4–6.
23. Captain Colomb, *Slave-Catching in the Indian Ocean* (London, 1873), 12.
24. *Illustrated London News*, 23 January 1858, p. 74.
25. Weinthal, op. cit., vol. 2, p. 339.

CHAPTER 4

1. Frank McKenna, *The Railway Workers, 1840–1970* (London, 1980), 142–53.
2. *Railway Magazine*, 8 (1901), 140.
3. Ibid. 6 (1900), 436.
4. Paul Theroux, *The Great Railway Bazaar* (Harmondsworth, 1977), 354.
5. William Vincent, *Seen from the Railway Platform* (London, 1919), 23.
6. On *Bradshaw* see G. Royde Smith, *The History of Bradshaw* (London, 1939), Charles E. Lee, *The Centenary of 'Bradshaw'* (London, 1940), John Partington, 'Bradshaw', *Railway Magazine*, 2 (1898), 243–50.
7. *Punch*, 29 July 1865.
8. Revd Reginald Fellows, 'Bradshaw's First Timetable', *Railway Magazine*, 76 (1935), 391–2.
9. John Pendleton, *Our Railways* (London, 1896), vol. 2, pp. 153–4.
10. R. E. Charlewood, 'The Public Time-Table Books of our Chief Railways', *Railway Magazine*, 17 (1905), 335–42.
11. J. Pearson Pattinson, 'Railway Timetables', *Railway Magazine*, 3 (1898), 478–82.
12. McKenna, op. cit. 31–4.
13. John A. Droege, *Passenger Terminals and Trains* (New York, 1916), 277–8.
14. Adrian Vaughan, *Signalman's Morning and Signalman's Twilight* (London, 1984), 197–9.
15. F. S. Williams, *Our Iron Roads* (1883; repr. Woking, 1981), vol. 2, p. 488.
16. Jack Simmons (ed.), *Memoirs of a Stationmaster* (Bath, 1974), 40.
17. Len Bedale, *Station Master* (Sheffield, 1976), 76–7.
18. Williams, op. cit. 300.
19. *Railway Magazine*, 5 (1899), 229.
20. T. Norman Chamberlain in J. H. Whitehouse (ed.), *Problems of Boy Life* (London, 1912), 151–62.

21. Michael Deakin and John Willis, *Johnny Go Home* (London, 1976), 85–6.
22. On the railway police see J. R. Whitbread, *The Railway Policeman* (London, 1961), and H. J. Prytherch, 'Our Railway Police', *Railway Magazine*, 6 (1900), 53–60, 134–41. Cf. H. S. Dewhurst, *The Railroad Police* (Springfield, Illinois, 1955) for the United States.
23. Whitbread, op. cit. 62.
24. Ibid. 175.
25. Ibid. 176.
26. Prytherch, op. cit. 137.
27. On the station in town planning, see J. R. Kellett, *Railways and Victorian Cities* (London, 1979); David Turnock, *Railways in the British Isles* (London, 1982); R. E. Dickinson, *The West European City* (London, 1961); J. H. Appleton, 'Railways and the Morphology of British Towns', in R. P. Beckinsale and J. M. Houston (eds.), *Urbanization and its Problems* (Oxford, 1970), 92–118; S. H. Beaver, 'The Railways of Great Cities', *Geography*, 22 (1937), 116–20.
28. Beaver, op. cit. 117.
29. Kellett, op. cit. 281–2.
30. J. M. and Brian Chapman, *The Life and Times of Baron Haussmann* (London, 1957).
31. Robert R. Taylor, *The Word in Stone: the Role of Architecture in the National Socialist Ideology* (Berkeley, 1974), and Jochen Thies, 'Nazi Architecture: a Blueprint for World Domination', in David Welch (ed.), *Nazi Propaganda* (London, 1983), 45–64.
32. Thies, op. cit. 59.
33. Albert Speer, *Inside the Third Reich* (London, 1970), 134–5.
34. Ibid. 138.
35. Kellett, op. cit. 2.
36. Ibid. 6.
37. Ibid. 293.
38. Kurt Norborg (ed.), *Proceedings of the IGU Symposium in Urban Geography* (Lund, 1962), 585–6, 597.
39. On British railway towns see W. H. Chaloner, *Social and Economic Development of Crewe* (Manchester, 1950); Sophie Andreae, 'Railway Towns', in Marcus Binney and David Pearce (eds.), *Railway Architecture* (London, 1979), 176–89; B. J. Turton, 'The Railway Towns of Southern England', *Journal of Transport History*, 2 (1969), 85–100.
40. A. I. Dmitriev-Mamonov and A. F. Zdziarski, *Guide to the Great Siberian Railway* (1900; repr. Newton Abbot, 1971), 263. The succeeding examples are taken from the same work.
41. *Railway Magazine*, 19 (1906), 440.
42. Ibid. 16 (1905), 111–12.
43. Ibid. 18 (1906), 180.
44. Ibid. 19 (1906), 443–4.
45. Ibid. 18 (1906), 182.

CHAPTER 5

1. Shepard B. Clough, *The Economic History of Modern Italy* (New York, 1964), 26.
2. John Pendleton, *Our Railways* (London, 1896), vol. 2, p. 30.
3. Ibid.

4. L. Girard, 'Transport', *Cambridge Economic History*, vol. 6 (Cambridge, 1965), pt. i, p. 238.
5. Eric Newby, *The Big Red Train Ride* (London, 1978), 54.
6. R. K. Narayan, speaking on Thames Television, *The South Bank Show*, 13 March 1983.
7. Paul Theroux, *The Great Railway Bazaar* (Harmondsworth, 1977), 206.
8. 'Brunel Redivivus', 'The Funeral of Queen Victoria', *Railway Magazine*, 8 (1901), 265.
9. *Hail and Farewell: the Passing of King George V* (*The Times*: London, 1936), 53.
10. Ibid. 54–5.
11. Ibid. 86.
12. M. Satow and R. Desmond, *Railways of the Raj* (London, 1980), 13. The *Illustrated London News*, 4 June 1853, none the less described the opening as an event which 'will be remembered when the battlefields of Plassey, Assaye, Meanee and Goojerat are seen as mere landmarks in our history'. The *Bombay Gazette* of 28 April 1853 went further: 'Every Englishman must have congratulated himself on being one of the dominant race that day. The scene was worth to England the addition of many regiments to its army.'
13. H. O. Arnold-Foster, *The Queen's Empire* (London, 1897).
14. G. F. Perera, *The Ceylon Railway* (Colombo, 1925), 54–7.
15. *Railway Magazine*, 18 (1906), 182.
16. Mortimer and Dorothy Menpes, *Durbar* (London, 1903), 20–1.
17. Correlli Barnett, *The Collapse of British Power* (New York, 1972), 153.

CHAPTER 6

1. *Railway Magazine*, 3 (1898), 365.
2. Charles E. Lee, *Passenger Class Distinctions* (London, 1943).
3. *Railway Magazine*, 71 (1932), 319.
4. John Pendleton, *Our Railways* (London, 1896), vol. 2, pp. 132–3.
5. John Aye, *Humour on the Rail* (London, 1931), 147–8.
6. Alan A. Jackson, *London's Termini* (Newton Abbot, 1969), 225, 231.
7. Murray's *Handbook* (1919), p. xxiv.
8. Ernest Protheroe, *Railways of the World* (London, 1914), 596.
9. Murray's *Handbook* (1919), p. xxv.
10. Mortimer and Dorothy Menpes, *Durbar* (London, 1903), 208–9.
11. Sir Sidney Low, *A Vision of India* (London, 1911), 73–4.
12. Ibid. 77.
13. Ceylon Railways, *General Regulations and Information for Passengers* (Royal Commonwealth Society collection, n.d., late nineteenth century).
14. Lord Edward Cecil, *The Leisure of an Egyptian Official* (London, 1921; repr. London, 1938), 241. Suspicion of ticket clerks was universal. Baedeker's *Guide to Southern Italy and Sicily* (1912), pp. xv–xvi, warned passengers: 'it is advisable to keep a sharp eye on the ticket-clerks, as "mistakes" are by no means infrequent, while no attention is paid to subsequent complaints'.
15. Cecil, op. cit. 241–2.
16. *Railway Magazine*, 18 (1906), 506.
17. Eric Newby, *The Big Red Train Ride* (London, 1978), 13.
18. *Railway Magazine*, 18 (1906), 328.
19. Jules Verne, *Around the World in Eighty Days* (London, n.d.), ch. 4.

20. J. N. Westwood, *Soviet Railways Today* (London, 1963), 8.
21. *Railway Magazine*, 4 (1899), 440–9.
22. P. Ransome-Wallis, *On Railways* (London, 1951), 180.
23. Anthony Croxton, *Railways of Rhodesia* (Newton Abbot, 1973), 217.
24. Plans of these and many other stations can be found in John A. Droege, *Passenger Terminals and Trains* (New York, 1916).
25. Pendleton, op. cit., vol. 1, p. 259.
26. Droege, op. cit. 29.
27. Ibid. 84.
28. Rudyard Kipling, *Letters of Travel (1892–1913)* (London, 1920), 29. Other quotations from Dee Brown, *Hear that Lonesome Whistle Blow* (London, 1977), 238–9.
29. Pendleton, op. cit., vol. 1, p. 260.
30. J. N. Westwood, *A History of Russian Railways* (London, 1964), 11.
31. G. N. Curzon, *Russia in Central Asia* (London, 1889), 99.
32. *Railway Magazine*, 18 (1906), 328.
33. Brian Fawcett, *Railways of the Andes* (London, 1963), 76.
34. We are indebted to Dr Rory Miller for this story.
35. *Railway Magazine*, 6 (1900), 129–33.
36. Ransome-Wallis, op. cit. 187.
37. R. W. Walmsley, *Nairobi, the Geography of a New City* (Nairobi, 1907).
38. Protheroe, op. cit. 650–1.
39. *Railway Magazine*, 6 (1900), 560.
40. Protheroe, op. cit. 622.
41. Howard W. Risher, *The Negro in the Railroad Industry* (Philadelphia, 1971).
42. *Railway Magazine*, 6 (1900), 123.
43. E. A. Pratt, *British Railways and the Great War* (London, 1921), 477.
44. Author's collection.
45. Marcel Peschaud, *Les Chemins de fer allemands et la Guerre* (Paris, 1927), 178.
46. Elizabeth Wilmot, *Meet Me at the Station* (Toronto, 1977), 1, 114.

CHAPTER 7

1. Charles Dickens, *American Notes* (London, 1842; repr. Harmondsworth, 1972), 113.
2. J. Horsley Denton, 'Private Stations', in H. A. Vallance (ed.), *The Railway Enthusiast's Bedside Book* (London, 1966), 86–91.
3. Jeffrey Lant, *Insubstantial Pageant* (London, 1979), 23–4.
4. George P. Neele, 'A Notable Private Railway Station: Gosport, Clarence Yard', *Railway Magazine*, 19 (1906), 513–16.
5. George P. Neele, *Railway Reminiscences* (East Ardsley, 1974), 473.
6. Ibid. 491–2.
7. *Illustrated London News*, 2 October 1858.
8. J. N. Westwood, *A History of Russian Railways* (London, 1964) 102.
9. On the railways, suburbia, and the rise of commuting, see David C. Thorns, *Suburbia* (London, 1972); F. M. L. Thompson (ed.), *The Rise of Suburbia* (Leicester, 1982); Alan A. Jackson, *Semi-Detached London* (London, 1973) and *London's Local Railways* (Newton Abbot, 1978); Harold Perkin, *The Age of the Railway* (Newton Abbot, 1971); J. R. Kellett, *Railways and Victorian Cities* (London, 1979); and Kate Liepmann, *The Journey to Work* (London, 1944).

10. Arnold Bennett, *Hilda Lessways* (London, 1911), 139–40.
11. John Stevenson, *British Society 1914–45* (Harmondsworth, 1984), 25.
12. T. W. H. Crosland, *The Suburbans* (London, 1905), 81, 35.
13. Eric J. Evans and Jeffrey Richards, *A Social History of Britain in Postcards* (London, 1980), 82.
14. Robert Thorne, *Liverpool Street Station* (London, 1978), 46.
15. Perkin, op. cit. 270.
16. John Betjeman, 'Metroland', in J. Guest (ed.), *The Best of Betjeman* (London, 1978). On the development of Metroland, see also Dennis Edwards and Ron Pigram, *The Romance of Metroland* (Tunbridge Wells, 1979) and *The Golden Years of the Metropolitan Railway* (Tunbridge Wells, 1983).
17. René Clozier, *La Gare du Nord* (Paris, 1940), 280–2.
18. Alan A. Jackson, *Semi-Detached London*, 173.
19. Katherine Chorley, *Manchester Made Them* (London, 1950), 114–15.
20. *Railway Magazine*, 18 (1906), 326–8.
21. Ibid. 328.
22. Ibid. 501–2.
23. Ibid. 425 6.
24. On the seaside and the railways see J. A. R. Pimlott, *The Englishman's Holiday* (London, 1947); J. Walvin, *Beside the Seaside* (London, 1978); J. K. Walton, *The English Seaside Resort: a Social History, 1750–1914* (Leicester, 1983).
25. M. V. Hughes, *A London Child of the 1870s* (Oxford, 1934; repr. 1978), 85–91.
26. John K. Walton, 'Railways and Resort Development in North-West England 1830–1914', in F. M. Sigsworth (ed.), *Ports and Resorts in the Regions* (Hull, 1980), 120–37.
27. S. Kirkwood, 'Railway Tourist Literature', *Railway Magazine*, 6 (1900), 510–16.
28. Alan Delgado, *The Annual Outing and Other Excursions* (London, 1977).
29. Ibid 118–20.
30. On country stations see Alexander Frater, *Stopping-Train Britain* (London, 1983), and David St John Thomas, *The Country Station* (Newton Abbot, 1976).
31. David St John Thomas, op. cit. 44.
32. G. A. Wade, 'The Prettiest Railway Stations', *Railway Magazine*, 6 (1900), 46–52.
33. Quoted in *Railway Gazette*, 46 (1927), 107.
34. Elizabeth Wilmot, *Meet Me at the Station* (Toronto, 1977), provides examples of all these community uses of the station.
35. James Stevens Curl, *A Celebration of Death* (London, 1980) and *The Victorian Celebration of Death* (Newton Abbot, 1972).
36. This 'receiving-station' is illustrated in *Commonwealth in Focus, 130 Years of Photographic History* (International Cultural Corporation of Australia, 1982), 66.

CHAPTER 8

1. On the role of railways in the economy of Britain and Europe see David Landes, *The Unbound Prometheus* (Cambridge, 1969); Patrick O'Brien (ed.), *Railways and the Economic Development of Western Europe* (Oxford, 1983); G. R. Hawke, *Railways and Economic Growth in England and Wales, 1840–70* (Oxford, 1970); Clive Trebilcock, *The Industrialization of the Continental Powers 1780–1914* (London, 1981); Carlo Cipolla (ed.), *Fontana Economic History of Europe*, vol. 4 (London, 1973); M. C. Reed (ed.), *Railways in the Victorian Economy* (Newton Abbot, 1969); T. R. Gourvish, *Railways and the British Economy, 1830–1914* (London,

1980); P. S. Bagwell, *The Transport Revolution from 1770* (London, 1974); L. G. Macpherson, *Transportation in Europe* (London, 1910); Michael Robbins, *The Railway Age* (London, 1962).

2. Quoted by M. C. Reed, op. cit. 28.

3. Rainer Fremdling, 'Railroads and German Economic Growth: a Leading Sector Analysis with a Comparison to the United States and Great Britain', *Journal of Economic History*, 37 (1977), 585.

4. Roger Price, *The Modernization of Rural France* (London, 1983), 296–7.

5. T. R. Gourvish, op. cit. 28.

6. Price, op. cit. 213.

7. A. C. Chauncey, 'The Whittlesea Brick Traffic', *Railway Magazine*, 5 (1899), 247–51.

8. Jacob Metzger, 'Railroad Development and Market Integration: the Case of Tsarist Russia', *Journal of Economic History*, 34 (1974), 529–49.

9. Peter I. Lyaschenko, *History of the National Economy of Russia* (New York, 1949), 11–12.

10. The effect of the railways on diet is studied in detail in John Burnett, *Plenty and Want* (London, 1966).

11. Ibid. 159.

12. Philip Unwin, *Travelling by Train in the Edwardian Era* (London, 1979), 86.

13. On the milk trade see P. J. Atkins, 'The Growth of London's Railway Milk Trade c.1845–1914', *Journal of Transport History*, NS 4 (1978), 208–26.

14. Walter F. Downing, 'The Fruit Traffic of Evesham', *Railway Magazine*, 15 (1904), 404–8; P. Collins, 'The London and South-Western Railway and the Strawberry Traffic', *Railway Magazine*, 19 (1906), 71–5; Ernest Protheroe, *The Railways of the World* (London, 1914), 216–20.

15. Victor L. Whitechurch, 'Flowers and Vegetables from Cornwall and the Scilly Isles', *Railway Magazine*, 4 (1899), 311–18.

16. A. C. Chauncey, 'Histon Jam Traffic', *Railway Magazine*, 4 (1899), 277–80.

17. Richard Perren, *The Meat Trade in Britain, 1840–1914* (London, 1978); idem, 'The Meat and Livestock Trade in Britain, 1850–70', *Economic History Review*, 28 (1978), 385–400.

18. Victor L. Whitechurch, 'The London and North-Western Railway and American Meat', *Railway Magazine*, 5 (1899), 358–68.

19. Protheroe, op. cit. 222.

20. Ibid. 352–3.

21. Ibid. 214–15.

22. Ibid. 224–5.

23. *Railway Magazine*, 6 (1900), 193.

24. D. T. Timins, 'Important Railway Goods Depots, 1. Nine Elms', *Railway Magazine*, 6 (1900), 70–8.

25. Ibid. 76.

26. E. M. Bywell, 'Important Railway Goods Depots, 2. Forth, Newcastle-upon-Tyne', *Railway Magazine*, 6 (1900), 149–57.

27. D. T. Timins, 'Important Railway Goods Depots, 3. Paddington', *Railway Magazine*, 6 (1900), 193–200.

28. J. Medcalf, 'Important Railway Goods Depots, 4. King's Cross', *Railway Magazine*, 6 (1900), 313–20.

29. The full story of the Paris stations of the Nord network is told in René Clozier, *La Gare de Nord* (Paris, 1940).

CHAPTER 9

1. Albert Fishlow, *American Railroads and the Ante Bellum Economy* (Cambridge, Mass. 1965); Robert Fogel, *Railroads and American Economic Growth* (Baltimore, 1964).
2. Percy Martin, *Through Five Republics* (London, 1905).
3. Idem, *Mexico of the Twentieth Century*, 2 vols. (London, 1907), p. v.
4. G. N. Curzon, *Russia in Central Asia* (London, 1889), 58.
5. J. H. Patterson, *The Man-Eaters of Tsavo* (London, 1907).
6. W. S. Churchill, *My African Journey* (London, 1908).
7. Quoted in J. Martineau, *The Life and Correspondence of Sir Bartle Frere*, 2 vols. (London, 1895), vol. 1, p. 401.
8. Martin, *Through Five Republics*, 234.
9. Quoted in Curzon, op. cit. 191–2.
10. Dee Brown, *Hear that Lonesome Whistle Blow* (London, 1977), 254.
11. Harold A. Innis, *A History of the Canadian Pacific Railway* (1923; repr. Newton Abbot, 1972).
12. F. A. Talbot, *The Making of a Great Canadian Railway* (London, 1912), 33.
13. S. A. Pain, *The Way North* (Toronto, 1964).
14. Talbot, op. cit. 150–1.
15. Ibid. 151–2.
16. Ibid. 155.
17. Innis, op. cit. 132, 144, 159.
18. Ibid. 198.
19. Pain, op. cit. 105.
20. Talbot, op. cit. 93.
21. Harmon Tupper, *To the Great Ocean* (London, 1965), 98.
22. Curzon, op. cit. 156.
23. Frank H. Spearman, *The Strategy of Great Railroads* (London, 1905).
24. John A. Droege, *Freight Terminals and Trains* (New York, 1912), 8.
25. Carl Condit, *The Railroad and the City* (Columbus, 1977), *passim*.
26. Spearman, op. cit. 15–16.
27. Ibid. 17.
28. Droege, op. cit. 101.
29. John F. Stover, *The Life and Death of the American Railroad* (New York, 1970), 98.
30. Droege, op. cit. (1925 edn.), 531.
31. Norman Leys, *Kenya* (London, 1924), 354–6; idem, *Last Chance in Kenya* (London, 1931), 43–54.
32. Henry W. Cave, *The Ceylon Government Railway* (London, 1910).
33. George Hearn and David Wilkie, *The Cordwood Limited* (Victoria, 1967), 36.

CHAPTER 10

1. Details of working conditions in stations around the world appear throughout the book. So in this chapter we will concentrate on Britain and America in order to draw a cohesive, comparative picture. On workers and working conditions in British stations, see Frank McKenna, *The Railway Workers, 1840–1970* (London, 1980), P. W. Kingsford, *Victorian Railwaymen* (London, 1970), Henry Chappell, *Life on the Iron Road* (London, 1924), W. J. Gordon, *Everyday Life on the Railroad* (London, 1892), Rowland Kenney, *Men and Rails* (London and Leipzig, 1913), John Farrington, *Life on the Lines* (Ashbourne, 1984). On conditions in the United

States, see Walter Licht, *Working for the Railroad* (Princeton, 1983), Benjamin C. Burt, *Railway Station Service* (New York, 1911), Marshall M. Kirkman, *Railway Service: Trains and Stations* (New York, 1878), J. F. Stover, *The Life and Decline of the American Railraod* (New York, 1970).

2. Kenney, op. cit. 149–50.
3. F. Jacqmin, *Railroad Employés in France* (New York, 1877), 9–11.
4. Sir George Findlay, *The Working and Management of an English Railway* (London, 1889), 22–3.
5. Burt, op. cit. 65.
6. Kirkman, op. cit. 221.
7. Burt, op. cit. 132.
8. D. B. Hanna, *Trains of Recollection* (Toronto, 1924), 26.
9. Licht, op. cit. 120.
10. E. B. Ivatts, *Railway Management at Stations* (London, 1885), 54.
11. Ibid. 58.
12. Jacqmin, op. cit. 7.
13. Kirkman, op. cit. 237.
14. Findlay, op. cit. 27.
15. Ivatts, op. cit. 41. The American equivalents by Burt and Kirkman are much less detailed and exhaustive.
16. Ivatts, op. cit. 2.
17. Ibid. 12.
18. Ibid. 47.
19. Ibid. 53.
20. As an example see the LNWR rules printed in Sir Francis Head, *Stokers and Pokers* (1849; repr. Newton Abbot, 1968), 86–7. Specific instructions on station cleaning are given in Ivatts, op. cit. 419–20.
21. Burt, op. cit. 67.
22. *Railway Magazine*, 2 (1898), 167–8.
23. W. Vincent, *Seen from the Railway Platform* (London, 1919), 91.
24. Jack Simmons (ed.), *Memoirs of a Stationmaster* (1879; repr. Bath, 1974), 83.
25. *Railway Magazine*, 15 (1904), 334; ibid. 16 (1905), 379, 383, 483.
26. Ibid. 8 (1901), 20–1.
27. Burt, op. cit. 238–40.
28. F. S. Williams, *Our Iron Roads* (1883; repr. Old Woking, 1981), vol. 2, pp. 317–18.
29. Burt, op. cit. 177–8.
30. McKenna, op. cit. 103.
31. Ernest Protheroe, *The Railways of the World* (London, 1914), 246.
32. Gordon, op. cit. 76.
33. Ivatts, op. cit. 445.
34. Ibid. 441–2.
35. Harry Aland, *Recollections of Country Station Life* (Blaby, 1980), 10.
36. Ibid. 26–7.
37. Arthur Randell, *Fenland Railwayman* (London, 1968), 11–12.
38. Aland, op. cit. 19.
39. Chappell, op. cit. 19. For an account of the involvement of station staff, particularly signalmen, in accidents see L. T. C. Rolt, *Red for Danger* (London, 1955), and J. A. B. Hamilton *British Railway Accidents of the Twentieth Century* (London, 1967).
40. Chappell, op. cit. 24–5.
41. P. S. Bagwell, *The Railwaymen* (London, 1963), 96; on the unions in Britain see

this work generally. For America see P. S. Foner, *History of the Labor Movement in the United States*, vol. 2 (New York, 1955), and Philip Taft, *Organized Labor in American History* (New York, 1964).

42. Licht. op. cit. 249.
43. Adrian Vaughan, *Signalman's Morning and Signalman's Twilight*, one volume edn. (London, 1984), 114.

CHAPTER 11

1. On the station in nineteenth-century warfare, see John Westwood, *Railways at War* (London, 1980), E. F. Carter, *Railways in Wartime* (London, 1964), and E. A. Pratt, *The Rise of Rail Power in War and Conquest, 1833–1914* (London, 1915). On the American Civil War, see G. E. Turner, *Victory Rode the Rails* (Indianapolis, 1953; repr. 1972), T. Weber. *Northern Railroads and the Civil War* (Columbia, 1952), and R. C. Black, *Railroads of the Confederacy* (Chapel Hill, North Carolina, 1952).
2. Pratt, op. cit. 9–10.
3. Turner, op. cit. 204.
4. G. N. Curzon, *Russia in Central Asia* (London, 1889), 47–8.
5. G. W. Steevens, *With Kitchener to Khartum* (Edinburgh, 1898), 2.
6. Ibid. 29–30.
7. Leo Weinthal (ed.), *The Cape to Cairo Railway* (London, 1923), vol. 2, p. 285.
8. Sudan Government, *Railways and Steamers* (Khartoum, 1910); Sudan Railways, *Visit the Sudan* (Atbara, 1912).
9. R. S. S. Baden-Powell, *The Matabele Campaign 1896* (London, 1897), 10–11.
10. E. A. H. Alderson, *Pink and Scarlet, or Hunting as a School for Soldiering* (London, 1900), 124.
11. Steevens, op. cit. 27.
12. E. P. C. Girouard, *History of the Railways during the War in South Africa, 1899–1902* (London, 1903).
13. Pratt, op. cit. 256.
14. *Natal Province Descriptive Guide and Official Handbook* (Durban, 1911), 194.
15. G. N. Curzon, *Problems of the Far East* (London, 1896), 314.
16. H. C. Thomson, *China and the Powers* (London, 1902), 3. Thomson provides a graphic account of the battle at the station at Tientsin, pp. 34–60.
17. Eric Newby, *The Big Red Train Ride* (London, 1978), 185.
18. *Railway Magazine*, 15 (1904), 504.
19. Percy Martin, *Through Five Republics* (London, 1905), p. x.
20. Ibid. 22.
21. Ibid. 22–3.
22. M. Frayn *et al.*, *Great Railway Journeys of the World* (London, 1981), 141–2.

CHAPTER 12

1. Marcel Peschaud, *Les Chemins de fer allemands et la Guerre* (Paris, 1927), 6.
2. On the role of the station in twentieth-century wars in general see John Westwood, *Railways at War* (London, 1980), and E. F. Carter, *Railways in Wartime* (London, 1964). Specifically on the First World War see E. A. Pratt, *British Railways and the Great War* (London, 1921), J. A. B. Hamilton, *British Railways in World War One* (London, 1967), Gabriel Lafon, *Les Chemins de fer français pendant la Guerre* (Paris,

1922), J. N. H. Henaff and Henri Bornecque, *Les Chemins de fer français et la Guerre* (Paris, 1922), F. Marchand, *Les Chemins de fer de l'Est, 1914–18* (Paris, 1924), Marcel Peschaud, op. cit. On the Second World War see R. Bell, *History of the British Railways during the War 1939–45* (London, 1946), O. S. Nock, *Britain's Railways at War 1939–45* (London, 1971), Bernard Darwin, *War on the Line: the Story of the Southern Railway in War-Time* (London, 1946), George C. Nash, *The L.M.S. at War* (London, 1946), Norman Longmate, *How We Lived Then* (London, 1973), 292–302.

3. Vera Brittain, *Testament of Youth* (1933; repr. London, 1979), 117–18.
4. Ibid. 177–8.
5. Ibid. 188–9.
6. Peschaud, op. cit. 104.
7. Henaff and Bornecque, op. cit. 262.
8. Harmon Tupper, *To the Great Ocean: Siberia and the Trans-Siberian Railway* (London, 1965), 393.
9. E. A. Pratt, op. cit. 394.
10. Ibid. 794.
11. Ibid. 378–9.
12. Nash, op. cit. 7.
13. R. Broad and S. Fleming (eds.), *Nella Last's war: a Mother's Diary 1939–45* (Bristol, 1981), 43.
14. Carter, op. cit. 176–7.
15. Nock, op. cit. 56.
16. Darwin, op. cit. 78–9.
17. Tupper, op. cit. 432.

CHAPTER 13

1. *Railway Magazine*, 68 (1931), 429.
2. Ibid. 17 (1905), 257.
3. John A. Droege, *Passenger Terminals and Trains* (New York, 1916), 259–60.
4. The slighted Begum of Oudh lived in the VIP waiting-room of New Delhi Station from 1972 to 1985, when she was offered accommodation in keeping with her status.
5. *Railway Magazine*, 71 (1932), 394.
6. Ibid. 68 (1931), 59.
7. F. S. Williams, *Our Iron Roads* (1883; repr. Old Woking, 1981), vol. 2, p. 314.
8. Droege, op. cit. 207–11.
9. Ceylon Railways, *General Regulations and Information for Passengers* (Royal Commonwealth Society Collection, n.d., late nineteenth century).
10. Droege, op. cit. 224–5.
11. John Aye, *Humour on the Rail* (London, 1931), 145–6.
12. Quoted in Williams, op. cit. 266.
13. Anthony Trollope, *He Knew He Was Right* (1869; repr. London, 1963), 351–2.
14. L. T. C. Rolt, *Isambard Kingdom Brunel* (London, 1971), 140.
15. Jack Simmons (ed.), *The Railway Traveller's Handy Book of Hints, Suggestions and Advice* (1862; repr. Bath, 1974), 69–70.
16. Sir William Acworth, *The Railways of England* (London, 1900), 157.

17. Charles Dickens, 'Mugby Junction', in *Christmas Stories* (London, 1871; repr. Oxford, 1959), 515–16.
18. Jack Simmons (ed.), *Memoirs of a Stationmaster* (1879; repr. Bath, 1974), 72.
19. Sir Francis Head, *Stokers and Pokers* (1849; repr. Newton Abbot, 1968), 86–7.
20. Robert Thorne, 'Places of Refreshment in the Nineteenth-Century City', in Anthony D. King (ed.), *Buildings and Society* (London, 1980), 228–53; Donald J. Olsen, *The Growth of Victorian London* (Harmondsworth, 1979), 104.
21. *Railway Magazine*, 8 (1901), 143.
22. Karl Baedeker, *Southern Italy and Sicily: a Handbook for Travellers* (Leipzig, 1912), p. xviii.
23. Karl Baedeker, *Norway, Sweden, and Denmark* (Leipzig, 1912), p. xix.
24. Acworth, op. cit. 157.
25. Henry W. Cave, *The Ceylon Government Railway* (London, 1910), 24.
26. Dee Brown, *Hear that Lonesome Whistle Blow* (London, 1977), 142.
27. Quoted in Elizabeth Wilmot, *Meet Me at the Station* (Toronto, 1977), 100.
28. Droege, op. cit. 376.
29. Brown, op. cit. 223–6.
30. Quoted in Droege, op. cit. 377.
31. The East India Railways, for example, employed thousands of water-carriers to supply the needs of its passengers: *Railway Magazine*, 18 (1906), 502.
32. Richard D. Altick, *The English Common Reader* (Chicago, 1957), 89.
33. Wolfgang Schivelbusch, *The Railway Journey* (Oxford, 1980), 66.
34. Charles Manby Smith, *The Little World of London* (London, 1857), 96.
35. Samuel Phillips, 'The Literature of the Rail', *Essays from The Times*, series 1 (London, 1855), 311–25.
36. Ibid.
37. Ibid.
38. Margaret Dalziel, *Popular Fiction 100 Years Ago* (London, 1957), discusses railway literature in general. On the role of W. H. Smith see Sir Herbert Maxwell, *The Life and Times of W. H. Smith, M.P.* (Edinburgh, 1893).
39. William Vincent, *Seen from The Railway Platform* (London, 1919), 83.
40. Ibid. 64.
41. Robert Roberts, *The Classic Slum* (Harmondsworth, 1977), 160.
42. P. G. Wodehouse, *Wodehouse on Wodehouse* (Harmondsworth, 1981), 264.
43. George Orwell, *Collected Essays, Journalism, and Letters* (Harmondsworth, 1970), vol. 1, p. 588.
44. Examples of the covers of these works are illustrated in M. Satow and R. Desmond, *Railways of the Raj* (London, 1980), 43, and Charles Allen, *A Scrapbook of British India, 1877–1947* (London, 1977), 31.
45. John Pendleton, *Our Railways* (London, 1896), vol. 1, p. 116.
46. Jeffrey L. Kieve, *The Electric Telegraph* (Newton Abbot, 1973).
47. Pendleton, op. cit. 120.
48. Ibid. 118.
49. Oscar Wilde, *The Works of Oscar Wilde* (London, 1965), 152.
50. George Arliss, *George Arliss by Himself* (London, 1940), 220.
51. Sir Sidney Low, *A Vision of India* (London, 1911), 77–8.
52. Head, op. cit. pp. 54–5.
53. Williams, op. cit. 257.
54. H. J. Prytherch, 'Modern Obliviousness as Exemplified in the Railway Lost Property Office', *Railway Magazine*, 2 (1898), 258–65.

55. Lucinda Lambton, *Temples of Convenience* (London, 1978).
56. *Railway Magazine*, 15 (1904), 251.
57. F. M. L. Thompson, 'Nineteenth-Century Horse Sense', *Economic History Review*, 29 (1976), 60–79.
58. *Railway Magazine*, 15 (1904), 332.
59. Ibid. 111–12.
60. *Railway Magazine*, 8 (1901), 271; Pendleton, op. cit. 113; Williams, op. cit. 267.

CHAPTER 14

1. Rudyard Kipling, 'The King', *The Seven Seas* (London, 1935), 56.
2. Samuel Carr (ed.), *The Poetry of Railways* (London, 1978), 69.
3. The best anthology of railway poetry is Kenneth Hopkins (ed.), *The Poetry of Railways* (London, 1966), which includes a fine selection on stations. But there are also useful selections in Samuel Carr, op. cit., and Bryan Morgan (ed.), *The Railway Lover's Companion* (London, 1963). The best work on railway art is Hamilton Ellis, *Railway Art* (London, 1977).
4. Hopkins, op. cit. 106–7.
5. The most celebrated of these are Thomas Talbot Bury's *Six Coloured Views of the Liverpool and Manchester Railway* (1831), I. Shaw's *Views of the Most Interesting Scenery on the Line of the Liverpool and Manchester Railway* (1831), James Wilson Carmichael's *Views on the Newcastle and Carlisle Railway* (1836), Thomas Talbot Bury's *The London and Birmingham Railroad* (1837), John Cooke Bourne's *Drawings of the London and Birmingham Railway* (1839), Arthur Fitzwilliam Tait's *Views on the Manchester and Leeds Railway* (1845), and J. C. Bourne's *The History and Description of the Great Western Railway* (1846).
6. Gareth Rees, *Early Railway Prints* (London, 1980).
7. Peter Conrad, *The Victorian Treasure House* (London, 1973).
8. Tom Taylor, *The Railway Station, Painted by W. P. Frith* (London, 1865), 3–5.
9. Andrew Turnbull (ed.), *The Poems of John Davidson* (Edinburgh, 1973), vol. 2, p. 436.
10. Ibid. 434.
11. Siegfried Sassoon, 'Morning Express', in *Collected Poems* (London, 1961), 44–5.
12. Hopkins, op. cit. 151.
13. Thomas Hardy, *Collected Poems* (London, 1962), 205.
14. Philip Henderson, *First Poems* (London, 1930), 64–5.
15. Frances Cornford, *Collected Poems* (London, 1955), 86.
16. Jean Cocteau, *Poésie 1916–23* (Paris, 1925), 231.
17. Hardy, op. cit. 487.
18. Karl Shapiro, *Poems 1940–53* (New York, 1953), 149–50.
19. M. Baroli, *Le Train dans la littérature française* (Paris, 1963), 153.
20. Léon-Paul Fargue, *Poèmes* (Paris, 1944), 24–5.
21. Ibid. 105–6.
22. Edward Thomas, *Collected Poems* (Oxford, 1978), 71–3.
23. Henry Maxwell, *A Railway Rubaiyat* (Cambridge, 1968), 1.
24. Jules Laforgue, *Poésies complètes* (Paris, 1970), 226–7.
25. U. Apollonio (ed.), *Futurist Manifestos* (London, 1973), 21–2.
26. James Thrall Soby, *Giorgio de Chirico* (New York, 1966).
27. On the station in the picture postcard see Eric J. Evans and Jeffrey Richards, *A Social History of Britain in Postcards 1870–1930* (London, 1980), R. J. Silvester,

Official Railway Postcards of the British Isles (Chippenham, 1978), Frank Staff, *Picture Postcards and Travel* (Guildford, 1979).

28. Jack Lindsay, *Gustave Courbet: his Life and Art* (London, 1977), 225.
29. Charles Wilson, *The History of Unilever*, (London, 1970), vol. I, p. 32. On the history of enamel advertising see Christopher Baglee and Andrew Morley, *Street Jewellery* (London, 1978).
30. *Railway Magazine*, 4 (1899), 350.
31. J. T. Shackleton, *The Golden Age of the Railway Poster* (London, 1976), 77.
32. On railway posters see Shackleton, op. cit., Bevis Hillier, *Travel Posters* (London, 1976), R. B. Wilson, *Go Great Western: a History of G W R Publicity* (Newton Abbot, 1970).

CHAPTER 15

1. There is no work specifically on the station in literature and film. But on the train in literature, see Frank P. Donovan, Jr., *The Railroad in Literature* (Boston, Mass., 1940), and Marc Baroli, *Le Train dans la littérature française* (Paris, 1963). On the train in film, see John Huntley, *Railways in the Cinema* (London, 1969), and David Gunston, 'Railways on the Screen', *Railway Magazine*, 104 (1958), 86–90, 128.
2. Emile Zola, *La Bête humaine*, trans. Leonard Tancock (Harmondsworth, 1977), 47.
3. Ibid. 44–5.
4. Ibid. 80–1.
5. Pierre Leprohon, *Jean Renoir*, trans. Brigid Elson (New York, 1971), 113.
6. Franc-Nohain, *Les Salles d'attente* (Paris, 1925), 59–60.
7. R. D. Blackmore, *Cradock Nowell* (London, 1866), vol. 2, pp. 200–1.
8. Marcel Proust, *Remembrance of Things Past*, trans. C. K. Scott Moncrieff and Terence Kilmartin (Harmondsworth, 1983), vol. 1, pp. 693–4.
9. Lawrence Durrell, *Justine* (London, 1963), 90–1.
10. Thomas Mann, *Death in Venice*, trans. H. T. Lowe-Porter (Harmondsworth, 1982), 44–5.
11. E. Nesbit, *The Railway Children* (1906; repr. Harmondsworth, 1983), 239.
12. Arnold Bennett, *A Man from the North* (London, 1914), 1–2.
13. Idem, *Whom God Hath Joined* (London, 1919), 44–5.
14. Idem, *The Matador of the Five Towns and Other Stories* (Leipzig, 1912), 180–1.
15. Keith Waterhouse, *Billy Liar* (1959; repr. Harmondsworth, 1983), 177.
16. Jerome K. Jerome, *Three Men in a Boat* (1889; repr. Harmondsworth, 1983), 47–8.
17. *Railway Magazine*, 2 (1898), 56.
18. Alphonse Daudet, *Fromont Junior and Risler Senior*, trans. Edward Vizetelly (London, 1894), 233–7.
19. H. H. Brindley, *Where was Mr. Carker killed?* (Cambridge, 1911).
20. Anthony Trollope, *The Prime Minister* (1876; repr. London, 1968), 231–3.
21. Leo Tolstoy, *Anna Karenina*, trans. Rosemary Edmonds (Harmondsworth, 1981), 800–1.
22. *Railway Magazine*, 71 (1932), 279–80.
23. *The Sunday Times*, 24 May 1936.
24. C. A. Lejeune, *Chestnuts in her Lap* (London, 1947), 162.
25. Ibid. 161.
26. Richard Winnington, *Film Criticism and Caricatures, 1943–53* (London, 1975), 48.

27. Reprinted in John Russell Taylor (ed.), *Masterworks of the British Cinema* (London, 1974), 336.
28. *Observer*, 1 July 1956.
29. *Daily Worker*, 30 June 1956.
30. *The Bioscope*, 23 September 1931.
31. An acount of the filming of *The Wrecker* and the subsequent *Oh, Mr Porter* on the same line can be found in Edward Griffith, *The Basingstoke and Alton Light Railway* (Farnham, 1970).
32. *The Bioscope*, 3 February 1932; *Picturegoer*, 18 June 1932.
33. The filming is described in Harry Watt, *Don't Look at the Camera* (London, 1974), 79–97, and Elizabeth Sussex, *The Rise and Fall of British Documentary* (Berkeley, 1975), 67.

EPILOGUE

1. John A. Droege, *Freight Terminals and Trains* (New York, 1925), 531–8.
2. Paul Theroux, *The Old Patagonian Express* (Harmondsworth, 1980), 142.
3. Ibid. 236.
4. Miles Kington, 'Three Miles High', in M. Frayn *et al.*, *Great Railway Journeys of the World* (London, 1981), 118.
5. Droege, op. cit. 531.
6. Report of the Federal Commission on a General Plan for the Cities of Ottawa and Hull, 1915 (Sir H. S. Holt, Chairman), 58–9.
7. Marcus Binney, 'Reusing Railway Buildings', in Marcus Binney and David Pearce, *Railway Architecture* (London, 1979), 206–8.
8. The front page of this issue of the *Portland Press Herald* is illustrated in the Educational Facilities Laboratories and National Endowment for the Arts *Reusing Railroad Stations*, vol. 1 (New York, 1974), 59.
9. Ibid. 42.
10. We are indebted to Omer Lavallée for cuttings from Canadian newspapers on these issues.
11. Jacques Dalibard, 'Getting on the Right Tracks', *Canadian Heritage*, Feb.–Mar. 1984.
12. Dane Sobat, 'Old Station was a Showpiece', *Calgary Herald*, 27 July 1983.
13. We are indebted to New Zealand Railways for cuttings from New Zealand newspapers.
14. Westrail, the Railways of Western Australia, sent us details of their recent station developments.
15. Information on reuse can be found in Binney and Pearce, op. cit. 206–29; the two volumes of the Educational Facilities Laboratories and National Endowment for the Arts *Reusing Railroad Stations* (New York, 1974 and 1975); and Elizabeth Wilmot, *Meet Me at the Station* (Toronto, 1977).

Sources

PRIMARY

The photographic collections of the Crown Agents, the India Office Library, and the Royal Commonwealth Society

The James Carmichael Smith Collection and other materials (press cuttings, ephemera, etc.) on colonial railways in the Royal Commonwealth Society Library

Report of the Federal Commission on a General Plan for the Cities of Ottawa and Hull, 1915 (Sir H. S. Holt, Chairman)

Plan for the National Capital: General Report (J. Gréber, Ottawa, 1950)

Railway Companies Report on the Modernization of Stations (April 1944)

The Illustrated London News
The Railway Gazette
The Railway Magazine

SECONDARY

Acworth, Sir William M., *The Railways of England* (London, 1900)

Adrian, Werner, *Speed: Cinema of Motion* (London, 1975)

Afinogenov, Alexander, *Distant Point* (London, 1941)

Aland, Harry, *Recollections of Country Station Life* (Blaby, 1980)

Aldcroft, Derek H., *Studies in British Transport History* (Newton Abbot, 1974)

Alderson, E. A. H., *Pink and Scarlet, or Hunting as a School for Soldiering* (London, 1900)

Alexander, Edwin P., *Down at the Depot* (New York, 1970)

Allen, G. Freeman, *Railways Past, Present, and Future* (London, 1982)

Allwood, Rosemary, *George Elgar Hicks: Painter of Victorian Life* (London, 1982)

Altick, Richard D., *The English Common Reader* (Chicago, 1957)

Andrews, Cyril B., *The Railway Age* (London, 1937)

Anon., *Indian Railways, One Hundred Years* (New Delhi, 1953)

—— 'The Natal Railways and the War', *Railway Magazine*, 6 (1900), 201–3

—— 'The New Montreal Central Station', *Railway Gazette*, 80 (1944), 571–3, 594–8, 620–1.

—— *The Railways of New South Wales, 1855–1955* (Sydney, 1955)

—— 'Rhodesia Railways', *Railway Magazine*, 6 (1900), 427–37

Anouilh, Jean, *Point of Departure* (London, 1950)

Apollonio, U. (ed.), *Futurist Manifestos* (London, 1973)

Appleton, J. H., 'Railways and the Morphology of British Towns', in R. P. Beckinsale and J. M. Houston (eds.), *Urbanization and its Problems* (Oxford, 1970), 92–118

Arliss, George, *George Arliss by Himself* (London, 1940)

Arthurton, Alfred W., 'The Day's Work at Paddington Station', *Railway Magazine*, 15 (1904), 330–8

Atkins, P. J., 'The Growth of London's Milk Trade, c.1845–1914', *Journal of Transport History*, NS 4 (1978), 208–26

Aye, John, *Humour on the Rail* (London, 1931)

Baden-Powell, R. S. S., *The Matabele Campaign 1896* (London, 1897)

Baedeker, Karl, *Egypt and the Sudan* (Leipzig, 1908)

—— *Norway, Sweden, and Denmark* (Leipzig, 1912)

—— *Southern Italy and Sicily* (Leipzig, 1912)

Baglee, Christopher, and Morley, Andrew, *Street Jewellery* (London, 1978)

Bagwell, P. S., *The Railwaymen*, 2 vols. (London, 1963, 1982)

—— *The Transport Revolution from 1770* (London, 1974)

Barman, Christian, *An Introduction to Railway Architecture* (London, 1950)

—— *Next Station* (London, 1947)

Baroli, Marc, *Le Train dans la littérature française* (Paris, 1963)

Baron, Wendy, *The Camden Town Group* (London, 1979)

Barrow, Kenneth, *Flora* (London, 1981)

Barzun, Jacques, 'The Imagination of the Real or Ideas and their Environment', in
    G. Anderson, S. Donadio, and S. Marcus (eds.), *Art, Politics, and Will* (New York,
    1977), 3–27

Beaver, S. H., 'The Railways of Great Cities', *Geography*, 22 (1937), 116–20

Bébout, Richard, *The Open Gate, Toronto Union Station* (Toronto, n.d.)

Bedale, Len, *Station Master* (Sheffield, 1976)

Bell, R., *History of the British Railways During the War 1939–45* (London, 1946)

Belloc, Hilaire, *On Nothing and Kindred Subjects* (London, 1908)

Bennett, Arnold, *Hilda Lessways* (London, 1911)

—— *A Man from the North* (London, 1914)

—— *The Matador of the Five Towns and Other Stories* (Leipzig, 1912)

—— *Whom God Hath Joined* (London, 1919)

Berridge, P. S. A., *Couplings to the Khyber* (Newton Abbot, 1969)

Betjeman, John, 'Metroland', in J. Guest (ed.), *The Best of Betjeman* (London,
    1978)

—— and Gay, John, *London's Historic Railway Stations* (London, 1972)

Biddle, Gordon, *Railway Stations in the North West* (Clapham, 1981)

—— *Victorian Stations* (Newton Abbot, 1973)

—— and Nock, O. S. (eds.), *The Railway Heritage of Britain* (London, 1983)

—— and Spence, Jeoffrey, *The British Railway Station* (Newton Abbot, 1977)

Binney, M., Hamm, M., and Foehl, A., *Great Railway Stations of Europe* (London,
    1984)

—— and Pearce, David (eds.), *Railway Architecture* (London, 1979)

Blackmore, R. D., *Cradock Nowell* (London, 1866)

Boag, G. L., *The Railways of Spain* (London, 1923)

Body, Geoffrey, *The Railway Era* (Ashbourne, 1982)

Bohi, Charles, *Canadian National's Western Depots* (Toronto, 1977)

Booth, Michael, *English Melodrama* (London, 1965)

—— *Victorian Spectacular Theatre* (London, 1981)

Bowers, Michael, and Watters, Patrick, *Railway Styles in Building* (London, 1975)

Brant, E. D., *Railways of North Africa* (Newton Abbot, 1971)

Brindley, H. H., *Where was Mr. Carker Killed?* (Cambridge, 1911)

Brittain, Vera, *Testament of Youth* (1933; repr. London, 1979)

Broad R., and Fleming, S. (eds.), *Nella Last's War: a Mother's Diary* (Bristol, 1981)

Brown, Dee, *Hear that Lonesome Whistle Blow* (London, 1977)

'Brunel Redivivus', 'The Funeral of Queen Victoria', *Railway Magazine*, 8 (1901),
    260–5

Buchler, Walter, 'The Newfoundland Railway', *Railway Magazine*, 76 (1935),
    166–8

Burge, J. Thornton, 'The Duties of a Country Stationmaster', *Railway Magazine*, 19 (1906), 536–43.

Burke, Thomas, *Travel in England* (London, 1942)

Burnett, John, *Plenty and Want* (London, 1966)

Burt, Benjamin C., *Railway Station Service* (New York, 1911)

Bywell, E. M., 'Important Railway Goods Depots, 2. Forth, Newcastle-upon-Tyne', *Railway Magazine*, 6 (1900), 149–57

Cairns, J. F., *Railways for All* (London, n.d.)

Cameron, Rondo, *France and Economic Development of Europe 1800–1914* (Princeton, 1961)

Čapek, Karel, *Intimate Things* (London, 1935)

Carr, Samuel (ed.), *The Poetry of Railways* (London, 1978)

Carter, E. F., *Famous Railway Stations of the World* (London, 1958)

—— *Railways in Wartime* (London, 1964)

Cave, Henry W., *The Ceylon Government Railway* (London, 1910)

Cecil, Lord Edward, *The Leisure of an Egyptian Official* (London, 1921; repr. London, 1938)

Cecil, George, 'Railway Settlements in India', *Railway Magazine*, 16 (1905), 111–13

Central Office of Information, *The Campaign in Burma* (London, n.d.)

Chaloner, W. H., *The Social and Economic Development of Crewe, 1780–1923* (Manchester, 1950)

Chang Kia-Ngau, *China's Struggle for Railroad Development* (New York, 1943)

Chapman, J. M. and Brian, *The Life and Times of Baron Haussmann* (London, 1957)

Chappell, Connery, *Trouble on the Line* (London, 1963)

Chappell, Henry, *Life on the Iron Road* (London, 1924)

Charlewood, R. E., 'The Public Time-Table Books of our Chief Railways', *Railway Magazine*, 17 (1905), 335–42

Chauncey, A. C., 'Histon Jam Traffic', *Railway Magazine*, 4 (1899), 277–80

—— 'The Whittlesea Brick Traffic', *Railway Magazine*, 5 (1899), 247–51

Chesterton, G. K., *Tremendous Trifles* (London, 1909)

Chorley, Katherine, *Manchester Made Them* (London, 1950)

Churchill, W. S., *My African Journey* (London, 1908)

Cipolla, Carlo (ed.), *Fontana Economic History of Europe*, vol. 4 (London, 1973)

Clough, Shepard B., *The Economic History of Modern Italy* (New York, 1964)

Clozier, René, *La Gare du Nord* (Paris, 1940)

Collins, P., 'The London and South-Western Railway and the Strawberry Traffic', *Railway Magazine*, 19 (1906), 71–5

Colomb, Captain, *Slave-Catching in the Indian Ocean* (London, 1873)

Compagnie des Chemins de Fer de l'Est, *La Gare de L'Est* (Paris, 1931)

Condit, Carl W., *The Railroad and the City* (Columbus, 1977)

Conrad, Peter, *The Victorian Treasure House* (London, 1973)

Cookridge, E. H., *Orient Express* (London, 1978)

Corbin, Thomas W., *The Romance of Modern Railways* (London, 1922)

Corbyn, Ernest, *All Along the Line* (London, 1958)

Cornford, Frances, *Collected Poems* (London, 1955)

Cowie, Peter, *The Cinema of Orson Welles* (London, 1965)

Crosland, T. W. H., *The Suburbans* (London, 1905)

Croxton, Anthony H., *Railways of Rhodesia* (Newton Abbot, 1973)

Curl, James Stevens, *A Celebration of Death* (London, 1980)

—— *The Victorian Celebration of Death* (Newton Abbot, 1972)

Curzon, G. N., *Problems of the Far East* (London, 1896)

—— *Russia in Central Asia* (London, 1889)

Dalziel, Margaret, *Popular Fiction 100 Years Ago* (London, 1957)

Darwin, Bernard, *War on the Line: the Story of the Southern Railway in War-Time* (London, 1946)

Daudet, Alphonse, *Fromont Junior and Risler Senior* (trans. by Edward Vizetelly) (London, 1894)

Day, John, R., *Railways of Northern Africa* (London, 1964)

—— *Railways of Southern Africa* (London, 1963)

Deakin, Michael, and Willis, John, *Johnny Go Home* (London, 1976)

Deane, Frank L., 'Notable Railway Stations: Flinders Street, Melbourne', *Railway Magazine*, 71 (1932), 1–9

Delgado, Alan, *The Annual Outing and Other Excursions* (London, 1977)

Denton, J. Horsley, 'Private Stations', in H. A. Vallance (ed.), *The Railway Enthusiast's Bedside Book* (London, 1966), 86–91

Dethier, Jean (ed.), *All Stations* (London, 1981)

Dewhurst, H. S., *The Railroad Police* (Springfield, Illinois, 1955)

Dickens, Charles, *American Notes* (London, 1842; repr. Harmondsworth, 1972)

—— *Christmas Stories* (London, 1871; repr. Oxford, 1959)

—— *Dombey and Son* (London, 1848; repr. Oxford, 1974)

Dickens, Charles (the Younger), *A Dictionary of London* (London, 1879)

Dickinson, R. E., *The West European City* (London, 1961)

Dmitriev-Mamonov, A. I., and Zdziarski, A. F., *Guide to the Great Siberian Railway* (1900; repr. Newton Abbot, 1971)

Dollfus, Charles, de Geoffrey, Edgar, and Baudry de Saunier, Louis, *Histoire de la locomotion terrestre: les chemins de fer*, 2 vols. (Paris, 1935)

Donovan, Frank P., Jr., *The Railroad in Literature* (Boston, Mass., 1940)

Downing, Walter F., 'The Fruit Traffic of Evesham', *Railway Magazine*, 15 (1904), 404–8.

Droege, John A., *Freight Terminals and Trains* (New York, 1912 and 1925)

—— *Passenger Terminals and Trains* (New York, 1916)

Durrell, Lawrence, *Justine* (London, 1963)

Dyos, H. J., and Aldcroft, D. H., *British Transport* (Harmondsworth, 1974)

Educational Facilities Laboratories and National Endowment for the Arts, *Reusing Railroad Stations*, 2 vols. (New York, 1974 and 1975)

Edwards, Dennis, and Pigram, Ron, *The Golden Years of the Metropolitan Railway* (Tunbridge Wells, 1983)

—— and —— *The Romance of Metroland* (Turnbridge Wells, 1979)

Eliot, T. S., *Collected Poems, 1909–1962* (London, 1963)

Ellis, Hamilton, *The Pictorial Encyclopaedia of Railways* (London, 1968)

—— *Railway Art* (London, 1977)

Evans, Eric J., and Richards, Jeffrey, *A Social History of Britain in Postcards 1870–1930* (London, 1980)

Falconer, John, 'Nineteenth-Century Photography in Ceylon', *The Photographic Collector*, 2 (1981), 39–53

Fargue, Léon-Paul, *Poèmes* (Paris, 1944)

Farrington, John, *Life on the Lines* (Ashbourne, 1984)

Fawcett, Brian, *Railways of the Andes* (London, 1963)

Fellows, Reginald B., 'Bradshaw's First Timetable', *Railway Magazine*, 76 (1935), 391–2

Findlay, Sir George, *The Working and Management of an English Railway* (London, 1889)

Fishlow, Albert, *American Railroads and the Ante Bellum Economy* (Cambridge, Mass., 1965)

Fitzgerald, R. S., *Liverpool Road Station, Manchester: an Historical and Architectural Survey* (Manchester, 1980)

Fogel, Robert W., *Railroads and American Economic Growth* (Baltimore, 1964)

—— *The Union Pacific* (Baltimore, 1960)

Foner, P. S., *History of the Labor Movement in the United States* (New York, 1955)

Ford, Colin, and Harrison, Brian, *A Hundred Years Ago* (Harmondsworth, 1983)

Forster, E. M., *A Passage to India* (1924; Harmondsworth, 1982)

Foxwell, E., and Farrer, T. C., *Express Trains English and Foreign* (London, 1889)

Franc-Nohain, *Les Salles d'attente* (Paris, 1925)

Fraser, W. Hamish, *The Coming of the Mass Market, 1850–1914* (London, 1981)

Frater, Alexander, *Stopping-Train Britain* (London, 1983)

Frayn, Michael, *et al.*, *Great Railway Journeys of the World* (London, 1981)

Fremdling, Rainer, 'Railroads and German Economic Growth: a Leading Sector Analysis with a Comparison to the United States and Great Britain', *Journal of Economic History*, 37 (1977), 583–604

Fry, H. W., 'A Railway of Brazil the São Paulo Railway', *Railway Magazine*, 8 (1901), 439–48

Fry, Roger, *Vision and Design* (London, 1937)

Fussell, Paul, *Abroad: British Literary Travelling between the Wars* (Oxford, 1980)

Gillis, John R., *The Development of European Society, 1770–1870* (New York, 1877)

Girouard, Sir E. P. C., *History of the Railways during the War in South Africa, 1899–1902* (London, 1903)

Gordon, W. J., *Everyday Life on the Railroad* (London, 1892)

—— *Our Home Railways*, 2 vols. (London, 1910)

Gourvish, T. R., *Railways and the British Economy, 1830–1914* (London, 1980)

Grant, E. M., *French Poetry and Modern Industry 1830–70* (Cambridge, Mass., 1927)

Green, Henry, *Partygoing* (1939; repr. London, 1962)

Green, Roger, *The Train* (Oxford, 1982)

Greville, H. D., 'A Railway Through Two Republics', *Railway Magazine*, 2 (1898), 143–7

Griffith, Edward, *The Basingstoke and Alton Light Railway* (Farnham, 1970)

Grillo, R. D., *African Railwaymen* (Cambridge, 1973)

Grow, Lawrence, *Waiting for the 5.05* (New York, 1977)

Guide to the Colombo and Kandy Railway (Colombo, 1867)

Gunston, David, 'Railways on the Screen', *Railway Magazine*, 104 (1958), 86–90, 128

Hail and Farewell: the Passing of King George V (*The Times*: London, 1936)

Hamilton, J. A. B., *British Railway Accidents of the Twentieth Century* (London, 1967)

—— *British Railways in World War One* (London, 1967)

Hanna, D. B., *Trains of Recollection* (Toronto, 1924)

Hardie, William, *Scottish Painting 1837–1939* (London, 1976)

Hardy, Ronald, *The Iron Snake* (London, 1965)

Hardy, Thomas, *Collected Poems* (London, 1962)

Harrison, Derek, *Salute to Snow Hill* (Birmingham, 1978)

Hawke, G. R., *Railways and Economic Growth in England and Wales, 1840–70* (Oxford, 1970)

Head, Sir Francis, *Stokers and Pokers* (1849; repr. Newton Abbot, 1968)

Hearn, George, and Wilkie, David, *The Cordwood Limited* (Victoria, 1967)

Henaff, J. N. H., and Bornecque, Henri, *Les Chemins de fer français et la Guerre* (Paris, 1922)

Hill, M. F., *Permanent Way*, 2 vols. (Nairobi, 1957)

Hillier, Bevis, *Travel Posters* (London, 1976)

Hitchcock, Henry-Russell, *Early Victorian Architecture in Britain* (London, 1972)

Hoare, John, *Sussex Railway Architecture* (Hassocks, 1979)

Holcroft, Harold, *The Railways of Germany During the Period 1939–45* (London, 1948)

Hollingsworth, Brian, *Atlas of the World's Railways* (London, 1972)

—— *The Pleasures of Railways* (London, 1983)

Hopkins, Kenneth (ed.), *The Poetry of Railways* (London, 1966)

Horsfield, Brenda (ed.), *Steam Horse; Iron Road* (London, 1972)

Huddleston, G., 'The East Indian Railway', *Railway Magazine*, 17 (1905), 481–8; 18 (1906), 177–82, 323–8, 425–9, 501–6; 19 (1906), 40–5, 262–6, 349–53, 440–4

Hughes, M. V., *A London Child of the 1870s* (Oxford, 1934; repr. 1978)

Hull, Raymond, *et al.*, *Vancouver's Past* (Vancouver, 1974)

Huntley, John, *Railways in the Cinema* (London, 1969)

Ilyin, M., *Moscow: Architecture and Monuments* (Moscow, 1968)

Innis, Harold A., *A History of the Canadian Pacific Railway* (1923; repr. Newton Abbot, 1972)

Irving, Robert Grant, *Indian Summer, Lutyens, Baker, and Imperial Delhi* (New Haven and London, 1981)

Ivatts, E. B., *Railway Management at Stations* (London, 1885)

Jackson, Alan A., *London's Termini* (Newton Abbot, 1969)

—— *London's Local Railways* (Newton Abbot, 1978)

—— *Semi-Detached London* (London, 1973)

Jackson, Herbert and Mary, *History of the Maryport and Carlisle Railway* (Maryport, 1979)

Jacqmin, F., *Railroad Employés in France* (New York, 1877)

James, Henry, *English Hours* (Oxford, 1981)

Jennings, Paul, *Just a Few Lines* (London, 1969)

—— *My Favourite Railway Stories* (Guildford, 1982)

Jerome, Jerome K., *Three Men in a Boat* (1889; Harmondsworth, 1983)

Johnston, Colin, and Hume, John R., *Glasgow Stations* (Newton Abbot, 1979)

Jones, Kenneth Westcott, *Romantic Railways* (London, 1971)

Kellett, John R., *Railways and Victorian Cities* (London, 1979)

Kennedy, Ludovic, *A Book of Railway Journeys* (London, 1981)

Kenney, Rowland, *Men and Rails* (London and Leipzig, 1913)

Kent, P. H., *Railway Enterprise in China* (London, 1907)

Kichenside, Geoffrey, *The Restaurant Car* (Newton Abbot, 1979)

Kieve, Jeffrey L., *The Electric Telegraph* (Newton Abbot, 1973)

King, Anthony D. (ed.), *Buildings and Society* (London, 1980)

Kingsford, P. W., *Victorian Railwaymen* (London, 1970)

Kipling, Rudyard, *From Sea to Sea*, 2 vols. (London, 1901)

—— *Kim* (London, 1908)

—— *Letters of Travel (1892–1913)* (London, 1920)

—— *The Seven Seas* (London, 1935)

—— *The Years Between* (London, 1919)

Kirkman, Marshall M., *Railway Service: Trains and Stations* (New York, 1878)

Kirkwood, S., 'Railway Tourist Literature', *Railway Magazine*, 6 (1900), 510–16

Klapper, Charles, *London's Lost Railways* (London, 1976)

Koebel, W. H., *Argentina, Past and Present*, (London, 1914)

Kubinszky, Mihaly, *Bahnhöfe Europas* (Stuttgart, 1969)

Lafon, Gabriel, *Les Chemins de fer français pendant la Guerre* (Paris, 1922)

Laforgue, Jules, *Poésies complètes* (Paris, 1970)

Lambton, Lucinda, *Temples of Convenience* (London, 1978)

Landes, David, *The Unbound Prometheus* (Cambridge, 1969)

Langdon, R., *The Life of Roger Langdon* (London, 1908)

Lant, Jeffrey, *Insubstantial Pageant* (London, 1979)

Lardner, Dionysius, *Railway Economy* (1850; repr. New York, 1968)

Lawrence, H. S., 'The South African Railways', *Railway Magazine*, 68 (1931), 173–83

Lawrence, John T., 'Railways in South India', *Railway Magazine*, 2 (1898), 307–15

—— 'The Railway System of Northern India', *Railway Magazine*, 3 (1898), 445–54

Lee, Charles E., *The Centenary of 'Bradshaw'* (London, 1940)

—— *Passenger Class Distinctions* (London, 1943)

Legg, Stuart, *The Railway Book* (London, 1952)

Legget, Robert F., *Railways of Canada* (Newton Abbot, 1973)

Leitch, David B., *Railways of New Zealand* (Newton Abbot, 1972)

Lejeune, C. A., *Chestnuts in her Lap* (London, 1947)

Leprohon, Pierre, *Jean Renoir* (trans. by Brigid Elson) (New York, 1971)

Lewis, Colin, *Railways of Argentina* (London, 1983)

Licht, Walter, *Working for the Railroad; the Organization of Work in the 19th Century* (Princeton, New Jersey, 1983)

Liepmann, Kate, *The Journey to Work* (London, 1944)

Lindsay, Jack, *Gustave Courbet: his Life and Art* (London, 1977)

Lloyd, David, 'Railway Station Architecture', *Industrial Archaeology*, 4, no. 3 (August 1967), 185–225; 4, no. 4 (November 1967), 293–310

Lloyd, Roger, *The Fascination of Railways* (London, 1951)

—— *Railwaymen's Gallery* (London, 1953)

Longmate, Norman, *How We Lived Then* (London, 1973)

Low, Sir Sidney, *A Vision of India* (London, 1911)

Lucie-Smith, Edward, and Dars, Celestine, *Work and Struggle: the Painter as Witness* (London, 1977)

Lyaschenko, Peter I., *History of the National Economy of Russia* (New York, 1949)

Lynch, Kevin, *The Image of the City* (London, 1960)

Lynd, Robert, *In Defence of Pink* (London, 1937)

Maas, Jeremy, *Victorian Painters* (London, 1978)

McKenna, Frank, *The Railway Workers, 1840–1970* (London, 1980)

Macpherson, L. G., *Transportation in Europe* (London, 1910)

Mann, Thomas, *Death in Venice* (trans. by H. T. Lowe-Porter) (Harmondsworth, 1982)

Marchand, F., *Les Chemins de fer de l'Est, 1914–18* (Paris, 1924)

Martin, Percy F., *Mexico of the Twentieth Century*, 2 vols. (London, 1907)

—— *Through Five Republics* (London, 1905)

Marzio, Peter C., *The Democratic Art: Pictures for Nineteenth-Century America* (London, 1980)

Masters, John, *Bhowani Junction* (London, 1954)

Maxwell, Henry, *A Railway Rubaiyat* (Cambridge, 1968)

Maxwell, Sir Herbert, *The Life and Times of W. H. Smith, M.P.* (Edinburgh, 1893)

Measom, George, *The Illustrated Guide to the Great Western Railway* (London, 1952)

—— *The Official Illustrated Guide to the South-Eastern Railway and its Branches* (London, 1958)

Medcalf, J., 'Important Railway Goods Depots, 4. King's Cross', *Railway Magazine*, 6 (1900), 313–20

Meeks, Carroll L. V., *Italian Architecture 1750–1914* (Cambridge, Mass., 1966)

—— *The Railroad Station* (New Haven and London, 1956)

Menpes, Mortimer and Dorothy, *Durbar* (London, 1903)

Metzger, Jacob, 'Railroad Development and Market Integration: the Case of Tsarist Russia', *Journal of Economic History*, 34 (1974), 529–49

Mills, W. F., *The Railway Service* (London, 1967)

Mitchell, W. R., *Life on the Settle–Carlisle Railway* (Clapham, 1984)

Morgan, Bryan (ed.), *Crime on the Lines* (London, 1975)

—— *Railways—Civil Engineering* (London, 1963)

—— (ed.), *The Railway Lover's Companion* (London, 1963)

Morris, Jan, with Simon Winchester, *Stones of Empire* (Oxford, 1983)

Mulligan, Fergus, *One Hundred and Fifty Years of Irish Railways* (Belfast, 1983)

Murray, *A Handbook for Travellers in India, Burma, and Ceylon* (London, 1906, 1919)

Nash, George C., *The LMS at War* (London, 1946)

Natal Province Descriptive Guide and Official Handbook (Durban, 1911)

Neele, George P., 'A Notable Private Railway Station: Gosport, Clarence Yard', *Railway Magazine*, 19 (1906), 513–16

—— *Railway Reminiscences* (East Ardsley, 1974)

Nesbit, E., *The Railway Children* (1906; repr. Harmondsworth, 1983)

Newby, Eric, *The Big Red Train Ride* (London, 1978)

Noakes, Aubrey, *William Frith: Extraordinary Victorian Painter* (London, 1978)

Nochlin, Linda, *Realism* (Harmondsworth, 1971)

Nock, O. S., *Britain's Railways at War 1939–45* (London, 1971)

—— *Continental Main Lines: To-day and Yesterday* (London, 1963)

—— *Railways of Asia and the Far East* (London, 1978)

—— *Railways of Australia* (London, 1971)

—— *Railways of Canada* (London, 1973)

—— *Railways of Southern Africa* (London, 1971)

—— *Railways of the USA* (London, 1979)

—— *Railways of Western Europe* (London, 1977)

—— *Scottish Railways* (London, 1950)

Norborg, Kurt (ed.), *Proceedings of the IGU Symposium in Urban Geography* (Lund, 1962)

O'Brien, Patrick (ed.), *Railways and the Economic Development of Western Europe* (Oxford, 1983)

Olsen, Donald J., *The Growth of Victorian London* (Harmondsworth, 1979)

Orwell, George, *Collected Essays, Journalism, and Letters* (Harmondsworth, 1970)

Osborne, George, 'The Sung-Wu Railway', *Railway Magazine*, 6 (1900), 557–60

Page, Martin, *The Lost Pleasures of the Great Trains* (London, 1975)

Pain, S. A., *The Way North* (Toronto, 1964)

'Palinurus', *The Unquiet Grave* (1944; repr. Harmondsworth, 1984)

Partington, John, 'Bradshaw', *Railway Magazine*, 2 (1898), 243–50

Patterson, J. H., *The Man-Eaters of Tsavo* (London, 1907)

Pattinson, J. Pearson, 'Railway Timetables', *Railway Magazine*, 3 (1898), 478–82

Paulian, Louis, *The Beggars of Paris* (London, 1897)

Pehnt, Wolfgang, *Expressionist Architecture* (London, 1973)

Pendleton, John, *Our Railways*, 2 vols. (London, 1896)

Perera, G. F., *The Ceylon Railway* (Colombo, 1925)

Perkin, Harold, *The Age of the Railway* (Newton Abbot, 1971)

Perren, Richard, 'The Meat and Livestock Trade in Britain, 1850–70', *Economic History Review*, 28 (1978), 385–400

—— *The Meat Trade in Britain, 1840–1914* (London, 1978)

Peschaud, Marcel, *Les Chemins de fer allemands et la Guerre* (Paris, 1927)

Pevsner, Nikolaus, *A History of Building Types* (London, 1979)

Phillips, Samuel, 'The Literature of the Rail', *Essays from the Times*, series 1 (London, 1855), 311–25

Pierre, W. A., *Canterbury Provincial Railways* (Wellington, 1964)

Pimlott, J. A. R., *The Englishman's Holiday* (London, 1947)

Pinto, Adolphus Augusto, *História da Viação Pública de São Paulo* (São Paulo, 1903)

'P.M.C', 'Mexican Central Railway', *Railway Magazine*, 6 (1900), 129–33

Pope, Robert Anderson, 'Grand Central Terminal Station, New York', *Town Planning Review*, 2, no. 1 (April 1911), 55–64

Porter, P. B., 'Across India by Train', *Railway Magazine*, 63 (1928), 425–7

Pratt, E. A., *British Railways and the Great War* (London, 1921)

—— *The Rise of Rail Power in War and Conquest, 1833–1914* (London, 1915)

Price, Roger, *The Modernization of Rural France* (London, 1983)

Protheroe, Ernest, *The Railways of the World* (London, 1914)

Proust, Marcel, *Remembrance of Things Past* (trans. by C. K. Scott Moncrieff and Terence Kilmartin) (Harmondsworth, 1983)

Prytherch, H. J., 'Modern Obliviousness as Exemplified in the Railway Lost Property Office', *Railway Magazine*, 2 (1898), 258–65

—— 'Our Railway Police', *Railway Magazine*, 6 (1900), 53–60 and 134–41

Pulbrook, Ernest C., 'The First Railway in China', *Railway Magazine*, 3 (1898), 430–4

Randell, Arthur, *Fenland Railwayman* (London, 1968)

Rannie, J. Allen, 'The Railway Journeys of Mr. Sherlock Holmes', in Peter Haining (ed.), *A Sherlock Holmes Companion* (London, 1980), 105–15

Ransome-Wallis, P., *On Railways* (London, 1951)

Read, Jan, and Manjon, Maite, *The Great British Breakfast* (London, 1981)

Reed, M. C. (ed.), *Railways in the Victorian Economy* (Newton Abbot, 1969)

Rees, Gareth, *Early Railway Prints* (London, 1980)

Reilly, Sir Charles, 'Our Big Railway Stations', in *Some Architectural Problems of Today* (London, 1924), 31–6

Reynolds, A. M., *The Life and Work of Frank Holl* (London, 1912)

Reynolds, Graham, *Painters of the Victorian Scene* (London, 1953)

Ridge, W. Pett, *On Company's Service* (London, 1905)

Risher, Howard W., *The Negro in the Railroad Industry* (Philadelphia, 1971)

Robbins, Michael, *The Railway Age* (London, 1962)

Roberts, Robert, *The Classic Slum* (Harmondsworth, 1977)

Rolt, L. T. C., *Isambard Kingdom Brunel* (London, 1971)

—— *Red for Danger* (London, 1955)

Ronaldson, T., 'Imperial Railways of North China', *Railway Magazine*, 4 (1899), 440–9.

Ross, Alan, *Colours of War: War Art 1939–45* (London, 1983)

Rous-Martin, Charles, 'New Zealand Railways', *Railway Magazine*, 5 (1899), 465–72; 6 (1900), 13–20

Rowe, Vivian, *French Railways Today* (London, 1958)

Ruskin, John, *The Seven Lamps of Architecture* (London, 1907)

Sala, George Augustus, *Twice Round the Clock* (London, n.d.)

Sassoon, Siegfried, *Collected Poems* (London, 1962)

Satow, Michael, and Desmond, Ray, *Railways of the Raj* (London, 1980)

Schivelbusch, Wolfgang, *The Railway Journey, Trains and Travel in the Nineteenth Century* (trans. by Anselm Hollo) (Oxford, 1980)

Schmied, W., *Neue Sachlichkeit und Magischer Realismus in Deutschland 1928–1933* (Hanover, 1969)

Scott, James, *Railway Romance and Other Essays* (London, 1913)

Scott, Paul, *The Raj Quartet* (London, 1966–75)

Seaton, Ray, and Martin, Roy, *Good Morning Boys: Will Hay, Master of Comedy* (London, 1978)

Sellwood, Arthur and Mary, *The Victorian Railway Murders* (Newton Abbot, 1979)

Shackleton, J. T., *The Golden Age of the Railway Poster* (London, 1976)

Sheehy, Jeanne, 'Railway Architecture—its Heyday', *Journal of the Irish Railway Record Society*, 12 (1975–6), 125–38

Sidney, Samuel, *Rides on Railways* (1881; repr. London, 1973)

Silvester, R. J., *Official Railway Postcards of the British Isles* (Chippenham, 1978)

Simmons, Jack (ed.), *Memoirs of a Stationmaster* (1879; repr. Bath, 1974)

——*The Railways of Britain* (London, 1968)

——(ed.), *The Railway Traveller's Handy Book of Hints, Suggestions and Advice* (1862; repr. Bath, 1974)

——*St. Pancras Station* (London, 1968)

Singleton, C. C., and Burke, David, *Railways of Australia* (Sydney, 1963)

Smith, Charles Manby, *The Little World of London* (London, 1857)

Smith, G. Royde, *The History of Bradshaw* (London, 1939)

——*Old Euston* (London, 1938)

Smithson, A. and P., *The Euston Arch and the Growth of the London, Midland and Scottish Railway* (London, 1968)

Soby, James Thrall, *Giorgio de Chirico* (New York, 1966)

Spalding, Frances, *Magnificent Dreams* (New York, 1978)

Spearman, Frank H., *The Strategy of Great Railroads* (London, 1905)

Staff, Frank, *Picture Postcards and Travel* (Guildford, 1979)

Staffan, L. C., *Railway Station Buildings, an Historical Survey* (New Zealand Institute of Architects, Wellington, 1965)

Statham, F. Reginald, 'The Railway System of Natal', *Railway Magazine*, 2 (1898), 64–9

Steevens, G. W., *With Kitchener to Khartum* (Edinburgh, 1898)

Stevenson, John, *British Society 1914–45* (Harmondsworth, 1984)

Stilgoe, John R., *Metropolitan Corridor: Railroads and the American Scene* (New Haven and London, 1983)

Stones, H. R., 'A Notable Railway Station in Buenos Aires', *Railway Magazine*, 63 (1928), 171–83

Stover, John F., *The Life and Decline of the American Railroad* (New York, 1970)

Sussex, Elizabeth, *The Rise and Fall of British Documentary* (Berkeley, 1975)

Taft, Philip, *Organized Labor in American History* (New York, 1964)

Talbot, F. A., *The Making of a Great Canadian Railway* (London, 1912)

Tatlow, Joseph, *50 Years of Railway Life* (London, 1920)

Taylor, Derek, and Bush, David, *The Golden Age of British Hotels* (London, 1974)

Taylor, John Russell (ed.), *Masterworks of the British Cinema* (London, 1974)

Taylor, Robert R., *The Word in Stone: the Role of Architecture in the National Socialist Ideology* (Berkeley, 1974)

Taylor, Tom, *The Railway Station, Painted by W. P. Frith* (London, 1865)

Theroux, Paul, *The Great Railway Bazaar* (Harmondsworth, 1977)

——*The Old Patagonian Express* (Harmondsworth, 1980)

Thomas, David St John, *The Country Station* (Newton Abbot, 1976)

Thomas, Edward, *Collected Poems* (Oxford, 1978)

Thompson, F. M. L., 'Nineteenth-Century Horse Sense', *Economic History Review*, 29 (1976), 60–79

——(ed.), *The Rise of Suburbia* (Leicester, 1982)

Thomson, H. C., *China and the Powers* (London, 1902)

Thorne, Robert, *Liverpool Street Station* (London, 1978)

Thorns, David C., *Suburbia* (London, 1972)

The Times Book of Argentina (London, 1927)

Timins, D. T., 'By Rail in Japan', *Railway Magazine*, 2 (1898), 230–6

——'Important Railway Goods Depots, 1. Nine Elms', *Railway Magazine*, 6 (1900), 70–8

——'Important Railway Goods Depots, 3. Paddington', *Railway Magazine*, 6 (1900), 193–200

Tiresias, *Notes from Overground* (London, 1984)

Tolstoy, Leo, *Anna Karenina* (trans. by Rosemary Edmonds) (Harmondsworth, 1981)

Tomsell, Ian, 'The Railways of Trinidad', *Railway Magazine*, 69 (1931), 275–9

Treacy, Eric, *Steam Up!* (London, 1950)

Trebilcock, Clive, *The Industrialization of the Continental Powers 1780–1914* (London, 1981)

Trollope, Anthony, *He Knew He was Right* (1869; repr. London, 1963)

——*The Prime Minister* (1876; repr. London, 1968)

Tupper, Harmon, *To the Great Ocean: Siberia and the Trans-Siberian Railway* (London, 1965)

Turnbull, Andrew (ed.), *The Poems of John Davidson* (Edinburgh, 1973)

Turner, George E., *Victory Rode the Rails* (Indianapolis, 1953; repr. 1972)

Turnock, David, *Railways in the British Isles* (London, 1982)

Turton, B. J., 'The Railway Towns of Southern England', *Journal of Transport History*, 2 (1969), 85–100

Union-Castle Line Guide to South and East Africa (London, 1911–12)

Unwin, Philip, *Travelling by Train in the Edwardian Era* (London, 1979)

——*Travelling by Train in the Twenties and Thirties* (London, 1981)

Vale, A., 'The Jaffa–Jerusalem Railway', *Railway Magazine*, 10 (1902), 321–32

——'The Transcaspian Railway', *Railway Magazine*, 12 (1903), 277–80 and 415–22

Vaughan, A., *Great Western Architecture* (Oxford, 1977)

Vaughan, Adrian, *Signalman's Morning and Signalman's Twilight* (London, 1984)

Verne, Jules, *Around the World in Eighty Days* (London, n.d.)

Vincent, William, *Seen from the Railway Platform* (London, 1919)

'Voyageur', 'The New Central Station at Wellington', *Railway Magazine*, 74 (1934), 100–5

——'Recent Railway Developments in New Zealand', *Railway Magazine*, 68 (1931), 368–73.

Wade, George, 'Famous Continental Railway Stations', *Railway Magazine*, 16 (1905); 379–84, 482–7; 17 (1905), 130–4, 489–98

——'The Prettiest Railway Stations', *Railway Magazine*, 6 (1900), 46–52

Waller, P. J., *Town, City, and Nation: England 1850–1914* (Oxford, 1983)

Walmsley, R. W., *Nairobi, the Geography of a New City* (Nairobi, 1957)

Walton, John K., *The English Seaside Resort: a Social History, 1750–1914* (Leicester, 1983)

——'Railways and Resort Development in North-West England 1830–1914', in E. M. Sigsworth (ed.), *Ports and Resorts in the Regions* (Hull, 1980), 120–37

Walvin, James, *Beside the Seaside* (London, 1978)

Wardle, John, 'A Tour over the Pioneer Railway of Canada (the Grand Trunk Railway)', *Railway Magazine*, 17 (1905), 226–35

Waterhouse, Keith, *Billy Liar* (1959; repr. Harmondsworth, 1983)

Watt, Harry, *Don't Look at the Camera* (London, 1974)

Watt, J. O. P., *Southland's Pioneer Railways* (Wellington, 1965)

Weber, T., *Northern Railroads in the Civil War* (Columbia, 1952)

Weinthal, Leo (ed.), *The Story of the Cape to Cairo Railway and River Route from 1887–1922*, 4 vols. (London, 1923)

Welch, David (ed.), *Nazi Propaganda* (London, 1983)

Westwood, John, *Railways at War* (London, 1980)

Westwood, J. N., *A History of Russian Railways* (London, 1964)

——*Railways of India* (Newton Abbot, 1974)

——*Soviet Railways Today* (London, 1963)

Whitbread, J. R., *The Railway Policeman* (London, 1961)

Whitechurch, Victor L., 'Flowers and Vegetables from Cornwall and the Scilly Isles', *Railway Magazine*, 4 (1899), 311–18

——'The London and North-Western Railway and American Meat', *Railway Magazine*, 5 (1899), 358–68

——*Stories of the Railway* (1912; repr. London, 1977)

Wilde, Oscar, *The Works of Oscar Wilde* (London, 1965)

Williams, F. S., *The Midland Railway: its Rise and Progress* (1888; repr. Newton Abbot, 1968)

——*Our Iron Roads*, 2 vols. (1883; repr. Old Woking, 1981)

Wilmot, Elizabeth A., *Meet Me at the Station* (Toronto, 1977)

Wilmot, Tony (ed.), *Beware of the Trains* (Hornchurch, 1981)

Wilson, Charles, *The History of Unilever* (London, 1970)

Wilson, R. B., *Go Great Western: a History of GWR Publicity* (Newton Abbot, 1970)

Winnington, Richard, *Film Criticism and Caricatures, 1943–53* (London 1975)

Wishaw, Francis, *Railways of Great Britain and Ireland* (1842; repr. Newton Abbot, 1970)

Wodehouse, P. G., *Wodehouse on Wodehouse* (Harmondsworth, 1981)

Wood, Christopher, *Victorian Panorama* (London, 1976)

Zola, Emile, *La Bête humaine* (trans. by Leonard Tancock) (Harmondsworth, 1977)

Index of Stations

General Index